DAVID FOSTER WALLACE IN CONTEXT

David Foster Wallace is regarded as one of the most important American writers of the twentieth and twenty-first centuries. This book introduces readers to the literary, philosophical and political contexts of Wallace's work. An accessible and useable resource, this volume conceptualizes his work within long-standing critical traditions and with a new awareness of his importance for American literary studies. It shows the range of issues and contexts that inform the work and reading of David Foster Wallace, connecting his writing to diverse ideas, periods and themes. Essays cover topics on gender, sex, violence, race, philosophy, poetry and geography, among many others, guiding new and long-standing readers in understanding the work and influence of this important writer.

CLARE HAYES-BRADY is Associate Professor in American Literature at University College Dublin. She is the author of *The Unspeakable Failures of David Foster Wallace: Language, Identity, and Resistance* (2016).

DAVID FOSTER WALLACE IN CONTEXT

EDITED BY

CLARE HAYES-BRADY

University College Dublin

CAMBRIDGE
UNIVERSITY PRESS

CAMBRIDGE
UNIVERSITY PRESS

Shaftesbury Road, Cambridge CB2 8EA, United Kingdom

One Liberty Plaza, 20th Floor, New York, NY 10006, USA

477 Williamstown Road, Port Melbourne, VIC 3207, Australia

314–321, 3rd Floor, Plot 3, Splendor Forum, Jasola District Centre, New Delhi – 110025, India

103 Penang Road, #05–06/07, Visioncrest Commercial, Singapore 238467

Cambridge University Press is part of Cambridge University Press & Assessment, a department of the University of Cambridge.

We share the University's mission to contribute to society through the pursuit of education, learning and research at the highest international levels of excellence.

www.cambridge.org
Information on this title: www.cambridge.org/9781316513323

DOI: 10.1017/9781009064545

© Cambridge University Press & Assessment 2023

First published 2023

A catalogue record for this publication is available from the British Library.

A Cataloging-in-Publication data record for this book is available from the Library of Congress
NAMES: Hayes-Brady, Clare, editor.
TITLE: David Foster Wallace in context / edited by Clare Hayes-Brady.
DESCRIPTION: Cambridge ; New York, NY : Cambridge University Press, 2022. | Includes bibliographical references.
IDENTIFIERS: LCCN 2022033905 (print) | LCCN 2022033906 (ebook) | ISBN 9781316513323 (hardback) | ISBN 9781009073516 (paperback) | ISBN 9781009064545 (epub)
SUBJECTS: LCSH: Wallace, David Foster–Criticism and interpretation. | BISAC: LITERARY CRITICISM / American / General | LCGFT: Literary criticism.
CLASSIFICATION: LCC PS3573.A425635 Z6624 2022 (print) | LCC PS3573.A425635 (ebook) | DDC 813/.54–dc23/eng/20220916
LC record available at https://lccn.loc.gov/2022033905
LC ebook record available at https://lccn.loc.gov/2022033906

ISBN 978-1-316-51332-3 Hardback

Contents

Figures

Contributors

ANTONIO AGUILAR VÁZQUEZ is a member of the David Foster Wallace Research Group. He obtained a BA in English literature from the National Autonomous University of Mexico, an MSc from the University of Edinburgh and a PhD from the University of Glasgow. He is currently finishing the Creative Writing MFA program at New York University.

LAURIE MCRAE ANDREW is an independent scholar and the author of The Geographies of David Foster Wallace's Novels: Spatial History and Literary Practice (Edinburgh University Press). Aside from Wallace, he works on literary geographies and contemporary fiction.

CORRIE BALDAUF is associate professor at Eastern Michigan University. Her art practice is based out of a shared studio space in Detroit, Michigan. She was an international resident artist at Griffin Gallery International Residency (West London, United Kingdom). Baldauf has shown her *Optimism Filter Project* in Detroit at *Art X* (2013) and in Lille, France, at *lille3000* (2014). Her interactive work has been exhibited at the Detroit Institute of Art, Museum of Contemporary Art Detroit, Songjiang Museum in Shanghai and the Museum Palazzo Barolo in Turin. Her art has appeared in *ART – Das Kunstmagazin*, *Fukt Magazine for Contemporary Drawing*, *Hyperallergic*, *Lufthansa Exclusive Magazine* and *HOHE Luft Magazine*.

JON BASKIN is the associate director of the Creative Publishing and Critical Journalism program at the New School for Social Research. He is also the editor of *The Point* and the author of *Ordinary Unhappiness: The Therapeutic Fiction of David Foster Wallace* (2019).

ALICE BENNETT is senior lecturer in English Literature at Liverpool Hope University, United Kingdom. Her most recent book is *Contemporary*

Fictions of Attention (2018). She is currently writing a book on alarms for Bloomsbury's Objects series.

MARSHALL BOSWELL is professor of English at Rhodes College. He is the author of three works of literary scholarship: *John Updike's Rabbit Tetralogy: Mastered Irony in Motion* (2001), *Understanding David Foster Wallace* (2004, revised and updated in 2020) and *The Wallace Effect: David Foster Wallace and the Contemporary Literary Imagination* (2019). He is also the author of two works of fiction, *Trouble with Girls* (2003) and *Alternative Atlanta* (2005). With Stephen Burn, he is the coeditor of *A Companion to David Foster Wallace Studies* (2013) and the editor of *David Foster Wallace and "The Long Thing": New Essays on the Novels* (2015).

RALPH CLARE is associate professor of English at Boise State University, specializing in post-45 American literature. He is the author of *Fictions Inc.: The Corporation in Postmodern Fiction, Film, and Popular Culture* (2014) and the editor of the *Cambridge Companion to David Foster Wallace* (2018). His latest book project is *Metaffective Fiction: Structuring Feeling in Contemporary American Literature*.

PHILIP COLEMAN is professor in the School of English, Trinity College Dublin, where he is also a fellow. He has edited *David Foster Wallace: Critical Insights* (2015) and contributed essays on Wallace to a number of edited collections. He has published extensively on US American poetry and short fiction.

ALLARD DEN DULK is senior lecturer in Philosophy, Literature, and Film at Amsterdam University College and Research Fellow at the Faculty of Humanities of the VU Amsterdam (The Netherlands). He is the author of *Existentialist Engagement in Wallace, Eggers and Foer: A Philosophical Analysis of Contemporary American Literature* (Bloomsbury 2015). Currently, he is working on a book, tentatively titled *Wallace's Existentialist Intertexts: Comparative Readings with the Fiction of Kafka, Dostoevsky, Camus and Sartre*. For more information and publications, see www.allarddendulk.nl.

MAUREEN ECKERT is professor of Philosophy at UMASS Dartmouth whose editorial works include *Fate, Time and Language: David Foster Wallace s Essay on Free Will* (2010), *Freedom and the Self: Essays on the Philosophy of David Foster Wallace* (2015) and *Theories of Mind: Introductory Readings* (2006). She is founder and codirector of the

PIKSI: Logic summer program, and an advocate of nonclassical logic, focusing on instructional methods for presenting it in undergraduate philosophy curricula.

MARTIN PAUL EVE is professor of Literature, Technology and Publishing at Birkbeck, University of London. He holds a PhD from the University of Sussex and is the author or editor of seven books. Martin is a recipient of the KU Leuven Medal of Honour and a winner of the Philip Leverhulme Prize.

TIM GROENLAND teaches in the School of English, Irish, and Communication at the University of Limerick. His first book, *The Art of Editing: Raymond Carver and David Foster Wallace*, was published in 2019 by Bloomsbury Academic. His writing has appeared in *Critique: Studies in Contemporary Fiction*, *The Los Angeles Review of Books* and *The Dublin Review of Books*, among other venues.

VINCENT HADDAD is Associate professor of English at Central State University. His academic writing has appeared *in Inks The Comparatist, ImageTexT, Post45* and a special issue on DFW in *Orbit*. His public writing has appeared in *Los Angeles Review of Books*, *Public Books*, *Black Perspectives*, *Middle Spaces* and *The Rambling*.

CLARE HAYES-BRADY is associate professor of American Literature at University College Dublin, and the author of *The Unspeakable Failures of David Foster Wallace*, published by Bloomsbury Academic (2016), out now in paperback. She is also the editor of the *Journal of David Foster Wallace Studies* and has published widely on contemporary fiction.

DAVID HERING is senior lecturer in English Literature at the University of Liverpool. His writing has appeared in publications including *The Los Angeles Review of Books*, *Orbit*, *Critical Engagements*, *The London Magazine* and *The Oxonian Review*. He is the editor of *Consider David Foster Wallace: Critical Essays (SSMG, 2010)* and author of *David Foster Wallace: Fiction and Form (Bloomsbury, 2016)*

EDWARD JACKSON is associate lecturer at The Open University. He is the author of *David Foster Wallace's Toxic Sexuality: Hideousness, Neoliberalism, Spermatics* (Bloomsbury Academic, 2020) and a coeditor of "Supposedly Fun Things: A David Foster Wallace Special Issue" for *Orbit: A Journal of American Literature* (2017).

PAUL JENNER is lecturer in English at Loughborough University. His essays on David Foster Wallace have appeared in *Consider David Foster Wallace* (2010) and *Fictional Worlds and the Moral Imagination* (2021). He is currently writing a book on David Foster Wallace, Marilynne Robinson and Stanley Cavell.

DANIELA FRANCA JOFFE has a PhD in English Language and Literature from the University of Cape Town. She earned her BA at Harvard University and her master's at the University of Oxford. She left academia in 2020 to pursue a teaching career and now works in early years education.

MATTHEW LUTER is on the English faculty at St. Andrew's Episcopal School in Jackson, Mississippi. He is the author of *Understanding Jonathan Lethem* (University of South Carolina Press, 2015) and coeditor, with Mike Miley, of *Conversations with Steve Erickson* (University Press of Mississippi, 2021). His work has appeared in journals including *Critique*, *The Southern Literary Journal*, *Genre* and *Orbit*. He is a founding board member of the International David Foster Wallace Society.

ÁINE MAHON is assistant professor in the School of Education at University College Dublin. Her primary research areas are Philosophy of Education and Philosophy of Literature. Áine's first monograph, *The Ironist and the Romantic: Reading Richard Rorty and Stanley Cavell*, was published by Bloomsbury in 2014. She is the coeditor of *Stanley Cavell, Literature and Film: The Idea of America* (Routledge, 2013) and *Philosophical Perspectives on Contemporary Ireland* (Routledge, 2020). Áine's forthcoming collection is entitled *Philosophical Readings of the Contemporary University: In Shadows and Light*.

PIA MASIERO is associate professor of North American Literature at Ca' Foscari University of Venice. Her research interests include modernist and contemporary literature, literary theory at the intersection of cognitive sciences and second-generation postclassical narratology. She has published, among others, on Philip Roth, William Faulkner, David Foster Wallace, George Saunders, Alice Munro, Jorge Luis Borges and Roberto Bolaño.

MIKE MILEY teaches literature at Metairie Park Country Day School and film studies at Loyola University New Orleans. He is the author of *Truth and Consequences: Game Shows in Fiction and Film* (University

Press of Mississippi, 2019) and coeditor of *Conversations with Steve Erickson* (with Matthew Luter, University Press of Mississippi, 2021). His writing has appeared in *Critique, Literature/Film Quarterly, Music and the Moving Image, Orbit* and elsewhere.

ALEXANDER MORAN is faculty chair for excellence in Undergraduate and Graduate Writing at Stanbridge University. He is the author of *Understanding Jennifer Egan* (University of South Carolina Press, 2021) and also the editor of *Conversations with Jennifer Egan*, which is under contract with the University Press of Mississippi. He has published widely on contemporary American fiction and currently serves on the board of *The Journal of David Foster Wallace Studies*.

TIM PERSONN teaches literature at the University of Victoria in British Columbia, Canada. He holds a PhD in English-CSPT (Cultural, Social and Political Thought) from the University of Victoria, and degrees in English and Philosophy from Universität Hamburg, Germany. His essays have appeared in Textual Practice, Post45, Hohe Luft Magazine, and Orbit, and he has a forthcoming monograph, Fictions of Proximity: Skepticism, Romanticism, and the Wallace Nexus.

JAMIE REDGATE is the author of Wallace and I: Cognition, Consciousness, and Dualism in David Foster Wallace's Fiction (Routledge, 2019) and a teacher in the School of Critical Studies at the University of Glasgow, where he is currently working on a second monograph, tentatively titled Meatfiction: Humanism, Animals, and Veganism in the Contemporary Novel. Jamie's essays have been published by English Literature, Electric Literature, Extra Teeth, and elsewhere, while his fiction has been longlisted for the Blinkpot Award, won third prize in the Imprint Writing Competition, and been chosen as the "Best of 2021" by The Rush. In 2022, Jamie was longlisted for the Moniack Mhor Emerging Writer Award. www.jamieredgate.co.uk.

JOEL ROBERTS is an Associate Lecturer at the Open University and Specialist Study Skills Tutor at Liverpool John Moores University. His research interests include nineteenth- and twentieth-century American Literature, the twentieth-century American road novel, literature and spatiality, and literature and urban development.

EMILY RUSSELL is professor of English at Rollins College in Winter Park, Florida. She is the author of *Transplant Fictions: A Cultural Study of*

Organ Exchange (2019) and *Reading Embodied Citizenship: Disability, Narrative, and the Body Politic* (2011).

COLTON SAYLOR currently lectures in the Department of English and Comparative Literature at San José State University. His research centers on issues of race, capitalism and the state in the twentieth century. His work has been published in *The Journal of David Foster Wallace Studies* and *The Journal for the Study of Radicalism*.

JEFFREY SEVERS is associate professor of English at the University of British Columbia, the author of *David Foster Wallace's Balancing Books: Fictions of Value* (2017) and the coeditor of *Pynchon's* Against the Day*: A Corrupted Pilgrim's Guide* (2011). His essays have appeared in *Critique*, *Textual Practice* and several other journals.

MARY SHAPIRO is professor of linguistics and chair of the Department of English and Linguistics at Truman State University in Kirksville, Missouri. She serves on the executive board of the Modern Language Association's Association of Departments of English. Her monograph *Wallace's Dialects* (Volume 3 in the Bloomsbury David Foster Wallace series) was published in May 2020.

PETER SLOANE is lecturer in English at the University of Lincoln, United Kingdom. He has published widely on British and US fiction and film, including *David Foster Wallace and the Body* (Routledge, 2019) and *Kazuo Ishiguro's Gestural Poetics* (Bloomsbury, 2021). He is currently coediting *Kazuo Ishiguro: New Essays* (Manchester University Press, 2022), while working on his third monograph, *Acts of Kindness: Altruism and the Arts* (Cambridge University Press, 2024).

DOMINIK STEINHILBER is a postdoctoral researcher at the chair of American Studies of the University of Konstanz. His first research project, "The American Epic Novel in the Ulyssean Tradition," investigated David Foster Wallace's *Infinite Jest* and Thomas Pynchon's *Gravity's Rainbow* with regard to their response to James Joyce's *Ulysses*. Apart from David Foster Wallace, his research interests include alternative ecologies in 19th century American writing as well as theories of sustainable reading. His articles have appeared in venues such as Ecozona, Critique: Studies in Contemporary Fiction, The Journal of David Foster Wallace Studies, and American Literature in the Era of Trumpism: Alternative Realites.

STUART TAYLOR teaches at Edinburgh Napier University and the University of Glasgow, where he completed his doctoral dissertation entitled "Encyclopedic Architectures: Mathematical Structures in the Works of Don DeLillo, Thomas Pynchon, & David Foster Wallace" in 2019. His writing features in *Lettera Matematica, Orbit, Postmodern Culture* and *The Encyclopedia of Contemporary American Fiction* (Wiley-Blackwell, 2022).

LUCAS THOMPSON is lecturer in English at the University of Sydney. He previously held Lecturer and Research Associate positions at the United States Studies Centre at Sydney, as well as working across various other teaching roles at the University of Sydney, the University of New South Wales and the University of Wollongong. He is the author of *Global Wallace: David Foster Wallace and the World* (2017), as well as numerous other publications on contemporary and twentieth-century US fiction.

CATHERINE TOAL is professor of literature and dean of the faculty at Bard College Berlin. She studied at Trinity College Dublin (BA) and Harvard University (MA, PhD) and held a Research Fellowship at Emmanuel College, University of Cambridge. In 2019, she was a visiting researcher at Sorbonne Université. In 2016, her book *The Entrapments of Form: Cruelty and Modern Literature* was published by Fordham University Press, with the support of a grant from the Modern Language Initiative of the Mellon Foundation.

Acknowledgments

It has been a strange time to gather and edit a book of essays. Between the development of the idea and team for the volume and its production, life took on a strange new shape, with the arrival of a new disease that made the world seem both infinitely smaller and infinitely larger. In the spirit of this strange, networked remoteness, it seems appropriate to highlight and thank the many people who have made this volume possible. Working through the pandemic has given me a renewed value for the yielding, fractal strangeness of Wallace's writing and a greater appreciation for the collaborative spirit of the community of scholars of his work. This community has worked through the strangest and most stressful period many of us can recall, producing scholarship full of insight, wit and enthusiasm. I am hugely indebted to them, and appreciative of the generosity of their writing, their thinking and their time.

Ray Ryan, editor at Cambridge University Press, approached me to edit this volume in 2018, while I was on maternity leave and casting about for my next project and a sense of purpose. What a piece of work to be offered! Ray's advice and support throughout this process have been invaluable, both to the book and to my own development as a scholar and academic. During the process of developing the volume, two reviewers provided rich and useful feedback; the book would be much inferior without their guidance, and I thank them for their time and expertise. Having gathered the essays, I realized I needed eyes sharper than my own to help assemble them to the best advantage. In this respect, I could not have had better collaborators than Dr. Edward Jackson, whose work on the bibliography has been impeccable, and Dr. Dara Downey, copy editor and proofreader extraordinaire, whose attention to both micro and macro levels of detail is unparalleled. They are wonderful colleagues and friends, and I thank them sincerely.

This book has occupied most of my professional attention and time since 2019, and my colleagues at University College Dublin have provided a collegial, supportive space, always ready with advice and cheer, and tea (either real or, latterly, virtual). In particular, I must thank Dr. Katherine Fama, Dr. Nerys Williams and Dr. Maria Stuart, whose unstinting support and friendship has been critical to my career and to the development of this volume. Lastly, my family has been a source of stalwart, if occasionally baffled, support throughout the many iterations of reading, shaping, editing and polishing, and so, to Maz, May, Ely and Leo, my unending love and gratitude.

Abbreviations

Page references in notes will be given using the following abbreviations:

BFN	*Both Flesh and Not: Essays.* New York: Little, Brown, 2012
BI	*Brief Interviews with Hideous Men.* Boston: Little, Brown, 1999
BS	*The Broom of the System.* New York: Penguin, 1987
CL	*Consider the Lobster.* New York: Little, Brown, 2005
DFWR	*The David Foster Wallace Reader.* Eds. Karen Green and Michael Pietsch. New York: Little, Brown, 2014
EM	*Everything and More.* New York: W. W. Norton, 2003
FTL	*Fate, Time and Language.* New York: Columbia University Press, 2010
GCH	*Girl with Curious Hair.* New York: W. W. Norton, 1989
IJ	*Infinite Jest.* Boston: Little, Brown, 1996
OB	*Oblivion.* New York: Little, Brown, 2004
SFT	*A Supposedly Fun Thing I'll Never Do Again.* Boston: Little, Brown, 1997
SR	*Signifying Rappers. With Mark Costello.* New York: Ecco Press, 1990
SS	"Solomon Silverfish." *Sonora Review,* 16 (Autumn 1987), 54–81
ST	*String Theory.* New York: Library of America/Penguin Random House, 2016
TIW	*This Is Water.* New York: Little, Brown, 2009
TPK	*The Pale King.* Ed. Michael Pietsch. New York: Little, Brown, 2011

Introduction

Clare Hayes-Brady

In the pantheon of writers of the late twentieth and early twenty-first centuries, few loom larger than David Foster Wallace. Fêted during his lifetime and outright worshipped following his death in 2008, Wallace's writing captured the zeitgeist of millennial anxiety and confusion. Bridging the gap between the postmodern and its uncertain aftermath, Wallace's dizzying prolixity and extraordinary mastery of form, combined with his strange and estranging visions of the contemporary world, drew breathless critical reviews and immense loyalty among his many readers. Indeed, the effects of his work extend far beyond his direct engagement with readers; Wallace's status as cultural icon is perhaps best captured by the number of people who own, but have not read, his masterwork, *Infinite Jest*, as well as by those who recognize its symbolic value. Wallace – and especially *Jest* – is a touchstone in contemporary popular culture, with references to his work appearing in popular television shows like *Castle* and *The Gilmore Girls*, while the mention of his name in long-form cultural think pieces is a common occurrence. There is a strange dichotomy in this renown. Wallace's name is a kind of popular synecdoche for the earnest, highbrow cultural engagement of a subset of (mostly) young, white, male consumers. In an episode of the television series *Roots*, for example, a white teenage boy begins reading *Infinite Jest* with the specific aim of impressing a girl. As this suggests, Wallace's work continues to signal the development of the earnest, emerging-hipster, mainly white intellectual youth. At the same time, Wallace continues to exert a significant and highly nuanced influence in the literary and cultural life of the twenty-first century, echoing in the work of some of the most innovative writers of his own generation and the generations since. Wallace is mentioned explicitly as an influence by many authors, including Jonathan Franzen, Zadie Smith, Porochista Khakpour and Ben Lerner. Whether directly acknowledged or otherwise, Wallace's legacy echoes in the work of these and many other critically acclaimed and commercially successful authors, as Marshall Boswell has elucidated in his recent book on "the Wallace effect."[1]

Critical work on Wallace emerged in tandem with his publishing career, which began in 1987 with *The Broom of the System*. He was the subject of scholarly attention even before the sensation that was *Infinite Jest*, published in 1996. The 1993 summer issue of *The Review of Contemporary Fiction* contained Wallace's now-famous interview with Larry McCaffery, and also included Lance Olsen's foundational "Termite Art, or Wallace's Wittgenstein," James Rother's essay on the overlooked story "Order and Flux in Northampton," and a short piece by Mark Costello on working with (or around) Wallace. With the publication of *Infinite Jest* came a greater intensity of critical and scholarly attention, including essays by Tom LeClair and Katherine Hayles that continue to resonate in more recent scholarship. Early in the twenty-first century, a clear sense emerged of Wallace as a truly significant writer, though he was largely assessed in the immediate context of postmodernism and its murky aftermath. Timothy Jacobs' 2001 essay on Hopkins, Wallace and order set the tone for a reading of Wallace's innovation within a longer historical context that has been picked up latterly by Lee Konstantinou and Lucas Thompson. Boswell's *Understanding David Foster Wallace*, originally released in 2003 and with a second edition published in 2020, has remained a touchstone for Wallace scholarship since its publication, as has Stephen Burn's *Infinite Jest: A Reader's Guide*, from the same year. Much of the reading undertaken by this early scholarship engaged closely with Wallace's own, quite directionist self-assessment and metacritical writing – Boswell, Burn and Jacobs were united, in their different critiques, in affording the essay "E Unibus Pluram" a central critical role as a kind of artistic manifesto. Subsequently, "E Unibus Pluram," along with these influential interpretations of it, became foundational to scholarly readings of Wallace. Nonetheless, the work of this first wave of scholarship was diffuse rather than dialogic, and tended, as much foundational criticism does, towards the hagiographic, highlighting the cultural importance of what was then a critically underworked author.

Wallace himself haunts these early works of criticism. As several of the essays in the current volume note, Wallace was an inveterate director of his own interpretation, both in the way he invited readers to read his work and in the critical eye he turned on other authors of his own time and preceding generations. As Lucas Thompson notes in Chapter 5, there is,

[1] See Boswell, *The Wallace Effect*.

among critics and scholars, "a sense that one's interpretations have been anticipated by Wallace himself."[2] It is notable too how frequently his observation of a particular skill or foible in one author's work is applicable to his own writing, such as his observation of Franz Kafka's radically literal humor, the "comedy-as-literalization-of-metaphor" whose lack of subtlety is its power, just as it is in Wallace's own writing.[3] Nevertheless, like many authors with such a powerful presence both in his own work and in contemporary culture at large, both the cultural and the critical discourses have wrestled with a tendency to over-biographize Wallace's outputs, which the present volume works to avoid, focusing instead on his writings and legacy. However, a brief note of biography for those readers unfamiliar with Wallace's background is useful to situate him in his contemporary context.

David Wallace was born into a family of words in Ithaca, New York, on February 21, 1962. His mother, Sally, from whom the Foster in his *nom de plume* would later come, would become an English teacher during Wallace's childhood. His father, James, was an academic – a graduate student at Cornell University when David was born, later a professor of philosophy at the University of Illinois. David was joined by a younger sister, Amy, in 1964. In his biography of Wallace, D. T. Max talks of the importance of "midwestern virtues of normality, kindness, and community"[4] and of a routine-based, serene upbringing, with Wallace's love of reading nurtured by his parents, especially his mother. Language and writing loomed large in Wallace's childhood, as an individual pursuit and a family passion. The rather sinister games played by the character Avril Incandenza in *Infinite Jest*, in which she pretends to asphyxiate in response to a grammatical error, was an exaggeration of Sally's own reaction to such errors. Wallace also fondly recalled his father's reading to them; the written word was a kind of magic that bound the family together in an idyll of education and edification. Besides the classics, and the highbrow collective literary engagement of the family, Wallace read the more common texts of his age – *The Hardy Boys* and, as Jamie Redgate productively explores in Chapter 19, J. R. R. Tolkien – and began to develop a prodigious appetite for television that would last into his adulthood and deeply shape his writing.

An athletic and sociable boy, Wallace was an able tennis player in his youth, playing throughout high school until his form began to taper off alongside faster-growing peers. Although he remained a gifted player long

---

[2] See Chapter 5, 65.   [3] Wallace, "Some Remarks," *CL*, 63.   [4] Max, *Every Love Story*, 1.

into his adolescence, Wallace lost his competitive edge, a struggle that would again be important to his writing, visible in the endless perfectionism of the students of Enfield Tennis Academy in *Infinite Jest*. As Max notes, this period coincided with Wallace's discovery of recreational drugs, and the return of a childhood anxiety, suggesting that the idyllic youth was not as straightforwardly tranquil as Max's account might imply. After high school, Wallace attended Amherst College in Massachusetts, where he double majored in English and Philosophy, and where the illness that would shadow and ultimately claim his life made its first clear appearance. Once again, Wallace excelled as a student, and was remembered as a dominant and able presence in the classroom, but late in his sophomore year, he suffered a debilitating period of depression, returned home to recover, drove a school bus for a period, read voraciously and began to develop his voice as a fiction writer. Returning to college with what his roommate Mark Costello described as a changed outlook, he wrote what would become *The Broom of the System* as his English major project, along with the Philosophy thesis that would be published after his death in the volume *Fate, Time and Language*, as well as beginning to publish in the college's literary magazine. An MFA at the University of Arizona was next, which would cement in Wallace a suspicion of creative writing programs and what he saw as their inauthenticity. The beginning of his career-long relationship with agent Bonnie Nadell and the publication in 1987 of *The Broom of the System*, his first novel, would launch him on to the American literary scene as a significant new voice, a significance that was amplified by subsequent publications, including, especially, the seismic *Infinite Jest*, in 1996. Meanwhile, though, Wallace struggled with his writing, applied to Harvard as a graduate student in Philosophy and spiraled into another depressive period, during which he withdrew from his studies to seek treatment at McLean psychiatric hospital in Boston. This stint saw him formally diagnosed and prescribed the antidepressant Nardil, upon which he would remain for most of the rest of his life. Having found some stability with this regime, Wallace began to return to his life, writing, teaching, dating and navigating fame. In 2001, he moved to Pomona College in California, where he would continue teaching until his death. Here he met and married artist Karen Green, adopted two dogs, and seems to have lived in relative serenity for seven years.

Wallace's death by suicide on September 12, 2008, sent shock waves through the literary world, and was followed by a deluge of memorials, reflections and think pieces on this "voice of a generation." Indeed, it is really since Wallace's death that a critical mass of scholarship and a sense of grounded discourse has emerged, building on the earlier touchstones. From being relatively understudied before his death, Wallace has become in danger of being overdetermined by critical attention. The sense of a cohering cluster of scholarship began to emerge around 2009, with the first single-author conferences on Wallace in Liverpool and New York, followed in 2010 by the first volume of collected essays on his work, *Consider David Foster Wallace*, edited by David Hering and based on the conference in Liverpool. Some eighteen volumes on Wallace have been published in the intervening years; that is to say, new books are emerging at an average rate of nearly two a year, and this shows no sign of slowing down, with numerous new monographs and collections under contract or in press. In the earlier wave of scholarship, *Infinite Jest* was often the central focus, along with "E Unibus Pluram" and the aforementioned interview with Larry McCaffery, both published in 1993 in the *Review of Contemporary Fiction*. These texts created a lasting axis of critical concentration on his outputs from the mid-1990s. More recently, scholars have taken a longer view, less committed to *Jest* as a creative fulcrum and more invested in creating critical accounts of sustained aesthetic and ethical concerns across Wallace's career. David Hering and Mary Holland's work on form, and Jeff Severs' interrogation of value in Wallace's work have articulated systematic, wide-ranging understandings of the writer's broad and complex corpus. The recent tide of critical work has built on the earlier scholarship while engaging in contemporary debates that situate Wallace's writing relative to global literary exchange, embodiment and environmental humanities. The current volume continues this expansion into ongoing debates, further embedding and reexamining Wallace's contemporary relevance and historical sweep, from the nineteenth century to the ongoing evolution of literature and popular culture. Bloomsbury Academic has established a series on Wallace, edited by Stephen Burn, that has moved the direction of scholarship away from the early terms of its dialogue, which was largely occupied with questions of narcissism, alienation and empathy, establishing Wallace in orientation to American postmodernism and as a cerebral, abstract thinker. By contrast, volumes in the new series have so far positioned Wallace's work firmly within its broader context, highlighting his embeddedness in global literature, his undeniable cultural and literary impact on the generations after him, and examining his use of language in its sociolinguistic context, thus reimagining his Americanness in more socially grounded ways. Such scholarly progress is assisted by the opening of an incomplete archive of Wallace's writing and papers at the Harry Ransom Center in Austin, Texas, which itself opens up new avenues for critical dialogue, both by offering new material for study and by recasting what we think we know from the published works. Tim Groenland's *The Art of Editing* and Jamie Redgate's *Wallace and I*, two excellent, widely different recent readings of Wallace's work, both depend on this archive in vital and various ways. As Ralph Clare recently pointed out, the archive "has complicated, if not outright disproven, a Unified Wallace Theory."[5] *David Foster Wallace in Context* will contribute to this continuing development of the field of Wallace Studies, challenging and deepening existing readings, while also drawing attention to underworked areas of exploration, including linguistics, poetry and racial capitalism, among others. Outside of traditional scholarly publications, Wallace is widely assigned, studied and discussed, and is a fixture on contemporary university reading lists and syllabi, in both positive and negative contexts. Conferences devoted to his work continue at a rate of two or so a year, while papers and panels on his writing proliferate at larger conferences on literature, the humanities and American Studies. Recent years have seen the establishment of the David Foster Wallace Society, set up in 2017, which runs the peer-reviewed *Journal of David Foster Wallace Studies*. All told, there is a sense that Wallace is experiencing a zeitgeist moment and, simultaneously, that his work has become an indisputable, if not uncomplicated, fixture in the contemporary canon.

This complication largely emerges from tensions between the literary and cultural legacies that have developed and been cemented since Wallace's death in 2008, tensions best described as grounded in a dissonance between the significance and value of Wallace's written works and the assessment of his public persona, along with what we know of his private life. Outside of the academy, Wallace has been a prominent cultural figure, surfacing in the public imagination as a sort of prophet, featuring in a *Jeopardy!* question in early 2021, and popping up twice in *The Simpsons*, the image of a wise writer gone before his time. Wallace is imagined as simultaneously of and reflecting his generation, coming of age at the zenith of postmodernism and in the period of rapid expansion of television at home, of which he acknowledged himself to be a heavy consumer, and which greatly influenced his work. He is, to contemporary eyes, in some sense the very incarnation of Kierkegaard's artist, portrayed as a genius too lofty and sensitive for this world. Along with his periodic appearance as a cultural symbol, there is a great deal of thoughtful and rigorous work on Wallace that emerges from non-academic sources, with

[5] Clare, "Introduction," *Cambridge Companion*, 6.

numerous amateur reading groups of *Infinite Jest* particularly (see
InfiniteSummer.org for an example of this phenomenon), social media
groups devoted to his work and numerous podcasts that address his writing
and life, including the long-running *The Great Concavity*. This diversity
reflects Wallace's unusual place in contemporary cultural dialogues and
particularly the "vibrant nonprofessional readership" that has marked his
cultural significance over the years.[6] This nonprofessional, fan-based,
globally dispersed community constitutes its own (largely online) research
nexus, complicating and contributing to more traditional scholarly dialogues. Of particular significance in this respect is the website www
.thehowlingfantods.com, run by Nick Maniatis, which has been acknowledged by numerous scholars as a significant resource for bibliographies,
reviews and information. Wallace-l, the long-standing LISTSERV community of fans run by Matt Bucher, is also a significant online gathering
space for readers, scholars and information-seekers. This body of "nonprofessional" research is particularly interesting since it helps to shape a
critical field that is also characterized by academic precarity, and in which
the boundary between scholarly and "casual" criticism is ever more
blurred. Within this context, after his death, opinion pieces and reflective
essays devoted to Wallace's genius flourished for a time in mainstream
media, followed more recently by an inevitable backlash on more than one
front. Specifically, the organic development of Wallace Studies scholarship
has moved from the early hagiography into a period of closer critical
examination, which included work on Wallace's flaws as a writer, most
frequently examining his complex and often unsatisfying approaches to
race and gender.

This critical conversation preceded the #MeToo movement, which
brought with it a reckoning of sorts in terms of Wallace's reputation.
Mary Karr's Twitter posts in 2018 regarding her troubled past relationship
with Wallace highlighted the sustained abusive behavior she experienced
throughout their acquaintance in the late 1990s, during a tumultuous time
for the young Wallace (which had already been mentioned in Max's 2012
biography).[7] While the allegations have never been formally disputed,
Wallace has naturally become the *Q* in this hideous interview, his inter-
jections subject to speculation and projection, the frustrating silence of the
dead forestalling any possibility of further clarity. Various other narratives
have emerged of Wallace's attitudes to relationships, though nothing as
troubling as Karr's account. More pertinently for the work of this volume,

---

[6] Ibid., 4.   [7] See Max, *Every Love Story*, 146–81.

recent years have seen greater attention paid to the profile of Wallace's readers, the "lit-bro" figure who has come to be associated with Wallace's cultural legacy. This character – or caricature, perhaps – is every bit as vibrant in the popular imagination as the Kerouac and Hemingway boys of earlier generations, and both preceded and survives the allegations of abusive and unsavory behavior that have shadowed Wallace's reputation over the past number of years. Emerging from the critical and cultural confluence of these strands of thought, an ongoing conversation both within and without the discipline of Wallace Studies has explored and continues to explore what it means to study a writer whose work engages so deeply with toxic masculinities. This thread of discussion is necessarily taken up by a number of the essays in the volume, situating these conversations in the broader context of work reflecting on the ethics of cultural engagement and consumption. While this is by no means the only – or even the most productive – facet of the discipline, scholarly conversations on Wallace's sustained interest in forms of masculinity and embodiment in contemporary America have contributed to an exception- ally vibrant period in Wallace Studies. This (perhaps natural) trajectory has moved the criticism toward more granular engagement on gender and the body, as well as on topics such as politics, geographies, ecocriticism, attention, disability and so on. After the ground-clearing work of earlier scholars, this movement is particularly interesting as it coincides with a broader cultural reexamination of the processes of canonization, the moral and ethical obligations of author and of reader and scholar, and the power of what we choose to read and study in an age of almost limitless choice.

Debates about the ethics and merits of assigning and reading Wallace have ramped up in recent years. The most obvious example, and one that has crossed academic and popular media, is that which followed Amy Hungerford's 2016 essay in the *Chronicle of Higher Education*, "On Not Reading," about the value and virtue of engaging with a cisgendered, white, middle-class American man – one, moreover, who was at best enmeshed in systems of toxic privilege, and at worst, allegedly, violent and abusive – with Wallace becoming a kind of synecdoche for this argument in wider cultural dialogue. Nonacademic articles by writers, including Deirdre Coyle and Jessa Crispin, concentrated in 2017 but emerging periodically in the intervening years, have sought to articulate a sense of why Wallace, in particular, is so central in this dialogue, and why his displacement is important. Partly because Wallace's position was so profoundly emblematic of these systems of toxic privilege, and partly because his work appears through its almost flagellatory self-consciousness to acknowledge and attempt to expiate this privilege (arguably in both author and reader), Wallace provides an especially rich case study for the reconfiguration of the contemporary canon. Unarguably influential but obviously and avowedly problematic, Wallace's work appears to offer an ideal discursive space for these broader contemporary questions.

In this vein, in light of the critical mass of scholarship on his work and his relevance to the broader cultural moment in terms of discourses surrounding ethical and aesthetic value and the canon, the time is ripe for a volume of essays that examine the contexts of Wallace's writing. Intended to work as a source for both novice readers and more experienced scholars, the thirty-four essays that follow this introduction reach across the full spectrum of Wallace's considerable creative range, exploring form, theme and interpretation from a wide variety of angles. The book's main work begins with Part I, *Contexts*, which explores the literary and cultural contexts within which Wallace operated, tracing how he engaged with these heritages in ways both implicit and explicit. Pia Masiero opens the volume with an assessment of Wallace's narratological strategies, which opens space for Marshall Boswell's examination of empathy – one of the primary themes in Wallace's work – and his debt to Nabokov. Broadening out to consider the historical and cultural milieux in which we can usefully understand Wallace, Ralph Clare considers his emergence in the context of literary cultures of the 1980s, Catherine Toal employs a nineteenth-century lens to look at resonances with Herman Melville, and Lucas Thompson situates Wallace's writing amid its European influences. Influences of form come to the fore in Philip Coleman's tour through the role of poetry, and Matthew Luter examines the complex role of entertainment, another sustained theme. This essay opens the way for Corrie Baldauf's exploration of visual cues, art and clothing, closing a section that offers important guidance for readers and scholars on reading Wallace as a deeply culturally embedded author.

Following this part, the volume focuses more specifically on some of the dominant themes and preoccupations of Wallace's work, with Part II on *Ideas*. Wallace's preoccupation with philosophy is well documented, both in criticism, beginning with Lance Olsen's early work on his interest in Wittgenstein, and in the publication of his own undergraduate Philosophy thesis on free will and determinism under the title *Fate, Time and Language*, and the range of references and influences in his work is wide and complex. Alice Bennett follows Baldauf's work on ekphrastic transfers with an essay that intriguingly teases out the theme of attention, both within Wallace's work and as a feature of the time at which he was writing.

Jon Baskin's exploration of sincerity opens into Aine Mahon's account of perfectionism and the challenge of balancing irony and sincerity, suggesting a kinship between Wallace and Stanley Cavell that associates sincerity with redemption and self-improvement. In a related discussion, Antonio Aguilar Vazquez offers a reading of Rortyan pragmatism in Wallace's writing that both extends and challenges existing readings of the author's pragmatic bent. Maureen Eckert then imagines a world in which Wallace had gone into Philosophy instead of fiction writing as a profession, and in so doing offers a survey of Wallace's work on modal logic and fatalism, which is followed by Paul Jenner's examination of free will as it is worked through in Wallace's writing, especially *Infinite Jest*. Also interested in ideas of limitation and boundary, Stuart Taylor examines Wallace's sustained interest in infinity, which is followed by Allard den Dulk's tracing of the influences of existentialist philosophy and how, like infinity, it elucidates both the form and the thematic occupations of Wallace's work. In keeping with the theme of systems of thought that influence both structure and content, this part closes with Tim Personn's meditation on the importance of religion and spirituality, leading into Jamie Redgate's analysis of Wallace's ideas about consciousness and the soul, which offers an unexpected avenue of connection between Wallace and Tolkien. While the essays have different focuses, they work in conversation to explore how Wallace investigated ideas of both attention and distraction, showing how positive and negative exist in tension within his imagined worlds – how attention (positive) slips into obsession (negative), how sincerity becomes simulation, how communication can collapse into spectatorship, and the productive oppositionality of mind and body.

The next part, *Bodies*, considers the contexts of embodied experiences depicted (and not depicted) in Wallace's work. In recent years in particular, Wallace's engagement with the body – especially the gendered body – has become a primary critical focus. This part traces the dominant critical conversations in this area, beginning with Emily Russell's sketch of sex as a preoccupation for Wallace. Daniela Franca Joffe picks up on this theme and extends it to consider questions of race, gender and changing readership, as well as what she sees as a conservative trajectory in Wallace's representations of gender. Edward Jackson turns his attention to masculinity and its figurative weight, complicating critical narratives of how Wallace recenters traditional masculinities. Dominik Steinhilber considers the representation of gender against a changing backdrop of cultural understandings of authorship and structural violence. Moving away from the role of the normative body, the final essays in this part see Peter Sloane outlining Wallace's persistent thematization of disability, and Vincent Haddad returning us to the nineteenth century for a consideration of queerness and addiction fiction.

Haddad's essay opens into Alexander Moran's work on opiate fiction and capitalist systems of criminalization, the first essay in the final part, entitled *Systems*, which is occupied with the systems and structures that prescribe and proscribe individual behaviors. Moran's essay is succeeded by Colton Saylor's account of racial capitalism as a structuring force throughout Wallace's writing, which is both enriched and challenged by Mary Shapiro's assessment of dialect and racial identity. Jeff Severs grounds his reading in place and systems of agriculture, leading into Laurie MacRae Andrew's exploration of the interdependence of humanity and environment, in an essay on the dominant economic and cultural concerns of Wallace's work. Picking up on the theme of dependence and society, Joel Roberts returns us to issues relating to dialogue and citizenship, an increasingly dominant concern in the later part of Wallace's career. David Hering's essay on Wallace and Ronald Reagan extends this appraisal, tracing an earlier concern with the systems and stories of political engagement. The final two chapters of the volume circle back to the creative systems that governed Wallace's life and career, with Tim Groenland's exploration of Wallace's encounters with the publishing industry and, lastly, Mike Miley's account of the system that dominated Wallace's own life, that of the author–reader relationship. Finally, the volume closes with a Bibliography section. It has not been possible to include every single piece of scholarship on Wallace's writing – at least, not without sorely testing the word count and the patience of the editorial team at Cambridge University Press – and so what is gathered here comprises all works referenced in the volume and a range of significant works beyond that category (with apologies to the many excellent works of criticism that we could not fit in). In gathering this material, we wish to acknowledge – and to direct readers to – the David Foster Wallace Research Group at Glasgow University, who scrupulously maintained a comprehensive bibliography of work on Wallace until late 2019.

There are, of course, limitations to the scope of this collection, and I hope that scholars will find new and provocative directions for their own research emerging from the essays here. Essays on film and television, on classics, on finance, on sport and on affect are all avenues of thought that I as editor – and, indeed, as a Wallace scholar – would wish to have included, but the space of a book is not infinite, even for Wallace. I hope, in keeping with Wallace's own avowedly infinity-directed, anti-teleological project, that this book marks an opening, rather than a closing, for the vibrant and vital scholarly and cultural discussions about Wallace that have developed over the past decades.

PART I

Contexts

CHAPTER I

David Foster Wallace and Narratology

Pia Masiero

As far as a broad notion of narratology is concerned, David Foster Wallace is typically mentioned in relation to two macro topics: his vexed relationship with postmodernism – explicitly disowned and formally relied upon – and his growing interest in the reader. One of the clearest articulations of this dual-faced objective comes from "The Salon Interview" (1996):

> The project that's worth trying is to do stuff that has some of the richness and challenge and emotional and intellectual difficulty of avant-garde literary stuff, stuff that makes the reader confront things rather than ignore them, but to do that in such a way that it's also pleasurable to read. The reader feels like someone is talking to him rather than striking a number of poses.[1]

I propose to consider the two topics – the legacy of postmodernism and the attention to the reader – as deeply imbricated: The experimental, ironic, self-referential ingredients typically associated with postmodernism, in fact, require some kind of weakening or tweaking to create room for the reader. Wallace's narratological choices are aimed at squaring this complex circle, by attending to the reader while employing the tools of the postmodernist trade, when needed, if needed.

The section devoted to Wallace's teaching materials in *The David Foster Wallace Reader* contains a list of narratological terms, such as Point of View, Narrative Omniscience, Unreliable Narrator and Voice that he wanted his students to define. In the same section, in the "Guidelines for Writing Helpful Letters of Response to Colleagues' Stories," Wallace suggests to his students a series of questions to guide their assessment of the work of their peers, such as "Is the story's point of view appropriate, and is it consistent?"; "Are the characters 3-D, human, complex, developed?"; "What [...] are the elements that have the strongest effect?"[2]

---

[1] L. Miller, "Interview," 61.   [2] Wallace, *DFWR*, 606, 620–21.

The list of terms and the fifteen questions attest to the fact that Wallace deemed these categories (and their effects) the blocks upon which aspiring writers had to build their narrative edifices in spite of their living in such nonclassical, postindustrial times. Acknowledging these classical ingredients as foundational does not imply that Wallace employs them classically. It implies that he was aware that they are a necessary point of departure for any writer.

As an aspiring writer himself, Wallace had to wrestle with the requirement to stick to narratological nuts and bolts, and he describes that early stage as a veritable "beating [his] head upon the wall" of the kind of structure required by his creative writing teachers – "straight, standard Updikean metaphor, Freytag's pyramid if you want."[3] Wallace's trajectory as a writer may well be described as a progressive liberation from this frustrating straitjacket into his own version of narratology. Even if fiction was for Wallace, at first, the springboard to play with "the four hundred thousand pages of continental philosophy and lit theory" in his mind[4] – most obviously with *The Broom of the System* – and to parody fellow writers by mimicking their styles – most notably with *Girl with Curious Hair* – he always had the reader in mind. Wallace enlisted himself among "those of us civilians" who "know in our gut that writing is an act of communication between one human being and another,"[5] "a living transaction between humans."[6]

The transaction is a *living* one, which is as much as to say that it is alive and not dead, dynamic and not static, dialogic and not monologic, in a relation of reciprocal negotiation and becoming, as the word "transaction" suggests. This dialogic dynamic is possible because the writer and the reader share the same postindustrially defined humanity: they "are stuck in here, in language [. . .] together," and they are both "marooned in [their] own skull" – that is, basically alone, and self-conscious.[7] These traits, coupled with Wallace's intellectualizing attitude, have triggered the rather typical reading of Wallace's prose as an instantiation of his cerebral disposition. And yet it could be argued that his passion for modal logic and mathematics represents his finding ways of living *only* in his head and that his decision to devote himself to fiction for good demonstrates the need for a rounder engagement with "what it is to be a fucking *human*

---

[3] See McCaffery, "Interview," 37, and Max, *Every Love Story*, 59–64.
[4] Lipsky, *Although of Course*, 35.   [5] Wallace, "Unibus," *SFT*, 144.
[6] McCaffery, "Interview," 41.   [7] Ibid., 22.

being" and for countering solipsism and loneliness with interaction.[8] But how?

There are ingredients that are typically associated with Wallace's prose: storylines that defy linearity; a consistent resistance to closure, which results in open-endedness and anti-teleology; the coexistence of multiple voices; perspectives that may be mutually deconstructive; the permeability of multiple narrative levels and the contextual employment of metafictional devices; the abundant reliance on materiality through an obsessive attention to descriptive details; the depiction of perceptual and existential instability; an all-encompassing interpretive ambiguity. Not all of them are unique to Wallace's fiction, and are variously connected with that experimentation with fictional structure that may be associated first with modernism and then with postmodernism. And yet, in Wallace's work, these established techniques stem from three distinctive factors: (1) the kind of realism he is interested in; (2) his need to communicate with the reader; (3) his profound faith in "experimental stuff."[9]

Wallace's narratology may thus be defined as porous and embodied, the latter as the necessary consequence of the former, the two mutually cross-fertilizing and informing every single ingredient we recognize as typically Wallacian. It is a porous narratology because it reflects the experience of postindustrial people who are transformed into battlefields of contending forces by information overload, a condition worsened and thus amplified by "the metastasis of self-conscious watching."[10] It is embodied, because, as the "twist" on the faces of the protagonists of Wallace's "Radically Condensed History of Postindustrial Life" makes perfectly clear, emotions happen and bear traces in the body – that is, we are in the world as bodies. His formal choices are the consequences of an attempt to capture "the cognitive texture" of postindustrial times – porous and embodied – in fictionally porous and embodied terms.[11] This amounts, as it will be clarified in the pages that follow, to the exploitation of a given formal device making the most of its affective dimension. It is an *attempt*, and, as the numerous examples of failed communication attest (most notably in *Brief Interviews with Hideous Men*), the effort does not guarantee any success.

Fiction is inhabited by human beings, and their stories can provide a way out of loneliness and marooning because they can be not only thought

---

[8] Ibid., 24. [9] Lipsky, *Although of Course*, 39. [10] Wallace, "Unibus," *SFT*, 34.
[11] Lipsky, *Although of Course*, 39.

about in our self-conscious skull but also inhabited imaginatively – that is, experientially. Wallace famously maintained,

> Fiction's purpose is to give the reader [. . .] imaginative access to other selves. Since an ineluctable part of being a human self is suffering, part of what we humans come to art for is an experience of suffering, necessarily a vicarious experience [. . .] if a piece of fiction can allow us imaginatively to identify with characters' pain, we might then also more easily conceive of others identifying with our own. That is nourishing, redemptive; we become less alone inside.[12]

Wallace's conception of the fruition of art seems an exemplary instantiation of the enactivist interpretation of cognition. Imaginative access (pertaining to the mental dimension) depends upon a vicarious experience of suffering (pertaining to the bodily dimension): enactivism promotes a vision of cognition that understands mind in a relational dynamic with (and not as separated from) sense perception and embodied action. According to an enactivist reading, "minds are embedded in the world" and should be thought of "as extensive embodied activities."[13]

For imaginative access to be redemptive, it has to bear on readers' lives; that is, it necessitates an experiential structure that allows recognition and attunement. Imaginative access is possible and, most importantly, is potentially a game changer when it is rooted in a bodily experience: It does not matter whether this experience is vicarious; it matters that the imagination is offered signposts to trigger embodied responses that allow a "bodily attunement."[14] Reading can shift the way readers perceive their here and now if their experience of reading goes beyond mere simulation and becomes enactment. This is possible if and when imagination is given textual places that readers may inhabit so as to undergo the emotion from within (the text and oneself). The redemptive thrust of the readers' imaginative access to other selves is what Wallace recognized in good art and – it is fair to assume – strived for in his own writing.

To touch on his readers' "nerve endings" and explore "what it feels like to live,"[15] Wallace activates his readers' experiential structure, building his storyworlds – realistically – on the postindustrial, porously mediated "world of and for appearance";[16] on embodied lives and selves that do not "feel like [sic] anything like a unified developed character in a linear narrative," [17] but are "very fragmented," inhabited by "a symphony of

---

[12] McCaffery, "Interview," 22.   [13] McKergow and Dierolf, "Enactivism," 45.
[14] Caracciolo, *The Experientiality*, 22.   [15] Lipsky, *Although of Course*, 36, 39.
[16] Wallace, "Unibus," *SFT*, 49.   [17] Lipsky, *Although of Course*, 39.

different voices, and voice-overs, and factoids, going on all the time and digressions on digressions on digressions."[18]

As a detailed narratological taxonomy of Wallace's choices goes beyond the scope of this contribution, the focus here will be on the narrating voice, as it may be considered as the blueprint for a host of other interrelated formal features. Wallace himself told David Lipsky that "the old tricks have been exploded, and I think the language needs to find new ways to pull the reader. And my personal belief is a lot of it has to do with voice."[19]

The novella "Westward the Course of Empire Takes Its Way," which closes Wallace's first short story collection, *Girl with Curious Hair*, is considered to be a turning point in his career, a moral (and literary) rite of passage that would open up the route for *Infinite Jest* and his mature phase. The novella is a rite of passage in terms of formal choices as well, pointing to a more stringently porous and embodied narrative disposition, away from the eminently reactive modes recognizable in *Broom* and *Girl*. Wallace himself admitted to McCaffery that the story ended up being "crude and naïve and pretentious," but he nonetheless stressed that "everything [he] wanted to do came out in the story."[20] It is easy to read the novella as gradually falling prey to its own parodying metafiction and turning upon itself, but traces of Wallace's attempt at finding ways of attending to the reader while using the tools of the postmodernist trade are unmistakably present.

The narrating instance is established straightaway with the opening sentence: "Though Drew-Lynn Eberhardt produced much, and Mark Nechtr did not, Mark was loved by us all in the East Cheasapeake Tradeschool Writing Program that first year, and D.L. was not."[21] A first-person narrator who presents himself as belonging to a "we" – "we in the writing program" – ushers us into the storyworld.[22] He retrospectively refers to "that first year," thus establishing the privileged knowledge that distance typically grants. The employment of the personal pronoun "you" is likewise evident, both in its impersonal usage – "she wasn't the sort of free spirit you could love"[23] – and in a more explicit address to the reader – "Professor Ambrose summed it up well [. . .]. You

[18] Paulson, "Interview," 132.   [19] Lipsky, *Although of Course*, 72.
[20] McCaffery, "Interview," 41.   [21] Wallace, "Westward," *GCH*, 233.   [22] Ibid., 234.
[23] The vestiges of this pair – the metafictional intrusions and the generic "you" – surface, for example, in the second part of section 15 of *IJ*: "This should not be rendered in exposition like this, but Mario Incandenza has [. . .]. Tennis's beauty's infinite roots are self-competitive, You compete with your own limits to transcend the self in imagination and execution" (82, 84).

don't want her facial reaction described."[24] The awareness of having an
audience, implicit in employing the nongeneric "you," does not belong
among the traits typically associated to first-person narrators. The obvious
exception concerns homodiegetic narrators who are writers – the example
of Nick Carraway in *The Great Gatsby* comes immediately to mind – and
this is clearly what we have here.

Macroscopically speaking, the novella is an explicit response to John
Barth's "Lost in the Funhouse": both stories are heavily metafictional and
revolve around the defamiliarization of the reading experience starting
from metalepsis, namely the breaking of narrative levels due to intrusions
by the narrator. But here lies the crucial difference: Barth's author intrudes
in a story that he is telling about others, whereas Wallace's author intrudes
in a story in which he is diegetically present (if nameless and essentially
invisible). The basic structure is the same, however, and the first-person
narrator is to be considered authorial in a very literal sense, as he authors
the story we are reading. This literalness overwrites porously the limited
privileges inherent in a first-person narrative situation and thus challenges
usual readerly expectations. Wallace is here creating a porous metafictional
setting that can be considered a formal instantiation of the necessity to
weaken experimental "stuff" so as to create a dialogic space for the reader to
inhabit. This space, however, is not an easy one to negotiate: the disrup-
tion of "the reader's encoded response[s]"[25] is part and parcel of Wallace's
need to take the transaction past "[her] cocoon of habituation."[26]

The deconstruction of the notion of narratological authoriality is up
front here and already concerns the dismantling of borders and their
potential cross-contamination, which goes a long way in explaining
Wallace's postindustrially realistic project. Wallace insists pervasively on
the mediated nature of the reality we live in: The inventing, and thus
mediating, mind is audible, but this mind comes through as present – that
is, embodied and not Olympically distant and disembodied.

The metaleptic porousness of narrative levels cannot be considered in
itself a novelty, since it was present in Barth's story too and is intrinsically
connected to any metafictional procedure, and yet the presence of a first-
person narrating instance endowed with authorial privileges creates a
rippling effect, which expands porousness to include the present and the
past, the here and the there, the inside and the outside. This expanded
notion of embodied porousness constitutes the key ingredient in Wallace's

---

[24] Wallace, "Westward," *GCH*, 234.   [25] Hayes-Brady, *Failures*, 52.
[26] McCaffery, "Interview," 29.

reinterpretation of classical narratology, which may take slightly different forms in this or that text, but maintains its experientially oriented core. An immediate collateral effect is the tendency to amplify perceptual instability. Formally speaking, this implies difficulties in discerning the source of information (problems of attribution) or the creation of a sort of echo effect because of free indirect discourse.[27] Footnotes, as well as open endings, point to a porous interpretation of forms too, as they attract our attention beyond the text and mimic the never-ending, daily transaction with meaningfulness that characterizes our embodied lives.

"Westward" therefore begins with a retrospective past tense. It then proceeds along the Barthian path – the account concerning the protagonists (and their pasts) and metafictional interruptions – until the time comes when the day of the scheduled Reunion "of everyone who has ever been in a McDonald's commercial" reaches central stage with J.D. Steelritter's waiting for the two final guests to arrive: "Jesus, Ocean City, in the past [. . .] Vs. Illinois, in the present, the here and now."[28] From here on, the two parallel threads are (mainly) in the present tense. This – again – sets "Westward" apart from Barth's handling of his metafictional piece, as in Wallace's text the main plotline is offered to the reader as a story to be shared in its progress, *both* in its being written (the authorial side of the *I*) and in its being experienced (the diegetic side of the *I*). The explicit spelling out of the time and place of the story as being "in the present, the here and now" activates a (so to speak) collateral effect of the porousness of narrative levels we are talking about, veritably crucial as far as readerly engagement is concerned. The representation of the events taking place in the novella, as presented by the narrator in his here and now, overlaps deictically speaking with the present tense, the here and now, of the reading moment. The deictics of the present are – to say the least – pervasive; here follow some examples *not* pertaining to metafictionally intrusive moments: "By the way, not too much of *this* is important. But it's true, and J.D. is *here* at the broad smeared C.I. Airport window"; "Sternberg is *now* officially sleep-deprived"; "It's undeniable that they

---

[27] This is not immediately the case here, but it can be easily detected in the many instances in which the dropping of graphical markers for direct speech creates a temporary indecision ("she says I do not care if you believe me or not, it is the truth, go on and believe what you want to. So it is for sure that she is lying. When it is the truth she will go crazy trying to get you to believe her. So I feel like I know" ["Everything Is Green," *Girl*, 229]), or in which a repetition produces a weird bouncing effect ("And so I did ask my husband, as we were driven in our complimentary limousine to join Ron and Charmian and maybe Lindsay for drinks and dinner across the river at NBC's expense, just what way he thought he and I really were, then, did he think" ["My Appearance," *Girl*, 201]).

[28] Wallace, "Westward," *GCH*, 235, 243–44.

don't even yet have transportation to the Funhouse, and that it's awfully slow going, *here*."[29] This pervasiveness creates a structural pattern that paves the way to reach beyond representation into experientiality. It can be argued that this pattern bespeaks Wallace's need to create textual pathways to communicate with the reader and invite him/her to move from consciousness attribution to consciousness enactment, namely from the stage of recognizing a certain real, emotional, conscious state and attributing it to a fictional character to the stage of "imaginatively '[trying] it on.'"[30] The lively transaction that Wallace strove for passes through the creation of textual traces that may be inhabited, and this starts from the most basic form of inhabiting the real world we know of – our bodily experience, which is always inherently rooted in the here and now of the present tense. Wallace may not be using this or that deictic consciously, but he senses like a rhabdomancer that single words themselves may do the trick of intersecting readers' lives, of fostering "the negotiating of the boundaries between self and other," and thus offer "a reprieve from the exhausted self-referentiality of contemporary subjectivity."[31]

Repeatedly returning to the deictic field of the here and now is one such strategy, which can be detected in many other texts, to be paired with the widespread employment of the personal address. The "you" that famously closes the novella – "You are loved" – is present all along. Metafictional intrusions cannot but be directed to the reader, but the distance between Barth's impersonal reader and this personalized one is enormous, because in "Westward," the personal address belongs *both* in the storyline – "By now Mark and D.L. were being seen together. Why? You can bet that question got asked" – *and* appears in the paragraphs that mimic Barth's famous asides: "OK true, that was all both too quick and too slow, for background – both intrusive and sketchy. But please, whether your imagination's engaged or not, please just acknowledge the propositions, is all."[32] In both textual situations – in the intrusions and in the storyline proper – Wallace's text indexes the "you" to the reader along porous lines, the ones along which Pop Quiz 9 of "Octet" is famously staged and the ones that baffle the reader in "Good Old Neon," where, in the folds of its Chinese box structure, the reader is addressed as if he/she were in the car with Neal on his way to commit suicide. These are, possibly, the two most obvious examples, but the presence of this "you" pops up everywhere, even in Wallace's footnotes.

---

[29] Ibid., 245, 253, 263 (emphasis added).　　[30] Caracciolo, *The Experientiality*, 49.
[31] Hayes-Brady, *Failures*, 55.　　[32] Wallace, "Westward," 237–38.

We can detect this same porousness in Wallace's handling of narratorial omniscience as well. *Infinite Jest* presents a rethinking of this category, subtly inviting an emotional alignment beyond its complex fractal structure, thanks to a mitigation of the omniscient narrator's privilege. The porous version of omniscience that Wallace needs is deftly prepared, as the first clear sign of omniscience comes at page 32 (chapter 4, section 8 if we consider Greg Carlisle's proposal[33]) when we stumble upon a gnomic present – that is, a statement claiming general validity. Sections 1–7 present an array of narrative situations: Wallace's masterpiece famously begins with a scene in which we are told what happens to Hal in his own voice in the present tense. Nothing could be (narratologically) more distant from omniscience, as the focus, in this first scene, is on the instant rendering of Hal's consciousness without any distancing perspective. In the following section, Wallace resorts to an internally focalized narration: Ken Erdedy is waiting and waiting for "the woman who said she'd come"[34] with the fifth of a kilo of marijuana, which should end his addiction for good. His sense of entrapment is formally amplified by the absolute restriction to his internal experiencing perspective, conveyed by the association of the past tense with deictics pertaining to the presentness of his waiting – here, now, this – which bespeak an opacity to any projection of future self. The third person, inherent in internally focalized narrations, however, introduces the presence of an external narrating instance, which is obviously absent from the first section. Our attention is not alerted to the authorial narrator's presence because it is limited to contextualizing glosses and because the descriptions are colored with Erdedy's idiolect, a clear example of linguistic porousness. We must go through another section, which quotes a dialogue in its entirety as if it were recorded (sounds included), to arrive at page 32 and encounter the narrator's presence in all his authorial capacity. At this point, the narrative situation is established: a polyphonic storyworld in which the authorial narrator may decide to disappear to make room for the individual subjectivities of characters whose existential and linguistic specificities deserve full-fledged status. More relevant, experientially speaking, is that the gradual display of the narrator's cognitive privileges introduces a peculiar way to be omniscient. This peculiarity is fully manifested in the following passage:

> Here's Hal Incandenza, age seventeen, with his little brass one-hitter, getting covertly high in Enfield Tennis Academy's underground Pump

---

[33] Carlisle, *Elegant Complexity*, 39.   [34] Wallace, *IJ*, 17.

Room and exhaling palely into an industrial exhaust fan. It's the sad little interval after afternoon matches and conditioning but before the Academy's communal supper. Hal is by himself down here and nobody knows where he is or what he's doing.[35]

The narrating voice handles this presentation porously: he *both* confirms his privilege by providing information not shared by others, and he seems to align himself with Hal's perceptual and emotional take through a reference to Hal's deictic field. As with the narrator in "Westward," the deictic field here activated provides an existential positioning – "down here" – that allows the reader to inhabit imaginatively Hal's consciousness from within.

The strategy – once again – is that of deconstructing a formal device and reconfiguring it along porous and embodied lines, which both allow and invite a potential emotional sharing: an omniscient-like kind of authority is needed to control the overabundant narrative material of which the novel is made, and to confer on it all, but this authority is rehumanized along embodied lines and thus – again – rendered experientially recognizable. The zooming in and zooming out of the lives and thoughts and feelings of many characters, both from their own limited perspectives and from a broader more knowledgeable perspective, constitutes the formal macroscopic skeleton of Wallace's masterpiece.

There are many situations of this kind in Wallace's fictional universe, many of them following the same pattern: offering access to a character's specific perceptual positioning and providing a key to rethinking otherness as depending on a specific emotional and existential configuration. This is part and parcel of what Stephen Burn defines as "a refined concentration upon characters."[36] The juxtaposition of voices that present, dialogically, each character's unique perspective in the first person (the case of "Here and There" is paradigmatic), or, conversely, the coexistence of two characters whose dialogue is orchestrated by an authorial narrator but whose peculiar take on the world is conveyed through their own respective mental idiolects (the Marathe and Steeply sections in *Infinite Jest* are the most obvious examples), or the presentation of two interlaced limited perspectives (as in the story "Think"[37]) go in the same porous and embodied direction. Porous and embodied paths cut across narrative levels and activate and manifest *both* the readers' and the author's engagement with characters.

---

[35] Ibid., 49.   [36] Burn, *Reader's Guide*, 12.   [37] See Masiero, "The Case of 'Think.'"

These are just some representative examples of the porousness of certain (formal) borders – the direction that Wallace tried to give to his ambitious fictional project. Whether his need to communicate with the reader and provide a textual space of encounter succeeded or not remains open to debate. This too is experientially determined and has to be felt at each reader's nerve endings.

CHAPTER 2

A Meeting of Minds
David Foster Wallace, Vladimir Nabokov and the Ethics of Empathy

Marshall Boswell

A uniquely competitive and combative writer, David Foster Wallace, from the beginning of his career, was vocal and unrestrained in announcing his desire to unseat his predecessors. As early as 1993, he infamously declared, "If I have a real enemy, a patriarch for my patricide, it's probably Barth and Coover and Burroughs, even Nabokov and Pynchon."[1] In that same interview, however, he singles out both Robert Coover and, significantly for this essay, Vladimir Nabokov as "real geniuses, the writers who weathered real shock and invented this stuff in contemporary fiction."[2] The "stuff" to which he refers here is metafiction, broadly speaking, which Wallace's fiction both employs and repurposes. In granting Nabokov the status of "inventor" of one of the key animating features of his own fiction, Wallace invites us to examine the various ways in which Nabokov's art overlaps with and departs from his own. This essay addresses that inter-textual and aesthetic overlap, an artistic affinity that, with the notable exception of Tore Rye Andersen's 2014 essay, has largely gone unnoticed by Wallace scholars. Although Wallace insistently equated traditional metafiction with solipsistic self-obsession, he nevertheless employed meta-fictional devices throughout his fiction. As with Nabokov, his various self-reflexive strategies seek to lead his readers *out of* their solipsistic cages and establish an empathetic relationship with the author's own consciousness. More importantly, Wallace achieves this paradoxical agenda by embracing many of Nabokov's own strategies. Much has already been written on the importance of empathy in Wallace's work, and this essay seeks to take nothing away from that important aspect of Wallace scholarship. The parallels with Nabokov's work do, however, clarify how Wallace imagined "empathy" to manifest in the reading process and how that experience might be squared with his work's hyper-self-consciousness.

[1] McCaffery, "Interview," 48.   [2] Ibid., 30.

Brian Boyd's pioneering work on Nabokov argues that our need to close read Nabokov's novelistic puzzle pieces models how Nabokov felt we should pay attention to the natural world and all its rich patterning. The amount of focus and close attention to detail required to "solve" the riddles embedded in his texts place at the forefront of his concerns what he regarded as "the marvel of consciousness," which he once rapturously described as "that sudden window swinging open on a sunlit landscape amidst the night of non-being."[3] Nabokov's own term for the state of alertness that his works inspire is "aesthetic bliss," which, as he puts it in his afterword to *Lolita*, "is a sense of being somehow, somewhere, connected with other states of being where art (curiosity, tenderness, kindness, ecstasy) is the norm."[4] For Nabokov, the intense curiosity engendered by the puzzles and anagrams and self-reflective mirrors in his novels also inspires "tenderness" and "kindness," emotions that are by definition other-directed – in this case, toward the world, toward creaturely reality and, by extension, other humans. The encompassing emotion for this heightened state of "aesthetic bliss" is "ecstasy," which, without discounting its sexual overtones, literally refers to a spiritual escape from the body ("ex stasis").

In rendering "the relationship between reader and text an image and an enactment of the tussle between the individual mind and the world," as Boyd puts it, Nabokov employs metafiction to create another layer of "ex stasis" that involves the transcendent interaction between author and reader.[5] Nabokov conceived of this interaction as similar to the relationship between the composer of a chess problem and its solver. As he famously explains in *Speak Memory*, "Competition in chess problems is not really between White and Black but between the composer and the hypothetical solver (just as in a first-rate work of fiction the real clash is not between the characters but between the author and the world)."[6] That final term in the quotation he later amended to "reader," since, as he explained, his original formulation was meaningless given that "a creative artist makes his own world."[7] In short, the world of a Nabokov novel is a playing field, one designed to plunge the reader into a competitive one-to-one relationship with the invisible but invoked author, whose elaborate puzzles spur the reader to a state of curiosity and tenderness, kindness and ecstasy.

---

[3] Boyd, *Vladimir Nabokov: The Russian Years*, 11.   [4] Nabokov, *Annotated Lolita*, 314–15.
[5] Boyd, *Nabokov's Ada*, 43.   [6] Nabokov, *Speak, Memory*, 290.
[7] Nabokov, *Strong Opinions*, 183.

Close readers of Wallace's work and his various directives about the purpose of fiction and art will hear many echoes, and some key divergences, in this thumbnail account of Nabokov's aesthetic model. In "Pay Attention! David Foster Wallace and his Real Enemies," Tore Rye Andersen touches upon one such echo, namely Wallace's late focus on attention and boredom, as articulated in *This Is Water* and *The Pale King*. Drawing primarily upon Richard Rorty's reading of *Lolita* in *Contingency, Irony, and Solidarity*, Andersen, like Rorty, focuses on a stray moment in Nabokov's text wherein Humbert Humbert, bored by a voluble barber, fails to notice that the son the barber brags about "had been dead for the last thirty years."[8] Rorty argues that this failure of attention "epitomizes Humbert's lack of curiosity – his inattentiveness to anything irrelevant to his own obsession," which failure Rorty goes on to argue invokes the novel's "moral," that is, "not to keep one's hands off little girls but to notice what one is doing, and in particular to notice what people are saying."[9] Andersen goes on to provide a convincing catalog of places in Wallace's *oeuvre* that fulfill what he articulated as one of *The Pale King*'s "2 Broad Arcs," namely "Paying attention, boredom, ADD, Machines vs people at performing mindless jobs."[10] But the affinities are deeper even than the one Andersen has helpfully teased out, as they touch also upon Wallace's abiding interest in human consciousness, metafiction, puzzles, reading and even ghosts. Perhaps just as importantly, the places where Wallace diverges from Nabokov, namely in his focus on solipsism, narcissism and encagement, also help illuminate the concrete particulars of his art.

Wallace set up the terms of his conflict with metafiction in his 1989 novella, "Westward the Course of Empire Takes Its Way," where his narrator declares that "metafiction is untrue, as a lover. It cannot betray. It can only reveal. Itself is its only object. It's the act of a lonely solipsist's self love."[11] In this formulation, the lovers are author and reader. But buried here is Wallace's admission that some sort of "betrayal" sits at the center of this author/reader relationship. What's more, the passage cited earlier appears in the context of the narrator speculating about the kind of art that the story's apprentice writer, Mark Nechtr, will one day compose, which Nechtr imagines as "something that stabs you in the heart."[12] That projected work of art will "*use* metafiction as a bright smiling disguise, a

[8] Nabokov, *Annotated Lolita*, 213; quoted in Andersen, "Pay Attention!," 21.
[9] Rorty, *Contingency*, 163–64; quoted in Andersen, "Pay Attention!," 21.   [10] Wallace, *TPK*, 545.
[11] Wallace, "Westward," *GCH*, 332.   [12] Ibid.

harmless floppy-shooed costume, because metafiction is safe to read, familiar as syndication, and no victim is as delicious as the one who smiles in relief at your familiar approach."[13] As such, Wallace's art is not itself metafiction; rather, it employs the tropes and strategies of metafiction to advance an agenda that is directed at the reader, an agenda that "stabs" the reader's heart.

For both Wallace and Nabokov, metafiction encompasses a wide range of narrative devices that all serve, as Wallace himself puts it, "to antagonize the reader's sense that what she's experiencing as she reads is mediated through a human consciousness, one with an agenda not necessarily coincident with her own," a component that, for Wallace anyway, distinguishes "art-fiction," from "'low' or commercial art."[14] Both authors affirm this antagonistic relationship as essential in establishing a dynamic relationship with the author. Alfred Appel, Jr., in his introduction to *The Annotated Lolita*, identifies seven recurring devices in Nabokov's art that affirm the work's total and self-proclaimed artifice: parody, coincidence, patterning, allusion, the work-within-the-work, staging and authorial voice, the latter of which Nabokov calls "an anthropomorphic deity impersonated by me."[15] Wallace's work, and *Infinite Jest* most significantly, employs almost all of the aforementioned devices. We note first the numerous film, television and pop culture parodies running through Wallace's signature work, many of which are described at great length, such as Incandenza's nun/biker/revenge drama, *Blood Sister: One Tough Nun*, along with literally dozens of others listed in the novel's exhaustive and minutely designed "filmography." Both *Infinite Jest* and the unfinished *The Pale King* teem with allusions to previous texts, both philosophical and literary, a dense web of intertextual markers that includes works by Søren Kierkegaard, William James, James Joyce, T. S. Eliot, Thomas Pynchon, Fyodor Dostoevsky and dozens of others. The title of Wallace's posthumous novel is itself likely an allusion to Nabokov's own *Pale Fire*, while, as I argue in *Understanding David Foster Wallace*, extended sections of *The Broom of the System* involving the character Rick Vigorous deliberately parody and allude to Nabokov's *Lolita*.[16] *Infinite Jest*, of course, gets its title from the film of the same name, the novel's primary "work-within-the-work," both of which allude to Shakespeare's *Hamlet*. And although Wallace's work de-emphasizes "patterning" in the Nabokovian sense, his novels and short stories amplify such paratextual device as endnotes,

[13] Ibid., 333, emphasis added.   [14] McCaffery, "Interview," 34.
[15] Nabokov, *Annotated Lolita*, xxvi–xxiii.   [16] See Boswell, *Understanding*, 25.

footnotes and scholarly bibliographies, all of which find analogs in Nabokov's playful use of a disingenuous Index in *Ada* and *Pale Fire*'s line-by-line "scholarly" exegesis of its title poem. All these devices, in Wallace's words, "prohibit the reader from forgetting that she's receiving heavily mediated data, that this process is a relationship between the writer's consciousness and her own, and that in order for it to be anything like a real full human relationship, she's going to have to put in her share of the linguistic work."[17]

Both authors make that "real full human relationship" between "the writer's consciousness" and the reader's even more explicit by their spectral appearances within the work itself. Of Nabokov's "staging" strategies, Appel explains, "Nabokov the protean impersonator is always a masked presence in his fiction: as impresario, scenarist, director, warden, dictator, landlord, and even bit player."[18] Just to cite one example of Nabokov's "masked presence," in *Lolita*, Humbert Humbert loses Lolita to a playwright named Clare Quilty, who pursues the two of them like a spectral vigilante throughout the novel's second half. Quilty's co-playwright is named Vivian Darkbloom, whose name is an anagram for Vladimir Nabokov. She also penned a biography of Quilty titled *My Cue*.[19] As such, each appearance of Quilty is Nabokov's "cue" to step on stage.

Wallace, too, makes protean appearances in both of his major novels, as well as in a late short story, ghostly presences that further link his work to Nabokov's. In *Infinite Jest*, Wallace's "Darkbloom" is James Incandenza, the filmmaker and creator of the lethal film *Infinite Jest*, who is referred to throughout that the text as the auteur. Incandenza makes a late posthumous appearance in the text as a "wraith," where he tells the novel's wounded hero, Don Gately,

> A wraith had no out-loud voice of its own, and had to use somebody's like internal brain-voice if it wanted to try to communicate something, which was why thoughts and insights that were coming from some wraith always just sounded like your thoughts, from inside your own head, if a wraith's trying to interface with you.[20]

The wraith's explanation deftly describes the process of reading a text, in which case the wraith stands in for the "writer's consciousness" entering into a "full human" act of communication with the reader. As I and other scholars have suggested, Incandenza's wraith might mark Wallace's

---

[17] McCaffery, "Interview," 34.   [18] Nabokov, *Annotated Lolita*, xxx.   [19] Ibid., 4.
[20] Wallace, *IJ*, 831.

engagement with Roland Barthes' "Death of the Author" theory, which gets revived here such that the "dead" author lives inside the book as a ghost.[21] It is also possible to argue that Incandenza's ghost is a controlling presence throughout the entire text, the ghost in the machine and the narrative voice behind the narrative voice. After all, the second paragraph of Wallace's gargantuan novel consists of one simple sentence: "I am in here."[22] Significantly, Nabokov's penultimate novel, *Transparent Things*, is also narrated by the ghost of a character who appears briefly in this already brief novel, a fact that John Updike, in his 1972 review of the novel, missed entirely.[23]

Wallace makes an even more overt appearance in *The Pale King*, via the series of "Author Here" chapters voiced by "the real author, the living human holding the pencil, not some abstract narrative persona."[24] That "living human" takes a job at the IRS during a forced suspension from Amherst College, Wallace's alma mater, where he was caught forging papers for money, a "service" Wallace also assigned to *The Broom of the System*'s "Antichrist," a Wallace-esque Amherst student and older brother of the novel's heroine, Lenore Beadsman. "David Wallace"'s suspension, though a fiction, has its real-life analog in Wallace's 1983 withdrawal from Amherst due to depression.[25] Wallace makes one additional, and significant, appearance in his celebrated late story, "Good Old Neon," where the ghost of the story's dead narrator – another authorial wraith – imagines how he might have appeared in the imagination of a one "David Wallace" who, since their shared high school years, had "emerged from years of literally indescribable war against himself with a bit more firepower than he'd had at Aurora West."[26]

These spectral presences, in both Nabokov and Wallace, place the reader in direct dialogue with the writer's consciousness. Similarly, the works' arsenal of metafictional devices deny the reader full immersion into the imagined world of the text and hence call heightened attention to the text's artifice, to the world outside the fiction, where the reader, like the comatose Don Gately, supine and immobile, becomes uniquely aware of herself as a reader whose consciousness has been temporarily "handed" over to another, her own "brain voice" now commandeered by an authorial wraith. Since Wallace wants his work to "stab [the reader] in the

---

[21] See, for instance, Boswell, *Understanding*, 96–97. [22] Wallace, *IJ*, 3.

[23] Updike opens the review thus: "Confession: I have never understood how they saw the woman in half. Any willful child can dumbfound me with card tricks learned from the back of a comic book. And I do not understand Vladimir Nabokov's new novel." See Updike, *Picked-Up Pieces*, 211.

[24] Wallace, *TPK*, 66. [25] Max, *Every Love Story*, 33. [26] Wallace, "Neon," *OB*, 181.

heart," as quoted earlier, he thus envisions his reader as a "victim" and his strategy as "like a betrayal. Like pulling out of what's supposed to let you inside."[27] The "betrayal" is grounded on the work's offer of empathy. As he acknowledged to Larry McCaffery, in setting up this reading process, Wallace is "at once allowing the reader to sort of escape self by achieving some sort of identification with another human psyche – the writer's, or some character's, etc – and [. . .] *also* trying to antagonize the reader's intuition that she is a self, that she is alone and going to die alone."[28]

As sketched out briefly at the beginning of this essay, in Nabokov, the purpose of these metafictional moves is to expand the reader's consciousness. Boyd describes the process via a dialectic of "resistance" and "solution." "Resistance" encompasses all the various ways Nabokov's text halt the reader's forward movement and immediate comprehension, including allusions, riddles, anagrams and obscure cross-references. All these features puncture the reader's immersion in the text and force a reckoning with the author, whose artistic decisions come under close scrutiny. This pattern of resistance compels the reader to solve the various puzzles, which Boyd likens to the ecstatic process of discovery experienced by close observers of the natural world, such as lepidopterists like Nabokov himself. "Nabokov's hiding things for the reader to find," Boyd argues, "is not the idle amusement of someone with nothing to say"; rather, it is Nabokov's way of "determining that his works will be apprehended in the same way he apprehends the world," which involved an insatiable craving for "the excitement of discovering what remains unknown just behind the apparent – and what remains behind *that*, and so on."[29] At the same time that Nabokov compels his readers to press against the limits of their consciousness, he "is also fascinated by the possibility of there being something beyond these limits, something outside human time and the blindness of human self-interest."[30] The undercurrent of cross-reference and allusions in a Nabokov text, which the reader must tease out in a confrontation with the author that replicates the relationship between chess-problem composer and its solver, allegorizes those moments when, as Boyd posits, we "may seem to feel, at rare peaks of consciousness, a strange promise of significance behind the visible world, an intimation of transcendental sense pressing through the fabric of space and time."[31]

Wallace's text practices a similar form of resistance, which he characterizes as "cruelty." As his narrator explains in "Westward," the reader of

[27] Wallace, "Westward," *GCH*, 334.   [28] McCaffery, "Interview," 32.
[29] Boyd, *Nabokov's Ada*, 43.   [30] Ibid., 45.   [31] Ibid.

his texts "tries to traverse: there is the motion of travel, except no travel [. . .] There'd be the illusion [sic] of both the dreamer's unmoving sprint and the disco-moonwalker's backward glide"; the narrator acknowledges that it "would take an architect who could hate enough to love enough to perpetrate the kind of special cruelty only lovers can inflict."[32] We see this "cruelty" in the arduous demands that *Infinite Jest* makes on its readers, and in its own dense pattern of allusions, cross-references and unresolved mysteries. The disco-moonwalker's backward glide provides a vivid metaphor for the novel's forward-backward crosscut plot, and the back-and-forth process of navigating the body text and the endnotes. Boyd notes that Nabokov stocks his narratives "with the disruptive, the digressive, the fantastic and the unnecessary while imparting to it a rapid motion that provides the illusion of a harmonious whole," a formulation that also applies to Wallace's major texts.[33] Works such as this cannot be comprehended in one reading, a fact that both Nabokov and Wallace not only accepted but also affirmed. Amy Hungerford, in her argument against reading *Infinite Jest*, cites as one compelling reason Wallace's "arrogance" in believing, as he explained to his frustrated editor Michael Pietsch, that "it was OK to make a reader read the book twice."[34] But "arrogance" isn't the whole story by any means. As with Nabokov, the purpose behind these disruptive strategies is to compel the reader to acknowledge the reading process as it is happening, and, ultimately, to elevate to primary importance not her immersion in the text but rather her interaction with the writer's consciousness. In this regard, rereading the text becomes not only a necessary part of its design but also a measure of its generosity, owing to the surfeit of hidden clues and problem-solving pleasures the author has planted there for readers to experience.

Although Wallace has been generally read as a posthumanist – or, in Paul Giles's term, a "sentimental posthumanist"[35] – with a decidedly materialist conception of human existence more generally and of human consciousness specifically, that reading fails to acknowledge what Jamie Redgate has recently shown to be a surprisingly Cartesian conception of the self, which includes not only the possibility of a soul but also, as already noted here, ghosts and the prospect of an afterlife. Citing Wallace's famous dictum that "fiction's about what it is to be a fucking *human being*," Redgate goes on to demonstrate that Wallace conceived of that "human

---

[32] Wallace, "Westward," *GCH*, 332.   [33] Boyd, *Nabokov's Ada*, 17.
[34] Max, *Every Love Story*, 199; quoted in Hungerford, *Making Literature Now*, 157.
[35] Giles, "Sentimental," 329–30.

being" as possessing a nonmaterial self, and possibly even a soul (see Chapter 19), citing Wallace's ghosts as the clearest metaphor for this conception of a transcendent self. He pays particular attention to a scene midway through *Infinite Jest*, in which a character named Lucien is murdered by the wheelchair assassins, after which "he finally sheds his body's suit" and is "free, catapulted home over fans and the Convexity's glass palisades at desperate speeds."[36] Similarly, Incandenza's wraith, now freed of its own bodysuit, can "whiz around at the invisible speed of quanta," while "Good Old Neon"'s ghost explains that "the internal head-speed or whatever of these ideas, memories, realizations, emotions and so on is even faster [. . .] when you're dying."[37] The point is clear: once freed of its body, the spirit is free, and operates outside of human time.

This last aspect of Wallace's art crystallizes where he differs from Nabokov. Whereas Nabokov's frustration with consciousness rests on its limitations, Wallace's frustration lies with its horrible isolation in a human body. Whether or not Wallace actually believed in ghosts is immaterial here. Ghosts convey his abiding desire to help his readers *escape from their heads*. If consciousness for Nabokov is a "marvel," for Wallace, as he declares in "The Suffering Channel," it is "nature's nightmare."[38] "Freedom from one's head" is in fact one of the major themes of James Incandenza's entire body of work, "self-forgetting as the Grail."[39] Whereas Nabokov wants us to realize how much of the concrete world we don't, but with effort could, comprehend, Wallace foregrounds consciousness and the arduous act of reading in order to help us escape our heads and, possibly, imagine consciousnesses other than our own. In short, Wallace's agenda, as many other scholars have already affirmed, is grounded in a terror of solipsism and a hope for increased empathy. Although he "betrays" his reader into this encounter with the invisible author, the payoff is this otherwise impossible-to-achieve encounter with another person's consciousness.

Wallace scholars have justifiably made much of his famous declaration that "a big part of serious fiction's purpose is to give the reader, who, like all of us is sort of marooned in her own skull, to give her imaginative access to other selves," a process he calls "nourishing, redemptive"; yet in the same breath, he reminds us that "true empathy's impossible."[40] As such, the empathy a reader might feel while reading his work is not only an illusion but also fleeting. Most importantly, the text's insistent self-

---

[36] Wallace, *IJ*, 488–89.   [37] Ibid., 831; Wallace, "Neon," *OB*, 150.
[38] Wallace, "Suffering," *OB*, 282.   [39] Wallace, *IJ*, 742.   [40] McCaffery, "Interview," 20–21.

reflexivity always calls the reader back to herself, which is not a bug but a feature. Ultimately, as with Nabokov, the other "self" to which the reading process gives the reader access is the *writer's*. As he explained to Laura Miller, following the publication of *Infinite Jest*,

> In fiction I think we can leap over that wall [of self] in a certain way. But that's just the first level, because the idea of mental or emotional intimacy with a character is a delusion or a contrivance that's set up through art by the writer. There's another level that a piece of fiction is a conversation. There's a relationship between the reader and the writer that's very strange and very complicated and hard to talk about [. . . .] There's a kind of Ah-ha! Somebody at least for a moment feels about something or sees something the way I do.[41]

That "somebody" isn't the character who might have had an emotion you share but the writer who described it in a way that resonates. Hence it is not entirely accurate, or at least an incomplete formulation, to assume that, in reading Wallace's work, one can have that nourishing and redemptive experience described by Nabokov as feeling "empathy" for his broken characters. That experience in reading Wallace is a mere metaphor for the primary meeting of minds that occurs between the reader and the writer's consciousness, a synergy that, as in Nabokov, happens when we are not immersed in the imagined world of the novel but rather contesting with the magician who conjured that world, the ghost of its machine. Reading Wallace is tantamount to teasing out and locating these ghostly traces, which reveal themselves only after repeated readings, and which, taken altogether, constitute his most direct communication with the reader, the message's true medium.

Introducing Nabokov as a model for Wallace's art, rather than as a "patriarch for his patricide," illuminates how we might square Wallace's paradoxical desire to write a fiction that enhances empathy while insisting on its artifice and mediation. The two agendas are ultimately one. As with Nabokov, Wallace's metafictional devices will always shatter whatever fleeting empathy a reader might feel for a character. Yet that punctured illusion discloses an even more important, supplemental and transcendent dialogue that occurs between that reader and the writer's authorial consciousness.

---

[41] L. Miller, "Interview," 62.

CHAPTER 3

Writing in a Material World
David Foster Wallace and 1980s Fiction

Ralph Clare

There are a number of ways to consider Wallace's relationship to 1980s American literature. Wallace began writing and publishing in the 1980s, and his major works of the decade – the novel *The Broom of the System* (1987) and story collection *Girl with Curious Hair* (1989) – make aesthetic statements that set them apart from the literary trends of the time. Marshall Boswell thus weighs Wallace's apprentice works against other critically acclaimed works of the period, teasing out their various influences, homages and parodies.[1] While such comparative criticism is fruitful, however, it neglects considering some significant forces at work in shaping the production and reception of 1980s literature. To this end, Kasia Boddy reads Wallace's early work in light of what Mark McGurl has dubbed the "Program Era" a period in which, by the 1980s, institutionalized creative-writing programs came to shape writers in particular ways. Boddy thus examines the stories in *Girl With Curious Hair* as creative-writing work-shopped pieces, since Wallace wrote them as a student in the University of Arizona's MFA program, which he attended from 1985–87.[2] Furthermore, in McGurl's view, Wallace is the quintessential program writer, whose reliance on institutions in life is mirrored thematically in his work.[3] The story of Wallace's relationship with 1980s fiction, then, is not exclusively aesthetic or "literary" and is certainly not that of the isolated genius furiously writing himself to inevitable success. Wallace's engagement with 1980s fiction is instead the story of a young writer attempting to navigate several institutional networks and relationships, and making writerly, career-oriented and personal life decisions within the institutional horizons of the time.

This essay therefore treats Wallace as an author working with and against certain institutions during the 1980s to show how, early on in

---

[1] Boswell, *Understanding*, 13–67.   [2] Boddy, "A Fiction of Response."
[3] McGurl, "Institution."

his career, they helped shape his understanding of literature, literary history, and his place within it. Pierre Bourdieu has conceived of what he calls "the field of cultural production" as "a field of position-takings" that agents continually take and retake within a structure that creates the positions to begin with."[4] This field has a "specific economy" in which agents and institutions – through the play of cultural, symbolic and/or actual capital – constantly struggle to legitimize or authorize what counts as, or is the value of, say, literature.[5] Indeed, Wallace was well aware of the lay of the literary field, carefully positioning himself in it throughout his career, often announcing his aesthetic and ethical principles in essays and interviews.[6] Nowhere is this truer than in Wallace's direct competition with one of his earliest and most pressing literary rivals of the 1980s: the diverse array of successful young writers branded as the Brat Pack. Early in his career, as we shall see, Wallace loosely associated himself with academia, publishing key works in semi-scholarly venues and storing up cultural capital, whereas writers such as Brett Easton Ellis, Jay McInerney, Tama Janowitz and others were swept up and packaged by an unprecedented literary marketing machine, with varying results. During the 1980s then, Wallace can be seen as preparing a space for his work to be accepted (with no guarantee that it would) beyond its eventual readerly and hyped popularity. The results of Wallace's efforts would become clear by the 1990s: While much of the Brat Pack's fortunes and fame declined as its hipness wore off, Wallace was able to survive his own subsequent ascendance as a literary phenomenon, thanks, in part, to the wider network he had created for the reception of his work. Instead of aspiring toward and embracing the literary celebrity so visible in the 1980s, Wallace would, in keeping with his work's themes, eschew the lure of media and its promises of fame, and aim toward creating the heady, lasting stuff of literature itself.

Youth and Brat Pack-aging in the 1980s

Wallace was clear about his feelings on the state of American literature in the 1980s, lambasting just about all of it in "Fictional Futures and the Conspicuously Young," a 1988 essay originally published in *The Review of Contemporary Fiction*. In the essay, Wallace complains of "a certain numbing *sameness* about much contemporary young writing,"[7] which he ruthlessly divides into three groups: "Neiman-Marcus Nihilism," "Catatonic

---

[4] Bourdieu, *Cultural Production*, 30.   [5] Ibid., 35.
[6] See Konstantinou, "Wallace's 'Bad' Influence."   [7] Wallace, "Fictional Futures," *BFN*.

Realism, a.k.a. Ultraminamalism, a.k.a. Bad Carver" and the "Workshop Hermeticism" of creative-writing programs.[8] According to Wallace, most of this straightforward, mimetic fiction suffers from "anti-intellectualism" and a willful ignorance of the postwar "loss of innocence about the language that is its breath and bread."[9] Further, Wallace is highly critical of the manic marketing of young writers, condemning the "shameless hype" in which "writers' proximity to their own puberties seemed now an asset."[10] Wallace specifically calls out the packaging of the Brat Pack, even describing the cover of a 1987 *Village Voice* that satirizes the group. Lastly, Wallace claims that although "1987's America is not a nice place to be," it is "*imperative* that art *not* be nihilistic" by simply reproducing or capturing the despair of the times.[11] Fiction had to respond to this state of affairs.

"Fictional Futures" also condemned literary minimalism itself, the *genre de l'age*. Indeed, Wallace's own work recalled the out-of-fashion postmodernist literature of the prior two decades. Thus, for all the essay's present-tenseness and hand-writing-wringing about the future, Wallace pointedly returns to the postmodern past to counter minimalism's naïve view of representational language.[12] Yet Wallace, believing even postmodernism was at a dead end, announces his frustration with postmodern metafiction via Mark Nechtr, the main writer-character in *GCH*'s novella "Westward the Course of Empire Takes its Way." The story critiques John Barth's kind of metafiction, and expresses Mark's desire to write fiction that moves beyond it: "Maybe it's called metalife. Or metafiction. Or realism. Or gfhrytytu. He doesn't know."[13] How Nechtr will make his "mark" (his name) is essentially Wallace's chief concern too.

That "Fictional Futures" remarks upon the "assets" and "futures" of well-marketed young writers in a decade in which, as Wallace notes via Oliver Stone's *Wall Street* (1987), "Greed is good," implies that Wallace detected, like Bourdieu, the cultural economics at work in the literary marketplace. In this sense, "Fictional Futures" reads something like a series of stock tips or market predictions and urges a remarkable long-term view of literary investment, which perhaps did not interest the brokers – editors and publishers – of the high-flying 1980s. After all, author stocks were surging, and the industry was benefiting. For Wallace, however, aesthetics, the market and youth culture were mixing in troubling and unsustainable ways. In short, Wallace's work didn't jibe well with the 1980s. The

[8] Ibid., 39–40.   [9] Ibid., 63, 65.   [10] Ibid., 37, 39.   [11] Ibid., 67.   [12] Ibid., 63–65.
[13] Wallace, "Westward," *GCH*, 333.

celebrity and marketing of the Brat Pack disturbed Wallace, who worried that commercial hype disguised a lack of depth, sacrificed the lasting and later for the here and now.

Wallace's broad market predictions on 1980s writers' stocks or styles proved fairly accurate, particularly if we consider success beyond that of bestsellers and instant fame but instead as sustained readerly, critical and eventually academic acceptance. The fortunes of the "core" Brat Pack members – Ellis, McInerney and Janowitz – the hottest lit-product there was at the time, best demonstrate the 1980s boom-and-bust cycle of literary reception that might serve as an allegory of the 1980s economy itself, characterized by its leveraged buyouts, corporate raiders, and short-term bull market thinking – all punctuated with the market crash of 1987. The Brat Pack itself – a loose collection of aesthetically divergent writers working with different publishers, none of whom claimed the mantle – was a disparaging term originally used to describe a bunch of young Hollywood actors.[14] Yet the literary Brat Pack would become a brand, part of an unstoppable marketing machine in keeping with the times.[15]

Today, the Brat Pack's moment appears limited chiefly to the latter half of the 1980s. Jay McInerney, having published the mildly innovative second-person minimalism of *Bright Lights, Big City* (1984), would, after two more tepid novels, turn even more traditional with *Brightness Falls* (1992), a realist novel *still* about the 1980s that employs the rocketing stock market and 1987 crash as an allegory for the publishing industry. Ironically, McInerney's fame or critical reception would never again reach the heights he attained in his early career. Tama Janowitz, who would also continue to publish, would similarly never recapture her initial fame and critical praise. Decades later, Janowitz would release a memoir, *Scream: A Memoir of Glamour and Dysfunction* (2016) that, as the title suggest, fits the inevitable and ironic celebrity genre of the once-famous talking about their past by still trading on their now-erstwhile fame. Some writers would later appear in articles about how they "survived" the Brat Pack, including Jill Eisenstadt and Donna Tartt, both of whom would find firmer success decades later, *despite* their earlier association with the Brat Pack.[16]

Only Bret Easton Ellis has achieved both popular and, to a fair degree, academic acclaim for his work. Ellis was probably Wallace's true, if only, target when he disparaged "Neiman-Marcus Nihilism." *Girl with Curious Hair* is an obvious parody of Ellis' work, though Wallace claimed not to

[14] Blum, "Hollywood's Brat Pack."   [15] Ferguson, "Youth Culture on the Skids."
[16] Diamond, "Sex, Drugs, and Bestsellers."

have read Ellis.[17] Wallace also admired Ellis' early use of popular culture in his fiction.[18] The ambitious Wallace, then, clearly saw Ellis as his closest competitor for the "future" of American literature. It is thus telling that Ellis would expand and maintain a busy social media persona – he's on Twitter, has a podcast and has had a majority of his books turned into films – while Wallace, post-*Infinite Jest* (1996), showed little interest in this kind of media cultivation or in continuing his early career critical shots at Ellis.[19] If nothing else, Ellis' efforts show a keen awareness, à la Bourdieu, that his relevance depends, in some part, on keeping up (not avoiding) an aggressive "personalized" social media presence to supplement his work.[20]

Instead of pursuing (or succumbing in the 1990s) to Brat Pack-style fame, popularity and financial recompense, Wallace would focus his efforts on long-term reception and success, shunning the short-term boom he suspected characterized 1980s fiction. It is important to note, for example, that Wallace wrote "Fictional Futures" after returning from his first stay at Yaddo, the writer's colony. As D. T. Max suggests, the trip serves as a case in point regarding Wallace's struggle with imagining his future as a writer. At Yaddo, he struck up an acquaintance with McInerney, who drove a Porsche and was dating a model at the time.[21] McInerney's kind of success served as a potential prototype for Wallace, as Wallace got an up-close glimpse of what a best-selling author gained via financial security. Wallace, as Max relates it, was considering the "wages" of such success in true Bourdieuean fashion: What was lost and/or gained by a writer's finding fame and financial stability through the marketplace? Was true art sacrificed on the market's altar?[22] During his stay, Wallace even came across a "who's hot" article in *Esquire*, in which he landed an up-and-coming spot on the tier below McInerney. Wallace was clearly tempted, in Yaddo's ego-irritating, competitive environment, to cave in to the buzz and frivolous pop-cultural "lists" that equated success with media consecration.

As Max shows, Wallace provided an interesting, if conflicted, answer to the question of how to define and pursue success when he agreed to join a photo session for a spread in *Us* magazine for Janowitz's latest book. Wallace left Yaddo, hightailed it to NYC, hobnobbed and name-dropped with the other writers, dressed up and joined the shoot, only to drop out at

---

[17] Max, *Every Love Story*; Boswell, *Understanding*, 46–47.   [18] Ibid., 60–61.
[19] See McCaffery, "Interview," 130–32.
[20] For a portrait of the "relationship" between the two ambitious and antithetical authors, see one-time Wallace and Ellis editor Gerry Howard's "I Know Why Bret Easton Ellis Hates David Foster Wallace."
[21] Max, *Every Love Story*, 96–97.   [22] Ibid., 97.

the last second.[23] Today, it is nearly impossible to imagine Wallace captured in such a group-publicity shoot, posing with other authors, so against this kind of marketing did Wallace's career prove itself. McInerney, Ellis and Janowitz, however, were frequently captured enjoying NYC's nightlife, basking in their newfound celebrity, and garnered plenty of magazine covers, spreads and gossip columns. Both Ellis and McInerney were invited to, and attended, the 1985 MTV Video Music Awards (the MTV phenomenon being another youth-cultural coup). And Janowitz was friends with Andy Warhol, made a promotional video for one book and appeared on *Letterman*, as well as in a 1987 print ad for Rose's Lime Juice. The sudden, and peculiarly 1980s, pop-cultural fame of these writers, whether or not it was deserved or courted, could certainly make any aspiring writer feel that they might be missing the party – or, at least, actual partying.

Consider also the startling number of novels by core Brat Pack writers that were made into movies at the time, including Ellis' *Less Than Zero* (1987), McInerney's *Bright Lights, Big City* (1988) and Janowitz's *Slaves of New York* (1989) (David Leavitt's *The Lost Language of Cranes* would appear in 1992).[24] Wallace too would flirt with the idea of a film adaptation but would balk at following through. After Alliance Entertainment optioned *Broom* for $10,000, he found himself unable to write a treatment.[25] Years later, respected non-Hollywood filmmaker Gus Van Sant wanted to option *Infinite Jest*, though even then Wallace was still "worried it seemed whorish" to agree.[26] That nearly twenty years later Wallace would consent to John Krasinski's film version of *Brief Interviews with Hideous Men* (2009) suggests a more mature decision by Wallace, one that could be made free from the early-career pressures. Instead of giving in to an easy ego boost and a tidy payday with the chance of a larger exposure of his work, Wallace kept his focus on writing fiction and non-fiction. Throughout his career, his medium would remain the literary, not the treatment or script.

After Yaddo, Wallace even toyed with the idea of getting a high-powered New York agent.[27] Wallace may have been thinking of McInerney's friend and agent, Gary Fisketjon. Fisketjon was a hip NYC agent, a mover and shaker, whose tastes in fiction would help to shape the

---

[23] Ibid.

[24] A crossover between Brat Packs even occurred when Ellis and Judd Nelson hung out in Los Angeles for a *Vanity Fair* piece that Ellis wrote. See Ellis, "Looking for Cool in L.A.," 90–93, 118–19.

[25] Max, *Every Love Story*, 82.   [26] Ibid., 225, 322, n. 24.   [27] Ibid., 97.

decade's literary pulse. *Esquire* even profiled him. He had recently launched the Vintage Contemporaries series with the release of 1984's *Bright Lights, Big City*, the wild bestseller (moving over three hundred thousand copies) that would send McInerney soaring into fame. Fisketjon curated his list of authors to include young and established writers and many a minimalist. He was, moreover, a marketing genius, overseeing the visual branding of the series, which some ridiculed as "yuppiebacks." *Bright Lights*, for instance, benefitted from "a shrewd marketing campaign that presented it as a cross between a compact disc and a SoHo restaurant."[28] Yet publishers would emulate Fisketjon's model of success.

Had he gone with Fisketjon or someone similar, Wallace's work might have ended up on a popular and briskly selling list, backed by a publisher and agent with major cachet and promotional might. But what kind of pressure, in terms of sales and marketing, might that have brought? Wallace, in the end, stayed with Bonnie Nadell. The trust he had in Nadell through the friendship they had formed better suited his temperament. Nadell clearly understood how to pitch and place Wallace's work, and excelled at dealing with his concerns and anxieties, warranted or not. Wallace's choice to stay with Nadell provides yet another tacit answer to Wallace's question of what real literary accomplishment entailed: a steady faith in and commitment to the work itself, one that renounced the flash and glitz of 1980s literary fame.

Institutions with Something

With this commitment in mind, one of the most important ways that Wallace (with Nadell) established his work for the long term was in choosing where to publish. Indeed, Wallace would amass a good deal of symbolic or cultural capital by forging connections with key journals, scholars, and writers. Wallace could therefore overcome the feeling of being overlooked critically and focus his energies on writing a new kind of fiction. This is especially true of Wallace's relationship with *The Review of Contemporary Fiction* (see Chapter 33 for more discussion of this). Wallace, for instance, penned "Fictional Futures" for a mere $250 at the behest of the *Review*'s editor Steven Moore, who had reached out to Wallace. *Review* writers around this time included a who's who of young and old, experimental and postmodernist writers, featuring the likes of Kathy Acker, Harry Matthews, Lynne Tillman, Lance Olsen and Cristine

---

[28] Hertzberg, "The Short Happy Life of the American Yuppie," 105.

Brooke-Rose. It also occasionally featured important scholars who were advocates of postmodern literature, including Brian McHale, Larry McCaffery, Moore himself and Tom LeClair (who would later write an important early essay on Wallace's work). The 1988 *Review* issue, "The Novelist as Critic," in which Wallace's "Fictional Futures" appears, for instance, also contains work by Matthews, Gilbert Sorrentino, Robert Creeley, Brooke-Rose and an essay by Barth, titled "Postmodernism Revisited."

The *Review* also gave Wallace a space in which to write and explore longer-form criticism with academic leanings that simply would not get ink in major magazines. Not only did "Fictional Futures" appear in the *Review*, but so did the first version of one of Wallace's most famous essays, "E Pluribus Unum: Television and US Fiction," which clocked in at forty-seven pages. Only an academically inclined journal would be willing to publish Wallace's ideas at length and before his work became more successful, after which point his essays could be included and expanded in collections whose sales projections were not incredibly risky, such as *A Supposedly Fun Thing I'll Never Do Again* (1997), which contained a revised "E Pluribus Unum." In a venue such as the *Review*, then, Wallace could develop complex intellectual arguments about fiction and language, account for his work that drew upon critical theory and expect a like-minded and engaged audience.

So too is it significant that Wallace's work appeared in editor Brad Morrow's *Conjunctions*, which published "John Billy" in 1988 (and the uncollected "Order and Flux in Northampton" in 1991). *Conjunctions* is committed to an aesthetic similar to that evident in the *Review*, mixing the work of an older avant-garde, postmodernists and contemporary writers whose work continues in that vein. John Ashbery and William H. Gass were, at the time of Wallace's publications, two of several notable contributing editors, and over the years its pages have featured the likes of Barbara Guest, Joyce Carol Oates, Robert Coover, Lydia Davis, Lyn Hejinian, Rick Moody, Carole Maso, Mary Caponegro and Jonathan Lethem. Wallace's "John Billy," for example, appeared in a 1988 issue with William T. Vollmann, Matthews, Joseph McElroy, Sorrentino and Creeley.

Clearly, the *Review* and *Conjunctions* plugged an emerging Wallace directly into the tradition that his work drew upon, the postmodern and experimental, and associated him with writers who took seriously poststructuralist notions of language. This connection helped counterbalance the sway of the minimalist and realist fiction that the literary market

was promoting. Indeed, Nadell, keenly aware of the intricacies and potential of Wallace's audience, had indicated to Wallace that some, if not all, of
his work would probably not appeal to mainstream magazines such as *The
New Yorker, Esquire* or *The Atlantic*.[29] Wallace desired the exposure and
cachet that these publications would lend his work – and he would publish
in *Playboy* (which published "My Appearance" under the title "Late
Night") and in the mainstream-for-writers *Paris Review* (which published
"Little Expressionless Animals") – but the fact was that he was simply not
going to land stories regularly in the largest magazines.

Publishing in smaller venues such as the *Review* and *Conjunctions*, while
it wouldn't lead directly to big paydays and commercial success, would
allow Wallace to publish more formally challenging work while simultaneously establishing a meaningful reputation with influential people and
readers. Wallace could thus gain a larger readership in more popular,
widely read publications that could be fairly remunerative, but, just as
importantly, these mainstream publications were supplemented by
university-affiliated journals whose readership largely consisted of scholars
and writers with a special kind of high-cultural capital.

The *Review*, furthermore, served to support and inspire Wallace in
many other ways. Wallace became friendly, and held a long correspondence, with Moore and Morrow. It was also in the *Review* that Wallace
first saw an ad for David Markson's *Wittgenstein's Mistress* (1988), which
would be a pivotal read for the young writer and a novel that would have a
major influence on him. In his long review essay, "The Empty Plenum"
(1990), Wallace finds in Markson's novel what could be a manifesto for his
own work, praising it for "reminding us of fiction's limitless possibilities
for reach and grasp, for making heads throb heartlike, and for sanctifying
the marriages of cerebration & emotion, abstraction and lived life; transcendent truth-seeking & daily schlepping."[30] Among a number of tiny
epiphanies, Wallace also seized upon the fact that "people who write need
to do so as a mode of *communication*."[31]

In fact, some of Wallace's favorite 1980s novels around this time reflect
his desire to bring together postmodern aesthetics with a literature of
feeling: Two were by established postmodernists – Sorrentino's
Aberration of Starlight (1980) and Markson's *Wittgenstein's Mistress* – and
two were by younger writers – Jonathan Franzen's *The Twenty-Seventh
City* (1988) and William T. Vollmann's *The Rainbow Stories* (1988). In the
case of Franzen and Vollmann, here were younger writers whose work was

[29] Max, *Every Love Story*, 87.   [30] Wallace, "Empty Plenum," *BFN*, 74.   [31] Ibid., 83.

not in step with 1980s minimalism (both were non-MFAs too); in the case of Sorrentino and Markson, here was an older postmodern generation that nevertheless helped to show the way forward.

Moreover, Markson's novel was published by Dalkey Archive Press, which also published the *Review*, and held to a similar literary aesthetic. Housed at the Illinois State University, whose English Department was postmodern-friendly and would later offer Wallace his full-time teaching gig and allow him to return to the Midwest, the Press had saved Markson's unpublished novel from obscurity. In turn, the university and press would help Wallace. Thus, Wallace's inroads with the *Review* in the 1980s introduced him to a small academic community that was committed to reading, teaching and publishing work like his. This modest network eventually expanded to include Wallace himself when he joined the ISU English department in 1993 and made lifelong friends. Wallace ultimately found himself surrounded and supported by both institutions and people who provided the kind of stable environment in which he best thrived.

The *Review* and *Conjunctions* thus served as nodal points in a wider institutional network that helped Wallace to establish a critical reputation upon which his later more commercial success would, in part, rest. That Wallace would, during the 1980s, candidly prepare a path for the reception and success of his work – with no promise that it would be so – indicates that his ideas about fiction mattered as much as the fiction itself, especially in terms of where they would be published. Call it, after Bourdieu, establishing cultural or symbolic capital, but there is nothing cynical about a writer carefully positioning his work to avoid the dictates of pure market forces or the trends of the times. Bourdieu points out that one is always playing the game, even if one claims not to be or tries to opt out. Literature never simply speaks for itself. Wallace, if anything, was earnest and forthright about his beliefs and openly fought for them in his non-fiction and fiction. His so-called canonization ultimately arises, as it necessarily must, thanks to both popular readership *and* institutional support, not due to some locatable genius or mystical charisma. Wallace's version of fiction, it should be remembered, was not guaranteed at the time to overcome the hegemony of 1980s publishers and the literary market. The fact that it did speaks as much to Wallace's ability to negotiate various institutions, to engage and employ them, as it does to the value and prominence of his work.

CHAPTER 4

Confidence Man
David Foster Wallace and the American Nineteenth Century
Catherine Toal

"It's when people begin to fancy that they actually know something about literature that they cease to be literarily interesting, or even of any use to those who are." So opines the protagonist of David Foster Wallace's first novel *The Broom of the System* (1987), as he tries to persuade his girlfriend, who has been working on the switchboard of his publishing company, to begin reading manuscripts.[1] Wallace's essays offer a version of the same sentiment. His discussion of the poststructuralist concept of the "death of the author" in "Greatly Exaggerated" (1992) observes that "for those of us civilians who know in our gut that writing is an act of communication between one human being and another, the whole question seems sort of arcane." "One thing which [the erasure of the author] cannot mean," Wallace insists, citing William Gass, "is that *no one did it.*"[2] In a short story that is also a theory of literature, "Westward the Course of Empire Takes its Way" from *Girl with Curious Hair* (1989), the novelistic counterpart to poststructuralism, metafiction, is unfavorably compared, in its bloodlessness and solipsistic self-referentiality, to "meatfiction," a type of writing that wants to "fuck" and even kill the reader, "to perpetrate the kind of special cruelty only real lovers can inflict."[3]

Wallace's skepticism about literary theory has, of course, not stopped the absorption of his work into scholarly schemes of classification, even as these acknowledge his uniqueness.[4] Equally, Wallace's hostility to poststructuralism is complicated by his own use of metafictional

---

[1] Wallace, *BS*, 308.   [2] Wallace, "Greatly Exaggerated," *SFT*, 144–45.
[3] Wallace, "Westward," *GCH*, 310, 331–32.
[4] Boswell identifies Wallace as "a nervous member of some still-unnamed (and perhaps unnamable) third wave of modernism" in *Understanding David Foster Wallace*, 1. Hayes-Brady has teased out the complexities of Wallace's affiliation to the label "postmodernism," focusing on the problems raised by any implication of historical succession, the pluralism of the work designated by the term and the possibility that Wallace is part of a generation which surpassed this movement. See *Failures*, 2, 27, 45.

techniques. His advocacy of "sincerity" in contrast to postmodern "irony" seems compromised by layers of reflexive commentary.[5] Recently, another problem has arisen in the reception of Wallace's work, one that bears directly on his repeated insistence that literature is an act of communication – of whatever tenor – between two people. Largely because of his commencement address *This Is Water* (2005), Wallace had achieved by the time of his death by suicide in 2008 the status of a kind of secular saint, who championed the capacity for "attention and awareness and discipline, and being able to truly care about other people and to sacrifice for them."[6] *Infinite Jest* (1996) had already diagnosed the damage caused by indifference and distraction. The testimonies of some of those who knew Wallace in private have raised the specter of hypocrisy in his injunction to selflessness, and of pathology in his evocation of vulnerability.

When theoretical debates and contemporary reputations pass out of memory, literary history remains to clarify their place in a larger story. Wallace has not often been situated within the longer legacy of the national tradition to which he belongs. He drew an opposition between his own work and the "Howells/Wharton/Updike school of US Realism," thereby linking one of his avowedly Oedipal *bêtes noires* to "Gilded-Age" and early twentieth-century portraits of American society.[7] Invocations by his interpreters of the so-called American Renaissance (compassing the period from the 1830s to the Civil War) are local and thematic – for example, the echoes of Herman Melville's "Bartleby, the Scrivener: A Story of Wall Street" identified in *The Pale King* (2011).[8] A recent "global" contextualization of Wallace's work includes a nineteenth-century pedigree for him, but it is Russian, not American.[9] There is, however, another Melville text that directly illuminates Wallace's strategies and preoccupations: *The Confidence Man: His Masquerade*, first published on April Fools' Day in 1857.

General affinities with the most monumental of American writers are already apparent in Wallace's formation as well as his ambition. His father read *Moby-Dick* aloud to him when he was eight years old.[10] An intriguing poetic counterpart to the didactic guidance of *This Is Water*, the title of which refers to an older fish introducing two young fish to the concept of the element they live in, emerges through Wallace's reference to the epic of

---

[5] Several studies have sought to resolve this tension. See, for example, Konstantinou, "No Bull" or Kelly, "New Sincerity."
[6] Wallace, *TIW*, 120.   [7] McCaffery, "Interview," 36.
[8] Shapiro, "From Capitalist to Communist Abstraction," 1249–71.
[9] Thompson, *Global Wallace*, 89–116.   [10] Harry Ransom Center, "Biographical Sketch."

the whale in "A Supposedly Fun Thing I'll Never Do Again." There, he tells us that "in school I ended up writing three different papers on 'The Castaway' section of *Moby-Dick*, the chapter where the cabin boy Pip falls overboard and is driven mad by the empty immensity of what he finds himself floating in."[11] With a rather different pedagogical emphasis from his commencement address, Wallace goes on to say that he teaches Stephen Crane's "horrific" story "The Open Boat" in order to inculcate "the same marrow-level dread of the oceanic I've always felt, the intuition of the sea as primordial *nada*, bottomless depths inhabited by cackling tooth-studded things rising toward you at the rate a feather falls."[12] Pursuing the connection to Melville unveils the disquieting elements that lurk beneath the moral authority of the 2005 graduation speech.

In an assessment that resonates with the ambivalent response of well-known critics to *Infinite Jest*, contemporary reviewers objected that Melville's *The Confidence Man* was not a novel.[13] The action of the plot is interspersed with theories of literature that operate as disruptive effects under the guise of argument and prescription. Melville's experimental, digressive interventions confirm the long-standing role of "metafiction" in the genealogy of the form. As Doris Lessing – a twentieth-century writer caught like Wallace between modernism and its subsequent hyphenated prefix – once commented, "the debate about the novel has been going on since the novel was born."[14] In the American context, eighteenth-century styles of dismantling and questioning the genre persisted long after European societies had developed the classic "realist" mode. Though their conception of antebellum literary culture as a whole has since been challenged, theorists of American literary emergence gave an accurate account of the alternative concerns of the texts that they helped to institutionalize as canonical. F. O. Matthiessen emphasized the importance of "myth-creation" for Emerson and his circle;[15] Leo Marx stressed the impact of a decisive contest between industrial advance and pastoral wildness;[16] Lionel Trilling upheld the work of Poe, Hawthorne and Melville against the claim that it did not represent social reality: the American tradition was an invention of the "mind."[17]

Wallace was fond of criticizing American postmodernist writers for having contributed to the formation of an empty, ubiquitous cultural discourse of advertising, one that extended far beyond the marketing of

---

[11] Wallace, "A Supposedly Fun Thing," *SFT*, 262.   [12] Ibid.   [13] Parker, *Herman Melville*, 339.
[14] Lessing, "Preface," 13.   [15] Matthiessen, *American Renaissance*, 626–28.
[16] Marx, *The Machine in the Garden*.   [17] Trilling, "Reality in America," 14.

actual consumer goods.[18] But this criticism ignores the degree to which a complex, elusive narrative style had already developed in American letters, signaling a separation between a popular audience and literary endeavor. Such a division is thought to have emerged in the European context with the advent of early twentieth-century modernism,[19] but it was manifest in nineteenth-century America due to the primacy of the market as the sole means of support for literary production.[20] During the Cold War, a canon was established from these retroactively "high cultural" works in order to claim a "cultural capital" commensurate with US global power.[21] The 1950s onward witnessed a flowering of novelistic hyper-intricacy under the influence of this canon, and in continuation of a fissure between mass entertainment and linguistically rich literature. A quest resumed for the "Great American novel" to represent the nation.[22] *The Confidence Man*, with its multitude of references, studied humor and insistence that the reader assemble its intelligibility, must be regarded as a progenitor of this line of fictional descent, from William Gaddis, through Thomas Pynchon, to Wallace himself.

If Melville's text is one avatar of postwar "metafiction," another source has been identified for the lineage of the twentieth-century US novel, which is not irrelevant to the illumination *The Confidence Man* casts on Wallace's work. Ernest Hemingway famously claimed that "all modern American literature comes from one book by Mark Twain called *Huckleberry Finn*."[23] The voice created by Twain might be seen as the direct opposite of the self-referential theoretical narrative, inaugurating a tradition of innocent, socially critical perspectives such as those of Scout Finch and Holden Caulfield. Wallace's affiliation to this genealogy has not attracted (and has perhaps not required) interpretative attention. But the appeal of his writing, especially among younger readers, seems partly attributable to its combination of hefty intellectual credentials with this no-nonsense, colloquial, apparently wholly candid American lingo. The voice rings out clearest in his interviews ("I guess maybe, but it's developed in an awful clunky way"),[24] and in the offhand confessions of his essays: "I formed this view of [Bill] Pullman the actor as a kind of good and decent but basically ineffectual guy, an *edgeless* guy";[25] "what I discovered as the tournament wore on was that I can be kind of a snob and an asshole."[26]

[18] McCaffery, "Interview," 48–49.   [19] Jameson, *Postmodernism*, 2.
[20] Gilmore, *American Romanticism*, 54.   [21] Pease, "*Moby-Dick* and the Cold War," 113–55.
[22] Buell, *Dream*, 56–57.   [23] Hemingway, *Green Hills of Africa*, 17.
[24] McCaffery, "Interview," 32.   [25] Wallace, "David Lynch Keeps His Head," *SFT*, 186.
[26] Wallace, "Michael Joyce's Professional Artistry," *SFT*, 227–28.

As might be expected, Wallace's fiction adds a further stratum of complication to the aural note. The twentieth-century writer to whom he is most flatteringly compared is Nabokov,[27] and one basis for the link resides in their shared "imitation" of American vernaculars. In Wallace's case, this appears, for example, in his ventriloquism of William F. Buckley in *Girl with Curious Hair*" and of an immigrant idiolect in "John Billy." *The Confidence Man* represents a forerunner to Wallace in being not only a theoretically elaborate and experimental text but also in its use of a form frequently found in Wallace's narratives, and which relates to his aesthetic of "communication": a dialogue between two interlocutors, but not necessarily two distinct voices.

Reviewers of *The Confidence Man* did not accept that it was a novel precisely because it seemed only to be a series of dialogues. Like Wallace's novels, it introduces a landscape that is half geographical reality, half fictional staging, with the theme of the story literally signaled in the first chapter by placards held up or posted on the deck of a ship traveling down the Mississippi.[28] Thereafter we are privy to a sequence of mainly two-party exchanges – occasionally involving the chorus of a crowd – with each interaction appearing to feature the same central protagonist in a different disguise, before his final incarnation as "the cosmopolitan," a synonym for the devil.

In Wallace's work, a putative dialogue form proliferates throughout, most notoriously in *Brief Interviews with Hideous Men* (1999), where the eponymous males are questioned by an unnamed female interlocutor indicated by "Q." Other formats bearing the same quality of formal interaction yet lacking genuine exchange include the Letterman show theorized in "My Appearance," the Jeopardy quiz of "Little Expressionless Animals," the radio-show aggression of "Host," the focus-group dynamics of "Mr. Squishy" (from *Oblivion*), the recurring ritual of therapy from *The Broom of the System* to the AA meetings of *Infinite Jest* to "The Depressed Person." Even when a – possibly empty – structure of an interlocution is not the genre of the piece, it represents the central focus, as in the description of John McCain's encounter with a Republican-Presidential-nomination campaign-rally audience member in "Up, Simba," or the interpretation of the many messages issued to customers by the services of the cruise ship in "A Supposedly Fun Thing I'll Never

[27] Boswell, *Understanding David Foster Wallace*, 147; Severs details Wallace's references to Nabokov in *David Foster Wallace's Balancing Books: Fictions of Value*, 282,n. 35.
[28] Melville, *The Confidence Man*, hereafter *CM*.

Do Again." Most strikingly, in his essay on September 11, "The View from Mrs. Thompson's," Wallace understands the planes crashing into the World Trade Center as a message addressed to himself and his generation, rather than to the Midwestern housewives in whose homes he views the event.

The overwhelming affinity between Wallace and Melville lies in the relentless concern with the question of genuineness in dialogic exchanges. *The Confidence Man* is dominated by the possibility of financial donation or transaction. A "negro cripple" denounced as a "painted decoy" cries out to be accounted honest; a man in mourning solicits charity from a merchant who has given money to the beggar, claiming, with the support of arcane details, that they are acquainted. The mourner then urges a student he sees reading Tacitus to "drop" this ancient purveyor of cynicism.[29] A collector for the "Seminole Widows and Orphans Society" demands not only contributions but also credulity from his benefactors.[30] The representative of a coal company asks investors made eager by rumors he seems himself to have spread, how they can wish to do business with him in such an informal setting.[31] A herb doctor proclaims that his medicines will work only if the ailing believe.[32] A "philosophical" employment agent defends human nature from a jaded frontiersman who would rather have machines than human males as workers.[33] The last figure, the "cosmopolitan," repeatedly argues the case – in a series of discourses that range through the question of whether one can have trust in the quality of wine, or in the morality of laughter, Shakespeare or beauty – for lending money to a friend in need.[34] He tries to persuade the barber to provide services without immediate payment, dissuades a rich old gentleman from precautions for safeguarding his money, and questions the degree of authority accorded the Bible.[35] Throughout these interchanges, both mistrust and confidence are represented as species of contagion, and identity becomes a matter of assertion and suspicion.

Wallace's dialogues are more concerned with whether people can be sincere in speech. In his representations of popular culture or advertising, the distortion of authenticity by money is a secondary or prerequisite element. At times, his narratives search for a core of genuineness that does not exist, or which the search itself will destroy (for instance, in the interrogations of therapy). On occasion, the very ruthlessness of the fixation on sincerity clings to the ideal it has already abandoned – as in

---

[29] Ibid., 15, 26.   [30] Ibid., 33.   [31] Ibid., 56.   [32] Ibid., 83.   [33] Ibid., 114–28.
[34] Ibid., 162, 164, 172, 190.   [35] Ibid., 235, 248–49.

the long analysis in "Up, Simba" of John McCain's perhaps faked exchange with a worried supporter.[36] At times, Wallace even seems to entertain a belief in misguided forms of political sincerity that are mere ideological ruses or clichés. For example, he produces a pointless analysis of the vitriol directed at a Black caller by right-wing shock-jock John Ziegler on the subject of O. J. Simpson: "If a white person gets angry about a black person's 'pretending to be white,' doesn't the anger come off far less as sympathy with the person's betrayed race than as antipathy for somebody who's trying to crash a party he doesn't belong at?"[37] The 9/11 essay, "The View from Mrs. Thompson's," seems to believe in purely religiously inspired convictions on the part of the terrorists as much as in the simplicity of the Midwestern housewife – and to feel indicted by both.[38]

The Confidence Man exhibits a similarly obsessional attachment to the very quality that it undermines. The satanic protagonist articulates an insistent plea for trust, while corrupting it utterly. Dismissing the plea opens no viable alternative. The figure most starkly juxtaposed with the "cosmopolitan" is that of a notorious "Indian-hater" ruthlessly committed to a policy of extermination.[39] Among the devil's interlocutors, Emerson, parodied as "Mark Winsome," and Thoreau, depicted as Emerson's slavish disciple, "Egbert," propose a worldview so transcendent of practicality as to be inhuman. Rejecting the appeals of charity would also turn the primordial crimes of the American polity – slavery and indigenous genocide – into mere chimeras. The narrative lacks any stable moral landing place, since the steamship setting is used like a stage, occluding motive and changes of dress as characters appear from and disappear onto shore.

The Confidence Man clearly formulates a general critique of American society, contrasting the religious principles supposedly important to it with the effects of the struggle to survive in a capitalist polity. With its westward orientation and multifarious throng, the steamship journey also conjures the tension between ideals of community and the anonymity necessarily generated by endless expansion. In a strangely close affinity with Wallace, Melville creates physical descriptions that estrange as much as familiarize, seeing his characters as scraps of fragments gathered from a wide variety of sources, yet defined by signature traits in a manner typical of costumed disguise. Wallace encounters individuals as uncanny layers of reference, for instance, in his remark that the tennis player Thomas Enqvist "looks eerily like a young Richard Chamberlain, the Richard Chamberlain of

---

[36] Wallace, "Up, Simba," CL, 224.   [37] Wallace, "Host," CL, 334.
[38] Wallace, "The View from Mrs. Thompson's," CL, 140.   [39] Melville, CM, 144.

The Towering Inferno, say, with this narrow, sort of rodentially patrician quality."[40] The coach Charles Tavis in *Infinite Jest* is not the reproduction of a televisual image but contagiously *reproducible*, his "compulsive hand-movements" and "pathological openness of manner" leaving him so vulnerable to mimicking imitation that this has to be prohibited among his students in order to safeguard his authority.[41] In the yet-vaster America conjured by Wallace in that novel, one that has enlarged into the "ONAN" conglomerate, a sociopolitical condemnation is also sketched. The near future it mocks exists between two extremes: consumerist addiction and terrorist sacrificial willpower.

Wallace's disgust with the effects of American overindulgence finds expression, too, in "A Supposedly Fun Thing I'll Never Do Again" when he records the experience of watching his fellow citizens "waddling in expensive sandals into poverty-stricken ports," realizing that his country has produced a new type of creature: "the world's only known species of bovine carnivore."[42] In his polemics against selfish solipsism and his defenses of sincerity, he ought to be regarded as a true inheritor of the religious core of nineteenth-century US reformist thought, and specifically of the Calvinist sensibility that historian Ann Douglas identified as the foundation of the American conscience.[43] His awareness of the question of race was perhaps (for his moment) *less* sophisticated than Melville's,[44] and his politics more naïve,[45] but this only confirms the primacy of the essentially religious worldview that animates his opposition between temptation and self-control, falsity and authenticity.

The Confidence Man contains a further peculiarity that sheds light on Wallace's model of art as genuine communicative transmission. Melville's text shares not only a bizarre dialogue form in common with Wallace's work but also repeated recourse to the trope of the story-within-a-story. As in Wallace's case, these tales are commentaries on the persons engaged in the exchange and their situation. They ostensibly explain the dispositions of speakers, initially referencing nonpecuniary causes (sexual or existential). At the same time, they are fabrications designed to extort or justify withholding money – and thus variants on the essential logic of every interaction portrayed. Egbert (Thoreau) tells one such story, of particular

---

[40] Wallace, *ST*, 82, n. 61.   [41] Wallace, *IJ*, 519.
[42] Wallace, "A Supposedly Fun Thing," *SFT*, 310–11.   [43] Douglas, *Feminization*.
[44] As Thompson has shown, Wallace's awareness of his own "whiteness" did not prevent his considering other races as merely relative to this category. See "Wallace and Race," 204–20.
[45] D. T. Max quotes Wallace in *Every Love Story* rationalizing his decision to vote for Ross Perot in 1992 with the statement "you need someone really insane to fix the economy," 259.

interest to Melville's biographers, concerning "China Aster," a candle-maker prevailed upon against his better judgment to accept a loan from a friend, and who is then ruined when the friend demands repayment at exorbitant interest.[46] Hershel Parker argues that the tale shows Melville's view of himself as a "victim" of the generosity of his relative Tertullus D. Stewart, who had offered him the money to refurbish his farm at Arrowhead.[47] The entanglement took place at a phase of Melville's life when his hopes of consistent remuneration through literary success were permanently receding.

The biographical reference changes our perception of the dynamics of the novel. Continual duplicitous solicitation of financial donations could be regarded as a disguised allusion to the levying of interest by lenders, rather than an exposé of fake appeals to charity. On the other hand, both China Aster and the series of protagonists embodying the devil are in receipt of monetary gifts, and so are implicitly aligned. From this perspective, the antics of the mutating "cosmopolitan," extracting money from human passersby through sudden ambush, feint and rhetorical bamboo-zling, become a fantasy of obtaining funds without toil or trouble, an implication confirmed by the comic exuberance of these scenes. The hyper-inventiveness of this character even seems a plea for the opportunity to "get away" with continuing to write, as when his stratagems to persuade Egbert to give him financial assistance (storytelling, hypothetical role-playing, abstruse argument) end in a performance of the desperate cry: "Help, help!."[48]

Melville's theories of fiction in the narrative are also reducible both to the affirmation that financial calculation overshadows everything, and to an attempt to persuade the reader to accept and approve ("buy") the work of art he/she is being offered. The first metafictional intervention, on "consistency" of character, explains the figure called Charlie Noble's sudden indulgence of a fit of despair in human trustworthiness as a sign of the general complexity of humanity – when the novel in fact only offers two attitudes: confidence or incredulity. The second, on "reality" and fiction, suggests that the "devil" can be encountered anywhere; while the third, on "originality" of character, responding to the barber's view of the cosmopolitan as "quite an original," has much the same meaning, arguing that fictional works rarely have more than one such "original" figure, if that many.[49]

---

[46] Melville, *CM*, 208–20.   [47] Parker, *Herman Melville*, Vol. II, 278–81.
[48] Melville, *CM*, 206.   [49] Ibid., 237–39.

Far apart in David Foster Wallace's writing career appear two instances of stories-within-stories as dialogic performances. Toward the end of *The Broom of the System*, the protagonist Rick tells his girlfriend Lenore an elaborate story that reflects the triangular relationships he has arranged in their lives, and the combination of obsessive jealousy and faithless desire that animate his designs. When Lenore objects to the story, he launches a volley of sexist abuse.[50] The same kind of moment occurs at the end of the last "interview" with a "hideous man," in which the speaker tells Q a tale recounted to him by a woman he met at a festival, claiming that he fell in love with the woman, despite his low opinion of her otherwise, when she told him about having survived a violent rape by responding to her assailant's aggression with affection and compliance. Q is understandably skeptical, suspecting a creepiness, prurience, and hostility behind the act of telling the story as a strategy of seduction.[51] We infer this from the fact that the man ends his monologue with an abusive tirade, more vitriolic and obscene than Rick's sudden outburst.

In their structure, these vignettes thwart the ideal of "communication between one human being and another." They are also not so much examples or achievements of the passionate desire to shake up the reader articulated by Wallace's invocation of "meatfiction," with its visceral sexual or murderous aggression, the "special cruelty" of lovers. Instead, although always interpretable as "exposing" the tendency they enact, these stories-within-stories create a frame for a banal, everyday exercise of misogynist license: the right to say something simultaneously regarded as unsayable. To that extent, they represent not a "transaction," whether "erotic or altruistic or sadistic," but the gratification of a proclivity.

In Wallace's work, the canonical figures of nineteenth-century American literature appear only to confirm a process of cultural degeneration. Lyle in *Infinite Jest* is "going through a Whitman period, part of grieving for himself,"[52] a detail that signals the conversion of authentic quest into lifestyle choice. A similar connotation attaches to Wallace's reference to Emerson in "E Unibus Pluram," his essay on television. Genuineness becomes mere pose in the comparison between the bearing of the modern actor – aware of an audience but pretending not to be – and Emerson's evocation of the kind of man whose inner "moral quality" makes him "fit to stand the gaze of millions."[53] The demand for cash

---

[50] Wallace, *BS*, 433.   [51] Wallace, "B.I. #20," *BI*, 313.   [52] Wallace, *IJ*, 254.
[53] Wallace quotes Cavell's reference, in *Pursuits of Happiness*, to Emerson's 1844 essay "Manners" in "Unibus," *SFT*, 25.

dressed up in outlandish physical and rhetorical costume in *The Confidence Man* shows that there is venerable nineteenth-century precedent for personal fixation masquerading as literary communication, just as Wallace shares with his forefathers their imposing projects of moral diagnosis and formal experimentation.

CHAPTER 5

David Foster Wallace and European Literature

Lucas Thompson

How exactly will David Foster Wallace and his work be remembered? What kinds of readers will be drawn to his writing over the coming decades, and what will they make of it? In 2022, we are at a critical point in negotiating Wallace's cultural and literary legacy, with scholars and general readers alike reconsidering their investments in both his fiction and his non-fiction, but also rethinking the complex connections between the life and the work. As a clearer picture of Wallace's biography emerges, many readers have been prompted to consider what it might mean to engage with the writing of someone with troubling political positions or patterns of behavior, and a lively discourse has sprung up around denouncing both Wallace and those who defend him. Such backlash is somewhat predictable, given the breathless enthusiasm on the part of critics and readers in earlier decades. The culture has made a correction – perhaps an overcorrection – but a more measured and less fanatical approach to Wallace's work, on the part of both lay readers and professional interpreters, was always inevitable. Recent years have seen a thoroughgoing reconsideration of Wallace's work and legacy, and it is not yet clear what the final consensus will be.

Of course, professional readers have an important part to play in such negotiations. Even though the loudest and most polemical voices often come from mainstream, online venues of one kind or another, the ongoing scholarly conversation about the meaning and value of Wallace's work continues apace. Critics will still sift through Wallace's drafts and archives, as well as tracing his stylistic innovations, philosophical investments and influence on later generations of writers, among many other lines of enquiry. But what about in terms of "placing" Wallace? In what terms will he be understood as a late twentieth- and early twenty-first-century US writer? Will his readership primarily view him as an insular American figure, as does his German translator Ulrich Blumenbach, who sees him as

"US-centric and sealed off"?[1] Will they emphasize his parochial identifications to the Midwest, or his leanings toward literary traditions from elsewhere? In this chapter, I want to argue that Wallace was in fact a complex and conflicted cosmopolitan, who in spite of a lifelong aversion to international travel and a deep antipathy toward translation, was always attempting to situate himself in relation to literary traditions from well beyond the United States. In earlier work, I have shown how our collective understanding of Wallace's fiction and non-fiction can be fruitfully opened up by situating it in light of literature from elsewhere.[2] I have revealed the ways in which Wallace's work, despite appearances, and despite his occasional willingness to be conceived as a regional, Midwestern novelist, actually fits within a broad conception of world literature, revealing how Wallace looked beyond the United States for aesthetic models and intellectual sparring partners at every point in his career. I have situated Wallace's writing in relation to Latin America (tracing his substantive connections to writers such as Gabriel Garcia Márquez, Manuel Puig, Jorge Luis Borges, Carlos Fuentes, José Donoso, Octavio Paz and Julio Cortázar), Russia (predominately Fyodor Dostoevsky and Leo Tolstoy, but also Nikolai Gogol, Anton Chekhov, Ivan Turgenev, Alexander Pushkin, Ivan Goncharov, Daniil Kharms and other twentieth-century Russian absurdists), France and particularly French Existentialism (notably Camus and Sartre, which he understood in large part in reference to earlier US novelists, such as Flannery O'Connor and Walker Percy, who had found ways to Americanize existentialist insights), and African (American) culture (which he engaged with via his long-standing interest in comparative mythology and a passionate advocacy of late-1980s hip-hop.) Here, though, I want to stress Wallace's relation to European literature, broadly conceived, or what he himself characterized as "the tradition of Western letters." This characterization comes from a 1993 interview in which Wallace listed many complaints about the culture of MFA creative-writing programs, based on his own student experience in the MFA program at the University of Arizona, along with his teaching in similar programs at Amherst College and the University of Illinois. MFA curricula, according to Wallace, was often depressingly insular in their approach to fiction, emphasizing US models and precedents instead of encouraging a more expansive vision of literary endeavor. "One of my big complaints about Arizona," explained Wallace, "was that though I liked a lot of the students, and I liked a lot of the regular faculty, I didn't much like the creative

[1] Brinkbäumer, "Interview by Klaus Brinkbäumer."   [2] Thompson, *Global Wallace*.

writing faculty. They really disparaged the idea of learning how to write as part of learning how to take part in the tradition of Western letters."[3] Mark McGurl, in his authoritative account of US creative-writing programs, *The Program Era*, has noted their tendency to function "as shrines to vivacious American individualism," but for Wallace, their US-centered ideologies went much deeper.[4] As well as criticizing MFA programs for their shallow presentism, in their tendency to emphasize contemporary fiction over earlier forms, he also found their insularity irksome, as noted above. In a later essay, Wallace wondered why "Homer and Milton, Cervantes and Shakespeare, Maupassant and Gogol – to say nothing of the Testaments – have receded into the mists of Straight Lit," while writing instructors instead prioritize a tradition of twentieth-century US realism largely limited to "[J.D.] Salinger," "[John] Updike," "[Raymond] Carver," "[Ann] Beattie" and "[Jayne Anne] Phillips."[5] For Wallace, such a curriculum was reductively nationalist, needlessly cordoning off global literature from the interests and aspirations of emerging US writers. In response, he constructed his own impressively globalist reading list, which contains many surprising and unexpected inclusions. I have listed many of the specific novelists that Wallace engaged with across his career in *Global Wallace: David Foster Wallace and World Literature*, but Wallace's reading included examples from Japan, Poland, Finland, Austria, Italy, Denmark, Latvia and the Netherlands, to name just a few. He regularly seized on opportunities in interviews to recommend beloved non-American writers and novels, and in 2000, gave one interviewer, Eduard Lago, a revealing response to a question about his reading habits. "I read less contemporary American fiction than I do anything else," Wallace said.[6] It is worth emphasizing how unlikely it is for a mainstream US novelist of this period to have such profound investments in fiction from elsewhere. While Wallace might not have quite been in the same category as the American essayist, editor and translator Eliot Weinberger – a undisputed paragon of world literature, with multilingual, polymathic credentials – we might nonetheless think of him as being somewhat akin to a writer like Susan Sontag, whose advocacy and enthusiasm for global writers of all kinds often wove its way through her own work. Like Wallace, Sontag herself conceived of world literature as a correction to her own experiences of "provincialism" and "inane schooling":

---

[3] Kennedy and Polk, "Looking," 15.   [4] McGurl, *Program*, 368.
[5] Wallace, "Fictional Futures," *BFN*, 62.   [6] Lago, "Interview."

> To have access to literature, world literature, was to escape the prison of national vanity, of philistinism, of compulsory provincialism, of inane schooling, of imperfect destinies and bad luck. Literature was the passport to enter a large life; that is, the zone of freedom.[7]

Notwithstanding Weinberger's own strident critique of Sontag's alleged "Eurocentrism," a shortcoming perhaps only evident to someone with Weinberger's global literary credentials and standing, Sontag's devotion to global authors may well have been an influence on Wallace.[8] (It is worth noting that the Wallace archives at the Harry Ransom Centre contain a heavily annotated edition of Sontag's debut essay collection *Against Interpretation* [1966], with its expansive interests in art and ideas from outside the United States, with essays on Simone Weil, Eugène Ionesco, Nathalie Sarraute, Cesare Pavese, Michel Leiris, Jean Genet, Jean-Luc Godard and Robert Bresson, among others.) While he may not have been such an outspoken advocate for non-US writers, nor as obvious a cosmopolitan as Sontag, I want to suggest that Wallace is nonetheless far closer to her end of the literary spectrum than he is routinely taken to be.

Scholars still routinely understand Wallace as having had serious aspirations to be part of a high-postmodern cohort of US writers, placing his work in relation to figures such as John Barth, William Gaddis, William H. Gass and Donald Barthelme. But we are still in need of a richer sense of the ways in which Wallace was always aspiring – both successfully and otherwise – to participate within much larger literary traditions. Together with a general ambition to be a globally recognized writer (the kind of writer, as he told Mark Costello in the 1980s, whose fiction would still be "read 100 years from now"), he was particularly concerned with situating himself in relation to a European lineage, as his reference to "the tradition of Western letters" in the aforementioned interview reveals.[9] Part of this ambition likely came from his time serving as Associate Editor for Dalkey Archive's *Review of Contemporary Fiction*, a role he held as part of his appointment at the University of Illinois at Bloomington-Normal, from 1991 through to 2002. In this role, Wallace edited a vast number of international short stories and essays, frequently finessing translator's renderings into prose that a mostly American audience would find more readable.

Wallace worked on *RCF* issues that presented Danish, Finnish and Latvian fiction, as well as those devoted to the work of Raymond

---

[7] Sontag, "Literature," 207.   [8] Weinberger, "Notes."   [9] Max, *Every Love Story*, 23.

Queneau (France) and Milorad Pavić (Serbia), to name just a few. During the years of Wallace's involvement, as now, the *RCF* presented an astonishingly diverse array of global writers, acting as impresario to many obscure figures who might not otherwise have found an American audience. Indeed, there is a lengthy list of writers whose work would have passed across Wallace's desk in his Associate Editor role. Even if we limit this selection to writers from Europe, such a list includes Maria Němcová Banerjee, Georges Perec, Claude Ollier, Luigi Pirandello, Jacques Roubaud, Juan Goytisolo, Danilo Kiš, Tadeusz Konwicki, Knud Holst, Franco Ferruci, Felipe Alfau, Paulo Valesio, Josef Škvorecký, Alessandro Carrera, Claude Simon, Lubomír Dorůžka, Antonio Tabucchi and Jens Christian Grøndahl, among countless others. We know that Wallace was an avid reader of the *RCF*, even after leaving Illinois for a chaired position at Pomona College, and it seems likely that a fair portion of his exposure to non-US writers came from these pages – particularly from those he worked with in producing the triannual publication. His involvement at the *RCF*, as Ralph Clare writes in Chapter 3 of this volume, gave him access to a very different literary world to that of both his own literary peers and the mainstream US publishing industry. Indeed, he was always a little in awe of the genuine literary cosmopolitanism of his editorial board colleagues, along with the unapologetically avant-garde predilections of the journal, next to which his own fiction – even at its most experimental – often appeared relatively conventional. Indeed, in an interview with the *LA Weekly*, Wallace self-deprecatingly revealed that his colleagues at Dalkey considered him to be "almost the house realist," thinking of him "as a quaint *New Yorker*ish, sort of [John] Cheeverish figure."[10]

Such exposure fundamentally altered Wallace's sense of literary ambition, and it is not by accident that his own fictional doppelgänger in *The Pale King*, David Wallace, "dream[s][. . .] of becoming an immortally great fiction writer à la Gaddis or Anderson, Balzac or Perec, &c."[11] Revealingly, Wallace here pairs two US giants with two French counterparts, with one representative in each case taken from a broadly realist or naturalistic genre, and one from a more avant-garde or postmodern tradition. The signature "&c." stands in, I think, for the wider literary world outside France and the United States, but it is telling that Wallace here uses two canonical European signifiers of literary greatness in formulating his own literary ambitions. And while we now have a fairly good sense of how Wallace's work relates to a twentieth-century US lineage of fiction, which

10 Weissman, "Sleek and Brilliant."   11 Wallace, *TPK*, 73.

includes Gaddis and Anderson (though Anderson's influence on Wallace is somewhat less visible), we still lack a way of situating his work alongside the European literary tradition that these twin references gesture toward.

To begin with, it is worth noting that there are countless references to Europe within Wallace's fiction and non-fiction, many of which are telling in what they reveal about his attitude and approach to European literary culture. Europe often functions as a signifier of elegance and style, as in David Cusk's description, in *The Pale King*, of a "heart-stoppingly pretty girl" with "an almost European hauteur about her," along with the Jesuit taxation lecturer who wears a "stylish" hat that strikes the narrator as distinctly "European-looking."[12] Such generalizations also take more intellectual forms: As Adam Kelly rightly notes, the long conversations on political philosophy between Marathe and Steeply in *Infinite Jest* pit American ideas of liberty – phrased in terms of negative liberty in the formulation "freedom-from" – against a European, positive alternative, in the form of "freedom-to."[13] Elsewhere, Wallace uses references to European culture and norms to offer visions of utter alterity, indicating ideological positions and ways of thinking that are entirely alien to the US psyche, such as when Gerhardt Schtitt says that, "like most Europeans of his generation," he finds contemporary US culture at once "hilarious and frightening."[14] It is curious that individual European countries are rarely isolated, but are far more frequently conflated within a broader, continental category, as in Schtitt's love of "excruciatingly loud European opera," or the claim, in "Consider the Lobster," that live crustacean cooking "is big in Europe."[15] When Wallace does attempt more precise distinctions, they tend to be comically clichéd, as when he characterizes the contest between Roger Federer and Rafael Nadal as pitting "the passionate machismo of southern Europe [against] the intricate clinical artistry of the north," or when he describes the Dutch tennis player Richard Krajíček, in "String Theory," as possessing characteristically "phlegmatic Low Country cheer."[16]

As these examples imply, Wallace's image of Europe is in many ways deferential and always slightly idealized: There is something willingly subordinate about his view of European superiority over American crassness, a view at odds with a long legacy of US writers. The widespread perception of American inferiority was something that the Transcendentalists of the mid-nineteenth century, for instance, had little

---

[12] Ibid., 235, 332. [13] Kelly, "Development," 274. [14] Wallace, *IJ*, 82.
[15] Ibid., 756; Wallace, "Consider," *CL*, 250. [16] Wallace, "String Theory," *ST*, 220.

time for (Henry David Thoreau famously proclaimed, "I must walk toward Oregon, and not toward Europe," since that is the "way the nation is moving"[17]). Wallace's sense of cultural and literary inferiority might be slightly more complex than the kind that most troubled Thoreau and Ralph Waldo Emerson, but it nonetheless often inhabits a similar logic of yearning and displacement. Taken together, such invocations of Europe, as incidental as they might appear within the texts themselves, are highly revealing. More importantly, though, how did Wallace use and situate himself in relation to European literature? My own earlier work has argued that he frequently used his encounters with European literature to get outside – in one way or another – American paradigms and cultural assumptions (not in the sense of *transcending* such paradigms, but in momentarily sidestepping or defamiliarizing them), Crucially, he also incorporated and responded to the work of European novelists in order to try and stake out a position for himself within literary traditions broader than contemporary US fiction.

I want to give just one example to highlight the complexity of Wallace's literary debts to European literature: the portrayal of the recovering drug addict Randy Lenz in *Infinite Jest*. There are some US intertexts present in this characterization as well: Lenz carries with him a hollowed-out copy of William James's *The Varieties of Religious Experience*, for instance, which he clearly read at least part of before using it as a decoy for his cocaine stash, since he uses one of James's theories to articulate his own "*Catharsis* of resolving."[18] But there are two European references that I see as carrying more weight. The first is to Georg Büchner's 1835 novella *Lenz*, which Wallace drew on heavily in his own characterization of Randy Lenz: Both characters are constantly walking or in motion, use a disjointed syntax that stems from psychological disintegration, are noticeably ugly, and have confidants to whom they divulge their innermost thoughts at great length. Wallace also gives his own Lenz Polish ancestry, perhaps in a nod to the supposedly European Romantic proclivities he is exhibiting, and is playfully ironic with Lenz's name, an obvious homonym for *lens*, which is not exactly fitting for a character who is constantly distracted, unfocused and opaque to himself. But the most obvious instance of rewriting occurs through the precarious and dangerous inner lives of both characters: Both are attempting to detox and nurse themselves back to health (Jakob Lenz in Ban de la Roche, after episodes of psychosis, and Wallace's Lenz at Ennet House, where cocaine withdrawals cause him to develop several

---

[17] Thoreau, "Walking," 234.   [18] Wallace, *IJ*, 544.

obsessive-compulsive disorders) and both try to redeem themselves
through violence. For Büchner's Lenz, violence takes the form of grotesque
acts of self-harm, which are formulated as a form of purging – such as
"bang[ing] his head against the wall or caus[ing] himself keen physical pain
in some other way" and "scratching himself with nails" in the hope that
"pain [might] beg[i]n to restore his consciousness" – while Randy Lenz
expresses his own pain by torturing animals, which he finds sadistic
pleasure in killing with garbage bags (at one point, he also briefly contemplates killing a homeless man, but is repulsed by the thought).[19] But the
latter Lenz's strategies, as disturbing as they are, are only a subtle exaggeration of Jakob Lenz's hatred for nonhuman animals. During one of his
diatribes in *Lenz*, he argues both that humanity is "among the higher forms
of creation" and that no other life-form can experience emotion:

> He expressed himself in even more detail: how, in all things, there is an
> ineffable harmony, a sound, a supreme happiness which, among the higher
> forms of creation – endowed with a greater number of organs – reaches out
> beyond its own limits, ringing out, resounding and understanding, though
> as a result, all the more deeply affected; whereas among the lower forms,
> everything is more repressed, more limited, yet displays a greater degree of
> inherent calmness. He elaborated upon the theme.[20]

Wallace, too, elaborates upon the themes of Büchner's novella in his
characterization of Randy Lenz, extending certain lines of characterization
in new directions and using Jakob Lenz as a template for his own character.
Moreover, Lenz's representation of fractured psychology states would
surely have appealed to Wallace, since Büchner's groundbreaking novel
incorporates syntactical fragmentation, disjointed transitions between
scenes, dreamlike imagery, all while using predominately vernacular
German.

   And yet these very tangible forms of appropriation are made more
complex once we perceive another European intertext, Witold
Gombrowicz's *Kosmos* [*Cosmos*] (1965). Wallace characterized this
Polish-language novel as a "work of genius" in "The Empty Plenum," in
which he listed *Cosmos* with four other high-art European novels –
Hermann Hesse's *The Glass Bead Game* [*Das Glasperlenspiel*], Voltaire's
Candide, Sartre's *Nausea* [*La Nausée*] and Camus's *The Stranger*
[*L'Étranger*] – as examples of what he helpfully labeled "INTERPRET-
ME fiction," by which he meant works that "not only cry out for critical

[19] Büchner, *Lenz*, 57, 80.   [20] Ibid., 65.

interpretation but actually try to direct them."[21] Clearly, placing his compatriot David Markson in such lofty company allowed for the possibility that another ambitious contemporary US author – Wallace himself – might join the same European heights of greatness. As for his idiosyncratic definition of literary "genius," as someone who has written at length on Wallace's fiction and non-fiction, I am well aware of the way he himself both preempted and subtly tried to "direct" his critics. There is often a sense that one's interpretations have been anticipated by Wallace himself, and that the entire field is merely retracing his own footsteps (this intuition, incidentally, is one of the reasons why the usual prohibitions around the intentional fallacy have largely and perhaps rightly been suspended by Wallace scholars, as the number of arguments that rest heavily on his own interviews and non-fiction attest). Gombrowicz's novel features another macabre, self-hating antihero, who, like Lenz, finds catharsis and aesthetic release in killing small defenseless animals (such as cats and sparrows), and whose feeble grip on reality becomes even more tenuous across the course of the novel. Witold, the character at the heart of *Kosmos*, is another recovering addict, attempting to detox but only succeeding in tangling himself within increasingly paranoid fantasies, just like Randy Lenz. His obsession with solving what he thinks is a mystery leads only to the further devolution of his soul, and his confused search for answers only further reinforces his confusion.

In these twinned points of reference to European literature, Wallace's literary strategy here recalls his memorable formulation of what he called "Eastern-European literature" as offering a solution to some of the representational challenges of US postmodernism. In a brief piece on Zbigniew Herbert's *Pan Cogito* [*Mr Cogito*], Wallace wrote, "It seems significant that only writers from Eastern Europe and Latin America have succeeded in marrying the stuff of spirit and human feeling to the parodic detachment the postmodern experience seems to require."[22] Across his career, Wallace was always on the lookout for ways of appropriating technical devices and narrative strategies from elsewhere (particularly from Europe – specifically Eastern Europe – and Latin America) as a way of both advancing the tradition of US postmodernism he saw himself as having inherited, and of making a case for his own fiction as a serious participant within broader literary culture and traditions.

What this brief survey of just a few of Wallace's European literary engagements ultimately reveals is a very different angle on his work than

---

[21] Wallace, "Empty Plenum," *BFN*, 75.   [22] Wallace, "Mr. Cogito," *BFN*, 122.

that which is commonly used by both critics and general readers. What emerges, as we pay close attention to Wallace's career-long interest in literature from elsewhere, is a picture of a contemporary US writer unusually invested in global literary traditions, who often required deep and sustained engagements with the work of others in order to write his own. Wallace borrowed extensively from European and other non-US writers, often Americanizing, depoliticizing and engaging in various forms of what Michel de Certeau would call aesthetic "poaching" [*la perruque*].[23] (None of this is meant as a criticism, merely a description: I explore these various strategies in far more detail in *Global Wallace*.) He thus fits neatly within Daniel Medin's helpful characterization of J. M. Coetzee, Philip Roth and W. G. Sebald – all writers with whom Wallace has been compared – as writers "for whom immersion in others was crucial to their own fiction."[24]

Furthermore, a richer sense of Wallace's literary intertexts throws up many important questions and hints at new ways of reading his work. What changes when we understand Wallace's fiction as a self-conscious response not only to the work of certain obvious US postmodern precursors but also to a much more global tradition of literature and thought? What are we prompted to see anew in his work once we understand his ambition to write within the "tradition of Western letters"? And how might contemporary writers from outside the United States, who have read (perhaps in translation) and internalized Wallace, begun building on his technical innovations and approaches to further their own fiction? Marshall Boswell has given us a compelling theorization of "the Wallace effect" on a younger and contemporaneous generation of US writers, but what of his no doubt equally substantial – though perhaps more difficult to trace – effect on writers from elsewhere?[25] Of course, these are just a few of the questions we might be prompted to ask in the light of Wallace's engagements with the European literary tradition. But my sense is that it will alter his legacy considerably if we are able to sustain a sophisticated approach to his fiction and non-fiction that takes seriously their investments in world literature alongside their more readily apparent connections to earlier US fiction. The fact that his work looks both outward (to Europe, and other parts of the literary globe) as well as inward (to fellow Americans) marks him as a complex and conflicted cosmopolitan, a dimension of his work that we need to find ways of registering in order to gain a fuller sense of Wallace's artistic achievements.

---

[23] Certeau, *Practice*, 25.   [24] Medin, *Three Sons*, 14.   [25] Boswell, *The Wallace Effect*.

CHAPTER 6

David Foster Wallace and Poetry

Philip Coleman

Who is the "fifty-six-year-old American poet" – "the fourth most anthologized poet in the history of American belles lettres" – David Foster Wallace writes about in "Death Is Not the End," the second piece in *Brief Interviews with Hideous Men*?[1] Not quite as hideous as some of the men who appear later in the collection, the portrait Wallace paints is nonetheless that of a man who is hard to like in part because the banal details of his private self – from the "modest swell of his abdomen" to the "simulated-rubber thongs on his feet"[2] – feel somehow at odds with the description of him as "a poet two separate American generations have hailed as the voice of their generation" and "the first American-born poet ever [...] to receive [...] the coveted Nobel Prize for Literature."[3] The listing of the poet's awards and prizes in the opening sentences of the piece place him on a cultural pedestal against which Wallace's positioning of him "lying in an unwet XL Speedo-brand swimsuit in an incrementally reclinable canvas deck chair" creates an uneasy tension.[4] A sense of solipsistic smugness is suggested that reaches its culmination in the minutely observed features of the poet's body, his "forehead dotted with perspiration, his tan deep and rich, the insides of his upper legs nearly hairless, his penis curled tightly on itself inside the tight swimsuit, his Vandyke neatly trimmed."[5]

Wallace's description of the poet in "Death Is Not the End" creates an expectation of recognition. This is prefigured and reinforced by his fictional engagement with "real-life" figures in stories such as "Lyndon," for example, in *Girl with Curious Hair*, but it is undermined by the author's insistence, in the unnumbered preliminary pages of *Brief Interviews with Hideous Men*, that "[t]he characters and events in this book are fictitious."[6] While it may be tempting to use the details given in the text to guess at the

---

[1] Wallace, "Death," *BI*, 2. [2] Ibid. [3] Ibid., 1. [4] Ibid. [5] Ibid., 3. [6] Ibid., n.p.

poet's identity – we are told that he was born in September 1938 and will celebrate his fifty-seventh birthday in 1995, the year when the story is set – Wallace ultimately has bigger fish to fry. In the first sentence, we are informed that he is "known in American literary circles as 'the poet's poet' or sometimes simply 'the Poet,'" but Wallace's narrator is not being merely sarcastic.[7] The figure of "the Poet" is known not just in "American literary circles" but more generally in the cultural history of the United States as an Emersonian construct through which, from the nineteenth century onward, the nation's artistic efforts have often been brought into what Albert Gelpi (after Ezra Pound) has called "a coherent splendor" that is born out of "the imaginative fashioning of the unruly and resistant materials of experience."[8] For Gelpi, this is the "goal" of the American modernist poet, but it has its origins in the nineteenth-century writings of Ralph Waldo Emerson and his disciple Walt Whitman, for whom the relationship between disparate aspects of experience was the focus of intense artistic investigation.

In "Death Is Not the End," Wallace gives us the figure of "the Poet" in a late-twentieth-century vignette that recalls Emerson's insistence that "[w]e were put into our bodies, as fire is put into a pan, to be carried about; but there is no accurate adjustment between the spirit and the organ."[9] Wallace's portrait of the prizewinning contemporary "poet," in other words, is "complexly shadowed"[10] by the figure of the (Emersonian) "Poet": Notwithstanding the comic absurdity of the image of the man presented before us, he is a member of Emerson's "new nobility [. . .] conferred in groves and pastures, and not in castles, or by the sword-blade."[11] The "fire" and "spirit" are not the same thing as "the organ" or the physical body –one is merely the carrier of the other. In short, the "poet" is not the "Poet" and the distinction between these lies at the heart of "Death Is Not the End." The story may then be read as a text that expands on what W. B. Yeats described as "The Choice" in his poem of that title, between "Perfection of the life, and of the work."[12] Here is a poet, Wallace infers, whose "work" has achieved the highest levels of aesthetic excellence and recognition. However, unlike the artist who "is forced to choose" between a "heavenly mansion" and "an empty purse,"[13] Wallace's poet seems to have it all. He has it all, moreover, because he is a "Poet" and, as such, he is a kind of ideal figure for Wallace, who was in his midthirties when "Death Is Not the End" was written.

---

[7] Ibid., 1.   [8] Gelpi, *Splendor*, 2.   [9] Emerson, *Prose and Poetry*, 447.
[10] Wallace, "Death," *BI*, 3.   [11] Ibid., 467.   [12] Yeats, *Poems*, 296.   [13] Ibid., 296–97.

Wallace was interested in the problem of artistic success throughout his career, but it was primarily a question of aesthetic fulfillment, specifically to do with this sense of the relationship between content and form. Indeed, the best description of it he could find came from a letter Yeats wrote to Dorothy Wellesley in 1936, which Wallace paraphrased in his interview with Larry McCaffery in 1993 in response to a question about his "approach to form/content issues."[14] Describing his pursuit of "a special sort of buzz" that he likens to "an epiphany in Joyce's original sense" and to certain kinds of mathematical "proof-completion," he says, "It was really an experience of what I think Yeats called 'the click of a well-made box.' Something like that. The word I always think of it as is 'click.'"[15] This is an important moment in Wallace's account of his practice as an artist, but it is also crucial to an understanding of the central role that poetry played in his development. Wallace was concerned with the question of genre – the difference between fiction and non-fiction, for example, or the relationship between the short story and the novel: These are issues he explored throughout his work.[16] His reference to Yeats in the McCaffery interview, however, suggests that for him there is something "special" (his word) about poetry, and he acknowledges it in the works of a wide range of poets, including John Donne, Gerard Manley Hopkins and Philip Larkin.[17] He tells us that "[t]he first fictional clicks [he] encountered were in Donald Barthelme's 'The Balloon'" and in "Don DeLillo's stuff [. . .] almost line by line," but he does not hear it in the work of John Updike. It is also there, he says, in the work of Argentine author Manuel Puig – who "clicks like a fucking Geiger counter" – as well as the work of Puig's compatriot, Julio Cortázar.[18]

In his original letter to Dorothy Wellesley, Yeats used the idea of the "click" to distinguish between prose and poetry. "The correction of prose," he wrote, "because it has no fixed laws, is endless, a poem comes right with a click like a closing box."[19] Yeats is writing here about writing itself, not about interpretation, but in his reference to the Irish poet, Wallace breaks down the distinction between poetry and prose (indeed, assuming he did

---

[14] McCaffery, "Interview," 34.   [15] Ibid., 34–35.
[16] See, for example, Wallace's essay "Deciderization 2007," in which he analyses the differences between fiction and nonfiction (*BFN*, 299–317). "Westward" is a frustratingly good example of Wallace's explorations in the interstices between the short story and the novel/novella forms (*GCH*, 231–373). The title of "Westward," indeed, is worth noting in the context of Wallace and poetry because it is taken from a poem of the same title by George Berkeley. See Berkeley, *Works*, 373.
[17] McCaffery, "Interview," 35.   [18] Ibid.   [19] Yeats, *Letters*, 22.

not read Puig and Cortázar in their original Spanish, his claim also has some bearing on his understanding of what can be achieved in translation). Barthelme, DeLillo, Donne, Hopkins, Larkin, Cortázar, Puig: what unites them all, novelists and poets, is the "click." Problematically, of course, what unites them too is the fact that they are all men, and Wallace's sense of a poetic pantheon, so to speak, is predominantly male.[20] In another interview, with Laura Miller in 1996, he praises Donne and Larkin again – Larkin "more than anyone else" – but also Louise Glück and Mary Karr.[21] These references are fleeting, however, and one longs for Wallace to slow down and engage with the poets he mentions, male and female, with the attention to detail he uses when he writes about the work of David Markson, say, or the films of David Lynch.[22] Wallace's short essay on Polish poet Zbigniew Herbert's *Mr. Cogito* – described by him as the "best book of 1994" when it was published in translation into English that year – also provides a brief glimpse into the young American author's clear interest in contemporary poetry and poetics outside the United States, as Thompson has illustrated in the preceding chapter.[23]

On one occasion when he does write about poetry in some depth, interestingly, it is to the intergeneric form of the so-called prose poem that he turns his attention, in a review of the December 2001–March 2002 issue of *The Prose Poem: An International Journal*.[24] Wallace's review contains little to recommend the anthology or its contents: He suggests that only 31 of the anthology's 204 prose poems are "good/alive/powerful/interesting enough to persist in [the] reader's mind more than 60 seconds after completion" and only one author (David Ignatow) is said to have created works that are "so totally beautiful and merciless that you can't forget them even if you want to."[25] In the course of his discussion, however, Wallace considers "the Prose Poem per se" in a way that gives some insight into his sense of poetry itself, no matter who it is written by, and what it meant to him:

> Like all self-consciously transgressive poetic forms, the p.p. [i.e. the prose poem] is, by both definition and intent, anti-formal. That is, it is distin-guished as a form primarily by what it lacks, viz. stuff like line breaks,

---

[20] To put it another, less polite way: What unites them all is not just the "click," but the *dick*. For an extended analysis of Wallace's failings in relation to the ways that he wrote, or did not write, about gender and sexuality, see Hayes-Brady, *Failures*.
[21] See Burn, *Conversations*, 63.
[22] See "Empty Plenum," *BFN*, 73–116, and "David Lynch Keeps His Head," *SFT*, 146–212.
[23] Wallace, "Mr. Cogito," *BFN*, 121–22.   [24] Ibid., 243–56.   [25] Ibid., 249.

enjambment, formal rhyme- or metrical schemes, etc. At the same time, a prose poem very consciously calls itself a *poem*, which of course sends the reader a message, namely that this is a particular kind of literary art that demands a particular kind of reading – slow, careful, with extra attention paid to certain special characteristics. Not least of these special characteristics are the compression and multivalence of the poem's syntax and the particular rhythms and tensions of the poem's music. These are what give a poem the weird special urgency that both justifies and rewards the extra work a reader has to put into reading it. And see that it's nearly always *formal* features that create and convey this poetic urgency: e.g., the tension of the line breaks against the lines' own punctuation and meter, the use of breaks and enjambment and metrical scheme to control speed, emphasis, multivalence of expression, etc.[26]

In this passage, we get a very clear sense of Wallace's appreciation of poetry and the particular demands it makes not just on the reader but also on the writer of poems. Moreover, this passage, and the various and often impassioned references to individual poets he makes in interviews, combine to give the impression that poetry mattered a great deal to Wallace as he sought to fine-tune his craft and define his sense of his own work's "weird special urgency" in prose.

Wallace's appreciation of the "special characteristics" of poetry is reflected in the many references to individual poets that are not only scattered throughout his works but that also, at times, serve specific structural and thematic functions in a wide range of his texts. He often refers to well-known poets for comic effect. In *The Broom of the System*, for example, Larkin's "This Be the Verse" – a poem widely known for its mordant comedy – is dropped into a conversation between LaVache and Lenore when we are told that Gramma Lenore would "go on and on about Auden and Wittgenstein, who she thinks are like jointly God."[27] Much has been written about the philosophical side of this conjunction in Wallace's work, but the role of two major English poets here, and others elsewhere, has not been examined in any detail. In terms of the relationship between poetry and comedy, indeed, it is hard to read Emily Dickinson's poems in a "serious" way once one reads, in *Infinite Jest*, that "every single one of Ms. Dickinson's canonical poems could by [*sic*] sung without loss or syllabic distortion to the tune of 'The Yellow Rose (of Texas).'"[28] Orin Incandenza's metrical observation is echoed and developed later in the text when we read that Hal "taps his fingers in a little

---

[26] Ibid., 253–54 (emphases in original).   [27] Wallace, *BS*, 249, 328.   [28] Wallace, *IJ*, 1005.

anapestic gallop" over a "console's power unit" while they are talking.[29] Moments such as these demonstrate Wallace's sense in which the structures and patterns of formal poetry permeate our existence, not just in terms of lines remembered from the poets we may have read – such as Larkin or Dickinson – but in the way that we create the rhythms of our own individual lives.

In *Infinite Jest*, Hal is not the only character who seems to embody poetry in this way. Joelle van Dyne, too, has a keen interest in American poetry. The name of her alter ego, Madame Psychosis, alludes to "Madame Sosostris, famous clairvoyante," in T. S. Eliot's *The Waste Land*.[30] On one occasion, she reads a poem by Amiri Baraka, the important late twentieth-century African American poet, on her radio show, but she is also an obsessive metricist who will observe, for example, that a caller to the station "pronounced *beautiful* like the earlier *interested* in four syllables, splitting the diphthong, betraying her class and origin."[31] "You will be poetry in motion, Jim," James Incandenza Senior tells his son in an important early scene in the novel.[32] Throughout the text, however, poetry and the idea of it as a kind of linguistic system through which an author can "control speed, emphasis, multivalence, etc" (as Wallace says in his ruminations on the prose poem) are used to describe disparate aspects of individual and intersubjective experience, from speech to tennis. "Tell all the truth but tell it slant," Dickinson famously insisted,[33] but Wallace revises this injunction in *Infinite Jest* and writes, in a scene where Don Gately is desperately trying to get at "the truth" at a Boston AA meeting, that this cannot be "a calculated crowd-pleaser": rather, "it has to be the truth *unslanted*, unfortified. And maximally unironic."[34] Wallace reaches toward an understanding of the meaning of "truth" by considering a range of personal experiences and fictional scenarios – from his own encounters with individuals in Alcoholics Anonymous to the creation of the unforgettable character Don Gately – but the notion of "the truth unslanted" comes into focus precisely because the encyclopedic novel that is *Infinite Jest* is placed in a dialogic relation to an eight-line lyric poem written in 1872. Wallace's methods of engaging with poetry throughout his fiction provide important interpretive touchstones that can aid deeper understandings of his work and working methods, therefore, but they are not always obvious. Is there an allusion to John Berryman's Dream Song 153 ("I'm cross with god who has wrecked this generation") when Hal tells

---

[29] Ibid., 1021.   [30] Eliot, *Selected Poems*, 52.   [31] Wallace, *IJ*, 186, 230.   [32] Ibid., 158.
[33] Dickinson, *Poems*, 1872.   [34] Wallace, *IJ*, 369 (emphasis added).

Mario Incandenza that he has "administrative bones to pick with God" early in *Infinite Jest*, for example, or a further, extended reference to Eliot's *The Waste Land* in the description of the Great Concavity's cycle from "Wasteland to lush"?[35]

More explicit references, like when we are told that Lyle "was going through a Whitman period" or Kate Gompert is "reading somebody called Sylvia Plate" (i.e. Plath), are easier to be sure about.[36] The clearest example of Wallace's direct engagement with poetry across his œuvre may be in his short story "Little Expressionless Animals," the first story in *Girl with Curious Hair*. In the preliminary pages to that book, we are told that "[p]art" of the story "makes use of the third stanza of John Ashbery's 'Self Portrait in a Convex Mirror' from John Ashbery's *Selected Poems* (Viking Press, 1985, 192–93)."[37] The bibliographical specificity is interesting here, but we are not told which lines, in particular, from Ashbery's long poem are used, or to what "use" they have been put: The readers must figure these things out for themselves by reading Wallace's story with the same kind of "slow" and "careful" attention he believed poetry demands. Toward the end of "Little Expressionless Animals," in one of the tenderest moments in Wallace's early fiction, the character Julie tells Faye, her lover: "That's when I love you, if I love you, [. . .] when your face moves into expression."[38] In the scene that follows, Julie tries to explain what she means not only by referring to poetry and how it has informed her sense of self – "'You asked me once how poems informed me,' she says" – but she works phrases from Ashbery's "Self-Portrait in a Convex Mirror" into her account of her relationship with Faye:

> "Oceans are only oceans when they move," Julie whispers. "Waves are what keep oceans from just being very big puddles. Oceans are just waves. And every wave in the ocean is finally going to meet what it moves toward, and break. The whole thing we looked at, the whole time you asked, was obvious. It was obvious and a poem because it was us. See things like that, Faye. Your own face, moving into expression. A wave, breaking on a rock, giving up its shape in a gesture that expresses that shape. See?"[39]

[35] Ibid., 40, 573; Berryman, *Dream Songs*, 172.

[36] Wallace, *IJ*, 254, 593. Lyle is also a William Blake fan. At one point in the novel, we learn that he "often brought some Blake out, as in William Blake, during these all-night sessions, and read Incandenza Blake, but in the voices of various cartoon characters, which Himself eventually started regarding as deep" (*IJ*, 379).

[37] Wallace, *GCH*, n.p. [38] Wallace, "Little Expressionless Animals," *GCH*, 41.

[39] Ibid., 40–42.

In this passage, Wallace takes lines from Ashbery's poem – "Like a wave breaking on a rock, giving up/Its shape in a gesture that expresses that shape"[40] – and sets them moving in a new context, not just that of his story but in an intimate exchange between two women at a moment of particular intensity in their relationship. In an important sense, Ashbery's poem is taken over by Wallace. However, Wallace's reworked text affirms a belief in the force of the poetic that comes into being and "expresses a shape" in (human) form.

Wallace's sense of literary form is complex and multifaceted, and it could be suggested that one does not need to acknowledge his engagements with poetry to appreciate this. Indeed, to a great extent, his reputation firmly rests on the work he produced as a writer of prose: three novels, three collections of short stories, three collections of essays, and a number of other works of non-fiction that explore aspects of contemporary music, mathematics and philosophy. In each of these works, however, in different and often unexpected ways, Wallace turns to specific poetic examples in a manner that suggests he had more than a passing interest in the genre. "Rappers are Miltonic devils," Mark Costello says in *Signifying Rappers*, the book on early rap music he co-wrote with Wallace in 1990, and in one section of the book, Wallace describes how "the best raps are usually operating in a high gear of poetical efficiency *against* the almost Eliotically strenuous limitations of both complex rhythmic demand and the requirements of near-cognate rhyme."[41] Wallace's point here is not only that rap should be taken seriously as verbal art, but that it is perhaps more complex and critically amenable to "close listening" than much of what passes for what he calls "good serious poetry" in the late twentieth century.[42] Costello and Wallace insist that the reader/listener must pay attention in order that the "energy, wit, and formal ingenuity of the rap" [*sic*] can be fully appreciated.[43] They appreciate this, however, because they understood what Yeats called "The fascination of what's difficult."[44] In his philosophical work on Richard Taylor, Wallace argues that "if Taylor and the fatalists want to force upon us a metaphysical conclusion, they must do metaphysics, *not* semantics."[45] In those instances where he speaks of the work of individual poets, however, Wallace is often less troubled by semantics – what certain lines or phrases in their poems might "mean" in a literal sense – than he is by the possibility that poetry gives "shape" to more profound, metaphysical meanings.

---

[40] Ashbery, *Selected Poems*, 73.   [41] Wallace, *SR*, 97, 132 (emphasis in original).
[42] Ibid., 96–97.   [43] Ibid.   [44] Yeats, *Poems*, 142.   [45] Wallace, *FTL*, 213.

Some of Wallace's works of fiction may be read as attempts to get at these deeper significations in particular poetic texts by playing with their formal shapes and structures. His story "Death Is Not the End," for example, can be seen as an extended fictional meditation on the following lines from William Carlos Williams's "Asphodel, that Greeny Flower," from which Wallace's title appears to be taken:

> I have learned much in my life
>> from books
>>> and out of them
>> about love.
>>> Death
>>>> is not the end of it.[46]

What does anyone learn "from books" about love or death? It is clear that Wallace learned a great deal about life, and art, from reading poetry. Whether he was writing short stories or novels, essays or reviews, it was rarely far from his mind.[47] In his important essay "E Unibus Pluram," he says that he identifies the poets James Cummins and Bill Knott by "Plucking from [his] shelves almost at random," but his comments about their work, and the work of other poets elsewhere, suggests a more strategic and sustained engagement with modern and contemporary poetry.[48] *The Pale King*, Wallace's posthumously published novel, alludes to John Keats's poem "La Belle Dame sans Merci" in its title, as Clare Hayes-Brady has discussed,[49] and it takes as an epigraph a quotation from a prose poem by contemporary American poet Frank Bidart: "We fill pre-existing forms and when we / fill them we change them and are changed."[50] There is a playful reference here to the fact that many of the characters in *The Pale King* spend their lives literally filling in "pre-existing forms" on behalf of the Internal Revenue Service of the United States. In a more serious way, however, Wallace is also suggesting that poetry may be the best "form" we have to "fill in" the metaphysical gaps that remain when the work of semantics is done.

---

[46] Williams, *Poems* II, 314.
[47] It is worth noting, too, that Wallace's earliest writings, composed when he was six or seven years old, are poems. See Wallace's "Viking Poem" at www.theawl.com/2010/03/david-foster-wallace-viking-poem/.
[48] Wallace, "Unibus," *SFT*, 45.   [49] See Hayes-Brady, "'Palely Loitering,'" 142–56.
[50] Wallace, *TPK*, xii.

CHAPTER 7

David Foster Wallace's "Non"-Fiction

Martin Paul Eve

In addition to his voluminous fictional output, David Foster Wallace wrote a large quantity of work that can be deemed non-fiction. The subject matter of this material is diverse and ranges from rap music and race, through the philosophy of mathematics, US electoral politics, and animal welfare in the gastronomic space, up to prescriptivist grammar. It is partly Wallace's reputation in the non-fictional space – perhaps as a "philosopher-novelist" of sorts – that has led to more general claims for his "genius" and literary canonization.[1] For indeed, the symbiosis of the essay form with the career of the contemporary novelist is undeniable.[2]

Before considering Wallace's non-fictional writing, it is first worth querying the strict division between "fiction" and "fact" that structures this binary. For, in essays such as "A Supposedly Fun Thing I'll Never Do Again," Wallace introduces humorous set pieces that add to the comic timbre of the work in general, but that seem unlikely, actually, to have occurred. As an example, there is the instance where Wallace claims in this essay that he believes he is surveilled while aboard the cruise ship, thus allowing the cabin crew to conduct their cleaning activities only when he is out of his cabin for more than thirty minutes. And certainly this episode provides Wallace with some humorous material:

> So now for a while I theorize that somehow a special crewman is assigned to each passenger and follows that passenger at all times, using extremely sophisticated techniques of personal surveillance and reporting the passenger's movements and activities and projected time of cabin-return back to Steward HQ or something, and so for about a day I try taking extreme evasive actions – whirling suddenly to check behind me, popping around

[1] For more on this, see Severs, *Balancing Books*, 3.
[2] For just one example, see Childs and Gigante, *The Cambridge History of the British Essay*.

corners, darting in and out of Gift Shops via different doors, etc. – never one sign of anybody engaged in surveillance.[3]

But a fundamental question remains: Is this passage *non-fiction*? Do readers really believe that Wallace took these actions? I would argue not. Instead, portions of Wallace's journalistic and essayistic outputs should be thought of as "creative non-fiction." That is, in keeping with the near-term literary-historical field in which he was working – postmodernism – Wallace's non-fiction is not straightforwardly *non*, but instead blurs the creative-critical boundary. I further contend here that Wallace's non-fiction writing, using many of the same metafictional techniques as in his fiction, needs to be understood in relation to poststructuralist philosophies of text that ask *what we mean by fiction vs non-fiction*. Does non-fiction really mean "writing that refers to an extra-textual reality"?

Since the high point of poststructuralist theory in the 1970s, it has been a literary-philosophical commonplace to state that there is no absolute difference between literary and nonliterary writing. That is, there is nothing a work of fiction or non-fiction can do within its own language to persuade a reader absolutely of its own factuality or fictionality. John Searle and Jacques Derrida have both claimed this at various points. For Searle, "The utterance acts of fiction are indistinguishable from the utterance acts of serious discourse," while for Derrida, "No exposition, no discursive form is intrinsically or essentially literary before or outside of the function it is assigned."[4] The only problem for such a view is that Andrew Piper shows that machine classification *can* distinguish between fact and fiction with over 95 percent accuracy using just a 1,250-word stretch of text.[5] For the sake of clarity, this computational approach is not checking whether a text is true. It verifies only the work's "intended truth claims" within language.[6] While future work may wish computationally to examine the linguistic traits of Wallace's fiction against his non-fiction, the remainder of this chapter is devoted to a representative descriptive sampling of Wallace's non-fiction across his career, mostly drawn from *Signifying Rappers* (1990); *A Supposedly Fun Thing I'll Never Do Again* (1997); *Everything and More: A Compact History of Infinity* (2003); *Consider the Lobster* (2005); *This Is Water* (2009); *Fate, Time, and Language: An Essay*

---

[3] Wallace, "A Supposedly Fun Thing," *SFT*, 256–353.
[4] Searle, "The Logical Status of Fictional Discourse," 68; Blanchot and Derrida, *The Instant of My Death*, 28.
[5] Piper, *Enumerations: Data and Literary Study*.
[6] Ibid., 98. Portions of this paragraph are drawn from Eve, "Review of Andrew Piper."

on Free Will (2010); and *Both Flesh and Not* (2012). For the sake of expediency, rather than because it is the only classificatory system or because these works can neatly be so carved, I divide the rest of this chapter into the headings of "Philosophy," "Experiential Argument" and "Politics." It is worth admitting, up front, that this schema perhaps accords less attention to one area of Wallace's practice than it might. For Wallace also wrote works of literary criticism. Some of these pieces, such as his 1997 review of John Updike's *Toward the End of Time*, have become influential in their own right, particularly in this instance for introducing the phrase "the Great Male Narcissists" to refer to Norman Mailer, Updike and Philip Roth.[7] Such work can, also, however, often fall under the rubric of "politics," rooted as they usually are within sociological paradigms. Hence, despite its tendency to oversimplify, I stick to the aforementioned mapping for this chapter's cartography. Finally, for this introduction, it would be remiss not to note that there are, on occasion, differences between the versions of Wallace's non-fiction essays that were published in the original serial venues (journals, magazines and so forth) and the editions that appear in subsequent anthologies.[8] Thus, it is always worth comparing sources when working with Wallace's non-fiction writing.

Philosophy

It is no secret that his father was a philosophy professor and that Wallace's undergraduate degree was a joint major in English and philosophy. Indeed, it is often reported that it was the philosophical element of Wallace's intellectual purview that dominated, with one commentator remarking that he "knew him as a philosopher with a fiction hobby."[9] This comes across in Wallace's non-fiction writing, which has a strong philosophical strand, embracing the histories of mathematics, logic and other areas, and most strongly embodied in *Everything and More* and *Fate, Time, and Language*. There have also, to date, been at least two volumes solely dedicated to exploring Wallace's philosophical output.[10] It could be said, in fact, that much of Wallace's non-fiction writing is philosophical in its content. It is worth noting up front, also, that Wallace's philosophical writings bend problematically toward appropriation for self-help

---

[7] Wallace, "John Updike, Champion Literary Phallocrat," *CL*.
[8] See, for instance, "Tense Present" in *Harper's Magazine* vs. "Authority and American Usage" in *CL*.
[9] Wallace, *Fate, Time, and Language*, 3.
[10] Bolger and Korb (eds.), *Gesturing toward Reality*; Cahn and Eckert (eds.), *Freedom and the Self*.

purposes.[11] In particular, the publication of his almost-schmaltzy Kenyon commencement address as *This Is Water* has tended, in the popular imagination, to overshadow Wallace's actual philosophical work. It is debatable whether Wallace would even have classified this text as "philosophy," filled, as it is, with "didactic little stor[ies]."[12] Wallace's only formal contribution to philosophical literature is the published version of his undergraduate philosophy honors thesis, *Fate, Time, and Language*. This work is a response to a 1962 essay in *The Philosophical Review* by Richard Taylor called "Fatalism."[13] In "Fatalism," Taylor presents a novel argument for fatalistic thinking – that is, the notion that all actions are predetermined and cannot be modified. Taylor does this by presenting six widely accepted propositions from contemporary philosophy and showing them to be logically incompatible with the idea of free will. The basic twist that Taylor achieves is to show that, while we accept that our actions in the present cannot influence the past (and, indeed, are constrained or determined by them), the same can be said of *future events*. That is, that a gun barrel is cool in the future, for Taylor, can be shown to determine the fact that the gun was not fired in the present. Taylor's article prompted grave disquiet, as evidenced by the number of direct responses, which are collected in *Fate, Time, and Language*. Yet, while there was consensus that Taylor's conclusions were undesirable – that either the universe is fatalistic or that there are major problems with some of the core propositions of contemporary philosophy – there was no agreement among respondents as to precisely *what* was wrong with Taylor's reasoning. For Wallace, as well as for Steven Cahn, who edited the Wallace volume, one of the core problems with the respondents was that many of them argued that Taylor's piece could not be correct *because* it ended up showing that fatalism was indeed how the universe works.

Wallace's award-winning thesis and posthumous book argued that the problem in Taylor's logic required a new formal language that could express what he calls the intensional-physical-modality system. Reading this system is not for the fainthearted (the first rule of the system is: "$[[t_n p]]_w = 1$ iff $[[p]]_w,^{t/n} = 1$"). The basic gist of Wallace's argument is easier to grasp, though, and concerns situated truths with respect to physical embodiment ("situational physical modality"). It asks questions of "impossibility" with respect to the placement of an individual at any particular time; what does it mean to say that one *can* do

---

[11] D. T. Max, "Why David Foster Wallace Should Not Be Worshipped as a Secular Saint."
[12] Wallace, *TIW*.   [13] Taylor, "Fatalism."

something – or has the possibility to do something – when that person is situated at a particular geo-temporal coordinate? Others have explored more thoroughly the extent to which Wallace's contribution marks a serious philosophical intervention, with Columbia University Press insisting that the book underwent thorough peer review, while the paratexts in the edited edition tactfully sidestep an appraisal of the correctness of his argument. Wallace's other philosophical contribution, though, was through his work on the philosophy of mathematics.

In *Everything and More: A Compact History of Infinity*, Wallace turns his attention to Cantorian mathematical philosophies. This is not a work of original philosophy or history, but rather a piece of "pop technical writing" that explores some of the ways in which mathematical paradoxes can be resolved within specific paradigms of understanding "infinity." It is also a work that has attracted some scathing denunciations from mathematicians. As Amir D. Aczel put it, "this book is very disappointing. I found mathematical misinterpretations [. . .,] many mathematical statements that are patently wrong [. . . and] Wallace is not the right expositor of these ideas."[14] Michael Harris, another professor of mathematics, wrote that Wallace's book was "laced through and through with blunders of every magnitude."[15] Elsewhere, a further well-qualified commentator called *Everything and More* "a train wreck of a book, a disaster."[16] The Wallace fansite, *The Howling Fantods*, even contains a mathematical errata document that runs to three A4 pages in length of corrections to Wallace's math.[17] Readers of this work should, therefore, be careful in approaching Wallace's history of infinity as a work of mathematics. Instead, as Roberto Natalini has shown, this work perhaps better serves as a key to understanding certain formal decisions made in the crafting of Wallace's novels, including his indebtedness to other math-centric works, such as Don DeLillo's *Ratner's Star* (1976).[18] Yet the question remains: If the book is so bad as a work of mathematics, what does this say for our use of such explication as a backdrop against which to situate Wallace's fiction? Wallace was, to some extent, skeptical of such uses of his philosophical writings to underscore his fictional work. In an oft-quoted 2006 interview, he disarmingly said, "If some people read my fiction and see it as fundamentally about philosophical ideas, what it probably means is that these are pieces where the characters are not as alive and interesting as I meant

[14] Aczel, "Good Novelists."　　[15] M. Harris, "A Sometimes Funny Book."
[16] Rucker, "Infinite Confusion," 313.　　[17] Ragde, "Mathematical Errata."
[18] Natalini, "David Foster Wallace and the Mathematics of Infinity."

them to be."[19] Yet the very idea that Wallace might be a "therapeutic" writer is indebted to his association with Wittgensteinian philosophy and the idea that "doing philosophy" might or should itself be a therapeutic activity.[20] It is, therefore, worth noting that Wallace's philosophical writing does overlap with his fiction. For instance, the "Eschaton" game in *Infinite Jest* (1996) relies on various philosophies of mathematics and representational/critical reality.[21] Likewise, *The Broom of the System* has an explicitly Wittgensteinian theme. In all, though, it is clear that Wallace's formal philosophical and mathematical texts are, in themselves, relatively slight and not well regarded by those outside of his fictional fanbase, bucking the critical trend that Thompson identified in a previous chapter of following Wallace's implicit (and explicit) directions for interpretation (and not even well regarded by mathematicians who enjoy his fiction). Where his non-fiction writing becomes stronger, though, is in his experiential creative non-fiction.

Experiential Argument

Wallace's non-fiction really comes into its own when he writes in magazines about his experiences, be they aboard cruise ships ("A Supposedly Fun Thing"), watching Roger Federer play tennis ("Roger Federer as Religious Experience"), and visiting lobster festivals ("Consider the Lobster"). These pieces allow for his expansive prose style to work its humor without the threat of inaccuracy within the contents that plagues his technical works on philosophy and mathematics. That said, as noted earlier, there *are* inaccuracies in these works that cast some doubt on the definition of "non-fiction." Consider Wallace's description of a Federer shot:

> Federer's still near the corner but running toward the centerline, and the ball's heading to a point behind him now, where he just was, and there's no time to turn his body around, and Agassi's following the shot in to the net at an angle from the backhand side … and what Federer now does is somehow instantly reverse thrust and sort of skip backward three or four steps, impossibly fast, to hit a forehand out of his backhand corner, all his weight moving backward, and the forehand is a topspin screamer down the line past Agassi at net, who lunges for it but the ball's past him, and it flies straight down the sideline and lands exactly in the deuce corner of Agassi's

---

[19] Karmodi, "A Frightening Time."   [20] See Baskin, *Ordinary Unhappiness.*
[21] Wallace, *IJ*, 321–41. For more on this, see Eve, "Equivocationary Horseshit."

side, a winner – Federer's still dancing backward as it lands. And there's that familiar little second of shocked silence from the New York crowd before it erupts, and John McEnroe with his color man's headset on TV says (mostly to himself, it sounds like), "How do you hit a winner from that position?"[22]

Yet, in the age of YouTube, a quick verification search shows that McEnroe's comment applies to a shot that is barely anything like the one described by Wallace. As with many religious experiences, seeing Federer play tennis was clearly deeply personal for Wallace and difficult to correlate with any extratextual, shared reality. Wallace's non-fiction certainly comes with fictional embellishments. More positively, though, perhaps what works best with Wallace's experiential essays is that they are also all driven by an argumentative thrust. In the case of Federer, Wallace states that "The specific thesis here is that if you've never seen the young man play live, and then do, in person, on the sacred grass of Wimbledon, through the literally withering heat and then wind and rain of the '06 fortnight, then you are apt to have what one of the tournament's press bus drivers describes as a 'bloody near-religious experience.'"[23] Elsewhere, the arguments that drive Wallace's non-fiction are arguably more extreme. When it comes to the Maine Lobster Festival, for example, Wallace argues that we should consider the sentience of the animal that is boiled alive, and even takes this so far as to compare the festival with the Holocaust.

Time and again, Wallace crafts his essayistic experiential pieces into argumentative propositions that deliberately contrast two extreme poles for humorous effect. So while Wallace claims, in "A Supposedly Fun Thing," that he has been hired to write "a directionless essayish thing," with a "paucity of direction or angle," he repeatedly distrusts such commissions. "They keep saying – on the phone, Ship-to-Shore, very patiently – not to fret about it," he writes. Yet Wallace also says that "They are sort of disingenuous, I believe, these magazine people. They say all they want is a sort of really big experiential postcard – go, plow the Caribbean in style, come back, say what you've seen." Wallace instead turns his experiential postcard into an argument about how the "pampered" living style, marketed as featuring on board a seven-night cruise, is transformed into a "kind of death-and-dread-transcendence."[24] It is, of course, the bathetic differences between these poles – a seven-night luxury cruise and "death-and-dread-transcendence"; a lobster festival and the Holocaust; Roger Federer and religious experience – that drive Wallace's creative non-fiction.

[22] Wallace, "Federer as Religious Experience," *BFN*, 6.   [23] Ibid.
[24] Wallace, "A Supposedly Fun Thing," *SFT*, 256–354.

Wallace gives us arguments, but they are often deliberately absurd. Wallace's extremity is not just achieved through wild juxtaposition of the everyday and the outlandish; his subject matter is often, itself, also unusual. Consider, for instance, Wallace's essay "Big Red Son," the subject of which is the pornographic film industry and its effect upon contemporary culture. This subject allows Wallace, once more, to create humor in his non-fiction writing. After all, when simply handed character/stage names such as "Dick Filth," there is barely any need for Wallace to return to the Pynchonian naming style that he deployed in his first novel, *The Broom of the System*. It's as though the gags come prepackaged. However, there is also a danger circling around this area. While Wallace takes care to highlight feminist perspectives on pornography and to draw attention to the toxic masculinity that inheres in such culture, as with mathematics, one has to ask whether he is always the right person to do so.[25] After all, as Edward Jackson has highlighted in the wake of D. T. Max's biography, and as later essays in this volume demonstrate, Wallace is intensely problematic with respect to gender and sexuality.[26]

All of which is to say that Wallace's experiential argumentative essays should always be viewed with a critical eye on his perspectivized position. Just as, in his philosophical work, Wallace argued for the importance of embodied positional takes, rather than transcendental subjects, I contend that reading Wallace's "non"-fiction requires us to situate his work in relation to the man, and to pay attention to what we know about his life. For the experiential angle that Wallace brings punctures any bubble of the intentional fallacy; the life and the writing cannot sit wholly apart from one another. Which brings us, finally, to politics in Wallace's writing.

Politics

Although, as Marshall Boswell puts it, "Wallace is not generally thought of as a political novelist," a complex personal politics are evident in his essayistic non-fiction.[27] Perhaps the clearest example of this is in Wallace's profile of Senator John McCain, collected as "Up, Simba" in *Consider the Lobster*. A nonpartisan piece that, in the collected version, comes with a self-situating statement that notes that, on this occasion, Wallace voted for the Democrat Bill Bradley, Wallace's article purports to be neither pro- nor anti- McCain.[28] While Boswell notes the importance

---

[25] Wallace, "Big Red Son," *CL*, 18–19. [26] Jackson, *Toxic Sexuality*; Max, *Every Love Story*.
[27] Boswell, "Trickle-Down Citizenship," 211. [28] Wallace, "Up, Simba," *CL*, 157.

of this essay for the discussion of civics in *The Pale King*, I would personally also draw attention to the humor that Wallace again brings to the
piece, for example, that the press buses are known as "Bullshit 1" and
"Bullshit 2."[29] Perhaps more importantly, though, I would like to highlight that politics in Wallace's non-fiction are to be found in the least likely
of places (although this is perhaps to be expected. Defining "politics" is a
notoriously difficult task, as it encompasses all kinds of interpersonal
interactions, as evidenced in the aforementioned note on Wallace's literary
criticism).[30] One of Wallace's most political, but also, surprisingly, most
readable and ranging essays is his "Authority and American Usage," a
review of a dictionary.[31]

Specifically, Wallace's review of Bryan A. Garner's *A Dictionary of
Modern American Usage* is even subtitled "or, 'Politics and the English
Language' is redundant." This work, which actually unites all the strands
that I have here covered, roves from explications of Wittgenstein's private
language argument to giving a "thesis statement" – the argumentative
trope for which I advocated earlier.[32] Wallace's essay also dedicates a
substantial portion of its rhetoric to the different political stances that
dictionaries can hold. Namely, it argues that those who advocate for
grammatical dictionaries can be either prescriptivist or descriptivist, with
the former camp specifying how language *should* be used, while the latter
describe how language *is* used. This, in itself, represents different polarities
of political opinion in the United States. Wallace goes further than this,
though. In a highly controversial move, he extends the analogy between
prescriptivism and descriptivism to discuss women's reproductive rights in
the context of US democratic tolerance and the *Roe vs. Wade* ruling.[33]
Wallace is cautious and equivocationary here, though. Instead of taking
any kind of principled stance, he instead argues that it is necessary to be
both "Pro-Life and Pro-Choice," in a sort of rejection of binary logic.
Wallace uses a type of rational logic to argue for the respect for life in the
case of doubt as to whether a fetus should be deemed a living human,
while also arguing that he cannot infringe upon the reproductive and
bodily autonomy of a pregnant woman. The answer that Wallace comes
to is, however, mealymouthed and allows him to worm out of the situation
without ever answering the ethical call: One has to pick one's side on the
basis of an individual moral decision that involves a hard choice, not to
evade the choice by claiming that we can take *both* options. And it is on

[29] Ibid., 171.   [30] See, for a good example, Markovits, *The Politics of Sincerity*.
[31] Wallace, "Authority and American Usage," 66–127.   [32] Ibid., 72.   [33] Ibid., 82.

this note that I will close this chapter. Wallace's non-fiction writings – however we choose to define them – provide a rich ground for scholars and fans of his fiction, or as works standing alone. I have sought here to challenge notions that these writings are discrete because they are purely factual, and that they can be separated from Wallace's fiction by a distinction between truth and fabrication. I have also suggested that some artificial groupings – philosophy, experiential argument and politics – can provide frames that help us categorize Wallace's non-fiction writings, to some extent. In all, though, Wallace's non-fiction writings present sources that are not just informative for and generative of his fiction, but that work in symbiosis with those other writings. As such, they deserve and reward close attention in their own right, not necessarily as non-fictions but more as "non"-fiction.

CHAPTER 8

"Thanks Everybody and I Hope You Like It"
David Foster Wallace and Entertainment

Matthew Luter

In many discussions of David Foster Wallace's work, entertainment can get a bad rap. This may seem an odd assertion, given that Wallace's best-known work is centered around a so-called fatal entertainment, the title film within *Infinite Jest* that captivates viewers to the point of paralysis and death. With entertainments like those, who needs enemies? But I want to suggest instead that, throughout Wallace's body of work, neither the creation nor experience of entertainment in itself, as creator or as audience, is a bad thing. The act of bringing something into the world for the purpose of bringing joy or diversion to another person – whether a faceless mass viewership or an intimate loved one – can be an expression of appreciation, even an act of love. Entertainment becomes sinister and threatening, however, when it becomes a means to an end, something that views its audience not as a recipient of a gift but as an opportunity to pursue one's own goals without regard for the feelings of others. Some of Wallace's essays and much existing Wallace criticism subscribe to the Frankfurt School theorists' assumptions that popular entertainment is seductive but potentially oppressive. For instance, in his 2009 memorial essay on Wallace, Jon Baskin asserts that in exposing the dangers of empty, cooler-than-thou satire, "Wallace draws a line from the Frankfurt School to the metafictionists to *The Simpsons* to *The Daily Show*."[1] The ephemeral pleasures of entertainment may threaten to blind viewers to deeper political, existential or spiritual ills, the argument goes.

Be that as it may, Wallace's fiction still holds out the possibility – specifically in a key scene from *Infinite Jest* on which I'll focus here – that entertainment can transcend the forces of mere commerce and the dehumanizing effects of viewing one's audience as a customer only. After glancing at the conventional wisdom in existing criticism regarding how Wallace viewed entertainment, I'll address briefly what we know

---

[1] Baskin, "Death Is Not the End."

biographically about Wallace's own consumption of popular entertainment – and what he saw as its potential value. Then I'll explain how Wallace borrows some of his skepticism toward entertainment from Marxist critics like Fredric Jameson, Max Horkheimer and Theodor Adorno. But crucially, he also tries to imagine a use value for entertainment as an act of communication from creator to recipient. Wallace's fiction certainly critiques those forces that turn artworks into commodities to be traded. It also offers a few examples, even if tentative ones, of a better way.

In his 2010 state-of-the-field essay on Wallace Studies, Adam Kelly coined the term "essay-interview nexus" to describe the centrality of two pieces of writing to an entire generation of scholarship on Wallace.[2] "E Unibus Pluram: Television and U.S. Fiction" and a wide-ranging interview with Larry McCaffery originally ran side by side in a 1993 edition of *The Review of Contemporary Fiction*, and read together, they make clear Wallace's skepticism toward the surface pleasures of entertainment, particularly irony-laden television of the 1980s and early 1990s. In suggesting that many Americans, at their own peril, choose empty entertainment that does not nourish them intellectually or spiritually, Wallace echoes Frankfurt School theorists like Horkheimer and Adorno while also adumbrating Steeply and Marathe's recurring conversation about free will in *Infinite Jest*. Kelly argues that this understanding of Wallace's project had, by 2010, become "established orthodoxy" in critical circles.[3]

But it's important to keep in mind just how admittedly susceptible Wallace was to even the most surface pleasures of entertainment. In the McCaffery interview, for instance, even as he praises artists generally perceived as high-culture icons (such as Leo Tolstoy and Anton Chekhov), he also claims to "revere" the *Terminator* films.[4] He admits that such "Commercial entertainment" often "smooths everything over" in a way that encourages "passive spectation," but he positions himself as no less vulnerable that anyone else to that form of viewership.[5] Several years later, in the book-length conversation with David Lipsky published as *Although of Course You End Up Becoming Yourself*, Wallace speaks highly of several films that, while artistically successful, were also profitable wide-release mainstream movies. He states that "Spielberg's first few things were *magic*," recalls seeing *Blue Velvet* as "[t]he biggest, most important movie experience of my life," and describes *Glory* as "a great movie" and

---

[2] Kelly, "Death of the Author." [3] Ibid. [4] McCaffery, "Interview," 33, 50. [5] Ibid., 33.

"ingenious."[6] Kitschier movies show up too, most prominently the action flick *Broken Arrow*, which prompts Lipsky to note that "he likes movies where things blow up."[7] References to Wallace's soft spot for the musician Alanis Morissette recur through Lipsky's book as well. And in one 1996 profile, Wallace even admits to weaknesses for *Baywatch* and *The Love Boat*.[8]

In the Lipsky conversation, Wallace refers frequently and approvingly to the longtime *New Yorker* film critic Pauline Kael, who insisted that popular film is rarely great art, and that the value of its purpose as amiable entertainment should not be underestimated. Wallace shares with Kael, he says, a sense that "the *predictability* in popular art, the *really* formulaic stuff, the stuff that makes *no* attempt to surprise or do anything artistic, is so *profoundly soothing*."[9] While admitting that "a narrative that will take *care* of you, and won't in any way challenge you" could still be "artwise not the greatest art [...] the function it provides is *deep* in a certain way."[10] In other words, to be entertained – or perhaps more importantly, to *feel* entertained – can be an experience of great warmth and solicitude.

The primary obstacle to such solicitude, though, comes via the interference of consumer culture. The anti-consumerist argument that late capitalism has turned all art objects – even those that take experimental or ostensibly noncommercial forms – into mere products has been most prominently articulated by Fredric Jameson. The key claim to his *Postmodernism: or, the Cultural Logic of Late Capitalism* is the assertion that "aesthetic production today has become integrated into commodity production generally."[11] By that logic, artworks that try to entertain, especially as an act of care, might still manage to meet an audience's emotional needs, but in order to do so, they must first enter a marketplace that will inevitably cheapen them by commodifying them. Decades before Jameson, Horkheimer and Adorno made a similar claim, but their grievances with the culture industry add a real fear of popular entertainment's potential to oppress.

"The culture industry perpetually cheats its consumers of what it perpetually promises," Horkheimer and Adorno assert.[12] Popular entertainment might pretend to offer its audiences some sort of uplift potentially associated with great art, but it fails inevitably. No popular

---

[6] Wallace, quoted in Lipsky, *Although of Course*, 166, 169, 209.
[7] Lipsky, *Although of Course*, 122.   [8] Bruni, "The Grunge American Novel," 41.
[9] Wallace, quoted in Lipsky, *Although of Course*, 199 (emphases in original).   [10] Ibid., 199.
[11] Jameson, *Postmodernism*, 4.   [12] Horkheimer and Adorno, "The Culture Industry," 139.

entertainment can truly be art, they contend, emphasizing that the film and radio productions of the early twentieth century are only business ventures, with the same hierarchies and inequalities of any other profit-making venture: "They call themselves industries; and when their directors' incomes are published, any doubt about the social utility of the finished products is removed."[13] Since they exist in the same marketplace as any other product, pop-culture products become homogenized, as "culture now impresses the same stamp on everything," and such conformity of expression is dangerous, because it limits the imagination of working-class audiences.[14] They become passive, "helpless victims to what is offered them."[15] Taken together, the culture industry "ruins the fun" that we might want to associate with the joys of entertainment, "by allowing business considerations to involve it in the ideological clichés of a culture in the process of self-liquidation."[16] Simply put, popular entertainment is a political and artistic dead end, but that is to be expected, Horkheimer and Adorno assert, since democratic societies under capitalism are headed to their own dead ends as well. The Frankfurt School argument finds some articulation in *Infinite Jest* in Marathe's awareness that many Americans, if given the opportunity to watch an entertainment that leads to their own demise, will accept being entertained to death – especially if they have been convinced that the choice has emanated naturally and entirely out of their own free will.

At least within the text of the novel, Wallace does not fully endorse interpreting James Incandenza's film *Infinite Jest* so negatively via an overly theoretical reading of what entertainment can and cannot do. Wallace has film-studies graduate student Molly Notkin voice to Rodney Tine a reading of "the entire perfect-entertainment-as-*Liebestod* myth" that reads as a parody of anti-capitalist academic discourse, right down to a citation of a nonexistent Deleuze monograph.[17] At the level of plot, however, Marathe and Steeply's conversation about the fatal entertainment – let alone the activity of the AFR throughout the novel – certainly positions the *Infinite Jest* cartridge as a weapon of political terrorists. But it's also vital to note that Wallace positions any harm that comes upon a nation as a result of the cartridge as a partially self-inflicted harm. When Marathe asks Steeply the extended rhetorical question, "forget for a moment the Entertainment, and think instead about a USA where such a thing [as accepting a fatal entertainment by choice] could be possible enough for your Office to fear: can such a USA hope to survive for a much longer

---

[13] Ibid., 121.   [14] Ibid., 120.   [15] Ibid., 133.   [16] Ibid., 142–43.   [17] Wallace, *IJ*, 792.

time?," he also suggests that a nation of people so willing to accept their own oppression – however pleasurable it may be – is a nation that was already too far gone before the cartridge ever existed.[18] Wallace has Marathe echo the apocalyptic tone of Horkheimer and Adorno's assertion that capitalist societies were already on the road to ruin, but he casts the problem less in economic terms and more in terms of a self-centered spiritual malaise. As a result, the film *Infinite Jest* becomes one of many examples of entertainment objects in Wallace's *oeuvre* that turn destructive when they become mere tools. They cease to attempt to entertain positively and instead treat other people simply as a means to an end.

But within Wallace's novel, the *Infinite Jest* cartridge is not only that. Its creator saw it as an invitation to connection. Well before it became a tool for those seeking to dominate and neutralize their opponents, James Incandenza intended the film to be an expression of care for Hal. As James's wraith reveals to the hospitalized Don Gately late in the novel, he saw his introspective son turning "blank, inbent, silent, frightening, mute" and "spent the whole sober last ninety days of his animate life working tirelessly to contrive a medium via which he and the muted son could simply *converse*."[19] *Infinite Jest* was a "last resort," as he tried to "[m]ake something so bloody compelling it would reverse thrust on a young self's fall into the womb of solipsism, anhedonia, death in life."[20] Notably, the original intent for the film was not merely to entertain Hal passively but to summon Hal's positive and participatory reaction. The wraith's reflection on James's intent as a filmmaker ends by bemoaning how awfully he has been misunderstood by most of his viewers: "The scholars and Foundations and disseminators never saw that his most serious wish was: *to entertain*."[21] With this confession in mind, James's decision to ignore all other observers, critics or collaborators, in favor of gearing his production to one other person – and someone he perceives as suffering, in great need of care – becomes even more poignant.

As dismissive as Wallace seems toward the Jameson/Horkheimer and Adorno school of thought, through Molly Notkin's pseudo-intellectualism, he seems equally affirming of the artistic theory of Lewis Hyde. Wallace has endorsed Hyde's *The Gift* with an approving blurb, and some of his comments in interviews are indebted to Hyde's fundamental proposition that all artworks (including popular entertainments, which I would extend Hyde's claim to include) are most fruitfully understood as gifts to their audiences. In a possible nod to Jameson, Hyde allows that "a

---

[18] Ibid., 318.   [19] Ibid., 838.   [20] Ibid., 839.   [21] Ibid. (emphasis in original).

gift can be destroyed by the marketplace."[22] But even as he uses economic metaphor to characterize the dissemination of art, he asserts that mere products cannot be art. "[T]he primary commerce of art is a gift exchange," Hyde explains, and "unless the work is the realization of the artist's gift and unless we, the audience, can feel the gift it carries, there is no art."[23]

In the McCaffery interview, Wallace speaks of "the agenda of the consciousness behind the text," which he says has "something to do with love."[24] He continues, "One of the things really great fiction-writers do [. . .] is *give* the reader something. The reader walks away from real art heavier than she came to it. Fuller."[25] Wallace's earliest attempt at positioning his fiction as a gift to the reader comes at the end of *Girl With Curious Hair*. The collection's heavily metafictional final story, "Westward the Course of Empire Takes Its Way," ends with the sentence, often interpreted as direct address to the reader, "You are loved."[26] Furthermore, the final page includes other sentences that seek to remove the story from the system of commodity exchange that Jameson and Horkheimer and Adorno so decry. Following a use of the phrase "without purchase" that leverages a double meaning – not only meaning *loss of grip* but also *free of charge* – the narrator tells the reader, "Absolutely no salesmen will call" and "I want nothing from you."[27] Wallace has characterized this story as an attempt to take metafiction to its logical extreme of "Armageddon" and "then out of the rubble reaffirm the idea of art being a living transaction between humans."[28] Yes, Wallace characterizes a creator's relationship with an audience as a transaction, but he also emphasizes that it is hardly an exchange of capital or product.

"Westward," then, attempts to enact care for its audience – or, at least, it attempts to clear an imaginative space for it. Yet within *Infinite Jest*, James Incandenza's cinematic act of care for his son fails. It's well documented that Wallace's working title for *Infinite Jest* was *A Failed Entertainment*, and in the Lipsky book, Wallace interprets this discarded phrase: "The idea is that the book is structured as an entertainment that doesn't work. Because what entertainment ultimately leads to" is the fatal cartridge.[29] Given the way that its fractured chronology and complex structure require an unusually active reader to keep an immense amount of information straight, the novel might fail as entertainment by the definition that

[22] Hyde, *The Gift*, 356.   [23] Ibid.   [24] McCaffery, "Interview," 50.   [25] Ibid.
[26] Wallace, "Westward," *GCH*, 373.   [27] Ibid.   [28] McCaffery, "Interview," 41.
[29] Lipsky, *Although of Course*, 79.

equates being entertained with passivity. But understood differently, the title is apt because the novel's central act of creation fails: James's film does not lead to connection with his son, and eventually, a whole continent is at risk as a result.

Infinite Jest does, however, give us a close and sustained look at an act of entertainment that succeeds, because it exists outside of commercial exchange and seeks to please a mutually appreciative audience. That entertainment is Mario Incandenza's filmed puppet show, an adaptation of *The ONANtiad*, his father's film about the creation of the Organization of North American Nations, itself described as "a four-hour piece of tendentiously anticonfluential political parody long since dismissed as minor Incandenza."[30] Traditionally shown each year at Enfield Tennis Academy's Interdependence Day banquet, Mario's version has become "way more popular with ETA's adults and adolescents than it is with the woefully historically underinformed children it had first been made for."[31] Additionally, "Mario's big public yearly moment at ETA" occurs when he introduces his work, in this case with the brief and direct, "Thanks everybody and I hope you like it."[32] His quick acknowledgment of gratitude for his audience's attention and desire for them to be pleased stands in sharp contrast to the cerebral and even hostile relationships to audience that the novel associates with Mario's father. And indeed, the room seems entertained. Except for ETA's youngest, the viewers are "having a rousing good time," treating Mario's film as an old-time participatory melodrama, "occasionally heckling or cheering ironically, every so often throwing sweets that stick to the screen."[33] When Johnny Gentle appears, "There is much cracking wise and baritone mimicry of a President roundly disliked," almost as if he were a mustache-twirling villain made to be booed.[34] Even as multiple characters feel anxious over the surely impending consequences of that afternoon's Eschaton fiasco, the screening of Mario's film – on a day off from compulsory practices, no less – comes across as relaxed and mirthful. It's tough to imagine this kind of joy and camaraderie taking place at a screening of one of James's films.

Wallace draws this contrast indirectly but intentionally. From start to finish, the scene centered on Mario's film at the banquet runs to just over sixty pages, but it's interrupted by Hal's own musings on his father's less conventionally entertaining work. Hal knows of James's "middle-period"

---

[30] Wallace, *IJ*, 380–81.   [31] Ibid., 380.   [32] Ibid.   [33] Ibid., 385.   [34] Ibid.

films that were "obsessed with the idea of audiences' relationships with various sorts of shows," most prominently *The Medusa v. The Odalisque* and *The Joke.*[35] In the former, an onscreen theatrical audience sees a battle between two dangerous mythical creatures and are gradually turned to stone one by one, but since viewers of the film don't get to see the battle or its participants up close, "the film's audience ends up feeling teased and vaguely cheated."[36] *The Joke* is a conceptual work wherein the film's viewers see only a projection of the viewers themselves in real time. Easily the "most hated Incandenza film," when exhibited, its viewers "saw row after row of itself staring back at it with less and less expectant and more and more blank and then puzzled and then eventually pissed-off facial expressions."[37] Both films are aggressively un-entertaining in their perverse denial from audiences the pleasures of passive spectation, one by refusing to show what seems to be the most interesting thing onscreen, the other by refusing to show anything at all not already visible in the space of the theater. As a result, Wallace sets the coldness of these films against the warmth of Mario's less polished but much better received effort, which actively brings together a community in shared enjoyment. James's high-art, legacy-focused cinematic work is thus clearly marked as less successful – both as entertainment and as communication – than Mario's less cerebral work.

Aside from Hal's rumination on this difference, the other major interruption in the description of Mario's film explains how broadcast and cable television in *Infinite Jest*'s America have both been largely replaced by InterLace's system of cartridges and teleputers. The bellwether for this shift was the fictional advertising firm Viney and Veals, known for viscerally grotesque TV ads for aspirin, liposuction clinics and tongue scrapers. These commercials moved tons of product for their clients, but they so disgusted viewers that they wound up lowering the ratings of the shows on which they appeared. As a result of such drastically lowered viewership, networks started to fold, until InterLace executives imagined, "what if the viewer could become her/his *own* programming director; what if s/he could *define* the very entertainment-happiness it was her/his right to pursue?"[38] For many readers, InterLace's solution famously predicts on-demand and streaming video services to come years after this novel's publication. But also, this digression emphasizes entertainment that is

[35] Ibid., 396.   [36] Ibid., 397.   [37] Ibid., 397–98.   [38] Ibid., 416.

driven by the needs of advertisers and the whims of passive viewers whose choice is illusory. Unlike Mario's film, still being enjoyed by an appreciative audience – even though, Wallace allows, "everybody's sugar-crashing a bit" – InterLace's technocratic model removes any possible gift value from the experience of an artwork as entertainment.[39] InterLace rejects the idea that cable TV customers experience "empowerment" through access to a vast number of channels, because to watch prepro-grammed cable is "just the invitation to choose which of 504 visual spoon-feedings you'd sit there and open wide for."[40] But an InterLace subscriber still chooses a spoon-feeding – just from a greater variety of options. And even if InterLace's programming is ad-free, meaning that the viewer is no longer being aggressively accosted by third-party corporations, viewers remain customers of InterLace and of the producers of their preferred entertainment. Wallace continually casts the shift from cable to InterLace in terms of inside-baseball industry deals; in so doing, he emphasizes that the interests driving this new model think only in terms of commerce, never in terms of art or content.

In discussing entertainment's complexities in Wallace's body of work, I've focused my argument on *Infinite Jest*, but I would assert that it holds true elsewhere in Wallace's fiction. His stories and novels include several images of overconsumption of entertainment that might be characterized as addiction, or of unusually heightened and personal sensitivities to what entertainment may have to tell the listener. Steeply's father in *Infinite Jest* develops an attachment to *M*A*S*H* that threatens his relationships with his family (and suggests a difficulty telling reality from fantasy). The narrator of "Good Old Neon" feels attacked by a throwaway joke on a rerun of *Cheers*. And Chris Fogle's conversion narrative in *The Pale King* is animated by a sudden realization that watching *As the World Turns* is not the best use of his time.

But crucially, in none of these scenes is the entertainment in question presented as an inherently sinister force. These characters may have allowed themselves to be amused to death, to borrow Neil Postman's phrase, but Wallace does not lay the blame at the feet of the creators of sitcoms or soap operas. That said, the creators of the InterLace teleputer systems, the AFR, the television networks in "Tri-Stan: I Sold Sissee Nar to Ecko," and the executives of The Suffering Channel in the story of the

[39] Ibid., 438.   [40] Ibid., 416.

same name all come in for heavy critique in Wallace's fiction. That's because their attitudes toward entertainment – and their positioning of it as product, not as gift – result in attitudes toward their audiences that are only transactional in a consumerist sense, defined by profits, Nielsen ratings and political domination. Those actions, not the desire to entertain or to be entertained, constitute the greater sin within Wallace's body of work.

CHAPTER 9

David Foster Wallace and Visual Culture

Corrie Baldauf

Pop Culture as Magic

On the trail marked with pollen may I walk

With grasshoppers about my feet may I walk

With dew about my feet may I walk[1]

Throughout his writing, Wallace invokes, often obliquely, a wide assortment of visual artworks, generally as a means of bringing the reader into the narrative. Many moments of ekphrasis punctuate his writing. In *Infinite Jest*, he references myths of tapestry-weaving in Leutze's mural of Manifest Destiny, as well as referencing Bernini and Escher. *The Pale King* includes the St. Louis Arch, *The Thinker*, and the thousands of terra-cotta soldiers buried in Emperor Qin's Tomb. Using ekphrasis, Wallace is able to help us see art; using pop culture, he is able to help us connect to art. Theatrically appropriating Bertolt Brecht, Wallace guides us to hear him as an artist and entertainer capable of breaking through the space between the stage of the text and the space we occupy as readers in the audience. He reminds, "One of the things the artist has to do is take a lot of this familiarity and remind people that it's strange."[2] This chapter explores the ways in which Wallace uses descriptive language of images in his writing, situating narrative in conversation with visual stimuli and reaching beyond language to image, color and texture. *The Pale King* includes some of his most innovative ekphrastic cues. By moving between descriptions of pop culture, fine art, and nonart, Wallace reveals affective experiences in ordinary life. The first instance in *The Pale King* is an unexpected form of art: a logo. After an evocative list of sensory images, he writes, "Your shoes' brand incised in the dew. An alfalfa breeze. Socks' burrs."[3] The reader

---

[1] Paramananda, *Change Your Mind.*   [2] McCaffery, "Interview," 19.   [3] Wallace, *TPK*, 6.

becomes someone who has agency over the world Wallace has created, just by stepping in it.

This shoe print is one of multiple "ekphrastic transfers" that Wallace employs. In this chapter, ekphrastic transfer is defined as ekphrastic description applied to objects and landscapes not traditionally considered art. This goes against the origin of ekphrasis as a vivid description of real or imagined works of art. By doing so he asks readers to create art out of their surroundings, just as the logo on the bottom of your shoe stamps the ground beneath it. Wallace describes how "The whole way that the world acts on my nerve endings is bound up with stuff [. . .] pop stuff [. . .] what I mean by it is nothing different than what other people mean in writing about trees and parks [. . .] It's just the texture of the world I live in."[4]

In personal correspondence and in interviews, Wallace expresses a distinction between serious and commercial art. Wallace writes to Didier Jacob: "art is where difficult complex questions get made urgent and human and real. Serious art makes people uncomfortable."[5] While art is "uncomfortable," television, cartoons and ads provide a comfortable introduction. Yet Wallace has a distrustful relationship with the easiness of entertainment. In *Infinite Jest*, Wallace incorporates names of familiar products as commercial-like headings representing specific years. Through this participatory game, a form of conversation begins between author and reader. The particularity of the chapter headings includes product names, for instance, Glad or Dove, allowing readers to pull in their own experiences as content. Wallace describes this with brevity: "Particularity births form; familiarity breeds content."[6] Ads' easy familiarity breeds nostalgia, bringing us away from commercial associations to personal memories if we connect with them as art. A holiday greeting card that Wallace wrote to David Markson says, "May you ignore the ads and see the faces."[7] In other words, he wishes Markson something beyond a commercial holiday: an awareness that one could look past the hype of the season and find real connection.

Real connections require the author and reader to work, as numerous other chapters in this volume point out. Wallace brings a conversational and often gamelike approach to this. In *The Pale King*, as Chris Fogle ruminates on his labor, he begins to see more artful aspects of the job. Wallace's choice of a stereotypically boring profession in a typically

---

[4] L. Miller, "Interview," 60.   [5] Wallace, "Letter to Didier Jacob," Harry Ransom Center.
[6] Wallace, "Empty Plenum," *BFN*, 106.
[7] Wallace, "Greeting Card to David Markson," Harry Ransom Center.

disliked federal agency makes a forceful point that all work has personal rewards. Fogle sets out upon this path with a fondness for advertisements that echo Wallace's branding of "Subsidized Time" in *Infinite Jest*. A rotating foot sign makes the point playful. Fogle uses the position of the sign to decide whether to study or go to a bar called "The Hat."[8] A cult symbol located in Los Angeles, the sign is transplanted into Illinois' urban landscape in *The Pale King*. While Fogle describes looking back at his student self as a wastoid, he can remember every article of clothing, down to his untied Timberlands. At a time when shoes were a valuable portion of his identity, the rotating foot sign held convincing meaning for him. While Fogle sees "that enormous, sudden, dramatic, unexpected, life-changing experiences are not translatable or explainable,"[9] Wallace asks readers, through ekphrastic description of the sign, to learn to share the experience itself. Pedestrian art, above all art forms, is powerful in its relatability. We touch it, stand in it and pass through it.

Throughout *The Pale King* Wallace makes numerous references to hats, shoes and feet. Hats and shoes emphasize the upper and lower limit of our body, the edges of our ability to experience art and the world. In Joseph Frank's *Dostoevsky*, Frank quotes Dostoevsky, and in his copy, Wallace adds emphasis in black felt pen: "'All of contemporary youth is stupid and backward!' Dostoevsky once shouted. 'shiny boots are more valuable for them [nihilists] than Pushkin!'"[10] Fogle's character alludes to Dostoevsky's descriptions of contemporary youth and places Fogle's father in Dostoevsky's shoes. Fashion is more familiar to Fogle, and therefore more personal than poetry. Parallel to his father's connection with poetry, Fogle finds rhythm in signage.

Later in the book, an animated logo of a globe turning and the introductory audio from the soap opera *As the World Turns* spark Fogle's understanding of his role as an observer in a world he is not participating in. He sees his watching as "a nihilistic art form."[11] Fogle's pop-culture-induced epiphanies lead to his newfound respect for work in the IRS. Here is the magic of pop culture: It allows us to see the art of standing in our shoes, beneath our hats, and within the landscape around us.

"The singular art," as Plato defines it, is not about a stagnant object; it is about the art of our actions. Pop images like the rotating foot sign and references to shoes and feet are allusions to Plato's philosophy. In Wallace's

---

[8] Wallace, *TPK*, 165. [9] Ibid., 216.
[10] Frank, *Dostoevsky*, 23. Wallace's copy held at Harry Ransom Center.
[11] Wallace, *TPK*, 224–25.

copy of Adams' *Critical Theory Since Plato*, he emphasizes this quote: "the poet who introduces a shoe into his poem copies the shoemaker's copy of the Platonic 'idea' or 'form' of a shoe."[12] This reveals two keys to understanding *The Pale King* and the multiple roles that art embodies in Wallace's writing. First, it implies that *The Pale King* could be read as a poem, in keeping with the suggestion of the previous chapter. Second, each of Wallace's descriptions of Fogle and his father "squeezing his shoes" is intentional and verse-like, a running gag version of a refrain in poetry. Wallace was more willing to have the reader assume that "squeezing my shoes" is a redundant tic in the writing than risk the disappointment a reader might feel if he explains the connection; in "The Empty Plenum," Wallace asserts that unveiling the source would be "for me weak and disappointing because it's an explanation."[13] He begins "The Empty Plenum" with a quote by Stanley Cavell that highlights the potential significance of foot and shoe references in *The Pale King*. "But what other philosopher has found the antidote to illusion in the particular and repeated humility of remembering and tracking the uses of humble words, looking philosophically as it were beneath our feet rather than over our heads?"[14]

Wallace implies that Fogle's nihilistic ritual of the foot sign exists outside of his father's and Plato's shoes because the foot is bare. The ritual aligns Fogle with his father's path in public service. Rachel Barney describes Plato's emphasis on a shoemaker's ability "to understand what is good for feet; ultimately this requires understanding the good of the body, which means understanding the good of the soul." Barney adds in parenthesis, "It follows [. . .] that only the philosopher-king can be a truly expert shoe maker."[15] A supervisor at the IRS practicing awareness and attention is referred to as "The Pale King" and seems to be an allusion to the philosopher-king. Rosamond Kent Sprague states that "According to Plato, the ideal ruler is one who possesses 'the singular art' [. . .] if the cobbler produces shoes, what does the philosopher-king produce? [. . .] good men."[16] To be a good citizen, Wallace asks the reader to place more emphasis on being present in the world and less emphasis on status. As readers leap between depictions of entertainment and clothing to descriptions of famous works of art, their expectations of each shrink and expand nearly simultaneously. This active change in perception, to see that

---

[12] Adams, *Critical Theory Since Plato*, 3.   [13] Wallace, "Empty Plenum," *BFN*, 107.
[14] Ibid., 73.   [15] Barney, "The Carpenter and the Good."
[16] Sprauge, *Plato's Philosopher-King*, 115.

thoughtful reflection and striving for excellence are as essential as breath-
ing, is Wallace's *cri de coeur.*

The reader does not have Chris Fogle's depth of perception in the
beginning of *The Pale King*; Wallace places readers in a landscape suddenly
and seemingly without plot. They find themselves in a cascade of words
describing the native and alien blooms of Illinois. In *Paul Valéry Revisited*,
Walter Putnam describes the Greek translation of "to make," or poïein, as
"capturing the nascent poetic moment and crafting it into a work of art."
As Putnam reflects on Valéry's poetry, he determines that "a degree of
obscurity itself was essential to them [Valéry's poems]. In summary, he
thought poems were for making us 'become' not for making us 'understand.' The process first of making a poem, then of the reader's taking it in,
was in many senses the poem itself."[17] We might reflect on *The Pale King*,
and Wallace's use of diffuse ekphrastic descriptions, in this glow.
Ekphrastic transfers help readers "become;" we cocreate artful sensory
experiences with Wallace, allowing us to engage our world with meaning
rather than taking meaning from others.

Art and Fame

In many of his works, Wallace struggles with ideas of fame. Wallace often
omitted the names of famous artworks in his texts. I propose he did this to
help us as readers move past barriers of art-historical fame and expectation
to actively engage and reconstruct, through our own memories, the
described works of art as we read. He faces similar expectations, through
fame as a writer, about style and intent that keep readers from having a
personal experience with a narrative. To counteract this, Wallace uses
ekphrasis, ekphrastic transfer, and repetitive allusion. There are multiple
instances in *The Pale King* where famous artworks are invoked but never
named. Instead, through ekphrastic description, the reader comes to realize
what is being referenced, participating in the narrative by completing the
process of seeing the work. Wallace communicates an experience to the
reader rather than a name.

Wallace uses statues' concrete stillness to represent the effect of fame
and status. David Markson, with whom Wallace corresponded, references
the character Incandenza from *Infinite Jest* in his book *Reader's Block*.
Markson reveals the process by which worshipping removes agency by
refusing to see the individual beneath the fame, "Heraclitus did say that

---

[17] Putnam, *Paul Valéry Revisited*, 16–17.

praying to statues of the gods was like talking to a house instead of to its owner."[18] Wallace writes "All That" as his fame is being solidified. The narrative reads, at first, as one where the parents trick their son, telling him that a toy cement mixer turns when he is not looking.[19] The more Wallace experienced fame, the more difficult he found it to move forward with his work; he could only create when no one was looking. In *The Pale King*, Wallace works to free himself from his own notoriety. Fame and status are embodied as famous art, including the St. Louis Arch, *The Thinker*, and the terra-cotta soldiers buried in Qin's Tomb. Described in scant but recognizable detail, the works could easily remain on the periphery of a reader's awareness. Wallace both conceals and reveals the fame and status of the statues in *The Pale King*. The physical weight of a statue is repeatedly used to remind the writer, character and reader of a more valuable theoretical weight.

In "Fictional Futures and the Conspicuously Young," Wallace points to a power reserved for art: "Entertainers can divert and engage and maybe even console; only artists can transfigure."[20] This power is then applied to what most do not consider art: our own actions. For example, characters in *The Pale King* transfigure their childhood neuroses into artful methods for handling the monotony of working for the IRS. Wallace describes an IRS employee as "posted at the St. Louis Service Center, literally in the shadow of the strange, scary giant metal arch thing."[21] Being enigmatic makes room for readers to realize their capacity to fill in the blank.

Through diffusion and occlusion, Wallace describes art's ability to help people identify with others, disregarding their status. In the interview with Larry McCaffery, he states that "if a work of art can allow us imaginatively to identify with a character's pain, we might then also more easily conceive of others identifying with our own."[22] Art transforms only when fame has not frozen its power. There is one statue that Wallace repeatedly placed in his writing as a reminder of fame's ability to immobilize. In "Good People," Sheri Fisher and Lane Dean are figuring out whether or not they should have an abortion when, in Lane's glance, Sheri suddenly appears "in a pose of thinking, almost like that one statue."[23] Like reproductions of Auguste Rodin's *The Thinker*, originally titled *The Poet*,[24] Wallace reproduces Sheri and Lane's story in *The Pale King*. The statue solidifies Lane's

[18] Markson, *Reader's Block*, 23. Markson and Wallace were friends; see note 5.
[19] Wallace, "All That."   [20] Wallace, "Fictional Futures," *BFN*, 53.   [21] Wallace, *TPK*, 21.
[22] McCaffery, "Interview," 127.   [23] Wallace, "Good People."
[24] Rodin, "The Thinker." When conceived in 1880 in its original size (approx. 70 cm) as the crowning element of *The Gates of Hell*, seated on the tympanum, *The Thinker* was entitled *The Poet*.

ability to identify with Sheri's pain and his own. Whatever they decide, their current identity is immobilized just as Wallace felt himself to be immobilized by his fame. Wallace, Sheri and Lane fear being labeled by what they produce.

Wallace makes *The Thinker* particularly strange in "The Suffering Channel." Brint Moltke makes art through excretion, landing reproductions of famous artworks, one of which is *The Thinker*, in the toilet. Journalist Skip Atwater conspires with Brint's wife to show off the artist's skill.[25] Wallace alludes to this in *The Pale King*: "You just need to get Mel ready for this, so he doesn't come and see where they put him and start shitting little green men about it."[26] Wallace shows that the reproduced statues, like *The Thinker*, with time's patina and accumulated fame, are as basic and familiar as plastic, patina-green army men.

Wallace may have identified with Rodin as an artist and *The Thinker* as a famous icon. *The Thinker* is a portrait of the artist and athlete stopped from action by his thoughts. Originally 70 cm in height, it was enlarged and then repeatedly reproduced, more than doubling in scale as it gained notoriety.[27] Through Wallace's multiple ekphrastic descriptions, the reader gains an empathetic insight into the position of the famous artist. In an interview with Terry Gross, Wallace describes his thoughts as a roadblock between himself and his athletic performance when playing tennis: "I would choke. I would begin thinking [...] drooling on the baseline."[28] In "Good Old Neon," Neal is a seemingly cool student who sees his notoriety as necessitating an arduous and constant tending to a statue of himself. He remembers being called out when he fakes meditating. He says, "Master Gurpreet, although he kept his facial expression inscrutable, gave me a deep and seemingly respectful bow and said that I sat almost like a living statue of mindful repose."[29] He finds himself stuck, "condemned to a whole life of being nothing but a sort of custodian to the statue."[30] Notoriety is an act, and Neal believes he must kill himself to escape it. The statue is coolness, his worship and his ability to enact an ideal in every group of which he is a part. In Wallace's writing, statues are immobilized icons, allowing characters and readers to identify their own status or immobility.

[25] Wallace, "The Suffering Channel," 316.   [26] Wallace, *TPK*, 354.
[27] Rodin, "The Thinker."   [28] Gross, "The Fresh Air Interview."
[29] Wallace, "Good Old Neon," *OB*, 159.   [30] Ibid., 161.

Uncomfortable Art

Difficult art, according to Wallace, might not be the over-conceptualized art films he excerpts in the endnotes of *Infinite Jest*. Difficult art is learning to live with daily challenges. For students at Enfield Tennis Academy, handling the constant push to excel becomes an art for some and a hell for most. In an art-as-coping example, Wallace has Pemulis, a cerebral student with a sense of humor, design a "highly amusing low-memory TP game, whose graphics featured a picture of de Lint [his tennis coach] and a mock-up of the hell panel from H. Bosch's triptych 'The Garden of Earthly Delights'"[31] Posters, prints or reproductions of famous paintings and photographs line the walls of difficult situations in Wallace's writing.

Both prints and pain are democratic. Art waits while characters and readers determine what they can take on. Art helps because it is something to engage with outside the self. In "Good Old Neon," Neal pauses in juggling his emotions and criticism of his therapist to describe the prints on Dr. Guftason's wall.[32] The reproductions are not in themselves difficult. The art provides distance from, or perspective on, what is difficult for the patient. Neal feels labeled, locked in stasis by Dr. Guftason. Neal uses the print to escape this feeling; the reproduced art becomes a means for him to take control of his environment by judging the art and his doctor who owns the art instead of looking at himself. The experience of remembering pain is reproduced in Neal's therapy session. Rather than use the opportunity to become self-aware and present in his pain or in his experience of the art, he escapes his pain by placing his doctor in the same stasis of fame that the art is in as a reproduction. People can travel between present experience and painful stasis. Wallace remembers the role of art to shift a person out of stagnation, "I had a teacher I liked who used to say good fiction's job was to comfort the disturbed and disturb the comfortable."[33] People's perception of art reflects this shift. Famous art enters the sphere of pop culture through reproduction, inching it closer to stasis. Yet all art, including pop art, can bring us back to our senses. Transformation through authentic experience is in the working of our bodies, not the artwork. In *Infinite Jest*, the veterans of Alcoholics Anonymous speak in the slogan language of motivational posters. Don Gately asserts that "the slogan means there's no set way to argue intellectual type stuff about the Program [AA]. Surrender to Win, Give it Away to Keep It. God As You Understand Him. You can analyze til you're

---

[31] Wallace, *IJ*, 999. [32] Wallace, "Neon," *OB*, 146. [33] McCaffery, "Interview," 21.

breaking tables with your forehead and find cause to walk away from it, back Out There."[34] Wallace's difficult art is less about analyzing and more about being.

Jeffery Severs uses Wallace's story "Westward the Course of Empire Takes Its Way" to bring attention to Wallace's "fondness for low gags."[35] He shows how Wallace mocks Emanual Leutze's mural theme of Manifest Destiny to examine human obsession and struggle stemming from capitalist expansion.[36] Wallace points out that each person chooses something to worship. Worship includes addiction, consumption, or, in this example, an obsession with progress. The mural is a reminder to be critical; through humor we are able to ease past our obsessions.

Wallace places Leutze's mural in an airport lounge, compares cathedrals to shopping malls in *The Pale King*,[37] and in *Infinite Jest* shows an art film of Cornaro Chapel and Bernini's "The Ecstasy of St. Theresa."[38] In each example, something revered is equated with a subject of worship or obsession. The last builds a telescopic series of obsessions; the reader voyeuristically watches an actress watching a film of a filmmaker watching a still image of a commercialized icon. The repetition of this theme in his *oeuvre* helps readers connect instances of obsession across Wallace's narratives and use his writing as a surrogate to reflect on their own patterns of worship.

Just as art provides perspective, ekphrastic description can help people gain objective distance. Multisensory input reaches further into the reader's awareness. No matter how still or inaudible a work of art is, ekphrastic description has the potential to imbue it with movement (action), rhythm (sound) and credibility (realness). In "Church Not Made with Hands," Wallace transfers Cézanne's painterly style to the sunrise: "A dead Cézanne does this August sunrise in any-angled smears of clouded red, a blue that darkles."[39] Author, character and reader are in this moment Cézanne himself, seeing the landscape. A character in "Yet Another Instance of Porousness of Certain Borders" acts as proxy, using the seeming simplicity of color to practice the difficult art of appreciation: "I'm super conscious of my eyesight and my eyes and how good it is to be able to see colors and people's faces and know just where I am, and how fragile it all is [...]"[40] These ekphrastic transfers give readers space to

---

[34] Wallace, *IJ*, 1002. [35] Wallace, "Letter to Michael Pietsch," 1988, Harry Ransom Center.
[36] Severs, *Balancing Books*, 73. [37] Wallace, *TPK*, 269. [38] Wallace, *IJ*, 740.
[39] Wallace, "Church Not Made with Hands," *BI*, 194.
[40] Wallace, "Yet Another Instance," *BI*, 35.

notice, to bring into awareness the magic of making something routine, profound. Strange details in ekphrastic descriptions and ekphrastic transfers allow readers to inhabit the environments of Wallace's narratives in a way that feels textured. Objects and art are built onto a page as if they are both hinged (grounded) and upright (raised). A reader sees what is in motion in their lives and what exactly they worship that has the potential to immobilize them.

Wallace revels in asking readers to explore depths, external and internal. By doing so, the reader and author can turn a printed word into physical experience, and pushing through the narratives becomes a shared labor of creation. In *Infinite Jest*, AA members drive on urban roads with confusing signs that are referred to as "Escherian."[41] M. C. Escher's hand drawing a hand actively embodies the strange loop of continually working on ourselves. By taking in the details, seeking out the extraordinary information in everyday experiences, readers can find text in the texture of the physical world. Don Gately makes his sobriety endurable by building an imaginary and internal room, reminding himself to take life one heartbeat at a time: "he had to build a wall around each second just to take it."[42] Wallace makes learning new information experiential instead of just instructional. In the final pages of *The Pale King*, Wallace leaves us with an affirmation, reminding us one last time of our capacity to create meaning through experience:

> You are a trained observer [. . .]. You have declined to take off your shoes. The knob beside the dimmer is your chair's control; it reclines and the feet go up. It is important that you be comfortable.
>
> "You have a body you know."[43]

Thinking of Gately and my role as a trained observer, I remember that learning the intricate steps of building a wall include first laying out the framework. Narrow wooden or metal lengths of material are assembled in formations that resemble roman numerals, II, III, IV, letters even: "TTTTT." I am reading the building material as I do words. From the aforementioned, while the wall is still on the ground, I notice you could lay on your back and fit between two of the bare whale-scaled skeletal verticals in the spine of the wall. This careful looking shows me how buildings are made to fit our bodies. After raising the wall and covering it in sheets of plywood, I notice the same dimensions as I lay in bed. Tomorrow, as I drive to work, I might think about the fit of my shoes or Plato. A raised

---

[41] Wallace, *IJ*, 1034. [42] Ibid., 860. [43] Wallace, *TPK*, 539.

word above a billboard, when viewed closely, mirrors our experience of driving across a bridge, its vertical trusses also resembling roman numerals, seeing through them to water, sky and space that the bridge, made of letters and numbers, keeps you from falling through.

Art is not comfortable. Art is comforting.

PART II

Ideas

CHAPTER 10

David Foster Wallace and Attention

Alice Bennett

It is tempting to see "attention" as the unified and unifying theme that runs across Wallace's whole career. Readers have consistently understood Wallace's writing as an inquiry into aspects of attention that intersect with his interests in philosophy,[1] politics,[2] economics,[3] information,[4] education[5] and cognitive neuroscience,[6] and return continually to a complex aesthetic-ethical framework with "attention and engagement" at its heart.[7] Attention itself therefore becomes something like the rimless hub of the tax offices in *The Pale King* – a central routing point through which many of Wallace's other principal interests are funneled. But is there a coherent definition of what attention is in Wallace's work? And does attention have a single "context" from the second half of the twentieth century to the beginning of the twenty-first? In this chapter, I am interested in laying out some of the discontinuities and contradictions in "Wallace's attention," and in identifying the extent to which these complexities are also reflective of a historical period in which attention and distraction have been highly scrutinized and charged with cultural meaning.

Wallace's lifetime spanned almost half a century – a period in which the cultural conceptions of attention not only changed substantially, but also a

---

[1] On Wallace, attention and philosophy, see, for instance, Bennett's "Inside David Foster Wallace's Head" and Den Dulk's "Boredom, Anxiety and Irony."

[2] On Wallace, attention and politics, see Clare, "The Politics of Boredom," and Santel, "On David Foster Wallace's Conservatism" (particularly on "the link between solipsism and distraction," 626).

[3] The notion of the attention economy as an alternative source of value runs throughout Severs' *David Foster Wallace's Balancing Books*, but emerges most explicitly in the sixth chapter. My *Contemporary Fictions of Attention* also deals with some of these questions in the second chapter (on Wallace).

[4] On Wallace, attention and media, and particularly information overload, see Houser's "Managing Information" and Letzler's *The Cruft of Fiction*.

[5] On Wallace, attention and education, see O'Sullivan, "David Foster Wallace, Loneliness."

[6] On Wallace, attention and neuroscience, see Burn, "'Webs of Nerves Pulsing and Firing.'"

[7] Turnbull gives a very full account of the ethical significance of attention in Wallace's aesthetics in his essay "*This Is Water* and the Ethics of Attention." For more on Wallace, art and attention, see also Andersen's "Pay Attention!"

period in which attention was consistently an object of social concern. A very rough cultural history of attention might divide the era 1960–2010 into two, with each period manifesting some distinct differences in the way attention's psychological, social and political status was imagined. The first period might run from the 1960s to the 1980s, taking us from *The Society of the Spectacle* (1967), through the emergence of the concept of the attention economy in the 1970s, and on to Neil Postman's *Amusing Ourselves to Death* (1985). The second period, from the 1990s to the 2000s, amplified what came before in areas such as the attention economy's intensification and expansion. In other ways, however, this period was markedly different, as control of attention came to be a synecdochal representation of an individual's responsibility for developing and disciplining their own cognitive capacity in the modes of neoliberal subjectivity theorized by, for instance, Wendy Brown, in *Undoing the Demos* (2015). I make the case here, therefore, for not one but two contexts for Wallace's attention, with a specific date in the mid-1990s – 1996 – as the moment of transition.

Period One: Engagement

Wallace's work up to and including *Infinite Jest* has been understood through modes of attention that include passive watching, the rapt consumption of entertainment and the head-turning attention demands of advertising under consumer capitalism.[8] This is the context of early Wallace stories such as "My Appearance" and "Little Expressionless Animals," in which TV's culture of spectatorship is turned inside out by a view from inside. The most explicit aspect of Wallace's own attention-theorizing in this period is the essay "E Unibus Pluram" (1993). The essay should be understood in the context of a decades-long debate about the attractions of television, which takes in media analysis from Marshall McLuhan's *Understanding Media* (1964) to Postman's *Amusing Ourselves to Death* (1985), the latter of which was a key touchstone of Wallace's theorizing of entertainment in the 1990s. In the broader literary context, novels such as Thomas Pynchon's *Vineland* (1990) and Don DeLillo's *Mao II* (1991) made manifest anxieties about the addictive properties of

---

[8] These framings begin in 2003 with Boswell's and Burn's readings of "Unibus" in *Understanding David Foster Wallace* and *Infinite Jest: A Reader's Guide*, respectively. For some more recent contextualizing of Wallace's work among postmodern consumerism and TV culture, see Fitzpatrick's *The Anxiety of Obsolescence*, which also offers an important broader literary context for Wallace's attitudes to watching.

the "tube" and its potential to make the book redundant. Wallace's work of the late 1980s and early 1990s therefore emerges into a particularly acute moment of literary concern about television, but it's a moment with a long tail back to at least the 1960s.

"E Unibus Pluram" and its recognition of the genuine fun and pleasure of television is an important corrective to depictions of TV as a deadening addiction. Nevertheless, Wallace argues in the essay that television is a solace for people who love to watch but hate to be watched themselves; those who want a one-way relationship with attention, to "receive without giving" because TV "engages without demanding."[9] Wallace's 1993 interview with Larry McCaffery contains the well-known passage in which he first lays out his own artistic philosophy of attention, explaining, "All the attention and engagement and work you need to get from the reader can't be for your benefit; it's got to be for hers."[10] Good art in any medium thus does not simply engage "without demanding," but it also doesn't only demand "attention and engagement" for itself and its cleverness (which is the implicit critique of postmodern metafiction). Wallace's play with failures of dialogue and interaction – culminating eventually in the one-sided conversations of *Brief Interviews with Hideous Men* (1999) – can therefore be placed within a broader context of twentieth-century concerns about what media does to and with an audience's attention.[11]

In its exploration of the influence of television on the generation of writers who came to prominence in the 1980s, "E Unibus Pluram" also reminds us that it was the formative period of the 1960s and 1970s that shaped Wallace's own cognitive terrain. As he explains, television taught a way of attending to the world beyond it: "Those of us born in like the sixties were trained to look where it pointed."[12] But the finger pointing from the television to the real stopped maintaining its referential function "in the summer of 1974" when Watergate allowed TV's inherent irony to come to the fore with enough clarity for "even a twelve year old, sitting there, rapt."[13] By the late 1980s and early 1990s, these rapt children had learnt a new kind of self-protective apathy, which manifested itself as Generation-X slacker nihilism and hip irony.[14] As Wallace explains in

[9] Wallace, "Unibus," *SFT*, 37.   [10] Wallace in McCaffery, "Interview," 50.
[11] Hering's *Fiction and Form* contains the fullest account of these dialogic aspects of Wallace's work, and it is also a foundational concept for Hayes-Brady's *Failures*, from which I have taken this notion of failed dialogue.
[12] Wallace, "Unibus," *SFT*, 33.   [13] Ibid., 36.
[14] Boswell's "Slacker Redemption" gives more detail on the role of political apathy, especially in Wallace's conception of the development of an adult attention for Gen X.

the essay, this jaded posture should be understood as a particular cultural manifestation of (in)attention:

> Indifference is actually just the 90s version of frugality, for US young people: wooed several gorgeous hours a day for nothing but our attention, we regard that attention as our chief commodity, our social capital, and we are loath to fritter it.[15]

Postmodern irony thus becomes a sort of protective charm against being pulled into the processes of consumer capitalism. But it is a buffer that dulls and numbs the self to the pleasures of wholehearted absorption and the rapt attention of childhood. This entrapping conflict between the seductive dangers of one-way "ogling" and the deadening safety of irony, underpinned by a memory of childish absorption, is similarly evident in the depiction of the Entertainment in *Infinite Jest*, which casts its viewer in the position of a baby to simulate an experience of rapt attention that is not just infantile but also disarmingly innocent and unguarded. The Entertainment is a stealth weapon that can only function because giving one's attention over to something fascinating is such a profoundly human pleasure.

The context for Wallace's conceptualization of attention as "our chief commodity" is the emergence of the notion of the attention economy, expressed as early as 1971 by the economist Herbert Simon:

> What information consumes is rather obvious: it consumes the attention of its recipients. Hence a wealth of information creates a poverty of attention and a need to allocate that attention efficiently among the overabundance of information sources that might consume it.[16]

Simon's "attention economy" is best understood as the counterpart of information overload – the thrift that responds to its excess. Wallace recognizes from the outset, however, that economizing the attention by cultivating a hip indifference is not a sufficient response to too much information. An alternative is to think of *Infinite Jest* as a novel that encourages the reader to train their attention to manage information overload and, as David Letztler has comprehensively argued, to "develop our abilities to filter information to their maximum capacities."[17] In "E Unibus Pluram," Wallace describes Mark Leyner's writing as, like television, creating the experience of "too many choices and no chooser's manual": *Infinite Jest* is that "chooser's manual."[18]

[15] Wallace, "Unibus," *SFT*, 64.   [16] Simon, "Designing Organizations," 40–41.
[17] Letzler, *The Cruft of Fiction*, 92.   [18] Wallace, "Unibus," *SFT*, 80.

From his analysis of the attention-grabbing techniques of advertising and the distractions of mass media entertainment to the modes of passive spectatorship and dead-end irony cultivated within audiences in response to this environment, Wallace's picture of late capitalism can only be understood with reference to the notion of the attention economy, and his fiction as an attempt to bypass or short-circuit its conventional modes of engagement and absorption. Nevertheless, TV's consumerist overload of "too many choices and no chooser's manual" eventually increases in ubiquity and intensity over the next decade. By the time of "Deciderization – 2007," Wallace comments on the "Total Noise" of the "culture and volume of info and spin and rhetoric and context that I know I'm not alone in finding too much to even absorb."[19] Wallace's strategies of choosing and deciding therefore began to come under extreme pressure in a rapidly shifting attention ecology.

Period Two: Focus

In one of the usage notes that he wrote for the 2004 *Oxford American Writers' Thesaurus* (reprinted as "Twenty-Four Word Notes" in *Both Flesh and Not*), Wallace observed that the verb "to focus" had taken over from "to concentrate" as the preferred terminology for referring to the act of attention.[20] The examples that he offers to illustrate the word's usage identify the place of "focus" in the discourse of business and management ("Our focus is on serving the needs of our customers"; "He's the most focused warehouse manager we've ever had"), but also in the language of self-help and spirituality, associated with what he terms the word's "somewhat jargony New Age feel."[21] Wallace's examples place us in the terrain of self-improvement and the mindful self-regulation and optimization of cognitive capacity. "Focus" therefore signifies a new regime of attention that has supplemented (if perhaps not supplanted) the old attention-grabbing techniques of the height of postmodernity. We should place this change within the context of the intensification of a knowledge, information and attention economy, with its demand for immaterial labor, that contributes to a distinct era of "cognitive capitalism" whose perpetual

---

[19] Wallace, "Deciderization – 2007," *BFN*, 301.
[20] Wallace, "Twenty-Four Word Notes," *BFN*, 273.   [21] Ibid., 272.

demand is for the attending subject to commodify their own cognitive capacities.[22] "Focus," Wallace indicates, is the word for this demand.

If "E Unibus Pluram" has become the rubric for interpreting Wallace's responses to the discourses of attention circulating in the culture of the late 1980s and early 1990s, the 2005 Kenyon College Commencement Address is the equivalent text for his later work. The speech (and its subsequent publication as the 2008 book *This Is Water*) has seen Wallace enlisted as a champion for attentional discipline. Specific passages from the piece are easily taken out of context (something invited by the sentence-per-page motivational mantra formatting of *This Is Water*) and are amenable to regurgitation in the macro-genre of popular self-help, management and spirituality books.[23] Lines such as "The really important kind of freedom involves attention, and awareness, and discipline" and "'Learning how to think' really means learning how to exercise some control over *how* and *what* you think" almost write themselves in bridesmaid font onto a motivational coaster.[24] This Wallace is a champion for the self-disciplining of the attention – a kind of productivity guru for a new era of cognitive capitalism.

The other context into which Wallace's writing about attention emerges in the latter part of the 1990s and in the early twenty-first century is the perception of the period as an "age of distraction" caused by digital media and the Internet, and especially their perceived threat to reading and its concomitant forms of attention. In his 1994 book, *The Gutenberg Elegies*, Sven Birkerts offers one of first versions of this argument, which in the following two decades launched a thousand think pieces. Birkerts suggests that print lends itself to "sustained attention," while the "electronic order" has created ripple effects, which mean that "our students are less and less able to read and comprehend their required texts."[25] By the time of his introduction to the 2006 edition, Birkerts was identifying how "[c]hip and screen" had "put single-track concentration, the discipline of reading, under great pressure" and replaced it with "the restless, grazing behavior of clicking and scrolling."[26] The previous thirty years of discourse around television and its passive viewers have seamlessly transferred into condemnations of reading the Internet as a somehow degraded and degrading form

---

[22] Moulier-Boutang's *Cognitive Capitalism* gives an overview of the socioeconomic concepts, with the section on attention in chapter 3 particularly relevant. Terranova's essay "Attention, Economy and the Brain" offers more specific investigation of the digital economy.

[23] Some examples of many: Werner, *Gospel Brokenness*; Newton, *The Little Book of Thinking Big*; Smith, *You Are What You Love*.

[24] Wallace, *TIW*, 53, 120.   [25] Birkerts, *The Gutenberg Elegies*, 122–23.   [26] Ibid., xiv.

of reading. Wallace, notably, departs from this standard hand-wringing about the kids and their attention spans. In an interview with Michael Goldfarb in 2004 (just before the Kenyon College Commencement Address), he takes pains to attribute the degradation of attention span to his *own* generation, identifying the need for "a willingness to pay a certain kind of attention" in order to deal with an overwhelming media landscape, but specifically observing that younger people – "in their twenties and thirties" – are "more accustomed" to these forms of attention and don't find them such a "big deal" as he does.[27] Wallace's position therefore seems to be quite distinct from those defenders of liberal arts education, who see it as developing a capacity for sustained and disciplined attention in young people to act as a bulwark against digital media.

Wallace's late fiction is similarly ambivalent about attention as a faculty to be worked upon and disciplined. In "The Soul is not a Smithy," for instance, the forms of attention demanded by schooling are shown to batter and force attention into a particular shape amenable to future work. "Smithy," with its daydreamy central protagonist, seems to operate in part as a defense of mind-wandering, as the boy in the story uses distraction to escape both everyday classroom discipline *and* an unfolding and potentially traumatizing hostage situation. Elsewhere in *Oblivion* are other instances of inattention that are self-protective but also tragic, such as the child in "Incarnations of Burned Children" who has "learned to leave himself" and disincarnate into oblivious non-presence, his body that "walked about and drew pay and lived its life untenanted."[28]

Wallace's ambivalence about the control and disciplining of attention finds its most extreme contradictions in *The Pale King*. Initial responses to the novel billed it as a dramatization of the ideas in the Kenyon College address, and identified both the novel and the speech as endorsing pre-vailing self-help and personal productivity advice surrounding the control of attention, under the heading of "mindfulness."[29] The IRS agents who must be "in a word, unborable," become, in this interpretation, heroes of productivity, grinding out attentive labor even though everything in them

---

[27] Wallace in Goldfarb, "The Connection," 141–42.   [28] Wallace, "Incarnations," *OB*, 116.

[29] For instance, this early *Washington Post* write-up before publication: "The characters in *TPK* are Internal Revenue Service agents working at an IRS facility in the Midwest. The intense tediousness of their jobs and their attempts to transcend boredom reflect Wallace's preoccupation with the concept of 'mindfulness' – the idea, as he put it in a 2005 commencement speech, that you should be 'conscious and aware enough to choose what you pay attention to and to choose how you construct meaning from experience'" (Thompson, "*New Yorker*").

would prefer not to.[30] Nevertheless, that the novel identifies so many of the struggles and personal tragedies involved in reshaping the attention into a form that will allow productive labor in an ultimately deadening setting – as the agents learn to "function effectively in an environment that precludes everything vital and human. To *breathe, so to speak, without air*"– is surely more of a testament to the brutality of the demand for optimized and disciplined attention than a celebration.[31] Jeff Severs' analysis of the imagery of boredom as "boring a hole" into the self in *The Pale King* is instructive as a register of the kinds of self-harm that are engendered by the attempt to master and discipline the attention. Severs writes of *The Pale King* as a novel about the revaluation of work, or an attempt to try and reimbue work – and especially the kinds of "cognitive labor" associated with new kinds of capitalism – with a lost "spiritual potency" that Wallace was experiencing himself as a result of his own difficulties with writing.[32] Creating a novel full of paper workers attempting to regulate their own boredom for the greater good can therefore be seen as a way for Wallace to try to recapture some of the experiences of his own early writing when states of "flow" were easier to encounter and the work felt less like work.[33] Nevertheless, as Wallace realized as early as his 1998 essay, "The Nature of the Fun," the pleasure of meaningful work is not transactional. "Fun" returns to work not as something ground out and reached through effort, but by grace: "a gift, a kind of miracle."[34]

1996

"Paying attention, boredom, ADD, Machines vs. people at performing mindless jobs."[35] These notes, left by Wallace toward the writing of *The Pale King* and collected at the end of the published version of the novel, describe one of the book's "2 Broad arcs."[36] I am placing the transition between the two configurations of attention that I outlined at the start of this essay in 1996, and suggesting that this transition is entangled with most of the items on Wallace's list. 1996 was the year in which Shire Pharmaceuticals received FDA approval for Adderall, their branded blend of amphetamine salts, which was intended for the treatment of ADHD. Alan Schwarz suggests that the brand name was inspired by the phrase

---

[30] Wallace, *TPK*, 440.   [31] Ibid.   [32] Severs, *Balancing Books*, 203.
[33] Bennett's "Inside David Foster Wallace's Head" considers Wallace's annotations on his copy of Cziksentmihalyi's *Flow* as part of his analysis of boredom in the writing and in Wallace's own struggle to maintain interest and attention.
[34] Wallace, "The Nature of the Fun," *BFN*, 199.   [35] Wallace, *TPK*, 547.   [36] Ibid.

"ADD for all," with the implication that if everyone's attention is in some way deficient, then everyone is a potential customer whose "focus" can be improved.[37] Adderall was a significant drug because it represented the massification of a deficit of attention – a social diagnosis rather than an individual one. Year 1996 was also the year in which the Personal Responsibility and Work Opportunity Reconciliation Act (PRWORA) was passed in the United States, fulfilling Bill Clinton's campaign pledge to "end welfare as we know it" by removing entitlement to aid, setting lifetime limits on the receipt of welfare, and introducing work requirements and a system of sanctions for those who failed to comply. PRWORA, with its language of "personal responsibility," wrote self-discipline into law and introduced penalties for people who failed to submit themselves to work, however boring or bullshit it might be.[38] 1996 was also, of course, the publication year of *Infinite Jest*.

Kiki Benzon finds that Wallace's characters and their individualized difficulties "identify the psychological and spiritual effects of a culture governed by neoliberal principles."[39] The precise effects of neoliberalism on Wallace's characters change across his work, from the 1980s to the 2000s. In the early work, the deadening, emptying passivity of TV watchers and entertainment zombies, as well as the nihilism of snarky ironic detachment, are the psychological effects of a particular form of consumer capitalism. But in the later work, we see a character like Chris Fogle have an epiphanic moment that takes him out of passive spectatorship and into another role in the IRS, in which his ability to reshape his cognitive capacities and submit to extreme boredom for a greater social good makes him heroic. Between the 1980s' free markets and financialization, and the psychological consequences of that neoliberalism finding their target in the twenty-first century's demands for complete self-optimization, the 1990s were a period of transition between two key historical moments. In a literary context, they also represent a transitional period between postmodernism and whatever is coming after. I see 1996 as a convenient dividing-line between these two distinct but connected attention-contexts. Loosely, the movement is from a predominant concern with the attention of groups or masses or audiences as spectators, to a predominant interest in attention as a faculty to be managed and

---

[37] Schwarz, *ADHD Nation*, 96.
[38] Carcasson, "Ending Welfare"; Carcasson traces instances of the "ending welfare as we know it" slogan back to an address to students at Georgetown University in 1991. "Bullshit jobs" is Graeber's phrase, from the book *Bullshit Jobs*.
[39] Benzon, "Millennial America," 32.

disciplined as part of a personal responsibility for the care of the self. Both should be understood as treating attention as part of an economic transaction: In the first, attention is a resource to be traded (information or entertainment in exchange for the capture of attention to for advertising); in the second, attention is a personal resource to be cultivated, and the control of attention is a skill more or less problematically developed by education.

As William James wrote, "Everyone knows what attention is."[40] Throughout his work, Wallace was able to bring some of the biggest and most difficult questions of his lifetime down to the level of readers' personal experience by inviting them to notice their own attention, in all its fluctuating and flitting and filtering. Joshua Cohen writes of that William James line that it "arrests your attention, then lets it loose."[41] This is often the effect of reading Wallace, and especially his final lines, which pull in a drifting reader's attention and then turn it loose out onto the world: "So decide," "Now go do the right thing," "Try to stay awake."[42]

---

[40] James, *Principles*, vol. 1, 381.   [41] J. Cohen, *Attention!* 1.
[42] Wallace, "Octet," *BI*, 160; "Twenty-Four Word Notes," 280; "Up, Simba," *CL*, 234.

After Analysis
Notes on the New Sincerity from Wallace to Knausgaard

Jon Baskin

In his essay "Dialectic of Sincerity,"[1] the critic Adam Kelly helpfully locates Wallace in a conversation about sincerity that goes back to Trilling's classic work of cultural criticism, *Sincerity and Authenticity*. In that book, Trilling had identified a major shift in cultural sensibility. The ethic of sincerity, which he defined as the "congruence between avowal and actual feeling,"[2] had given way to the ethic of authenticity, a more introspective and philosophical value that was focused less on the communication of feeling than on the investigation of "being."

Already in 1972, Trilling was able to foresee some of the risks and limitations of this newly regnant sensibility. But as Kelly lays out, by the time Wallace came on the scene a generation later, the ethic of authenticity had become entrenched to the point of decadence. Following two decades of postmodern art and theory, irony, self-consciousness and a pose of what Wallace called "hip nihilism" had become the methods and products of a search for authenticity that no longer believed in itself. It was this condition that set the stage for Wallace and other artists at the time to call for a return to sincerity, or – granting that "return" was probably impossible – for the aesthetic innovation that came to be known as the "new sincerity."[3]

Kelly, writing in 2014, traces some of the ways in which Wallace's "reconstruction of new forms of sincerity" provided a model for future fiction writers like Dave Eggers, Jennifer Egan, George Saunders and Jeffrey Eugenides. I agree with Kelly that Wallace's essays and fiction influenced the way the next generation of American writers thought about sincerity. But a difference in how I view Wallace's approach to sincerity – and the extent to which his own fiction demonstrates the limitations of

---

[1] Kelly, "Dialectic."   [2] Trilling, *Sincerity and Authenticity*, 2.
[3] To my knowledge, Wallace never used this exact term, and its currency in the culture – beginning by most accounts in alternative music circles in the late 1980s – predated his writing about sincerity. Still, he was considered the "movement's" center of gravity in literature.

that approach – leads me to a different conclusion about where we might see Wallace's influence most clearly in today's literary fiction.

I begin this essay by offering my own interpretation of Wallace's attitude toward sincerity, informed by a reading of Wallace's mature fiction that I developed in my book-length study, *Ordinary Unhappiness*. I argue there that Wallace's mature fiction is best understood as a form of "philosophical therapy" – a term inflected by Wittgenstein's description of philosophy, in the *Philosophical Investigations*, as being like "different therapies" – which he used for differing purposes depending on what kind of problem – or "habit of thought" – he was trying to address in his readers. This background is important to the argument here because I read Wallace's fiction not as providing a "new theorization of the concept of sincerity" – as Kelly describes it[4] – or even as offering a replicable model for it. Rather, I read his fiction as an intervention – in the therapeutic sense of the word – in the discourse around sincerity as it manifested itself in 1980s and 1990s America.

The discourse around sincerity today is quite different, I believe, from that one, and even in some respects from the one Kelly confronted in 2014. In the second half of the essay, I describe some contemporary expressions of sincerity that Wallace could only gesture toward in his own time, with a particular focus on the fiction of the popular Norwegian novelist Karl Ove Knausgaard as an example.

***

The natural place to start for anyone thinking about Wallace and sincerity is with his 1993 essay on television and American fiction, "E Unibus Pluram." There, Wallace famously calls for a new crop of literary "anti-rebels," who, "eschew[ing] self-consciousness and hip fatigue," would be willing to "risk the yawn, the rolled eyes, the cool smile, the nudged ribs, the parody of gifted ironists, the 'Oh how banal.'"[5] But what would this anti-rebellious art, which risked being "too sincere,"[6] look like? Some critics who have searched Wallace's fiction for clues, pointing to the fact that much of it is famously convoluted and self-conscious, have argued that he failed to take his own advice. In a sense, I think they are right. But I want to look briefly at two pieces of Wallace's fiction, both of which thematize art and communication, as a way of understanding *why* Wallace might have chosen to write the way he did.

[4] Kelly, "Dialectic."   [5] Wallace, "Unibus," *SFT*, 193.   [6] Ibid.

The first is a short story, "Octet," in the middle of Wallace's 1999 collection, *Brief Interviews with Hideous Men*. "Octet" is as convoluted and self-referential as anything Wallace ever wrote. The story begins as a series of "pop quizzes," with each quiz depicting interpersonal situations (such as a woman who has to choose between raising her baby in poverty or abandoning it to her ex-husband's repugnant but incredibly wealthy family), that call for a moral "decision" on the part of one or more of the protagonists. Eventually the quiz is broken off and the writer turns to the reader, asking what she would do if she wanted to find out whether "other people deep inside experience things in anything like the same way you do" – which the author says had been the purpose of the quiz (but which he now worries the quiz is failing to do).[7] What follows resolves into an investigation into the strategies available to a writer who wishes to engage in sincere communication with their audience.

The author cycles through the various postmodern strategies – all of them employing forms of self-reflexivity and irony – including the popular method of metacommentary, the practice of the author interrupting their own text to speak "directly" to the reader, which is what is happening in the story itself. But the strategy is far from foolproof, as the author acknowledges; it can and has been used manipulatively, and it might in fact make you look like "just another pseudopomo Bullshit Artist."[8] The key to avoiding this fate, suggests the narrator of the story, is that "you're going to have to eat the big rat and go ahead and actually use terms like *be with* and *relationship* and use them sincerely – i.e. without tone-quotes or ironic undercutting or any kind of winking or nudging."[9] In other words, you're going to have to be really sincere, even "naked," in your employment of metacommentary. Yet this nakedness opens you to the opposite danger: not of being seen as a bullshit artist but of coming across as overly credulous and sentimental. At *best*, the quiz (and the story) concludes,

> It's going to make you look fundamentally lost and confused and frightened and unsure about whether to trust even your most fundamental intuitions about urgency and sameness and whether other people deep inside experience things in anything like the same way you do ... [it's going to make you look] more like a reader, in other words, down here quivering in the mud of the trench with the rest of us, instead of a *Writer*, whom we imagine to be clean and dry and radiant of command presence and unwavering conviction as he coordinates the whole campaign from back at some gleaming abstract Olympian HQ.
>
> So decide.[10]

---

[7] Wallace, "Octet," *BI*, 136.   [8] Ibid., 135.   [9] Ibid., 132, n. 9.   [10] Ibid., 136.

In his first essay on Wallace and the new sincerity, published four years before the one I quoted above, Kelly reads "Octet" as key to Wallace's "theorization" of sincerity.[11] Relating him again back to Trilling, and setting him up as an inheritor of ideas he finds in Derrida about the impossibility of communication, Kelly alleges that Wallace was looking for a concept of sincerity that could exist "without maintaining an outdated commitment to expressive subjectivity that fails to acknowledge present realities."[12] What Kelly means by "present realities" is that, in his view, for sincerity to survive as an artistic value in a culture like ours – a culture suffused by self-consciousness and skepticism – it cannot depend on some kind of anachronistic faith in the uncorrupted communication of the pure or innocent self.

Kelly is right that this task, of finding a way for sincerity to exist within an age of authenticity, takes on some urgency in Wallace's fictional universe. But if I am right about what Wallace was doing, the language Kelly uses of "theorization" is both significant, and significantly misleading. According to my reading, Wallace's fiction does not provide us with a new "theory" of sincerity but rather therapeutically "treats" – in the Wittgensteinian sense – our tendency to turn the problem of communication into a theoretical or metaphysical question, rather than a practical and moral one. This is a tendency that someone like Derrida clearly shares, and thus cannot help us chart our way beyond.

The words with which "Octet" ends, "So decide," constitute a reminder in the form of a command. The command is for the reader, imagining themselves as a writer, to decide on a strategy of communication, but the reminder behind the command is that problems of communication are in the first place problems of the will, as opposed to of the intellect. The therapeutic recommendation is to confront our doubt and skepticism about the possibility of sincere communication without denying or trying to "solve" them – not to stop thinking but to stop denying the limitations of what a certain form of thinking can decide for us. This means recognizing the role that decision and mutual dependency inevitably play in modern human relationships, including in the relationship between a writer and a reader of an experimental collection of stories. Sincerity will always be vulnerable to the risks of fraudulence as well as those of sentimentality: To "decide" to be sincere anyway, or to accept a writer's sincerity, is to decide to take those risks, not to discover some way around them.

[11] Kelly, "Dialectic."   [12] Ibid.

Having established at the end of "Octet" that sincerity is an everyday challenge to be met, rather than a theoretical problem to be solved, one might still ask Wallace: How do we meet that challenge in modern society, when we have all become so unprecedentedly aware of its complications? It is for the answer to this question that I turn to *Infinite Jest*. The action in *Infinite Jest* is split between an elite tennis academy and a halfway house in a near-future Massachusetts town. Among other things, the two settings reflect a contrast in communicative norms and expectations. Whereas originality, skepticism and sarcastic humor are prized among the students at the tennis academy, what the AA community privileges in terms of communication is encapsulated by the name of their nighttime public gatherings: "Commitments." At a Commitment, addicts take turns going to a podium and telling their stories. The stories, we are told, are governed by a reliable formula, and the speakers are encouraged to "Keep It Simple." The audience, meanwhile, learns to view jokes, irony and sarcasm with suspicion – not for aesthetic or literary reasons, but rather because they are so familiar with their danger. The addicts are all well-acquainted with the risks of "sly disingenuous manipulative pseudo-sincerity," not least because they have employed it themselves in their past to get by as addicts.[13]

Although commentators have often portrayed the AA sections of *Jest* as anti-philosophical or sentimental,[14] I believe they constitute the fullest expression of the philosophical impulses Wallace shares with Wittgenstein. The Commitments are presented as a language game that has evolved, in contrast to the pervasive cultural commitments that create addicts – to status, control, the American cult of greatness and genius – with the explicit intention of checking the habits of thought that privilege irony, sarcasm and other "self-presenting fortifications."[15] In so doing, these stringent rules and conventions represent an acknowledgment that there is nothing simple about "Keeping it Simple." Indeed, we might say that this is what is "new" about the new sincerity. It is not that Wallace offers a new theory of sincerity, different from the one embraced by Rousseau, or described by Trilling, but that his writing is suffused by a consciousness of how *hard* it is to achieve sincerity in the age of authenticity and irony.

Hard, but not hopeless, enigmatic or anachronistic. It is possible to get better at "committing" to what one says, to achieving a congruence between avowal and feeling. It is especially possible if one is part of an institution with norms and practices that are engineered to deprogram us,

---

[13] Wallace, *IJ*, 369.   [14] Cf. Holland in "Heart's Purpose"; and McGurl, "Institution."
[15] Wallace, *IJ*, 369.

as a character in the novel says AA has done for him, from what Wallace pictures as a self-defeating addiction to questions of fraudulence and authenticity. It was this deprogramming – a way of achieving peace from a certain kind of philosophy (as Stanley Cavell once described the aim of Wittgenstein's writing)[16] – that I believe is the philosophical and ethical aim of Wallace's fiction.

Yet, as I suggested earlier, Wallace can be credibly accused of not having had the courage to ever fully "eat the rat" and be earnest without "tone quotes."[17] Although the Recovery Center in *Infinite Jest* may be an "irony-free zone,"[18] there is still plenty of irony in the novel. This choice may be justified by Wallace's desire to appeal to a thoroughly programmed readership, and Kelly is not alone in taking it to indicate the potential, and even the necessity, for sincerity and irony to learn how to coexist in contemporary literature. I take the persistence of irony in Wallace's fiction more straightforwardly, as a failure – even if a strategically motivated one – to live up to his own ideals about the need for the writer to make himself fully vulnerable. It is not only Wallace's success at achieving sincerity, but also his failures, that previewed the ways in which the new sincerity might develop in the years that followed his death.

***

In order to see the full significance of the forked path that the new sincerity has taken in contemporary writing, it is helpful to return to Trilling. Throughout *Sincerity and Authenticity*, Trilling draws from Hegel, and particularly from Hegel's reading of the dialectic of the "honest soul" (representing the ethic of sincerity) and the "disintegrated consciousness" (representing the ethic of authenticity, and bolstered by the art of self-conscious irony) in Diderot's *Rameau's Nephew*.[19] In this dialectic, irony is a tool that becomes attractive in an age of authenticity (as a protection against the risk of fraudulence), whereas it is an enemy of the ethic of sincerity (which accepts the risk). For Hegel, who was one of the great philosophers of authenticity, the victory of the disintegrated consciousness over the honest soul – and therefore of authenticity over sincerity – was preordained: It represented a forward step in spirit's progressive destiny of self-knowledge and self-consciousness. Curiously enough, however, Trilling says nothing about the evident costs of that victory, from the

---

[16] Cavell, *Little Did I Know*, 100.   [17] Wallace, "Octet," *BI*, 132, n. 9.   [18] Wallace, *IJ*, 369.
[19] Trilling, *Sincerity and Authenticity*, chapter 2.

point of view of *art*, within Hegel's dialectic. The triumph of authenticity in Hegel occurs historically toward the end of the Romantic period, which is the same period in which art becomes, according to Hegel's famous pronouncement, "for us, a thing of the past."[20]

What exactly Hegel means by saying such a thing – his "end of art" thesis – is notoriously controversial. For our purposes, I want only to emphasize that, for Hegel, the end of art was synonymous with its transition from delivering a full emotional and sensory experience, to being something that "invites us to intellectual consideration."[21] In the modern period, that is, art becomes a partner of philosophy in the journey toward full self-consciousness or self-knowledge (it is as a fully autonomous activity, distinct from philosophy, that it can be said to "end").

Wallace's fiction is undeniably invested in the project of self-knowledge, as the term I used in my book, "philosophical therapy," implies.[22] But I believe the hoped-for outcome of his therapy, in its most ambitious form, was to bring the project to an end – at least *within art*. Sincerity was, for Wallace, a concept that signified the path out of the dead end of intellectualized art, the decadent products of which he reacted so strongly against in his own time. But while Wallace was able to see the need to make the turn to sincerity – and even offered suggestions for how institutions might encourage and help us to make that turn – he did not ever fully make that turn himself.

Moreover, the artists who *have* most fully made it, in the wake of Wallace's death, are not the ones who tend to be most closely associated with him. To be sure, many American writers in the generation after Wallace's have endeavored to take their readers, as Ben Lerner says at the beginning of his novel *10:04*, "on a journey from irony to sincerity."[23] But while Lerner, Eugenides, Eggers, Egan, Jonathan Lethem, Maggie Nelson, Teju Cole and Leslie Jamison – among many others – can all be said to have questioned the social and aesthetic value of irony and detachment, none of them have "eaten the rat" either: None of them, that is, have truly risked being accused of banality and sentimentality. In large part, they have protected themselves from this criticism by combining rhetorical earnestness with a rhetorical self-consciousness that successfully disarms the risks of that earnestness (as one critic perceptively put it of Lerner, his fiction arrives already armed with "its own critique, and its own defense,"[24] an account not unlike that given of Wallace by many critics).

---

[20] Hegel, *Aesthetics*, 13.   [21] Ibid.   [22] Ibid.   [23] Lerner, *10.04*, 1.
[24] Krishnan, "A Fine, Exacting Nvel."

Although at times this may be seen as merely a strategy for self-protection – to avoid the ridicule of fellow sophisticates – it also appears to be the product of deeper commitments. The end of Lerner's most recent novel, *The Topeka School*, in which the poet-narrator arrives at an ICE protest in downtown Brooklyn with his wife and daughter, gives a sense of what many of these writers are committed to producing: social and political self-consciousness, which is offered to us as the fruit of historical experience. These artists are, like Wallace, committed to a Hegelian conception of modernity, in which art contributes alongside philosophy to our moral, political and intellectual progress. It is not easy to break with such a project, so deeply engrained is it in the ethos of the institutions that educate, encourage, and publish most of our artists and critics. Yet some contemporary artists have broken with it.

Karl Ove Knausgaard's six-volume *My Struggle*, the best-selling novel on either side of the Atlantic of the past decade, is classified often as a work of "auto-fiction." This is a genre defined by its hovering – as the name implies – between autobiography and fiction. The genre is far from new – Proust's *Remembrance of Things Past* could be called a work of auto-fiction – and it can be employed for diverse purposes. But as the critic David Shields has pointed out, many of the past decade's auto-fictional novels are united by certain qualities of voice or sensibility. Besides blurring the lines between fact and fiction, they tend to employ a style that emphasizes "deliberate unartiness" and a tone of unusual "emotional urgency and intensity."[25] Besides *My Struggle*, this description fits several other of the most powerful works of contemporary literature in recent years: Sheila Heti's *How Should a Person Be?* and *Motherhood*, Elena Ferrante's *Days of Abandonment* and *Neapolitan* tetralogy, and Rachel Cusk's *Outline* trilogy.[26]

The ascendency of auto-fiction has occurred alongside a renewed emphasis on literary sincerity: It might therefore be compared to the rise of the literary autobiography that, Trilling pointed out, accompanied the original turn to sincerity in Rousseau's time. But the best of these books are in no way "naïve," either in tone or in the sense that they attempt to go back to preexisting conventions (say of "realism" or classicism). None of the authors I mentioned pretend that the aesthetic effects they are after can

---

[25] Shields, *Reality Hunger*, 5.
[26] Lerner's, Cole's and Nelson's novels, which combine sincerity with notes of detachment and skepticism, are also works of auto-fiction. This only proves that the genre is capacious; while it may be especially hospitable to certain sensibilities, it is hardly limited to them.

be achieved merely by purity of intention or innocence of heart. Nor do they ever claim to have honest souls; quite the opposite. Common to all of them is an explicit thematization of the struggle to write – and to live – as coextensive with a struggle to moderate their tendencies toward over-intellectualization and self-consciousness, which they equate with insincerity, not to mention bad art. In this, these writers heed the lessons of Wallace's therapy even as they move beyond the model he offered of art as a form of therapy, or of philosophical self-improvement. In his literary and art criticism, Knausgaard has interviewed other contemporary artists he admires, all of whom place great value on sincerity. At one point in his book on Edward Munch, he speaks to the painter Vanessa Baird, who tells him, "Art isn't a therapeutic project, at least not to me it isn't. It's a way for me to get away from being therapeutic."[27]

Appropriately, Knausgaard has also presented his struggle toward sincerity as involving a broader revaluation of values. In Book One of *My Struggle*, Knausgaard describes staring late one night at an oil sketch by Constable from 1822, and feeling within himself a conflict between two different ways of looking at art, one of which comes naturally to him from his time studying painting and literature in graduate school, and one that comes from somewhere else. "It was as if two different forms of reflection rose and fell in my consciousness," he writes, "one with its thoughts and reasoning, the other with its feelings and impressions, which, even though they were juxtaposed, excluded each other's insights." At the end of an hour staring at the sketch, he says, "I focused my gaze on the picture again, all my reasoning vanished in the surge of energy and beauty that arose in me. *Yes, yes, yes,* I heard. *That's where it is. That's where I have to go.* But what was it I had said yes to? Where was it I had to go?"[28]

Properly viewed, Wallace's art can be seen as encouraging us to take a step in this direction. He hoped his fiction would therapeutically release us from the malaise of "analysis-paralysis," in part by showing us the direness of its symptoms (Hal, locked up in himself and unable to communicate at the beginning of *Infinite Jest*, is only the most dramatic example). One of these symptoms was that sincerity had come to seem, rather than an everyday social problem, like a theoretical and even a metaphysical conundrum, which it would take elaborate steps to solve. Given this fact, perhaps Wallace was right that, for his historical moment, "deprogramming" was

---

[27] Knausgaard, *So Much Longing*, 170.
[28] I'm grateful to Toril Moi for directing my attention to this passage, which she wrote about at length in her essay "Describing My Struggle."

the best that could be hoped for. As it has turned out, Wallace's combination of irony and earnestness has proven attractive for many of his
literary followers.

But in a historical period that appears very different from that one,
when irony has finally receded as a regnant cultural value, a few artists have
recognized the possibility of more fully inhabiting the artistic ideal Wallace
could only gesture toward. Knausgaard's project seeks to be post- or even
anti-therapeutic: It is a model for a literature that comes after analysis. And
one that offers, perhaps, a model for the kinds of artistic experiences we
might have when the end of art finally ends.

CHAPTER 12

Perfectionism and the Ethics of Failure

Áine Mahon

As Baskin has argued in the previous chapter, a core theme in David Foster Wallace scholarship is the tension in the writer's work between irony and sincerity. Critics point in this context to Wallace's troubled relationship with postmodernism; they argue that he embraces pastiche and play in the wake of epistemic uncertainty and metaphysical loss, and yet holds a concomitant desire to communicate all that might be meaningful and humane.[1] Writing in this vein, Marshall Boswell has suggested that Wallace ironizes irony itself in his attempt both to recognize and to overcome our postmodern condition. On Boswell's understanding, the purpose behind such stylistic somersaulting is to place a deeply ethical pressure upon the Wallace readership – to acknowledge the death of all gods and metanarratives and still to create a space "where direct, 'single-entendre' principles can breathe and live."[2]

I take this critical scholarship as an important starting point for any consideration of Wallace's work and suggest, moreover, that the irony/sincerity thematic might helpfully be explored with reference to contemporary American philosophy. Specifically, I want to argue in what follows for the kinship between Wallace's work and that of Stanley Cavell. This kinship is a matter of style as well as substance as the philosophical concerns of writer and philosopher bleed into a characteristically frantic or overwrought prose. The writings of Wallace and Cavell intimidate as they invite; they *insist* on their reader's attention. And yet, for all this spiraling self-consciousness, Cavell and Wallace unite importantly in the distinctive humanism of their work. Theirs is a thoroughgoing commitment to sincere and serious speech – to old-fashioned humanist promises, in other words, that literature and philosophy might help us become better people.

---

[1] See Boswell, *Understanding*; Kelly, "New Sincerity"; and Giles, "Sentimental."
[2] Boswell, *Understanding*, 207.

In bringing Wallace and Cavell together in this way, my intuition is that both figures can grant the constitutive solitudes of the human condition and yet both can labor to point a way beyond them. This potentially redemptive moment involves something like a return to "the ordinary," in Cavell's somewhat misleading phrase, a return that involves the potential of sincerely expressed language to foster and maintain human connectedness. In its invocation of the Ordinary Language Philosophy of J. L. Austin and the later Wittgenstein, "the ordinary" in the Cavellian lexicon captures the potential of sincerely expressed language to return us to the shared contexts of our lives. "The ordinary" in this most available sense is a move away from theorizing or abstraction, a turn instead to everyday behavior and sense. It emphasizes continually those common words and gestures that hold us all together. However, and most crucially, "the ordinary" in the Cavellian construal is just as extraordinary as it is familiar. It is "uncanny," it is "fantastic," and it is always already "strange." It is part of the burden of Cavell's corpus to show that we don't always recognize what we have in common on that most basic human level – that we don't always acknowledge the "uncertain necessity" of our lives. Thus, the humanity of ourselves and those around us must be *won back* in every encounter.

If the ordinary for Cavell is something we are continually questing after – not a benign or settled space but a difficult and even painful undertaking – Wallace, similarly, is working in a linguistic landscape where the lack of necessary connection between words and world places a marked responsibility on users of language. If there is no necessary connection between words and the world outside them, then it is incumbent upon us to assume a much greater responsibility for everyday gesture and speech. It is incumbent upon us to acknowledge the ordinariness of our lives as the only framework that might hold us together; in the absence of metaphysical certainties, there is simply nothing more. Recognizing in this way the centrality of *really meaning what we say*, Wallace and Cavell are united by a philosophical/literary anxiety that is importantly Wittgensteinian at root. Both philosopher and writer suffer the consuming solitude of what Cavell terms "a state of inexpressibility, of words not matching our needs"[3] and both respond in kind by reigniting what it might mean to express oneself fully. Thus, each in their distinctive way has been forced to shun convention in order to stay true to their philosophical

[3] Cavell, *Day after Tomorrow*, 220.

or literary voice. And within this effort at sincere and individual expression, I would argue, lies the promise of their work for moral education.

***

> When they were introduced, he made a witticism, hoping to be liked. She laughed extremely hard, hoping to be liked. Then each drove home alone, staring straight ahead, with the very same twist to their faces.

> The man who'd introduced them didn't much like either of them, though he acted as if he did, anxious as he was to preserve good relations at all times. One never knew, after all, now did one now did one now did one.[4]

As exemplified in the short story, "A Radically Condensed History of Post-Industrial Life," Wallace's writings probe and oftentimes parody the sickening duplicity of contemporary relationships. Again and again, what is offered in these fictions are inner lives that are isolated and irritated and hyper-confessional. Typically, these lives are male and American and privileged and sex-obsessed; they are lonely and unsympathetic and *deeply*, gut-wrenchingly sad. On reading these stories, it can be an intellectual struggle to ascertain anything at all of interpersonal worth, let alone any promise of redemption or grace, as Wallace's characters suffer from being relentlessly ambushed by his now-characteristic obsessions – from loneliness to depression, from self-loathing to solipsism, from the paralyzing fear of fraudulence to the tragic inability to transcend the self and enjoy community. The intellectual gifts of these young Americans are profoundly problematic, because they enable them, as Jon Baskin frames the point, "to interrogate, but not to escape, a corrosive solitude."[5]

Take Neal, the central narrative voice of Wallace's story "Good Old Neon." When Neal contemplates his own suicide, a sizable proportion of his worry relates to others' perception of this suicide as showy or inauthentic. So concerned is Neal that others won't read his own killing of himself as intentionally spectacular or dramatic – that they won't find in his final act any aspect of performance – that he contrives to crash his car in as isolated a spot as possible. Neal insists that he wants few witnesses to his suicide, and he insists furthermore that this absence of audience is for his own benefit as much as anyone else's. He simply does not want, in his own words, "to spend my last few seconds trying to imagine what impression the sight and sound of the impact might make on someone watching."[6] Fully aware of his own self-sabotaging proclivities and fully aware

---

[4] Wallace, "Radically Condensed," *BI*, 0.   [5] Baskin, "Coming to Terms."
[6] Wallace, "Neon," *OB*, 177.

that these are highly unattractive proclivities to frame the taking of one's life, Neal identifies in his ongoing rumination a putrifying self-obsession pityingly representative of our contemporary age. As he confesses in the afterthought of his many overwrought explanations, "this is the sort of shit we spend our lives thinking about."[7]

In the pleas and paranoias of its fraught protagonist, "Good Old Neon" joins a long tradition of unhappy American narrative, from the unreliable storytelling of Edgar Allan Poe to the unheroic revelation of Philip Roth or Saul Bellow. And yet, in the depth and breadth of his emotional pain, Neal has no full forebear in American prose literature. Haunting Wallace's character from the first to the final line is the fact and "the paradox" of fraudulence, the hard-won yet frightening realization that "the more time and effort you put into trying to appear impressive or attractive to other people, the less impressive or attractive you felt inside."[8] It is the paradox of fraudulence that brings Neal to the office of his therapist, and it is the paradox of fraudulence that postpones full honesty or disclosure within these therapy sessions. Of course, for Wallace, the therapist/patient relationship is itself an extreme parody of contemporary relationships – supposedly intimate and supposedly open but in actual fact fully contrived and fully artificial. In Neal's struggle to become intelligible to himself – to explain himself *to himself* let alone to another – the therapist/patient relationship works not to occasion but to postpone intimacy.

"Becoming intelligible to oneself" is, of course, a key Cavellian motif. In the philosopher's extensive writings on the theme of Moral Perfectionism, such intelligibility can only be forged in concert with another; "the self is not obvious to the self," as he phrases it in *The Claim of Reason*.[9] Cavell's account of Moral Perfectionism is complicated, but it involves at the very least a drive toward self-improvement and ethical progress. Perfectionism is an ongoing and iterative repetition of self-discovery – "a process of moving to, and from, nexts"[10] – that is explored throughout the philosopher's work but with particularly detailed reference to a core group of thinkers (among them Augustine, Emerson, Nietzsche, Kierkegaard, Mill, Rousseau, Kant and Wittgenstein).

Uniting the work of these philosophers, on Cavell's reading, is a picture of the self on a continuous quest of perfectibility; here the self is drawn on a journey to a higher or more cultivated state. The same journey commits one to the moral necessity "of making oneself own intelligible

---

[7] Ibid.   [8] Wallace, "Neon," *OB*, 147.
[9] Cavell, *Claim*, 312.   [10] Cavell, *Conditions*, 12.

(one's actions, one's sufferings, one's positions)"; the emphasis above all is on becoming understandable both to oneself and to others, "as if we were subject to demands we cannot formulate, leaving us unjustified, as if our lives condemn themselves."[11] Thus, with such a focus on understanding and right orientation, Moral Perfectionism embodies an almost Platonic aspiration toward the ideal. The aim in its simplest form is to recover from lostness and confusion, and to find one's way toward a new and personally won reality that establishes, in the same achieved moment, a firmer footing for others.

Ironically, what critics sometimes interpret as an "aversiveness" or even as an "obfuscation" in Cavell's own style is partly explained by this emphasis on perfectionism – by the philosopher's guiding idea that we are morally responsible for making ourselves understood by each other and that therefore we must continually *fight* for expressiveness.[12] Mindful of this moral responsibility, written expression in the perfectionist mode cannot merely signify the clear formulation of texts and ideas, but must enact, in Richard Shusterman's words, "a deeply personal, deeply ethical work of self-critique and self-transformation."[13] Cavell's own writing, as a consequence, holds itself to the most testing conditions and standards. His most sensitive critics have long explored the characteristic difficulty of this prose (which is at times as condensed and as unparaphrasable as poetry);[14] it is thus, at least in Richard Poirier's words, "*necessarily hard work*, a wriggling, a screwing, a turning of words."[15] Cavell's prose battles continuously, not exactly to move forward, but more to maintain the complexity of his thought. Such labor is captured nicely in *Philosophy the Day after Tomorrow*, where the philosopher urges that the ambition of philosophy transcends mere problem-solving or progression. It is "not to get anywhere (else)," he writes, "but to find itself, where it is."[16]

It is at this juncture that the commonalities between Cavell and Wallace are most evident. I would argue that the antiteleological impetus of Cavell's prose overlaps importantly with Wallace's drive to preserve complexity and contradiction. If Cavell's writing is marked by a resistance to paraphrase – by an irreducibility to single argument or thesis – then characteristic of the Wallace *oeuvre* is a similar employment of key words,

---

[11] Ibid., 4.
[12] See, for example, Gould, *Hearing Things*; Norris, "Claim to Community"; Shusterman, "Ethics of Democracy."
[13] Shusterman, "Ethics of Democracy," 209.
[14] See, for example, Gould, *Hearing Things*; Eldridge, *Cavell and Literary Studies*.
[15] Poirier, *Poetry and Pragmatism*, 129.   [16] Cavell, *Day after Tomorrow*, 98.

themes and patterns, recurring conceptual emphases often only apparent to the initiated reader.[17] Wallace's prose is endlessly complex and spiraling, with signature qualifications and reversals and contradictions, and with the postponement, primarily, of straightforward thesis or position. There is a marked desire in his work not to resolve tensions but to foreground what they might reveal about the human condition.

To take an example from Neal, in "Good Old Neon," here is a headlong expression never quite getting there as Neal makes a bigger and bigger deal of where "there" actually is. There is a furious inadequacy in the rush and tumble of Neal's words, a momentum that keeps promising and yet keeps denying satisfaction. The whole story might be read as a thorough railing against language – a railing at least against language's limitation and our inability to communicate. As Neal captures the problem in the latter part of the story:

> As though inside you is this enormous room full of what seems like everything in the whole universe at one time or another and yet the only parts that get out have to somehow squeeze out through one of these tiny keyholes you see under the knob in older doors. As if we are all trying to see each other through these tiny keyholes. [...] But at the same time it's why it feels so good to break down and cry in front of others, or to laugh, or speak in tongues, or chant in Bengali – it's not English anymore, it's not getting squeezed through any hole.[18]

This idea of English not being quite good enough, or not quite honest enough, is a recurring motif in Wallace's fiction. In "Good Old Neon," Neal bemoans the reality of "words and chronological time" creating "all these total misunderstandings. And yet at the same time English is all we have to try to understand it."[19] Meaningless babble "is somehow less false than real English";[20] and "it's interesting if you think about it, how clumsy and laborious it seems to be to convey even the smallest thing."[21] This first-person narrative, of course, becomes itself radically in question as, in the final stages of the story, it is revealed that the narrative voice is not in fact "Neal" but someone called "David Wallace" who comes across Neal's photo in his high school yearbook and tries to imagine "through the tiny little keyhole of himself" what caused Neal to take his own life "in the fiery single-car accident he'd read about in 1991."[22] "Good Old Neon," then, is a "nested narrative," in Cory Hudson's words, where Wallace deliberately introduces confusion and contradiction to muddy the storytelling levels.[23]

---

[17] See Mahon, *The Ironist and the Romantic*.   [18] Wallace, "Neon," *OB*, 178.   [19] Ibid., 151.
[20] Ibid., 157.   [21] Ibid., 153.   [22] Ibid., 180.   [23] Hudson, "Fraudulence," 297.

This muddiness confounds and disorientates his reader. It causes them to fundamentally distrust everything they have read thus far. There are definite parallels here with the prose of Cavell. To take an example from *In Quest of the Ordinary*, Cavell concludes a typically complex essay – one that brings together the work of Descartes, Emerson and Poe, among others – with the line "This is said on tiptoe."[24] This line is deeply frustrating for the Cavellian reader in its dual purpose as disclaimer ("I'm stretching here. You might have to stretch with me") and encouragement ("You might have to re-read this essay to see if you agree").

Similar to the reader of Wallace's fiction, the initiated reader of Cavell's philosophy must be on alert for sudden changes in tone, perspective and narrative voice. As the relationship between writer and reader – one that Wallace had been working so diligently to cultivate (or so it seemed) throughout the painstakingly introspective voice of Neal – is brought so radically into question, so too is the very promise of human relationship in general. Indeed, "Good Old Neon" might be read as one long list of aborted human connections and human communities. Several pages are invested in exploration of Neal's dishonesty with his therapist, Dr. Gustafson, but Neal's story is haunted at a deeper level by the impossibility of intimacy with multiple characters major and minor: He perceives only fraudulence and self-disgust in his relations with his parents, his sister, his work colleagues, his churchgoing community, his meditation teacher and even, in retrospect, with his adolescent classmates. With Angela Mead, a teenage girlfriend, he "*put up a very good front* as somebody who could have deep conversations and really wanted to know and understand who she was inside."[25]

If it is clear from Neal's narrative that Wallace wishes to lampoon the excesses of self-reflection and introspection, it is clear also that he places just as little faith in therapeutic discourse. Indeed, as Jon Baskin points out, no other writer "has ever presented more scenes of *failed* talk therapy than David Foster Wallace," Hal Incandenza from *Infinite Jest* being the signature example.[26] But if introspection fails, and therapeutic discourse fails, more worrying still is Wallace's suggestion that human relationship itself might fail – that human relationship itself is *constitutionally* doomed to fraudulence. Certainly, in his construction of Neal – one of the many "hideous men" of Wallace's middle and later short fiction – this is a live and suffocating possibility. Even the reader's relationship with Neal is

[24] Cavell, *In Quest*, 129. [25] Wallace, "Neon," *OB*, 142 (emphasis added).
[26] Baskin, "Untrendy Problems," 145.

denied any semblance of conclusion as the narrative perspective switches suddenly to "David Wallace"; after pages and pages of investment, the climactic moment of Neal's suicide is never described.

Such disappointment returns us in interesting ways to Cavell's idiosyncratic picture of the human and of human relationships. It is central to the philosopher's writings on skepticism to suggest that our lives with other selves are fully risky and fully fraught, and that we stand constantly to be missed or mired or actively denied by those around us. Throughout his extensive *oeuvre*, Cavell urges that it is a human tendency not to embrace our shared uncertainties but to avoid them, to close our eyes to other human persons in all their separateness and in all their complexity; such closure marks not only an ignorance but also an outright *annihilation* of the other person. Moreover, it is in the undramatic and the daily that these tragedies are most damagingly played out. In Cavell's words:

> in the everyday ways in which denial occurs in my life with the other – in a momentary irritation, or a recurrent grudge, in an unexpected rush of resentment, in a hard glance, in a dishonest attestation, in the telling of a tale, in the believing of a tale, in a false silence, in a fear of engulfment, in a fantasy of solitude or of self-destruction – the problem is to *recognize* myself as denying another, to understand that I carry chaos in myself. Here is the scandal of skepticism with respect to the existence of others; I am the scandal.[27]

Thus for Cavell, the perfectionist writing of the self has epistemological as well as ethical implications. Continually mindful of our relationships with other persons as always and essentially in question, it is of the highest importance that we present our own selves as fully authentic, fully open, fully sincere. What is implied is the need to take responsibility for one's own words, the need to rescue words and sentences from usages long ossified and obsolete. The task here is to *really mean what we say*, to redirect a patient and comprehensive interest to the everyday words we share in common. Such effort lies at the beginning of any perfectionist journey.

For the characters in Wallace's fiction, however, such possibilities of perfectionism are simply not available. The ability to develop from one self to another – "a process of moving to, and from, nexts,"[28] in Cavell's words – is consistently blocked in these characters' trajectories because of a characteristic *stymying* of dialogue, a refusal to grant other people a

---

[27] Cavell, *Day after Tomorrow*, 151.   [28] Cavell, *Conditions*, 12.

complexity akin to one's own. In one of his direct appeals to his reader, Neal grants that "all this time you've probably been noticing" [the overarching paradox of fraudulence], but the granting of this insight or ability still fails to keep Neal and his implied reader in sympathy for very long; a few lines later, he will assert, "That's OK, it doesn't really matter what you think."[29]

Wallace and Cavell may unite in their awareness that it is characteristic of the human to deny the human, but the key difference, on this reading, is where this awareness ultimately leaves them. For Cavell, such constitutional denial can be resolved or overcome or somehow moved onward through our labors with language and our perfectionist efforts to make ourselves intelligible to each other. For Wallace, the same possibilities simply aren't alive. The limitations of ordinary English lead beyond disappointment to devastation and silence – to "Not another word", in "Good Old Neon"'s parting shot.[30]

***

In bringing Wallace and Cavell together in this piece, I am conscious of the very real biographical connections yet to be fully explored between the pair. Wallace knew of Cavell's philosophy before the writer began his graduate work at Harvard, and, at least according to D. T. Max, Cavell was a philosopher "who held a special place in Wallace's esteem. Indeed Cavell may have been one of [Wallace's] literary models."[31] On finding himself a student in Cavell's classroom in the fall semester of 1989, however, it seems that this esteem quickly dissipated. Wallace dropped out of Cavell's classes on finding the latter's teaching incomprehensible and his students sycophantic. To Wallace, "Cavell seemed to be talking only to himself and his initiates." In exasperation at this perceived self-indulgence, Wallace interrupted Cavell while teaching (as one of his peers recounted) "and asked him to 'make himself intelligible please,' a snarl on his face."[32] Eventually, Wallace stopped attending Cavell's classes before dropping out of his graduate program altogether. He subsequently suffered a serious breakdown of his mental health, leading to a recovery period in psychiatric hospital, a stint in a halfway house and a lifelong association with AA.[33]

---

[29] Wallace, "Neon," *OB*, 152.   [30] Ibid., 181.   [31] Max, *Every Love Story*, 132.
[32] Ibid., 132–33.
[33] For these insights into the relationship between Cavell and Wallace, and the aftermath of Wallace's time at Harvard, I am grateful to Adam Kelly and his unpublished conference paper, "Sincerity, Discipline, and Good Posture: David Foster Wallace at Mid-Career." Kelly's paper is particularly interesting for the attention it draws to Cavell's reading of Emerson's "Self-Reliance" and how this reading might have impacted, in turn, on Wallace's developing idea of genius.

Notwithstanding the complications and difficulties of this personal history, the impulse to bring Wallace and Cavell into productive dialogue stems from the obvious overlaps in their distinctively American inheritance of the later Wittgenstein. Wallace and Cavell are importantly united in their shared recognition that everyday language is not a matter of intellectual certainties but a matter of vulnerable attunements. It is based not on the fixed meaning of our words but on our willingness, as wielders of words, to *remain* in tune with each other.

I have been arguing that it is on the level of style that this unity is most obviously played out. Cavell's difficult style testified to the manifold perils of expressiveness and exposure. That as humans we are condemned to a disappointing finitude – that we are never fully settled in our attitudes toward other people and are always entirely vulnerable to their rebuke or denial or grievance – destines our every attempt at writing to the self-conscious and the unsure. For Cavell, of course, a compensatory power prevails. This is the perfectionist self-transcendence that emerges from expressions fully honest and fully sincere, the perfectionist self-transcendence persistently giving voice to intuitions fugitive, risky or only partly complete. For Wallace, disappointingly, such perfectionist ambitions collapse into failure. There simply isn't the same sense, as we get in the work of Cavell, that effortful expression will bridge the gap between self and other. Cavell would say that we might never *know* the other person, but this isn't to say that we can't *acknowledge* them. Indeed, it is in the possibility of acknowledging another's humanity – the possibility that we might recognize them as persons just as complex and just as contradictory as ourselves – that Cavellian skepticism moves from disappointment to hope. For Wallace, sadly, the same personal and ethical progress simply cannot be achieved because our lack of certainty in language moves us beyond disappointment and vulnerability to radical isolation and self-doubt. In the end, Moral Perfectionism can never take full flight in Wallace's prose because he is far less hopeful than Cavell. He is far less convinced that any investment in responsive dialogue will return us ultimately to the ordinary.[34] In this same lack of conviction, Wallace situates his characters in lifeworlds of failure and fraudulence – in unceasingly solipsistic realms of pain.

---

[34] I have argued elsewhere that the American philosopher tonally closest to Wallace is not Cavell, in fact, but Cavell's contemporary, Cora Diamond. See Mahon, "Difficulties."

CHAPTER 13

The Pragmatist Possibility in David Foster Wallace's Writings

Antonio Aguilar Vázquez

Western philosophy is a key part of David Foster Wallace Studies. Proof of this are publications such as *Gesturing Toward Reality: David Foster Wallace and Philosophy* and *Freedom and the Self: Essays on the Philosophy of David Foster Wallace*. The central focus of both texts is the presence and influence of philosophy in Wallace's writings, but also Wallace's mention of philosophical authors and concepts in interviews. The American pragmatist Richard Rorty is among the constellation of philosophers who appear most often in academic work on Wallace. In this essay, I hope both to expound some core concepts of Rorty's philosophy and to demonstrate their capacity to interpret Wallace's literature. I'll begin with a reading of *Infinite Jest* based on Rorty's distinction between epistemology and hermeneutics, followed by an interpretation of Wallace's "Philosophy and the Mirror of Nature" that moves away from the eponymous book by Rorty. I explain Rorty's philosophical concepts as I use them to read Wallace, and argue that Rorty's concepts could be used to approach any of Wallace's texts (with varying degrees of utility) and his literature as a whole.

To better grasp Rorty's philosophy, it's useful to place him within the tradition of American pragmatism. This is a line of thinking begun by Ralph Waldo Emerson in the nineteenth century and is considered unique to the United States. To describe this tradition in a clear and succinct manner, I'll use Cornel West's genealogical study of the American Pragmatist tradition, *The American Evasion of Philosophy*, where he states that the "common denominator" of the tradition is a "future-oriented instrumentalism that tries to deploy thought as a weapon to enable more effective action."[1] West's study places Rorty at the tail end of American pragmatism; his study ranges "from Emerson to Rorty,"[2] and we can say that, by reading Wallace through Rorty, we are also, in general terms,

---

[1] West, *American Evasion*, 5.   [2] Ibid., 5.

placing Wallace's literature in conversation with the pragmatist tradition. I show here that Wallace wielded this American weapon in his writings, and it is through Rorty that we can best understand what he accomplished with it.

If, as Rorty suggests, the "chief task" of epistemology "is to mirror accurately [. . .] the universe around us,"[3] what happens once we discard epistemology? What task is left for philosophy and the human mind if it no longer looks to discover the true nature of the universe? What remains is the "romantic notion of man as self-creative";[4] the conclusion of *Philosophy and the Mirror of Nature* departs from this notion, and it constitutes my hermeneutical interpretation of Alcoholics Anonymous's[5] discourse and of Don Gately in Wallace's *Infinite Jest*. Rorty uses the term "edifying philosophy" to describe the hermeneutic act of self-creation, the "project of finding new, better, more interesting, more fruitful ways of speaking."[6] Here we notice the future-oriented characteristic of pragmatism: Once the belief in and the search for a "permanent neutral matrix for all inquiry or history" is abandoned,[7] then we should be less concerned over what is true and beyond doubt, and more interested in finding what is useful to us, new ways of speaking, and "a new and more interesting way of expressing ourselves, and thus of coping with the world."[8]

What is the clearest link between Wallace and Rorty? To my knowledge, Wallace never mentioned Rorty's name in interviews or in writing. However, there is a glaring reference to Rorty in the collection *Oblivion* (2004), where one of the stories, "Philosophy and the Mirror of Nature,"[9] takes its title from Rorty's book. This was Rorty's first publication, where he argued for the abandonment of "The notion that philosophy should provide a permanent matrix of categories into which every possible empirical discovery and cultural development can be fitted without strain" – in other words, the end of epistemology. The title itself is a reference to the "overambitious conception of philosophy" that "stem[s] from the same set of seventeenth-century images," and it announces the book's intention to engage with the West's philosophical tradition.[10]

However, there is something of a double bind in the role of "Mirror" for Wallace Studies. If it catalyzed Rortyan approaches to Wallace's writing, it also restricted these readings to *Philosophy and the Mirror of Nature*. This is

---

[3] Rorty, *Mirror*, 357.   [4] Ibid., 358.   [5] For the rest of this essay, I refer to this as "AA."
[6] Rorty, *Mirror*, 360.   [7] Ibid., 179.   [8] Ibid., 365.
[9] For the rest of this essay, I refer to this story as "Mirror."   [10] Rorty, *Mirror*, 123–24.

somewhat problematic since the anti-epistemological proposal of that book is really the point of departure for his philosophy, rather than its acme. Consider that the first two parts of *Philosophy and the Mirror of Nature* (around 75 percent of the book) are devoted to presenting the history and consequences of the concept of the human mind becoming an accurate mirror of nature (capable of perceiving the essence of reality) and to present arguments from both analytic and continental philosophy to show that this concept reached a dead end. It's only in the last section of the book that Rorty makes a proposal, that philosophers should give hermeneutics the place that epistemology once held, and Rorty didn't publish his full engagement with this proposal until ten years later in 1989, with the publication of *Contingency, Irony and Solidarity*. Another quotation by Cornel West can help to explain this differently; if "the evasion of epistemology-centered philosophy [...] results in a conception of philosophy as a form of cultural criticism," then we can consider *Philosophy and the Mirror of Nature* as the "evasion" and *Contingency, Irony and Solidarity* as the "cultural criticism," which is, as I will show, more fecund for reading Wallace.[11]

This is not to say that the work done on Wallace and Rorty in, for example, Thomas Tracey's "The Formative Years," Marshall Boswell's "The Constant Monologue Inside Your Head," or Clare Hayes-Brady's *The Unspeakable Failures of David Foster Wallace* (which is not all about Wallace and Rorty but does contain the most extensive published work on the topic) should be ignored or discredited. I do think, however, that they've done all that could be done within a limited bibliographical space. In this sense, Hayes-Brady is right in stating that "For Rorty, the most important thing is to keep the conversation going," but for Rortyan readings in Wallace Studies to move forward, I believe they must focus on *how* and *why* this conversation should continue.[12]

As mentioned, I examine here the presence of and preference for the hermeneutical approach over the epistemological one (that is, anti-essentialism over essentialism[13]) in the novel *Infinite Jest*. I do so by analyzing the discourses of the novel's two protagonists, Don Gately and Hal Incandenza, as representations (but not as allegories) of hermeneutics and epistemology, accordingly. I also focus on the impact caused by the

---

[11] West, *American Evasion*, 5.   [12] Hayes-Brady, *Failures*, 85.

[13] Or, as Rorty states at the start of *Contingency, Irony and Solidarity*, "the idea that truth was made rather than found" (3). For those interested in the topic, I suggest a slow plunge into this book, but if a shorter text is needed, I suggest the essay "Relativism: Finding and Making" by Rorty, which opens his book *Philosophy and Social Hope* (1999).

two institutions they inhabit: Ennet House Drug and Alcohol Recovery House [sic] and Enfield Tennis Academy.[14] By discourse, I mean the commandments of AA around Ennet, which are geared at guiding people away from their addictions; and the tennis-training programme at Enfield, which is developed to create professional players.

I read ETA's discourse and training system as operating on a "classic picture of human beings"[15] and with it an epistemological system that justifies a set of beliefs and a consequential way-of-being, that of the successful tennis player. Although the importance of steering through a "goal-based culture of pursuit" and transcending tennis is present in the Academy's discourse,[16] the institution still focuses on making players that attain and maintain a level of success (consider that the students are constantly aware of their place in the school rankings), and not so much on the life that lies beyond it; Hal's situation at the end of the novel demonstrates the consequences of this. On the other hand, at Ennet, the rules are more like communally agreed contingent guidelines. Contingency and routine become the key characteristics of a method that must adapt to the near-infinite variety of the recovering addict's experience.

Hal and Don never meet in any scene dramatized in the novel, although it is twice suggested that they meet during the unwritten events that occur between the last and first sections of the novel.[17] Near the end of the novel, there is a parallelism between their situations and, despite the aforementioned plot distance, we can find both textually present on page 902, where Hal's section ends and Don's begins. Their narrations remain separated, but we can notice important similarities: Both characters are horizontal, Don lies on a hospital bed, Hal is lying on his "back on the carpet of Viewing Room 5";[18] both characters are engrossed in their minds, rediscovering lost memories and trying to understand their present situation; both are battling to stay away from their drug of choice, marijuana for Hal and Demerol for Don. The protagonists are linked through resemblance, and the differences that occur within the parallel establish ETA as epistemological and Ennet's AA as hermeneutical.

One of the key differences between both protagonists is their experience of present time. Before lying down on the carpet floor, Hal has a panic attack, which, somewhat like Don's painkiller-free pain, sharpens his senses. Hal can manage this fear on the tennis court but not outside of it: "Lyle's [the academy's guru] counsel had been to turn the perception

---

[14] I'll refer to these institutions as Ennet and ETA, respectively.   [15] Rorty, *Mirror*, 357.
[16] Wallace, *IJ*, 680.   [17] Ibid., 17, 934.   [18] Ibid., 902.

and attention on the fear itself, but he'd shown us how to do this only on-court, in play."[19] Unrestrained by the court's limits, this perception spreads out into the world: "What didn't seem fresh and unfamiliar seemed suddenly old as stone." And so the repetitions of the past and the future are accounted for in Hal's present time: "The familiarity of Academy routine took on a crushing cumulative aspect [...]. I reexperienced the years' total number of steps, movements, the breaths and pulses involved."[20] Hal also imagines the amount of food he'll consume and the excrement he'll exude. The training of ETA fails, even betrays, Hal: He's unable to make use of his skills beyond the court, and his cumulative view of the past is reminiscent of the ranking system that determines your present skill on the summary of your previous games. His view of the future as an enumerated set of actions speaks of a worldview based on the predetermined and the commensurable.

Don endures his present and his pain differently. Although he suffers from the gunshot wound in his shoulder, the pain is less than that which he endured during the first two weeks of not taking Demerol: "but the hurt was nothing like the Bird's hurt was." He faces the pain of the wound with the same technique he used when he went cold turkey: "Living in the Present between pulses [...] living completely In The Moment."[21] Don considers the possibility that this is how the veterans of AA think he should live, present in between each heartbeat. It is certainly the way he faces the pain in his shoulder, and consequently, his reaction is the opposite to Hal's; the junior tennis player considers the measurable quantities in his past and future, while Don turns away from this type of thinking and chooses to remain in between heartbeats: "Here was a second right here: he endured it. What was undealable-with was the thought of all the instants all lined up and stretching ahead, glittering."[22] Don describes Hal's panic attack while avoiding it, and, like Hal, Don is also going through a kind of withdrawal. Both AA veterans and the hospital's medical staff strongly approve and recommend painkillers to Don, yet he refuses them because he craves the drug for more than the relief it offers:

> No single second was past standing. Memories of good old Demerol rose up, clamoring to be Entertained. The thing in Boston AA is they try to teach you to accept occasional cravings, the sudden thoughts of the Substance [...]. It's a lifelong Disease: you can't keep the thoughts from popping in there.[23]

[19] Ibid., 896.   [20] Ibid., 896–97.   [21] Ibid., 860.   [22] Ibid.   [23] Ibid., 890.

Don suffers both from extreme pain and from withdrawal, his problems are worse than Hal's, and he deals better with his situation. A further difference between the two protagonists is their relative willingness to communicate with others. As Hal lies horizontal, various characters appear and try to talk to him, getting no reply: "some more heads came and awaited response and left."[24] We last see Hal on the floor of his room, remembering his childhood and his father, finally conjuring an image of his mother having sex with ETA's top-ranked player John Wayne.

Don becomes (unwillingly) the receptor of the AA confessionals when paralyzed in bed: "It seems like Don G.'s gotten way more popular as somebody to talk to since he's become effectively paralyzed and mute."[25] Various characters visit Don and open up to him; they use him as an audience at an AA meeting. However, Don is not passive: Given his ailment, he can barely talk back to the visitors; he does pay attention and try to get his point across, even attempting to write his questions. In other words, Don tries to establish conversations with other beings despite his limitation. In their common horizontality, this is what differentiates Hal from Don. This comparison shows that the ideology of AA offers more than ETA's; while the former trains one in a sort of outward movement that attempts to establish conversations, the latter invites you to establish limits and reside comfortably within your own mind.

Returning to "Mirror," I find it telling that in David Hering's chapter on *Oblivion* in the *Cambridge Companion to David Foster Wallace*, the only mention of the story is the following: "in ["Mirror"] a mother and a son's lengthy ride inside a bus with a 'flesh-colored' interior prompts a series of reflections on failed litigation and personal, vengeful, unhappiness."[26] I take this as a sign of the constraint created by only reading "Mirror" with *Philosophy and the Mirror of Nature* and not with a broader use of Rorty's philosophy. A more critical reading is available that is not concerned with solipsism or the loss of truth but with the suffering of others.

"Mirror" is an eight-page, one-paragraph monologue in which the protagonist and narrator talks about his life while accompanying his mother on the bus. The mother has had two botched facial cosmetic surgeries and so her "her face was a chronic mask of insane terror."[27] They take the bus to visit the attorney carrying out the lawsuit against the mother's latest cosmetic surgeon. The narrator is a man of "imposing size" who wears "goggles" and "specially constructed gloves," and collects and

[24] Ibid., 906.   [25] Ibid., 828.   [26] Hering, *Fiction and Form*, 99.
[27] Wallace, "Mirror," *OB*, 182.

breeds black widows in his home garage.[28] He was incarcerated for negligence because a child fell through the roof of his garage, crashed on the widows' habitat, and died from their bites.[29]

In my Rortyan reading, the narrator's obsessions are the root of his mother's sufferings, yet he is unable to recognize this connection. In other words, the crux of my reading lies on what the character ignores and the manner in which he does it. The mother paid for her first botched operation with "a small product liability settlement" from an insecticide company: "her original liability was that a worker at the assembly plant actually glued a can's nozzle on facing backward."[30] Some of the academic readings of this story acknowledge the "liability settlement," but none press the issue as to why she was spraying insecticide in the first place. I find that the narrator provides a clear answer: "Her fear of the phylum arthropodae is long-standing which is why she never ventured in the garage [. . .]. Ironically also hence her constant spraying of R – – d© despite my repeatedly advising her that these species are long-resistant to resmethrin and trans-d allethrin."[31] The mother fears the spiders her son keeps and breeds, so she constantly uses insecticide in her home. She also tries to take the insecticide with her when visiting the attorney: "The phobia becomes so extreme she will carry a can in her bag of knitting until I always find it before leaving and say firmly, No."[32] This may sound like an exaggeration on her part, but there are two factors that the narrator mentions but doesn't link. First, the mother is the narrator's "custodian" since he is on parole, and so must be accompanied by her at all times, and he also protects her "throughout the long ride" on the bus.[33] Protection is necessary for the extreme reactions other bus passengers have to her "chronic mask." Second, the son carries a briefcase "at all times," which is filled with black widows.[34] This means that the mother is never far from the creatures she fears. Their relationship is both of codependence and of legal necessity. I will return to this later on.

Marshall Boswell looks at "Mirror" in his essay "The Constant Monologue Inside Your Head." Boswell suggests that the stories in *Oblivion* are not just united by joint publication but also through style, since "the entire volume appears on the page as a vast, unbroken wall of

---

[28] Ibid., 183, 189.
[29] It's worth noting that this story is an amalgam of three sources: O'Connor's "Everything That Rises Must Converge," Gordon Bryce's *The Red Hourglass: Lives of the Predators*, and Rorty's eponymous book.
[30] Wallace, "Mirror," 182, 188.   [31] Ibid., 185.   [32] Ibid., 186.   [33] Ibid., 183.
[34] Ibid., 184.

text" as if to represent the character's "hermetic isolation."[35] This connection between content and form is a strategy for the effect the narratives aim to create: "Each story locates the reader in the protagonist's word-drunk interior and traps her there for the story's grueling duration."[36] "Mirror" is no exception to the interior voice and to the shared style of the collection that abandons "narrative action in favor of dense description."[37] However, this story does not fully fit into Boswell's reading of *Oblivion*. Consider the proposal that each protagonist is "at the mercy of [his] mind."[38] Is this accurate for the narrator of "Mirror"? Not unless we stretch the definition of that statement to include any character whose thoughts and voice are part of the narrative. I don't read the narrator of "Mirror" as troubled; he may be the only character who makes jokes in *Oblivion*. He does seem beyond redemption, but does he yearn "for a release from the prison-house of interiority"? It is doubtful.[39]

My reading sees the protagonist as someone who believes their judgments to be irrefutable, and this blinds him to the suffering he metes out to others. In a Rortyan framework, I take the protagonist to believe in epistemological truths, in concepts that are eternal and fixed. The complexity of the story lies in its hermetic quality; the only voice in this story is of the protagonist; he is our only source of narrative. The widow's venom, the mother's fear, the child's death: should these be disregarded because there is no epistemological system with which to judge them?

As mentioned, Rorty develops his proposal from *Philosophy and the Mirror of Nature* in the book *Contingency, Irony and Solidarity*, where he analyzes "works of fiction which exhibit the blindness of a certain kind of person to the pain of another kind of person."[40] The narrator's "blindness" is such that he laments the loss of "rare specimens" that escaped during the accident leading to the child's death, and he doesn't notice the torment that the spiders cause his mother. It is by analyzing the protagonist's relation to the pain of others that we open the Rortyan reading of this story.

To construct this reading, let's place the story in the Rortyan classification of books that "ask the question 'What sorts of things about what sorts of people do I need to notice?'"[41] This query provides a pragmatic and contingent departure point from which to read Wallace's short story and

---

[35] Boswell, "Constant Monologue," 151.   [36] Ibid., 152.   [37] Ibid., 153.   [38] Ibid.
[39] Ibid., 165.
[40] Rorty, *Contingency*, 141. Nabokov's *Lolita* and Orwell's *1984* are Rorty's main examples.
[41] Ibid., 143.

its indolent narrator. It also highlights Wallace's capacity to write books that could lead us to consent and establish communal and individual values, for "such books show how our attempts at autonomy, our private obsessions with the achievement of a certain sort of perfection, may make us oblivious to the pain and humiliation we are causing."[42] Rorty details the relationship between private creation and the pain of others in the chapter "Private Irony and Liberal Hope," and through them he presents the concept of vocabularies.[43] These are the linguistic contingencies for describing reality. Since there is no singular and true language with an absolute and privileged understanding of reality, how we describe the world defines how we understand it. Rorty labels the people aware of how these constraints determine the individual's own self-creation and their relationship with others as the "liberal ironist."

The "liberal ironist" fulfills three concurrent conditions: They're skeptical of the vocabularies they use, they know that arguments constructed with their vocabulary "can neither dissolve or underwrite these doubts," and they know that their vocabulary is not "closer to reality than others" nor is it "in touch with a power not herself."[44] Here, I'll only make use of the first one, since it's the most apt for my argument, and because without it the other two conditions cannot be met. The Rortyan "ironist" "has radical doubts about the final vocabulary she currently uses, because she has been impressed by other vocabularies, vocabularies taken as final by people or books she has encountered."[45] If one has "radical doubts" about their vocabulary and understands that the self-description resulting from that vocabulary is not the "True" one but simply one among many, then an experimental attitude of redescription is adopted, either to expand one's vocabulary or to adopt a new one: "We ironists hope, by this continual redescription, to make the best selves for ourselves that we can." This means that ironists are interested in "enlarging our acquaintance" and the "easiest way of doing that is to read books."[46] If we depart from the belief that "pain is nonlinguistic," then we only know someone is suffering if it's communicated to us.[47] In this reading, the protagonist is a metaphysician; he is with those who "tell us that unless there is some cruel sort of common ur-vocabulary, we have no 'reason' not to be cruel to those whose final vocabularies are very unlike ours."[48] Since the protagonist never doubts his vocabulary, he cannot comprehend his mother's aforementioned "long-standing" fear "of the phylum arthropodae." He knows that this is why

---

[42] Ibid., 141.   [43] Ibid., 73–95.   [44] Ibid., 73.   [45] Ibid.   [46] Ibid., 80.   [47] Ibid., 94.
[48] Ibid., 88.

"she never ventured in the garage," yet he does nothing to comfort her or assuage her fear.[49] The hermeneutical Don Gately is again useful, since his attentiveness toward the suffering of others sets him apart from the arachnophile protagonist, although both are comparable in girth and size. Don does not read much, but he does not consider his knowledge of AA to be eternal and all-knowing, nor does he consider his interests to be above the pains of others.

The Rortyan "ironist" knows that their vocabulary is limited and contingent, that it is not all-encompassing, nor is it near a true or eternal language. The protagonist of "Mirror" does not meet this condition; in this sense, the short story can be seen as a sort of snapshot of a vocabulary devoid of any Rortyan "radical doubts" about its capacity. In other words, it's the description of someone who believes their private vocabulary *is* a "mirror of nature."

Despite its brevity, "Mirror" shows us both the depth of Rorty's American pragmatist philosophy and how its application to Wallace's literature results in profuse and detailed readings. Moreover, this analysis demonstrates the depth and sophistication of Wallace's construction of both character and vocabulary, as well as his engagement with philosophical developments. These readings show the possibilities to be garnered by reading Wallace's *oeuvre* with a robust understanding and application of Rorty's American pragmatism.

---

[49] Wallace, "Mirror," 185.

CHAPTER 14

A Tale of Two Theses
System J and The Broom of the System

Maureen Eckert

Another Possible World

The posthumous publication of philosopher David Foster Wallace's novel and undergraduate honors thesis in English, *The Broom of the System*,[1] in 2010, has generated excitement among academics and the general public. While Wallace's philosophy colleagues were not surprised that he had written a full-length novel given the wide range of his publications (numerous short stories and inventive, award-winning essays), they were challenged regarding its Wittgensteinian theme. It is difficult to reconcile the philosophical interests found in his earliest philosophical work, "Richard Taylor's Fatalism and the Semantics of Physical Modality,"[2] with this early, and apparently equal, fascination with Wittgenstein. Was this, in some way, a return of the repressed? Wallace's undergraduate work in formal logic grounded his thriving research and publications in areas including Non-Classical Logic, Metaphysics, Philosophy of Mind, Ethics and Public Philosophy.[3] Literary critics have reviewed the thesis novel positively, often expressing regret that Wallace's potential and aptitude for fiction writing had been overshadowed by his work in logic and academic

---

[1] David Foster Wallace, *The Broom of the System*, ed. Mark Costello, afterword by Dale E. Petersen (New York: Columbia University Press, 2010). Dale Petersen was Wallace's advisor for his honors thesis in English at Amherst College. Mark Costello indicates that Wallace had always wanted to have this manuscript published, especially after editing it during his brief time in the MFA Program at the University of Arizona; however, he never got around to it.

[2] David Foster Wallace, "Richard Taylor's Fatalism and the Semantics of Physical Modality," *Journal of Philosophy*, 84.9 (1987), 538–64. In this essay, page numbers for quotations and paraphrases refer to the copy of the thesis held in the library at Amherst College, given that we are exploring his earliest philosophical work.

[3] Wallace's essay, "A Supposedly Fun Thing I'll Never Do Again," published in *Harper's* magazine in 1985, brought his writing to the attention of a broad audience, much like his essays on tennis playing, such as "Tracy Austin's Beyond Center Court: My Story," *The Philadelphia Inquirer*, 1992, and on the events of 9/11 in "The View from Mrs. Thomson's," The *NYT Literary Supplement*. Wallace was a founder and chair of the Public Philosophy Committee of the American Philosophical Association in 1998.

philosophy. The popular "cult" following which *The Broom of the System* quickly earned made it impossible to ignore Wallace's status as a literary figure of some kind.[4] There were clearly two roads that Wallace could have taken, and it is interesting to imagine that a literary trajectory was just as possible. This essay investigates the context and composition of Wallace's earliest philosophical work on Richard Taylor's argument for Fatalism. Once established, we will see how events surrounding the start of his doctorate at Princeton and the publication of his undergraduate philosophy thesis sealed his "fate" – in our actual world.[5]

Part 1: Earliest Steps on the Road Taken

As an undergraduate at Amherst College (1980–85), Wallace completed two honors theses, one in philosophy and the other in English. While encouraged by one of his thesis advisors, Jay Garfield, to pursue philosophy, he was very attracted to the idea of completing an MFA in writing.[6] Mark Costello, his college roommate, lifelong friend and collaborator notes that Wallace was strongly convinced that his choice between paths was contingent and could be otherwise – that had he not gone to Princeton for his doctorate, "he might have been a journalist, and a good one; a high school teacher, and a good one; a writer, and a very good one,

---

[4] Michiko Kakutani's review in the *New York Times Review of Books, Books of the Times*, "Cleveland Rocks: Fiction, Philosophical and Otherwise," March 31, 2011, spurred international interest in the book as she suggested that the posthumous publication amounted to "the defeat of philosophy at the hands of the philosopher himself." Articles by professional philosophers responding to this claim were published in *The Stone Blog* of the *NYT*. The reignition of the "ancient war" between poetry and philosophy (Plato, *Republic*, 607) struck a nerve. Interest in Wallace's philosophical works grew as new readers discovered a philosophical writer known for his exceptional prose and readable texts (outside the formalisms). Recordings of his lectures and conference presentations have continually surfaced and posted on YouTube by colleagues and former students, fueling interest.

[5] Bear in mind that, for a modal realist like Wallace, there are an infinite number of possible worlds, each of which is as real as ours, although inaccessible. From the perspective of another possible world at which Wallace took the path of becoming a writer and fulfilled the promise of *The Broom of the System*, that world is the actual world and ours is a possible one from that world's perspective. Although Wallace and his dissertation supervisor disagreed on the status of impossible worlds and, ultimately, the place of contradictions in logical systems, Wallace enjoyed Lewis' modal realism and the infamous "incredulous stares" that this position elicits.

[6] It should be noted that Wallace briefly left his graduate studies at Princeton after applying to – and being accepted into – the MFA program in writing at the University of Arizona in the fall of 1989. It was there that he polished The Broom of the System before leaving and returning to resume his studies at Princeton. The desert landscape of Arizona, he later told colleague John Perry at Stanford University, kept reminding him too much of Quine in a nettlesome way (philosopher W. V. O. Quine, arch-opponent of Modal and Non-Classical Logics, famously preferred "desert landscapes" or metaphysical nominalism).

and perhaps he wouldn't have been a philosopher."[7] Richard Taylor's argument in favor of Fatalism sang a philosophical siren song that Wallace found irresistible. As an apex of philosophical challenges, Taylor's work has the annoying feature of being an apparently airtight argument that is, simultaneously, incredibly wrong.

People sometimes express fatalistic ideas to the effect that everything that happens must happen "for a reason" or on account of a cosmic force. This type of fatalism does not follow from a set of premises regarding logical principles; it expresses people's sense of destiny and helplessness against forces larger than themselves. Personal philosophies are very different from the views articulated by professional philosophers. The questions philosophers engage frequently are not quite what they seem to be. It is helpful to think of an argument for fatalism as a test of a certain kind. Fatalist arguments have posed challenges to the limits of logic from a very early point in Western philosophy. Aristotle, who codified the first set of texts in Western logic (the *Organon*), presents a fatalist argument in Book 9 of *De Interpretatione*. When it came to understanding how future contingent statements could be understood, there appeared to be a hard choice – the Law of Excluded Middle (LEM) *or* fatalism (but not both) – but Aristotle found that a multivalued logic, one in which there are more than only the two truth values of true and false, would solve the problem: a statement regarding contingent events in the future was *neither true not false*. A statement could be true (1), false (0) or neither (null). Logic *requires expansion* in this approach; we may need better and/or different intellectual resources to capture reasoning in natural languages. Taylor, following Aristotle, rejected the LEM – the very first "presupposition" (premise) in his own argument.

Although authoring a fatalist argument, Taylor was not a fatalist. Wallace's undergraduate thesis made the error of presenting Taylor as if he were. In preparing his manuscript for publication in the *Journal of Philosophy*, an anonymous reviewer, later revealed to be Steven M. Cahn, wrote written in his report:

> It should be emphasized at the outset that Taylor's article is not an argument for Fatalism as such. Rather, he claims that certain assumptions adopted almost universally in contemporary philosophy yield a proof of Fatalism. Taylor leaves it an open question whether to accept Fatalism or make adjustments in these assumptions. He himself suggests modifying some of these assumptions, and in particular the law of excluded middle.[8]

---

[7] Mark Costello, "David Foster Wallace at Amherst," Amherst College website, 2009.
[8] Steven M. Cahn, private correspondence.

Wallace figured out the identity of his enthusiastic blind reviewer was, post-publication, and they met at the annual Eastern American Philosophical Association conference in the winter of 1989, where he presented the paper – an impressive achievement for a third-year graduate student. By doing so, Wallace mirrored Cahn, who had also published his work on Taylor in the *Journal of Philosophy* while still a graduate student at Columbia University. This early success in publication guaranteed Wallace a welcoming prodigal return to work on his doctorate at Princeton. It may also have been with Taylor's blessing that Wallace tried his hand at fiction writing. Taylor writes in his article, "Time and Life's Meaning" (1987):

> The thought of a world altogether devoid of music or literature or art is the thought of a world that is dark indeed, but if one dwells on it, the thought of a world lacking a single one of the fruits of creative genius that our world actually possesses is a depressing one. That such a world would have been so easy, so inevitable, but for a solitary person, at a single moment is a shattering reflection. This is the verdict of philosophy [...]. That a world should exist is not finally important, nor does it mean much, by itself, that people should inhabit it. But, that some should, in varying degrees, be capable of creating worlds of their own and history – thereby creating time in the historical sense – is what gives our lives whatever meaning they have.[9]

It is, perhaps, at this juncture of Wallace's life, deciding between philosophy and literature, that we can perceive the importance that world-building has in his work in formal semantics and in literature. As an undergraduate, he had been unaware of the bloodless, often vicious intellectual warfare taking place over world-building in philosophy. The very legitimacy of possible-worlds semantics was still in question, as were questions of impossibility, contradiction and how they are to be understood (if at all). In his undergraduate work, we find him creatively constructing a logical system – System J – to solve the fatalist problem, *completely unaware* that his methodology and system were by no means acceptable in mainstream philosophy at that time (indeed, he would have to join forces with logicians across the globe to earn acceptance for his perspective on logic in mainstream Anglo-American philosophy).

Part 2: Taylor's Fatalist Argument and System J

Section I of Wallace's thesis sets up the problem and identifies the philosophical "moves" that he believes are open to him. He presents Taylor's argument; an analysis of the situation provided in the argument;

[9] Richard Taylor, "Time and Life's Meaning," *The Review of Metaphysics*, 40.4 (1987), 686.

and a discussion of the modalities (the types of possibility and necessity) involved.[10] The heart of the thesis concerns "situational physical modalities," which Wallace advances (provides a semantics for) to challenge the validity of the argument, presenting what he calls the "Taylor Inequivalence." As Wallace clarifies, there is a distinction between logical (alethic) and causal (physical) modalities of necessity and possibility. He further contends that there is a difference between general and *situational* physical necessities and possibilities (modalities). He states:

> What is situationally physically possible and necessary at any given moment is a function both of the general physical laws that govern the operations of our world, and of the particular set of relevant physical conditions and considerations (situations) that obtain at that moment [. . .] and situations change from moment to moment.[11]

The "big deal" here is that, while physical modalities concern invariant physical laws and are atemporal, situational physical modalities are *not at all*. Not only are the physical laws under consideration, but so also are the sets of circumstances that prevail at specific times and places.[12]

Section II presents a review of the literature regarding Taylor's fatalist argument.[13] In this section, Steven Cahn is represented as one of Taylor's defenders.[14] Wallace determines, as Cahn suggests, that attempting to refute Taylor's fatalist argument by claiming that it is wrong due to its consequence of fatalism is simply not going to suffice. Wallace introduces the premise of his thesis, "The Taylor Inequivalence," in the next section, Section III.[15] Perhaps the best way to grasp this premise of modal inequivalence is through Wallace's example. There is a difference in holding that:

(a) The absence of an event today (say, no Sea Battle), entails that *yesterday* it was impossible to command the battle.

as opposed to

(b) The absence of an event today (no Sea Battle) entails it was impossible *yesterday* to command the battle.

---

[10] See chapter 15, David Foster Wallace, *Fate Time and Language*, edited by Steven Cahn and Maureen Eckert, 3–4. 4–6. 7–10.
[11] Ibid., 25.   [12] Ibid., 8.   [13] Ibid., 10–19.
[14] Steven M. Cahn, "Fatalistic Arguments," *The Journal of Philosophy*, 61.10 (1964), 295–305. In this paper, Cahn refutes an array of Taylor's critics' arguments. In fact, Cahn's article not only demonstrates the strengths of Taylor's argument but also goes one step further: Cahn constructs arguments for fatalism, which do not have LEM as a premise.
[15] Wallace, "Fatalism," 19–28.

Note where the "yesterday" falls in each sentence. In (a) the impossibility regards the command at that time, yesterday, and in (b) the impossibility regards yesterday. Wallace argues that Taylor's argument yields (b) and that (a) cannot be derived from (b). Reasoning through the nature of physical modality will show that (b) doesn't yield fatalism. Only (a) would, but this is not the output of Taylor's argument.

Wallace's insight lies in perceiving that the fatalist arguments trades not only on what is called "scope ambiguity" but also on a problem of "under-description" in available formal languages: a richer formal language must be developed through establishing a formal system and providing a semantics for this system. What is meant by "formal system" includes the symbols (alphabet), the rules (grammar) as well as the axioms and rules of inference through which well-formed formulas can be produced. The "semantics" of a formal system is an "interpretation" of the system, and regards the assignment of meanings to the symbols and the provision of truth-values to its sentences (its well-formed formulas, or WFFs).

In Section III, Wallace further explains the unique position he occupies with respect to developing his argument:

> Since there exists in the philosophical literature to date no real semantic device for handling the sorts of modalities we are concerned with here, this essay will attempt to introduce and formalize some of the features I believe such a semantic device should include. Intuitive use will be made of some aspects of the modal semantics introduced by Saul Kripke and extended by Richard Montague's work in intensional logic. The tense-operator terminology will be that used by Robert MacArthur (following A.N. Prior).[16]

Wallace brings together a number of views then-current in the literature to develop this semantic device. In Section V, Wallace explains some difficulties in applying Kripkean and Montaguesque semantics that are ironed out with his System J. His grasp of what is needed to develop the model and semantics for analyzing situational physical modality is significant.

Once Wallace establishes his formal framework, he returns in Section IV to formalize his earlier discussion of his attack on Taylor's argument, "Argument for the Taylor Inequivalence."[17] He is then ready to work through the details of the semantics of situational physical modalities, which he has developed in Section V: "Formal Device for Representing and Explaining the Taylor Inequivalence: Features of the Intensional-Physical-Modality System J."[18] In this section of his thesis, Wallace applies as well as defends System

[16] Ibid., 26.   [17] Ibid., 28–37.   [18] Ibid., 37–62.

J. According to Wallace, System J improves upon some difficulties with Kripkean and Montaguesque semantics. Montaguesque semantics gives us a way to evaluate modalities at certain times, but is still insufficiently fine-grained. It cannot account for the difference between (a) the evaluation of a modality at a time (the time at which a modality is evaluated), and (b) the evaluation of modality-at-a-time (the time to which the modality asserted is said to apply).[19] On page 45, Wallace begins to set out a visual representation of how System J provides interpretations of propositions (i.e., assigns truth values) to future contingent statements. System J may have some unusual features, yet Wallace defends his view of situational physical modalities and how they are interpreted under System J, writing:

> Physical modalities are understood as sensitive to time and sensitive to world situations causally joined in mother-daughter relationships, as part of causal paths. And this understanding of physical modality seems to point to a way to solve the Taylor problem, to show that even under the most generous acceptance of his premises and reading of his argument, the fatalist conclusion he wants to "force" upon us does not validly follow.[20]

The complexities involved in laying out System J and analyzing future contingent statements may, at first glance, seem overly complicated. It is crucial to keep in mind that these sorts of statements in ordinary language *are* fairly complicated. When we consider the way that things will possibly be, there is an array of possibilities, although these possibilities are far from infinite. Wallace uses System J to map out these various sets of possibilities at each of the distinct times *when they were possible*.

Wallace argues that, furthermore, System J better captures physical-modal expressions in our natural language:

> If, for example, I am now on a train to St. Louis and I say, "I could just as easily be on a train to Chicago right now," I am talking about the compatibility of my presence on the Chicago-train with certain physical conditions. What conditions is it asserted to be compatible with? Certainly not the conditions that obtain right now, for then I would really be saying I could be on both the St. Louis-train and the Chicago-train at the same time. The conditions I am referring to here are most plausibly characterized as those obtaining at some point in the past – say, when I was on the train platform [. . .] with me deciding where I wanted to go. It is just this sort of construal of "I could just as easily be on the Chicago-train right now" that System J captures.[21]

[19] Ibid., 42.   [20] Ibid., 51.   [21] Ibid., 61.

There are interesting reasons to take System J seriously. Section VI of the thesis discusses further applications of System J (62–74), and there is a final concluding section, Section VII: "Implications for the Modern Fatalist Argument" (74–76).[22] Most intriguingly, his achievement is not so much disproving Taylor's argument, but demonstrating that *logic is an active research area* – one that is open to new techniques, operators and semantic considerations. His work resists the hegemony of classical logic. In all naiveté, the system he developed has the function of increasing the expressive power of logic. While the majority of professional philosophers at that time saw classical logic as a settled matter, and approached it as a sacrosanct organon, Wallace had failed to get the memo.

Part 3: The Road Almost Taken

After submitting both his philosophy and English honors theses in the early spring of 1985, Wallace remained on campus. Had he returned home, it is likely that many things might have been different. We know that, at this point in 1985, Wallace was leaning toward pursuing an MFA in fiction. He had taken time off from his studies at Amherst the year before, returning home and discovering that he had a talent for writing fiction and got more out of it creatively and expressively than he got out of philosophy.[23] Of course, the philosophy faculty working closely with him were entirely supportive, if not surprised by his change of heart. Jay Garfield (Hampshire College at that time) pressed Wallace about his flagging philosophical ambition. "Are you out of your mind?" is how Wallace recalled him responding to the news that he might abandon philosophy after achieving such stellar work on his thesis: "You can get this thing published, and you can get a *job*, while you're still in grad school. You're . . . totally stupid."[24]

If not for an encounter with logician Charlie Donahue, a graduate student at UMass Amherst, we might very well be exploring the

---

[22] Ibid., 62–76.

[23] In his introduction to *The Broom of the System*, Costello notes that it had seemed that Wallace had lost his passion for philosophy. "The world, the reference, of philosophy was an incredibly comfortable place for young Dave," he writes. "It was a paradox. The formal intellectual terms were cold, exact, even doomed. But as a place to be, a room to be in, it was familiar, familial, recognized." Fiction, Costello states, was the "alien, risky place." Luckily for us, Wallace came to see that there was nothing cold nor doomed about logic.

[24] From a 2007 interview with Robert Marshall in the online cultural magazine *3 AM.*, Marshall regularly interviews philosophers in order to bring their ideas to public attention; his first question is typically, "How did you get into philosophy?"

circumstances of a posthumous publication of Wallace's philosophy thesis. Donahue, a legendary logic instructor and advocate of Non-Classical Logic, had only begun his work in this area. At UMass Amherst, he studied modal logics but had just discovered the works of more radical logicians. He saw no principled reason that logicians should police their explorations of logical systems. Having become acquainted with Wallace in an Amherst coffee shop, Donahue urged him to consider graduate study in a program suited for his interests: Princeton's graduate program where not only Saul Kripke taught but also David K. Lewis. Richard Sylvan had received his doctorate at Princeton working with Lewis in 1980. It was possible to participate in the Non-Classical revolution from Princeton. Donahue warned Wallace against attending Harvard University, "the cursed house of Quine."

These insights from Donahue proved invaluable. Wallace visited Princeton, a long pilgrimage from Amherst, Massachusetts, where his faith was rewarded. Lewis was teaching a graduate seminar focused on his latest as-of-yet-unpublished manuscript, *On the Plurality of Worlds*.[25] Lewis utilized graduate seminars to present his research, inviting criticism and input from the graduate students. Wallace's glimpse into the intellectual community at Princeton during his visit was critical to his choice to pursue his doctorate there. The xeroxed copy of *On the Plurality of Worlds* that he received the day he sat in on the seminar was also crucial. Footnote no. 3 of the text, where Lewis rejects the very notion of impossible worlds, so irritated Wallace that it became the grain around which the pearl of his dissertation research formed. The rest, as they say, is history.

Part 4: The Road Not Taken

Wallace's tragic suicide in 2008 left the philosophical community devasted. The publication of *The Broom of the System* was, in a sense, a gift for all of us. One of its most intriguing features is that it brings to the light an interest in the work of Wittgenstein that Wallace had never taken up during his career as a philosopher. *The Broom of the System* is in some ways a play space for Wallace's struggle against closed systems as well as the operations-and-rules language games. Literary critics were quick to pick up on these facets of the work. Marshall Boswell noted in the *LA Review of Books*:

---

[25] David K. Lewis, *On the Plurality of Worlds* (Oxford: Blackwell, 1986).

> Hence for Wallace, the job of the post-Barth novelist is not to honor the
> master's insight into the inherent artificiality of novelistic conventions but
> to overturn the related insistence that texts are "closed systems" that
> produce their own meaning through endless self-reference. Rather, the
> self-conscious metafictional novel, in David Foster Wallace's hands,
> becomes an open system of communication – an elaborate and entertaining
> game – between author and reader.[26]

For Boswell, it is obvious that the (often problematic) devices of literary
metafiction might have been challenged and transformed, had Wallace continued writing fiction. In her review for the *London Review of Books*, Clare
Hayes-Brady discussed the significance of (later) Wittgenstein's notions of
language games (and family resemblances) in Wallace's novel, writing:

> The two antinomies that appear in the text, for example, the linguistic
> puzzles that appear at important points in the novel, are distinct nods to
> language games that function as signposts on Lenore's meandering path.
> [. . .] Lenore's progress towards comprehending the rules of various games
> by which she lives her life maps on to the philosopher's journey towards
> understanding the workings of language.[27]

Arguably, the message here may very well be that it is much better to
perform Wittgensteinian philosophy. The activity of writing, of creating a
fictional world permitted Wallace to challenge the terms of the language
games at work in fictional world-building. It is only through actually
playing and participating in such games that its rules and conventions
can be developed and changed. Writing about writing is, itself, its own
game. One cannot change the object-level game and how it is played from
outside of it because iterations leave this level untouched. Understood this
way, it makes sense that Wallace would explore Wittgenstein's ideas
through writing fiction instead of writing *about* Wittgenstein. Likewise,
we can see how Wallace's engagement in developing logical systems – even
from the very start with System J – were inspired moves in exploring ways
to change and develop alter and advance the rules of formal systems *tout
court* from the inside. We can only imagine how Wallace developed the
"game" of literature as he continued practicing it in some possible world.
From our position, unfortunately or otherwise, that world remains evocative yet inaccessible.

---

[26] Marshall Boswell, "Understanding Broom of the System," *New York Times Sunday Book Review*,
January 2012.
[27] Clare Hayes-Brady, "The Book, the BS and the Ladder: The Philosophical Grounding in *Broom of
the System*," *London Review of Books*, 33.25, December 2011.

CHAPTER 15

Free Will and Determinism

Paul Jenner

Where might readers hope to find something approaching free will in David Foster Wallace's work? A tempting answer would seem to be just this: deep down inside. This is less a place, however, than a complex sentiment, an intimate affect closer to vulnerable and embarrassing fantasy than to the resolute autonomy we might associate with free will. Or is free will in Wallace's work more akin to a kind of enlightened conformity with public virtue made one's own, as in *The Pale King*? Is free will manifest as performance, or is it instead the ability to keep silent or still? Has free will degraded to mere lifestyle or image conjured in association with specific consumer goods, or with the act of consumption itself? Conversely, what forms does determinism take in Wallace's work? Is determinism now a matter of existential individuality undone by statistical, demographic predictability (not to mention the predictableness of the ways in which the demographically typical individual will push against such typicality)? Is determinism the effect of addiction, whether to substances or to consumer capitalist entertainment? Or does determinism take more familiar forms, whether religious and metaphysical, or materialist and natural? Is determinism even the source of or thematized as a certain kind of diversionary comfort in Wallace's writings, a mappable intellectual concern or puzzle keeping less cerebral dreads, sub-dreads and responsibilities at bay? Perhaps this is one way to understand *Infinite Jest*'s reflection: "American experience seems to suggest that people are virtually unlimited in their need to give themselves away, on various levels."[1]

The thought is returned to later in the novel: "We are all dying to give ourselves away to something, maybe. God or Satan, politics or grammar, topology or philately – the object seemed incidental to this will to give oneself away, utterly. To games or needles, to some other person. Something pathetic about it. A flight-from in the form of a

[1] Wallace, *IJ*, 53.

plunging-into."[2] A temptation or will to determinism would become another level on which the self might be experienced as wanting to give itself away. We might think here of *Infinite Jest*'s mention of the

> quiet tales [that] sometimes go around the Boston AA community of certain incredibly advanced and hard-line recovering persons who have pared away potential escape after potential escape until finally, as the stories go, they end up sitting in a bare chair, nude, in an unfurnished room, too advanced to stomach the thought of the potential emotional escape of doing anything whatsoever, and just end up sitting there completely motion- and escape-less until a long time later all that's found in the empty chair is a very fine dusting of off-white ashy stuff that you can wipe away completely with like one damp paper towel.[3]

It is hard not to recontextualize these quiet tales as stark parables of reading and writing, and as something more than a *reductio ad absurdum* because of their persistence as a felt imperative; there is a characteristic raising of the stakes in Wallace's work, whereby free will or agency comes to demand a next-to-impossible act of self-overcoming.

The clash between free will and determinism should be seen as a perennial and abstract philosophical problem with numerous historical, cultural and social inflections, each asking whether the self is significantly free or rather in some sense predestined. Wallace's relentlessly analytical writings explore both the abstract and experiential elements of the clash. Wallace's fiction and non-fiction alike are of course deeply preoccupied with canonical, even traditional philosophical concerns such as solipsism and epistemology; even as, inevitably, his fiction reframes philosophical problems – including the very notion of philosophy as consisting of a series of isolatable and a-historical problems. His undergraduate philosophy dissertation, "Richard Taylor's 'Fatalism' and the Semantics of Physical Modality," for which Maureen Eckert imagines a rich alternative life in the previous chapter, sought to affirm the reality of free will against Taylor's intuition-bending argument that our actions and possibilities in the present are radically constrained by the future – a future upon which present actions hold no sway. "A fatalist," Taylor summarizes,

> thinks of the future in the manner in which we all think of the past. For we do all believe that it is not up to us what happened last year, yesterday, or even a moment ago, that these things are not within our power, any more than are the motions of the heavens, the events of remote history or of China.[4]

---

[2] Ibid., 900.   [3] Ibid., 998.   [4] Taylor, "Fatalism," 41.

As James Ryerson notes, the worldview implied by Taylor's paper was one "of a world without human agency, without the notion of what might have been, with only the certitudes of history's one and only possible path."[5] Although Wallace's response was informed by and contributed to technical, mathematical-logical strains of contemporary analytic philosophy, it can also be heard as chiming with an American tradition of philosophy best represented by the pragmatism of William James. In his Gifford lecture series, *A Pluralistic Universe*, marshaling arguments against monistic idealism, James decried what he dubbed "vicious intellectualism," whereby logic is used "privatively" to "make nature look irrational and seem impossible." James noted a process whereby concepts, "first employed to make things intelligible, are clung to even when they make them unintelligible."[6]

The Jamesian echo here consists in Wallace's picking apart of Taylor's fatalist argument that reflection upon the very logic of statements about the future is sufficient to establish the truth of fatalism in the world. The world is then contorted to conform to the apparent necessities of logic (as Wallace puts this in his dissertation: "doing violence to our belief that parts of the universe enjoy at least some degree of causal contingency and that persons enjoy at least some control over what does and will happen to them").[7] Wallace's argument reaches the following conclusion: "If Taylor and the fatalists want to force upon us a metaphysical conclusion, they must do metaphysics, *not* semantics. And this seems entirely appropriate."[8] As my initial rehearsal of the different forms that the conflict between free will and determinism might assume in Wallace's writing indicates, however, his undergraduate philosophy thesis is significant here not for, as it were, resolving the problem of fatalism once and for all in his texts, but rather for anticipating what will be at stake: how problems of agency and free will recur in his work. It is interesting to note Taylor's (gendered) portrait of a fatalist: "It would [. . .] be pointless for him to deliberate about what he is going to do, for a man deliberates only about such things as he believes are within his power to do and forego, or to affect by his doings and foregoings."[9] It is safe to say that, in Wallace's work, the restoration of deliberation does not present as the restoration of power.

Reflecting on his eventual decision to write fiction rather than philosophy, Wallace focused on a certain kind of aesthetic experience or "click"

---

[5] Ryerson, "Introduction: A Head That Throbbed Heartlike," 6.
[6] James, *A Pluralist Universe*, 219. [7] Wallace, "Richard Taylor's 'Fatalism'," 142.
[8] Ibid., 213. [9] Taylor, "Fatalism," 41.

that he prized in philosophical work informed by mathematical logic – an experience he would also come to find in some fiction:

> One teacher called these moments "mathematical experiences." What I didn't know then was that a mathematical experience was aesthetic in nature, an epiphany in Joyce's original sense. These moments appeared in proof-completions, or maybe algorithms. Or like a gorgeously simple solution to a problem you suddenly see after half a notebook with gnarly attempted solutions. It was really an experience of what I think Yeats called "the click of a well-made box." Something like that. The word I always think of it as is "click."[10]

It is tempting to listen for a similar click when sounding the relationship between philosophy and fiction in Wallace's work. Leland de la Durantaye suggests that Wallace's undergraduate philosophy thesis contains "the most important idea of all, the one that links together all his works [. . .] the question of how to be truly free."[11] Thinking in terms of Wallace's fiction as possessed of philosophical foundations or underpinnings only takes us so far, though, not least because the very idea of modern philosophy as foundational is itself philosophically questionable, albeit internal to professional philosophy's self-image in one form or another. A further strategy is to attribute to Wallace a broad "project" at once cultural and philosophical, thereby allowing writings of various forms and genres to find unity in their shared contribution to this wider *telos*. This *telos* is moreover commonly redemptive in character and aspiration at both cultural and individual levels, limning the necessity, for example, for a post-ironic and ethical sensibility. An alternative perspective is provided by Amy Hungerford in *Making Literature Now*, which sharply interrupts critical narratives constructing Wallace's work as redemptive:

> a selfless chivalric nobility [. . .] caught on as a narrative about Wallace: it is remarkable how often his work is said either to be about, or to demonstrate, love. But Wallace, it seems to me, did not need the reader's love because he was already his own greatest love and his own work's most devoted fan – which was perhaps the obverse of the ordinary-guy self-deprecation that characterized his public manner.[12]

After Hungerford, the significance of free will in relation to Wallace becomes less an inquiry into what his work has to say *about* free will than a prior *act* of readerly free will in the form of a principled intellectual

---

[10] Quoted in Ryerson, "Introduction: A Head That Throbbed Heartlike," 5.
[11] de la Durantaye, "The Subsurface Unity of All Things," 21.
[12] Hungerford, *Making Literature Now*, 148.

refusal to read his work: "to put it in the very terms of Wallace's erotics of reading: Wallace proposes to fuck me. [...] I can refuse the offer, and so *I will.*"[13]

   Wallace's first novel, *The Broom of the System*, explores Wittgenstein's philosophy, particularly the late Wittgenstein of *Philosophical Investigations*. Although taking a fictional rather than a directly philosophical approach, *The Broom of the System* has also been interpreted as thinking through a threat to human agency. This threat stems not now from fatalism, with human agency rendered impossible through logical analysis of the truth value of statements about the future, but rather from a particular way of seeing late Wittgenstein's picture of human understanding as configured and elaborated through grammar, criteria and language games. Drawing in part on some of Wallace's own remarks, the novel can be read as a fictive elaboration of worries arising from a horizontal and anthropological reading of these language games. On this loosely poststructuralist reading, language games are restrictive and confining, since they carry the implication that we never reach an extralinguistic referent or reality beyond linguistic convention. Worries about solipsism, so recurrent in Wallace's writing, and of just the sort that Wittgenstein's private language argument were meant to alleviate, reemerge here in a linguistic guise. They help to shape a threat of linguistic determinism suffusing *Broom*, best exemplified by protagonist Lenore Beadsman's meta-fictionally ironic anxieties about being a linguistic construct. As Marshall Boswell puts it, "Lenore is 'controlled' from without by the language-games she inhabits, like it or not."[14] Contesting Boswell's reading, however, Stephen Mulhall has argued that neither Wittgenstein's *Philosophical Investigations* nor Wallace's *Broom* needs to be taken as a philosophical or literary argument for linguistic determinism and/or anti-realism. Lenore's Gramma, the novel's missing character and Wittgensteinian voice, reworks the example of a broom from *Philosophical Investigations* to establish one of late Wittgenstein's fundamental philosophical claims: that meaning is use. The truly essential portion of the broom – brush or handle? – cannot be established without reference to the use to which the broom is to be put, with breaking a window or sweeping a floor yielding different perspectives on the broom's true essence. As Mulhall notes, the moral here is far from deterministic:

---

[13] Ibid., 152 (emphasis added).   [14] Boswell, *Understanding*, 32; quoted in Mulhall, *Shadows*, 288.

both Gramma and Wittgenstein use their brooms to represent the grammar
of language-games as translucent to reality and as ultimately determined by
rather determinative of the autonomous choices of language-users. For
them, participation in language games requires neither the sacrifice of
contact with non-human reality nor the subordination of inter-personal
communication to the external, impersonal control of predetermined grammatical rules.[15]

A late Wittgensteinian vision of language, then, need not be taken as
motivating a linguistic determinism in Wallace's work.

An alternative way in to considering the relevance of Wittgenstein's
philosophy for Wallace's writings in relation to free will and determinism
is offered by Stanley Cavell's work on Wittgenstein. Wittgenstein's writing, Cavell observed, "is deeply practical and negative, the way Freud's is.
And like Freud's therapy, he wishes to prevent understanding which is
unaccompanied by inner change. Both of them are intent upon unmasking
the defeat of our real need in the face of self-impositions which we have
not assessed, or fantasies which we cannot escape."[16] In the case of
(Cavell's) Wittgenstein, understanding unaccompanied by inner change
would amount to overlooking the importance of Wittgenstein's writing by
assimilating it as so many contributions to a static problem-solution
philosophical format, rather than implicating his words with lived existential questions. Cavell's perception of self-impositions unassessed and fantasies unescaped finds a distinct relevance for Wallace's work, offering a
fruitful way of understanding the analytical momentum of his prose.
Wallace's fiction and non-fiction might be reliably described as invested
in uncovering the defeat of real needs by false necessities. In the fiction and
non-fiction alike, further, this takes the form of analyses of self-impositions
as yet unassessed and fantasies unescaped, co-articulated at cultural and
individual levels. Since these excavations amount to therapeutic work of
recovery, they should not be expected therefore to dislodge once and for all
the necessities they disclose as constituting the psychic life of power (deep
down inside). Tracing the defeat of our real need, however, is a central way
in which Wallace's work can be seen as bound up with the question of free
will (a focus and perspective that leave his work open to charges of
voluntarism, as if the recovery of the self were not just necessary but
sufficient for broader forms of redemption and as if, paradoxically, it is
up to us whether or not we have free will).

---

[15] Mulhall, *Shadows*, 294.   [16] Cavell, "Availability," 72.

The title of Wallace's final short story collection, *Oblivion*, hints at bad news as far as free will goes. "It's called free will, Sherlock," exclaims the narrator of "Good Old Neon," but the implied obviousness here concerns the obvious *difficulty* of free will, registering its entanglement with Wallace's characteristic concerns of interiority, expression, knowing and being known.[17] By the time the reader comes across an "I" in *Oblivion*'s first story, "Mister Squishy," they are more likely at first to puzzle over it as yet another addition to the story's dense flurry of acronyms before recalling its traditional, first-person referent. The story's protagonist, "Target Focus Group Facilitator" Terry Eric Schmidt Jr., reflects that to allow oneself truly to be known by another might involve "pouring out the most ghastly private fears and thoughts of failure and impotence and terrible and thoroughgoing *smallness* within a grinding professional machine you can't believe you once had the temerity to think you could help change or make a difference or ever be more than a tiny faceless cog in."[18] For Schmidt, marriage might allow for this kind of knowledge, but ordinary marriage cannot bear such a burden of knowledge (Wallace raising the stakes again) without becoming for him a disconcertingly corrosive ideal or downcast horizon: "not as a goal to expect ever to really achieve but as a kind of navigational star, as in the sky, something high and untouchable and miraculously beautiful in the sort of distant way that reminded you always how ordinary and unbeautiful and incapable of miracles you your own self were" (33). What looks like a movement here toward the extraordinariness of the ordinary (marriage) collapses back upon itself as another take on Schmidt's thoroughgoing smallness. Schmidt's sexual fantasies about one of his colleagues, Darlene Lilley, have a similar affective trajectory, his passivity within these fantasies disclosing to Schmidt his essential meekness: "his apparent inability to enforce his preferences even in fantasy [. . .] make him wonder if he even had what convention called a Free Will at all, deep down."[19] What convention calls free will, convention expects to find deep down, with "Mister Squishy" both endorsing and exploring this latter assumption.

Sianne Ngai's brief discussion of "Mister Squishy" takes up the story to help establish her contemporary aesthetic category of the cute.[20] Ngai focuses on the logo of the fictional confectionary brand from which Wallace's story takes its title: "a plump and childlike cartoon face of indeterminate ethnicity with its eyes squeezed partly shut [. . .]. The icon

---

[17] Wallace, "Neon," *OB*, 179.   [18] Wallace, "Mister Squishy," *OB*, 32.   [19] Ibid., 55.
[20] Ngai, *Categories*, 8.

communicated the sort of innocuous facial affect that was almost impossible not to smile back at or feel positive about in some way."[21] These qualities of mimetic response and near-coercive interpellation ("almost impossible not to smile back") Ngai analyses as signature features of cuteness. Schmidt himself is less conscious of the Mister Squishy character's cuteness than he is disturbed by resemblances between its formless innocuousness and his own sense of being "thunderingly unexceptional": more shapeless than shaped and more determined than free, of his being neither different nor able to make a difference.[22] Focusing on the story's sustained interest in difference, a case could be made in fact that its narrative also shares properties with the aesthetic described by Ngai under the category of the interesting. It is not just that the story explores cuteness but is itself interesting, but that the story takes up what Ngai identifies as "the serial, epistemological, essentially comparative style of the interesting" and shares this style's preoccupation with questions of "the routinization of novelty, the tension between individualization and standardization."[23] The case for "Mister Squishy" as interesting in Ngai's sense might also find encouragement in the discursive properties of Wallace's prose more generally, its implicit and sometimes explicit incorporation of theoretical and philosophical discourse aligning with "the new intimacy between art and criticism," which the interesting both embodies and contends with.[24] The stories in *Oblivion* are perhaps as close as Wallace's prose (with its overwhelming, maximalist momentum) would get to the dialed down, cool emotional tones Ngai associates with the interesting.

Questions of free will and determinism in the story are explored as the narrative puts into play notions of discerning differences, being different, product differentiation, and making a difference. Although the young Terry Schmidt forms a "determination to make a difference in the affairs of men someday in the future," that future has now arrived; "time had indeed slipped by, just as in popular songs, and revealed Schmidt fils to be neither special nor exempt."[25] Schmidt now has "very nearly nothing left anymore of the delusion that he differed from the great herd of the common run of men."[26] As Schmidt summarizes his job: "The whole problem and project of descriptive statistics was discriminating between what made a difference and what did not."[27] Although Schmidt intuits his own unimportance, he also underestimates it, insofar as he is entirely unaware of the true (in)significance of his latest assignment as a Test

---

[21] Wallace, "Mister Squishy," *OB*, 4.   [22] Ibid., 43.   [23] Ngai, *Categories*, 38.   [24] Ibid., 38.
[25] Wallace, "Mister Squishy," *OB*, 42.   [26] Ibid., 47.   [27] Ibid., 12.

Group Facilitator. On Schmidt's understanding, his task is to research the feelings of a particularly prized (youthful, male) consumer demographic about *Felonies!* – a new confectionary aligned with nebulous associations of transgression and rebellion. Schmidt is unaware that the assignment has been intricately designed to establish the superfluous nature of his job – and to establish this, further, by quantifying ways in which the very presence of a Facilitator makes *too much* of a difference when it comes to determining consumer habits and preferences that might be tracked more stealthily online ("even the unnecessary variable of consumers even *knowing* they were part of any sort of market test was excised").[28]

The dense administrative layering adumbrated in "Mister Squishy" suggests a determinism not out of place in a naturalist novel. Resistance to this determinism, from Schmidt's perspective at least, takes two forms, neither of them especially promising. The first involves Schmidt's desperate fantasy and apparent resolve to make a negative and sinister difference by experimenting with ways to inject deadly chemicals into Mr Squishy products. The second form, one that is remarkable but cruelly inconsequential, involves the metaphysical fact of subjectivity, which cuts across but never quite transcends the story's statistical discourse of differences. Schmidt is fascinated by his ability to be elsewhere in thought, to "as it were take a step back inside his own head," "simultaneously fascinated and repelled at the way in which all these thoughts and feelings could be entertained in total subjective private."[29] Complicating Wallace's position in *This Is Water*, Schmidt's ability to choose what he pays attention to does not prevent his being "totally hosed."[30] His subjective elsewhere, it turns out, is never very far from his work ("as if merely being employed, however ephemerally, in the great grinding US marketing machine had somehow colored his whole being"), and reinscribes the experiential, metaphysical privacy of thought.[31] Schmidt, after all, has been "trained by the requirements of what seemed to have turned out to be his profession to behave as though he were interacting in a lively and spontaneous way while actually remaining inwardly detached and almost clinically observant."[32] An individual if culturally shared fantasy, moreover, albeit one that has begun to sour for Schmidt, sustains a fantasy of exceptionality precisely by extrapolating from this (notably Cartesian) perspective on the metaphysical contours of subjectivity:

---

[28] Ibid., 63.   [29] Ibid., 17, 31.   [30] Wallace, *TIW*, 55.
[31] Wallace, "Mister Squishy," *OB*, 25.   [32] Ibid., 9.

a large percentage of bright young men and women locate the impetus behind their career choice in the belief that they are fundamentally different from the common run of man, unique and in certain crucial ways superior, more as it were central, meaningful – what else could explain the fact that they themselves have been at the *exact center* of all they've experienced for the whole 20 years of their conscious lives?[33]

If Schmidt has gained some perspective on this fantasy, it remains nonetheless a fantasy unescaped.

Many of the questions posed by "Mister Squishy" are already underway, of course, in *Infinite Jest*. Don Gately anticipates Schmidt, for example, in his queasiness over a determinism of demographic typicality: "People turned out so identical in certain root domestic particulars it made Gately feel strange sometimes, like he was in possession of certain overlarge private facts to which no man should be entitled."[34] Given the novel's interest in addiction and compulsion, *Infinite Jest* has its own way of pursuing these questions. As a resident of Ennet House's addiction recovery program puts it:

> your personal will is the web your Disease sits and spins in, still. The will you call your own ceased to be yours as of who knows how many Substance-drenched years ago. [...] You have to [...] surrender your will. This is why most people will Come In and Hang In only after their own entangled will has just about killed them. You have to want to surrender your will to people who know how to Starve The Spider. You have to want to take the suggestions, want to abide by the traditions of anonymity, humility, surrender to the Group conscience. If you don't obey, nobody will kick you out. They won't have to. You'll end up kicking *yourself* out, if you steer by your own sick wills.[35]

These words provide a fitting way of summarizing what is at stake in Wallace's work as far as free will goes. The will is not coterminous with the self but is sick, steering and entangling, and standing in need of education, therapy and community. Free will for Wallace is less an impossible illusion than a burdensome, next to impossible responsibility.

---

[33] Ibid., 20.   [34] Wallace, *IJ*, 57.   [35] Ibid., 357.

CHAPTER 16

David Foster Wallace's Mathematics of the Infinite

Stuart J. Taylor

Wallace's interest in mathematics is regularly traced back to his under-graduate philosophy studies, and his philosophy dissertation is an early example of his interest in the liberating potential of logico-mathematical language systems. "For most of my college career," he told Larry McCaffery in 1993, "I was a hard-core syntax wienie, a philosophy major with a specialization in math and logic."[1] From this background, Wallace came to appreciate "that a mathematical experience was aesthetic in nature."[2] In his writing, Wallace developed and deployed a certain math-ematical aesthetic to explore related metaphysical issues, such as existence, space and time. While a growing band of critics continue to explore various types and instances of mathematics in Wallace's writing, it is the mathematics of the infinite that is a perennial feature in his *oeuvre*.[3] Although Roberto Natalini notes that mathematics "was not [Wallace's] systematic approach" to everything that he wrote, it is possible to chart the development of the mathematical infinite in Wallace's *oeuvre* from his early undergraduate work to his unfinished, posthumously published novel, *The Pale King*.[4]

The adjective "infinite" describes something "Having no limit or end (real or assignable); boundless, unlimited, endless; immeasurably great in extent, duration, or other respect. Chiefly of God or His attributes; also of space, time, etc., in which it passes into the mathematical use."[5] In *Everything and More*, his popular-science history of the mathematical

---

[1] McCaffery "Interview," 34.   [2] Ibid., 34–35.
[3] Mullins, "Theories of Everything and More"; Woods, "Early-Morning Uncertainties"; and Severs, *Balancing Books*. These studies are preceded by Natalini's "David Foster Wallace and the Mathematics of Infinity." Natalini also edited a special edition of the journal *Lettera Matematica International* in December 2015.
[4] Natalini, "David Foster Wallace and the Mathematics of Infinity," 43.
[5] "infinite, adj., adv., and n." *OED Online*.

infinite, Wallace defines the Hellenic term *to apeiron* as describing "infinitely long/large [. . .] undefinable [. . .] unbounded natureless chaos."[6]

In modern mathematics, however, common everyday words like "infinite" are used in different, precise ways. The mathematical definitions of "infinite" retain the Hellenic sense of "a quantity without limit," and include the geometric understanding of something *at* infinity that is at "infinite distance, or that portion or region of space which is infinitely distant."[7]

This geometric infinite is also a major feature of Wallace's writing, from his early creative non-fiction about the Midwest planes to *Infinite Jest*'s unlimited capaciousness, and is perhaps the clearest example of the aesthetic nature of mathematical experience that Wallace described. In "Derivative Sport in Tornado Alley," Wallace notes that "Tornadoes, for me, were a transfiguration [. . .] the dimensionless point at which parallel lines met and whirled and blew up."[8] He also compared the end of *Infinite Jest* to the geometrical infinite of "Certain kind of parallel lines [that] are supposed to start converging in such a way that an 'end' can be projected by the reader somewhere beyond the right frame."[9] The novel's optical limitlessness also complements its fractal qualities. Wallace has described his magnum opus as "structured like something called a Sierpinski gasket, which is a very primitive kind of pyramidal fractal" – a Matryoshka-doll nesting of triangles, whose lines trace an infinite distance (Figure 16.1).[10] Furthermore, the novel's tennis academy is structured as a "cardioid," the dominant shape of another famous fractal, the curve described by the boundary of the Mandlebrot set: a special set of complex numbers whose infinite sequence remains bounded, in a similar way to Sierpinski's triangular fractal (Figure 16.2).[11] As Brian Clegg notes, the geometry of fractals "demonstrates quite painlessly that it is possible in principle to have something infinitely long drawn in normal, finite space."[12]

Yet, still more precisely (and more frequently), the "infinite" features in the branch of mathematics known as analysis. Analysis studies "topics that involve the use of limiting processes," including "the summation of infinite series, which involve 'infinite' processes," indefinitely continued without ever coming to an end.[13] From his earliest publications, Wallace frequently used the analytical infinite to elaborate his discussions of the metaphysical

[6] Wallace, *EM*, 44.   [7] "infinity, n." *OED Online*.   [8] Wallace, "Derivative Sport," *SFT*, 17.
[9] Max, *Every Love Story*, 319, n. 19.   [10] Silverblatt, "David Foster Wallace: *Infinite Jest*."
[11] Wallace, *IJ*, 983, n. 3; the term "Mandelbrotian math" appears on 994, n. 34.
[12] Clegg, *Infinity*, 230.   [13] "analysis, n." *OED Online*.

Figure 16.1 Sierpinski gasket

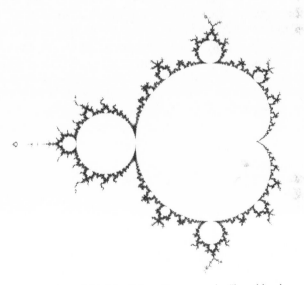

Figure 16.2 Boundary of the Mandlebrot Set – note the "heartlike shape of the largest part"
(Gowers et al., Mathematics, 507.)

infinite, especially to reconcile various infinites: the infinitely expansive and the infinitely dense.

Between 1879 and 1884, Georg Cantor, a major subject of *Everything and More*, demonstrated that the finite did not empty out into a chaotic infinity (∞), but instead a distinguishable "Transfinitum" in which one could, with "transfinite" numbers ($\aleph$, ω), comprehend both the size (cardinality, $\aleph$) and organization (ordinality, ω) of infinite mathematical objects.[14] The transfinite numbers of Cantor's set theory "showed that it was possible to go on in a structured, an ordered, way beyond infinity."[15] In so doing, Cantor completed the shift from considering the "infinite" as the unbounded disorder of *apeiron* to a concept explainable by so-called *ordered structures*. This latter consideration offers us another avenue of considering the mathematics of the infinite in Wallace's writing, particularly in *Infinite Jest*.

Beyond the specific mentions of Cantor in *Jest*, the most extensive way in which Wallace engages with mathematics of the infinite in the novel is through set-theoretical hierarchies of narrative containers that resemble ordered structures. In mathematics, ordered structures utilize "common tools for comparison like 'greater than or equal to' and 'less than or equal to'" for the purposes of ordering or comparing all or some elements of a set, including infinite sets.[16] It was Cantor's Diagonal Proof that established set theory's authority and ultimately alleviated the Classical anxiety over *apeiron* (boundless infinity). More generally, we can consider an ordered structure as characterized by a "binary relation $\leq$ defined on a set."[17] For example, by comparing sets A and B, we might find that not only is A *greater than* B ($A > B$) but that every element of B is also an element of A. This means that B is subset of A ($B \subset A$), meaning B is *inside of* A: in other words, A *contains* B.[18] Similar containers feature throughout *Jest* – from Hal's declaration "I am in here," through plots concerning the Great Concavity/Convexity and the cranium of James Incandenza, to the various formal features of the novel, including non-numerical calendar of Subsidized Time – in a nonlinear arrangement of narrative data that contribute to the novel's encyclopedic quality.[19] Containers as ordered structures also describe the formal arrangements of the novel's narrative at an overarching level. The formal containers of *Infinite Jest* resemble set $>$ subset ordered structures where the main text of

---

[14] Cantor, *Unendliche*, 85, 129.   [15] Clegg, *Infinity*, 171.   [16] Mashaal, *Bourbaki*, 82.
[17] Burris and Sankappanavar, *Course*, 4.   [18] English, *Mathematical Reasoning*, 40–42.
[19] Hayles refers to the Concavity/Convexity as a "dump" representative of a "widening circle of toxicity" and a "failure to *contain* damage within a prophylactically enclosed area" ("The Illusion of Autonomy and the Fact of Recursivity," 686, emphasis added). This ecological model resists any encyclopedic enterprise that seeks to encircle, and hermetically seal, such generative sites. As these sites are often characterized by information overload, however, the geographic setting maps a cognitive arena, with Wallace representing consciousness as striving to escape its cranial confines and, in this way, connect with others.

the novel (*IJ* 3–981) is distinguished from the endnotes collected as the "Notes and Errata" appendix (*IJ* 983–1079).[20]

In the novel, the Cantorian infinite is most overt, however, in Coach Gerhardt Schtitt's conception of mathematically beautiful tennis. Early in *Infinite Jest*, it is revealed that the major philosophical understanding of tennis at ETA is mathematical. James Incandenza founded the tennis academy "from a background in math-based optical science" while "Schtitt approached competitive tennis more like a pure mathematician than a technician."[21] Schtitt's coaching philosophy emphasizes the belief that "real tennis was really about not the blend of statistical order and expansive potential that the game's technicians revered, but in fact the opposite – *not*-order, *limit*, the places where things broke down, fragmented into beauty."[22] It is important to keep in mind here the competing conceptions of "limit." One is defined by "statistical order," the Attic "condition in which everything has its correct or appropriate place."[23] The other, more-precisely mathematical sense of "order" indicates the ordered structures that enable mathematicians like Cantor to deal with infinity. In the Classical sense of a universe of "statistical order," limit was an ordering boundary, while "no limit means no form, and no form means chaos, ugliness, a mess."[24] The other sense is used in calculus when discussing functions. For example, following the predictable curve of the function $y = 1/x$, we can see that, as x *approaches* 0, y *approaches* a *limit*: an exponentially increasing value that gets ever closer to infinity (Figure 16.3). It is this notion of a *limit* that Schtitt locates in mathematically messy, or "*not*-order[ed,] places where things broke down."

Despite his "knowledge of formal math" being "equivalent to that of a Taiwanese kindergartner," Schtitt intuited "that locating beauty and art and magic and improvement and keys to excellence and victory in the prolix flux of match play is not a fractal matter of reducing chaos to pattern":

> it was a matter not of reduction at all, but – perversely – of expansion, the aleatory flutter of uncontrolled, metastatic growth – each well-shot ball admitting of n possible responses, 2^n possible responses to those responses, and on into [. . .] a Cantorian continuum of infinities of possible move and response.[25]

[20] Nadel, "Consider the Footnote," 224.   [21] Wallace, *IJ*, 81.
[22] Ibid., 81 (emphasis in original).   [23] "order, n.," *OED Online*.   [24] Wallace, *EM*, 44–45.
[25] Wallace, *IJ*, 82.

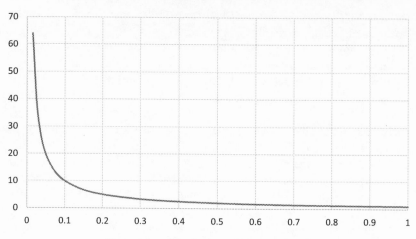

Figure 16.3   The Reciprocal Function $y = \frac{1}{x}$

Endnote 35 in *Infinite Jest* extrapolates upon this important exposition of Cantor – the first mention of the mathematician in Wallace's published writing. Most notably, it stresses that his "Diagonal Proof demonstrated that there can be an infinity of things between any two things no matter how close together the two things are." In this view, the n in question is $\aleph_0$ – the smallest infinite number. This permits the reader to regard "Enfield" not only as n-field, a number field where actions are rendered as mathematical operations, but also as an *in*finite field of play. The endnote then bends back to relating mathematics to tennis, revealing that Cantor's Diagonal Proof "deeply informed Dr. J. Incandenza's sense of the transstatistical aesthetics of serious tennis."[26] Shortly thereafter, Schitt's limited articulation is succeeded by the more advanced mathematical language of James Incandenza:

> a Cantorian continuum of infinities of possible move and response, Cantorian and beautiful because *in*foliating, *contained*, this diagnate infinity of infinities of choice and execution, mathematically controlled but humanly *contained*, bounded by the talent and imagination of self and opponent, bent in on itself by the containing boundaries of skill and imagination that brought one player finally down, that kept both from winning, that made it, finally, a game, these boundaries of self.[27]

[26] Ibid., 994, n. 35.   [27] Ibid., 82.

In Cantor's transfinite mathematics, if n denotes a set, then 2^n denotes its power set – the number of possible arrangement of elements within the container of the set.[28] In *Infinite Jest*, the expansive, unraveling infinite of $\aleph_0$ is shown, here, to be secondary to the ordinal infinite $2^{\aleph_0}$ *"contained"* within "boundaries of self"; in so doing, Wallace expresses the geometrical infinite of Sierpinski and Mandelbrot fractals in Cantorian analytical terms.

Moreover, through this switch in perspective from Schtitt to Incandenza, the narrative enacts the level-elevation of ordered structure that it describes, a technique that Wallace used in his other writings. The "Cantorian continuum" also features prominently in the hardest parts of *Everything and More*.[29] One section that particularly resonates with mathematically infinite descriptions of tennis, like Schtitt's and Incandenza's earlier, is the discussion of Cantor's demonstration that "every point on a 2D plane" – such as a tennis court – "can be put into a 1-1C [one-to-one correspondence] with a point on the R.L. [Real Line]" – that is, with every real number: the integers, the fractions, and the irrationals such as π. Cantor's technique regarding planes can furthermore "be used to show that a 3D cube, a 4D hyper cube, or actually any n-dimensional figure's total point-set has the same cardinality as the R.L.'s set of real numbers, namely c," the continuum.[30] Yet, combined with the modifier "Cantorian," "continuum" also evokes the Continuum Hypothesis, which is discussed at the climax of *Everything and More*. The Continuum Hypothesis is Cantor's conjecture that there is no set whose cardinal number – the value designating its size – is *greater than* the cardinal number of the natural numbers ($\aleph_0$) but *less than* the cardinal number of the real numbers (c, a.k.a. $2^{\aleph_0}$). Since Cantor's death, this conjecture has been shown – by Kurt Gödel and Paul Cohen in the middle of the twentieth century – to be undecidable: formally neither true nor false.[31] Wallace describes current "speculative systems" that attempt to deal with the Continuum Hypothesis, post-Gödel-and-Cohen, as "among the most hyperabstract constructs in modern math," which use "rarefied terms like 'Cantorian' v. '1st-Order-Universes' [. . .] and many others that are fun to

[28] Clegg, *Infinity*, 185.
[29] For a discussion of the composition of the book, see S. Taylor, "Making."
[30] Wallace, *EM*, 263.
[31] Gödel's 1930 exploration of this problem in his *Incompleteness Theorems* are dramatized in Wallace's short story parable "Here and There," which is dedicated "For K. Gödel" (*GCH*, 149). See Gödel, *On Formally Undecidable Propositions*.

say even if one has no clear idea what they're supposed to denote."[32] In a footnote to this sentence, Wallace asserts that:

> A good deal of contemporary set theory seems to involve arguing about what these theoretical terms mean and just when and why they do (=mean what they mean, if anything (and, if not anything, then what that nothing might mean (and so on))).[33]

This demonstrative *et cetera* is, in the language of *Infinite Jest*, appropriately "*in*foliating, *contained*" within parenthetical marks.

As the example earlier shows, the interpolations of *Everything and More* constantly remind the reader of the constructed nature of the text and of the resultant mediation of material. One of the most insistent of such interpolations recounts an unverified dialogue between Wallace and Great Discoveries series editor Jesse Cohen concerning suggested revisions to Wallace's manuscript:

> IYI FROM SERIES EDITOR's LETTER OF QUERIES ON MS. VERSION OF BOOKLET: "p. 272, paragraph following graphic of 'Array #3': so, in other words, no matter how many subsets of I we come up with, we can always create new ones? If so, do you want to say something like that, just to spell it out?"
>
> FROM TESTY AUTH. REPLY: "No we do *not* want to say something like that because it's [. . .] deeply, seriously wrong: we're not *creating* new subsets; we're proving that there *do* exist and *will always* exist some subsets that no list or integral 1-1C can capture. W/ 'exist,' admittedly, requiring a wisesass 'as it were' or 'whatever that means' or something – but the reader'd have to be a radical-Shiite Kroneckerian to believe that what we're doing in this proof is really *creating* these new subsets."[34]

Thus, the entire structure of *Everything and More* emphasizes the analogous "chasmal terrain of self-reference" that haunts the paradoxes of Cantorian transfinite mathematics and set theory: In short, the book's form functions as a performative aspect of its content.[35]

While Wallace maintained his interest in narrative uses for mathematical ordered structures in his fiction writing after *Infinite Jest*, *Oblivion* is notable for a greatly diminished prominence of interpolative foot/ endnotes. Yet, while notes are used more sparingly in his later fiction, in stories such as "Good Old Neon," Wallace's palette of mathematical imagery continues to draw attention to models of the mind as conscious

---

[32] Wallace, *EM*, 303.   [33] Ibid., 303, n. 124.   [34] Ibid., 273, n. 70 (emphasis in original).
[35] Ibid., 275.

"interiors," represented by those embedded, nested narratives that are analogous to mathematical ordered structures.[36] Drafts of the short story in the archives of the Harry Ransom Center show that Wallace changed "therapy" to "analysis," an abbreviation of "psychoanalysis" that also suggests analogies with transfinite mathematics.[37] This brings therapy (or therapeutic communication and transformation) together with the mathematics of "limit[s] towards which the series converge[s]."[38] In Wallace's story, Neal takes as his mortal limit the irreconcilable axes of Fear and Love, those "exhaustive and mutually exclusive" domains comprising the "two basic, fundamental orientations a person could have toward the world." This limit would be marked by suicide: "I woke up having decided I was going to kill myself and end the whole farce."[39] Like the narrator of Wallace's debut, "The Planet Trillaphon As It Stands In Relation To The Bad Thing," Neal in "Good Old Neon" identifies the failure of language, whether natural or symbolic, to represent faithfully the infinitely extensive and infinitely dense experience of pain, instead preferring the "orderly" moment of death.[40] The representation of such a moment – and the movement into and description of the eternity of the afterlife – is approached, instead, through narrative ordered structures.

"Good Old Neon" features important dramatizations of narratives with similar order-types akin to those used in Cantor's mathematics. The first occurs early in the story, where the narrator lists "some of the various things" that he tried to end the fraudulence that defined his life:

> EST, riding a ten-speed to Nova Scotia and back, hypnosis, cocaine, sacro-cervical chiropractic, joining a charismatic church, jogging, pro-bono work for the Ad Council, meditation classes, the Masons, *analysis*, the Landmark Forum, the Course in Miracles, a right-brain drawing workshop, celibacy, collecting and restoring vintage Corvettes, and trying to sleep with a different girl every night for two straight months [...] In terms of the list, psycho*analysis* was pretty much the last thing I tried.[41]

Note here that "analysis" is listed initially as the eleventh item on the list, only to be revealed as "the last thing" or final item on the list. Here, then, two ordered structures are presented: the list of "various things" as narrated by the deceased (that is, from *outside time*), and the chronological sequence of the narrator using those "things" to try to end his fraudulence.

[36] Boswell, "Constant Monologue," 151.
[37] Wallace, "Good Old Neon," Handwritten Draft, Harry Ransom Center.
[38] Wallace, "Neon," *OB*, 167.   [39] Ibid., 164, 169.   [40] Wallace, "Trillaphon," 30.
[41] Wallace, "Neon," *OB*, 142–43 (emphasis added).

Juxtaposing these ordered structures suggests both the gap between both worlds and the means by which this gap is traversed through associative communication. This structural juxtaposition can also be seen regarding the story's only footnote. Signaled by an asterisk, this footnote contains the words "THE END": So the ordered structure of the story changes from {1,2,3, ...} to {1,3, ... 2}, with the second *infinite* gap permitting the structural-level shift to another order-type or ordered structure: David Wallace's consciousness.[42] With Wallace's dramatic use of a footnote – restricted to this one instance in the whole story – he performs the ordered structures of the mathematical infinite and their analogous relation to "the universes inside you, all the endless inbent fractals of connection and symphonies of different voices, the infinities you can never show another soul."[43]

While "Good Old Neon" dramatizes the difficulties of achieving sincere communication between individual minds, in Wallace's final, uncompleted work, he returned to larger institutional models of consciousness, inside of which readers continue to negotiate levels of mind. In *The Pale King*, chiropractor Doctor Kathy conceives of "the universe as an infinite system of neural connections."[44] Yet recognition of this is impeded by society's applied-mathematical calculations, in a world where "Routine, repetition, tedium, monotony, ephemeracy, inconsequence, abstraction, disorder, boredom, angst, ennui [...] are the true hero's enemies."[45] The proximity of "abstraction" and "disorder" suggests regression to Ancient Greek ideas of the infinite as *to apeiron*, antagonistic to Cantor's transfinite mathematics. There is significant irony, then, in the substitute Jesuit's claim that "the heroic frontier now lies in the ordering and deployment" of finite facts, and that bean counters should be lionized for "Riding herd on the unending torrent of financial data. The eddies, cataracts, arranged variations, fractious minutiae. You order the data, shepherd it, direct its flow, lead it where it's needed, in the codified form in which it's apposite."[46] For Jeffrey Severs, such emphasis of the "languages of workplaces and bureaucracies, often amoral or *meaninglessly mathematicized*, colonize the minds on display."[47] Developing this reading, we may see that ordered structures model Wallace's strategy for meaningful logistic resistance to such colonization, offering a means to appreciate the hierarchies of Wallace's "concrete model" of cognition.[48]

---

[42] Ibid., 179n.   [43] Ibid., 179.   [44] Wallace, *TPK*, 405.   [45] Ibid., 233.
[46] Ibid., 234–35.   [47] Severs, *Balancing Books*, 170 (emphasis added).
[48] Burn, "Paradigm," 383.

Thus, while Wallace's footnotes are conspicuously absent throughout much of *The Pale King*, his ordered structures can still be seen in what Simon de Bourcier describes as the novel's hypotactic hierarchies.[49] While Meredith Rand appears to be stuck in a "vicious circle ... going around and around inside the problem instead of really looking at the problem," within this infinite cycling, her personal anxieties are drawn to higher narrative levels through communication with Shane Drinion.[50] In analytical terms, Drinion has pulled Rand from her Vicious Infinite Regress into a communion, whose "'I' can be validly approximated by a convergent infinite series."[51] By moving from Vicious Infinite Regress to effective communication, Wallace continued to explore the redemptive analogies of mathematical analysis, specifically of ordered structures.

In his review of *Everything and More*, Michael Harris wrote that Wallace's "preoccupation with infinity here, and presumably in his fiction as well, is ultimately metaphysical."[52] That he continued to explore this metaphysics through the mathematics of the infinite throughout his career demonstrates Wallace's prodigious interdisciplinary intellectual energies. In an interview with Dave Eggers following the publication of *Everything and More*, Wallace suggests that the "real point" of the book was an attempt to address "one of the really significant problems of today's culture," namely the fragmentation of knowledge and its resultant suppression of connective, empathetic communication:

> We live today in a world where most of the really important developments in everything from math and physics and astronomy to public policy and psychology and classical music are so extremely abstract and technically complex and context-dependent that it's next to impossible for the ordinary citizen to feel that they (the developments) have much relevance to her actual life. Where even people in two closely related sub-sub-specialties have a hard time communicating with each other because their respective s-s-s's require so much special training and knowledge. And so on.[53]

The "hard time communicating" is one of the "things about the contemporary U.S. that make it distinctively hard to be a real human being," a diagnosis Wallace made to McCaffery in 1993. The "gooey" imperative to "find [...] ways for educated people to talk meaningfully with one another across the divides of radical separation" that Wallace attempted with his technical writing in *Everything and More* resonates with the "really human" characteristics articulated by Hal in *Infinite Jest*: of

---

[49] Bourcier, "Syntax," np.   [50] Wallace, *TPK*, 498.   [51] Wallace, *EM*, 195.
[52] Harris, "A Sometimes Funny Book," 634.   [53] Eggers, "Interview."

being "unavoidably sentimental and naive and goo-prone and generally pathetic," yet because of these attributes to be communicatively connected to others.[54] As this interdisciplinary reading has shown, by observing ordered structures and considering their place in the mathematics of Cantor's set-theoretical treatment of infinity, it is possible to draw important connections across Wallace's writing, especially between his most celebrated work of fiction and his most marginalized non-fictional text. Such an approach suggests both works as "infinite jests" – *jest < gest*: "a narrative of exploits" – tales about the infinite, which, through main-text/notes relations resembling mathematical ordered structures, evoke infinite tellings.[55]

[54] Wallace, *IJ*, 694–95.   [55] "jest, n.2." *OED Online*.

CHAPTER 17

David Foster Wallace and Existentialism

Allard den Dulk

This interpretation is "existential," Mario, which means vague and slightly flaky. But I think it may hold true in certain cases.[1]

Despite this somewhat dismissive statement by one of *Infinite Jest*'s characters, David Foster Wallace's work is perhaps best understood in light of existentialism, that is, as critically renewing ideas and concerns from existentialist philosophy and literature. Wallace repeatedly expressed his admiration of existentialist authors: He published articles on Fyodor Dostoevsky and Franz Kafka, stated his agreement with Søren Kierkegaard's critique of irony, referred to Albert Camus in several writings and interviews, while Jean-Paul Sartre is also known to have been a "great favourite" of Wallace.[2] This chapter provides an overview of the main themes and intertextual connections that his work shares with the existentialists. Reading Wallace in light of those connections will deepen our understanding of Wallace's literary project as both formally innovative and driven by traditional, moral themes such as virtue, empathy and selfhood.

This chapter situates Wallace's writing in conversation with several key existentialists, highlighting the structural commonalities of his fiction and the in-betweenness of philosophy and literature in existentialist writing, as well as suggesting that Wallace's writing does not necessarily realize its virtues "in" the texts, "by" the characters, but often – and more importantly – by the work of the reader.

Existentialism as Philosophy and Literature

While Wallace's writing has a clearly philosophical dimension, its exploration of philosophical themes, rather than being conceptual or theoretical,

---

This chapter therefore derives part of its content from some of my previous publications on Wallace, most importantly from *Existentialist Engagement*.

[1] Wallace, *IJ*, 765.   [2] Smith, "Difficult Gifts," 264.

is driven by a clear desire to express, and thereby allow the reader to experience, some of the most existentially urgent and painful aspects of contemporary human existence. The possibility of conveying these problems in this way motivated Wallace's occupational switch from philosophy to literature, and also explains his affinity with existentialism.

Simone de Beauvoir writes, "Existentialist thought claims to grasp the essence at the heart of existence; and if the description of essence is a matter solely for philosophy properly speaking, then the novel will permit us to evoke the original upspringing of existence in its complete, singular, and temporal truth." For existentialism, because of its emphasis on subjectivity and ambiguity as the "essence" of human existence, literature provides a legitimate mode of philosophical inquiry into "metaphysical experience" – which De Beauvoir defines as the individual "placed in one's totality before the totality of the world" – because it seeks to explore experience in its "singular and temporal form," not attempting to reduce it to a "universal meaning in an abstract language." De Beauvoir explains that "it is not a matter of exploiting on a literary plane truths established beforehand on the philosophical plane, but, rather, of manifesting an aspect of metaphysical experience that cannot otherwise be manifested." De Beauvoir describes Dostoevsky's writing as a prime example of existentialist literature, as "living discovery."[3] This formulation is strikingly similar to Wallace's praise of Dostoevsky's work for its "theoretical agenda w/ <u>living</u> characters" and as a "model" for writing "morally passionate, passionately moral fiction" that is also "radiantly human fiction."[4]

Wallace and Kierkegaard: The Existentialist View of the Self

In the existentialist view, starting with Kierkegaard, an individual is not automatically a self but has to become one. For Kierkegaard, there is no "true core" that an individual always already "is" or "has" and that underlies selfhood. Becoming a self is the task of human existence. In his essay on Kafka, Wallace formulates an almost identical view, remarking that nowadays it is a common mistake to think "that a self is something you just *have*." According to Wallace – who explicitly compares Kafka to Kierkegaard in this respect – we should keep in mind the central insight of existentialism, "that the horrific struggle to establish a human self results in

---

[3] De Beauvoir, "Literature and Metaphysics," 269–77.
[4] Wallace, "Joseph Frank's *Dostoevsky*," Handwritten Draft, Harry Ransom Center; Wallace, *CL*, 274.

a self whose humanity is inseparable from that horrific struggle. That our endless and impossible journey toward home is in fact our home."[5]

This is what Kierkegaard calls "becoming a self": A human being has to take up their individual facticity – their circumstances of birth, their limitations and their possibilities – integrating these into a unified existence, transcending one's given situation. If the individual does not take themself up in this way, they do not acquire a self. Such a human being does not "exist" but just "is."[6] Another way of formulating this is that such an individual is *alienated* from what it means to be human.

We can recognize this view throughout Wallace's writing. *Infinite Jest* describes its many addict characters as not having a self, as being "empty" inside. In the novel, addiction is a metaphor for not taking up responsibility for one's life, and, as a result, suffering from "internal emptiness." Conversely, the novel describes Don Gately, in his process of recovery, as "returned to himself."[7] In *The Pale King*, Lane Dean Jr.'s remark that he is "just broken and split off like all men" expresses the same view, that the self is not based on some preexisting unity but rather something that is constantly torn between freedom and facticity and, therefore, has to be made whole.[8] Additionally, in the chapter about the boy who wants to kiss every part of his body, the narrator remarks, "Every whole person has ambitions, objectives, initiatives, goals."[9] A person becomes whole, becomes a self, by giving direction to their own situation through choices and taking on responsibilities.

Wallace and Kafka: *Infinite Jest* and *The Metamorphosis*

One of the most famous existentialist portrayals of alienation and the struggle for selfhood is undoubtedly Kafka's *The Metamorphosis* (1915). In his Kafka essay, Wallace describes Kafka's fiction as employing a "radical literalization of truths we tend to treat as metaphorical."[10] Indeed, Kafka's novella provides a highly insightful comparative reading to the two opening sections of *Infinite Jest*: The first section introduces Hal Incandenza as locked in a seeming but unexplained state of catatonia; the second describes the mental breakdown of Ken Erdedy.

First of all, there are striking thematic resemblances: Similar to Gregor, Hal is described as nonhuman, even "*sub*animalistic" (related descriptions

---

[5] Wallace, *CL*, 64–65.   [6] Kierkegaard, *Either/Or, Part II*, 250–51.
[7] Wallace, *IJ*, 694–95, 860.   [8] Wallace, *TPK*, 42.   [9] Ibid., 394.
[10] Wallace, "Some Remarks," *CL*, 63.

later on in the novel call to mind reptiles or insects);[11] both characters are "imprisoned" in this state of being right from the start of the story; they have both become incapable of human speech; when they are forced by officials (the chief clerk, the university deans) to reveal themselves (by opening the door, or trying to speak up), they are both met with disgust and violently subdued. Furthermore, in Erdedy, we encounter an existential attitude similar to that of Gregor: one of reflective self-deception and denial of self-determining choice, leading to complete self-alienation; this state of being and its similarity to Gregor's are further emphasized by Erdedy's anxious identification with an insect in his living room. Furthermore, the structure of both texts also invites comparative reading. With the mysterious transformation of their main characters, *The Metamorphosis* and *Jest* both offer their narrative climax in, respectively, their first sentence and page (doubly so in the case of *Jest*, because its opening section describes the chronologically last events of the novel's narrative). As such, both texts employ "exformation" – that is, the exclusion of crucial information that forces the reader to make associations and connections – which, in the case of Kafka's stories, according to Wallace, tend to be of the "nightmarish" kind, "primordial little-kid stuff from which myths derive."[12]

In light of these connections, Wallace's description of Kafka's "literalization-of-metaphor" strategy encourages us to ask, what metaphor is literalized by Hal's fate? I contend that it's the fact that, in the society portrayed in the novel, alienation is the acceptable, default mode of existence, while "being really human" is regarded as being "not-quite-right-looking," "with big wet eyes and froggy-soft skin"[13] – in other words, as Hal is seen in the opening section: as disgusting and repulsive. Thus, whereas Gregor and Erdedy seem to embody alienation and despair, Hal might in fact be seen as having taken up the task of self-becoming. This question of lack of self and possible self-recovery brings us to Wallace's existentialist conception of self-consciousness.

Wallace and Sartre: Self-Consciousness

Wallace's fiction portrays many excessively self-reflective characters: Their constant introspection fosters a misunderstanding of the relation between thought and world. In its portrayal of processes of consciousness, Wallace's work displays a clear affinity with Sartre's existentialist-phenomenological

---

[11] Wallace, *IJ*, 14.   [12] Wallace, "Some Remarks," *CL*, 61–62.   [13] Wallace, *IJ*, 695.

view: For both, consciousness should be directed outward. In Sartrean terms, consciousness has to *transcend* itself toward the world. As Zadie Smith writes: "If Wallace insists on awareness, his particular creed is – to use a Wallacerian word – *extrorse*," that is, facing outward; "awareness must move always in an outward direction."[14]

According to Sartre, consciousness has no substance; it is solely a relation, an awareness of something other than itself: It is sheer intentionality, a directedness-at-something. Therefore, the self – in line with the above-described view – is not something that is already there, residing "in" consciousness; rather, the self is transcendent, it is constituted beyond consciousness, in the world. Sartre observes that self-reflective introspection attempts to turn consciousness into an object with a certain essence (an inherent self), while consciousness is sheer intentionality and thus has no such essence.[15] This objectification at the heart of self-reflection is the basic dynamic that underlies what Sartre famously describes in *Being and Nothingness* as forms of "bad faith," which all consist of trying to give oneself an essence.[16]

To return to *Infinite Jest*'s Erdedy: The novel's second section portrays this character's hyperreflexive mind as it spirals to the point of psychological breakdown. The section conveys how excessive self-reflection objectifies, distorts and completely estranges one from one's own thoughts and feelings: "[Erdedy] thought very broadly of desires and ideas being watched but not acted upon, he thought of impulses being starved of expression and drying out and floating dryly away, and felt on some level that this had something to do with him and his circumstances and [. . .] would surely have to be called his problem." Other passages in the novel, on Ennet House and Alcoholics Anonymous (AA), further illustrate how hyperreflexivity leads to a total alienation from the self, where "the cliché 'I don't know who I am' unfortunately turns out to be more than a cliché."[17]

Wallace and Dostoevsky: "The Depressed Person" and *Notes from Underground*

Another portrayal of hyperreflexivity, Wallace's short story "The Depressed Person" can be further understood in comparison with Dostoevsky's *Notes from Underground* (1864). Wallace expressed his admiration of Dostoevsky at length in his review of Joseph Frank's biography of

---

[14] Smith, "Difficult Gifts," 264, 268.   [15] Sartre, *Transcendence*, 1–7.
[16] Sartre, *Being and Nothingness*, 72.   [17] Wallace, *IJ*, 26–27, 204.

the Russian novelist. Wallace admired two main aspects of Dostoevsky's work that form an insightful comparative frame for "The Depressed Person," namely Dostoevsky's cultural critique *and* his ability to cast such critical-theoretical ideas into fictional form – that is, his ability to write "morally passionate, passionately moral" prose that is also "radiantly human fiction." Wallace mentions *Notes from Underground* as one of the best examples of these qualities.[18]

Both "The Depressed Person" and *Notes* portray their protagonists as a type, as an embodiment of the tendencies of their respective cultural formations. A footnote on the first page of *Notes* states that "such persons as the writer of such notes not only may but even must exist in our society."[19] Similarly, "The Depressed Person," because of its title and eponymous, nameless main character, demands to be read, not just as a portrayal of deep psychological despair but as the diagnosis of a type that is bound up with our specific time. Wallace writes that the power of *Notes* lies in its "admixture of the universal and the particular." That is, on the one hand, the novella and its protagonist are "impossible really to understand without some knowledge of the intellectual climate of Russia in the 1860s." On the other hand, the underground man's traits are recognizable to all of us: "we can all see parts of ourselves" in him, Wallace writes.[20] The depressed person offers a similar admixture of general and particular, with features recognizable through time, but also firmly rooted in her own historical period.

Furthermore, both texts describe these traits of their protagonists as a form of illness. In the opening sentence of *Notes*, the underground man states, "I am a sick man … I am a wicked man." He suffers from a "heightened consciousness" that imprisons him in an "inertia" of spiteful, "wicked" thoughts.[21] Wallace's story, too, starts by stating its protagonist's illness: "The depressed person was in terrible and unceasing emotional pain, and the impossibility of sharing or articulating this pain was in itself a component of the pain and a contributing factor in its essential horror."[22] Throughout, the depressed person constantly scrutinizes her thoughts and feelings *and* the attempts to formulate these, all of which seem insufficient, impeding all conclusions and actions (as none can be established over others), thus making her life meaningless.

---

[18] Wallace, "Joseph Frank's Dostoevsky," *CL*, 258, 274.   [19] Dostoevsky, *Notes*, 5.
[20] Wallace, "Joseph Frank's Dostoevsky," 256.   [21] Dostoevsky, *Notes*, 5, 10.
[22] Wallace, "Depressed Person," *BI*, 31.

However, while both the depressed person and the underground man are in deep despair, there also seems to be – to use formulations from *Notes* – something "crafty," a paradoxical "pleasure," in their expression of (that is, in their "moaning" about) their pain. This is what the underground man calls his "spitefulness" or "wickedness": Due to his heightened consciousness, all possible actions have become meaningless and the underground man is locked in inertia, filled with self-loathing about the emptiness he suffers as the result of his own conscious inertia.[23] At the same time, this heightened consciousness – his awareness of the full implications of the beliefs of his time – gives the underground man a feeling of superiority. The depressed person also seems to use her suffering manipulatively, in her interactions with her therapist and with the members of her Support System, in order to deepen her own humiliation – urging others to tell her exactly how loathsome she is – but also to somehow establish her superiority over them – constantly underscoring her own complete awareness and honesty, while questioning that of others.[24]

Wallace and Kierkegaard: Irony

The theme of self-consciousness leads us to irony (and Wallace's oft-misunderstood critique thereof): Constant self-reflection entails constantly distancing oneself from one's thoughts and, as a result, from one's words and actions; in other words, it leads to a permanent ironic attitude. Irony has been one of the main hermeneutic concepts in critical approaches to Wallace's work, often centered on the relation between the critique of irony formulated in "E Unibus Pluram" and the possible workings of irony in *Infinite Jest*. Wallace himself stated, "I too believe that most of the problems of what might be called 'the tyranny of irony' in today's West can be explained almost perfectly in terms of Kierkegaard's distinction between the aesthetic and the ethical life."[25] Wallace's irony critique resembles Kierkegaard's in several key aspects.

For Kierkegaard, irony is not just a verbal strategy, an indirect or ambiguous form of language use, but an attitude toward existence, which initially fulfills an important role in the development of the individual. Through irony, the individual frees themself from "immediacy," from what is "given" – the individual's upbringing, social background,

---

[23] Dostoevsky, *Notes*, 15.   [24] Wallace, "Depressed Person," 55.
[25] Quoted in Den Dulk, "Beyond Endless 'Aesthetic' Irony," 325–45.

culture – that is, their facticity – and realizes that they do not coincide with this. Through irony, the individual obtains a negative freedom, a freedom-*from*. As such, irony constitutes for Kierkegaard an indispensable step toward freely choosing a personal interpretation of one's moral life, an (ethical) positive freedom, a freedom-*to*. However, irony cannot be the source of that "positivity," because it is pure negation. Therefore, irony, in its liberating potential, should be employed only temporarily.[26]

In his essay "E Unibus Pluram," Wallace, too, acknowledges that irony can initially be a valuable means of freeing oneself from what have become standard, immediate ways of seeing things that do not hold true anymore. But Wallace also notes, quoting Lewis Hyde, that "Irony has only emergency use. Carried over time, it is the voice of the trapped who have come to enjoy their cage." To this, Wallace adds that irony "serves an almost exclusively negative function. It's critical and destructive, a ground-clearing. Surely this is the way our postmodern fathers saw it. But irony's singularly unuseful when it comes to constructing anything to replace the hypocrisies it debunks."[27]

Like Wallace, Kierkegaard recognizes the danger of the ironist getting wrapped up in their ironic freedom, and turning irony into a permanent attitude. This is the defining characteristic of the aesthetic life-view. The aesthete uses an endless irony to avoid all commitment and retain their negative freedom. Wallace's critique targets the same form of irony: an automated, total irony that is no longer a means to overthrow hypocritical, unquestioned truths, but rather an instrument of cynicism that leads to despair. The contemporary Western individual, confronted with endless possible ways of shaping their life and therefore with the feeling that they have to shape it into exactly what they want it to be, can easily come to resemble Kierkegaard's aesthete, wanting to retain their freedom and bring their life into accord with their fantasy. According to Wallace, this contemporary ironic attitude has become "poisonous," resulting in "the contemporary mood of jaded weltschmerz, self-mocking materialism, blank indifference" and, as such, is the cause of "great despair and stasis in U.S. culture."[28]

The addicts portrayed in *Infinite Jest* clearly resemble Kierkegaard's aesthetes.[29] The result of the addict's aesthetic ironizing of values and actions is the feeling of emptiness and despair that *IJ* describes as

[26] Kierkegaard, *The Concept of Irony*, 246–58.   [27] Wallace, "Unibus," *SFT*, 67.
[28] McCaffery, "Interview"; Wallace, "Unibus," *SFT*, 49, 63.
[29] See also Boswell, *Understanding*, 138.

"anhedonia" or depression (a term that Kierkegaard also uses): "a kind of emotional novocaine," "a hollowing out of stuff that used to have affective content."[30] In *The Pale King*, we can recognize the aesthetic life-view and its consequences in Chris Fogle's descriptions of his old life as a "wastoid," and when he considers "that I might be a real nihilist, that it wasn't always just a hip pose. That I drifted and quit because nothing meant anything, no one choice was really better."[31]

To overcome the empty despair in which this life-view runs aground, the negative freedom established through irony should be followed, as mentioned earlier, by taking up the responsibility to give shape and meaning to one's life, thereby realizing a positive freedom. This is the choice that, for Kierkegaard, characterizes the ethical life-view.

Wallace and Camus: Community, "Good Old Neon" and *The Fall*

Most of Wallace's characters suffer from alienation and despair, and some of them might be seen to find a way out. In response to alienating self-reflection and irony, Wallace's works and those of existentialism affirm the above-described need for outward-directed awareness (which can be fruitfully understood as the striving for "sincerity" oft-associated with Wallace's literary project)[32] and for meaningful choice and commitment (which includes enduring the "boredom" that comes with sustained attention to and repeated affirmation of one's responsibilities).[33] However, rarely are such portrayals unambiguous: Wallace's work also shows how the language of self-recovery can be falsely appropriated, and how the virtues of attention and choice are often not realized by characters in the text. This sometimes leads to a criticism of Wallace that has been leveled against the other existentialists as well – namely, that their portrayals fail to realize the authenticity they might be seen to advocate, and instead offer solely the failure of the virtuous, of the sincere and the committed. I think such criticisms are inaccurate. Actually, what the works of Wallace and the existentialists can be said to do is to prompt readers to become aware of their own role in the realization of (in)authenticity in response to the text.

A good example of this is Wallace's emphasis, in response to alienation and despair, on community, on the need for the other – an emphasis that Wallace's work shares, above all, with that of Camus. Wallace and Camus both emphasize the necessarily communal character of meaningful

---

[30] Wallace, *IJ*, 692–93.   [31] Wallace, *TPK*, 293.   [32] See also Den Dulk, "Good Faith."
[33] See also Den Dulk, "Boredom."

existence. Camus describes this as following from absurdity: Because the world lacks the meaning that the individual expects of it, the individual rebels to demand meaning and in this rebellion becomes aware of the connection to the other.[34] Wallace repeatedly expressed his admiration for Camus and refers to the French author in several of his works, including *Infinite Jest* and *The Pale King*. "It makes my soul feel clean to read him," Wallace wrote in a letter; and in an interview, he stated that "our job as responsible decent spiritual human beings" lies in the "existential engagement" that Camus advocates.[35]

Wallace's story "Good Old Neon" and Camus's novella *The Fall* (1956) similarly aim to generate such a cathartic reawakening to responsibility in their readers. The two texts display strong resemblances in content and structure. In *The Fall*, protagonist Jean-Baptiste Clamence describes to a silent interlocutor how, after years of being a Parisian lawyer specialized in "noble cases," he became aware of the "falsehood" of his virtue and retreated to Amsterdam, "indulging in public confession as often as possible. I accuse myself up hill and down dale."[36] In the opening sentence of "Good Old Neon," the main character Neal states, "My whole life I've been a fraud."[37] He explains that this has led him to kill himself, and that he speaks to his addressee from beyond death. The rest of the story catalogues Neal's self-diagnosed fraudulence, which consists of his actions being purely motivated by the positive impression they will create in other people, and his unsuccessful attempts – through therapy, church, meditation and so on – to overcome this fraudulence. Thematically, both fictions portray excessive self-critique, fueled by an absolutist self-reflection, involving feelings of both fraudulence and exceptionality. Formally, both are confession stories narrated from a first-person perspective (which, toward the end of both texts, turn out to have been "imagined," albeit to different extents); and both posit an interlocutor, outlined as a character in the text, that ultimately functions to make the reader the direct addressee of the text. As such, "Good Old Neon" and *The Fall* function as a *mise-en-abyme* of the act of reading.[38] Both in their stories of self-accusation – itself a form of "reading" one's own behavior – and in how they position the reader, these texts propose an idea of what it means to be a reader – what the importance and responsibility of the reader, as an "other," is with regard to the self-critique portrayed.

---

[34] Camus, *The Rebel*, 22.   [35] Max, *Every Love Story*, 298–99; Karmodi, "Frightening Time."
[36] Camus, "The Fall," 273–356.   [37] Wallace, "Neon," *OB*, 141.
[38] See also Ellison, "Camus and the Rhetoric of Dizziness," 322–48.

Wallace wanted to "reaffirm" that fiction is "about what it is to be a fucking *human being*," and that it's a "living transaction between humans," "that writing is an act of communication between one human being and another."[39] These statements reiterate how for Wallace, and in existentialism, philosophy and literature relate to each other. Wallace's fiction aims to contribute to our philosophical understanding of concrete human existence, not by offering conclusive truths about its characters, but, similar to Kierkegaard's "indirect communication" – which uses pseudonyms and fictional narrators to express different life-views from within – by requiring the reader to "put in her share of the [work]," working through the problems and perspectives presented therein, and thereby furthering our understanding.[40]

---

[39] McCaffery, "Interview," 131; Wallace, "Unibus," *SFT*, 144.　　[40] McCaffery, "Interview," 138.

CHAPTER 18

David Foster Wallace and Religion

Tim Personn

Among the many books David Foster Wallace suggested to friends and colleagues, Brian Moore's 1972 novella *Catholics* has a special significance. Wallace introduced it to Jonathan Franzen in 1992 as an example of the kind of sincerity he aspired to in *Infinite Jest* (1996).[1] Zadie Smith, who taught Moore's book upon Wallace's "impassioned" recommendation, saw in it evidence for the seriousness of her friend's faith.[2] Indeed, there is much in Moore's tale about a conflict between old and new church practice that makes it a touchstone for Wallace's own relationship with religion, even if, or perhaps precisely because, he failed to join Catholicism or any other organized religion.

Catholics pits a modern view of religion as spiritual practice devoid of doctrinal certainties against the traditional dependence on a private, even mystical relationship with a deity. The young Father Kinsella represents the former, pragmatic approach, emphasizing a "generalized community concept, a group gathered in a meeting," rather than any personal relationship to God. The old Abbot O'Malley, in turn, wants to know how such a modern person can still pray. This question is not merely theoretical for the Abbot, who describes himself as "a very secular man" and has not prayed in years for fear of hearing nothing but God's silence.[3] Neither, it seems, was it theoretical for Wallace, a "churchgoer trained in philosophy," whose work might in a different time have been called religious, but who depicted more often than not the challenge of a character's inability to pray.[4]

When Wallace scholars have turned their attention to the author's relationship with religion, from Marshall Boswell's 2003 reading of Wallace as a spiritual writer to the multiple contributors to a 2019 volume on *David Foster Wallace and Religion*, they often tried to hold these two

---

[1] Max, *Every Love Story*, 164. [2] Smith, "Zadie Smith," 14. [3] Moore, *Catholics*, 59, 83.
[4] Stein, "Letter to the Editor."

aspects of communal practice and individual experience in a balance. For many, however, Father Kinsella's view seems to have won out. This is especially true of critics who read Wallace as representative of postsecularism – the dominant paradigm in literature-and-religion studies today. Matthew Mullins and Ryan Lackey, for example, turn to Wallace's treatment of Alcoholics Anonymous (AA) and the IRS as evidence for the proposition that only surrender to the rules of a community can enable individual freedom and spiritual soundness. In his recent survey of Wallace's relationship with religion, Mullins aptly summarizes this "community view" in Wallace Studies: "True spirituality, for Wallace, is not a matter of going deep inside oneself and transcending this mortal coil into the blissful beyond. [...] We cannot worship without the support of community."[5] This "community view" captures something essential about Wallace's pragmatic stance on religion; it emphasizes that he regarded membership in a group as alleviating the atomizing, even solipsistic effects of modern life experienced by many of his characters. But it is noteworthy that Wallace never presented a straightforward endorsement of AA or any other quasi-religious community. Arguably, this hesitation reveals the risk of overstating Wallace's communalism at the expense of a focus on the human being's private capacity for doubt and desire, which, in Moore and Wallace alike, is figured through adherence to individual choice and the possibility of prayer.

One would do well at this point to remember Mark McGurl's dialectical reading of Wallace's thought on the individual's role in institutions. Such a dialectic, McGurl explains, views the self more as "a highly reflexive inhabitant"[6] than a mere cog in the institutional machine – a codependency of agency and subjection to power that is well-captured by the poet Frank Bidart, another Catholic who struggled with his faith background, in a line Wallace chose as the epigraph for *The Pale King* (2011): "We fill pre-existing forms and when we fill them we change them and are changed."[7] Religious community, as one such institutional form to be filled by individuals who change it and are thereby changed, is no exception here. This dialectic provides answers to the problem of authorization faced by any group that assumes power over its members. This is the same question confronted by Moore's Abbot – in the absence of knowing the ultimate value, God's will, what standard is there to decide whether to be

---

[5] Mullins, "Wallace, Spirituality, and Religion," 198. [6] McGurl, "Institution," 30.
[7] Wallace, *TPK*, 2.

obedient to the demands of Catholic leadership for modernizing the church?

Wallace's parents' generation had taken the skepticism underlying this problem to mean that such questions of moral rightness are *only* about institutional power. For his parents' "atheism" of the "'60s brand," Wallace explained, religion "equals central suppression from authority."[8] His own work, however, rejects this anti-institutional stance as much as the anti-individualist solution of completely surrendering one's will. Instead, it places its faith in the individual's ability to authorize itself, and thus constitute its community – even if this means continuing, like the Abbot, to invest in the possibility of private revelation, only to find doubt and skepticism. That is why Wallace's work so often shows characters on the brink of existentialist decisions about belief. Doing so captures the force of critical reason in returning the reader to key questions and concerns about faith and religion. In fact, belief and doubt in Wallace are two sides of the same dialectical coin, and while doubt initially seems to weaken belief, philosophical questioning of the kind present in Wallace has the paradoxical power to deepen it.

This makes his work one of the most vibrant contemporary examples of the age-old program of reconciling reason and belief, a project shared by a range of authors, from Thomas Aquinas to Leo Tolstoy. In typical Wallace fashion, however, this reconciliation does not come in the form of a ready-made solution to be adopted. The editors of *David Foster Wallace and Religion* report from the author's book collection at the Harry Ransom Center that Wallace "did not shy away from naming God or writing about God in his comments in the margins of these works."[9] Still, when he dramatized similar searches in his literary work, his apprentice years in philosophy ensured that he was much more ambivalent in doing so. This persistence of critical reason is reflected in his essay on Joseph Frank's biography of Fyodor Dostoevsky. In Wallace's hands, the review becomes a meditation on the relevance of the teachings of Jesus Christ in the spirit of the Russian novelist, who could "dramatize extremely heavy, serious themes without ever being preachy and reductive," Wallace writes – a model of fiction he explicitly contrasts with the moralism about faith in Dostoevsky's contemporary, Tolstoy.[10]

Zadie Smith has identified this kind of fiction as having an "extrorse focus," one that moves "in an outward direction, away from the self." This

---

[8] Arden, "David Foster Wallace," 99.   [9] McGowan, "Conclusion," 192.
[10] Wallace, "Joseph Frank's Dostoevsky," *CL*, 269.

investment in "generous, healthy interpersonal relationships," she notes, shows "the responsible moral philosopher" in Wallace, who seeks a Wittgensteinian-pragmatist solution to the effects of skepticism in the stabilizing force of community. In the same breath, however, Smith also calls attention to a different side of Wallace, and even of Wittgenstein himself. The "real mystery and magic," Smith writes, "lies in [the] quasi-mystical moments [in Wallace's work], portraits of extreme focus and total relinquishment."[11] These quasi-mystical moments complement Wallace's belief in institutional limits and shift attention to the other side of his religious dialectic: the individual self's experience, his dreams, doubts and desires.

What Smith equates with Wallace's brand of mysticism here – the author's ability to become immersed in the details of almost anything, from the names of Boston street drugs to the minutiae of the tax code – is a key feature of his maximalist fiction. But the place where Wallace combines this stylistic trait with the most consistently irony-free vocabulary of mysticism, grace and transcendence is his celebrated non-fiction work on tennis, collected by the Library of America as *String Theory* (2016). Here, in the collection's first essay, "Derivative Sport in Tornado Alley," the reader encounters a young Wallace growing up in late 1970s Illinois as a talented tennis player who notices a "true religious-type wind" sweeping the Midwestern plains.[12] "I'd established a private religion of wind," Wallace comments in 1991, echoing William James's concept of a personal religion, and implicitly alerting his reader to the inner-directed nature of religious experience.[13]

In James's *Varieties of Religious Experience*, a work Wallace often listed as an influence, mysticism appears as a private state, which, as such, replaces social religiosity with individual experience. The defining feature of this state for James is "a reconciliation," "as if the opposites of the world [. . .] were melted into unity."[14] That *Varieties* treats this union as the universal core of all religious experience not only allows James to reference Eastern traditions in his pluralistic account; it also marks a convergence with Wallace's early essay, which cites a "Taoist ability to control via non-control" and "a Zen-like acceptance of things as they actually were" as the reasons for his success in high school tennis.[15] In fact, the references to Eastern mysticism are key for Wallace's presentation of his private religion of wind: "by thirteen," he reflects, "I'd found a way not just to

---

[11] Smith, "Difficult Gifts," 266, 295.   [12] Wallace, "Derivative Sport," *ST*, 5.   [13] Ibid., 13.
[14] James, *Varieties*, 298.   [15] Wallace, "Derivative Sport," *SFT*, 11, 13.

accommodate but to *employ* the heavy summer winds in matches," making his capacity to coordinate with the wind gales so as to deliver winning shots an expression of the kind of life lived in harmonious union with the laws of nature that is characteristic of the Eastern sages.[16]

At the end of the essay, however, a tornado hits. The young player, who has just reached puberty, is swept off his feet and falls down on another court – no longer a "coconspirator" with the "whole elemental exterior," but cast out from his preteen fusion with the natural surroundings.[17] The metaphorical import of this literal fall from grace is a bit too perfect, and D. T. Max has helpfully reported that the tornado did not arise on the Midwestern plains but in the author's imagination.[18] Still, the idea that Wallace's game declines around the time of his entry into adult thought serves as a reminder of some metaphysical strictures associated with the human condition. In fact, Wallace's one-time collaborator Mark Costello makes this fall from grace the defining characteristic of his friend's mature aesthetic: "Because appreciation is a *branch of thought*, it is only in falling, in coming down from ecstasy, that we can know that we have briefly touched the ultimate,"[19] Costello describes the process whereby ecstasy emerges only after the fact, upon returning to what James calls "normal waking consciousness," and then by taking on the features of a dream.[20]

This adolescent dream of unity recurs in the 2006 essay "Federer Both Flesh and Not," where watching the tennis player Roger Federer causes the writer to have what he calls, quoting a bus driver at the US Open, a "bloody near-religious experience."[21] The features of mysticism are writ large all over his account here too. Federer, Wallace notes, exemplifies a "kinetic beauty" that has to do with "human beings' reconciliation with the fact of having a body" because he can "do by 'feel' what cannot be done by regular conscious thought."[22] Yet the analytical philosopher in Wallace also observes a "real metaphysical truth" that takes stock of the difference in perspective between Federer and his audience – an observation intended, like the tornado in "Derivative," to place such "Federer moments" in the realm of dreams and visions.[23]

Indeed, the one who is least likely to recognize the beauty of these moments is Federer himself: "Your experience, in play," Wallace explains, "will not be that you possess phenomenal reflexes and speed."[24] It is only from a slight distance that Federer's athletic grace emerges as part of

---

[16] Ibid., 13.   [17] Ibid., 14.   [18] Max, *Every Love Story*, 319–20.   [19] Wallace, *DFWR*, 654.
[20] James, *Varieties*, 298.   [21] Wallace, "Federer," *ST*, 119.   [22] Ibid., 119, 131.
[23] Ibid., 117, 128.   [24] Ibid., 128.

"things that the rest of us can only dream of."[25] Rather than a source of despair, though, in Wallace's work this insight is cause for hope. After all, it carries with it the possibility that the mystical unity he finds in athletic exceptionalism may also extend into the most unexceptional moments of ordinary life in ways that we, who are absorbed into them, usually cannot see – just like Federer is blind to his own beauty. Famously, Wallace expressed this possibility of redemption by taking the dream of mystical union into the most mundane of settings: a supermarket checkout line. Given the right focus, he told a group of college graduates in 2005, we might experience even this "crowded, hot, slow, consumer-hell-type situation as not only meaningful, but sacred, on fire with the same force that lit the stars – compassion, love, the subsurface unity of all things."[26] Moments like this in Wallace are invitations to step back from the central place of the self, in a transcendent vision of our own immanent part in reality, and to recognize what he once described as the punch line of Franz Kafka's "religious" humor: "we've been inside what we wanted all along."[27] "These dreams are important," Wallace counsels us in the Federer essay; "they make up for a lot."[28]

What they make up for is hinted at through the story of a boy named William Caines, a cancer survivor who does the coin toss for Federer on the court. This juxtaposition of athletic genius and sick child is characteristic for Wallace's work, where the body is not only a place of grace but also the site of suffering. Wallace imagines this suffering, of the child and of his mother, caring for her son during chemotherapy, and asks, "How did she answer her child's question – the big one, the obvious one? And who could answer hers? What could any priest or pastor say that wouldn't be grotesque?"[29] Wallace does not name it here, but the reference to clergy identifies it as the question of theodicy: How could an omnipotent deity let such suffering happen?

The centrality of this question for Wallace has been suggested before for example by Franzen who remarked that it was his friend's depiction of the most "hideous" aspects of existence that placed him most obviously in the tradition of Dostoevsky.[30] Another hint is Wallace's love for Cormac McCarthy's *Blood Meridian*, a novel that has been read as a theodicy, but which, for some critics, still tries to rescue a benevolent God amid the mayhem of frontier warfare. The same pursuit of grace as a way of meeting the fact of suffering is also at the heart of Wallace's literary project,

[25] Ibid., 119.   [26] Wallace, *TIW*, 92–93.   [27] Wallace, "Some Remarks," *CL*, 65.
[28] Wallace, "Federer," 119.   [29] Ibid., 132.   [30] Elie, "A Conversation."

including the non-fiction work on tennis. In fact, the Federer essay shows once more that, in carrying out this project, Wallace's education in philosophy enlisted him in an ancient tradition, reaching back to Lao Tzu and Aquinas, which avoided naming the sacred for fear of degrading it as merely one more "thing" among many. In order to depict the "Federer moments," Wallace explains, he does what "Aquinas did with his own ineffable subject – to try to define it in terms of what it is not."[31]

Wittgenstein once identified the religious impulse with a peculiar form of gesturing: The "thrust" of the human desire for transcendence, he believed, "*points to something.*"[32] In Wallace, indebted as his work is to Wittgenstein, we find a similar way of circumventing the reifying processes of propositional language by simply *pointing* to, rather than describing, mystical experiences. After setting the stage with the story of young William Caines, Wallace gestures past his own words, at the material body of Federer, now figured as an embodied rejoinder to theodicy: "the truth is that whatever deity, entity, energy, or random genetic flux produces sick children also produced Roger Federer, and just look at him down there."[33] Wallace's gesture at the tennis player here – "Look at that" – is, in Wittgensteinian terms, an ostensive definition, with Federer as paradigm. Its place in grammar has been prepared by the background figure of the sick child, against which the gesture becomes meaningful the way Aquinas had demanded, "in terms of what it is not."[34] For Wallace, this was a way of staying true to the impulse of critical reason without embracing the excessively skeptical conclusion of much deconstructive and postmodernist thought – that there is nothing "outside" of textuality. The tennis essays, then, articulate the crux of Wallace's dialectical philosophy of religion: that we need the dream of mysticism to stand against our doubts, just like we need doubts to feed our desire for the dream.

The fiction, too, occasionally features such deictic elements. But more frequently, it reveals a different, though related method that also arises from the assumed primacy of gestures: the presentation of embodied states. Kafka's presence looms large over this method. As Jeffrey Severs has noted, Wallace's usage of such embodied images – gestures, postures, attitudes – follows the model of the Czech writer's fables, where abstract ideas are compressed into figures like a talking ape or an executioner pierced by his own needled harrow: "Wallace's expressionist idiom, inspired by Kafka," Severs explains, "results from his attempt to find physical instantiations of

---

[31] Wallace, "Federer," *BFN*, 124.   [32] Wittgenstein, "Lecture," 13.
[33] Wallace, "Federer," 137.   [34] Ibid., 124.

metaphysical states."[35] Among all these Kafkaesque literalizations in Wallace's fiction, the most religiously resonant is perhaps §36 of *The Pale King*, the story of a boy who attempts to kiss every part of his body.

That we are to read this practice as a form of spiritual devotion is indicated by Wallace's choice to juxtapose it with the historical accounts of mystics like the levitating Bengali Prahansatha the Second and stigmatists like St. Francis of Assisi. As background figures, they function as a reminder of the same desire that speaks from the "Federer moments" – for transcending our physical limits in a way "the rest of us can only dream of." Like the Caines episode, their presence in the text primes us to read the boy's dream of kissing "the back of his neck," his "ears, nose, eyes," and even "the paradoxical 'ding an sich' of the lips themselves" as quasi-religious.[36] This suggests a kinship between religious desire and the contortions of a person whose lips are trying to kiss themselves. As metaphysical hope meets human finitude, however, the narrator refrains from joking. Rather, Wallace presents the boy's reverence for these inaccessible sites as an argument for the "somber dignity" of his improbable project.[37]

Once again, this echoes Wittgenstein, Smith's inspiration for reading Wallace as a mystic, who also saw dignity in the human desire for transcendence: "It is a document of a tendency in the human mind," Wittgenstein confessed, "which I personally cannot help respecting deeply."[38] What Wallace's debt to Wittgenstein reveals here is this: Religious desire is animated by a directionality that becomes meaningful only in the immanent context of the human form of life, bounded by a finitude that is biological as much as epistemological. Wallace's literary methods are testament to this dual focus, which accepts our finitude while still gesturing at the dream of transcendence. At times, he frames a part of being as significant without overdetermining it in propositional language: He says merely, "Look at that." At other times, he pits opposites against each other in the production of a dissonance that is paradoxical and yet meaningful – the contortionist's desire juxtaposed with his all-too-human body.

Early Wallace tends further to exploit similar paradoxes for ironic effect. Take, for instance, the character Norman Bombardini in *The Broom of the System* (1987), a morbidly obese financier who is depicted as longing to ingest the whole world in a parody of any attempt at transcending one's

---

[35] Severs, *Balancing Books*, 16, 64.   [36] Wallace, *TPK*, 406.   [37] Ibid., 407.
[38] Wittgenstein, "Lecture," 12.

physicality to gain absolute self-definition that does not also recognize the limitations imposed by our biology. Another example is a chapter in *Infinite Jest* that dramatizes the same "religion of the physical" celebrated in the tennis pieces.[39] The scene involves Jim Incandenza, who receives a tennis lesson from his father in the 1960s. The father's instructions, interrupted by sips from a flask, put the same emphasis on a mystical union with nature as Wallace did in "Derivative," and here, too, the account ends with the memory of a literal fall, as the father reminisces about a "religious moment" in his youth, when he reached for an impossible tennis shot "in the attitude of a mortified monk in total prayer": "I learned what it means to be a body, Jim," he remembers, "as I fell kneeling and slid toward the stretched net, myself seen by me."[40] The father's intoxication does not do much to inspire confidence in this account, and yet, in line with the dual nature of irony as *both* reiterative *and* critical, this "parody" of "contemplative prayer" gets close to the paradoxical core of Wallace's philosophy of religion.[41] As a failure, it conveys the metaphysical recognition that we are embodied beings, confined by bodily limitations, but as a prayer, it also represents the dignity of trying to transcend this condition. This ambiguity is characteristic of Wallace, who once considered attaching the title "A Failed Entertainment" to *Infinite Jest*. Failure becomes a harbinger of success here, as Jim's father is thrown back on himself – "myself seen by me" – in precisely the kind of union of immanent body and transcendent self-regard that his own "failed prayer" in this moment would seem to preclude.

That the attitude of prayer by itself already validates the desire underlying it is also the take-away of a vignette in *Brief Interviews with Hideous Men* (1999), entitled "Think." In the story, a man who is about to cheat on his wife suddenly falls to his knees in prayer as he recognizes that his affair with a much younger woman will not bring him the desired transcendence of his loneliness. In her commentary on "Think," Smith finds this gesture to be an embodiment of the central yearning that speaks from Wallace's work – "the 'self alone' prays for a relation,"[42] she explains. But she also indicates that what the story leaves unresolved – that is, the question of whether the man is successful at establishing a relation with something outside of himself – might ultimately be answered on a different ontological level, by the reader's process of "reaching out" through empathy.

[39] Wallace, *IJ*, 169.   [40] Ibid., 168–69.   [41] Ibid., 168.   [42] Smith, "Difficult Gifts," 272.

There are resonances here once again with Moore's *Catholics*, where the Abbot, another "mortified monk," ultimately faces his "fear and trembling" and leads the congregation in prayer: "His trembling increased. He entered null. He would never come back. In null."[43] This ending is as ambiguous as its mathematical reference insinuates. Does the Abbot, as he enters "null," feel empowered by staring down his fear about God's silence, or does he simply stare at nothingness? The concept of zero, which is either a "useful limit" or a "portal to the abyss," allows Moore to keep both connotations in play.[44] Doing so literalizes the human being's immanent condition as a creature with transcendent aspirations in an ambiguous gesture that resembles Wallace's own depictions of religious experience, where belief without guarantees becomes an end in itself.

This is the kind of "extrorse" ending that, as Smith has it, opens outward. It is in the reader, if not in the Abbot himself, that the gesture reveals something about the act of prayer in the absence of certainty. Moore prefigures this reading by depicting the monks who follow the Abbot in prayer. For them, the gesture is not ambiguous, but singularly significant as a sign – like Federer's beauty for Wallace – that they need to stand against their doubt. This points once more to the "community view" on Wallace's stance on religion: That is, the force of community in helping people mutually reinforce their faith through shared rituals. Note, however, that when Smith described the ultimate Wallace gesture to represent his *oeuvre*, she turned to an image that qualifies this support of the community in religious worship.

The image occurs in the story "Church Not Made With Hands" and features an old Jesuit who prays in a field next to an industrial park. It seems likely that Smith had Moore's book on her mind when picking out this gesture. As in Moore, the prayer of Wallace's priest is "unmoored," she comments, meaning "without its usual object, God."[45] What Wallace adds to this idea, though, is his characteristic self-reflexivity. Indeed, while the priest offers instruction to others, his own practice is more private: He faces a canvas that shows a picture of himself in prayer. Wallace's quintessential gesture therefore becomes the recursive image of a man praying to a picture of himself praying. This self-regard radicalizes James's claim of the personal nature of religious experience: The priest has nothing but himself to sustain his choice to pray. But it also offers him the possible

---

[43] Moore, *Catholics*, 89. [44] McGurl, "Institution," 39. [45] Smith, "Difficult Gifts," 295.

recognition that the desire that fuels his gesture – for reframing the nothingness experienced on the inside – can, on the outside, be seen as beautiful precisely because it is grounded by nothing but itself. It seems that it was this picture of pure belief, where recursivity is figured as an aesthetic form of self-authorization, that Wallace offered his readers in response to Moore's question of how a modern person might still be able to pray.

CHAPTER 19

Mr. Consciousness

Jamie Redgate

In *The Rise of the Novel*, Ian Watt argues that the ascendency of the novel form in the eighteenth century was made possible by René Descartes' and John Locke's foundational ideas about human consciousness. Under the microscope of an Enlightened new era, human beings were thought to be, first and foremost, thinking things, whose "individual experience" was a clearer route to truth than tradition, and it was the novel that "most fully reflect[ed] this individualist and innovating reorientation."[1] To trace the evolution of what David Lodge calls the "novel of consciousness" up the centuries – through Defoe and Richardson's self-conscious self-construc-tions, Austen and Eliot's free indirect style, Joyce and Woolf's streams-of-consciousness – is to put together a thinking person's canon: a literature of ever-deepening introspection and intellection, and a "record of human consciousness" that is assuredly highbrow.[2] If David Foster Wallace can be said to belong to any literary tradition, it is surely this one.

The son of academics, a student of philosophy at Amherst, and a fiction writer who claimed to "steer" by the light of the likes of Descartes, Kant, Wittgenstein, Melville, Pynchon and DeLillo, Wallace always aimed high.[3] As early as 2003, Marshall Boswell took Wallace's "confident" cue and held him aloft as the pioneer of a "third wave of modernism," the "direct heir" to a "tradition of aesthetic development" in twentieth-century thought and art, and the next link in the chain of minds.[4] Where the first wave of modernism at the beginning of the century had brought forth Joyce, Woolf and Faulkner, whose work emphasized the primacy (and unreliability) of subjectivity in the context of Freudian models of the unconscious and Bergsonian time, the second, postmodern wave of writers spoke to contemporaneous concerns about cybernetics, behaviorism and the idea that human beings were the "sum total of [their] data"[5] and eerily

[1] Watt, *Rise*, 13.   [2] Lodge, *Consciousness*, 10, 74.   [3] L. Miller, "Interview," 62–63.
[4] Boswell, *Understanding*, 1.   [5] DeLillo, *White Noise*, 165.

reprogrammable.[6] Beginning at the end of the century, the "third wave" was shaped by new findings in cognitive science and the increasingly shared "belief that human begins are essentially their brains."[7]

As Paul Giles has noted, Wallace's writing "developed under the intellectual sign of posthumanism"[8] – an umbrella term for a critical view of human consciousness as being neither divinely sparked nor in charge – and his work clearly speaks to his own generation's (and, more broadly, his own century's) skepticism toward old-fashioned humanisms. In the literature of consciousness in the twentieth century, consciousness itself, ironically, played an increasingly small role. Long gone is the enlightened, reliable narrator whose brain is a precise device and under their control: As the narrator of *The Pale King* says, the "human mind" just "doesn't work that way, and everyone knows it."[9] Wallace certainly did. In *Infinite Jest*, the Incandenza family's materialistic philosophy is underpinned by Gilbert Ryle's criticism of Cartesian dualism as "false," a fantasy and an "escape-route" for those clinging to the belief that the soul – which Ryle derisively calls the "Ghost" – still resides inside the human "Machine."[10] *The Pale King*, meanwhile, is directly informed by Timothy D. Wilson and Tor Nørretranders's "model of the mind in which we have access to only a fragment of our total cognitive activity."[11] Contemporary cognitive science tells us that we can better learn about ourselves by changing our focus of study from "what William James calls the 'warmth and intimacy' of our own consciousness" to the unconscious, "administrative structures" that underlie it and do all the work.[12]

That Wallace employed these models of consciousness across his fiction suggests that he had a clear sense of the tradition he was writing his way into. As Lodge explains, the "novel[s] of consciousness" – as opposed to more commercial ventures like genre fiction or films – tend to "neglect story" and plot and pace, because the "deeper you go [...] into the minds of your characters [...] the slower the narrative tempo becomes, and the less action there is."[13] *Infinite Jest*, which was published at the tail end of the century, plants its flag as the ne plus ultra of this lofty tradition by tending so much toward exhaustive detail that it comes to an absolute stop. Predicting, in its early pages, the emergence of the very "'post-post'-modern culture" that the novel itself would come to exemplify, *Jest* also

---

[6] Pynchon, *Gravity's Rainbow*, 104.   [7] Vidal and Ortega, *Neurocultures*, 7.
[8] Giles, "Sentimental," 329.   [9] Wallace, *TPK*, 259.   [10] Ryle, *Concept*, 17.
[11] Burn, "Paradigm," 385.   [12] Ibid., 386.   [13] Lodge, *Consciousness*, 74.

imagines a literature of "hero[es] of *non*-action, the catatonic hero,"[14] like those characters whose in-bent thoughts bring Wallace's plots to a halt.

After more than two decades of Wallace Studies, Wallace's place in the thought-ful canon seems both deserving and assured. With Wallace's work so firmly entrenched in that camp, however, it is easily forgotten now that when he described the literature of consciousness, it was often with an emphasis on how emotionally cold it could be. In an interview with Stacey Schmeidel for *Amherst Magazine* in 1999, Wallace was asked, "What writers move you?":

> The question's verb is tricky. I regard Cynthia Ozick, Cormac McCarthy, and Don DeLillo as pretty much the country's best living fiction writers [...]. But that's not quite what you're asking. [...] "Move" is tricky. I heard all kinds of sneery stuff about the book *Bridges of Madison Country* when it came out, and joined in the sneering, and then saw the movie version on an airplane and bawled my head off at the end, which was mortifying. [...] I find the end of *Lord of the Rings* when Frodo says "I have been too badly wounded, Sam" moving. Etc. There's some top-shelf literary fiction I find moving [...] but it's more a more complicated kind of "moving" because this stuff involves cerebration and aesthetic apprehension [...] it's not the kind of stomach-punching emotion I guess I associate with "move."[15]

Throughout his interviews Wallace consistently invokes a rigid dualism between "top-shelf" fiction, which is written for the reader's head, and fiction that moves their gut and heart. There is something fundamentally cold, in Wallace's formulation, about thought. Purely cerebral fictions are home to the kind of blasted, "neurasthenic" landscapes that Wallace sees in the works of David Markson and Descartes,[16] works which are of course very smart, but which are moving only insofar as they remind Wallace what it feels like to feel nothing. Indeed, according to Wallace's mind-body model of literature, it would be quite impossible for such cerebral work to really move a reader, since it aims above the reader's neck. Feeling is all in the body: It is the *emotions* that *move*.[17]

One of the problems for Wallace was how then to write fiction that reconciles the apparently irreconcilable and "make heads throb heart-like."[18] Wallace was under no illusions about the limitations of more

---

[14] Wallace, *IJ*, 142.   [15] Schmeidel, "Brief Interview," 63–64.
[16] Wallace, "Empty Plenum," *BFN*, 93.
[17] The word "emotions" has its origins in debates about mind–body dualism. As George Makari explains, it began to be used instead of "passions" in the seventeenth century, because it better articulated the new fact that feelings resulted from the "inner motion[s]" of a fundamentally *mechanical* body (*Soul Machine*, 89).
[18] Wallace, "Empty Plenum," *BFN*, 74.

commercial fiction. The way he associates "puberty" with the arrival of "abstract-capable thought" and "coldly logical cognition" implies that he sees "spoon-fe[d]" entertainment as inherently childish.[19] Where Wallace defined art film as that which tries to "'wake the audience up' or render us more 'conscious,'" entertainment merely "enable[s] various fantasies."[20] So how does one write smart, serious literature that has those qualities – old-fashioned devices like "plot," and "characters" who feel "*alive*" – which serious literature is typically neither "expert" nor "interested in"?[21]

Wallace's dualistic taxonomy of fiction is hardly original. Jonathan Franzen made a similar distinction between "Status" and "Contract" novels, the first being important and difficult works of (usually male) genius, the latter more concerned with their "connection" to readers who perhaps have less patience for brilliance.[22] Steven Moore sees the distinction as one between art (which serves the "muse") and entertainment (the "marketplace").[23] Boswell's essay in this volume also attends to Wallace's relationship with Status literature. In my view, what's unique about Wallace's approach to this problem is his treatment of it primarily at the level of character. Wallace had a way in his work of humanizing philosophical problems, perhaps because philosophical problems had a way of humanizing him: He was someone, he said, "whose beliefs inform his stomach's daily state."[24] Though Wallace Studies has, as a rule, sensibly tried to move away from Wallace's own statements about his work, Wallace's take on the "weird conflict" in his culture "between [. . .] the 'inner sap' – the part of us that can really wholeheartedly weep at stuff – and the part of us that has to live in a world of smart, jaded, sophisticated people and wants very much to be taken seriously"[25] is especially important because his characters, from their stomachs up, embody the theory.

Wallace's work has all the markers of his academic training, but there has always been something hideous about men like Wallace in Wallace's work: the self-conscious, overly educated man who intellectualizes "terms like *love* and *soul* and *redeem*."[26] The problem for someone young and smart like *Infinite Jest*'s Hal – "Mr. consciousness" himself – is that it is from such "world-weary and sophisticated older people" that one learns "how to be cool."[27] Note, again, the dichotomy that Wallace sets up here: the difference between "cool[ness]" and warm, "gooey sentiment."[28] While Gately and

[19] Wallace, *IJ*, 321–22, 416.   [20] Wallace, "Unibus," *SFT*, 169–70.
[21] Wallace, "Joseph Frank's Dostoevsky," *CL*, 264.   [22] Franzen, "Mr. Difficult," 240.
[23] Moore, *The Novel*, 8.   [24] Wallace, "Empty Plenum," *BFN*, 79.
[25] Paulson, "Interview," 134.   [26] Wallace, "B.I. #20," *BI*, 268.   [27] Wallace, *IJ*, 461, 694.
[28] Ibid., 694.

other addicts are saved by their ability to suspend their cynicism – to submit to the grace of the "Higher Power" that they don't necessarily "even believe in" – Hal cannot be saved because he is "too sharp to ever buy" into the AA's humanistic fantasy: Though it leaves him feeling like a "void inside," Hal has learned to sneer at such escapism.[29] He is too good a student of his posthuman culture ever to accept that survival requires you to be alive "In Here" instead of "Out There," to be a living soul "inside [your] own hull," not just a "robo[t]" but an "actual human being" who takes responsibility for the machine they are stuck inside.[30] All of Wallace's characters are animated by the same "Cartesian nightmare"[31] that plagued him as a writer. Hal just doesn't know it. He has been told he is machine only.

Despite the fact that the recovery community is set up in *Jest* as a counter to Hal's highbrow posthumanism, critical readings of Wallace's work have tended to corroborate Hal's view. N. Katherine Hayles, Paul Giles, Elizabeth Freudenthal and others' readings are grounded in certain assumptions, commensurate with decades of posthuman theory, about the errors in humanistic thinking: Wallace's work, they say, is anti-"autonomy,"[32] "anti-interiority,"[33] anti-"humanism."[34] Studied alongside other members of the literature of consciousness – which as a rule forgo the simpler plots, the moral clarity, the willful heroes of less serious fiction – Wallace is read as a writer who must be smart enough to know that, as Lodge puts it, "the Western humanist concept of the autonomous individual self is" historically contingent, a fantasy, a dead idea.[35] With that as our foundation, it's no surprise that the very idea that Wallace might have written his characters as if they had souls – that trope of fantastic, escapist fiction – is easily dismissed, if it's raised at all.

By framing Wallace's work solely in the context of what he called a cold tradition, the warmth that Wallace aimed at does not register so well on the lens. Our focus is too much on the head, and on the cold model of the mind as product of the mechanistic body, while we neglect Wallace's heartfelt fiction that we are more than just that. The machine is occupied: the body's emotions have to move *someone*. The machine is occupied. In his interview with *Amherst Magazine*, Wallace listed exactly two books that moved him: *The Velveteen Rabbit* when he "first read it," and J. R. R. Tolkien's *The Lord of the Rings*.[36] Margery Williams' charming children's

---

[29] Ibid., 218, 468, 1066.   [30] Ibid., 374, 694.   [31] Wallace, "Empty Plenum," *BFN*, 93.
[32] Hayles, "Illusion of Autonomy," 693.   [33] Freudenthal, "Anti-Interiority," 192.
[34] Giles, "Sentimental," 329.   [35] Lodge, *Consciousness*, 91.
[36] Schmeidel, "Brief Interview," 63–64.

book about a toy rabbit's Cartesian transformation into something more than the sum of its parts is a telling choice on Wallace's part, and worth exploring. Here, though, and in order to better understand the heart that pumps the blood through Infinite Jest specifically, I want to explore its significant debt to Rings.

This may seem a peculiar pairing. The contours of Tolkien's Middle-Earth, the mythopoeic version of England where *The Lord of the Rings* – a "fundamentally religious," "heroic romance"[37] – is set, do not readily correspond with our map of Wallace as highbrow novelist.[38] Yet there are references to Tolkien in each of Wallace's three novels: to Gollum in *The Broom of the System* ("'Oh very much so, don't we, precious,' the Antichrist hissed"[39]), to "Mount Doom" in *Infinite Jest*,[40] and to "Tolkien-like eyebrows" in *The Pale King*.[41] In an interview with David Lipsky, Wallace said that he read *Rings* "five times as a teenager,"[42] while in other interviews he continued to refer to the "Sauron-like eye of the culture" and to *Rings* as a "bitchingly good read, I think."[43] (Wallace also referred, for good measure, to "hobbits' feet" in an entry for the *Oxford American Writer's Thesaurus*,[44] while Frodo's description of "the pale king" is perhaps a source for the elusive title of Wallace's final novel.)[45] Only Marshall Boswell has noted the connection, briefly suggesting that the quest-structure of Tolkien's epic may be a "source narrative" for *Jest*, in which various characters are caught up in pursuit of the dangerously addictive Entertainment.[46] But there is quite a lot more to the link than that, especially where it concerns matters of mind and character.

The first point to make is a clarification of Boswell's argument about the two books' shared "quest" structure. *Rings* is, in fact, a subversion of the typical quest: It is "an anti-quest, whose goal is not to find or regain something but to reject and destroy something" in order to save the world.[47] Though Boswell is right that *Jest* is built on the same premise – the novel's various threads are tangled around a dangerously addictive device that is better off destroyed – Wallace subverts Tolkien's subversion. *Jest*'s characters are certainly all in pursuit of the Entertainment (or one of

[37] Tolkien, *Letters*, 172, 414.
[38] Though when asked to pick ten books for J. Peder Zane's *The Top Ten*, Wallace *did* choose C. S. Lewis's *The Screwtape Letters*, Stephen King's *The Stand* and Tom Clancy's *The Sum of All Fears*, each of which has a certain fantastic, Manichean sensibility.
[39] Wallace, *BS*, 244.   [40] Wallace, *IJ*, 886.   [41] Wallace, *TPK*, 360.
[42] Lipsky, *Although of Course*, 221.   [43] Scocca, "David Foster Wallace," 87.
[44] Wallace, *BFN*, 280.   [45] Tolkien, *Lord of the Rings*, 257.   [46] Boswell, *Understanding*, 123.
[47] Shippey, *J. R. R. Tolkien*, 114.

its self-obliterating analogues), but they have no heroic compulsions: It is an anti-anti-quest, if you will. As Stephen Burn puts it, Wallace's novel has an "antiteleological spirit [. . .] refusing or parodying the notion of resolution or goal-reaching on multiple levels."[48] The idea that *Jest*'s American characters would have anything like Tolkien's noble "Love of [their] nation [. . .] Something bigger than the self" is laughable.[49] Even if they did seek to destroy the Entertainment, the film is said to be so alluring that even those without any particular desire to watch it are fatally, inescapably hooked. There is no hope of this "great Shadow [. . .] depart[ing],"[50] only catastrophe on *Jest*'s horizon. A cold reading of Tolkien indeed.[51]

I want to suggest that the vital connection between the two works comes, rather, from their strikingly similar treatment of addiction. Though Tolkien does not use the word "addiction," Tom Shippey explains that it neatly characterizes the nature of the Ring, which critics have read as a confused device because it inspires violent jealousy in some characters and indifference in others. As Shippey says, one use of the Ring "need not be disastrous on its own, but each use tends to strengthen the urge for another."[52] Tolkien's "original [. . .] concept of the 'Ringwraith,'"[53] those beings who become so enslaved to the Ring that they literally "*fade*" from worldly existence,[54] speaks dramatically to the power of addiction and the half-life addicts lead.

Wallace describes precisely the same *wraithing* process in *Infinite Jest*. James Incandenza, the addict and creator of the Entertainment, whose ghastly self-lobotomization triggers the plot of the novel, haunts the book not as a "ghost" or "spirit" but very specifically – and in a striking echo of Tolkien's language – as a "wraith."[55] At one point in the novel, Gately wonders if the word "wraith" means "like a ghost, as in dead?"[56] and it is interesting to note that, in Gately's sections, the wraith is only ever called a "wraith" or "ghost*ish*,"[57] while at the tennis academy, James is never a wraith but "ghost" only.[58] This careful word choice suggests that, to jaded kids like Hal, for whom the "reality of the ghost" in *Hamlet* is cause for "doubt,"[59] a ghost is a concretely "dead" idea (rather like the "dead" author, which Boswell discusses in Chapter 2 of this volume). For Gately, there is no

---

[48] Burn, "Webs of Nerves," 61.   [49] Wallace, *IJ*, 107.   [50] Tolkien, *Lord of the Rings*, 1246.

[51] Tolkien's work is not unreservedly warm, of course. *Rings*'s bittersweet ending, whereby the very victory of the forces of Good is what causes the world's worsening Fall, supports Tolkien's insistence that Middle-Earth was never a "never-never land" (*Letters*, 220).

[52] Shippey, *J. R. R. Tolkien*, 119.   [53] Ibid., 121.   [54] Tolkien, *Lord of the Rings*, 61.

[55] Wallace, *IJ*, 838.   [56] Ibid., 833.   [57] Ibid., 809, 817, 828–30 (emphasis added).

[58] Ibid., 281, 394, 870, 943.   [59] Ibid., 900.

such certainty. He rightly doubts his doubt. The wraith (and the wraithing process) surely seem real enough to an addict in recovery.

This ghostly imagery is applied across the novel's many "gaunt gray spectral" addicts.[60] Lost in the machinations of his addiction to violent behavior, Lenz is said to move with a "wraithlike" quality and, later, to have a "pallor" with "an almost ghostly aspect."[61] Eric Clipperton, while in the nadir of his own unhealthy addiction to hollow victories, is said to be "so blackly haunted" that he looks "spectral."[62] The saga of Steeply's father becoming a television-addict is that of a man "withdraw[ing] from life," becoming increasingly "haggard and spectral."[63] Hal, too, is said to be "a steadily more and more *hidden* boy [. . .] disappearing right before [his family's] eyes."[64] Wallace's pattern of descriptions of addiction evokes the "fad[ing] to shadows of ghostly grey" that marks the boundary of Tolkien's own wraith-world.[65] His addicts have that same "transparency."[66]

This larger-than-life literalization of the addiction process is twinned with another fantasy: that you literally lose something when you become an addict. Though contemporary posthuman theory tells us that there is no interior, humanistic self, no *soul*, there's certainly something tangible about the "meaningful human activity" that is lost when addicts fall in Wallace's novel.[67] Perhaps Wallace takes his cue from the myth-making that goes on in the AA itself, whose members give addiction a shape when they call it "the Disease," a "fiendishly patient" entity that "chew[s] away inside [your] head,"[68] as the Ring in Tolkien's own myth "eat[s] up [your] mind."[69] There is more to the wraithing process than the materialist account of "*p*-terminals" being stimulated, and the spiritual damage the Disease inflicts is real enough.[70] Call it what Steeply, recalling his father's own addiction, calls the "eye-factor": Something vital is "Misplaced. Lost,"[71] when the *I* behind the eyes is devoured. *Something* has to have been in there in the first place to make becoming a faded being, an "empty shell,"[72] in any way a meaningful loss.

Like Tolkien's Ring, the Entertainment and the Disease are fantasies, but they emphasize that even the most willful, well-meaning people can succumb: Addiction, in other words, is not a moral failure. They also remind us what is at stake. Just as the Ring splits the minds of those who wield it – "He hated it and loved it, as he hated and loved himself"[73] – Wallace's addicts are

---

[60] Ibid., 355.   [61] Ibid., 587, 717.   [62] Ibid., 432.   [63] Ibid., 640, 646.   [64] Ibid., 838.
[65] Tolkien, *Lord of the Rings*, 277.   [66] Ibid., 291.   [67] Wallace, *IJ*, 548.   [68] Ibid., 274, 355.
[69] Tolkien, *Lord of the Rings*, 72.   [70] Wallace, *IJ*, 474.   [71] Ibid., 647.   [72] Ibid., 508.
[73] Tolkien, *Lord of the Rings*, 83.

torn in two by their dependence: "You find you finally want to stop more than anything on earth [...] but you *still* can't stop, it's like you're totally fucking bats, it's like there's two yous."[74] Two yous: you and the machine that you inhabit, you and what your machine is enslaved to. (As Alexander Moran's Chapter 26 in this volume makes clear, addiction causes both physical and psychic pain). The irony is that it is only because Wallace's characters have souls or selves or something in there that they can be so torn in two. Without souls to suffer the shocks that flesh is heir to, they would not have needed to self-obliterate in the first place: They would either be machines only, or wraiths already. But they are neither. They are *human beings*. There is, in the end, a kind of heroism in *Infinite Jest*, but it is in the willingness to believe in your own humanity, to occupy your own machine, to be, impossibly, both a soul and a body at once.

The paradox of *Jest* is that, while it is a very real kind of death to sacrifice one's soul to escape into the Entertainment's all-too-comforting fantasy, it is only the fantasy that you have some soul to abandon that gives that loss any meaning. Wallace's attempt to reconcile two very different kinds of art is twinned with his attempt to marry two warring conceptions of the self. He is indeed too smart to allow that the soul truly exists, as he is too smart to let his work melt into "humanistic syrup."[75] Yet despite the cold facts and his high brow, he clings to the warmth in the ashes. In Wallace's fiction, the soul is a melancholy image, the ghost of a dead idea. Where better for it, then, than in fiction? We get to decide to believe.

To the accusation of escapism, Tolkien suggested that his critics had confused the "Escape of the Prisoner with the Flight of the Deserter."[76] Fantasy, which is to say that genre which is invested in the possibility of "consolation," "grace," and redemption,[77] is therefore "really an adult genre," and one for which Tolkien believed "a starving audience exists."[78] Perhaps Wallace will be remembered in the end not for leading the third wave of modernism, nor for his contribution to the literature of consciousness, but because within those parameters he also moved his readers. Wallace doesn't reconcile the two kinds of art. He finds no happy middle ground. But then the spark of his characters' humanity might not mean so much, were it not fighting so hard for air.

---

[74] Wallace, *IJ*, 347.   [75] Wallace, "Empty Plenum," *BFN*, 89.   [76] Tolkien, *Monsters*, 148.
[77] Ibid., 153.   [78] Tolkien, *Letters*, 209.

PART III

Bodies

CHAPTER 20

No Ordinary Love
David Foster Wallace and Sex

Emily Russell

Like a child looking up dirty words in a parents' dictionary, those who search for sex in David Foster Wallace's writing will find themselves in odd and often troubling places. We find a "hideous man" who yells "Victory for the Forces of Democratic Freedom!" during climax.[1] We encounter another who experiments with bondage, another who responds to his own rape with misogynistic hostility. Avril Incandenza, the matriarch of *Infinite Jest*, is rumored to have "engag[ed] in sexual enmeshments with just about everything with a Y-chromosome,"[2] possibly including her own son, but definitely including an underage student at the tennis academy. Couples turn fantasies into secret compulsions, pickup artists use sincerity as a weapon, and porn starlets submit to gang rape for money, while one to two dozen US males are driven to auto-castration each year. As Jonathan Franzen remarks for *The New Yorker* in 2011, there is a strange, "near-perfect absence, in [David Foster Wallace's] fiction, of ordinary love."[3]

Critical approaches to sex in Wallace's work are often caught between the Scylla and Charybdis of biographical criticism on one side and abstraction on the either. Critics fall into critiquing Wallace's sexual practice and prejudices, or they perilously ignore materiality by reading sex in the fiction exclusively as a metaphor for formal or conceptual concerns.[4] This tension between metaphor and materiality on the part of critics is mirrored in Wallace's work as well. In some depictions, sex serves as a hopeful vehicle for human connection; he is both interested in our common "vulgarity" and in intimacy as an escape from solipsism. But sex is also threatening in his *oeuvre*, as we are in danger of collapsing into the compromising demands of the body, which entrench our separation

---

[1] Wallace, "B.I. #14," *BI*, 17. [2] Wallace, *IJ*, 791. [3] Franzen, "Farther Away."
[4] For examples of the former, see Garber, "Dangerous Romance of Male Genius"; Max, *Every Love Story*; and A. Miller, *Land of Men*; for the latter, see Himmelheber, "I Believed"; Diakoulakis, "Quote Unquote Love"; Rando, "David Foster Wallace and Lovelessness."

from the soul and from others. Given his characteristic complexity and embrace of meanings that can seem to point in two different directions simultaneously, sex then serves as an excellent focal point to better understand both Wallace's writing and his legacy.

Wallace was drawn to sex and vulgarity throughout his career. For over a decade, Wallace seriously considered pornography for a possible fiction or non-fiction project, first manifesting in print with "Neither Adult Nor Entertainment" for *Premiere* in 1998. Later collected as "Big Red Son," the essay has Wallace assuming the plural identity of "your correspondents" to report on the Adult Video News Awards weekend in Las Vegas. Pornography and its milieu were fascinating to Wallace as an extreme site of so many of his preoccupations. It uses the manipulative tactics of advertising and demonstrates the impossibility of an unmediated experience. But pornography is also interesting to Wallace because of its "unabashedness," its predictable vulgarity, and the ways that the "whole AVN Awards weekend comprises [...] an Irony-Free Zone."[5] As Wallace reminds us:

> *vulgar* has many dictionary definitions and [...] only a couple of these have to do w/ lewdness or bad taste. At root, *vulgar* just means popular on a mass scale. It is the semantic opposite of *pretentious* or *snobby*. It is humility with a comb-over. It is Nielsen ratings and Barnum's axiom and the real bottom line. It is big, big business.[6]

Pornography creates connections among people by being common and popular, but it also offers a lens (albeit one smeared with Vaseline) onto a purer realm of physicality. Wallace writes, "It is difficult to describe how it feels to gaze at living human beings whom you've seen perform in hardcore porn. [...] To have seen these strangers' faces in orgasm – that most unguarded and purely neural of expressions, the one so vulnerable that for centuries you basically had to marry a person to get to see it."[7] Vulnerability, intimacy, unguarded expression – these are all states Wallace sought and worried about the possibility of reaching.

Although Wallace ultimately finds the world of pornography enervating, his short story "Forever Overhead" suggests that there is also beauty and commonality in the physical demands of the body. In this story, the high-dive platform at a local public pool becomes a symbol for the liminal space of puberty. Wallace's language recalls Walt Whitman in its exuberance, lyricism and emphasis on the body (see Chapter 22): "For months there

---

[5] Wallace, "Big Red Son," *CL*, 7–8.   [6] Ibid., 8.   [7] Ibid., 16.

have been dreams like nothing before: moist and busy and distant, full of yielding curves, frantic pistons, warmth and a great falling."[8] His descriptions throughout the piece are strikingly grounded in physical, sensory experience, including the "bleached sweet salt" smell that characterizes both the swimming pool and wet dreams. Later in the story, he writes:

> And girl-women, curved like instruments or fruit, skin burnished brown-bright, suit tops held by delicate knots of fragile colored string against the pull of mysterious weights, suit bottoms riding low over the gentle juts of hips totally unlike your own, immoderate swells and swivels that melt in light into a surrounding space that cups and accommodates the soft curves as things precious. You almost understand.[9]

In these lines, the concluding phrase, "you almost understand," captures the hopeful, questing nature of what Wallace wanted from his fiction. In his 1998 review of David Markson's *Wittgenstein's Mistress*, Wallace describes the power of successful novels as "making the head throb heart-like" and "sanctifying the marriages of cerebration & emotion, abstraction & lived life, transcendent truth-seeking & daily schlepping."[10] Despite the more typically vile and trashy depictions of sex in his writings, it is important to hold a place for this more hopeful vision of sensual experience.

Perhaps because Wallace could imagine intimacy as a path out of solipsism, he most often viewed the pursuit of sexual connection with deep skepticism. In at least four striking examples – Orin Incandenza, "Good Old Neon," "Brief Interview #42" and "Brief Interview #20" – Wallace describes a pattern of men objectifying women, of using the performance of sincerity and honesty as a manipulative tactic of seduction, and the self-aware confession of these tactics as a bankrupt desire for absolution that becomes itself a form of manipulation. The sheer repetition of this pattern in Wallace's work, combined with details from his life, suggest that Wallace was in some ways mirroring this cycle of confession and seduction with his reader (typically figured in his interviews as female).[11]

Objectification of women in Wallace's fiction exists both from the male characters and at the level of Wallace's development of characters (or lack thereof). Two of his female characters – Joelle van Dyne in *Infinite Jest* and Meredith Rand in *The Pale King* – are beautiful to the point of disability. Of the "Prettiest Girl of All Time," other characters describe van Dyne as

[8] Wallace, "Forever Overhead," *BI*, 5.   [9] Ibid., 8.   [10] Wallace, "Empty Plenum," *BFN*, 74.
[11] See McCaffery, "Interview," 127.

"almost grotesquely lovely" and "almost universally shunned."[12] Orin
Incandenza refers to the women he seduces as "subjects," targets the
mothers of young children, and collapses the identity of one sexual partner
into the phrase "the Swiss hand-model."[13] According to a friend, one of
Orin's classic pickup lines was to approach a woman and say, "Tell me
what sort of man you prefer, and then I'll affect the demeanor of that
man."[14] This "strategy" falls along a Möbius strip of performance,
sincerity, manipulation and honesty that is characteristic of Wallace's
writing about sex and its pursuit. What distinguishes this line from dozens
of other clichéd approaches is its self-consciousness. It is a "pose of
poselessness" that manages to perform sincerity and be openly manipulative at the same time.[15] Such characterizations are particularly striking in
light of a scathing review that Wallace published of John Updike's *Toward
the End of Time* in 1997. In this essay, Wallace charges Updike's characters
with being "always incorrigibly narcissistic, philandering, self-
contemptuous, self-pitying [...] and deeply alone, alone the way only a
solipsist can be alone," and caught in the "bizarre adolescent idea that
getting to have sex with whomever one wants whenever one wants is a cure
for ontological despair."[16] This takedown of one of his literary antecedents
signals a tragic irony in which Wallace can name and see such pathologies
in others and himself, but cannot offer an alternative.

   A comparison between the men at the center of "Brief Interviews" #20
and #42 suggest an admittedly narrow spectrum between men who use
sincerity-as-self-aware-manipulation as a predatory tactic and those who
fumble with honesty without ever rising above the behavior about which
they claim to feel guilty. "B.I. #20" offers a complex unfolding of narrative
ventriloquy in which an interviewer, whose speech is never captured in the
text, hears a "love story" from Eric. The two threads of the plot are Eric's
self-aware seduction of a "Granola Cruncher," and his retelling of *her* story
of sexual assault at the hands of another man and of how she saves her life
by transcending the violence through radical empathy and the "quote
L-word."[17] Several critics, including Clare Hayes-Brady, Rachel
Himmelheber, David Rando, Robert McLaughlin and Christoforos
Diakoulakis have discussed the nested dynamics of sex, gender, violence
and language at play in this story.[18] Within the narrative, Eric significantly

---

[12] Wallace, *IJ*, 290.   [13] Ibid., 565.   [14] Ibid., 1048, n. 269.   [15] Ibid.
[16] Wallace, "John Updike" (emphasis in original).   [17] Wallace, "B.I. #20," *BI*, 293.
[18] In her article, Himmelheber offers a takedown of Diakoulakis' hopeful reading of this story, and the
striking omissions of the vulgar and misogynistic language of Eric's final speech required to make
such a reading possible.

uses the same terms to describe both his participation in the interview and the "tactic" that he used to pick up the Granola Cruncher: "if I'm really going to explain this to you as requested then I have no choice but to be brutally candid" and "the typology here dictated a tactic of what appeared to be a blend of embarrassed confession and brutal candor."[19] The recursive nature of the story sets up a series of mirrored or repeated behaviors, all with a sheen of self-consciousness. Eric also acknowledges parallels between his seduction tactics and the tactics/actions of the narrative's rapist, for example: "Nor is this of course all that substantively different from a man sizing up an attractive girl and approaching her and artfully deploying just the right rhetoric and pushing the right buttons to induce her to come home with him."[20] The speaker in "B.I. #42" is less explicitly predatory, but similarly uses confession as a path to both seduction and absolution. He tells the woman he has been seeing, "Almost every intimate relationship I get into with women seems to end up with them getting hurt, somehow. To be honest, sometimes I worry I might be one of those guys who uses people, women. [. . .] I'm going to be honest with you because you deserve it. Sweetie, my relationship record indicates a guy who's bad news."[21] Note the repetition of "honest," with the distancing, passive phrasing of "seems to end up" and "somehow." Later in this one-sided conversation, the male speaker says, "I'm not explaining it well enough,"[22] expressing frustration at the limits of language and the fantasy that an effective explanation will equal absolution.

All these characterizations of manipulative men suggest that predation-through-sincerity expresses a root problem with intimacy. The men themselves are transparently aware of this dynamic and deploy it as part of their techniques: "an all too obvious part of the reason for his cold and mercenary and maybe somewhat victimizing behavior is that the potential profundity of the very connection he has worked so hard to make her feel terrifies him"; "He's a predator, you believe, and he too thinks he's a predator, but *he's* the really frightened one, *he's* the one running"; and "maybe the real root of my problem was not fraudulence but a basic inability to really love."[23] Both the men within the narrative and the narrative choices made by Wallace consistently name the exact pathologies being enacted. As Hayes-Brady argues, however, "etiology is not cure."[24]

[19] Wallace, "B.I. #20," 289, 290–91.   [20] Ibid., 303.   [21] Wallace, "B.I. #42," *BI*, 91.
[22] Ibid., 98.   [23] Wallace, "B.I. #20," 304; Ibid.; Wallace, "Good Old Neon," *OB*, 65.
[24] Hayes-Brady, "Neutral," 168.

The self-awareness demonstrated by both the characters and Wallace himself falls along two sides of a thin line, one side tragic, one menacing. In "Good Old Neon," the central character, speaking after his death by suicide, explains his choice to kill himself as a powerlessness to stop the problematic behavior that he can nevertheless see: "I was killing myself because I was an essentially fraudulent person who seemed to lack either the character or the firepower to find a way to stop even after I'd realized my fraudulence and the terrible toll it enacted."[25] Himmelheber sees this dynamic throughout *Brief Interviews*, arguing "that education in the form of access to self-knowledge, the legacy of 'therapy culture,' does not necessarily give people the means to address the problems they are able to name."[26] Himmelheber also identifies a more menacing effect of the absolution sought by the men's confessions: an entrenchment of rape culture. In "B.I. #20," even as Eric confesses similarities between his behavior and the rapist's, he also seeks to establish his difference to his listener (and the reader), thereby saving himself from excess culpability. As Jonathan Franzen argues of Wallace throughout his writings, "he gave us the worst of himself: he laid out, with an intensity of self-scrutiny worthy of comparison to Kafka and Kierkegaard and Dostoyevsky, the extremes of his own narcissism, misogyny, compulsiveness, self-deception, dehumanizing moralism and theologizing, doubt in the possibility of love, and entrapment in footnotes-within-footnotes self- consciousness," but Franzen generously concludes, "we feel the love in the fact of his art, and we love him for it."[27]

These recurring characterizations begin to pull us toward the consuming swirl of biographical criticism. Following his death in 2008, literary biography and reminiscences from friends and acquaintances began to take up an increasing share of public attention. Characters who may have been secondary players in Wallace's narrative began to assert their own centrality as authors of their own stories, most notably Mary Karr and Adrienne Miller (the latter of whom published a 2020 memoir that details her romantic and professional relationship with Wallace). These voices, in particular, have been buoyed by the #MeToo movement. #MeToo has prompted a new reckoning with the legacies of men in the public eye, and the testimony of women and biographical accounts of Wallace's life suggest there is much to reckon with. D. T. Max's 2012 biography alleges Wallace's longtime promiscuity: his confession of sleeping with a girl who

[25] Wallace, "Neon," *OB*, 173.   [26] Himmelheber, "I Believed," 523.
[27] Franzen, "Farther Away."

was underage, his use of AA meetings as cruising grounds for meeting emotionally fragile women (including married women and young mothers, according to Miller), and his "affect[ing] not to care that some of the women were his students."[28]

These details of Wallace's life provoke (at least) two questions. First, as Miller phrases it, "what are we to do with the art of profoundly compromised men?"[29] And, second, are an author's biases and behavior relevant to our reading of the work? In his 2004 review of a literary biography about Borges, Wallace himself addresses the question of interpretive relevancy by rejecting the hunt for "personal stuff encoded in the writer's art."[30] He argues that "the stories so completely transcend their motive cause that the biographical facts become, in the deepest and most literal way, irrelevant."[31] In the case of David Foster Wallace – and perhaps for all authors – the frisson of recognition between behavior in life and depictions on the page may be pleasurable or disappointing, but it does not open a new layer of meaning previously inaccessible from the text itself. Literary biography can be interesting on its own terms without being relevant to critical interpretation. And to the first question – what are we to do with Wallace's legacy? – the answer is likely to be more personal and may have changed for readers in the wake of #MeToo. The canonization of authors always creates a fraught and impossible set of expectations, in this case likely grief-driven by fans and their sense of a genius gone too soon. As Miller wonders, "Who looks to the author's life for moral guidance anyway?"[32] Where details of Wallace's behavior are significant, though, is in our collective acknowledgment of the systems that enabled and brushed over such transgressions to protect masculine genius.

The turn away from these biographical or moralizing readings is sometimes accompanied by a more general neutering of the vulgar and material realities of the body in Wallace's work.[33] Sex in Wallace's writing is always both material and metaphor, an expression of the simultaneity of meaning he so often emphasizes. Throughout his writing, Wallace uses sex as a vehicle to carry concerns about the possibilities and failures of fiction, language, intimacy, and isolation, but also as an imaginative exploration of sex itself. In interviews and essays across his career, Wallace uses masturbation and seduction as metaphors for the act of writing. In "The

---

[28] A. Miller, *Land of Men*, 204; Max, *Every Love Story*, 233.   [29] A. Miller, *Land of Men*, 323.
[30] Wallace, "Borges," *BFN*, 287.   [31] Ibid.   [32] A. Miller, *Land of Men*, 323.
[33] See, for example, Rando, "David Foster Wallace and Lovelessness"; Diakoulakis, "Quote Unquote Love"; or (to a lesser degree) Frantzen, "Finding the Unlovable Object Lovable."

Nature of the Fun," Wallace lingers for whole paragraphs on this sexual analogy: "when you first start writing fiction. [. . . y]ou're writing wholly to get yourself off," but then "onanism gives way to seduction as a motive."[34] As is often the case in his fiction, he describes masturbation as "terrific fun," but also "empty and hollow."[35] Seduction, in its turn, is figured here as "hard work [. . .] offset by a terrible fear of rejection,"[36] "puerile and dependent,"[37] and characterized by a "familiar love-hate syndrome. [. . . where] you have tremendous power over me, and I fear and hate you for it."[38] Despite these negative characterizations, Wallace also understands writing for publication in its best form as an intimate relationship with his reader. He tells McCaffery, "It's got something to do with love. With the discipline to talk out of the part of yourself that can love instead of the part that just wants to be loved."[39]

In its highest form, writing, for Wallace, is an act of intimacy both between the author and reader, and between the author and imagined others. In the same breath that he admits he is "willing to sort of die in order to move the reader, somehow," Wallace also names this intimacy as an act of "courage," a vulnerability exacerbated by his self-aware fear of "how sappy this'll look in print."[40] Wallace's keen understanding of both the profound possibilities of love in fiction and his self-conscious apprehension of the paralyzing obstacles to true intimacy make loneliness a central concern of his work. Wallace classes himself among the "subforties" whose "horrors" consist of "anomie and solipsism and a peculiarly American loneliness: the prospect of dying without even once having loved something more than yourself."[41] Wallace is quick to charge others with solipsism in part because he was so concerned about the difficulties of moving beyond the isolated self. He said early in his career that "serious fiction's purpose is to give the reader, who like all of us is sort of marooned in her own skull, to give her imaginative access to other selves."[42] As Hayes-Brady argues, the gender dynamics of Wallace's fiction often compromise his ability to achieve the access to others he seeks; his awareness of gender difference, paradoxically, often "paralyzes his authorial capacity for empathy"[43] and "The absence or failure of relationships may be read as a literalization of Wallace's own ideas about the challenges of connection."[44]

---

[34] Wallace, "Nature," *BFN*, 196–97.   [35] Ibid.   [36] Ibid.   [37] McCaffery, "Interview," 127.
[38] Ibid., 130.   [39] Ibid., 148.   [40] Ibid., 148–49.   [41] Wallace, "John Updike," *CL*.
[42] McCaffery, "Interview," 127.   [43] Hayes-Brady, "'. . .,'" 132.
[44] Hayes-Brady, "Neutral," 168.

But this interest in "imaginative access to other selves" remains constant throughout Wallace's career,[45] despite both his self-awareness and his blindness to is limitations. Sexual intimacy – as much as any another strategy – offers a path toward crossing boundaries between self and other. In *The Broom of the System*, Dr. Jay's bizarre "membrane" theory reminds us that physical boundaries and "hygiene anxiety" are forms of "identity anxiety," keeping us safe and clean, but isolated.[46] If physical boundaries create isolation, crossing these boundaries suggests a possibility of communion. Mary Karr beautifully describes this exchange in her poem "Suicide's Note: An Annual," written after Wallace's death: "More than once you asked / that I breathe into your lungs like the soprano in the opera / I loved so my ghost might inhabit you and you ingest my belief / in your otherwise-only-probable soul."[47] Although Wallace's typical depiction of love and sex is bound in darkness, there are bright moments of reverence and hope in the fiction. The couple in "Adult World" cannot be understood as a model of intimacy, but the story includes moments where sex and marriage are imaged as profound connection: "binding them now is that deep & unspoken complicity that in adult marriage is covenant/ love"; and "[his facial expression] may have been the kind of revelational pleasure of coming together as close as two married bodies could come."[48]

Crucially, this last moment of recognized intimacy comes only with maturity and hindsight; in the moment, "the young wife" in fact mistakes her husband's pleasure for pain. As is more common in the marriage in "Adult World," the couple is isolated by perceived secrecy, "misconnection, emotional asymmetry."[49] The limits of language itself consistently thwart this couple's attempts to achieve connection. Sex is "indescribably great," and the husband "couldn't even describe in words how much he liked it."[50] Wallace's attempts to capture profound experiences in language are more voluminous and eloquent than those of this poor spouse, but his writing is no less characterized by a sense that, although language is one of the few tools we have to achieve connection, is also inadequate to the task. As the post-suicide narrator of "Good Old Neon" says: "What goes on inside is just too fast and huge and all interconnected for words to do more than barely sketch the outlines of at most one tiny little part of it at any given instant."[51] This sentiment echoes the Modernist concerns of

---

[45] In one attempt to achieve this intimacy with others, Wallace describes himself as "crosswriting" or "writing in a feminine voice" (Wallace, "Empty Plenum," *BFN*, 100).

[46] Wallace, *BS*, '303.   [47] Karr, "Suicide's Note."   [48] Wallace, "Adult World," 162, 188–89.

[49] Ibid., 184.   [50] Ibid., 162.   [51] Wallace, "Neon," *OB*, 151.

William Faulkner's Addie Bundren (another narrator from beyond the veil of death): "Words don't ever fit even what they are trying to say at."[52]

And but so we return to the tension between materiality and abstraction in Wallace's work. Since the language and form of Wallace's fiction are notoriously confounding, perhaps we can find a primer in his life and non-fiction. We might turn to the seductive pull of biography that whispers to us that the suicide plot of "Good Old Neon" makes it a kind of confession from its suicidal author. Or that, since Miller's memoir describes seduction techniques from Wallace that very closely parallel the patterns found in his fiction, we can locate him among his self-aware but nevertheless "hideous men." Or, if we find the vulgar sex in "Big Red Son" distasteful and the allegations of abuse by Mary Karr and others disappointing, we can redraw Wallace as a monkish philosopher, whose true interests are wholly cerebral. Sex in Wallace's work and life surfaces all these tensions. In response, it is perhaps best to proceed under the banner discovered by the adolescent protagonist of "Forever Overhead": "The lie is that it's one or the other."

---

[52] Faulkner, *As I Lay Dying*, 171.

CHAPTER 21

"The Limits of His Seductively Fine Mind"
Wallace, Whiteness and the Feminine

Daniela Franca Joffe

When I first read *Infinite Jest*, I was seduced by its aura as much as by its content: its formidable page count and notoriety as a difficult read, which appealed to my longing to be seen as an intellectual; the glowing peritext[1] of my copy of the book, which proclaimed its greatness and importance before you had even gotten to the story; and the circumstances of Wallace's death, which cast a mysterious shadow over the whole reading experience. I assumed the students in my seminar at the University of Cape Town would be similarly enthralled. But the majority could not afford the twenty-dollar paperback copy I had prescribed and were working with pirated, no-frills PDF versions of the book. And while many in the class were moved by the poetic accounts of Don Gately's recovery journey and Hal Incandenza's mental health burdens, I struggled to sell them on the rest of the book, which they found obtuse, inaccessible, boring, antagonizing, even unreadable at points, full of 1990s American pop-culture references that meant nothing to them. The characters' abundant racial slurs did not help matters.

My students' reactions and circumstances made me see that the book, whose universal, humanistic appeal I had so believed in, in fact had *specificity* (cultural, historical, socioeconomic, demographic), and that there might be more to Wallace than the feel-good qualities I had long affixed to his work. The seminar took place before Wallace's reappraisal in light of the resurfacing of Mary Karr's allegations of abuse in 2018 and other revelations of abusive and troubling behavior on Wallace's part, which would further complicate my own and my students' engagement with Wallace's writing and legacy.

---

[1] The term "peritext" refers to the textual and visual elements surrounding the main body of published text (for example, the preface, the introduction, the author's note, the blurb, the front cover, and so on). See Genette, *Paratexts*.

While I was grappling with these questions, the Rhodes Must Fall student movement was quite literally shaking the foundations of the University of Cape Town, demanding a full reckoning not only with the institution's racist past (including the removal of its colonial statues and symbols) but also with its current Eurocentric leanings and exclusionary fee structures.[2] Intersectional discussions around race, gender, sexuality, class and curriculum – and all the polarization that comes with them – quickly became the norm on campuses across South Africa, in much the same way that politicized debate has spread worldwide in recent years, buoyed by the historic Black Lives Matter protests and the related fall of many colonial-era effigies. Instead of "bringing Wallace to South Africa," as I had naively hoped to do with my seminar, it occurred to me that the better exercise might be to turn the literary gaze around and bring the fraught South African experience to bear on Wallace's texts and how I read them.

What I discovered by running a South African gaze over Wallace's writing career was that its backdrop, too, was a more-or-less-constant culture war. From the second-wave feminist and sexual harassment reforms that swept through American colleges and institutions in the 1980s, when he was a student at Amherst; to the multicultural turn in American publishing, and in the United States generally, in the 1990s, when he was drafting *Infinite Jest*; to the resurgence of white nationalism and cultural nostalgia in the wake of 9/11, when he released his later works, Wallace entered the literary fray in charged political times.

As it turns out, Wallace's books are filled with self-conscious awareness of the shifting discourses of his day. He frequently adverted to his (and his characters') reading of feminist texts, returned often to the meaning of civic engagement in the life of American youth, and grappled – largely unsuccessfully – with his own positionality as a white American. Indeed, he made a sustained effort to signal his political savviness and, through it, his distinctness from what he called the "Great Male Narcissists" of the previous literary generation (Updike, Mailer, Roth).[3] Yet he also seemed genuinely unable, or else stubbornly unwilling, to pay more than lip service to the inclusion of narratives, perspectives and representations that were not white, masculinist and ableist in their orientation, as a number of

[2] Nyamnjoh, "Phenomenology"; Bhalla, "#RhodesMustFall Founder Speaks Out."
[3] Wallace, "John Updike," *CL*.

other readers have pointed out.[4] This chapter addresses Wallace's entanglement in the political context of his time, especially in its constructions of gender, and argues that, for a writer who ostentatiously feminized his ideal reader and seriously attempted to create two women protagonists, the language of the feminine is still little more than background noise, with women characters typically tracing a regressive arc through his writing.

Reading Wallace's work through a political lens reveals a disjunctive body of work that layers sensitive, progressive rhetoric atop an undercurrent of unmistakable conservatism, with the former often masking the latter. Some instances of this layering feel particularly resonant in the wake of the #MeToo conversation and Karr's allegations of abuse and intimidation by Wallace. For example, there is the way that Lenore Beadsman, the protagonist of *The Broom of the System*, begins by bravely defending herself against dorm-room sexual assault and ends up with the very man who tried to assault her: Andrew "Wang Dang" Lang. Lang not only barricades Lenore and three other young women in a dorm room, demanding physical contact, but soon after is seen telling his wife that he is leaving her because he has "run out of holes" in her body and "things to stick in them" – before assuring her that his growing erection during the scene is "purely perverse excitement at seein' [her] upset."[5] By the end of the novel, he is cuddling with Lenore and reminiscing about his grandmother.[6] The reader is invited to accept his wholesale transformation into a sympathetic character and laugh the earlier scenes off as parody.[7] Doing so feels ominous and uneasy post-2018.

For those reading Wallace in postcolonial settings or by way of critical race theory, other instances of his rhetorical maneuvering might raise questions. *Infinite Jest*, for example, is shot through with statements about what it means to be a "human being," but the author's misguided use of race as a trope has the effect of humanizing certain characters more than others. The novel's co-protagonist, Hal Incandenza, who attends an elite tennis academy and is white, is nonetheless able to shake off some of his whiteness through his peculiar characterization. Wallace draws attention to Hal's "great-grandmother with Pima-tribe Indian S.W. blood," his "radiantly dark" skin, his "eyes blue but darkly so," and his status as the only

---

[4] Banner, "They're Literally Shit"; Russell, "Some Assembly Required"; McGurl, "Institution"; Cohen, "Whiteness"; Morrissey and Thompson, "Rare White"; Gandert, "Short Meditation."
[5] Wallace, *BS*, 176–78.   [6] Ibid., 416–17.
[7] See Boswell, *Understanding*, 48. For a more in-depth reading of the feminine in *BS*, see Joffe, "The Last Word."

family member "who looks in any way ethnic."[8] In other words, Hal is subtly "minoritized," to borrow Robyn Wiegman's phrase.[9] He becomes not-quite-white and, by implication, not-quite-privileged.

This implication is extended through the unfolding theme of maternal abuse that Wallace establishes early on through the portrayal of Hal's childhood experiences alongside the rather uncomfortable representation of a peripheral black character named Wardine. In two of the book's opening vignettes, Wardine is badly beaten by her mother with a hanger, and a toddler-aged Hal receives no support from a hysterical Avril Incandenza when he accidentally eats a piece of mold. Here, Wallace seems to assert a thematic equivalence between Wardine's situation and Hal's that is far removed from the two characters' material realities.

The use of the Wardine scene as a kind of set piece for the broader tale of Hal's demise (and the scene's narration in cartoonish Ebonics, no less)[10] is telling of the way that minority characters are generally deployed in the book. Whether it is the "Orientals" who people Gately's dreams in the final sequence, even holding up the mirror with which Gately sees himself on the very last page,[11] or the blackface personas that Hugh Steeply and his colleagues perform to carry out their role as undercover government agents,[12] *Infinite Jest* is redolent of Toni Morrison's famous observation about the American literary canon: "What became transparent were the self-evident ways that Americans choose to talk about themselves through and within a sometimes allegorical, sometimes metaphorical, but always choked representation of an Africanist presence."[13] The inclusion of minority characters does little more than frame the novel's central, injured whiteness, just as Wallace's nods to the feminist movement in *Broom* help get "Wang Dang" Lang (and those like him) off the hook.

Approaching Wallace in this way resists the canonizing impulse. Mark McGurl has suggested that Wallace's canonization over the years has relied precisely on an avoidance of the more difficult aspects of his work, and that this avoidance reflects a broader trend within literary studies.[14] As he writes, "Wallace's canonization is occurring in a time of widespread rejection of the negative in literary studies, a general foreclosure on the possibilities of dialectical thinking in favor of cheerleading."[15] In Wallace's case, the preference for positive readings is, according to McGurl,

[8] Wallace, *IJ*, 101.   [9] Wiegman, "Whiteness Studies," 126.
[10] See Shapiro's Chapter 28 in this volume for further discussion of this phenomenon.
[11] Wallace, *IJ*, 809, 828, 830, 981.   [12] Ibid., 149.
[13] Or an Orientalist presence, in Gately's case. Morrison, *Playing in the Dark*, 16.
[14] McGurl, "Institution," 49.   [15] Ibid., 48.

"magnified by the authenticating pathos of his suicide," with his literary canonization often taking on the aspect of religious canonization.[16] Within this intellectual climate, probing "the limits of his seductively fine mind, all the better to defend ourselves from it," as McGurl asks us to do, can feel almost like blasphemy.[17] But this probing is necessary if we are to arrive at a more nuanced understanding of who Wallace was as a writer and what his legacy is in the twenty-first century. The point is not to try to undo his canonization but to inject it with criticality, and to become better readers/ scholars/teachers for it.

On the other hand, certain information that we now have about who Wallace was as a person may erode the need to continue reading him at all. His legacy may already be a *fait accompli*, with no further probing required. While debate around this issue has been brewing in academic and online circles alike,[18] ultimately the decision to read or not read Wallace, and the reason for doing or not doing so, is a personal one. I do not wish to weigh in on it. Instead, I want to suggest what is at stake in our engagement or nonengagement with Wallace, by unearthing some of the hidden, competing political discourses at work in his texts. The remainder of this chapter models this principle with reference to the theme of redemption in Wallace's posthumous novel, *The Pale King*, demonstrating how an ostensibly innocuous theme such as this can in fact become a conduit for right-wing views around race and gender. It is a short piece of close reading, intended to be a springboard for further critical analysis.

The Pale King, based in the 1980s era of Reaganomics but written in the years following 9/11, straddles both the Reagan and the Bush administrations.[19] When the novel mentions a climate of tax cuts and increased defense spending, it is gesturing to the Reagan years, but it is also reflecting its own post-9/11 moment, which was marked by the very same political and fiscal mood.[20] Reviews of *The Pale King* usually mention its Reagan-era setting but have for some reason glossed over its more contemporary resonances, missing the fascinating interplay in the book between masculinity, the Midwest and post-9/11 tropes such as heroism, sacrifice and duty. I propose that this interplay is worth investigating for what it

[16] Ibid., 33. See also Franzen, "Farther Away." [17] McGurl, "Institution," 48.
[18] See Hungerford, "On Not Reading"; Price, "Brief on Hideous Things"; Paulson, "David Foster Wallace in the #MeToo Era"; Goldberg, "Do Books by Men Implicated by #MeToo Belong in the Classroom?"
[19] See Hering's Chapter 32 in this volume for further analysis of this period in Wallace's work.
[20] US Department of Defence, "National Defense Budget Estimates for FY 2015"; Greenberg, "Taxes on the Rich."

reveals about Wallace's personal politics in the last years of his life, and the complex, highly rhetorical way in which he communicated that worldview to his readership. If scholarly accounts of the novel tend to align Wallace with liberal critiques of the (neoliberal, capitalist) status quo,[21] my reading has the opposite alignment at stake. It asks, "What are the conservative investments of the novel, and how might these be linked to the racialized and gendered modes of nation-building that took hold after 9/11?"

The redemption thread of the novel is developed mainly through the character of "Irrelevant" Chris Fogle, a white Midwestern man whose sprawling one-hundred-page autobiographical account of how he ended up working for the IRS operates as a kind of *bildungsroman*-style novella within the larger novel, of which it occupies a huge chunk. Fogle describes his journey from "wastoid" stoner and serial college dropout to devoted IRS agent, a journey that pivots on an encounter he has with a substitute accounting lecturer one semester during college attempt number three. The vision of redemption that Wallace offers through Fogle leverages all the discourses of post-9/11 nation-building – heroism, nationalism, remasculinization[22] – but modifies them to suit the "white-nerd" figure around whom Wallace's aesthetic is built.[23] The author is able to shake off the conservative baggage of the discourses he employs by cleverly incorporating feminist and 1960s-era liberation language, all the while offering the white-collar Midwestern man (and, as it turns out, him alone) a shot at "true heroism."[24]

When Fogle accidentally stumbles into an Advanced Tax class at his college, he ends up staying put instead of slipping out because an air of reverence, almost religiosity, within the classroom compels him to. Fogle knows that this particular accounting course is usually taught by Jesuit professors,[25] so he refers to the substitute teacher in his story by a host of religiously themed names, among them "the substitute Jesuit" and "the substitute father."[26] While this last designation is intended simply to indicate that the teacher is substituting for the regular Catholic priest professor, it carries a double meaning. Fogle lost his actual father in a freak and gruesome subway accident the year before this episode in the

---

[21] See Pietsch, "Editor's Note," *TPK*, v–x; Kakutani, "Maximized Revenue"; Raban, "Divine Drudgery"; Boswell, "Trickle-Down Citizenship," 468; Clare, "The Politics of Boredom"; Godden and Szalay, "The Bodies in the Bubble."
[22] Frascina, "New Patriotism"; Butler, *Precarious Life*; Ross, "Whiteness after 9/11," 227; Frankenberg, "Cracks," 555; Toh, "Fireman," 4.
[23] See McGurl, "Institution," 44.   [24] Wallace, *TPK*, 232.   [25] Ibid., 190, 215, 220.
[26] Ibid., 176, 215, 217.

Advanced Tax classroom, and so he ends up looking to this inspiring accounting teacher as a kind of surrogate. The Catholic air surrounding the teacher is also significant – not only because Fogle's own father "was raised as a Roman Catholic" but also because the teacher's austere demeanor, appearance and belief-system reflect the same conservative values that Fogle's father embodied while he was alive.[27] The teacher is an obvious stand-in for the dead father, picking up where he left off, and pointing the way for the abandoned son. This alone should grab our attention: Wallace does not usually restore dead fathers or come to the rescue of abandoned sons. We are in new, redemptive territory here.

Importantly, Fogle clashed heavily with his father while he was alive. He tended to side with his radical-feminist mother in rejecting the old-school version of manhood that his father represented. Recalling his childhood, Fogle describes his mother's rebellion against the highly traditional structure of her family and marriage, a rebellion that led to his parents' divorce. The mother's "consciousness-raising" involvement with "the women's lib movement of the 1970s" saw her turning to lesbianism and moving in with a woman named Joyce, with whom she owned a feminist bookstore. The two women would smoke pot, talk openly about their "early childhoods," and offer each other extensive "emotional support." Fogle says of his teenage years: "'Male chauvinist pig,' 'women's lib,' and 'stagflation' all seemed vague and indistinct to me during this time, like listening to background noise with half an ear."[28]

While the younger Fogle felt awkward smoking pot with the lesbian couple and was not completely sold on their ideas, he was much more closely aligned to their political world than to his father's. He thought of his father as being "barely alive, as like a robot or slave to conformity [. . .] a hundred percent conventional establishment, and totally on the other side of the generation gap." His mother, on the other hand, possessed a "hatred of traditional institutions and authority," and Fogle remembers her "fighting the bureaucracy of the school district" when he had learning difficulties as a child. His father stands for institutionalism; his mother stands against it. His mother voted for Democratic candidate George McGovern against Nixon in 1976; his father voted for Reagan in 1980, "even sending their campaign a donation."[29]

The "business hat" that his father wore every day of his life was the ultimate symbol of his orthodoxy. "Hats were things to make fun of," Fogle tells us of this time: "guys were essentially uncool if they wore a hat."

[27] Ibid., 190.   [28] Ibid., 157, 160, 165–66.   [29] Ibid., 158–61, 167.

The father's dress sense was similarly old-fashioned: "his body seemed designed to fill out and support a suit. And he owned some good ones, most single-button and single-vent, understated and conservative."[30] In Fogle's adolescent worldview, conservatism is something a man wears on his body in the form of suits and hats. Patriarchy has a style.

Fast-forward to the Advanced Tax scene, where the description of the substitute teacher's appearance makes absolutely clear his function as a paternal double. The teacher "wore an archaically conservative dark-gray suit," as well as a "topcoat and hat," resembling "someone in an archaic photo or daguerreotype." Now, though, his father dead and his adolescence behind him, Fogle does not find this archaic and conservative way of dressing uncool. Instead, he sees in it a "box-like solidity" that he admires. Fogle proceeds to describe the substitute teacher in terms that highlight his authentic manliness: "One way to explain it is that there was just something about him – the substitute. His expression had the same burnt, hollow concentration of photos of military veterans who'd been in some kind of real war, meaning combat."[31] It is precisely the substitute's resemblance to manly, warring, *real* men that lends him his special aura in Fogle's eyes.

This association between the substitute teacher and military-style manliness runs through the entire scene. At one point, Fogle comments on the substitute's posture, which looks "something like the 'parade rest' military position," and on his ability to "look at you no matter what angle you faced him from," like "that trick in Uncle Sam posters" for military recruitment.[32] It seems more than accidental that, when Fogle eventually signs up to join the IRS, the recruitment station is located in the same office as a US Air Force recruitment station. As Chris speaks to the IRS recruiter, "martial music" from the air force station wafts through the room, which is covered in American flags.[33] In signing up for the IRS, then, Fogle also seems to be subscribing to a particular mode of masculinity. Tied to traditional gender roles, in which men fight, protect and serve, it is the same mode of masculinity that he and his mom had vehemently rejected in his father only years before.

The centerpiece of the Fogle vignette is a lengthy speech from the substitute teacher about the virtues of the accounting profession. Through it, Wallace develops a mythology of white Midwestern masculinity that transforms the nerdy civil servant into the nerdy civic hero who serves the nation with balance sheets and income statements.

---

[30] Ibid., 159, 175.   [31] Ibid., 217–20.   [32] Ibid., 227–28.   [33] Ibid., 243–44.

The speech, addressed to the "gentlemen" in the room, cites the words "heroism" and "heroic" no fewer than seventeen times, unavoidably registering the obsession with manly patriotic duty that defined the post-9/11 period.[34] But if the jingoistic patriot performs his masculinity outwardly, sacrificing his life and his body, the accountant hero-nerd performs it quietly, sacrificing his mind and "enduring tedium" for the greater good.[35] This redemption paradigm comfortably accommodates the type of figures we find in Wallace's books (anxious, cerebral, small-town, white), as well as the figure of Wallace himself.

That there is *only* space for those who look like Wallace is confirmed by the frontier/colonial imagery dispersed throughout the speech. "Yesterday's hero pushed back at bounds and frontiers – he penetrated, tamed, hewed, shaped, made, brought things into being," says the teacher. "In today's world, boundaries are fixed, and most significant facts have been generated. Gentlemen, the heroic frontier now lies in the ordering and deployment of those facts. Classification, organization, presentation." Yesterday's hero, in other words, was the pioneer, the pilgrim, the conquistador – the white man, expanding westwards. The new hero, by contrast, battles numbers and figures. As the teacher's choice of words makes clear, though, he is an extension of his forebears, and still overwhelmingly white: "You have wondered, perhaps, why all real accountants wear hats? They are today's cowboys. As will you be." His "you" is explicitly directed at the white men in the room, who alone can identify with the cowboy reference. As Fogle notes, "it was hard to imagine the remaining orientals making much sense of cowboys and pies, since they were such specifically American images."[36]

Of course, in the critical multicultural paradigm, the definition of "specifically American images" would not be limited to cowboys and pies. But the Americanness being constructed here is a conservative one, in which white cultural images are placed at the center of authentic national identity, and everything else is pushed out to the periphery. Wallace, perhaps despite himself, ends up mirroring the post-9/11 nationalist tide, in which the hyphenated, robust identities of critical multiculturalism are melting-potted into one patriotic, flag-bearing, terror-busting whole.[37] Crucially, while Fogle can identify the exclusionary nature of the teacher's philosophy, signaling that he is sensitive and aware, he ultimately does not hesitate to subscribe to it.

[34] Toh, "Fireman."   [35] Wallace, *TPK*, 231.   [36] Ibid., 232–33.
[37] Grewal, "Transnational America"; Salaita, "Beyond"; Toh, "Fireman."

On account of his socially ideal skin color and gender, Fogle's transformation from college slacker to civil servant is effortless. It is a simple matter of getting a haircut and trading his grubby clothes for "a dark-gray ventless wool suit with a tight vertical weave and double-pleat trousers," as he promptly does during his summer vacation.[38] He dons the proverbial hat of the cowboy accountant, the one he once thought was so uncool. Looking pretty much identical to his father and "substitute father," Fogle also starts listening to the same "dry, conservative" radio station that his father preferred, and it is here that he first hears of the IRS's recruitment program.[39] A few weeks later, he is in, with martial music providing the soundtrack to his entrance into civil service.

Significantly for my argument, when Fogle's father dies, his mother falls apart. She splits up with Joyce, sells her share of the feminist bookstore, moves back to her ex-husband's house, and becomes "a virtual shut-in."[40] Joyce, meanwhile, falls in love with a (male) attorney and has two children. Much like their literary predecessor, Lenore Beadsman in *The Broom of the System*, both women end up returning to heterosexuality and domesticity, and their affair, their pot-smoking, their feminist "consciousness-raising" are implicitly written off as a brief, trifling phase. Feminism, then, functions as nothing more than a colorful backdrop to the main event of Wallace's (white-men-only) redemption project. More cynically, one might argue that it functions as a rhetorical device: even the radical, raging feminists return to old-fashioned cultural values in the end, and are happier for it. The progression that Wallace appears to advocate in this section is from feminism to traditionalism, rather than the other way around.

In one of the last scenes of the novel, we get an actual image of redemption, almost religious in its grandiosity: A character named Shane Drinion becomes so immersed in a conversation with his IRS colleague Meredith Rand that he literally levitates off his barstool. Drinion is described as the IRS equivalent of "a cowboy or mercenary," and indeed this image of him levitating in a bar can be viewed as the embodiment of Wallace's hopes and fantasies about white masculinity.[41] Drinion is the nerd-cowboy that the substitute teacher described, and we see him here in all his heroic glory. But if we look a little closer at the scene, we see that the conversation between Drinion and Rand in this scene centers on *her* mistrust of "artificial," self-serving institutions, on *her* struggle to love her body in a society that views her only as "a piece of meat": "you'll

---

[38] Wallace, *TPK*, 218.   [39] Ibid., 238.   [40] Ibid., 207.   [41] Ibid., 459.

never get taken seriously and never, like, be the president of a bank or something," she tells him, "because no one will ever be able to see past the prettiness."[42] Rand talks, and Drinion listens, and as he listens, he ascends to spiritual heights (while she remains very firmly on the ground). The impassioned feminist and anti-institutional discourse in this section is nothing more than background noise, like the background noise of Fogle's mother shouting "women's lib" throughout his childhood, deployed as fuel for Drinion's moral and literal elevation. It signals that Drinion is the kind of modern cowboy who has sympathy for the plight of women and racial others, even as he leaves them behind on his way up. Drinion becomes a metaphor for the novel's vision of redemption, delivered by the substitute teacher and subscribed to by Fogle.

The main thrust of this chapter can be summarized in a single sentence: Someone who writes about the torments of mental illness, addiction and loneliness with extraordinary poignancy and intelligence can still be tone deaf (or, frankly, just plain backwards) when it comes to race and gender matters, just as someone who is canonized can still be an abuser of women. In the latter instance especially, we need only scroll through the list of canonized men of letters to verify that this is true. What we choose to do with this information, though, is finally up to us.

[42] Ibid., 484, 488.

CHAPTER 22

David Foster Wallace and Masculinity

Edward Jackson

Critical accounts of David Foster Wallace's depictions of masculinity often follow a narrative of recentering, whereby he is seen as trying to reestablish a discredited androcentrism in the aftermath and knowledge of anti-patriarchal critique. As Hamilton Carroll puts it, "Wallace's writing tends to recenter a conservative masculinist perspective that he, like many of his principal characters (both male and female), seems unable to escape from."[1] Catherine Toal, Kathleen Fitzpatrick, Clare Hayes-Brady, Olivia Banner and Daniela Franca Joffe all conduct engaging readings along these lines. In their different ways, these critics show how Wallace recenters patriarchal perspectives despite his awareness of the fact that they are objectionable. His writing in this regard is symptomatic of the more general cultural trend Sally Robinson explores in her 2000 book, *Marked Men*. Robinson argues that white American men have mobilized an "identity politics of the dominant" since the 1960s to carry out "the cultural work of *re*centering white masculinity by *de*centering it."[2] Her argument has become a touchstone in assessments of this phenomenon. Carroll, for instance, builds on her readings to explore how "white masculinity has responded to calls for both redistribution and recognition by citing itself as the most needy and the most worthy recipient of what it denies it already has."[3] With Joel Roberts, I too have followed Robinson, Carroll and the aforementioned critics to argue that *Infinite Jest* restores white men to positions of authority at the expense of its female and black characters.[4] To offer a broad summary, then, narratives of masculine recentering in Wallace criticism go like this: By anatomizing the problems experienced by his white male characters, Wallace, with varying degrees of self-awareness, ends up privileging white masculinity.

---

[1] Carroll, "Desire, Self and Other," 169.   [2] Robinson, *Marked Men*, 3, 12 (emphasis in original).
[3] Carroll, *Affirmative Reaction*, 10.   [4] Roberts and Jackson, "White Guys."

These narratives conceive of Wallace's gender politics horizontally. In other words, they account for his (often tortured) attempt to move men back to the center of cultural authority after their apparent relegation to the periphery. More readings can be carried out in this vein, but in this chapter, I change the axis of approach. I wish to analyze the same topic vertically, emphasizing Wallace's suggestion that traditional masculine attributes are too deep-rooted to change. To be more precise, I investigate how Wallace *adds weight* to his male characters and perspectives. Key to my argument is what Bonnie Mann theorizes as the "ontological weight" of gender.[5] In an intellectual context of gender lightness and mutability, where Judith Butler's theories of the "contingent groundlessness"[6] of gender seem to hold sway, Mann is interested in the persistence of "profoundly traditional notions of manhood."[7] As she asks, "despite all the deconstruction of gender, when I am living it, why does gender continue to matter, to make sense?"[8] Mann is primarily concerned with how ideas of national manhood justify themselves by borrowing ontological weight from "the lived experience of gender," which, for many men and women, still "anchors one's existence."[9] Drawing on Simone de Beauvoir and feminist phenomenology, she argues that "the ontological weight of gender is established through the process of sedimentation that turns contingency into necessity."[10] In other words, "that [which] makes gender heavy [. . .] which makes gender real, which makes gender matter"[11] are the many contingent habits, styles, gestures and so forth, which, by being repeated, become necessary to how subjects understand themselves. Gender is "heavy" therefore in that changing, or living it differently can often be very difficult; when such change is brought about through cruelty or violence, moreover, it is "often utterly devastating,"[12] and particularly for heteronormative, cisgendered men.

The strength of Mann's approach lies in her helpful reminder that, although gender might be a performative construction, it is one that is still fundamental for plenty of people. This certainly rings true for Wallace; his novels, stories and essays all display a concern with what it means to be a (white, heterosexual) man in late twentieth-century America. For Brian McHale, postmodern culture in the 1990s exhibited an "aspiration to weightlessness," whereby consumerism in particular meant that "solidity and gravity are leached away from the material world and replaced by

---

[5] Mann, *Sovereign Masculinity*, 1.   [6] Butler, *Gender Trouble*, 192.
[7] Mann, *Sovereign Masculinity*, 9.   [8] Ibid., 69.   [9] Ibid., 1, 10.   [10] Ibid., 83.
[11] Ibid.   [12] Ibid., 1.

weightless simulacra."[13] Contrary to this weightlessness, when it comes to masculinity, Wallace keeps his feet firmly on the ground.[14] This is despite the contemporaneous rise of what Susan Faludi calls "ornamental culture," in which traditionally masculine virtues such as "surefootedness, inner strength, [and] confidence of purpose" became images produced by "marketing and consumerism" for men to buy rather than embody.[15] Michael Kimmel also points to such phenomena as the "metrosexual," the sexualization of male bodies, and the introduction of Viagra as signs of a new lightness in attitudes to masculinity.[16] In other words, these phenomena contributed to the sense that American masculinity was more fluid, contradictory and susceptible to intervention than had traditionally been thought. Furthermore, the rise of critical masculinity studies in the 1990s, of which Faludi's and Kimmel's studies are indicative, helped to augment the notion that traditional masculinity was, in Bryce Traister's words, "beaten, flaccid, and uncertain."[17] As a writer invested in the ontological weight of gender, Wallace pushes against these popular and intellectual contexts. He remains attached to the belief that masculinity is – or, should be – something substantial.

I have argued elsewhere that Wallace consistently locates this substance in toxic sexuality, which he presents throughout his work as the immutable "fact" of heterosexual masculinity.[18] In what follows, I draw on Mann's theories to extend my analysis in relation to another, underexplored aspect of masculinity in his writing – social class. As Mann notes, "because 'national manhood' [. . .] cannot, properly speaking, be said to exist, it is constantly forced to borrow its ontological weight from someplace else";[19] namely, from subjects' lived experiences, wherein the contingencies of gender figure as necessities, without which they would fall apart. Applying this framework to class, and illustrating my analysis with examples from *Infinite Jest*, the rest of this chapter unfolds in two stages. First, I show how Wallace generates ontological weight for masculinity by denigrating moments of gender contingency, epitomized by the transgender character Poor Tony Krause. Second, I argue that Wallace mobilizes such weight to support a classist ideal of the benighted blue-collar man, of which Ennet House resident Bruce Green is a prime

---

[13] McHale, *Postmodernism*, 139–40.
[14] For a more literalist interpretation of images of weight in Wallace's work, see Severs' *Balancing Books*.
[15] Faludi, *Stiffed*, 35.   [16] Kimmel, *Manhood in America*, 245–51.
[17] Traister, "Academic Viagra," 293.   [18] Jackson, *Toxic Sexuality*.
[19] Mann, *Sovereign Masculinity*, 176.

example. My goal in tracing these dynamics is to offer a blueprint for how Wallace adds weight to masculinity across his work more generally. For although my focus is on Wallace's investment in stereotypical ideas of working-class men in *Infinite Jest*, there are other – perhaps equally problematic – ideals of masculinity circulating throughout his corpus.

Writing in 1996 on the "conflicting meanings assigned to transsexuality in recent theories of the postmodern," Rita Felski identifies two "diverging views of the transgendered subject as either apocalyptic or redemptive metaphor,"[20] evident in the thought of Jean Baudrillard and Donna Haraway, respectively. Published in the same year, *Infinite Jest* places transgender people on the apocalyptic side of this binary, as examples of a nightmarish breakdown in gender difference. At the end of the novel, for instance, when Don Gately remembers Whitey Sorkin's henchmen torturing his crime partner, we can assume the presence of "fags dressed up as girls, like as in transvestals [sic]"[21] is meant to contribute to the scene's sadism. More prominently, Wallace presents male-to-female spy Hugh Steeply, USS Millicent Kent's cross-dressing father, and transgender sex worker Poor Tony as instances of slapstick comedy at best, and of monstrous perversion at worst. I use the term "men" deliberately, for Wallace punctures these characters' cross-gender identifications to emphasize the heaviness of the masculinity they are trying to renounce. This conservative attitude reappears later in Wallace's career, in his essay "Authority and American Usage." Here he predicts (albeit humorously) that any responsible father would prevent their son from wearing a skirt to school.[22] When Wallace writes about transgender identity, then, he presents it as a form of grotesque ventriloquism, in which the apparent facts of masculinity always pull men who identify as women back down to earth.

The heaviness of masculinity is literal in the case of USS Millicent Kent's "Old Man."[23] When the eight-year-old Kent returns home early to find her "three meters tall and morbidly obese" father wearing her leotard, his "obscene mottled hirsute flesh had pooched and spilled out over every centimeter" of the garment.[24] However, for my purposes, Mann's theory of ontological weight is more useful than such obvious, literal instances of heaviness. In her explanation of this concept, Mann highlights the testimony of Dhia al-Shweiri, an Iraqi man tortured by US forces at Abu Ghraib. She relates how Shweiri "claimed that the effort to 'shatter' his manhood and make him 'feel like a woman' was the worst

---

[20] Felski, "Fin de Siécle," 569, 566. [21] Wallace, *IJ*, 977.
[22] Wallace, "Authority," *CL*, 94–96. [23] Wallace, *IJ*, 123. [24] Ibid., 123–24.

form of torture imaginable."²⁵ Building on the work of Catharine MacKinnon and Elaine Scarry, Mann argues that by "shattering his manhood," the torturers demonstrated just how heavy his masculinity – and the shame of being made to feel like a woman – was to his subjectivity. Furthermore, they were able to appropriate this ontological weight to support their own militaristic ideals of sovereign masculine power: for as Mann puts it, "as the sexually shamed prisoner loses his [. . .] ontologically heavy, gendered *place in being*, the regime gains its own."²⁶ One does not have to cast Wallace as a torturer to see how, in *Infinite Jest*, similar processes occur in moments of gendered shame. Descriptions of Poor Tony's seizure as he withdraws from heroin, for example, work to shatter his identity as a *man*.

As his seizure reaches its climax, Poor Tony experiences his pain as being abjectly feminine. When someone we can assume is a paramedic – but who Poor Tony hallucinates to be his late father – forces his mouth open to retrieve his tongue, he "bit down and took the gloved fingers clean off, so there was rubber-wrapped meat in his mouth again."²⁷ Though indicative of his activities giving "blow jobs[s]"²⁸ as a sex worker, this image is also evocative of a *vagina dentata*, or toothed vagina. That Poor Tony hallucinates his father, who worked as an obstetrician, compounds the association of abjection with feminization. Imagining someone "with a hand on his lace belly as he bore down to PUSH and he saw the legs in the stirrups they held would keep spreading,"²⁹ Poor Tony hits his lowest point when made to feel like a woman. One could take this as evidence that patriarchal societies, like the one Wallace depicts in *Infinite Jest*, instill a horror of the female body in all subjects, transgender women included. But the fact that Poor Tony is more (conventionally) masculine than feminine in this scene – as is clear in the failure of his façade, with facial hair spoiling the effect of his eyeliner, the female clothing "he could neither wear nor pawn,"³⁰ and simply by virtue of the masculine pronoun Wallace uses to refer to him – suggests the point is far less encompassing than this. In other words, by illustrating Poor Tony's abject feminization, Wallace implies the shallowness of his identification as female. What Poor Tony has repressed, and which rises back into his consciousness with devastating effect, is the heaviness of his identity as a man, and one for whom the prospect of having a vagina or giving birth is repulsive.

²⁵ Mann, *Sovereign Masculinity*, ix.   ²⁶ Ibid., 193 (emphasis in original).   ²⁷ Wallace, *IJ*, 306.
²⁸ Ibid., 128.   ²⁹ Ibid., 306.   ³⁰ Ibid., 301.

Ironically, Poor Tony's horror of being feminized during his seizure spotlights the weight of his masculinity, which in Mann's words seems "*really there, really significant*"[31] despite his attempts to live as a transgender woman. The question remains, though, that if Shweiri's torturers appropriate the weight of his shattered gender identity to support their own sovereign masculinity, then what purpose does Poor Tony's humiliation serve in the novel? Most obviously, the identity weighing heaviest on Poor Tony by the end of his seizure is his Jewishness. For as his (disavowed) masculinity crumbles into a perceived femininity, this process not only reveals the shallowness of his transgender identification but also the importance of his ethnic origins. Hence the appearance in his mind of "*Zuckung*, a foreign and possibly Yiddish word he did not recall ever before hearing,"[32] and the recollection of his father tearing his shirt in "symbolic shiva"[33] when Poor Tony comes out (as either homosexual or transgender – Wallace does not confirm which).[34] However, this scene also contains details of another, more general masculine ideal to which Wallace adds weight elsewhere. Specifically, he replaces Poor Tony's "comely habile-ments [sic],"[35] the most visible signs of his status as transgender, with "slacks and suspenders and tweed Donegal cap he'd had to cadge from a longshoreman's union hall"[36] – the cliché accoutrements, that is, of a blue-collar worker. Though a passing detail, this change of clothes is signifi-cant.[37] It points to how Wallace punishes examples of gender lightness so he can, in part, add weight to classist stereotypes of working-class men.

Critics have picked up on Wallace's classism before. Martin Paul Eve notes the "undercurrent of class prejudice"[38] that informs "Consider the Lobster," while David Hering generously describes Wallace's disdain for lower-class Midwesterners as "unedifying."[39] Yet Hering also observes Wallace's tendency to valorize and aestheticize poor people,[40] and this is particularly apparent in the depiction of working-class men in *Infinite Jest*. The obvious example is Don Gately, who Elizabeth Freudenthal describes as the "sweetly naïve, muscular, working-class hero with barely a high-

---

[31] Mann, *Sovereign Masculinity*, 2 (emphasis in original).
[32] Wallace, *IJ*, 303 (emphasis in original).   [33] Ibid., 301.
[34] Wallace's at times problematic representation of Jewishness can be traced from his early short story, "Solomon Silverfish," all the way to his posthumously published novel, *The Pale King*. For more on this topic, see Max's *Every Love Story*, 63–64; Thompson's *Global Wallace*, 199; and my own *Toxic Sexuality*, 151–53.
[35] Ibid., 301.   [36] Ibid., 300.
[37] For more on the importance of clothing in Wallace's work, see Chapter 9.
[38] Eve, "Preferential Consideration," 15.   [39] Hering, *Fiction and Form*, 47.
[40] Ibid., 47, 183, n. 30.

school diploma."[41] In the interests of shifting attention from this over-analyzed character – who is arguably the novel's prime example of mascu-line recentering – I will briefly consider how the minor figure Bruce Green embodies the same stereotypes. Notably, the idea of working-class mascu-linity that Bruce embodies, and which Wallace tries to add weight to, is characterized by simplicity, supporting Andrew Warren's remark that Wallace channels "class inequality [...] through divisions in education (a not untrue marker of class)."[42] Channeling inequality in this way does not mean trying to overcome it, for Wallace values the "blue-collar"[43] Bruce precisely for his dumbness. Indeed, the weight of working-class masculin-ity keeps this man in his place.

A high school dropout and recovering addict, Bruce emerges as one of the novel's quieter heroes, notably because of his actions in helping Gately to fight Randy Lenz' attackers. Additionally, incidental details of his moral rectitude, whether in his refusal to talk to the authorities about this fight, in lending the sociopathic Randy Lenz a nonjudgmental ear, or in keeping Charlotte Treat's childhood abuse secret, contribute to his being a "stand-up" guy.[44] Stereotypes of working-class ignorance are important to such stoicism (the "dumb animal suffering"[45] of Bruce's childhood trauma after accidentally killing his mother with a prank can of nuts notwithstanding). That "he has about one fully developed thought every sixty seconds," stirs sugar into his coffee using "his bare blunt finger," and "doesn't know his tree-names"[46] cements Bruce's status as a kind of noble savage. This condescending depiction of working-class people as admirably stupid is not exclusive to masculinity in Wallace's work. In "The View from Mrs. Thompson's," the essay he wrote in response to the September 11 terrorist attacks, Wallace looks for solace in the homely ignorance of his female "working-class Bloomington"[47] neighbors. That said, this essay is the exception that proves the rule; in *Infinite Jest*, stereotypes of working-class simplicity are central to how Wallace presents Bruce, for one, as a figure of male ontological weight.

With his partner Mildred Bonk and "the other couple they'd shared a trailer with," Bruce goes through a phase of crashing "various collegiate parties," and thus of mixing with "upper-scale collegiates [sic]."[48] At one "Beach-Theme Party," Bruce becomes transfixed by the Polynesian music (the aforementioned matricidal nuts being "Polynesian Mauna Loa-

---

[41] Freudenthal, "Anti-Interiority," 210, n. 20.   [42] Warren, "Wallace and Politics," 175.
[43] Wallace, *IJ*, 582.   [44] Ibid., 547, 819, 1044.   [45] Ibid., 578.   [46] Ibid., 582–83, 606.
[47] Wallace, "View," *CL*, 137.   [48] Wallace, *IJ*, 584.

Brand"), and drinks so much beer that he *"shit* his pants."[49] Having sneaked to a bathroom, he is forced to change into a grass skirt, which he has to wear on the train home. Though he had later "savagely torn it to shreds and sprinkled the clippings over [his roommate] Doocy's hydroponic-marijuana development in the tub, for mulch,"[50] this grass skirt signals Bruce's momentary – but for him, no less disturbing – feminization. He experiences a similar horror to Poor Tony, albeit (in the heteronormative imaginary at work here) more straightforwardly because he is a cisgendered man. This is another instance of Wallace denigrating gender mutability; that the skirt becomes mulch for a hydroponic plant suggests that one form of "unnatural" groundlessness suitably feeds another. Yet Bruce's feminization also confirms the heaviness of his gender in terms of class, given that donning the skirt leads to his exit from this crowd of wealthy students, among whom he "felt awkward and out of place"[51] to begin with. What Wallace only hints at in Poor Tony's getup as a longshoreman is made literal here: A moment of gender contingency registers as shameful, and buttresses the seeming necessity of class divisions as a result. Indeed, if in Poor Tony's case, his working-class garb is still somewhat ersatz (notably, his new slacks and suspenders are made of "synthetic-fiber"[52]), Bruce's moment of gendered shame compels him to return to what he feels is his proper place as a blue-collar man.

Bruce's conversations with Lenz also show how Wallace denigrates social mobility more directly, and in order to affirm stereotypes of male working-class simplicity. Having taken cocaine, Lenz regales Bruce with various anecdotes, each as madcap as the last. These include how he once regrew a severed fingertip, his expert aikido skills, his memories of being in the womb, and his knowledge of cults and secret societies (on one of these, the Québécois militant group *Les Assassins des Fauteuils Rollents*, he is actually correct).[53] Notably, Lenz is thus convinced that "he was somehow not like the run of common men, and began to accept his uniqueness and all that it entailed."[54] As a ridiculous figure with delusions of grandeur – and one who makes a habit of killing animals – Lenz stands in stark contrast to Bruce's rugged humility. Bruce's contributions to their exchanges are indeed limited to "No shit's" and "Fucking-A's," and in response to Lenz' speculations on the Great Concavity, "he literally says he's never given it one thought one way or the other."[55] Although Lenz is a reprehensible figure with ideas "above" his station – thinking of himself as

---

[49] Ibid., 578, 584–85 (emphasis in original). [50] Ibid., 585. [51] Ibid., 584. [52] Ibid., 300.
[53] Ibid., 557–60. [54] Ibid., 557. [55] Ibid., 547, 561.

a "sexy artist-intellectual," for instance, and a *free lance script writer* – at least he *has* such ideas.[56] If Wallace presents Bruce as the more admirable man in this odd couple, whose nonjudgmental listening goes some way to humanizing Lenz, it is in no small part because he knows his place. By ridiculing Lenz' sense of his own uniqueness, and so his belief (however ludicrously articulated) that he is not constrained by his background, Wallace adds weight to Bruce's position as an ignorant working-class man.

This investment in working-class masculinity is not constant in Wallace's work. Characters such as Johnny One-Arm in "B.I. #40," for example, demonstrate Wallace's readiness to cast lower-class men as figures of hideousness rather than veneration, while *Oblivion* and *The Pale King* are all-but-exclusively concerned with white-collar men. In her analysis of how Wallace uses language as a signifier for socioeconomic status, meanwhile, Mary Shapiro finds some evidence of upward mobility in the characters of *The Pale King*.[57] Nonetheless, by arguing that Wallace adds ontological weight to classist ideas of blue-collar simplicity in *Infinite Jest*, I hope to have complicated narratives of masculine recentering. These narratives posit that Wallace sets out with a critical attitude to masculinity, which he then restores to authority. They therefore presuppose an initial moment of Wallace's characteristic reflexivity, when he acknowledges the problems with traditional masculinity before endorsing it nevertheless. Approaching the topic vertically, and arguing that Wallace makes masculinity *heavier*, I have showed how his conservative gender politics also bypass this reflexivity to bolster traditional masculinity in a more straightforward way. If recentering implies movement, and so some level of contingency, the accrual of weight I have examined denigrates such motility. There is no need for Wallace to recenter men on a social grid that (apparently) marginalizes them, if he can remagnetize the grid itself around ideas of masculinity that, he suggests, are too heavy to budge. Hence, although it does not make sense to say that Wallace recenters Poor Tony to a position of white male privilege, his horror at being feminized is still indicative of the grip that misogynist conceptions of masculinity have on his identity; even as the rest of his subjectivity dissolves, his repulsion toward women remains. The benefit of this vertical reading then is that it shows how Wallace's attempt – whether deliberate or inadvertent – to recuperate a social power that formerly belonged to men is not the only insight to be drawn from his conservative gender politics.

[56] Ibid., 279.   [57] Shapiro, *Wallace's Dialects*, 103–8.

Indeed, by adding ontological weight to Bruce's masculinity, Wallace recuperates a position of social powerlessness; that of the admirably ignorant working-class man, too stupid to be anything but consigned to his lot. The process by which this occurs, whereby Wallace denigrates moments of gender-class contingency to affirm the "working-class hero with barely a high-school diploma,"[58] can possibly be mapped onto other areas of Wallace's work. How might his revivification of grey-flannel-suit masculinity in *The Pale King*, and the grueling necessities of office work that it entails, depend on his ridicule of IRS interloper "David Wallace"? To what extent are Rick Vigorous' gender insecurities in *The Broom of the System* resolved in the redemption of Andrew "Wang Dang" Lang as a soulful chauvinist? More abstractly, how might Wallace's chief virtue of sincerity, "new" or otherwise, be coded as a masculine overcoming of postmodern irony's indeterminacies? Asking how Wallace adds ontological weight to masculinity in these ways will open his gender politics up to fresh investigation. For although his conservatism in this area now seems undeniable, there is still much work to be done in understanding how and why masculinity is, arguably, one of the heaviest topics in Wallace's writing.

[58] Freudenthal, "Anti-Interiority," 210, n. 20.

CHAPTER 23

Theorizing the Other

Dominik Steinhilber

As several of the essays in this volume have demonstrated, Wallace is far from an unproblematic author. Paradoxically, however, the problems and weaknesses of his texts stem from his very "wokeness," that is how cultural criticism is *employed*, and not brushed over, in his writing. Wallace is explicitly, even ostentatiously, aware of inequality and structural violence. Rather than ignoring them, Wallace employs issues of race, gender and sexual identity as metaphors for the workings and negative effects of the solipsistic, postmodern irony he sees contemporary culture to suffer from. Wallace thereby acts from a privileged position, viewing his own (ultimately white, male, heterosexual) issues with postmodernism as universal. In the process, he ignores the lived reality of violence marginalized groups experience by turning it into mere cerebral metaphors for and symptoms of cultural irony. Criticism is co-opted into Wallace's project of moving beyond postmodernism. On the one hand, then, Wallace's knowledge and use of Theory complicates criticism as any foreshortened application of Theory to Wallace's work would simply reproduce the "realistic" portrayal of misogyny, racism and homophobia in Wallace's writing. On the other hand, it is this knowledge of Theory through which Wallace, from his universalistic, white, male, heterosexual position, problematically turns the hardships of these groups into Theory-inflected functions of an unspeakable alterity ultimately put into service of Wallace's own project. Theories of race, gender and sex in Wallace's writing are primarily not applied to criticize society as such but to further an aesthetic "therapy" of solipsism Wallace sets as his main goal.

In the last ten years after his death, Wallace's biography, public perception and *oeuvre* have come under increased scrutiny. The #MeToo movement has left its dent on "Saint Dave," the honest, erudite yet down-to-earth genius that would reply to every single piece of fan mail (literary) America's moral compass, therapist and beacon of spirituality in an age of hip irony, tragically lost to suicide. Not that the figure of

"Saint Dave" had ever been unproblematic; although they were spoken of, allegations of Wallace's personal "failings" – more clearly, claims regarding abusive and predatory behavior in personal and professional contexts – were until then successfully incorporated and thus neutralized into an almost hagiographic representation of the author's public figure as a tortured and humanly imperfect genius. D. T. Max refers to allegations made by the poet Mary Karr in his biography *Every Love Story Is a Ghost Story*, folding them into the construction of a narrative of troubled genius. In an interview with Eric Been promoting his biography of Wallace, Max talks about a letter Wallace wrote to the head of his halfway house apologizing for planning to murder Karr's husband. However, while the content of the letter is relegated to an em-dashed side remark, Max, as in his biography, prefers to marvel at "the craftsmanship of that letter," noting, worshipfully, that "[o]ne thing his letters make you feel is that he thought the word was God, and words were always worth putting down."[1]

Wallace's public persona was only really problematized after the change of cultural awareness following #MeToo. A number of articles by, for example, Molly Fischer or Deidre Coyle called Wallace's work "lit-bro shorthand"[2] and told of how Wallace's male, evangelizing fans made, in particular, female readers, "preemptively uninterested in your opinion about [Wallace's works]."[3] Similarly, in 2018, a piece in *The Guardian* portrayed Wallace as "the patron saint of elevating male bullshit"[4] and at the annual David Foster Wallace Conference at Illinois State University, posters advertising the conference were vandalized with graffiti referring to Wallace's tarnished reputation. The cult of Saint Dave shifted into its opposite, a complete dismissal of everything related to Wallace as misogynist and reactionary to the point that (female) scholars were attacked for studying Wallace's works,[5] such as when, in 2016, Yale professor Amy Hungerford published *Making Literature Now*, followed by a piece in *The Chronicle of Higher Education* titled "On Not Reading," in which she argued against assigning the author due to the controversies in his biography.[6]

---

[1] Been, "David Foster Wallace."   [2] Fischer, "Literary Chauvinists."
[3] Coyle, "Men Recommend."
[4] Spampinato, "How Does the Literary Canon Reinforce the Logic of the Incel?"
[5] Paulson, "David Foster Wallace in the #MeToo Era: A Conversation with Clare Hayes-Brady."
[6] Hungerford, "On Not Reading."

Anticipating Wallace's deconstruction as a public figure by about seven years, scholarship on Wallace entered a second, more critical period.[7] While scholarship and cultural commentary following Wallace's death was laudatory and mostly concerned with Wallace's relation to postmodernism and his project of succeeding a cultural form of irony he saw as solipsizing, once the work of establishing the field was complete, a second wave of works emerged. Spearheaded, among others, by the feminist critiques of Wallace's works by Mary K. Holland and Clare Hayes-Brady, "Wallace Studies" sought to establish itself as a field of its own by including diverse and more nuanced critical perspectives and problematizing the author on his way into the literary canon. Although at first centered around questions of gender, a current which is, understandably, in light of Wallace's biography and the recurring role such issues play throughout his writing, still predominant, this second wave of Wallace Studies started to expose the multiple problems of Wallace's work. Not only questions of gender but also investigations into issues of race such as those provided by Lucas Thompson and Tara Morrissey or the, still underexamined, homo- and transphobic currents in Wallace's body of work reveal the problematic aspects of his writing and continue to open up the field to new perspectives. As Hayes-Brady argues, "issues of diversity are one of the major weaknesses of [Wallace's] writing."[8] Although, as Mary Shapiro has argued, the use of AAE and regional dialect in Wallace's work are more complex than they may appear,[9] other scholars have attacked, for instance, *Infinite Jest*'s use of faux-ebonics or Wallace's dismissal of AAE in favor of the supposed "universality" of "Standard White English"[10] in "Authority and American Usage." Similarly, Wallace's repeated use of homo- and transsexuality for apparently only humoristic effects has been met with heavy criticism.

Criticism, however, is far from a straightforward project if it is to do with the complexity and problems of Wallace's work justice. This is because Wallace, writing from a Theory-infused late twentieth-century perspective, is acutely aware of matters such as misogyny, racism and LGBTQ+ issues and, even more importantly, the theoretical frameworks we would usually employ to deconstruct and criticize such issues. In fact, while Thompson, on the subject of race, remarks that "though Wallace

---

[7] In his talk for the 2018 *David Foster Wallace Between Philosophy and Literature* conference in Italy, Adam Kelly situated this second phase somewhere between 2009 and 2014.
[8] Hayes-Brady, *Failures*, 168.   [9] Shapiro, *Wallace's Dialects*.
[10] Wallace, "Authority and American Usage," *CL*, 108.

was highly self-aware about his own racial identity [. . .] this self-awareness was not enough to prompt him to rethink the role of race in his work,"[11] the opposite, with equally problematic results, seems to be the case: Wallace's use of gender criticism, critical race theory, or queer studies as intertexts creates dangerous pitfalls for the critic seduced by the striking parallels between what they find in Wallace's texts and what critical discourse describes. At the same time, it is this form of intertextuality, Wallace's (self-) awareness, that really produces the deep problems of his writing.

The challenge of framing the problematic aspects of Wallace's writing lies in the way Wallace's texts actively perform their own critique as they themselves self-consciously engage with critical discourse. In *Infinite Jest*, for example, the film auteur JOI's filmography provided in the novel's endnotes follows Laura Mulvey's description of the male gaze in cinema to a tee.[12] JOI's films appear as written as an exercise in different modes of misogyny in film as Mulvey describes them, to the point that the fictional auteur's filmography seems to mirror the structure of Mulvey's essay. Thus, whereas the earlier films bespeak a sadistic mode of presenting woman as the guilty object, emblemized in the name of their production company Latrodectus Mactans Productions, the black widow that eats its mate and thereby raises male anxieties, the fictional film-auteur's later work shifts into either an active homosexual eroticism that dispenses with the female altogether or a fetishistic scopophilia that stylizes her into a perfect, motherly object. JOI's filmography, culminating in the film *Infinite Jest*, reads as a tour de force of feminist psychoanalytic vocabulary, the work of a filmmaker who seemingly cannot help himself but (re-) produce misogynist imagery. This, however, does not automatically mean that *Infinite Jest*, the novel, applies a male gaze itself. Since Wallace uses feminist literature as intertexts to depict and challenge misogyny, it would be unconstructive to naively problematize his works from an angle that does not consider Wallace's own usage of critical discourse as such a procedure could only reproduce, rather than critically question, Wallace's positions.

Wallace's *use*, if not representation, of gendered figurations of the other is a product of his perspective on contemporary America and the influence of a postmodern irony turned cultural discourse in the 1980s. In Wallace's diagnosis, the postmodernism that American culture has internalized is a phallocentric, deeply misogynist discourse. Wallace depicts contemporary culture as one oppressed by the unshakeable heritage of postmodernism's

---

[11] Thompson, "Wallace and Race," 204.   [12] Mulvey, "Visual Pleasure."

"Great Male Narcissists," authors, as Wallace expounds in his damning review of Updike's *Toward the End of Time*, whose works bespeak a self-absorbed solipsism and "persist in the bizarre, adolescent belief that getting to have sex with whomever one wants whenever one wants to is a cure for human despair."[13] Rather than a co-occurring yet unrelated phenomenon, misogynist objectification of women is to Wallace integral to (contemporary) postmodernism and the solipsism it produces. As Boswell remarks, "Wallace [...] sees a direct correlation between Updike's preoccupation with his Self and the long-standing charge against Updike of misogyny."[14] The representatives of the Updikes, Mailers and Roths of our world in Wallace's writing such as the Incandenzas' grandfather in *Infinite Jest* thus teach a philosophy of presence and selfhood through the control of (implicitly sexualized) objects that "will lie back and part their legs and yield up their innermost seams to you."[15] Reverently appropriated by later generations of artists and media producers, that is, Wallace's generation, these authors' individual sexism is magnified into a cultural norm and irreductively connected to irony. Hence, whereas, for example, Lacan's sexualized categories – father, mother, phallus and so forth – are in theory mere concepts and not historically contingent figures, for Wallace's America, which replicates their outlook in its general discourse, they become "reality" and therefore appear reified in his writing.[16]

In mimicking the ironic art "produced by world-weary and sophisticated older people" as a "guide to inclusion" and being "Unalone,"[17] Wallace's characters also appropriate these postmodern Great Male Narcissists' objectification of women into sex objects as a questionable "cure for human despair."[18] In Wallace's reading of contemporary culture, the cultural appropriation of postmodernism's equation of appearance and reality in general, and a Lacanian model of selfhood in particular, both results in and is a function of the objectification of women. Wallace thus depicts his, to cite the title of his second short story collection, "hideous men" as heirs to the Great Male Narcissists' misogyny and self-consciousness. These men not only exemplify but also themselves employ Lacanian psychoanalysis and poststructuralism to justify and enable their coercive behavior toward women.

---

[13] Wallace, "Certainly," *CL*, 59.   [14] Boswell, *Understanding*, 44.   [15] Wallace, *IJ*, 158.
[16] Importantly, Wallace's criticism is chiefly directed against a 1980s second wave of postmodernism and irony's implementation into media, represented in the father generations in Wallace's writings he himself is part of, rather than the original, if also at times misogynist, postmodernists of the 1960s.
[17] Ibid., 694.   [18] Wallace, "Certainly," *CL*, 59.

Wallace's postmodern (grand-) fathers, his "Great Male Narcissists," pass on their solipsizing narcissism, and with it their objectification of women, to the next generation. A proverbial locker-room talk in *Infinite Jest* perhaps best illustrates Wallace's reading of postmodernism as a paternal, phallocentric and misogynist heritage. Utterly exhausted from their training, *Infinite Jest's* tennis students indulge in an ironic conversation, lamenting not merely their exhaustion but rather their incapability to express their exhaustion in the language of their fathers. In Wallace's diagnosis of contemporary America, the postmodernism of Barth's metafictional literature of exhaustion has turned into a cultural discourse. While their fathers' language of exhaustion could still allow for self-expression, the next generation, Wallace portrays, is faced with a "[w]ord-inflation."[19] Meta-language having itself become exhausted, their exhaustion is "out of *tired's* word range."[20] Unable to express themselves through irony, as their fathers' exhausted "tuckered out'll do just fine"[21] is no longer capable of communicating one's experience, *Infinite Jest's* male students reproduce the legacy of the Great Male Narcissists by seeking recourse in Wallace's triad of solipsistic anesthetics, sex, media, and drug consumption, as they dream of "enormous pink-white French-painting tits that sort of like *tumble* out."[22]

Male and female alike, Wallace's characters are entrapped in the Lacanian framework they inherit from postmodernism's phallocrats, the sexist authors whose views inform the discourse of Wallace's society. This framework is one that conceives of an implicitly male subject defining itself in opposition to an implicitly female Other as object. Identifying contemporary culture as structured by a Lacanian "system where appearance remains a 'picture' or 'map' of ontology,"[23] Wallace views the subject as forced into a model of selfhood, which can only understand the female as Other. The subject, male or female, is thereby doomed to a "parodic *masculinization*" in the Lacanian "Quest for the Absent Object, a desire for attainment w/r/t which *un*attainability is that desire's breath & bread."[24] The (implicitly male) subject being "alienated via agency from an Exterior we have to objectify [...] in order to remain subjects,"[25] the othering of femininity is to Wallace inherent to a cultural discourse founded on a postmodernist "ontology-thru-nomination."[26] Ultimately

---

[19] Ibid., 100.   [20] Ibid.   [21] Ibid.
[22] Ibid., 102. Note the specific reference to "painting" that bespeaks the postmodernist fixation on the surface image.
[23] Wallace, "Empty Plenum," *BFN*, 100.   [24] Ibid., 115.   [25] Ibid., 102.   [26] Ibid., 113.

unattainable, however, the self's quest for subjecthood through objectification of the Other becomes "a constant generation and frustration of desire."[27] The meaning of the self in the discourse contemporary culture employs, language creating reality, is deferred along a chain of signifiers without ever attaining the desired meaning. Lacan's misogynist model underlying postmodernism's phallocentric discourse leads into a solipsistic double bind.

Holland's otherwise extremely insightful critique (mentioned earlier) is thus foreshortened when she criticizes Wallace for implying that "the true ontology of the feminine arises only in relationship to this defining male" and viewing "the problems of self-definition as fundamentally masculine."[28] On the contrary, rather than arguing "in his Lacanian way,"[29] as Holland has it, Wallace criticizes Lacan from within Lacanian language as solipsizing. Wallace's overt misogyny, for example, the lack of female voices in his writing and his stereotypical use of female figures, should rather be understood as a highly self-aware male writer's "realistic" representation of the misogynist discourse in "the whitely male West"[30] and its "stock rubrics via which we guys *apparently* must organize & process fey mystery."[31] Using a Lacanian vocabulary, Wallace depicts the naturalization of a masculinist Lacanian model as leading into solipsism. This, however, does not mean that he holds it to be the only, or his way of conceiving of selfhood. To Wallace, this language is simply the only one available to him and his readership.

Wallace's representation of misogyny, a representation that implicitly already utilizes Theory, should not tempt one to criticize the act of representation itself as misogynist. In fact, Wallace criticizes the solipsizing effects of postmodernism's misogynist legacy, repeatedly referring to it as a form of parental abuse. For instance, the female protagonist of "Suicide as a Sort of Present" is driven into her existential despair due to "parental abuse," though the narrator stresses that "[h]er parents [...] did not beat her or even really discipline her, nor did they pressure her."[32] Such instances of an ominous parental abuse-that-is-not-abuse, mentioned repeatedly throughout Wallace's writing, can be read as parents' introduction of their children into the phallocentric discourse of postmodernism, thereby laying the foundation for their children's solipsism. Wallace is thus, contrary to the foreshortened problematizations of his works, aware

[27] Holland, "'By Hirsute Author,'" 67.   [28] Ibid.   [29] Ibid., 68.
[30] Wallace, "Empty Plenum," *BFN*, 113.   [31] Ibid., 105 (emphasis added).
[32] Wallace, "Suicide," *BI*, 241.

of misogyny. He identifies, depicts and criticizes its occurrence within the self-conscious, Theory-infused image culture he portrays.

However, rather than absolving his writing of its problematic aspects, Wallace's (self-) awareness constitutes the very core of his failings as his feminist criticism is employed for very un-feminist ends. Sexism and phallocentrism are not only portrayed and criticized but are also employed as a metaphor for the *oeuvre*'s central concern, solipsism. As Daniela Joffe shows, Wallace eagerly genuflects to the second-wave feminism that transformed the American climate during the time of his writerly maturation, yet his texts effectively remain centered on male characters and male topics and refuse to question the categories of masculinity and femininity that prove central to his aesthetics. "Wallace's concessions to feminism," Joffe remarks, "enable him to keep white masculinity center stage."[33] Like women in patriarchy then, disavowed and denigrated both as active subjects and passive objects of the male gaze, the solipsist subject is caught in a double bind of omni-responsibility as the subject that creates reality from its language on the one hand and complete determination by others as the object of their description on the other hand. Wallace intellectualizes misogyny into a, to him, "pan-human"[34] philosophical problem. He thereby critically ignores a marginalized group's actual lived experience of structural violence in favor of his own abstract interrogation of solipsism. Choosing to apprehend misogyny cerebrally as a manifestation of and metaphor for his main concern, solipsism, Wallace downplays real misogyny as he draws his (essentially white, male, heterosexual) solipsism as a universal, and more pressing, issue. As Hayes-Brady remarks, Wallace effectively sacrifices his "obvious consciousness of gender relations" for his "almost-obsessive fear of solipsism."[35] Rather than exposing and countering misogyny, then, Wallace's feminist critique ultimately serves the role of a solution in a highly intellectualized, philosophical equation.

In particular, the French Feminism of the likes of Irigaray, Kristeva and Cixous with which Wallace was deeply familiar appears to Wallace a useful countermeasure against postmodernism's phallocentrism.[36] The reason for this appears to be that like Wallace, the French Feminists build on

---

[33] Joffe, "The Last Word," 172.   [34] Wallace, "Empty Plenum," *BFN*, 106.
[35] Hayes-Brady, "'…,'" 134.
[36] "Quotations" from key French feminist texts like Cixous' "The Laugh of the Medusa" reappearing in a Medusa with a "pained face" (741) in *IJ* or the aforementioned structuring of JOI's filmography around Mulvey's seminal cinema-essay can be found throughout Wallace's works. See also Kelly's chapter on "Brief Interviews with Hideous Men" in *The Cambridge Companion to David Foster Wallace*.

Lacanian theory in order to dismantle its misogyny, operating from within a phallocentric, postmodern language, the only language available, in order to offer alternatives to it. This can, for example, be seen in Wallace's concept of "crosswriting," a mode of writing heavily influenced by the French feminist notion of écriture féminine. Wallace's "crosswriting," self-reportedly first employed in his debut novel *The Broom of the System* and further developed throughout his body of work,[37] is a mode of writing in which the male writer, similar to a cross-dresser, acts from a feminine perspective. Wallace suggests that, since masculine postmodernism's institutionalized oedipal rebellion leaves no room for true nonconformity and change – after all, if postmodernism's iconoclastic rebellion is set as the norm, actual revolt becomes impossible - only a shift toward a feminine perspective could resolve solipsism.

Thus, the redemption of *Infinite Jest*'s protagonist Don Gately, for example, is structured around him exchanging his stepfather's moniker "MP" with Madame Psychosis, yet another, this time feminine, MP in the novel. The name of Gately's military police stepfather, a literalized name-of-the-father that serves in Lacanian theory as the fundamental signifier of phallocentric discourse, is thereby replaced by an alternative MP as the name-of-the-mother in a feminine language of écriture féminine.[38] By assuming a feminine position in accepting Madame Psychosis's "MP" as an alternative, maternal fundamental signifier, Gately can resist relapsing back into drug addiction and solipsism.

However, this crosswriting is an intertextual reference to rather than an example of French feminism's écriture féminine. Aware of his position as a white, male author, Wallace self-consciously resists the attempt to give voice to his sexual and racial Other, instead opting for potent absences or a parodic writerly transvestism that leaves little doubt that there is a white, male, heterosexual author behind the words. Wallace's crosswriting thus produces some of his most controversial writings such as the racist faux-ebonics of the "Wardine be cry" episode or the transphobia of the yrstruly (the moniker already pointing toward the function of the author) section

---

[37] Wallace calls *The Broom of the System* a "coded autobio" that is "hidden under the sex-change" of featuring a female protagonist as his alter ego in a 1993 interview with Larry McCaffery. This strategy of feminine ventriloquism is further elaborated on throughout the rest of Wallace's works. Unlike in *The Broom of the System*, however, Wallace's later writings come to mobilize the feminine voice as a sigil of complete alterity and relegate the assumption of a feminine language to the reader, the most overt example for this gender ventriloquism being the omitted questions of the female interviewer Q in *Brief Interviews with Hideos Men* that the reader has to fill in.

[38] cf. Irigaray, "Body Against Body."

in *Infinite Jest*, both related in a first-person parody of racial or sexual ventriloquism. To the author Wallace aware of his position as a white, heterosexual man, these voices remain inaccessible, instead to be inserted outside the text by a reader assuming the Other's perspective such as when in *Brief Interviews with Hideous Men* the female interviewer Q's questions are left as blanks, their feminine language to be filled in by the reader. They are, to cite Hayes-Brady's work, "unspeakable" and remain so in order to signify alterity.

Nevertheless, although attempting to foster identification with and give voice to an Other that must remain silenced in the phallocentric paradigm Wallace knows he is writing from, Wallace's "wokeness" regarding issues of diversity paradoxically bespeaks his problematic position of toxic masculinity, heteronormativity and white privilege. The "redemption" Gately experiences in *Infinite Jest*, for instance, is one structured along the lines of a heroification of toxically masculine values such as a refusal to change behavior and a pathological persistence despite the awareness of failure, behavior Wallace also apparently exhibited in his personal life. The redemptive assumption of a feminine language thus gives the hospital-bed-bound Gately the "heroic" strength to persist in his (masculine) self-destructive refusal to accept the pain medication his doctors urge him to take.[39]

Wallace puts feminism into the service of his own, deeply oedipal, struggle with his postmodernist fathers. Similarly, Wallace's awareness of racial diversity is overridden by his urge for universal communication, promoting White English as standard although he knows that "non-SWE-type dialects have their own highly developed and internally consistent grammars."[40] Likewise, homo- and transphobia are ignored as real issues where Wallace treats nonnormative sexuality as quotations of Lacanian concepts. Wallace's white, male, heterosexual privilege turns these groups of real people into not just Others, but Theory-quotations of an unspeakable Otherness, mere literary functions in Wallace's highly cerebral philosophical equations. The only group for whom Wallace's therapy "works" are the white heterosexual lit-bros who, due to their privilege, can afford to conceive of misogyny, racism and transphobia as intellectualized metaphors for solipsism. Although Wallace reportedly conceived of his reader as

---

[39] Notably, Wallace seems to be partly aware of the problematic aspects of his use of Theory, such as when he references the male author urging an implied female reader to assume a feminine position as "lexical rape." Interestingly, it is these instances in which Wallace reverts to the preemptive self-ironization he otherwise criticizes.

[40] Wallace, "Authority and American Usage," *CL*, 98.

female, it is predominantly white, heterosexual and male society (not to mention the class privilege Wallace exerts in expecting his readership to be familiar with the critical discourses he plays on intertextually), which can even be called to shift their perspective to identify with the Other and for which this Other is unspeakable.

Although it is potentially successful on an aesthetic level, Wallace's project is rife with highly problematic theoretical failings. While these failures are inherently unspeakable to an audience that shares Wallace's position and privilege, the inclusion of more diverse and critical perspectives in the second wave of Wallace Studies has opened up gateways to more nuanced understandings of Wallace's aesthetics as well as their problematic aspects. Critical perspectives on Wallace must therefore account for Wallace's intertextual use of the Theory that dominated academia during the time of his writing and his depiction of a hyper-self-reflexive "whitely male West"[41] that complicate problematization if they want to better grasp the extent of the *oeuvre*'s many weaknesses. The major obstacle in problematizing Wallace is Wallace's own use of critical discourse in his aesthetics of succeeding postmodernism. It is Wallace's self-awareness of phallocentrism, white privilege, and heteronormativity coupled with a privileged claim to universality, his reduction of the experiences of marginalized groups to abstract literary functions, and not an overt display of misogyny, racism, or homophobia, which makes his writing problematic on so many levels.

[41] Wallace, "Empty Plenum," *BFN*, 113.

CHAPTER 24

David Foster Wallace and Disability

Peter Sloane

A leading figure in Anglo-American literature who is also credited with galvanizing a "new phase in contemporary global literature," David Foster Wallace is often regarded as "the most important and influential writer of his generation."[1] We can infer from his critical and popular success that Wallace was endowed with both a peculiar literary ability and with a gift for communicating the often-unspoken despair of life in postindustrial society, in so doing offering his reader some redemptive consolation. Indeed, the 1997 award of a John D. and Catherine T. MacArthur Foundation Fellowship, a.k.a. the "Genius Grant," is testament to his ability. However, despite the adoration and acclaim elicited by his art, Wallace also struggled with a neurochemical imbalance that manifested as a depression so profoundly disabling that it precipitated his 2008 suicide. Those romantically inclined might divine a link between his creative achievements and his psychological malady. The anecdotal interdependence of great art and despair is experimentally attested, as Leon S. Brenner notes, "creative hyper-activation is a major causal factor in the genesis and onset of depression."[2] Brenner's study seems to provide evidence for a deeply ironic trade-off between Wallace's heightened ability to console others and his dis/inability to console himself.

The categories of "abled" and "disabled" as descriptors of persons necessarily prompt (while presupposing resolutions to) wider questions about human freedom, the agency to choose to act, or perhaps as Wallace now famously proposed, "truly to care about other people and to sacrifice for them over and over in myriad petty, unsexy ways every day."[3] Free will's (non-)existence is possibly the foundational dilemma of both Western philosophy and Western religion, and so in this sense stands as a universal theological and metaphysical conundrum that continues to

---

[1] Severs, *Balancing Books*, 1; Boswell, *The Wallace Effect*, 2.
[2] Brenner, "Creative Hyper-Activation," 359.   [3] Wallace, *TIW*, 120.

spawn rich debates between determinists, libertarians and compatibilists. But these ostensibly theoretical concerns, with which Wallace grappled with precocious analytic virtuosity in his undergraduate philosophy thesis, take on greater pragmatic social urgency in neoliberal North America, a nation founded on the concept of individualistic self-reliance, where "the best good," as Rémy Marathe has it, "is each individual USA person's maximum pleasure."[4] For example, one might wonder how such a society could find a place for what Ralph Waldo Emerson, in his highly influential manifesto "Self-Reliance," refers to as "invalids in a protected corner."[5] One solution, as Emily Russell argues, is that adherents to Emerson's uncompromising "autonomous individualism" may simply "cast out their opposites from membership" of American political society.[6]

In political philosophy, these "opposites" are excluded as signatories from what Jean-Jacques Rousseau called the "social contract," a "form of association [...] through which each individual, while uniting with all, will nevertheless obey himself alone and remain as free as before."[7] Unfortunately, "each individual" is not considered equal. Opposites, or "outliers" as they are often termed, are individuals and groups "beyond the reach of equal justice," or in Emerson's terms, in need of "apology or extenuation of their living in the world."[8] As Anita Silvers and Leslie Pickering Francis comment, traditionally understood "as a process of bargaining for mutual advantage," "social contract theory [...] stands between people with disabilities and justice," because those with disabilities are deemed unable to "participate in cooperatively productive activities."[9] In the age of neoliberal self-reliance, such an exclusion may be even more operative, a fact with which Wallace plays when, in *Infinite Jest*, he facilitates a debate about these issues with wheelchair-bound Marathe, a political activist/terrorist in search of the "Entertainment," which represents precisely something to bargain with for the rights of his severely disabled wife.

The term "disabled," whether it refers to physical, emotional or cognitive incapacity, denotes persons who do not sit within the very limited spectrum of neuro- or corporeo-typicality. As Faye Ginsberg and Rayna Rapp have persuasively written, disability is "a profoundly relational category, always already created as a distinction from cultural ideas of

---

[4] Wallace, *IJ*, 424.   [5] Emerson, *Essential Writings*, 133.   [6] Russell, *Embodied Citizenship*, 5.
[7] Rousseau, *Social Contract*, 19.
[8] Silvers and Pickering Francis, "Justice through Trust," 41; Emerson, *Essential Writings*, 136.
[9] Ibid.

normality, shaped by social conditions that exclude full participation in society of those considered atypical."[10] The category "disabled" is constituted by a series of exclusionary practices in social and physical spaces, which are constructed by and for the typical, the "normal." This constructivist interpretation is referred to as the "social Model of Disability," which opposes essentialist definitions and holds rather that "it is society which disables physically impaired people."[11] In this understanding, physical impairment does not constitute "disability," but merely precipitates disabling spatial exclusion.

Rosemarie Garland-Thomson interprets this as a matter of "world building." She writes, "The premise of world building is that the shape of the material world we design, build, and use together both expresses and determines who inhabits it and how we use it to exercise the duties and privileges of citizenship within that world."[12] Garland-Thomson has in mind the often-exclusionary physical infrastructure and architecture of the ostensibly public domain. But literature too is a variety of worldbuilding, informed by and informing our ideas about the way the social world is or should be. Nelson Goodman reminds us that art plays "a prominent role in worldmaking; our worlds are not more a heritage from scientists, biographers, and historians than from novelists."[13] Wallace's worlds are built for the atypical; it is they that constitute the "norm" in his familiar yet subtly disturbed and disturbing text-spaces. What is also evident in Garland-Thomson's analysis is that disability can be read simultaneously as both "a problem and an opportunity for solutions."[14] In this chapter, I approach Wallace's engagement with physical and cognitive disability with this concept in mind, to argue that he is not so much a writer of the grotesque as he is a humanist who figures disability and the disabled person as opportunities to "forge" sincere interpersonal relations both between characters and between character and reader. In some ways, this means appropriating the disabled body as what David Mitchell and Sharon Snyder describe as an "opportunistic metaphorical device," a common tendency for the able-bodied writer.[15] Yet Wallace also gives voice to the socially and culturally excluded, partially, as I suggest below, because he does not experience the "aesthetic nervousness" that Ato Quayson sees as endemic to literature, an anxiety that arises because "the dominant

---

[10] Ginsburg and Rapp, "Disability Worlds," 54.   [11] Oliver, *Understanding Disability*, 22.
[12] Garland-Thomson, "Building a World," 52.   [13] Goodman, *Worldmaking*, 103.
[14] Garland-Thomson, "Building a World," 51.
[15] Mitchell and Snyder, "Narrative Prosthesis," 222.

protocols of representation within the literary text are short-circuited in relation to disability."[16] Wallace, however, deals equally with the abled and disabled, making a virtue of an apparent insensitivity that is, ultimately, perversely inclusive, leaving no outliers.

Physical Disability

Wallace's engagement with physical disability spans his career and typifies his most iconic characters, from one-legged LaVache Beadsman in his debut *The Broom of the System*, through *Infinite Jest*'s enigmatically disfigured Joelle Van Dyne, to *The Pale King*'s hyperhidrotic David Cusk. It is in *Infinite Jest* that his interest in anomalous embodiment features most centrally, or, as Jeffrey Severs remarks, that the "imagery of bodies is rendered more grotesquely than anywhere else in Wallace."[17] While Severs' observation about the foregrounded atypical body is accurate, as Garland-Thomson suggests, it is in fact the ableist "stare [which] sculpts the disabled subject into a grotesque spectacle."[18] I want here to pay attention to Mario Incandenza and Gertraud Marathe, two of his most explicit examples of extreme physical disability. While evidencing Wallace's penchant for finding humor in the most unlikely places, these characters also demonstrate a persistent concern with the lived experience of disability and living with the disability of others. Giving expression to the experiential reality of disability, Gertraud and Mario present other characters with opportunities for meaningful interpersonal connection otherwise unavailable to them.

Mario is a permanent fixture at Enfield Tennis Academy (ETA), an elite school for gifted junior players founded by his late father James. A "kid with some lifelong character-building physical challenges," Mario is among Wallace's most profoundly corporeally impaired characters.[19] Brother to Hal, a talented junior tennis player, and Orin, a gifted football player, Mario is unable to aspire to achieve in the same way, although Hal suspects that their mother Avril "sees Mario as the family's real prodigy" (*IJ* 317). Wallace devotes several lengthy paragraphs to describing Mario's numerous "abnormalities," including "withered-looking and bradyauxetic arms," "nonprehensile fingers [. . .] unable even to grip a regulation stick or stand unaided behind a boundaried space."[20] Excluded from participation in

---

[16] Quayson, *Nervousness*, 15.   [17] Severs, *Balancing Books*, 95.
[18] Garland-Thomson, *Extraordinary Bodies*, 26.   [19] Wallace, *IJ*, 313.   [20] Ibid., 313–14.

ETAs athletic regimen, Mario's primary role, in a novel fascinated with the art of "interface," of conversation, is to listen:

> Mario is basically a born listener. One of the positives to being visibly damaged is that people can sometimes forget you're there, even when they're interfacing with you. You almost get to eavesdrop. It's almost like they're like: If nobody's really in there, there's nothing to be shy about. That's why bullshit often tends to drop away around damaged listeners, deep beliefs revealed, diary-type private reveries indulged out loud; and, listening, the beaming and brady-kinetic boy gets to forge an interpersonal connection he knows only he can truly feel, here.[21]

Mario serves a vital function for others, but this also enables him to forge (an interesting word if we think of "The Soul is not a Smithy") meaningful "interpersonal connections." There are some possibly troubling implications here, about the self-absence of those whose bodies resist "cultural ideas of normality."[22] This moment also acts at first sight as a contradictory counterpoint to Joelle van Dyne, whose motivation to support the Union of the Hideously and Improbably Deformed (UHID) is the shame that arises because the "improbably deformed" are highly visible, "the object of stares."[23] As Ema Loja and colleagues remark, the "non-disabled gaze [is] driven by curiosity, perceived as a 'right' to intrude, inquire, appropriate impairment as a public spectacle."[24] However, there is no inconsistency, but a subtle distinction between the heightened physical presence and the occluded self-presence of the "visibly damaged"; Mario's extraordinary body creates the illusion of paradoxical absence, and so Mario is perceived by his interlocutor to be emotionally or agentively transparent precisely because of the almost aggressive material presence of his body. Despite the apparently positive implications in this "interface," Wallace concludes with Mario's essential isolation, the fact that "only he" can feel any "interpersonal connection" because, for his conversation partner, Mario is simply not "really in there," a fact of which he is aware, but unconcerned.

Enfield is a total institution built by the Incandenzas' father James, "a towering figure in optical and avant-garde film circles" (once again highlighting the fascination with watching and being watched).[25] Mario occupies a privileged position at the center of ETA, a community devoted to sporting acumen that would, otherwise, exclude him by definition: Enfield's contract is predicated on the highly functioning body as currency

[21] Ibid., 80.   [22] Ginsburg and Rapp, "Disability Worlds," 54.   [23] Ibid., 534.
[24] Loja et al., "Stories of Resistance," 190.   [25] Wallace, *IJ*, 30.

in the exchange of athletic capital for education and sustenance. Nevertheless, Mario finds a place by following in his father's footsteps and developing a talent for filmmaking:

> Mario's facility with the head-mount Bolex attenuates the sadness of his status here, allowing him to contribute via making the annual ETA fundraising documentary cartridge [...] plus producing more ambitious, arty-type things that occasionally find a bit of an àclef-type following in the ETA community.[26]

It is remarkable that in a space so unconducive to the disabled, Wallace demonstrates that even the most extreme physical impairment need not result in social exclusion. Mario develops a passion for participation in his cloistered community, which in turn leads to a passion for filmmaking, for worldbuilding, for self-expression. Indeed, his films become cult classics for the junior tennis players, Mario becoming Enfield's artist in residence. And so, if it is his perceived absence that grants him a quasi-place at Enfield, this in turn facilitates for Mario an opportunity for personal growth, self-realization. Regardless of the role he plays as a listener for certain characters, there remains an element of the "pity, fascination, repulsion" that characterizes the able-bodied encounter with the disabled, for other characters and for the reader.[27] In literary terms, this confrontation often gives rise to Quayson's "aesthetic nervousness," in which literary representations of the disabled body provoke aesthetic-ethical dilemmas. Perhaps it is this anxiety that leads to the repeated (euphemistic) descriptions of disabled bodies in Wallace's works as "grotesque."[28] One might also suggest that, in celebrating Mario's ability to "contribute" (despite impairment), Wallace reinforces the social-contract theory, in which citizen's rights and responsibilities are determined by their capacity to participate in what John Rawls calls "social cooperation among equals for mutual advantage."[29] Mario creates a place for himself by bargaining, cooperating in the economy of value, and so ETA ultimately acts as a microcosm of wider US neoliberal political reality.

Mario is not, however, the most physically impaired character in the novel; that honor goes to Marathe's wife, Gertraud, who was "born as an infant without a skull" as a result of exposure to US pollution.[30] Wallace pays acute attention to Gertraud's "ablated" body and its various

---

[26] Ibid., 315–16.   [27] Garland-Thomson, *Extraordinary Bodies*, 12.
[28] One particularly influential example is Marshall Boswell's troubling description of *Infinite Jest's* "grotesque cripples," in *Understanding David Foster Wallace* (2003), 122.
[29] Rawls, *Theory of Justice*, 210.   [30] Wallace, *IJ*, 429.

incapacities, drawing our gaze to precisely those aspects of her anomalous body that are most likely to repulse:

> There were progressive decays of circulation and vessel, which calls itself restenosis. There were the more than standard accepted amounts of eyes and cavities in many different stages of development upon different parts of the body. There were the fugue states and rages and frequency of coma [. . .]. Worst for choosing to love was the cerebro-and-spinal fluids which dribbled at all times from her distending oral cavity.[31]

Her profound impairments are portrayed in a language and with a degree of attention usually absent in literary representations of disability. Marathe himself is wheelchair-bound, but in the spectrum from able-bodied to profoundly disabled, he is comparatively "normal." Wallace's description playfully crosses boundaries between scientific terminology in almost clinical precision and the outright absurdity of the proliferating eyes and cavities. In this instance, the balance possibly leans toward the grotesque, involving, as Paul Thomson suggests, "the co-presence of the laughable and something which is incompatible with the laughable."[32] There is little here to suggest that Gertraud is limited by social space; rather, her physical impairments are so severe that she is entirely dependent upon technology (Mario too is augmented by the prosthesis of head-mounted camera). Marathe is in search of the forbidden film so that he can barter for the "advanced Jaarvik IX Exterior Artificial Heart," with which Gertraud "can live for many more years in a comatose and vegetated state."[33] Playful, yes, even grotesque, but for Marathe, Gertraud stands as a challenge and an opportunity to love the unlovable precisely because of the extremity of her disabilities.

Shortly after their first meeting, Marathe realizes that he is unable to forget Getraud, and that he is in fact in love with her despite the obvious "heart- and head-difficulties." He says, "I had to face: I had chosen. My choice, this was love. I had chosen I think the way out of the chains of the cage. I needed this woman. Without her to choose over myself, there was only pain and not choosing."[34] Marathe does not really "choose," despite claiming that "the chains are of my choice";[35] rather, he has to accept cognitively that on some profound level below conscious agency, a decision has been made for him to "truly to care about" Gertraud and to sacrifice his wishes for care of her. It is no surprise for a writer so preoccupied with giving "imaginative" access to the suffering of others

[31] Ibid., 779.   [32] P. Thomson, *Grotesque*, 3.   [33] Ibid., 780.   [34] Ibid.   [35] Ibid., 781.

"marooned" in their skulls that a character so deeply in need of care is born without a skull, the contents of her soft head oozing beyond the porous borders of her vulnerable body in such a way as to act as a (sincere) plea for care. Gertraud does not simply provide Marathe with a single discrete purpose (caring for her); it is only because of the "love" inspired by her that his life is imbued with a system of meaning that extends beyond her: "Without choice of her life there are no other choices."[36] Because both he and she are disabled, he can overcome the "autonomous individualism" so prevalent throughout the book and the world in which Wallace's novel sits. Mario and Gertraud offer others a possibility for meaningful sacrifice of self, a kind of overcoming of solipsism in the service of precisely the sincerity for which Wallace advocates. As Timothy Jacobs has commented, Mario is "the only character in the novel who is neither cynical nor ironic," "the type of person with whom all the characters speak sincerely."[37] Once more, however, Wallace's use of disability is problematic, seen as an opportunity for others' self-development; in this way, the disabled body is reduced to little more than Mitchell and Snyder's "opportunistic metaphor." One might also ask for whose benefit Gertraud will live those "many more years in a comatose and vegetated state" that Marathe seeks to secure in the quest from which he derives personal worth, identity, value.

Cognitive Disability

Not all disabilities are physical, of course, and Wallace is equally, if not more, attuned to the subtle degrees of cognitive and emotional disability that often go unnoticed. As Benjamin Fraser observes, "cognitive disabilities, when juxtaposed with the increased theoretical, social, and cultural visibility of physical disabilities, have tended to remain disproportionately unseen."[38] As I have argued elsewhere, "for Wallace, *all* bodies are physically and metaphysically disabled and disabling," and so in this sense we each have, indeed *are* an invisible disability.[39] Wallace construes invisible impairment as being as equally debilitating and pervasive as the visible. We might think here of one of his most successful short pieces, "The Depressed Person." Unlike materially evident physical disabilities, invisible disabilities invite speculation about emotional and psychological resilience, sufferers "often seen by others as having succumbed too easily to the challenges and trials of life."[40] In Mario's case, it is clear that he is impeded

[36] Ibid.   [37] Jacobs, "Brothers Incandenza," 272.   [38] Fraser, "Cognitive Disability," 29.
[39] Sloane, *Wallace and the Body*, 7.   [40] Davis, "Invisible Disability," 186.

in various profound ways. For the invisibly disabled, however, the "impossibility of sharing or articulating" the experience of a nonmaterial impairment compounds the trouble itself.[41] As Davis continues, and Wallace illustrates, "the depressed person is mired in despair and unable to overcome doubts about his or her efficacy," leading to further "excruciating feelings of shame and inadequacy."[42] If the disabled body acts as a plea for care, for concern, the impaired mind has no such manifestation, and the sufferer must give voice to their own experience.

If depression is associated with an excess of feeling, certain cognitive atypicalities are associated with an absence of affect and empathy. Autism Spectrum Conditions (ASC) have traditionally been seen as synonymous with "difficulties developing empathy," partially because they result in "reduced attention to faces" and expression.[43] Wallace features autism in "Little Expressionless Animals," a story whose title hints at its concerns with the valence of faces and expression. The story recounts the tale of siblings Julie and Lunt Smith, abandoned as children by the side of a busy road by their mother and her partner. Left only with encyclopedias, both have an uncanny ability to recall facts, which has seen Julie become a longstanding Jeopardy champion, while supporting Lunt's medical expenses. Described as "Autistic to where this was like a mannequin of a kid instead of a kid," Lunt "cannot live in the world."[44] However, Lunt also presents an opportunity very similar to that provided by Gertraud:

> Taking care of him took incredible amounts of time. He wasn't company, though; you're right. But I got so I wanted him with me. He got to be my job. I got so I associated him with my identity or something. My right to take up space. I wasn't even eight.[45]

Interestingly, Julie once more suggests an absence as opposed to presence, implying that being with Lunt was, essentially, to be alone. Nevertheless, he constitutes for her a reason to be in the world much as Gertraud acts as Marathe's. Ultimately, she and he become a single entity; "If I'd been without him right then," she remarks to Faye, "I don't think there would have been any me left," [...] "*I'd* have been in hospitals all this time, instead of him."[46] In caring for Lunt, Julie has a reason to overlook her own trauma and to instead focus on the care of another, in this case a child in many ways immune to the emotional trauma that stays with Julie. This relationship does not simply involve an able person making personal

[41] Wallace, "Depressed Person," *BI*, 31.   [42] Ibid.
[43] Baron-Cohen et al., "Emotion Recognition," 3567–68.   [44] Wallace, "Little," *GCH*, 20.
[45] Ibid., 11.   [46] Ibid.

sacrifices for a disabled person, but rather a meaningful and equitable exchange, because Lunt justifies Julie's presence in the world. Gertraud and Lunt elicit what is interpreted as a kind of love – self-sacrifice – but which is instead a variety of dependence upon the disabled "other" for meaning. This sense occurs elsewhere, when we are told that Mario continues to ask Hal for help "bathing and dressing at thirteen," but "wanting the help for Hal's sake, not his own."[47] If there is any bargaining here, it is the subject being cared for that contributes most to the exchange, acting paradoxically as a kind of prosthesis, appendage, which brings to mind LaVache Beadsman's conception, in *The Broom of the System*, that he, in an odd reversal of roles, is "supporting [his] leg."[48]

Wallace's final novel, *The Pale King*, is equally interested in corporeality and disability. As Clare Hayes-Brady has remarked, it is "full of bodies, most of them somehow in distress."[49] ASC traits are present in the less extreme form of Shane Drinion, who shares many characteristics with his more cartoonish predecessor Lunt. The connection is made to the earlier story with the descriptions of Drinion as "expressionless unless someone tells a joke that's somehow directed at everyone around the table, at which time Drinion will smile briefly and then his face will go back to being expressionless."[50] Drinion is the novel's hero, an "immersive" (a person immune to boredom) projected in Wallace's notes to do battle on behalf of the human examiners in competition with the machines scheduled to replace them precisely because "typical" human examiners experience boredom, which impacts on processing efficiency. Wallace seemingly adopts the idea that people with ASC, as Baron-Cohen has argued, have "advance abilities in 'systematizing,'" which is "the drive to analyze or build systems, allowing one to predict the behavior of the system and control it."[51] This is an ideal characteristic for rote exams, but once more a possibly reductive and stereotypical portrayal of autism as akin to being a savant (most famously like *Rain Man*'s Raymond Babbitt).

Like Mario, Drinion is a good listener, and it is he who allows Meredith Rand, "pretty but a yammerer of the most dire kind," to tell her story of childhood despair.[52] As Adam S. Miller has written, "Drinion can pay attention to what she's saying without her charms making him defensive or distracted."[53] However, Drinion does not simply act as a passive point of interface; he too derives something like pleasure from listening:

---

[47] Wallace, *IJ*, 317.   [48] Wallace, *BS*, 239.   [49] Hayes-Brady, *Failures*, 185.
[50] Wallace, *TPK*, 450.   [51] Baron-Cohen et al., "Emotion Recognition," 3568.
[52] Wallace, *TPK*, 546.   [53] A. S. Miller, *Gospel*, 29.

Drinion is actually levitating slightly, which is what happens when he is completely immersed; it's very slight, and no one can see that his bottom is floating slightly above the seat of the chair. One night someone comes into the office and sees Drinion floating upside down over his desk with his eyes glued to a complex return, Drinion himself unaware of the levitating thing by definition, since it is only when his attention is completely on something else that the levitation happens.[54]

Drinion, invisible in various ways, forges precisely the kind of "interpersonal connection" that Mario enables, allowing his interlocutor to express things that otherwise remain unspoken. In return, Drinion derives energy from these encounters, feeding on interface, on information in the same way that Lyle feeds on perspiration. It is an exchange then, a bargaining of various kinds of good. The IRS, in the novel, is a society that privileges as opposed to excludes the neuroatypical. In this sense, it is like Enfield, only its opposite – Enfield is a total institution that fetishizes athletic superability; the Peoria IRS does the same with ASC traits and figures these as a heroic ability, even a superpower. Disability is indeed determined by space, community, society: in certain circumstances, apparent disabilities become heightened abilities. This is something we see recently in film, in *A Quiet Place* (2018), for example, or *Bird Box* (2018), where deafness and blindness are presented, respectively, as peculiarly useful and beneficial to survival in reimagined societies.

Conclusion

Disabilities, both cognitive and physical, proliferate in Wallace's fictional worlds. Often read simply as "grotesque," Wallace was profoundly interested in the fact of disability, its impact on lived experience, and the manner in which it both necessitates and enables care. It is predominantly an opportunity to rethink interpersonal relationships and for sincerity to emerge in the absence of irony. As I suggested in the opening, disability is perceived as both an impediment and an opportunity, and Wallace views the impediments produced by impairment as assets. We might think here of *Brief Interviews*' Johnny-One-Arm, who explicitly refers to his "flipper" arm as "the asset"; comical, yes, but also an important gesture toward challenging typical understandings of difference as disability. Disability is entirely relational, determined not by brute materiality but by the social

---

[54] Wallace, *TPK*, 487. Levitation occurs frequently in Wallace's writing, most notably with Lyle in *IJ* and Chick Nunn Junior in "John Billy."

and material spaces in which persons live. In the right community, ETA or the Peoria IRS, for example, an impediment is an asset, a possibility for engaging in the sincerity so fundamental to Wallace's project and his ongoing influence on contemporary global literature. Unavoidably, the disabled character often becomes a metaphor in ways with which disabilities theorists like Garland-Thomson, Quayson, Davis, Mitchell and Snyder have taken issue. One might suggest, however, that this is the fate of all literary characters; they are not facsimiles of persons, abled or disabled, but manifestations of their world's themes and concerns. Importantly, Wallace's willingness to address disability, to approach the impaired body and mind without "aesthetic nervousness," gives him, and the reader, the opportunity for an encounter often absent from literature.

CHAPTER 25

Queering Wallace
On the Queer History of Addiction Fiction

Vincent Haddad

In her controversial argument on not reading David Foster Wallace, Amy Hungerford aligns Wallace's writer-reader relationship with that described by Mark Nechtr, one of Wallace's first of many writer-figures: "a story, just maybe, should treat the reader like it wants to [,]... well, fuck him."[1] Buoyed by a swath of related articles of "Wallace backlash," Hungerford's framing of Wallace's writer-reader relationship as an erotic invitation, albeit arguably a misogynistic and toxic one, certainly resonates;[2] as does Hungerford's response to this invitation: "Wallace proposes to fuck me [...] I can refuse the offer and so I will."[3] Hungerford's response is warranted given her argument about Wallace's positioning of women in his texts. Yet, following Hungerford's noting of the "possibly queer, and certainly aggressive, resonances of Nechtr's male pronoun for the reader," we might reframe this proposal for Wallace's male readers, who he identified consistently as his primary audience, and who rarely conceptualize themselves as accepting an erotic offer by Wallace whatsoever.[4] Wallace's fiction cultivates this contradiction, often figuring its images of masculinity in opposition to male homosexuality, and therefore disavowing the intimacy between heterosexual men as a manifestation of desire. Embracing the transparent queerness of this invitation is crucial in fully understanding the most widely agreed-upon central function of Wallace's fiction as a literary-therapeutic salve for addiction, loneliness and depression.

Despite the pervasive preoccupation with sex in Wallace's work, critical analyses of sexuality in his fiction are rare, and analyses that explore

---

[1] Hungerford, *Making*, 141; Wallace, "Westward," *GCH*, 331.
[2] For analysis of these articles, see Hayes-Brady, "Reading Your Problematic Fave"; Boswell, *The Wallace Effect*, 125–48.
[3] Hungerford, *Making*, 152.   [4] Ibid., 141; Lipsky, *Although of Course*, 273.

sexuality through the lens of queer theory are even rarer.[5] This is surprising given the attention paid to Wallace's upbringing in the academy, and the concurrent rise of queer studies, to which a theory-obsessed Wallace was almost certainly exposed to as a MFA student.[6] Yet it is more surprising given the fact that queer theorists such as Sara Ahmed, Jack Halberstam, Lauren Berlant and Ann Cvetkovich have provided some of the clearest critical insight on the very content we associate with Wallace's fiction, such as how the optimistic aspirations and happiness that we invest in the idea of the good life function dialectically and recursively with shame, addiction, failure and suicidal ideation.[7] Without a consideration of queer theory, one can neither critically deconstruct nor affirmatively illuminate the potentiality of how Wallace's fiction figures sexuality. However, the losses do not end with analyses of sexuality in his fiction, but a host of coexisting and indeed contingent themes and ways of seeing in Wallace's fictional worlds.

This contribution explores how adopting this lens can alter how we understand the most fundamental function associated with Wallace's fiction: as a form of therapy. Timothy Aubry has effectively demonstrated how *Infinite Jest* serves this function, as well as how his fiction's contingent relation to addiction and recovery stories enabled Wallace to reinject what he saw as a dispassionate and exhausted postmodern form with moral and affective urgency.[8] Building on this argument, Jon Baskin persuasively contends that Wallace's therapeutic intervention is primarily philosophical and "addresses a readership he presumes to be in pain and one whose pain is connected to, and possibly a function of, a certain way of thinking."[9] Reading into the protagonist of Wallace's early story "The Planet Trillaphon," Baskin rightly points out that Wallace identifies this pain as "not just a function of the boy's personality or his immediate cultural or demographic environment, but [as] rooted in a *philosophical* confusion."[10] For Baskin, this enables Wallace's attempt to translate, from Sigmund Freud, "hysterical misery into ordinary unhappiness."[11] Thus, in *Jest*, the portions of the novel dealing with Alcoholics Anonymous typify how Wallace "offers not a way out of or around ratiocination but rather access

[5] Jackson's *Toxic Sexuality*, along with his contribution in this volume, are useful examples of the work that is being done in this field.

[6] For analysis of the impact of the "Graduate Seminar in Theory," including queer studies, on Wallace, see Boddy, "Fiction of Response."

[7] See Ahmed, *Promise*; Halberstam, *Queer Art*; Berlant, *Cruel Optimism*; Cvetkovich, *Depression*.

[8] Aubry, *Reading as Therapy*, 97–126.   [9] Baskin, *Ordinary Unhappiness*, 8.   [10] Ibid., 9.

[11] Ibid., 19.

to a non- or perhaps an antitheoretical *form* of reason."[12] Yet Wallace's appeal to the philosophical, beyond "demographic environment" and thereby toward the universal and ordinary, masks the history of queer therapeutic addiction narratives upon which he depends. In the next chapter, Alexander Moran draws attention to the roles of pain in Wallace's addiction narratives; it is instructive also to consider the roles of queer intimacy in these narratives. In conversation with this section's other chapters on gender and sexuality, this chapter explores the ways in which Wallace's writing occupies queer spaces in its representation of the fractured contingency of the addicted self in recovery.

Specifically, the chapter draws a comparison with Walt Whitman, another writer who once described the impetus for his writing as "sex, sex, sex: sex is the root of it all: sex."[13] As some may already know, Wallace's email address, "ocapmycap@ca.rr.com," was a reference to Whitman's famous poem "O Captain! My Captain!"[14] But Whitman's impact on Wallace goes much deeper than this. Scholars have cited Whitman as an influence on Wallace as an antecedent for his penchant for maximalism and for "defying conventional rules of good writing as a technique for connoting sincerity."[15] Whitman's conceptualization of (queer) sex is also a spectral presence in Wallace's fiction. In *Jest*, the "oiled guru" Lyle reads *Leaves of Grass* while "going through a Whitman period, part of grieving for Himself" – that is, for James O. Incandenza.[16] This Whitman devotee fittingly breaches the supposed boundaries of strict heteronormativity in the novel, and thus reveals how the novel problematically addresses and represses queerness. Describing how Lyle's tongue is "rough but feels good" when he licks sweat off him, Hal heads off a homosexual panic by assuring the reader "it isn't like a faggy or sexual thing" and that "[Lyle's] harmless as they come."[17] Despite the fraught protestation of Lyle's asexuality, Lyle's use of Whitman in mourning James is the most direct inference to a homosocial, if not queer, desire between Lyle and James. When alive, James would get "libated late at night with Lyle" and "pour his heart's thickest chime right out there," while Lyle, licking the sweat off James's skin, "would start to get tipsy himself as Himself's pores began to excrete bourbon" and read him poetry "during these all-night sessions."[18] As I have discussed elsewhere, given this

---

[12] Ibid., 62. [13] Traubel, *With Walt Whitman in Camden*, vol. 3, 452–53.
[14] Warren, "Wallace and Politics," 174.
[15] Hoberek, "Wallace and American Literature," 43. See also Giles, "Sentimental."
[16] Wallace, *IJ*, 254. [17] Ibid., 128. [18] Ibid., 379.

relationship and the queer threat posed by James' wraith in the novel, it is likely that Lyle chooses *Leaves of Grass* precisely because Whitman's poetic use of ghosts enabled one man to project himself, through language, beyond the grave to meet, and be intimate with, another man.[19]

Here, I will focus my attention on Whitman's temperance novel *Franklin Evans or The Inebriate: A Tale of the Times* (1842) to expand on the historical relationship between addiction narratives and sexuality to which Wallace's aesthetic strategy is indebted. Lesser known to today's readers than his masterful poetry collection *Leave of Grass* (1855), *Franklin Evans* was by far Whitman's largest commercial success during his lifetime despite being, like Wallace's *Broom*, a first novel he would later disavow.[20] The novel was published in full by *The New World*, a story-paper that mixed literary and nonliterary fiction, poetry and news from American and non-American writers, and as a result, the editors "found themselves defending both their patriotism and respectability."[21] In Whitman's short novel, the eponymous Franklin travels from Long Island to New York City in an attempt to make a life for himself. However, he becomes enthralled by the nightlife, including alcohol, music and (male) camaraderie, and hits a series of increasingly far-fetched rock bottoms. Ostensibly, *Franklin Evans* is an overly didactic warning against the dangers of alcoholism, with themes and modes of address immediately recognizable to readers of the AA scenes in *Infinite Jest*. The reader and Franklin listen to several warning stories of others' social and moral decline from alcoholism. These scenes mirror the moments in *Jest* when the Ennet House counselors ask Don Gately, and by extension the reader, to "sit right up at the front of the hall where they can see the pores in the speaker's nose and try to Identify instead of Compare."[22] However, this act of empathetic identification is not all that *Franklin Evans* will ask of its readers.

The temperance movements working at the time of *Franklin Evans* publication, as Michael Warner argues, "*invented* addiction."[23] In so

---

[19] See Haddad, "Conjuring David Foster Wallace's Ghost."
[20] Wallace readers will immediately recognize an affinity in Whitman's self-deprecating, yet not altogether accurate, comments on *Franklin Evans* later in life:

> I doubt if there is a copy in existence: I have none and have not had one for years [. . .] Their offer of cash payment was so tempting – I was so hard up at the time – that I set to work at once ardently on it (with the help of a bottle of port or what not). In three days of constant work I finished the book. Finished the book? Finished myself. It was damned rot – rot of the worst sort – not insincere, perhaps, but rot, nevertheless. (Traubel, With Walt Whitman in Camden, vol. 4, 323)

[21] Castiglia and Hendler, "Introduction," xxviii.   [22] Wallace, *IJ*, 345.
[23] Warner, "Whitman Drunk," 32.

doing, temperance connects to a broader shift in reform movements that identified so-called perversions that "turn actions (drinking alcohol, making pornography, stealing) into identities" like "alcoholic," "hoodlum," "pornographer," or, later, "homosexual."[24] This entanglement between behavior and identity is a wide-ranging feature of Wallace's fiction, including Hal's secretive use of marijuana in *Jest*, Neal's phoniness in "Good Old Neon," or even the difference between being a hideous man and a man acting hideously in *Brief Interviews*. Whitman's early temperance novel helpfully complicates the relationship between literary therapy, addiction and sexuality that will later become so prevalent in Wallace's fiction. Through this connection, my purpose is twofold: first, to recontextualize the fantasy of pre-postmodern and even pre-realist novels imagined by Wallace to be better-suited to the aesthetic project of therapy and recovery in a post-postmodern America; and second, to bring Wallace's aesthetic practice in closer contact with issues of sexuality that the universalizing gesture of fiction-as-therapy generally permits. While the contribution does not argue that Wallace was a queer writer, it elucidates the disruptive potential of queer readings within the context of late postmodernist constructions of self.

At the time of writing *Franklin Evans*, Whitman participated in the Washingtonian Temperance Society, whose population skyrocketed from six to half a million members between 1840 and 1842, and even included Abraham Lincoln among its ranks. Like Wallace, who while in recovery at the Granada House, "understood from the beginning that his fall from grace was a literary opportunity [. . .and] was alive to the new information he was getting,"[25] Whitman relied on these first-hand experiences with the Washingtonian Society in writing *Franklin Evans*. Citing Charles J. G. Griffin's research on the Washingtonian Society, Castiglia and Hendler explain that this particular temperance society was markedly different from the many competing ones of the time because, "while previous temperance drives had been led by abstemious middle-class men, often clergy, the Washingtonians were led by working men and women who were themselves suffering drinkers."[26] Other temperance societies preached to the pure about how to avoid becoming an irredeemable outcast, whereas the Washingtonians adopted "liberalizing Christian revival rhetoric of

---

[24] Castiglia and Hendler, "Introduction," xliv. For more on the invention of homosexuality, see Foucault, *History of Sexuality, vol. 1.*

[25] Max, "Recovery."

[26] Castiglia and Hendler, "Introduction," xxxiv; Griffin, "The Washingtonian Revival," 70–73.

individual salvation and human perfectibility to encourage 'fallen' drinkers to reform themselves and each other."[27] In this sense, the Washingtonian Society is an early predecessor of AA, founded nearly a century later.

Wallace readers will no doubt mark the echoes of Don Gately's experience in AA in Whitman's personal writing on attending a Washingtonian meeting:

> This man gave his "experience," descanted in enthusiastic terms on the great blessing the temperance cause had been to him. He was a very uncouth speaker. Yet, how all the boundaries of taste, all the laws of conventional usage, are leaped over, in oratory, by deep feeling and ardent sincerity. Every hearer in the room, assuredly, was thrilled to the heart by portions of this uneducated man's remarks. For our own part, we were never more interested in our life.[28]

For Wallace, the "ardent sincerity" that Whitman attributes to the speaker in this moment would become a worthy aesthetic and, indeed, therapeutic goal for fiction in the late twentieth century. Wallace's theory of fiction can also be heard in Franklin's anger toward the impulse of many of current reform movements to stand in judgment:

> The pure and virtuous cast scorn upon such as I have been, and as thousands now are. But oh, could they look into the innermost recesses of our hearts, and see what spasms of pain – what important attempts to make issue with what appears to be our destiny – what fearful dreams – what ghastly phantoms of worse than hellish imagination – what of all this resides, time and again, in our miserable bosoms – then, I know, that scorn would be changed to pity. It is not well to condemn men for their frailties. Let us rather own our common bond of weakness, and endeavor to fortify each other in good conduct and in true righteousness, which is charity for the errors of our kind.[29]

The capacity of fiction to represent "the innermost recesses of our hearts" was one such capacity called into question by the postmodern turn toward irony and metafiction. Reacting to these developments, Adam Kelly identifies Wallace as spearheading what he terms as New Sincerity, in which "The author and reader really do exist, which is to say they are not simply *implied*, not primarily to be understood as rhetorical constructions or immortalized placeholders. The text's existence depends not only on a writer but also on a particular reader at a particular place and time."[30] This strategy was actualized in a variety of ways, including the construction of

---

[27] Ibid.   [28] Whitman, *Journalism*, 91. Qtd. in Castiglia and Hendler, "Introduction," xxxv.
[29] Whitman, *Franklin Evans*, 55–56.   [30] Kelly, "New Sincerity," 206.

an ontologically ambiguous authorial presence through his endnotes in *Infinite Jest.*[31]

In its apparent straightforwardness and effort "to endorse and instantiate single-entendre principles," *Franklin Evans* could thus stand in for the fictionalized ideal of the "form of the novel in place before even the rules of realism were fully formulated," which Andrew Hoberek notes was attractive to authors like Wallace who were invested in developing a so-called "post-postmodern novel."[32] As was the consensus among critics of *Franklin Evans*, the novel certainly risks, as Wallace lauds, "the yawn, the rolled eyes, the cool smile, the nudged ribs, the parody of gifted ironists, the 'Oh, how *banal.*' To risk accusations of sentimentality, melodrama. Of overcredulity. Of softness".[33] However, shot through the didacticisms and clichés that constitute the novel are innuendos and double entendres that would later become a hallmark of his poetry. As Warner points out, "when he is talking about alcohol in *Franklin Evans* Whitman often seems to be thinking about something else."[34] For Whitman, masking his exact intention to connect with the (male) reader in his poetry, as well as through this addiction and recovery novel, was the very mechanism by which he could construct the queer intimacies that were socially and politically foreclosed during his lifetime.

The evidence of this development is both contextually present in Whitman's biographical engagement with the Washingtonian Society and textually present in *Franklin Evans*. Whitman was "only an occasion drinker who apparently never consumed to inebriation."[35] Instead, we can see a hint of something more motivating his interest in the temperance movement following his description of Washingtonian parades, where Whitman describes "a company of fine looking young firemen [who] variefied the experience with a temperance glee."[36] Finding even more descriptions of these firemen and other men in Whitman's journalism at such meetings in the same month, Castiglia and Hendler note further that his fascination with Washingtonian parades "[give] a glimpse of the 'adhesive' enjoyment of male beauty that would later inspire the [queer]

---

[31] See Aubry, *Reading as Therapy*, 97–126.

[32] Wallace, "Unibus," *SFT*, 81; Hoberek, "After David Foster Wallace," 220.

[33] Wallace, "Unibus," *SFT*, 8; For a litany of negative reviews describing *Franklin Evans* as banal schmaltz, see "Introduction," xxxviii–xl.

[34] Warner, "Whitman Drunk," 31.

[35] Hendler and Castiglia, "Introduction," xxxii. Citing the biography Holloway, *Free and Lonesome Heart*, 28.

[36] Whitman, *Journalism*, 91; quoted in Castiglia and Hendler, "Introduction," xxxv.

poems of *Calamus*."[37] A young Whitman attended these meetings in part to listen to "dirty" stories, including same-sex encounters; in this sense, Washingtonian meetings were a counterintuitive prelude to Whitman later immersing himself fully in the Bohemian lifestyle concentrated in bars and taverns, like Pfaff's basement beer cellar at 647 Broadway.[38]

Wallace was sensitive to the potential for and danger of entertainment in AA storytelling, particularly as it impacts the process of empathic understanding. As the narrator asserts,

> Again, *Identify* means empathize. Identifying, unless you've got a stake in Comparing, isn't very hard to do, here. Because if you sit up front and listen hard, all the speakers' stories of decline and fall and surrender are basically alike, and like your own: fun with Substance, then very gradually less fun, then significantly less fun.[39]

Indeed, with temperance fiction making up an astonishing 12 percent of all novels published in the 1930s, Castiglia and Hendler, calling on previous work by James Hart, explain that their effect was as much to "[titillate] audiences with immorality" as it was to provide tidy morals.[40] Yet the editors at the *New World* understood well that maintaining, or elevating, their reputation meant setting certain expectations that no doubt impacted the writing and reception of *Franklin Evans*, asserting that their "ample pages are unsoiled by profane or improper jests, vulgar allusions, or irreligious sentiments."[41] Though close readers of *Franklin Evans* can quickly identify all these so-called licentious components in Whitman's novel, it was nonetheless strategically advertised as a novel "written expressly for the NEW WORLD, by one of the best Novelists in the country, with a view to aid the great work of Reform, and rescue Young Men from the demon of Intemperance."[42] This dynamic required Whitman to begin developing his poetic craft of writing with multiple imagined audiences and intentions at play.

In the novel, the subject of alcohol addiction and its attendant settings permits Whitman to fictionalize an almost entirely masculine world – not entirely dissimilar from *Jest*'s Enfield Tennis Academy – and "ubiquitous homoeroticism – if not overt homosexuality."[43] Franklin's descent notably

---

[37] Castiglia and Hendler, "Introduction," xxxv.
[38] Levin and Whitley, "Bohemianism," 136–45. For more on the relationship between emerging discourses on sexuality and temperance, see Moon, *Disseminating Whitman*, 19–23.
[39] Wallace, *IJ*, 345.   [40] Castiglia and Hendler, "Introduction," xxx.
[41] Mott, *A History of American Magazines*, 361; quoted in Castiglia and Hendler, "Introduction," xxviii.
[42] Castiglia and Hendler, "Introduction," xxviii.   [43] Ibid., xxiii.

begins with the queer invitation from Colby to "go out and cruise a little," and the narrative continues to be structured around intense, homoerotic bonds between Franklin and the men he meets.[44] Routinely saved by these relationships with economically stable men, the consequences of his intemperance and homoerotic excess are often displaced, with an astonishing degree of cruelty, onto the novel's female, Native, and African American characters – a prioritizing of "white male positionality" over a racialized other that Colton Saylor and Samuel Cohen have noted in Wallace's work as well.[45] In one representative example, after securing a release from prison in fairly unbelievable fashion and signing a temperance pledge, Franklin is out for a walk and stops "to admire some rare plants that stood in pots" when "a middle-aged gentleman came out of the entrance, and saluting me courteously, entered into conversation."[46] This "somewhat lonely" bachelor and slave-owner named Bourne "brought out some excellent wine, before we parted, and we finished a couple bottles together [. . .] and only allowed me to depart under a strict promise, that I would visit him again on the morrow." Within the space of two pages,

> so intimate did we at length become, and so necessary to one another's comfort, that I took up residence in his house [. . .]. Bourne and I, during the day, were much of the time together, and night always found us over a bottle of wine [. . . The] occasions were not a few wherein I was forced to have assistance, in order to reach my chamber.[47]

The queer subtext of this relationship is hardly hidden but must be displaced through dramatic plot devices. During one such binge, Franklin decides to marry one of Bourne's "Creole" slaves, Mary. Filled with immediate regret, Franklin overtly courts a white mistress who demands that he purchase Mary's brother as a sign of Franklin's affection. This unconscionable show of devotion to his mistress achieves the intended goal of enraging Mary and initiating an elaborate murder-suicide plot that leaves Franklin himself unscathed.

The end result of such maneuvers is a strange novel that hardly fulfills what we would expect from Wallace's fantasy of a pre-realist, sincerely written addiction novel. Taking up reviewers' scoring of the novel as "wobbly" and "incoherent," Hendler and Castiglia persuasively argue that "the novel's ruptures reflect central cultural ideologies that, in the state of

---

[44] Whitman, *Franklin Evans*, 27.
[45] Saylor, "Loosening the Jar," 121; see also Cohen, "Whiteness."
[46] Whitman, *Franklin Evans*, 77.   [47] Ibid., 79.

emergence, were themselves 'incoherent,' even conflicted."[48] Especially relevant for contemporary readers of Wallace, Michael Denning writes of such populist moralizing literature of the 1840s that "questions about the sincerity of their purported beliefs or the adequacy of their political proposals are less interesting than questions about the narrative embodiment of their political ideologies."[49] Whether in its "incoherent" account of the ideological formation of sexuality, or indeed the other primary ideological formations that the novel takes up, such as nation building or speculative commerce, *Franklin Evans* and its fractured protagonist in recovery ultimately share much with the postmodernist ethos with which Wallace wrestled in the 1990s. This point is especially necessary to underscore as Wallace critics begin to appreciate Whitman's influence on his fictional conception of maximalism, sentimental posthumanism and, indeed, sincerity itself.

By way of conclusion, we might return to Wallace's intent to reaffirm writing, specifically in the form of a physically demanding, encyclopedic novel, as an act of (therapeutic) communication between the (male) author and the (male) reader. Anticipating this aesthetic urgency by over a century, Whitman similarly conceived of the book as a contact point between reader and author: "Camerado! This is no book / Who touches this, touches a man; / (Is it night? Are we here alone?)/ It is I you hold, and who holds you; / I spring from the pages into your arms."[50] As a Wallace reader, we might see this as a familiar description of the book as a material, physical exchange between author figure and reader. However, given this contextual understanding of *Franklin Evans*, we can see Whitman's appeal was equally expressive of a minority and marginalized queer experience, if not subversive precisely in its ability to enlarge this queer experience as imagistic of the nation itself. As *Franklin Evans* is but one example, Whitman's poetic double entendres would allow him to be understood by some (gay, male) readers, and missed by others who would censor his work through obscenity laws or, more seriously, persecute him for his sexuality.[51] Thus, reading into Whitman's words quoted earlier, we see not the universalizing and nostalgic ethos of bookish intimacy, but quite the opposite. We see the book as a desperate call into the future, where two

---

[48] Castiglia and Hendler, "Introduction," xl.
[49] Denning, *Mechanic Accents*, 103; quoted in Castiglia and Hendler, "Introduction," xl.
[50] Whitman, "So Long!," *The Portable Walt Whitman*, 235.
[51] For more on Whitman and obscenity laws, see Erickson, "Erotica."

men – ("Is it night? Are we here alone?") – can actualize an intimacy socially foreclosed in their historical present.

Is it a stretch to say that Wallace's fiction is likewise a desperate call into the future where two men can actualize their intimacy together? Even as his novelistic strategy shares so much with Whitman's, significant obstacles may prevent Wallace readers from recognizing this encounter as intimate or erotic as such. Yes, a number of queer, and potentially queer, characters populate Wallace's fiction. For example, Sara Ahmed's four queer figures of rebellion appear across Wallace's fiction. The "granola cruncher" in "B.I. #20" recalls Ahmed's feminist killjoy who poses a threat to the speaker not only because she "might not be happily affected by the objects that are supposed to cause happiness but that [her] failure to be happy is read as sabotaging the happiness of others."[52] One can draw connections as well to Ahmed's unhappy queer ("Lyndon" in *Girl With Curious Hair*), the melancholy migrant (Rémy Marathe in *Infinite Jest*), and the numerous radical revolutionaries in Wallace's fiction who refuse to align their desires with the collective order (most notably John and even Hal Incandenza in *Jest*). Yet these representations often appear threatening to the narrative – a threat diffused with elbow-nudging, homophobic jokes, as we see in the queer couplings of Orin Incandenza and the cross-dressing Hugh/Helen Steeply, the oiled guru Lyle and James Incandenza, or even Don Gately with multiple wraiths. Queering Wallace offers the vocabulary to critique these representations. So too, does it offer a way of understanding Wallace's entanglement, not only with Whitman but also with a longer, queer history of addiction narratives. Situating Wallace in the context of this history can delimit the fundamental queerness of his writer-reader relationship and the therapeutic function it promises.

[52] Ahmed, *Promise*, 66.

PART IV

Systems

CHAPTER 26

Infinite Jest *as Opiate Fiction*

Alexander Moran

Critics have discussed drug addiction in *Infinite Jest* as a metaphor for broader philosophical issues regarding freedom, popular entertainment and capitalism.[1] This is unsurprising, as Jacques Derrida notes that drugs and drug addiction raise "a number of highly philosophical concepts, concepts that philosophy is obliged to consider as priorities: 'freedom,' 'dependency,' 'pleasure' or 'jouissance.'"[2] Indeed, Wallace himself noted to David Lipsky that "the book isn't supposed to be about *drugs*, getting off drugs. Except as the fact that drugs are kind of a metaphor for the sort of addictive continuum that I think has to do with how we as a culture relate to things that are alive."[3] However, as criticism moves away from Wallace's own definitions of his work, the historical context of *Infinite Jest* is increasingly coming into focus. For instance, Marshall Boswell defines the "Wallace Effect," referring to the ways in which Wallace's pronouncements about his literary context have distorted our understanding of literary history, and seeks to correct these misinterpretations.[4] Mary K. Holland points out that, while many parts of the novel "were reasonable exaggerations of the cultural threats and technological developments of the 1990s [. . .] twenty years later, however, the novel feels quaint."[5] Similarly, Lee Konstantinou argues that "For all the efforts to suggest that Wallace predicted dimensions of Internet culture, it might be most accurate to say [. . .] that Wallace was a figure who reached his peak influence in the late 1990s."[6] As well as these studies, Daniella Joffe notes in her discussion of *The Broom of the System* that there is a growing critical turn in which critics seek "to decouple Wallace's writing from the largely ahistorical, universalist discourse that has surrounded the author since his death."[7] Wallace's

---

[1] For instance, see Aubry, *Reading as Therapy*, or Den Dulk, "Beyond."
[2] Derrida, "The Rhetoric of Drugs," 228.   [3] Lipsky, *Although of Course*, 81.
[4] Boswell, *The Wallace Effect*, 1.   [5] Holland, "*Infinite Jest*," 134.
[6] Konstantinou, "Wallace's 'Bad' Influence," 59.   [7] Joffe, "The Last Word," 155.

depictions of drugs, and of opiate addiction in particular, are more than just metaphors; they reflect a specific historical moment, and are part of a long-standing literary tradition regarding drug use.

In 1996, the year *Infinite Jest* was published, Purdue Pharma made the opiate analgesic OxyContin available as a prescription drug. Partly as a result of the availability and overprescription of this drug, 2016 saw the average life expectancy of Americans falling for the first time since the AIDS crisis, and 2017 opiate-related deaths far exceeded the record for fatalities from car accidents in a single year.[8] *Infinite Jest* was therefore published at a key moment in what is now known as the opioid crisis, as is evident in the encyclopedic knowledge that many characters have of brand-name prescription drugs, and indeed the many who are recovering from opioid abuse. In this chapter, I offer a materialist reading of Wallace's engagement with opiate use, and trace the connections between Wallace's text and a literary tradition I name "opiate fiction." As Derrida notes, "the concept of drugs supposes an instituted and an institutional definition: a history is required, and a culture, conventions, evaluations, norms, an entire network of intertwined discourses, a rhetoric, whether explicit or elliptical."[9] Wallace's novel reflects the new institutions that developed around opiates in the 1990s, and, in the near future in which it is set, a new rhetoric for opiate use has developed in response to their commercialization under late capitalism. Jeffrey Nealon accounts for this late-capitalist moment – which he renames "just-in-time-capitalism" – as being defined by an "intensification of existing biopolitical resources."[10] Wallace's text depicts just such an intensification of, rather than a departure from, the three defining features of opiate fiction that have accumulated over the last 200 years: chronic pain, the criminalization of the addict, and the gradual commercialization of synthetic opioids. I develop this argument by discussing Wallace's work as part of a history that includes the writings of Thomas De Quincey, Frank Norris' early short stories and William Burroughs's *Junky*. In doing so, I situate some of the less-frequently noted aspects of Don Gately's existence within this history, particularly regarding the onerous conditions of his probation.

Opiates have appeared in literature since at least *The Odyssey*, and, as Peter Sloane suggests, the Lotus Eaters in Homer's epic may be a model for the fateful narcotizing effects of the *Infinite Jest* film cartridge.[11] In his

---

[8] Katz and Sanger-Katz, "'Numbers"; DeWeerdt, "Tracing."
[9] Derrida, "The Rhetoric of Drugs," 229.   [10] Nealon, *Post-Postmodernism*, 31.
[11] Sloane, *Wallace and the Body*, 152.

history of writers and drug use, Marcus Boon notes how opiates are found in the work of Edmund Spenser, Geoffrey Chaucer and Shakespeare's *Othello*.[12] As well as the classics, heroin plays a central role in Nelson Algren's *The Man with the Golden Arm* (1949), William Burroughs' *Junky* (1953) and *Naked Lunch* (1959), the Vietnam War fiction of Tim O'Brien, the memoirs of Iceberg Slim (cited by Irvine Welsh as an influence on *Trainspotting* [1993]), Hubert Selby Jr.'s 1978 novel *Requiem for a Dream*, and L. Ron Hubbard's shlocky and enormous ten-book series *Project Earth* (1985–87).[13] There have also been novels since *Infinite Jest*, such as Tao Lin's *Taipei* (2013), that further develop the relationship between opiates and capitalism in a post-OxyContin world. While there have been many texts focusing on opiates and addiction, Boon asserts that "there has been no major advance in the narcotic literature since the 1950s – or even the 1930s. The same genres, confession, addiction, and disintoxication narratives, continue to be written."[14] *Infinite Jest* is definitively representative of such a "disintoxication" narrative, which, as Boon points out, has been described many times before. However, Boon's overarching description of such texts misses the differences between them. What has changed are the material conditions in which these drugs have been packaged, sold, distributed and consumed. Consequently, the point here is not to find all the citations to opiates throughout literary history and connect them to Wallace's text; rather, the focus is on the material context of Wallace's work. By depicting opiate use so extensively, Wallace not only engages with how late twentieth-century Americans consume and discuss drugs, but also with a literary tradition, that has catalogued the changes in attitudes and policies to drugs over the course of modernity. In doing so, *Infinite Jest* can be seen to reach back to some of these tropes – namely, as noted earlier, chronic pain, the criminalization of the addict, and the gradual commercialization of synthetic opioids – and also to advance this tradition by updating many of its features to the realities of opiate use in the United States in the 1990s.

To begin with the history of chronic pain and opiate addiction, this is a clear feature of Wallace's text. Gately is advised by the older AA members that while he may now feel "sober pain," at least this was "pain with a purpose."[15] Indeed, Gately's heroism toward the end of the novel is framed as resisting opiates; it is precisely his ability to experience intense, chronic pain, to deny himself the painkilling drugs that his doctor

---

[12] Boon, *The Road of Excess*, 19.   [13] Welsh, "Up From the Street."
[14] Boon, *Road of Excess*, 84.   [15] Ibid., 446.

recommends, that Wallace holds up as being admirable. How chronic pain is defined and coped with is one of the key themes of the novel, and this connects Wallace's text to a longer tradition. To return to the earliest instance of opiate fiction, Boon notes that Thomas De Quincey's *Confessions of an English Opium Eater* (1821) "invented the concept of recreational drug use." He clarifies that De Quincey was not the first person to take opium recreationally, but that he was "the first person to write about it in this way."[16] As De Quincey himself proclaims, "I have indulged in it to an excess, not yet *recorded* of any other man."[17] The story of opiate fiction, then, begins in the early nineteenth century, and it must be emphasized that opium and its derivatives are, at root, painkillers, and so in each era of opiate fiction, writers cite different forms of chronic pain. De Quincey cites opium as the only successful remedy for an unrelenting stomach ailment, and Algren's main character, Frankie Machine, becomes addicted after being treated with morphine for a shrapnel wound in World War II. However, in *Infinite Jest*, opiates are rarely a means of escaping from physical pain; indeed, one character describes them as a means of treating "psychic pain."[18] The young woman who spent her childhood watching her father rape her disabled sister notes that she experiences psychic pain, and that she tried to "numb it with opiates."[19] If, from its earliest moments, opiate fiction has been concerned with chronic pain, Wallace inverts this tradition; in a world where all is "numbed," the heroism that Gately portrays is of someone who can endure chronic pain, and not resort to opiates as a means of numbing or escape. Moreover, Wallace transfers this pain from the physical to the mental; *Infinite Jest* is replete with attempts to numb or escape from psychic anguish, whether through opiates, tennis, entertainment or other means.

That said, Wallace also differentiates his drug addicts in particular by foregrounding how their compulsive behaviors are othered, through a combination of classism, racialization, and criminalization. Indeed, this feature fits *Infinite Jest* into a broader history of opiate fiction, as this genre has charted the gradual criminalization of the addict. Eve Sedgwick argues that throughout the twentieth century, habitual behavior has increasingly become synonymous with notions of addiction, compulsion and a lack of self-control.[20] The reasons for this moralism are essentially bound to class and race; as David Courtwright points out, the early twentieth century witnessed "a shift in the addict population, from one that was

---

[16] Ibid., 37.   [17] De Quincey, *Confessions*, 2.   [18] Wallace, *IJ*, 373.   [19] Ibid.
[20] Sedgwick, *Tendencies*, 138–39.

predominantly middle-class, female, and medical to one that was lower-class, male, and nonmedical, [a change which] served as the critical precondition for the criminalization of American narcotic policy."[21] In Frank Norris' early short stories, published in *Wave* magazine around the turn of the twentieth century, one can see the early signs of this moral panic. Karen Keely discusses how a fear of the almost certainly apocryphal phenomenon of "white slavery" – the imprisonment of white women by Chinese immigrants in opium dens – plays a key part in Norris' stories "Bandy Callaghan's Girl" (1894) and "The Third Circle" (1897).[22] Partly fueled by the Chinese Exclusion Act of 1882 – which was not repealed until 1943 – Norris' stories reflect a widespread moment of racial panic. Indeed, Norris connects opium to a foreign threat, and this trait has continued throughout opiate fiction. Racialized othering is central to how Wallace depicts opioid addiction; heroin is purchased by Bobby C., Yrstruly, and Poor Tony Krause from a man called Dr. Wo in Chinatown, who provides the Drano that kills C. One of the characters who tries to tempt Gately out of his stoicism at the end of the novel is a Pakistani doctor, who emphasizes his "Moslem" heritage as he tries to tempt Gately into taking opioid painkillers.[23] Perhaps most obviously, one of the final words in the main narrative – in which Gately and Gene Fackelmann are higher than ever on Dilaudid – is the racial slur "Oriental," which Gately uses to describe one of Dr. Wo's henchmen.[24] The racialized othering of drug use has been a longtime feature of opiate fiction, and in his depictions of Dr. Wo and Gately's doctor, Wallace continues this tradition. *Infinite Jest* therefore represents a modern world of drug addiction, one defined by the commercialization of addiction, but also continues to perpetuate a long-held literary trope – an orientalist idea of who provides such drugs. In othering those who provide these drugs, Wallace's novel displays a troubling racial dynamic regarding who controls the supply of drugs, and, interestingly, this racial dynamic is evident in many works of opiate fiction dating back to the nineteenth century. Wallace therefore not only pushes forward the history of opiate fiction but also continues to draw on representations from earlier instances of this tradition. That Dr. Wo is the head of an organized-crime syndicate and that the Pakistani doctor is a medical physician also connects this orientalism to the other aspects of opiate fiction – namely, the criminalization of the addict, and the medicalization of addiction seen in late capitalism.

[21] Courtwright, *Dark Paradise*, xi.   [22] Keely, "Sexual Slavery."   [23] Wallace, *IJ*, 887.
[24] Ibid., 981.

The criminalization of the addict is another trope that can be traced back to the beginning of the twentieth century. Partly due to the racial panic seen in Norris' stories (which helped lead to Prohibition), America passed the Harrison Act in 1915, beginning the criminalization of addiction that persists to this day. Perhaps the finest exploration of this transition can be found in William Burroughs' *Junky*. His protagonist, William Lee, largely based on himself, is arrested in New Orleans, and decides to leave for Mexico. He leaves with a parting shot of anger that stands out in a text largely devoid of such moralizing:

> When I jumped bail and left the States, the heat on junk already looked like something new and special. Initial symptoms of nationwide hysteria were clear. Louisiana passed a law making it a crime to be a drug addict. Since no place or time is specified and the term "addict" is not clearly defined, no proof is necessary or even relevant under a law so formulated ... This is police-state legislation penalizing a state of being.[25]

This scene in Burroughs' text captures a transitional moment in the history of opiate fiction, whereby the addict has been criminalized. In *Infinite Jest*, Wallace makes the relationship between addiction and criminality clearest in how characters such as Gately, Tony Kraus, Gene Fackelmann and others are seen to rob, make forgeries and assault people to acquire drugs. However, what is perhaps most insidious about the criminalization of the addict in *Infinite Jest* is the administrative terror inflicted upon those in recovery, a development of what Burroughs discussed forty years before the publication of Wallace's novel:

> Once every couple months now, still, he has to put on his brown dress slacks and slightly irregular green sportcoat from Brighton Budget Large 'N Tall Menswear and take the commuter rail up to selected District Court venues on the North Shore and meet with his various PDs and POs and caseworkers and sometimes appear briefly up in front of Judges and Review Boards to review the progress of his sobriety and reparations.[26]

The criminalization of the addict creates a world where, to borrow Burroughs' term, Gately's "state of being" is policed. The reason for Gately needing to clean the disgusting Shattuck house showers is that he will "be paying court-scheduled restitution until well into his thirties if he stays straight, and needs the work."[27] Wallace's novel is reflective of a new

---

[25] Burroughs, *Junky*, 140.   [26] Wallace, *IJ*, 462.   [27] Ibid., 436.

administrative policing of the body in late capitalism, and therefore it can be seen to develop this aspect of opiate fiction.[28]

As represented by the Pakistani doctor, the history of opiate fiction also demonstrates the shifting role of the medical profession. This relationship is evident in both the European history of opiate fiction – De Quincey and Samuel Coleridge received their opium from a doctor – and after heroin was first created in 1898, it was marketed by Bayer Pharmaceuticals in the United States as a wonder drug for many everyday ailments.[29] There was also a period after the invention of the hypodermic needle when it was mistakenly believed that injecting opiates rendered them nonaddictive. Burroughs describes the role of "croakers," the doctors who write morphine prescriptions for addicts.[30] The modern iteration is the "pill mill," where opioids such as OxyContin, like heroin before it, are provided by exploitative doctors who use their credentials to make a lot of money. The absurd marketing of OxyContin sounds like Wallacean satire, as after the drug's release in 1996, Purdue enticed healthcare professionals to begin prescribing it with "branded promotional items such as OxyContin fishing hats, stuffed plush toys, and music compact discs."[31] *Infinite Jest* emphasizes the importance of medical professionals to addiction. One particularly notable scene is when a narrator describes the role of "Boston AA's Sergeant at Arms," who "stood casually checking its cuticles in the astringent fluorescence of pharmacies that took forged Talwin scrips for a hefty surcharge," where "strung-out nurses who financed their own cages' maintenance with stolen pharmaceutical samples, in [. . .] the storefront offices of stooped old chain-smoking MD's whose scrip-pads were always out and who needed only to hear 'pain' and see cash."[32] When in hospital, Gately remembers "the strung-out nurses he X'd and copped samples from," once again showing the relationship of addiction to medical professionals.[33] Courtwright notes: "Prior to 1900 most addiction resulted from the activity of physicians; it was, to use a shorthand term, iatrogenic," meaning an illness caused by medical treatment.[34] Wallace suggests that the relationship between unscrupulous physicians and addiction is as inextricable as ever. What is specifically new in the world of the novel, though, is the

---

[28] The ever-increasing criminalization and policing of addicts connects opiate fiction to what Michel Foucault calls biopolitics, which he situates as beginning during a similar period of the nineteenth century to opiate fiction. Foucault suggests that this was a period where "the biological came under State control" (*Society Must Be Defended*, 240). Opiate fiction is an interesting means to chart the development of biopolitical policies in American culture.

[29] Booth, *Opium*, 77.   [30] Burroughs, *Junky*, 24–25.   [31] Van Zee, "Oxycontin," 222.
[32] Wallace, *IJ*, 359.   [33] Ibid., 911.   [34] Courtwright, *Dark Paradise*, 2.

explosion of synthetic opioids, which has led to a commercialization of pain.

While Stefano Ercolino argues that the psychopharmacological language of *Infinite Jest* suggests its encyclopedic nature, this vocabulary misses the details of what Wallace cites, and the drugs that his characters use to treat their psychic pain.[35] The psychopharmacological intake of Wallace's characters is based on a commercialization of pain, both physical and mental, in contemporary America. In a world where even time is commodified, Wallace presciently imagined a future where the treatment of pain produces a new market. This commercialization of pain is represented through the new language of opioid addiction, which is demonstrative of the novel's publication at the pivotal moment when America's opioid crisis was about to worsen exponentially. It also points to the commercialization of pain as being one of the reasons for this opiate crisis. Nearly every drug that is sought by those addicted has been produced by a private company. Most obviously, Gately, Mike Pemulis and Joelle all seek and consume pharmaceutical-grade drugs (Gately opioids, Joelle cocaine and Pemulis anything). Gately cites the trust he has in the pills that he takes because of "Sanofi-Winthrop Co.'s very-soon beloved trademark."[36] He also moves to Demerol from Percocets, as it is "easier to get, being the treatment of medical choice for mind-bending post-operative pain."[37] These synthetic opioids and the brand names of the companies who make them become symbols of excellence to addicts, not to patients. Moreover, the language of addiction has shifted from the street names "smack," "brown" and "dope" to the veritable encyclopedia of possible opioids, of varying strengths, that are available in ONAN. Indeed, in Wallace's imagined future, ONAN has formed its own laws to codify these varying strengths, such as "the Continental Controlled Substance Act of YTMP," which outlines "ONANDEA's hierarchy of analgesics/antipyretics/anxiolytics." These laws define the drug-classes from "Category-II through Category-VI, with C-II's (e.g. Dilaudid, Demerol) being judged the heaviest w/r/t dependence and possible abuse, down to C-VTs that are about as potent as a kiss on the forehead from Mom."[38] One of the first undertakings of the new nation is to redefine the drugs many of the characters are addicted to, which has the unintended consequence of charting exactly which drugs should be most sought after.

---

[35] Ercolino, *The Maximalist Novel.*   [36] Wallace, *IJ*, 891.   [37] Ibid.   [38] Ibid., 984.

Another aspect of this commercialization can be seen in what these trademarks are attached to; specifically, the fourteen real pharmaceutical companies that Wallace cites as producing these drugs.[39] To focus on just a few, SmithKline Beecham is a name that resulted from a merger in 1989 (and is now GlaxoSmithKline after another merger), Wyeth-Aherst and Parke-Davis have since been purchased by Pfizer, and Du Pont Pharmaceuticals has become DowDuPont, for a brief time the world's largest chemical company, which has now split again.[40] The point of noting all these mergers is to show the multinational nature of the commercialization of pain, and the rapid growth of the industry before Wallace's novel was published, a pattern which has continued since. His focus on listing all these companies reflects a transition in how drugs are made, packaged and sold. In the world he depicts, addicts rather than patients place trust in drug trademarks, which have come to saturate the whole of society. In this transition to a culture defined by chronic psychic pain, capital has responded with a market to treat it. The near-future America is shown to be replete with opioids, and a new vocabulary of drugs and addiction has developed.

While Boon asserts that there have been few changes in "narcotic literature" since the 1930s, what this analysis of *Infinite Jest* shows is that what has changed are the material conditions in which these drugs are consumed. Moreover, although the type of pain that opioids are used to treat and the ways that addicts are policed and monitored may be similar throughout the history of opiate fiction, the scope and detail of these features of the genre have radically changed in the last fifty years. *Jest* stands as a document of a crucial moment in the history of America's relationship with opioids. When looked at in the context of the history of opiate fiction, the novel reflects the new institutions and rhetoric that defined drug use in America in the late twentieth century, and Wallace advances, inverts and complicates the central tenets of this literary tradition. Finally, reading *Jest* from a historical-materialist perspective allows us to account for how it reflects a specific moment in the history of opiate use – namely, the beginning of the opioid crisis in the United States, which from 1999 to

[39] These are Sandoz Pharmaceuticals, Bristol Laboratories, Knoll Laboratories, Sanofi-Winthrop Laboratories, SmithKline Beecham Pharmaceuticals, Marion Merrell, Dow Du Pont Pharmaceuticals, Wyeth-Aherst Labs, Parke-Davis Pharmaceuticals, Pfizer-Roerig Roche Inc., Schwarz Pharma, Kremers Urban, Inc., McNeil Pharmaceuticals and Lilly Pharmaceuticals.
[40] Abbott, "Merger"; Matthews, "A Different Dow."

2018 claimed approximately 450,000 American lives.[41] In this regard, *Infinite Jest* – despite its futuristic setting, absurdist humor, and byzantine form – is a deeply social novel, which can be plumbed for further insights into how opiates and other drugs have spread throughout contemporary America.

[41] The Centers for Disease Control and Prevention, "Understanding the Epidemic."

CHAPTER 27

David Foster Wallace and Racial Capitalism

Colton Saylor

In a 2006 interview with Ostap Karmodi, David Foster Wallace shared his fears of the consumer-capitalist-driven future facing the United States:

> My personal belief is that because technology and economic logic has gotten so sophisticated, cruelties can be perpetrated now that would have been unimaginable two or three hundred years ago. Therefore we are under more of a moral obligation to try very very very hard to develop compassion and mercy and empathy.[1]

Wallace's warning embodies what many have identified as his greater literary project: to contest the affective gaps induced by hyper-consumerism and produce empathetic narratives capable of reminding one "what it is to be a fucking human being."[2] This "technological and economic logic" references what the author sees as a "celebration of commercialism and consumerism and marketing that is not really balanced by any kind of shame."[3] This turn, which Wallace identifies as emerging in the 1980s and 1990s, coincides with the rise of a neoliberal economic order that thrives under the ability to sublimate exploitative practices with the outward appearance of mobility and freedom. In essence, what Frederic Jameson identifies as the logic of late capitalism, the ubiquitous yet undetectable capitalist logic that seeks to commoditize at the cost of the historical and the real, becomes anathema to our capacity to truly engage with one another, leaving open the possibility for new, "unimaginable" waves of exploitation.[4]

But if this 2006 interview is illustrative of his larger project against the alienating forces of late capitalism, it is also an encapsulation of Wallace's incapacity to imagine economic subjugation as simultaneously a matter of race. Just before his dire warning of late capital's "sophisticated" logic, Wallace explains:

---

[1] Karmodi, "Frightening Time."   [2] Ibid., 26.   [3] Ibid.   [4] Jameson, "Postmodernism."

And in some ways America has made progress in realizing as a culture for instance how terribly black Americans have been treated, how unfairly women have been treated [...] What you see in America right now, though, is yet another backlash. It's so expensive and so difficult to try to be fair to everybody, and it ends up with so much litigation and so many people howling for their rights, that many on the right wing and many in business simply want to throw up their hands and say "Fuck the whole thing and let's just go back to the state of Nature and war of all against all."[5]

Wallace's "backlash" echoes what we in a post-Trump United States recognize as a condemnation of "identity politics," a pragmatist-facing ideological movement that sees discrimination as ahistorical, singular events rather than entrenched cultural and national ways of doing business. While seemingly taking a critic's objective stance over this phenomenon, Wallace perpetuates a similar distancing between the late capitalist forces he recognizes as so harmful and the treatment of marginalized communities. As a result, the aforementioned backlash involves corporate America's resistance to the "expensive" and "difficult" process of social justice as opposed to that same economic logic's direct role in the racialization and continued subjugation of communities of color.

Pinpointing a comment made during an interview runs the risk of parsing too finely for any slippage in the author's empathetic purview and the racial realities it denies. But if his larger literary project is indeed about reclaiming a universal humanity from the jaws of consumerism, then that "human being" category, for Wallace, is untroubled and monolithic as opposed to socially constructed and influenced by racial discourse. With that in mind, his description of America's "progress" and its "backlash" becomes symptomatic of his understanding of late capitalism and its dangers, which seem separate to matters of racism and racial difference. In discussing the logic of capitalism writ large as already also a form of racist subjugation, I invoke what Cedric Robinson refers to as "racial capitalism." Influenced by the work of post-Apartheid South African intellectuals, Robinson introduces the term in *Black Marxism*, where he traces the origins of capitalism – the feudal systems of Europe – as relying upon racialized subaltern subjectivities through which the economy was able to function.[6] In an interview in *Perspectives on Anarchist Theory*, Robinson clarifies race's role in the accumulation of capital:

---

[5] Karmodi, "Frightening Time."

[6] For further reading on racial capitalism, including how more recent scholars have extended Robinson's work, see Melamed, *Represent*; Lowe, *Intimacies*; Johnson and Kelley, *Race Capitalism Justice*.

capital never develops according to pure market exigencies or rational calculus. Whatever the organization of capitalism may be and whoever constitutes its particular agencies, capitalism has a specific culture. As Aristotle first revealed, capital accumulation is essentially irrational. And as was the case in his time, race, ethnicity, and gender were powerful procedures for the conduct of accumulation and value appropriation.[7]

Per Robinson, the supposed complication of identity politics is in fact a foundational element of the capitalistic system. As such, those hardened racialized categories created through the perpetuation of racist discourse and white supremacy serve as cultural elements that influence the accumulation and circulation of capital.

A closer examination of key entries in Wallace's bibliography reveals his inability to include race as part of his critical calculations against the impacts of late capitalism, an absence that blunts his writing's political projects. Most telling across this examination is the author's refusal to interrogate how his own position as disaffected white critic of consumer capitalism is itself a product of racial capitalism's need for strict, racialized categories. Consequently, his discussions of late capital's horrors, which deny race's key role in the current economic order, are themselves perpetuations of the color-blind ideology needed to support racial capitalist discourse. Much has been said of Wallace's whiteness, from Samuel Cohen's astute overview of the writer's brief but telling literary encounters with racial others,[8] to Joel Roberts and Edward Jackson's critique of his New Sincerity as inherently white and male.[9] What remains to be seen is how this acknowledged discomfort with the realities of race and racism impacted what Wallace had to say about the scope of capitalism and our capacity to resist it.

Wallace's early non-fiction work, starting with his co-authored project *Signifying Rappers* (written with Mark Costello) in 1990, showcases his attempts to establish the narrative voice present in much of his celebrated essays: the inside-while-still-outside observer, the unwilling participant of mainstream social rituals with enough smarts to understand why one should be unwilling and enough empathy to see why others might be. In these expeditions, Wallace shows an intimate knowledge of the way capitalist logic fills in the invisible gaps behind seemingly carefree consumerism; at the same time, he demonstrates a misunderstanding of race's direct role in that same process.

---

[7] Robinson, *A Theory of Global Capitalism*, 7. [8] Cohen, "Whiteness."
[9] Roberts and Jackson, "White Guys."

In his attributed sections in *Rappers*, Wallace builds on rap's important function as a mirror to the lived realities of the Black community. Wallace – along with Costello – situates his examination of rap as Black art form from the edge of his own bubbled existence as white, male twenty-something living in post-busing Boston, which involved transporting students to other districts in the city in an effort to desegregate schools. But what begins as a clear acknowledgment of privilege, along with an apparent honest fascination with the inner workings of a cultural community, quickly becomes an opportunistic glance through an adjacent racial window into the capitalist anxieties of post-Reagan America. Wallace's interest in rap as it pertains to late capitalism has more to do with the unique cultural space from which it originates, one devoid of the white, "yuppie" hang-ups with consumerism and wealth. As the author himself reasons, "There's a real and marvelously unmeant beauty to the rap Scene's materialism, today. In no other music for no other audience can we see the Supply Side Republican vision of America's '80s so carefully decocted, rendered, *loved*."[10] In describing this love for the ideology behind rap's intimate relationship to consumerism, he writes, "What individuals really need and deserve most is the money to buy things that determine their 'class,' aka their 'face,' aka their freedom, aka their power, aka the degree of credulity and regard bestowed on them by one huge marching column that All Thinks Alike."[11] Here, Wallace presents one of his clearest descriptions of the same logic he references in his 2006 interview that opened this section. Crucial here is the fact that, according to the author, this consumerist logic supersedes race as a factor in manipulating the Black community. Many of his later concerns about the intersections of consumerism, human connection, art and sincerity come to bear here, but race only functions as an experimental space to think through these ideas. And that, for Wallace, is the point: Rap, and the Black experience from which it derives, offers a unique perspective into capitalism and consumer culture, an opportunity that the white listener would be wise to take, not to pass on the chance to see how capitalist logic has gone to work on *them*. Exploitation under capitalism, then, becomes the unifying factor behind the Us and Them of *Rappers*, the force that brings us to the "window" of racial difference. Wallace takes his idea of rap as synecdoche for the singular experience of the Black community too literally, thereby missing the way it also serves as a synecdoche for the movements of late capitalism and its inherent racist logic.

---

[10] Wallace, *SR*, 150 (emphasis in original).   [11] Ibid.

Commonly paired with *Rappers* in discussions of Wallace and race, "Ticket to the Fair" (later retitled "Getting Away from Already Being Pretty Much Away from It All") similarly demonstrates an awareness of race and space's connection. Also similar is the article's inability to conceive of that racialization as part and parcel to the unabashed consumerism that it targets for critique. Unique to "Ticket," however, is its divide between Wallace as East-Coast Outside Anthropologist and Wallace as Critic of Rampant Consumerism. Regarding the first voice, critics have called attention to the author's inability to observe without the aid of group binaries, what Cohen refers to as the essay's "hyper-attention to group identity, to Us vs Them."[12] Indeed, Wallace displays an awareness of the stratified hierarchy within the Illinois State Fair, made up of belittled carnies and city visitors, as well as more normative fair attendees. But in turning to depictions of the fair's gleeful participation in commerce, the author relies on discussions of spectacle and crowd mentality, critical turns that erase the observations of difference that he notes in other parts of the essay.

Part of what makes "Ticket" such a common launchpad for discussing Wallace and race is his observation deep into the article of the fair's inherent *whiteness*. When visiting the Twilight Ballroom, he takes in a clogging performance, a traditional folk dance that originated in Appalachia. As he observes the dance, Wallace takes in the space's racial aura: "There's an atmosphere in the room – not racist, but aggressively white. It's hard to describe – the atmosphere is the same at a lot of rural Midwest events. It is not like a black person who came in would be ill-treated; it's more like it would just never occur to a black person to come here."[13] Important here is the location of this observation, both in the fair itself and within Wallace's article. Triggering Wallace's race-consciousness is the cognitive dissonance induced by these white cloggers dancing to Aretha Franklin's "R-E-S-P-E-C-T." The author observes that "there's no hint of racial irony in the room; the song has been made this people's own, emphatically."[14] Similar to *Rappers*, the author's cues of racial difference arise only in matters of cultural production, where the Eurocentric clogging and Franklin's Afrocentric demand for equality create an easy contrast. But this attention only seems to last in the space created by the cloggers' performance and the un-ironic white spectacle that ensues, and while instructive in pointing to the passive racism at work in the construction of the tent's version of "Us," the scene

---

[12] Wallace, "Ticket", *SFT*, 49.　　[13] Ibid.　　[14] Ibid.

remains noticeably apart from Wallace's other observations of the fair as mass collective consumerism.

When the author does attempt to represent the phenomenon of late capital's grip on the Midwestern fairgoer, he does from the perspective as one of the mass, a positionality that simultaneously groups Wallace into that same collective whiteness of the Twilight Ballroom. As he and his companion navigate the fair's barrage of sensory overload, he relates a series of images in quick succession. The overstimulation of the fair's many attractions and commodities coincides with an inability to make sense of these same spectacles in any coherent, rational way. The author's observation in this same passage of three more African Americans among the sparse population of Black fairgoers is, tellingly, buried in this same overload of information: "Tottery Ronald McD. is working the crowd at Club Mickey D's 3-on-3 Hoops. Three of the six basketball players are black, the first I've seen since Mrs. Edgar's hired kids. Pygmy Goat Show at Goat Barn. Native Companion has zinc oxide on her nose. I'm sure we'll miss something."[15] Like the zinc oxide on his companion's nose, the Black attendees are one element within a stream of sights meant to work on the fairgoer's psyche. The author's brief attention to racial difference demonstrated in the Twilight Ballroom dissipates; instead, hyper-consumerism's spectacle of information blinds Wallace from connecting matters of racial difference with the fair's construction as a space for whiteness.

The author's final observation at the article's conclusion underscores this inability to relate capital with the construction of race. In submitting his final thesis on the fair's appeal, Wallace explains that "The faces in the sea of faces are like the faces of children released from their rooms [. . .] The real spectacle that draws us here is us."[16] Despite his attempts to differentiate himself from those Midwesterners that surround him, Wallace cannot help but group himself as part of the event's bigger "Us." To highlight the fair's ongoing fight for the attention and eventual business of each white attendee is to buy into that process's same efforts to erase the "problem" of race. Becoming a happy site for commerce here requires a safe place for whiteness to merely *be* without the antagonizing presence of racialized others. Without meaning to, Wallace falls for this phantasmagoria, the fair's ultimate trick: to censor the reality of race for the sake of good business.

These early failures to confront capitalism and its inherent connection to race help inform Wallace's fictional confrontations with late capital's

[15] Ibid., 44.   [16] Ibid., 54.

"sophisticated" logic. The most famous of these confrontations occurs in *Infinite Jest*, which takes place in a kind of late-capital wasteland. Much has been said of the novel's few characters of color and their distinctive narrative voice (see Shapiro's discussion of this in the next chapter), but said responses often focus on Wallace's mishandled treatment of race and dialect, and do so separately from its other more political critical targets. These criticisms hinge on the text's tendency to treat race as more a kind of communicative inconvenience as opposed to a societal marker of subjugation. To that point, as Jackson and Roberts argue, scenes such as Joelle's problematic meditation on the Black speaker's testimony at Cocaine Anonymous see race as a hindrance to identifying with the speaker, a hurdle meant to be navigated around in the quest for true, universal empathy – a universal empathy that, according to Jackson and Roberts, is decidedly white and male in perspective and ideology.[17]

Another of the novel's few direct mentions of race confirms this assimilative tendency: during the meeting between Marathe and Steely, the Québécois separatist asks, "And also why do they never send you into the field as yourself, Steeply? This is to say in appearance. The last time you were – what is it I hope to say – a Negro, for almost one year, no?," to which Steeply replies, "I was Haitian. Some negroid tendencies in the persona, maybe."[18] The dialogue paradoxically views race as both a performance – a costume used for camouflage – and a biologically essential characteristic. This episode, and the dialect-heavy "yrstruly" passage and other brief scenes of racialized difference, operate as found oddities in the larger, sterilized backdrop that is the Organization of North American Nations. That is, *Jest* sees race as one of many forms of identity politics that one must navigate to assume a more authentic, sincere mode of humanity; however, as the "negroid" example illustrates, this particular brand of difference lacks any context as to its societal construction or larger role in the buttressing of power.

In the novel's representation of consumer capitalism run amok, Wallace eschews matters of difference in favor of the universal. Such a move seeks to underscore capitalism's totality as a power regime, but it does so at the

---

[17] In a footnote to their article, Jackson and Roberts observe that this same assimilationist turn plays out in Wallace's "Authority and American Usage," in which he instructs his African American students to take up Standard Written English in order to participate in larger national conversations. Again, we see Wallace's complicated understanding of racism: a displayed knowledge of discrimination in standard (white) discourse coupled with a reluctant acceptance of that same discrimination masked in the form of pragmatism.

[18] Wallace, *IJ*, 126–27.

cost of seeing how such hegemony actually works through the crystalliza-
tion of racial categories. The book's temporality – that is, its usage of the
subsidized corporate calendar system – seeks to cohere all of society under
the banner of hyper-commercialization and loss of experienced time.
Stefan Hirt connects this new calendar system with the postmodern
condition of presentism, a constant emphasis on the now at the expense
of any real temporal teleology. He reasons that, in the world of *Jest*, "each
year no longer denotes a succession in time from one fixed point in the
past to an end point in the future, but simply a product of consumption
unrelated to either past or the future [. . .]. For Wallace, a lack of teleology
in a society guided by a narcissistic pursuit of happiness poses a grave
danger."[19] But in providing this vision of late-capital temporality, Wallace
envisions an oppressive state that applies equally to all ONAN subjects, a
universalized place of coercion. Alienation via capitalist logic is something
we (subjects living under this socioeconomic system) experience together.
As a narrative device, this congealing of space and time allows the book to
focus on its many white characters without having to call attention to the
complications of racial discourse. In effect, *Infinite Jest* creates a literary
space to interrogate consumerism and personal happiness as it pertains to
whiteness, thereby perpetuating the late capital order that sublimates racist
discourse in order to uphold the tenants of consumption.

　　Wallace's later fiction is characterized by a desire to stage new encounters with the spectacle of late capital. These literary encounters, like his
early non-fiction and *Jest*, seek a shared experience of capitalism that closes
any gaps due to racial or cultural difference. This is Wallace's empathy
project, his commitment to upholding the experience of being human, but
it also illustrates his need to erase race to do so. The most direct of these
stagings arises in the first story in *Oblivion* (2004), "Mister Squishy." The
short story takes up the world of advertising through the labyrinth that is
the Targeted Focus Group at the Reesemeyer Shannon Belt Advertising
Firm. The multilayer network of deception and false appearances within/
created by the TFG and the various executives at the firm are paralleled by
the spectacle playing out at the high-rise across the street: A man is
climbing the building using suction cups to adhere himself to its surface.
The climb attracts the attention of the many passersby below, culminating
in the figure's revelation, upon reaching the summit, that he is in fact
costumed as the mascot Mister Squishy.

---

[19] Hirt, "Existentialist," 28.

The story's attention to consumerism pertains mainly to its various levels of deception that it inflicts both on consumers and producers: a series of false referents building to the piece's final description of an executive's mind as mirroring a "great flat blank white screen."[20] Race again appears as a piece of data – meant to be mined for utility, but ultimately another piece of the endless stream of information. To wit, the narration's mentioning of the non-white focus-group members emulates the crowds of the Illinois State Fair:

> There were two African-American males in the Targeted Focus Group, one over 30, the one under 30 with a shaved head. Three of the men had hair classifiable as brown, two gray or salt/pepper, another three black (excluding the African-Americans and the Focus Group's lone oriental, whose nametag and overwhelming cheekbones suggested either Laos or the Socialist Republic of Vietnam – for complex but solid statistical reasons, Scott Laleman's team Profile grids specified distributions for ethnicity but not national origin).[21]

Removing national origin from the recording of ethnicity represents the focus on superficial exterior difference at the expense of contextual cultural identity. In one sense, then, the story records capitalism's alienating gestures toward the individual, seeking to flatten personal history and senses of self in order to produce easy-to-manipulate consumers. Later on, Wallace will use a similar burying of ethnicity by mentioning that one of the many onlookers of the climber is an "older African-American woman,"[22] a detail that echoes the same dehumanizing categorization as the Focus Group. As a result of all this attention to the flattening of experience, the climb's culmination leaves the group of individuals as a crowd – they cease to exist as a series of unique perspectives and histories and instead function as a mass group of consumers. Wallace writes, "the face's array of patternless lines rounding to resolve into something that produced from 400+ ground-level US adults loud cries of recognition and an almost childlike delight."[23] Mister Squishy's reveal produces a congealing of the many "US adults" into a single demographic, a collection of consumers capable of being entranced by the allure of the product fetish. The reveal symbolizes what for Wallace is capital's most dangerous "sophisticated" logic – the deep-seated quest for uncritical engagement with media that erases one's sense of history and empathy.

---

[20] Wallace, "Mister Squishy," *OB*, 66.   [21] Ibid., 11.   [22] Ibid., 39.   [23] Ibid., 53.

The categorization of these many individuals as crystallized ethnic groups with identifiable outward features is treated as a given fact of this consumer landscape, a blip of racial difference that only serves to identify the omniscient third-/first-person narrator (the story slips into the perspective of one of the male focus group members at various moments) as unraced and therefore, according to the story's own logic, white; that is, other than those people of color in the group, every other member is described through a series of nonracial factors, including head shapes, facial hair and clothing. We are afforded this supposed behind-the-curtains glimpse into advertising due to this same whiteness, which allows its narration to remain beyond racial categories while being deeply embedded in the many complex mechanisms at work.

There is much to be gained from engaging with Wallace's failed literary encounters with racial capitalism; perhaps the most edifying is how his bibliography, not limited to those works mentioned here, is so illustrative of those of other white authors of the past late twentieth/early twenty-first century seeking to represent the postmodern condition. His final novel, *The Pale King*, and its many variations of whiteness stratified through the lens of class, is a fitting culmination to that project; its attempts to depict late capitalism's alienating and oppressive effects on the human psyche, where one is locked in a constant *now* with no path to thinking historically, are serviced by a tendency toward colorblindness, a denial of race's social influence. But these depictions – both Wallace's and those of his peers – commit a shared error in reasoning: the assumption that not accounting for the reality of race is the same as wishing to do away with the discrimination that accompanies racial discourse. On the contrary, the field of racial capitalism calls for a deeper examination into the shared logic of race and capital, to cease discussions of whiteness as an identity category rather than a position of power in a capitalist social order. Through this lens, the author's work, despite its blind spots, continues to be instructive, both in showcasing how capitalist ideology is perpetuated and in reminding us of the many fraught racial underpinnings behind the "human" Wallace that was so intent on recovering.

CHAPTER 28

Language and Self-Creation
David Foster Wallace's Many Ways of Sounding American

Mary Shapiro

Those who knew David Foster Wallace speak of him as a "gifted mimic,"[1] and critics have mostly agreed. Samuel Cohen said Wallace had a "perfect ear not only for the way other people talk but also for the way other writers write."[2] When Steven Moore credited Wallace with capturing "the way modern America sounds in all its cacophony better than any of his contemporaries,"[3] he may have been referring to Wallace's penchant for invented onomatopoeia, but part of the discordant blend is undeniably a multitude of voices with different ways of speaking. Wallace's representation of dialects in both his fiction and non-fiction is a logical extension of his deep and abiding interest in the philosophy of language, directly related to his view of sincere communication as the basis for human connection and the only way to avoid the traps of narcissism, solipsism and stasis. Given Wallace's love of language and his drive to define, represent, even catalog all that is American (what Lucas Thompson calls "Wallace-as-national-metonym"),[4] it was inevitable that he would find different dialects of the English irresistible.

The inclusion of specific dialect features roots many of Wallace's characters in a real linguistic and semiotic framework, increasing the realism of his fiction, but also often working against stereotypes that might otherwise be associated with these dialects. The performances discussed in this chapter are, in fact, *idiolect* portrayals informed by dialects, taking into account a whole host of other projected identity characteristics. The quirky and individual nature of these "not-me" voices stand out from the pervasive background of Wallace's soundalike alter ego characters and narrators. These portrayals may not always be sociolinguistically accurate, but they are not employed as shorthand "dog-whistles" to evoke negative

---

[1] Lipsky, "Lost Years," 176; Cf. Costello, quoted in Max, *Every Love Story*, 21.
[2] Cohen, "To Wish," 75.   [3] Moore, "In Memoriam," 2.
[4] Thompson, "Wallace and Race," 4.

stereotypes of particular communities. While Wallace's characters are often in difficult social and economic circumstances, their use of dialect features is never intended to display a lack of intelligence or deficiency of moral character. After a brief discussion of literary dialectology, this chapter will consider Wallace's most salient presentations of ethnic and regional dialects, while also noting salient absences, groups whose speech Wallace chose not to mark.

There is little evidence that Wallace did any formal research on dialects, how regional and ethnic variables might interact with linguistic projections of gender, sexual orientation, class, or other aspects of identity, or how these markers are deployed differently in different situations. Beyond his "History of English" class in college, he never formally studied linguistics. He was nevertheless well aware which dialects (including his own) have prestige in our society and which are stigmatized, as he discussed at length in the *Harper's* essay "Tense Present."[5] Wallace's "spiel" to African American students in the writing courses he taught at Illinois State University about why he insisted on a more "standard" variety drew complaints from students at the time and continues to inspire critical commentary probing his attitudes toward race and ethnicity, as discussed in Chapter 23 of this volume.[6] However, this example also indicates that Wallace clearly had thought deeply about how pernicious stereotypes (i.e. "poor," "uneducated," "unintelligent," "obnoxious," "rude") are triggered in the minds of listeners and readers when they encounter particular uses of language, along with more accurate ideas of what group(s) speakers belong to, or aspire to, and how speakers are reflecting their awareness of the context of utterance.[7]

Readers are so habituated to the sanitization of dialogue in fiction that a more realistic encoding of dialect, not to mention all the disfluencies of normal conversation, would require hard work to decode, as well as reflecting negatively on the characters.[8] When authors depict dialects other than their own, they risk misrepresenting them, or being accused of cultural appropriation. If authors represent their own "nonstandard" dialect, the work may be seen as "dialect literature" (restricted to readers from that dialect group) rather than "literary dialect."[9] It is thus not surprising

---

[5] Wallace, "Tense Present," retitled "Authority and American Usage" in *CL*.
[6] For example, Mura, "White Writing Teachers," and Thompson, "Wallace and Race."
[7] On the use of jargon for community building, see also Warren, "Narrative Modeling."
[8] Hodson, *Dialect in Film and Literature.*   [9] Shorrocks, "Non-Standard Dialect."

that literary dialect portrayals have become less common in recent decades.[10]

A linguistic variable may simultaneously index a variety of identities. For instance, African American English (AAE) and various US East-coast regional dialects (Boston, Rhode Island, New York, New Jersey, inter alia) tend toward deletion of /r/ after vowels (so-called r-lessness); both AAE and working-class regional dialects may use multiple markers of negation within a clause; and for obvious historical reasons, AAE in any region shares many features with Southern white dialects. In the hands of an unskilled author, direct representation of a character's speech, without narrative commentary to help readers identify it, risks failing to evoke the intended identity characteristics, resulting only in negative evaluation of the character. As David Crystal points out, for dialect literature generally, "Outsiders find it difficult to know [. . .] whether the style is a representation of a genuine local dialect or whether it is an authorial stylistic manipulation to achieve a particular effect."[11]

Wallace's frequent attempts to capture dialects may have been motivated by a belief that this cacophony of voices is a core and desirable part of American identity, despite the dominance in his work of young, white, male focalizing characters (usually transparent alter egos for the author), as well as his delight in playing with language, his confidence in his "good ear" and desire to play linguistic provocateur. Nevertheless, even Wallace's more realistic dialect portrayals were strategically and sparingly deployed to underline his themes, and his choice to misrepresent dialect features in a few cases (when he was certainly aware that he was doing so) therefore demands particular scrutiny.[12]

Wallace's most discussed (and criticized) dialect representation occurs in a short section of *Infinite Jest* featuring the stream of consciousness of a very young Clenette Henderson. Clenette's language is certainly intended to trigger racial identification; along with a couple of lexical items that would be recognized by white readers but associated mainly with African Americans (such as "crib" for a residence, "jump[ing] double dutch"), Clenette's internal monologue includes salient and well-known markers of AAE, such as unmarked third-person singular present verb forms (e.g., "he say") and unmarked possessors (e.g., "Wardine momma").

---

[10] Hodson, *Dialect and Literature in the Long Nineteenth Century* provides an instructive survey of the proliferation of dialect representations in literature of the nineteenth century.

[11] Crystal, *Language of Stories*, 503.

[12] See Shapiro, *Wallace's Dialects*, for further exploration of this.

It does not, however, include many other AAE features of which Wallace was certainly aware, such as negative concord and inverted structures, and it misrepresents the use of invariant "be" (which in AAE is a marker of habituality, not a grammatical copula or auxiliary verb).[13] The important point (which white readers may miss) is that Clenette's thoughts are incoherent *by the standards of AAE*. As such, this section is less a statement of ethnic identity than an indication of trauma, an impression heightened by the amount of frantic repetition. If we read these deviations from AAE grammar (e.g., "Wardine be sit," "she be cry," intended as simple present tense)[14] as Clenette's errors rather than Wallace's, then this passage is all the more poignant: She sounds like no one else because she has no community to support her. If this were the only representation of AAE in the novel, McGurl's judgment that this echoes "the long tradition of disrespectful mimicry in US culture"[15] would be more understandable. The direct speech of both Yolanda Willis and Roy Tony in that same novel, however, as illustrated later, shows that Wallace recognized AAE as a continuum, not a single uniform dialect.

An unattributed piece of dialogue on page 180 is presumably from Yolanda; it uses negative concord and epenthetic pronoun ("they didn't none of them start till 11") and the invariant negative auxiliary "ain't" ("if I ain't been trying"), consistent with Yolanda's later speech. In this later section, Yolanda initially avoids AAE structures ("I didn't even tell you yet how ..."), but when Don Gately tries to get her to confirm who has been sexually harassing her, she code-switches ("I ain't use no names in here. All I say [...]"),[16] expressing heightened emotion. Unsurprised by the harassment, what upsets Yolanda is the implication that she is snitching. Although this entire scene occupies only half a page, it shows that Wallace was capable of capturing not only more realistic AAE dialogue, including code-switching, but also the power of such subtle shifts to convey a great deal of information.

Roy Tony, another background character whose ethnicity is consistently foregrounded, is identified by Clenette as a murderer and child molester, and by "yrstruly" as a drug dealer and violent gang leader. Wallace could have exploited readers' linguistic prejudices here, triggering negative evaluation of Roy Tony, by loading his speech with AAE dialect markers. Instead, Roy Tony does not speak directly until years (and hundreds of pages) after he is introduced, when he has become sober and is sincerely

[13] Green, *African American English*, 54, 93, 207.   [14] Wallace, *IJ*, 37.
[15] McGurl, "Institution," 43.   [16] Wallace, *IJ*, 565.

invested in his recovery. Despite his loathsome past, Roy Tony is the role model in this scene, as opposed to the insincere, white middle-class Ken Erdedy. Wallace's choice to incorporate some AAE features into Roy Tony's speech (for example, the completive "dən" ("done")) at this later point in the novel would seem to provide evidence that ethnic identity and morality are in no way related.

It is evident from the handwritten drafts and hand-corrected manuscripts archived in the Harry Ransom Center collection of Wallace's papers that he struggled with how to represent AAE phonology in these characters. For the most part, he avoided it, except for using italics to represent stressed syllables, perhaps because it would have been too difficult for readers to decode altered spellings, or perhaps because English orthography does not easily capture the more subtle phonological distinctions in intonation, vowel quality and partially glottalized or devoiced final-stop consonants. In an early version of the Clenette passage, which Wallace asked his agent to send out as an independent story titled "Las Meninas," the typed original had "goin" hand-corrected to "going,"[17] but the final version in *Jest* changed this again to "gone."[18] (The less ethnically marked informal "gonna" receives a variety of vowel pronunciations in contemporary American English, but the "gone" spelling would seem to rule out several of these, favoring an elongated "aw" /ɔ/.)

Wallace's most extended dialect experiments occur in his shorter fiction and non-fiction. In the early story "Solomon Silverfish," both the Jewish American English of the title character and the AAE of "Too Pretty" have been criticized as overly stereotyped.[19] The Jewish American dialect of the elderly friends Mr. Labov and Mrs. Tagus in "Say Never," however, has largely gone unremarked upon. Linguistic features represented include topic fronting, calques of Yiddish syntax (resulting in nonstandard placement of adverbs and relative clauses) and Yiddish phrasal verbs (such as "making with" and "knowing from"), but there are no outright borrowings of Yiddish words, no reference to Jewish religion and few to culture, no altered orthography to represent pronunciation or intonation. Late in *Jest*, Hal notes that he "was trying to make my intonation Jewish-motherish, that melodic dip-rise-dip,"[20] but Hal does not project this speech pattern onto all, or even most American Jews – it's associated, as indeed it is throughout Wallace's *oeuvre*, only with an older generation performing a specific social function. Mr. Labov and Mrs. Tagus are treated with dignity

[17] Wallace, *IJ*, Draft Materials, Harry Ransom Center.   [18] Wallace, *IJ*, 38.
[19] Hayes-Brady, *Failures*; Thompson, "Wallace and Race."   [20] Wallace, *IJ*, 908.

and sympathy, although the choice of Mrs. Tagus' sons to affiliate themselves with different identities is also portrayed as unsurprising. The elder
son, Leonard, an academic, has standard (and pompous) speech, even in
his internal monologue: "I will wait for the arrival of those whose orbits
I've decayed."[21] The younger son, Mikey, sounds like a working-class
white Chicagoan: "she just said how she didn't want to go out no more."[22]
Assimilation from Jewish immigrant to native "white" identity can be
completed within a single generation, the story suggests, but this is
not inevitable: Leonard's spurned wife Bonnie sounds much like the
older generation: "Joshua looks at me he's about to cry almost the poor
love [. . .]."[23]

Of course, like ethnic dialects, regional dialects also carry social weight
and may be highly stigmatized. In real life, these constructs interact in
fascinating and complicated ways – but not in Wallace's work, where
anyone noticeably regional is white, and characters of color do not employ
any salient markers of regional identity. In this way, Wallace appeared to
construe whiteness as an absence of ethnicity rather than affirming it as a
social construct. There is similarly an inverse relationship between regional
identity and social class in Wallace's representations, with working-class
characters much more likely to display regional dialect features. One
notable exception to this is the proud Texan dialect of both "Lyndon"
and *The Broom of the System*'s Andy Lang, although Lenore Beadsman
comments that Lang's dialect comes and goes, and he concedes that
"I guess maybe we all talk differently with different people. The good
old boy stuff is what I grew up on, and then at school I was from Texas and
so everybody expected this sort of talking, and so it kind of became my
thing, at school."[24] Just as with ethnic dialects, Wallace took care to
differentiate the speech associated with different regions, not representing
any dialect as monolithic.

Southern dialects are especially stigmatized, as Wallace well knew. Of all
the hundreds of characters in Wallace's work, *Infinite Jest*'s Joelle Van
Dyne is the only one who deliberately loses her native accent. "I now have
no accent except under stress," she claims, although the narrator comments that Gately finds her accent "just barely Southern and with a strange
and it turns out Kentuckian lapse in the pronunciation of all apicals except
s."[25] Earlier drafts had Joelle coming from Arkansas, and it is not clear that

---

[21] Wallace, "Say Never," *GCH*, 223.   [22] Ibid.   [23] Ibid., 214.   [24] Wallace, *BS*, 465.
[25] Wallace, *IJ*, 234, 366. Apicals is a technical linguistic term that Gately certainly would not use,
referring to consonants articulated with the tip of the tongue, including /t,d,n,l/.

Wallace changed anything about the way the character spoke when he changed her home state.[26]

One of Wallace's most interesting experiments with a nonstandard dialect occurs in "John Billy" set in Minogue, Oklahoma. Ellerhoff viewed this story as "inflating lyric voices found in the literature of the American South, from William Faulkner to Cormac McCarthy."[27] The eponymous narrator of "John Billy," who claims a white identity by distinguishing himself from both a "nigra" on the visiting football team and the "neighboring reservation's Native Americans,"[28] demonstrates both an enormous, erudite vocabulary and a very strong regional dialect, including pervasive use of some highly stigmatized features such as multiple negation with and without "ain't" (e.g., "never got seen no more," "ain't no difference"), nonstandard past-tense forms ("we/they was" throughout, "growed," etc.),[29] indefinite *a* before nouns with initial vowels throughout (e.g., "a ambulance," "a animal") and frequent deletion of preposition "of" (e.g. "hanging right out his head"). Nor is this combination seen as extraordinary in the context of the story: Another local, Glory Joy, intersperses lofty lexical items used correctly ("recalcitrant") with others that don't really apply ("threnodic"), along with the regularized-but-stigmatized reflexive pronoun "hisself."[30] A third character, T. Rex, casually specifies "macrocosmic speculation" as the intended direct object of the nonstandard "We done some together," although it's not entirely clear whether his pun of "meadow-physics" in the previous line is intentional.[31] The point is not that these are "authentic" Oklahoman performances, but that it should not be surprising if intelligent and educated people continue to use native dialects that encode their affiliation to a local area. Wallace evidently understood how his readers would respond to the nonstandard grammar, and aggressively and persistently challenged their stereotypes. If the juxtaposition of "highbrow" words with "lowbrow" grammar and vulgarity strikes readers as incongruous or amusing at first, the consistency of the presentation over twenty-six pages overcomes that response. Boswell says, "The gag here is that neither Glory Joy nor John Billy would be aware of such terms as 'mythopoeic'"[32] – but Wallace's jokes were often simultaneously deep and dark. The sad truth underlying the "gag" is that people are routinely discouraged from higher education because of their dialect;[33]

---

[26] Wallace, *IJ*, Draft Materials, Harry Ransom Center.   [27] Ellerhoff, "Proteus Bound," 120.
[28] Wallace, "John Billy," *GCH*, 122, 125–26.   [29] Ibid., 136, 144.   [30] Ibid., 131, 136.
[31] Ibid., 143.   [32] Boswell, *Understanding*, 87.
[33] There is a large body of research on critical race theory and higher education. For dialect discrimination in grading practices, see especially Wheeler, "Attitude Change."

Wallace understood that there is no reason, other than social pressure, why these linguistic features should not coexist.

Many Bostonians are proud of their regional distinctiveness, and as *Jest* is set in the Boston area, Wallace had ample opportunity to differentiate characters' use of regional dialect features, distinguishing between "Metro Boston," "North Shore," and "southie" pronunciations and slang. (The traditionally prestigious upper-class variety known as "Boston Brahmin," associated with the Kennedy family or John Kerry, is not mentioned in the novel). Members of the Incandenza family have no distinct regional dialect; Avril and Jim, not native to the region, apparently raised their children not just in relative isolation from the surrounding population, but literally and figuratively above it (up the hill). When Joelle has dinner with the Incandenza family, she thinks, "Everybody Please-and-Thank-You'd in a way that was sheer Yankee WASP."[34] Michael Pemulis, who uses local references and the regional intensifier "wicked," and whose "errors" Hal comments on, is not represented as r-less after vowels, though this is the main stereotype associated with Boston-area accents. Joelle mocks Gately's r-lessness ("*Harrd. Harrrrd.* Sound it out"),[35] but this feature is not directly included in the representation of his speech or his thoughts, except for thinking of the character "Norm" (in the sitcom *Cheers*) as "Nom."[36] Freudenthal argues that Gately is defined by "clichéd contradictions of working-class identity," but that readers forgive these clichés because they find Gately "so dang likeable."[37] This, however, raises the question of whether they would find him so likeable if his working-class Boston dialect were represented directly in the text. Or would they judge him as harshly as they do yrs truly, whose interior monologue not only encodes such a dialect but is also consistently misspelled and mispunctuated (with apostrophes consistently misplaced, and commas absent entirely, e.g. "Its' a fucking bitch of a life dont' let any body get over on you diffrent")?[38] It is significant, given the critical interest in Wallace's racial representations, that his only use of "eye dialect" (manipulations of written conventions that wouldn't affect pronunciation and are solely intended to trigger perceptions of ignorance) is reserved for a working-class white drug addict. Even this representation, however, does not directly encode r-lessness, which might prove too challenging for readers over the eight-page stretch focalized by yrstruly. The security guard who arrives on the scene after Gately has been shot illustrates how Gately, Pemulis, and yrstruly might

---

[34] Wallace, *IJ*, 745.   [35] Ibid., 563.   [36] Ibid., 834, 836, 883.
[37] Freudenthal, "Anti-Interiority," 191.   [38] Wallace, *IJ*, 129.

really sound: "Secyotty! Hold it right thaah.[...] I'm *oddering* desis until who's in chahge that I can repot the si*chation*."[39]

All of Wallace's dialect performances are implicitly contrasted with the white, male, Midwestern "Dave Wallace" narrator, which is at its most overt in the non-fiction, but gradually emerges across his fiction as well, culminating in the "Author Here" section of *The Pale King*, as detailed by Boswell.[40] Although Hayes-Brady maintains that "there are striking differences between [Wallace's] fictional and nonfictional voices,"[41] she is looking specifically at his narrative and rhetorical strategies; the strictly *sociolinguistic* performance across Wallace's works is much more consistent. This narrator's repeated (and false) claim of being from "Philo, IL"[42] is a tongue-in-cheek counterpart to the bumper-sticker slogan "I (heart) NY." In reality, of course, his ambivalence about the Midwest was much more interesting than a wholehearted investment in that identity. Wallace claimed a fondness for "the hard-earned Rural Midwestern of most of my peers," one of his two "native dialects," along with "the SWE [Standard Written English] of my hypereducated parents."[43] Growing up there himself, Wallace knew better than to fall prey to what Timothy Frazer called "One of the grossest misconceptions about the Midwestern United States": "that it is home to 'General American,' a bland, deregionalized variety of English spoken by everyone in the region."[44] Wallace's admittedly "elitist and snotty" description of "Kmart people" in "Getting Away From Already Pretty Much Being Away From It All"[45] notably does *not* include a description of the way they speak; it is a social, but not a linguistic, critique. David Lipsky represents Wallace's own Midwestern dialect as full of /z/-stopping before nasals ("wudn't," "dudn't," "idn't"), alveolar pronunciation of -ing suffixes ("willin'," "droppin'"), adverbial "near" and "real."[46] Wallace's personal papers contain notes about "Midwesternisms" in multiple locations, as well as a notebook devoted entirely to these.[47]

Even with the diverse dialects that Wallace included in *Jest*, there are notable gaps: There are few Latinx, South Asian Americans or Arab Americans, and no hybrid or blended ethnic identities. We get only passing glimpses of other ethnically marked background characters, who are not even given names, like the "tired Cuban orderly" who gets the last

[39] Ibid., 618–19. [40] Boswell, "Author Here." [41] Hayes-Brady, *Failures*, 137.
[42] See Hering, *Fiction and Form*, 144. [43] Wallace, "Tense Present," 50.
[44] Frazer, "Introduction to Midwest English," 102. [45] Wallace, "Getting Away," *SFT*, 120.
[46] Lipsky, *Although of Course*. [47] Wallace, "Midwesternisms," Notebook, Harry Ransom Center.

word in the opening section of the novel, the Pakistani manager of Store24, or the Irish immigrant who speaks at an Alcoholics Anonymous meeting. Wallace, who was not a fluent speaker of any language but English, typically showed great respect in his writing for speakers of other languages who learn comprehensible English, while delighting in the distinct phonology and syntax of those who, like Austrian coach Gerhart Schtitt, maintain non-native features. Thompson comments on the "ESL solecisms" of the Hungarian waiter and Asian cleaner in "A Supposedly Fun Thing," but also acknowledges that "Wallace's affection toward them is palpable."[48] It is difficult to tell, in many of *Jest*'s short, dense portrayals of dialect, often presented in a kaleidoscopic flux without attribution, whether a given speaker is a foreigner in America, an immigrant on the way to assimilation, or an American who maintains a non-white ethnic identity, and it seems clear that this was a line that Wallace either deliberately blurred or did not care about, raising questions about relationships between nationality, citizenship, and ethnic identity. Apart from Rémy Marathe, a main character who speaks a version of English clearly influenced by his native Québécois French, dialect representations in *IJ* are fleeting, but nonetheless generally sympathetic, as outlined earlier. They contribute to Wallace's celebration of heteroglossia in America while subtly reinforcing the idea that America is dominated by (and for) those of Western European descent.

It is with this understanding that we might interpret the marked lack of identifying dialect traits in *Brief Interviews with Hideous Men*, although the majority of that text consists of direct speech, encouraging the identification of those men as "(likely white)"[49] and obscuring any regional identity. In the absence of an omniscient narrator, or other characters who could share their observations of the men, the use of dialect would have helped trigger all kinds of implicit social knowledge about characters' regional, ethnic and socioeconomic identities. Yet Wallace rejected this strategy, and for good reason: The psychopathy that makes such men hideous has nothing to do with ethnicity or region. They are more alike than not, regardless of linguistic identity features that would have distinguished them. The overwhelming whiteness of *The Pale King* is equally interesting, as Araya has noted.[50] The IRS agents in Wallace's last, unfinished novel are not "hideous" (or at least no more so than anyone else), but their individual identities are subsumed into the larger organization; they have

---

[48] Thompson, "Wallace and Race," 213.   [49] Coughlan, "Sappy," 163.
[50] Araya, "Why the Whiteness?"

become cogs in the machine, to the extent that their identity *as* IRS agents erases any previous affiliation.

Wallace's vision of America does not appear to be a "melting pot" (which, as he shows, is not an option for people of color), but a healthier ideal, one in which different ethnicities, national origins, regional and other identities can be expressed and enjoyed, while individuals are judged as individuals. People from different backgrounds can do more than just coexist; they can actively cooperate to create a better community, as the addicts from different backgrounds support one another in *Infinite Jest*. Viewed in this light, Wallace's practice of assigning "half-Americanized" names (for instance, *Jest*'s LaMont Chu and Tony Nwangi, or Eric Yang in "(Church Not Made With Hands)"), none of whom have ethnic or non-native speech patterns, appears to be tacit recognition that one can be both typically "American" and still affirm one's heritage.

In the wake of Wallace's death, it seems less important to ask whether *he* was racist, classist, sexist, homophobic or ableist (although my reading of his work suggests sadly common internalized levels of these), than to explore whether his work can speak across these divides, whether readers of his work might find their own prejudices and unconscious biases confirmed or challenged. If Wallace had used his unusual facility with language just to impress or dazzle readers, it would be a rather sad "self-own," an illustration of the narcissism against which his work explicitly warns. If he had simply used language in startling and fresh ways in order to defamiliarize the world around us and the language itself, this would have been noteworthy. But Wallace did not stop there: He took the risk of representing a variety of dialects, in order to illustrate and explore the complex interplay of nationality, citizenship, race, ethnicity, region and social class in ways that we might continue to explore for years to come.

CHAPTER 29

Very Old Land
David Foster Wallace and the Myths and Systems
of Agriculture

Jeffrey Severs

> Quartz and chert and schist and chondrite iron scabs in granite. Very
> old land. Look around you. The horizon trembling, shapeless. We are
> all of us brothers.
>
> —*The Pale King*

D. T. Max reports that David Foster Wallace's home from the age of
seven, in Urbana, Illinois, was "a few blocks [from] fields of corn and
soybeans, prairie farmland extending as far as the eye could see," and the
teenage Wallace, before leaving for Amherst, "spent the last couple of days
wandering around the neighboring cornfields saying goodbye."[1] When
Wallace later writes the words in the epigraph above about "untilled fields"
to begin *The Pale King*, the short sentence fragments, the awestruck tone
and a sermonizing sentence about connection suggest an appreciation of
farmland's mythical resonances.[2] The atmosphere is one of ancient ritual,
of personified if not animistic land that, holding big truths, needs to be not
just bid farewell but revered. By this section's end, the gaze is directed from
the encircling horizon to the seeming religious symbols etched into animal
waste fertilizing this fallow soil: "the shapes of the worms incised in the
overturned dung and baked by the sun all day until hardened, there to
stay, tiny vacant lines in rows and inset curls that do not close because head
never quite touches tail." We are told to "Read these,"[3] and I have argued
elsewhere that they conjure the heated oracle bones of ancient China, with
their cracks read for prophecy.[4] Amid all this imagery of enduring cycles
and ancient mindsets, though, there are also hints of the narrative to come,
a story of the most modern of bureaucratic systems, carried out in built,
enclosed environments by pale servants. "Blacktop graphs" on the roads,
insects that are "all business all the time," and the dung's "lines in rows"
evoking the examiners' paperwork and ordered desks – all these indicate

---

[1] Max, *Every Love Story*, 1, 14.   [2] Wallace, *TPK*, 5.   [3] Ibid., 6.
[4] Severs, *Balancing Books*, 228.

that Wallace saw both myth and system, somehow intertwined, when he looked closely at farmland.[5]

Farmland fascinated Wallace throughout his career, I argue, because in these materials of his native ground he could bring together two capacious ways of accounting for the world – to be at once an analyst of myth in the school of the works by Joseph Campbell that he studied[6] and a writer of postmodern systems fiction in the vein of Thomas Pynchon and Don DeLillo. Farming as practiced in his native Illinois (where he lived again from 1993 to 2002, teaching at Illinois State University) wed two vectors for him: on the one hand, his myth-driven appreciation of the millennia-long worship of symbols of fertility, cultivation and abundance, and, on the other hand, his systems-driven understanding of highly rationalized contemporary agribusiness and the political and economic issues with which it intersected. Definitions of sustainable growth and productivity in a manically consumerist and financialized United States were on Wallace's mind almost always, and investigating farming, as well as biotechnology in food and fertilization, allowed him to ponder postmodern complexity, artificiality and control alongside the contingencies projected onto pre-Enlightenment myths and rituals of plenitude and lack. Farming thus offers a window on the "old traditional verities" Wallace said that his work, counterintuitively, used "postmodern technique[s]" like systems analysis to uncover.[7]

As Patrick O'Donnell has shown, Wallace, particularly in *Infinite Jest*, was a systems writer in the tradition of DeLillo, Pynchon, Gaddis, and Coover, authors of encyclopedic novels critically anatomized by Tom LeClair in *In the Loop: Don DeLillo and the Systems Novel* (1988) (a copy of which, heavily annotated by Wallace, is at the Ransom Center) and *The Art of Excess: Mastery in Contemporary Fiction* (1989). Such novels, O'Donnell writes in summary of LeClair's findings, tackle "systems of all kinds: scientific, linguistic, mechanical, psychological, cybernetic" and often, in their "encyclopedic nature," have an "investment in bringing together and connecting diverse forms of knowledge as critical elements of the story, thus enacting a narrative world that simulates the complexity, epistemological entanglements, and open- or closed-ended possibilities of the real one, or ones."[8]

For the Wallace who found interconnected complexity in large-scale agriculture, the essay that lays out some of his methods is his treatment of the Illinois State Fair, "Getting Away From Pretty Much Already Being

---

[5] Wallace, *TPK*, 5.   [6] Severs, *Balancing Books*, 207, 265, n. 21.
[7] Dazzle Communication, "Le Conversazioni 2006."   [8] O'Donnell, "Beyond," 114.

Away From It All." There, Wallace writes of farming as huge, systematized endeavor, the indifferent "agribusiness of weight and meat":[9]

> Illinois farmers [. . .] are not poor. Just the amount of revolving credit you need to capitalize a fair-sized operation – seed and herbicide, heavy equipment, crop insurance – makes a lot of them millionaires on paper. Media dirges notwithstanding, banks are no more keen to foreclose on Midwestern farmers than they are on Third World nations; they're in that deeply.[10]

As O'Donnell also notes, for Wallace, systems on very different scales are often "conflated entities (body, mind, school, nation are homologous)," leading to representations of the systematic bodies into and through which individual human ones are often organized and processed.[11] Thus there is a pun in Wallace's description of a well-capitalized farm as a "fair-sized operation," since the Illinois State Fair itself runs like a giant farm for processing humans, with the attendees playing the mechanistic part of cogs in a body-like system, not consumers of snacks but the things consumed (and excreted). "The Main Gate's maw admits us, slow tight-packed masses move peristaltically along complex systems of branching paths, [. . .] and are finally [. . .] expelled out of exits designed for heavy flow," Wallace writes, while other images liken fairgoers to the fatted cattle they have come to see.[12] Less muted critiques of agribusiness systems arise a decade later in "Consider the Lobster" (which I have characterized as a rewriting of "Getting Away"),[13] where Wallace, inching toward animal-rights views, asks whether "future generations will regard our present agribusiness and eating practices in much the same way we now view Nero's entertainments or Mengele's experiments."[14]

At the same time, though, the more memorable and explicit elements of "Getting Away" evince Wallace's quest in Midwestern farmland to uncover its premodern ritual subtexts and associations, the way that human perception invests the vastness of the landscape with awed and communal meanings (see McRae Andrew in the next chapter for more on this subject). The Fair is thus occasion for Wallace to contemplate growth beyond a childish, self-centered relationship to community rituals ("special ritual public occasions drive a kid right out of his mind," with the world around him "present[ing] itself as *Special*-For-Him"[15]) and the sense that some "communitarian" possibility might be latent in the fair, some sense of "state-as-community, a grand-scale togetherness" that may transcend

---

[9] Wallace, "Getting Away," *SFT*, 96.   [10] Ibid., 105.   [11] Ibid., 118.
[12] Wallace, "Getting Away," *SFT*, 131.   [13] Severs, "Wallace's Nonfiction," 119.
[14] Wallace, "Consider the Lobster," *CL*, 253.   [15] Wallace, "Getting Away," *SFT*, 90.

those systematic capitalist flows of consumption.[16] These non-fiction analyses bear some relation to the sudden insight in *The Pale King*: "Look around you [...] We are all of us brothers," and together such writings pose the implicit question germane to much of Wallace's work: is it merely massive twentieth- and twenty-first-century capitalist systems and their advertising and products that bind people together, or is some simpler, more lasting story of human provision and togetherness (and, in the later Wallace's terms, civic bonds) being played out?

Wallace's first title, *The Broom of the System*, receives no clear explanation in the novel itself, but he claims in an interview that an unexpected overlay of body, food and the language of systems is the source, further confirmation of O'Donnell's point about Wallace's body/system homologies: "the title comes from my mother's pet name for roughage [...] and fiber," Wallace says, "the broom of the system."[17] Food systems that feed the human system, for good or ill, run throughout *Broom*, where the setting is a "wasteland" created by "Industrial Desert Design"[18] on the orders of a Governor Zusatz (the name means "food additive" in German) intent on creating a counter-myth to Ohio's history of agricultural order, what he calls "hewing."[19] Consumables in this self-created hellscape are not products of the earth but of the lab. The careful appetite-cultivating processes behind high-sugar snack cakes would be Wallace's focus in "Mister Squishy," but the biotechnology of food was on his radar from the time of *Broom*'s miraculous Stonecipheco baby food and the Bombardini Company, "a firm involved in some vague genetic engineering enterprises."[20] In plot points that never really come clear, Bombardini mentions while eating his massive steak dinner, "No one had ever been able to give butter life either."[21] Is Bombardini's growth into some emblematic mythical beast of consumption tied to his synthetic food products, or maybe a backfired "Infant Accelerant" that he consumed?[22] Much speculation surrounds the question of whether Hal, in events following the end of *Infinite Jest*, has ingested the designer drug DMZ or seen the title film; but similar scrutiny might be brought to the yet more irresolute plot details of genetic modification, food and drugs in *Broom*.

Artificial food systems rule in *Broom*, but it is in the Illinois setting of "Westward the Course of Empire Takes Its Way," his next long narrative, that Wallace's distinctive approach to the meanings of contemporary agriculture first emerged fully, setting a template on which later works

---

[16] Ibid., 91.   [17] Kennedy and Polk, "Looking," 12.   [18] Wallace, *BS*, 54.   [19] Ibid., 53.
[20] Ibid., 47.   [21] Ibid., 91.   [22] Ibid., 153.

would build. While the mysterious drug sampling on Corfu (a frequent site in Greek mythology) figures only sketchily in *Broom*, in "Westward," Wallace creates a historical context for dense Illinois cornfields that cues reader to associations with the ancients: "Fact: all Illinois communities, from well-built Chicago down to Little Egypt, have their origin and reason in the production of nourishment. The soil of Illinois is second only to the Nile delta in terms of decayed-matter percentage, fertility."[23] Climactic scenes of Mark Nechtr in a rainy, muddy cornfield conjure what I have argued[24] is the community ritual – a "mythopoeum"[25] and rain dance – evident in "John Billy," an earlier story in *Girl with Curious Hair*. "Westward" in general seems keen to juxtapose a sense of an ancient appeal to the forces of fertility with the frustrating contradictions that modern systems of money, absolute profit extraction (by corporations like McDonald's) and biological control have brought into agriculture. The cornfield mud ("so fertile it stinks") in which Mark stands "beseeching," a "supplicant," is "milky" with "Pest-Aside," a pesticide to which hungry bugs have formed immunity.[26] Meanwhile, with "agron-ometric bitterness in her voice" as they drive through vast amounts of tall corn, Magda "explains that the usually awfully generous US government won't reimburse Illinois farmers for leaving their fields fallow – the soil's too rich here, and the macroeconomics of the nation's richest fields dictate maximum tillage – and but that, in the dark screw microecon drives into the agricultural picture, that very fertility produced so much corn [...] that it's literally worthless."[27] System abstractions and supply and demand thus trump an obvious cornucopia.

Mythology usually calls for gods and goddesses, and Wallace would certainly at other times make specific classical gods and demigods collide with modern technological systems, the best example being his Barthian parody of TV and film stars, "Tri-Stan: I Sold Sissee Nar to Ecko." But with his agricultural writing, there is usually more of an attempt to fashion a new, often degraded mythology appropriate to a world in which systems seem (but only seem) to control nature's innate contingencies. "Westward" is rife with mythological identifications and can seem at times an allegory of classical gods: Mark Nechtr not only has a name redolent of nectar, the food of the Olympian gods,[28] but is, with his archery and surgeon's shirt, a modern Apollo, god of, among other rationally ordered things, medicine

[23] Wallace, "Westward," *GCH*, 257.   [24] Severs, *Balancing Books*, 71–72.
[25] Wallace, "John Billy," *GCH*, 136.   [26] Wallace, "Westward," *GCH*, 347.   [27] Ibid., 299.
[28] Boswell, *Understanding*, 105.

and agriculture. Opposing him (in the Nietzschean terms "Westward" explores) is the god of consuming lusts, Dionysus, or J. D. Steelritter, whose orgiastic, deadly reunion expresses the absolutely dark subtext of hyper-consumerism's systematization of 60 billion McDonald's burgers – no real "provision of nourishment" by river deltas of dead matter there. Wallace underscores his point about new gods by having a Lord (Jack, the *Hawaii Five-O* actor) be a major participant in J. D.'s reunion. In nostalgic longing for an earlier generation's values typical of Wallace, Dionysian J. D., devoted to fast food and murder, seems a degraded contemporary god in relation to his mother, whose 1930s car accident and subsequent life in the wreckage, leading to an economy of rose-farming that overcomes the Great Depression, has the ring of a foundation myth. Is she, in her dedication to stillness, a Buddha? An earth goddess? Wallace seems flexible and syncretic in his use of sacred figures of agriculture in a way that the later TV critique in the more pedantic "Tri-Stan" would not allow for.

This same nostalgia for old gods of the old land arises in "Westward"'s present-tense scenes in the character of the overweight, overalled farmer, first seen at the Avis counter trying to pay for a car rental not with money but the grain of ancient barter. Near the end, Wallace positions Dionysian McDonald's glut and this old, small-time farmer, a giant totemic presence himself, as two alternatives for economy and, indeed, awed worship. On one side of the moving car, "the very tops of the two giant arches glint, just visible, inclined like a child's severe eyebrows just over the countertop line between land and the baby-blue iris of a sky that looks down all day at food"[29] (an image adapted from a previous creation of a modern god for a fallen world, the T. J. Eckleburg ad looming over the valley of ashes in *The Great Gatsby*). J. D. tellingly chooses to look at those arches, scene of his dark ceremony, while "the other five are all looking [out the car's other side] at the big farmer, hitching, motionless, a statue rushing toward them. He's huge; his thumb casts a shadow."[30] Eventually his tractor will slowly pass burger-clown DeHaven's broken-down, mudbound car, showing where Wallace's sympathies ultimately lie.

One has the sense fifteen years later, reading "The Suffering Channel," that "Westward" has been rewritten: a novella-sized narrative ending a story collection, about anorexic young women from the east coast whose writing is disparaged (as D. L.'s was), a range of rural Midwesterners of ample girth (here, Indianans) and a looming disaster that will befall the characters but not be directly narrated (here, 9/11). Wallace also rewrites

[29] Wallace, "Westward," *GCH*, 311.   [30] Ibid.

the scene of Mrs. Steelritter's car accident (where, staying all those years, she must have had the sex with the rose peddler that produced J. D.) when the obese Amber Moltke damages Skip Atwater's car in their lovemaking. Amber's first name suggests she has been preserved for many years, and Skip (his real first name is Virgil, suggesting that his whole account of the Moltkes is an investigation of modern myth) observes her "huge smooth calves [...] the overall size and hue of [...] museum grade vases and funeral urns of the same antiquity in which the dead wore bronze masks and whole households were interred together."[31] Is she, like the Nile delta in "Westward" that this description recalls, emblematic of Midwestern plenitude, another earth mother of sorts, in contrast to Laurel Manderley and the frivolous New York *Style* interns? Or do the ominous funereal associations and death of a household in that description, combined with a recurrent sense that Amber wants to cash in on her husband's art and potential celebrity, tell a different story?

This novella's evocation of agricultural symbols through the ages offers one answer, illuminating what is at stake in this meditation on fragile fecundity. As I have argued,[32] Brint's "miraculous poo"[33] sculptures are Wallace's way of pondering an ancient Egyptian symbol of fertilization, the dung beetle that feeds on waste (signaled by the "anodized cameo" of "some kind of beetle" on the Moltkes' doorframe[34]), as well as the larger miracle of renewal, of dead waste feeding new life, represented by the nitrogen cycle (also a key issue in my later interpretation of *Infinite Jest*). Brint's meditative calm also seems a positive model for the agitated Skip. But Amber's ceremony of betraying, crushing seduction is, by contrast, presided over by a symbol of modern agricultural systems, for she directs Skip to "a kind of crude mesa whose vantage overlooked a large nitrogen fixative factory, whose complex and emberous lights at night were an attraction county-wide."[35] Systems attempting to overcome natural limits to growth always interest Wallace, and mass-produced nitrogen fixative is an antidote for fallow fields, speeding up nature's course of renewal for impatient agribusiness. This earth-exhausting technique is in fact a recurrent Wallace image: in "Derivative Sport in Tornado Alley," he writes of learning to "play tennis on the blacktop courts of a small public park carved from farmland that had been nitrogenized too often to farm anymore."[36]

[31] Wallace, "Suffering," *OB*, 251.   [32] Severs, *Balancing Books*, 192–93.
[33] Wallace, "Suffering," *OB*, 262.   [34] Ibid., 247.   [35] Ibid., 259–60.
[36] Wallace, "Derivative Sport," *SFT*, 3.

With *The Pale King* incomplete, the scope of Wallace's ambitions with it remains unknown, but there are hints that the opening's "very old land" might have functioned throughout the novel as a foil to modern IRS systems, a means of pondering the fact that taxes – now manipulated paper abstractions, the exact amounts subject to so much moral scrutiny – were once paid in agricultural products like grain (the farmer's currency in "Westward"). Tim Groenland's painstaking genetic criticism of the many *Pale King* drafts left out of the published book shows that "Cede," a narrative set in first- and second-century Rome, was once interspersed with the stories of Chris Fogle and the contortionist boy. Starvation is a key theme of "Cede" (a punning evocation of the farmer's seed?), including of people who, in a mythical opening sequence, grow so paper-thin they float away on the wind, before descending to gorge themselves in an apple orchard.[37] Writing about the modern agriculture surrounding Peoria is somewhat sparse in *The Pale King* as originally assembled by editor Michael Pietsch, but there is one intriguing draft scene added to the 2012 paperback edition, on the childhood of systems expert Merrill Lehrl (here called "Charles Lehrl"), who, in the published novel-proper, is an unseen but powerful presence promoting computers over humans at every turn. The scene of Lehrl's upbringing is the agribusiness hub of Decatur, Illinois, actual home of food-processing giant Archer Daniels Midland, here rendered (or misread by Pietsch from Wallace's manuscripts?) as "Archer Dentists Midland." It seems likely that Wallace might have used a fleshed-out Lehrl to connect the agribusiness systems he witnesses as a boy – Decatur air that "stank either of hog processing or burnt corn depending on the wind," "weeds gone hypertrophic in the outwash of nitrogen fertilizers," cows and pigs being led into a rendering plant – with his adult attempts to regularize tax examination by excluding from it the faulty, messy bodies and minds that Wallace so prizes (see Sloane elsewhere in this volume for more on this subject).[38]

I have saved for my final reading surely the most complex and absurd example of Wallace's investigations into agricultural systems, the Great Concavity of *Infinite Jest*. The novel's primary setting of metro Boston leaves Wallace without any obvious way to explore farming realistically, but he still arranges an opportunity to describe a fantastical unintentional experiment in hyper-fertilization played out on a massive international scale. While literal forms of nitrogen-injected fields and overfertilized soil intrigued Wallace elsewhere, in the Great Concavity he has free rein to

---

[37] Groenland, "The Fragment," 135.   [38] Wallace, *TPK*, 9.

imagine such techniques in gargantuan, satiric excess, as metaphors for the toxic and uncontrolled implications of an economy hell-bent on constant growth and unlimited energy. He does so by making the fertilizer in this case the nuclear waste from James O. Incandenza's annular fusion, expelled from the United States by gigantic catapults, the result in the Concavity being an "environment so fertilely lush it's practically unlivable," populated by giant, feral hamsters and other fauna – at least part of the time.[39] As Michael Pemulis explains at length to Idris Arslanian, such rain forest lushness alternates over time with desert conditions, an equally unlivable extreme. This cyclical process, one that, as Pemulis also explains, "can produce waste that's fuel for a process whose waste is fuel for the fusion,"[40] is in effect one in which ambitious human-wrought systems attempt, disastrously, to displace the nitrogen cycle, that ancient, abiding process whereby dead plant and animal matter, along with the dung seen in the *Pale King*'s opening, will naturally serve as fuel for new growth if patiently deployed. Where Zusatz took only the nihilistic step of creating a wasteland to psychologically spur further growth in *Broom*, in *Infinite Jest*, wasteland creation has grown autonomous and utterly unstable. When Pemulis simplifies the whole cycle as "nothing but a huge right triangle,"[41] connecting Montpelier, Methuen and Loring Air Force Base, Wallace evokes the infamous Triangle Trade that sustained slavery in the Americas – with Americans now enslaved to their massive energy needs, in parallel with drug users' addictions. Systems would seem to offer greater control over environmental contingencies, but as O'Donnell argues, the Great Concavity is an exemplary case of Wallace's work "explor[ing systems] for their inherent contradictions," with the cycle sustainable "only if the black hole of the Great Concavity can grow beyond its bounds."[42]

In Arslanian's mnemonic for hyper-growth's deceleration of time, "Wasteland to lush: time's in no rush,"[43] and in Pemulis's mention of the "barren Eliotical wastes of the western Concavity,"[44] Wallace invites readers to compare his grim postmodern creation to that of T. S. Eliot – whose general diagnosis of the sterility of twentieth-century life in *The Waste Land* I think Wallace finds unconvincing, or simply limited. For one thing, as with the Great Concavity, Wallace sees the problem of postmodernity as no lack of fertility or productivity – it is too much of both, too much exploitation of long-standing cycles of organic renewal in order to serve a sickening glut, too much deference to monetary valuation.

---

[39] Wallace, *IJ*, 573.   [40] Ibid., 572.   [41] Ibid., 570.   [42] O'Donnell, "Beyond," 117.
[43] Wallace, *IJ*, 573.   [44] Ibid., 574.

In Wallace's work, too, premodern myths (like the Fisher King, hinted at throughout "Westward") are not salvific antidotes for technological systems; rather, these two elements are thoroughly intertwined explanatory models. With mechanized systems having achieved such dominance in Wallace's era, new myths have to be written in light of that dominance and of whatever was salvageable from the old myths. All that would be done, too, with little of Eliot's solemnity, and with parody and irony for the old myths (especially before the voice Wallace developed in *The Pale King*) riskily maximized. Thus when the Great Concavity inevitably leads to its own new, degraded mythology of growth – "[w]hole NNE [New New England] cults and stelliform subcults Lenz reports as existing around belief systems about the metaphysics of the Concavity,"[45] including various acts of worshipping "infants the size of prehistoric beasts [. . .] keening for the abortive parents who'd left or lost them" in the evacuation[46] – a reader paying attention to the long arc of *Infinite Jest* will see that such figurations represent no salvific, mythical outside to Wallace's insidious, dystopian structures. Rather, these overgrown, abandoned Concavity children reflect the young tennis players of ETA, themselves subjected to a proliferative series of controlling systems, a putative American worship of talented youths that ends up, in Wallace's consistent estimation, using and damning them (a similar outcome occurs for the wise, messianic child in "Another Pioneer").

Early in *Infinite Jest*, Hal has a nightmare in which he sees a gigantic tennis court with lines "going every which way, and they run oblique or meet and form relationships and boxes and rivers and tributaries and systems inside systems."[47] This scene, where geometry's order devolves into confusion, offers a master image for all the inchoate, interlocking systems in Wallace's work, as Taylor also shows in Chapter 16 here. And while the tennis court is the appropriate hewn landscape for Hal to map, the writing echoes the geometrically precise Illinois farmland that Wallace evoked in "Derivative Sport": "I'd grown up inside vectors, lines and lines athwart lines"[48] – or "systems inside systems." The "arrayed fields" of his youth, Wallace says, were "furrowed into lines as straight as only an Allis Chalmers and sextant can cut them," made ready not just for systems of pesticide, nitrogen and reliable yield, but for giant games of tennis too.[49] As I have demonstrated here, especially when he assembled narratives of at least novella length and complexity, farmland – as arranged by large-scale

[45] Ibid., 561. [46] Ibid., 562. [47] Ibid., 67. [48] Wallace, "Derivative Sport," *SFT*, 3.
[49] Ibid., 6.

agribusiness – was a site to which Wallace returned as his ur-system, his native environment but also an illustration of the postmodern claim that nature was thoroughly artificial, constructed according to the appetites of unbridled consumer capitalism. To this potent tool for understanding a post-1960s existence, though, he added a sense that a new agricultural mythology should be written, connecting the decades of his lifetime to the many more millennia over which humans had, with greater humility, worked, worshipped and partaken of very old land.

CHAPTER 30

David Foster Wallace's Ecologies

Laurie McRae Andrew

One of the best-known lines from David Foster Wallace's 1993 interview with Larry McCaffery is his blunt insistence that "Fiction's about what it means to be a fucking *human being*."[1] But this rallying cry leaves open the question of the world *beyond* the "human being": Does Wallace's rein-scribed literary humanism entail a redoubled anthropocentrism, or is there also room for a relationship between fiction and the more-than-human sphere? Wallace's life and career took place in a period increasingly dominated by concerns about human relationships with ecological envi-ronments, especially in the United States, where the formative years of Wallace's life coincided with a series of major environmental reforms following the establishment of the Environmental Protection Agency in 1970. The foundations of his career were built in the 1980s, a decade that saw membership of US environmental organizations increase from 2 mil-lion to 6.3 million.[2] By the time he died in 2008, recognition of the damage being wrought on the planet's environment had coalesced into an "awareness that the entire Earth's climate is affected by all nations, and that the United States [...] bears some special responsibility for possible environmental collapse later" – as Wallace himself reflected in a 2006 interview.[3] Environmental and ecological issues, then, form a prominent contextual backdrop to his work.

It's not surprising, therefore, that ecology formed one of the earliest major strands in Wallace criticism.[4] And yet, despite his late lamentation of climate crisis, the alignment of Wallace's writing with environmentalism is hardly straightforward. In *Infinite Jest*, he proves happy to turn his satirical lens onto "socially hyperresponsible overpriced" whole-food stores "full of Cambridge Green Party granola-crunchers."[5] More darkly,

[1] McCaffery, "Interview," 26.   [2] Patterson, *Restless*, 117.   [3] Karmodi, "Frightening Time."
[4] See Hayles, "Illusion of Autonomy"; Foster, "A Blasted Region"; Houser, "Disgust."
[5] Wallace, *IJ*, 478.

environmentalism is harnessed to the "Clean US Party" of President Johnny Gentle, in its union of "ultra-right jingoist hunt-deer-with-automatic-weapons types and far-left macrobiotic Save-the-Ozone, -Rain-Forests, -Whales, -Spotted-Owls-and-High-pH-Waterways ponytailed granola-crunchers"[6] – a fictionalized version, perhaps, of the Federation for American Immigration Reform, a far-right offshoot of the 1970s wave of environmentalism. Moreover, the prospect of nature in any genuine and untarnished form is not much in evidence in his writing. On the contrary, one of the major gags in *The Broom of the System* is that of the "Great Ohio Desert" (or "G.O.D."): the thoroughly artificial theme park wilderness that has sprung from the State Governor's desire for a return to nature as "a savage point of reference [...] An Other for Ohio's Self."[7] The result, ironically, is a thoroughly commercial operation overseen by the shadowy "Industrial Desert Design," a multinational corporation whose initials, continuing the Governor's pseudo-psychoanalytic terminology, suggest *id* – the unbound libidinal forces of late capitalism given free rein in this artificial state of "nature." Visitors to the resulting tourist attraction are obliged to "buy a Wander Pass at any gate" and negotiate crowds of people "hawking black tee-shirts"; an enterprise that, as the character Andrew Lang complains, "is just gettin' too goddamn commercialized."[8]

On the one hand, the G.O.D. is a very 1980s joke: an encapsulation of the brash commercialism of that decade, and an echo of Fredric Jameson's diagnosis of postmodernism as "the moment of a radical eclipse of Nature itself [...] irredeemably and irrevocably destroyed by late capital," such that it can no longer serve – despite the Governor's scheme – as "the other of our society."[9] But the G.O.D. also signals a longer history of America's desire for unspoilt wilderness – embodied in the conservationist movement that emerged in the late nineteenth century, after the closing of the western frontier had squeezed out the last areas of continental territory free of Euro-American habitation – and the ambivalent relationship between this desire and capitalist development. The origin of the G.O.D. is placed pointedly in 1972, a neat 100 years after the foundation of one of conservationism's great monuments: Yellowstone National Park, the first of America's national parks to be established. As Ted Steinberg explains, conservationism – far from opposing American civilization with an autonomous nature – always involved the application of the rationalizing logic of industrial capitalism to the physical environment. Steinberg connects conservationism with the scientific theories of industrial labor and

---

[6] Ibid., 382.   [7] Wallace, *BS*, 54.   [8] Ibid., 143, 421.   [9] Jameson, *Postmodernism*, 77.

production management associated with Frederick Winslow Taylor, also developed during the late nineteenth century: "Taylorism controlled workers, conservation controlled nature, and both relied on the principles of scientific management to do so." Yellowstone itself, as Steinberg makes clear, was as much the work of railroad capital sensing profit from tourism as of Congressional action, and the "wilderness" that resulted has always been a work of artifice: "In getting back to nature in the national parks [...] tourists actually bore witness to an engineered environment."[10] In practice, American "wilderness" has long been a product of capitalist development, and of the tourism industry in particular; that the G.O.D. displaces the real-world Wayne National Forest thus seems less an irony than an apt historical progression.[11]

Attention to tourism, then, allows Wallace to uncover a long-running paradox in America's relationship to its ecological environment: the stronger the desire for separate and untarnished natural landscapes, the more intensified the commodification of nature becomes. This is a paradox upon which Wallace plays in his journalistic essays. In his report on the 1993 Illinois State Fair, he tries to shake his "East Coast cynicism" by placing the fair in opposition to the industrial-scale agricultural landscape of the Midwest, as both Severs and Saylor have noted in earlier chapters, whose inhabitants are "alienated from the very space around [them ...] because out here the land's less of an environment than a commodity." He comments, "It's probably hard to feel any sort of Romantic spiritual connection to nature when you have to make your living from it."[12] The fair, despite its "garish and [...] aggressively Special" appearance, purportedly provides a momentary alternative: "the sheer *fact* of the land is to be celebrated here, its yields ogled and stock groomed and paraded, everything on decorative display."[13] What's notable, though, is the way that Wallace's sentence turns on itself: the italicized insistence on facticity making way for the language of "yields" and "stock," whose immediate reference is agricultural, but which also merges with the financial terminology likely familiar to readers of the "swanky East Coast magazine" (*Harper's*) for which the piece was written.[14] The promise of a decommodified and non-alienated relation to the land devolves mid-sentence back into the lexicon of late twentieth-century capitalism. Something similar happens in Wallace's famous account of a Caribbean cruise,

---

[10] Steinberg, *Down to Earth*, 139, 146, 153.   [11] Wallace, *BS*, 54.
[12] Wallace, "Getting Away," *SFT*, 89, 92.   [13] Ibid., 91–92 (emphasis in original).
[14] Ibid., 83.

"A Supposedly Fun Thing I'll Never Do Again": the trip affords Wallace "a chance to realize that the ocean is not one ocean," a line followed by a series of close descriptions of the varied seas encountered in the course of the cruise – a glimpse of autonomous and authentic nature.[15] But the passage resolves into Wallace's identification of the "only real constant" to this "nautical topography": "something about its unreal and almost retouched-looking prettiness [...] the closest I can come is to say that it all looks: *expensive*."[16] This is the irony that Wallace finds in the practice of tourism: It is precisely when the autonomy of ecological environments is posited that these environments become co-opted as commodities, their inherent value reframed in economic terms.

This critique of tourism as a mode of relating to ecologies is expressed even more explicitly in a footnote to "Consider the Lobster" – an account of the 2003 Maine Lobster Festival originally written for *Gourmet* magazine, which Wallace mischievously uses as an opportunity to question the ethics of animal consumption. "To be a mass tourist," he writes, "is to become a pure late-date American [...]. It is to spoil, by way of sheer ontology, the very unspoiledness you are there to experience [...] you become economically significant but existentially loathsome, an insect on a dead thing."[17] This closing image harnesses the practice of tourism to the imagery of the grotesque – an imagery that plays a key role in the essay, as Wallace explores the "deliberate collision, joyful and lucrative and loud" between Maine's tourism and lobster industries, and as the touristic consumption of commodified nature opens onto the literal consumption of the animal body.[18] Wallace raised economic and ethical relationships with animals as a concern alongside climate collapse in his 2006 interview, calling factory farming "one of the great unspoken horrors of modern capitalism," a system in which "every moment of [animals'] lives is suffering and torture" – "a monstrosity."[19] This horror manifests in "Consider" as, converted into an object of consumption (in both economic and physical senses), the materiality of the lobster takes on a thoroughly grotesque aspect: festival participants "sit cheek by jowl, cracking and chewing and dribbling" in an environment characterized by "smells [...] strong and only partly food-related" and "grotesquely inadequate Port-A-San facilities"; lobsters themselves contain "a redolent gout of water that [...] can sometimes jet out lemonlike and catch a tablemate right in the eye."[20] Where "A Supposedly Fun Thing" had explored the

---

[15] Ibid., 306.   [16] Ibid.   [17] Wallace, "Consider," *CL*, 240, n. 6.   [18] Ibid., 235.
[19] Karmodi, "Frightening Time."   [20] Wallace, "Consider," 239, 241.

commodification of an improbably attractive "nature," here the mass consumption of the lobster conversely produces a vulgarized animal form. And, in this disgusting instantiation, the animal body is also brought into association with the throwaway detritus of mass consumption: "styrofoam trays," "coffee in more Styrofoam," "plastic" utensils.[21] This association with waste makes its way into Wallace's potted taxonomy of the lobster itself: "they are garbagemen of the sea, eaters of dead stuff."[22] This essay, then, pinpoints a conjunction between the grotesque debasement of the animal and the mass waste production of late-stage consumer capitalism.

This conjunction of waste with the grotesque points to another major ecological strand in Wallace's writing, and these themes link up with the toxification of natural environments to form a counterpoint to the touristic simulacrum of nature that the G.O.D. represents. In *Broom*, these factors are worked through the novel in a scattered but insistent series of references to the toxification of the Midwestern environment: "clouds with pollutant bases" and "some kindly chemical cloud around the Erieview blackness"; and Lake Erie, which is "kind of a funny color" because its surviving water content is "unfortunately quite small."[23] The lake, in particular, forms a focal point for this toxification, and it's here that the connection with consumption, waste and the grotesque is manifested: Rick Vigorous likens the lake's appearance to "rotten mayonnaise [. . .] squelching brown and white between the pudgy fingers of the wind" – and the revolting image seems to stick, recurring twice more in the novel.[24] A fore-echo of "Consider," this "hideous view" explicitly connects ecological destruction with the decaying waste left over from physical consumption,[25] an image that kicks off the deployment of disgust as a mechanism for environmental engagement in Wallace's writing. As Heather Houser has pointed out, disgust forms the "emotional core" of Wallace's environmental themes, facilitating an effort to overcome "forms of detachment" (like the commodification of tourism) "that block environmental and social investment."[26] It's in this grotesque mode that the concrete fact of ecological environments, in their damaged and degraded late twentieth-century forms, starts to become visible in Wallace's work.

Waste, toxification and ecological destruction take on still more prominence in *Infinite Jest*, in which the disaster zone of the "Great Concavity" forms a dark sequel to *Broom*'s G.O.D. The Concavity is, we hear, a product of the "hideous redolent wastes" of late-stage capitalism;[27] a "toxic

---

[21] Ibid., 239.   [22] Ibid., 237.   [23] Wallace, *BS*, 46, 69, 261–62.   [24] Ibid., 300, 306, 353.
[25] Ibid., 300.   [26] Houser, "Disgust," 120.   [27] Wallace, *IJ*, 382.

horror" that unfolds in the northeastern United States and results in the "ecological gerrymandering" through which the poisoned territory – already damaged beyond repair – becomes a "designated disposal area" into which "all national refuse and waste" is channeled.[28] If Yellowstone is an antecedent to the G.O.D., then the vast rubbish dumps of late twentieth-century America – like New York's Fresh Kills, apocryphally visible from space, or Pennsylvania's GROWS landfill with its improbably Wallacean acronym – are the models for *Jest*'s cartographic reconfiguration. At the same time, the Concavity plot channels a series of high-profile domestic and international environmental disasters beginning in the late 1970s: the toxification of Love Canal, New York (explicitly named as a precedent for the Concavity in the novel), the partial nuclear meltdown on Three Mile Island in 1979, the Bhopal disaster in India in 1984, and the Chernobyl disaster in 1986. By the 1990s, cultural concern about these incidents had crystallized into what Lawrence Buell called the "metaphor of apocalypse": "the single most powerful master metaphor that the contemporary environmental imagination has at its disposal."[29] *Jest*'s Concavity, then, reflects an ecological consciousness increasingly dominated by images of toxic catastrophe.

And yet *Jest*'s environmental apocalypse tends to feel like a rather oddly contained and distant one. This is partly a result of the simple fact that none of the events that take place in and around the Concavity are directly narrated in the course of the novel; it signals a disaster kept both geographically and narratively distant, apparently fulfilling the remit of keeping the problem of excess waste at arm's length from America's social consciousness. In fact, the novel's environmental plot is related almost entirely through Mario Incandenza's homemade puppet show movie, a medium that presents the catastrophe in a resolutely unserious mode, complete with inexplicable "doo-wopping Motown cabinet-puppets."[30] The general tone of silliness continues even as the toxic disaster and its consequences unfold, the relocation of refugees from the uninhabitable territory envisioned in terms of "Snowmobiles and cross-country skiers and roller-skaters on those strange-looking roller-skates with just one line of wheels down each skate [. . .] BMW war-surplus motorcycles with sidecars and guys in goggles and leather helmets" – but not "demographically significant hang-gliding," and not "anything you could call true refugees."[31] The juxtaposition of the comic details with the suggestion of "true

---

[28] Ibid., 399, 403, 405.   [29] Buell, *Environmental Imagination*, 285.   [30] Wallace, *IJ*, 400.
[31] Ibid., 404.

refugees" – the latter indicating the possibility of genuine human consequences to this ecological disaster – serves to underscore the gap between
the predominant tone of the scene and the real impact of environmental
damage. Environmental collapse is encountered through a mediating lens
that disjoins it from its own facticity, turning it into de-realized
comic entertainment.

From our own position of heightened awareness of climate crisis and its
consequences, this devolution of the "metaphor of apocalypse" into a series
of increasingly outlandish gags sits a little uncomfortably – but it also
reflects what Buell called the "environmental doublethink" prevalent at the
end of the twentieth century, a condition in which "Awareness of the
potential gravity of environmental degradation far surpasses the degree to
which people effectively care about it."[32] The cultural situation that
Wallace describes in his manifesto "E Unibus Pluram: Television and
US Fiction," in which a generation reared on commercial entertainment
has been trained "to relate to real live personal up-close stuff in the same
way we relate to the distant and exotic, as if separated from us by physics
and glass, extant only as performance,"[33] seems to constrain the representational possibilities for dealing with ecological apocalypse. Where tourism
has historically converted nature into a commodity at exactly the moment
when ecological autonomy is posited, the dominant entertainment industries of the late twentieth century preemptively reframe environmental
catastrophe as a detached spectacle. The spatial, narrative and tonal distancing of the Concavity's disaster is a reflection on a society that recognizes the fact of waste-generated toxification resulting from the excesses of
advanced capitalism, but remains structurally incapable of taking this
fact seriously.

But, as we hear amid the chatter of Molly Notkin's graduation party,
"Filth by its very nature it is a thing that is creeping always back."[34] Thus,
though the Concavity itself is couched in terms of light entertainment, the
semantics of the grotesque seep into the occasional descriptions of a real
American landscape that appear around the dialogues between Hugh
Steeply and Rémy Marathe on their Arizona mountainside: the sky "was
the faint sick pink of an unhealed burn," and light "ran over everything in
a sickening yellow way like gravy."[35] Within the novel's primary geographical frame, the consequences of the Concavity's toxicity leak into Boston
through the Charles River, described briefly and without explanation as

[32] Buell, *Environmental Imagination*, 4.   [33] Wallace, "Unibus," *SFT*, 64.   [34] Wallace, *IJ*, 233.
[35] Ibid., 530, 646.

"florid-purple" and "Magic Marker-type blue," before we eventually learn that this lurid discolouration originates in the Concavity, and the "annulated Shawshine River" that "feeds the Charles and tints it the exact same tint of blue as the blue on boxes of Hefty SteelSaks";[36] the effects of ecological poisoning flow back through the novel's narrative geography initially unremarked, establishing themselves as a naturalized fact of its spatial environment.

These aspects form part of the novel's exploration of, as N. Katherine Hayles puts it, "the underground seepages and labyrinthine pathways through which the abjected returns in recursive cycles of interconnection."[37] For all its promise of containment, the boundaries of the Concavity turn out to be hopelessly porous, the toxification it is supposed to keep at a distance leaking back into the novel's field of vision. Waste itself turns out to be particularly uncontainable; despite President Gentle's promise to "rid the American psychosphere of the unpleasant debris of a throw-away past,"[38] detritus of various kinds seems to be ingrained everywhere in the novel's topography. Joelle van Dyne encounters alleys filled with "green IWD dumpsters" and sidewalks covered with "sodden litter";[39] Randy Lenz stalks a district in which "garbage from the overfull receptacles [. . .] becomes part of the composition of the street," and later encounters an alleyway "which smelled of ripe waste and rotting skin."[40] Trash, overflowing and unmanageable, is deeply embedded in the shared experience of the city's ordinary spaces.

The novel's fascination with the ubiquity of garbage echoes the prominence of waste and its disposal as an ecological issue in the late 1980s and 1990s, heralding a "new incarnation of environmentalism," which, "By linking toxicity with escalating consumer wastes and social and economic injustice [. . .] expanded to include issues of class, race and labor," according to Heather Rogers.[41] Waste formed a pivot around which ecology turned toward questions of environmental justice, recognizing that the human effects of ecological damage are far from evenly felt – it's fitting, then, that interactions with waste in *Jest* also form indicators of social status. For the elite Enfield Tennis Academy's "Tunnel Club," the journey into underground tunnels in search of rats is tinged with the transgressive thrill of defying Avril Incandenza's "violent phobic thing about vermin and waste and insects and overall facility hygiene," consummated in the

---

[36] Ibid., 184, 237, 561.   [37] Hayles, "Illusion of Autonomy," 687.   [38] Wallace, *IJ*, 382.
[39] Ibid., 221.   [40] Ibid., 583, 729.   [41] Rogers, *Gone Tomorrow*, 165.

discovery of a fridge full of decomposing food.[42] For the homeless heroin addict Poor Tony Krause, on the other hand, withdrawal necessitates a hiding place "in a dumpster complex [...] in Fort Point downtown," soon contaminated with Poor Tony's own bodily effluvia, a more intimate and degrading form of waste that "stayed there, on the summer dumpster's iron floor [...] not going anywhere."[43] The disgust that waste provokes is not a singular phenomenon in this novel; its psychological contours are shaped by social conditions, and thus relationships to waste become signifiers of the entrenched hierarchy of privilege that the novel portrays, providing an intersection between social and ecological contexts.

At the same time, the more intimate stories of the novel's characters also involve relationships to the waste associated with consumer capitalism, connecting in particular with the novel's central themes of addiction and recovery. Joelle, on her way toward an intentional overdose on crack cocaine – a way out of the "cage" of her addiction – buys "a .473-liter Pepsi Cola in a blunt plastic bottle" before immediately pouring the contents down a storm drain and watching it "pool there foaming brownly and stay put because the drain's gate is clogged solid with leaves and sodden litter."[44] This is a moment that presents us, at the lowest point of Joelle's despair, with a disordered relationship to the normative flow of consumption and waste: The disposable plastic receptacle that holds the product intended for consumption has become the valued item (since it's used in the ingestion of the drug, an intentional act of personal toxification), the product itself discarded among the garbage collecting in the drain.

This moment is echoed later in the novel as Don Gately recovers from his gunshot wound in St. Elizabeth's Hospital, struggling to resist the offer of narcotic painkillers that would jeopardize his hard-won sobriety. This is the occasion for the visitation of James Incandenza in the form of a "wraith,"[45] who brings with him a "good old can of Coke" – but one with "alien unfamiliar Oriental-type writing on it instead of the good old words *Coca-Cola* and *Coke*"; "the unfamiliar script on the Coke can is maybe the whole dream's worst moment."[46] Like Joelle's Pepsi bottle, the Coke can is both a ubiquitous symbol of American consumer capitalism and a material object marked for disposal on the other side of consumption – one that aptly reflects how thoroughly the mass generation of waste is integrated into the American economy and culture of the late twentieth

---

[42] Wallace, *IJ*, 671, 673.   [43] Ibid., 301.   [44] Ibid., 222–23, 222.   [45] Ibid., 829.
[46] Ibid., 832.

century. As with Joelle, Gately's moment of acute personal crisis is marked by a discomforting alienation from this familiar object that in turn indicates an instance of disjunction from the familiar cycle of waste. For Rogers, "trash is the visible interface between everyday life and the deep, often abstract horrors of ecological crisis"[47] – and in both characters' alienated and defamiliarizing relationships with these iconic forms of disposable packaging, the dysfunctional large-scale relationship to waste that the Concavity represents is folded into the novel's personal narratives of addiction and despair, and given an immediate and experiential content that counteracts the structural distancing of the Concavity itself.

If there is strategy for overcoming environmental doublethink in Wallace's work, it lies partly in this effort to chart lines of continuity between individual experience and ecological calamity. While the grotesque and disgusting make the debasement of animals and the toxification of the environment viscerally manifest, these moments of defamiliarization promise to open up a vital critical distance from our own practices in everyday life – a gap within which the ecological consequences of these practices might become tangible. There are few straightforwardly didactic lessons about ecologies to be found in Wallace's work, and he was never so naïve as to offer anything like the consolation of a recoverable nature beyond the sphere of human action. Indeed, his writing is perhaps most valuable in ecological terms for the way it gives expression to the thought and feeling of a generation thoroughly disabused of any such notion, conscious of the distorting prisms of tourism and entertainment but also of their inescapability, in the transition between the American environmentalism of the 1970s and 1980s and the impending planetary crisis of the twenty-first century. Wallace's writing doesn't offer immediate solutions the ecological dilemmas that we face now – but it does show us how our relationships to the environment have been constructed through the dominant economic and cultural practices of our recent history, and the kind of work that is required if we are to change them.

[47] Rogers, *Gone Tomorrow*, 3.

"I Could, If You'd Let Me, Talk and Talk"
Institutions, Dialogue and Citizenship in David Foster Wallace

Joel Roberts

Introduction: Wallace Studies and Citizenship

Citizenship is a defining theme of David Foster Wallace's literary and journalistic work. While this might be most explicit in the posthumously published *The Pale King* (2011), which focuses, as a number of scholars have explored, on the shifting relationship between taxation and civic identity in 1980s America, citizenship is nonetheless a thread that runs through Wallace's *oeuvre*.[1] *The Broom of the System* (1987) contains critical depictions of characters with civic leadership responsibilities, such as the manager of the nursing home David Bloemker and the televangelist Reverend Sykes, while the Canadian students' anger at the geographical-ecological mistreatment of Canada by the United States in *Infinite Jest* (1996) evidences a civic-mindedness that is notably absent in Enfield Tennis Academy's American students. Elsewhere, Wallace's short story collections contain a sense of a tragically degraded or absent public sphere, which is apparent in their oscillation between narratives of isolated, privatized lives and stories of political deception and failure. The theme of citizenship, then – of responsibility to a polity – runs through Wallace's fiction. Similar can be said of his non-fiction, where he regularly highlights the existential absurdities of the (de)regulatory civil society of neoliberal capitalism, such as in "A Supposedly Fun Thing I'll Never Do Again" in the collection of the same name, as well as intervening more explicitly in civic debates, such as with his profile of John McCain, "Up, Simba," in *Consider the Lobster* (2005).

The theme of citizenship in Wallace's work thus merits further exploration. Scholarly work to date has productively explored Wallace's "turn" to the question of citizenship in *King*, with Marshall Boswell arguing that Chris Fogle's story is a civic conversion narrative that challenges the

---

[1] See, for example, Boswell, "Trickle-Down Citizenship," and West, "Observacion."

corporate approach to taxation and citizenship in the 1980s.[2] Mark West picks up on this theme to argue that *King* engages with 1970s discourses of citizenship that themselves draw on the Puritan foundations of the first Anglo-American colonies.[3] Elsewhere, Robert Chodat reads Wallace's work, particularly from *Infinite Jest* onward, as a meditation on the relationship between language and civic identity. Chodat traces the influence of Stanley Cavell, James Wallace and John Dewey on what he understands as Wallace's exploration of "bad citizenship" – the different ways that the collective capacity of a polity to form and understand normative concepts has been degraded by what Wallace views as a rampantly individualistic consumer-capitalist culture.[4] Finally, Emily Russell argues that, via the incompleteness of the textual and corporeal body, *Jest* advocates for a form of citizenship that acknowledges the interdependence of the bodies of its citizens in the functioning of its polity.[5]

Wallace's work is consistently engaged with the question of citizenship, be it through his exploration of the role of language in shaping selves, the effects of mass entertainment on populations or his more overt interventions in public political discussion. This chapter outlines a key dynamic in the concept of "citizenship" in Wallace's writing. It argues that his work advocates for the renewal of a republican model of citizenship rooted in civic participation and dialogue. This is evident in the dialogic form of Wallace's fiction, which seeks to create the possibility of civic dialogue that it argues for, and which mirrors the narrative forms of the texts of the ancient republics that stand at the mythical foundation of the contemporary United States. Following this, the chapter then analyses one of the most explicit discussions of citizenship in Wallace's fiction: the elevator scene in *King*. I argue that it demonstrates that the dialogic norm of citizenship in Wallace is circumscribed in a number of limiting ways. This circumscription, I argue, evidences a wider anxiety in Wallace's work about institutionalization, the exclusions that occur in this process and the role of writing in facilitating it. The chapter concludes by suggesting that Wallace's novels seek to make "citizens" of their readers, who are required to have a certain amount of knowledge of them before they can enter into dialogue about them, and that his short fiction offers an alternative to this, where the kind of un- or pre-institutional chatter that sustains his novels' minor characters can occur.

---

[2] Boswell, "Trickle-Down Citizenship," 474.   [3] West, "Observacion," 230.
[4] Chodat, *High Words*.   [5] Russell, *Reading Embodied Citizenship*, 178.

"Always with You This Freedom!": Liberal and Republican Theories of Citizenship

Readings of citizenship in Wallace to date can arguably be understood through liberal and republican theories of it. Iseult Honohan's intellectual history of citizenship usefully traces the convergence and divergence of these two ideals. Honohan begins by outlining, "Citizenship has three distinct dimensions: legal status and rights, activity, and membership," and notes that "different conceptions of citizenship interpret, connect, and prioritise these differently." The divergence in these two traditions, Honohan suggests, is related to the concept of freedom. She continues, "Risking oversimplifying, we may say that the liberal conception focuses more on legal status and rights, and the republican conception relatively more on activity." For citizens of a liberal state, freedom is something that they have and that the law and its institutions protects against the infringement of; for citizens of a republican state, freedom is produced through the political process of collective deliberation and lawmaking, and is embedded in the wider concept of the common good.[6] Honohan outlines that the liberal tradition "focus[es] primarily on structures that protect individual rights, seen as pre-political," and that "as far as the state is concerned, freedom represents more a constraint on government than a goal it should promote." Consequently, liberal citizenship has a tendency to "rule out the state's promoting any particular idea of the good life."[7] In this sense, liberal citizenship upholds what Isaiah Berlin described as "negative liberty," where the freedom that citizens enjoy is legal protection from state interference – and undue interference from other citizens – in their life.[8]

Numerous critics have identified critiques of negative liberty in Wallace's fiction, and by extension of liberal citizenship.[9] Indeed, one understanding of Wallace's *oeuvre* could be that it moves from a critique of the degradations of liberal citizenship (*Jest*, *Brief Interviews*, *Oblivion*) to an appeal for the renewal of republican citizenship (*King*). In this reading, Wallace's work advocates for a polity wherein citizens are aware, as DeWitt Glendenning puts it in *King*, that "they were part of Everything, that huge Everybody Else that determined policy and taste and the common good," which is "made up of a whole lot of individuals."[10]

---

[6] Honohan, "Conceptions," 90–91. [7] Ibid., 87. [8] See Berlin and Harris, *Liberty*.
[9] See Hayes-Brady, *Failures*, 197; Kelly, "Development"; and Williams "'Something Real American.'"
[10] Wallace, *TPK*, 135.

§19 in *King* is perhaps the most explicit discussion of citizenship in Wallace's fiction, and it thus offers a useful lens through which to consider the wider functioning of this concept in his writing. Edmund Waldstein has observed that the dialogue in the scene laments that an active citizenry collectively formulating an agreement about what constitutes the common good, has all but vanished because of the negative liberty of liberal citizenship.[11] The founding fathers "cared more about the nation and the citizens than about themselves" and "were geniuses of civic virtue."[12] However,

> in the 1830s and '40s [...] states started granting charters of incorporation to larger and regulated companies [(...] [de Tocqueville] says somewhere that one thing about democracies and their individualism is that they by their very nature corrode the citizen's sense of true community, of having real true fellow citizens whose interests and concerns were the same as his.[13]

Republican civic virtue, then, has been eroded by liberal citizenship. "Individual citizens," Glendenning laments, "have adopted a corporate attitude."[14] The confluence of "liberal individualism" and "consumer capitalism" has created a situation where individuals seek only to protect their own interests and freedoms, with little sense of responsibility to a wider polity.[15]

Adam Kelly notes that the "unattributed quality of the dialogue" in this passage, coupled to Wallace's refusal to divide "the positions of his characters into traditional liberal/conservative or left/right binaries," means that the scene "can be read as Wallace's depiction of what an informed and open conversation about American political and intellectual history might look like."[16] The point, then, is not so much what any individual character says, but rather that they conduct this dialogue with one another and that their idea of citizenship develops as a consequence.[17] Arguably, this assessment of the scene does not undermine the observation that Glendenning's contributions represent the civic ideal of the novel. Indeed, Matthew Ryan Stewart observes that Glendenning "offers a representation of something fairly close to the ideal citizen for Wallace," and that "Wallace-the-character yearns for approval and comradery from Glendenning," as is evident in the fantasy where Wallace meets Glendenning and they bond over their shared frustration with Lehrl.[18] To this, it can be added that the dialogic ideal of the chapter is mirrored in

---

[11] See Waldstein, "The Dialectics of Individualism."   [12] Wallace, *TPK*, 135.
[13] Ibid., 135, 143.   [14] Ibid., 139.   [15] Ibid.   [16] Kelly, "Development," 278.   [17] Ibid.
[18] Stewart, "Modern Myth," 46–47.

Glendenning's pining for a citizenry that realizes that "they were part of Everything, that huge Everybody Else." The active, responsible citizenship of Glendenning's republican ideal is played out through the dialogic structure of the chapter (although, again, the overwhelming whiteness of *King*'s imaginary complicates this ideal, as Saylor points out in Chapter 27).

Wallace's fiction also embodies this deliberative, participatory citizenship in its form. As Kelly has outlined, his novels offer "a dialogic context in which both sides of the argument can be offered to the reader, without a clear authorial conclusion drawn," as with the famous Marathe-Steeply dialogue in *Infinite Jest*, where Wallace gives "full due" to both sides of the argument.[19] This, Kelly argues, is also structurally true of *Jest* and *The Pale King*, with the former "concerned to ask how technological developments should alter our political commitments" and the latter concerned with "the rise of the corporation [. . .] placing historic ideas of citizenship under crushing pressure."[20] *Jest* and *King* engage in extended dialogue about these ideas, with pronouncements such as Glendenning's, that he doesn't "want to put the issue in political terms when it's probably irreducibly political," demonstrating that there is "no master discourse" in Wallace's fiction, thus inviting the reader into the conversation.[21] The multiple registers of Wallace's fiction invite the reader to dialogue with these texts about the social and political questions they raise.

Iain Williams pushes this evaluation of the republican civic form of Wallace's fiction further, insinuating that it mirrors the texts of the Athenian republic that underpin the republican notion of citizenship. Williams observes that Wallace's fiction often mimics the questioning format of "socratic" dialogue (as with the Marathe-Steeply dialogue in *Infinite Jest*, and the elevator scene in *The Pale King*), since he was "most interested in the moment of potential that is created when differing ideas meet and compete."[22] The emphasis on dialogue in and the dialogic form of Wallace's fiction thus draws on the truth seeking of Socratic dialogues, which, as Kelly explains, "are constructed on the assumption that '[t]ruth is not born nor is it to be found inside the head of an individual person, it is born *between people* collectively searching for truth.'"[23] The dialogic form of Wallace's fiction is an invitation to collectively search for truth via dialogue.

[19] Kelly, "Development," 275.   [20] Ibid., 279.
[21] Wallace, *TPK*, 138; Kelly, "Development," 279–80.
[22] Williams, "'Something Real American,'" 10.   [23] Kelly, "Development," 269–70.

Beyond the Socratic form of Wallace's fiction, his texts have other formal qualities that mirror those of the ancient literature of the republican ideal. For example, *Jest* might be understood as an epic in the mold of Homer's *Iliad*, detailing the tragic failure of government in its polity and lamenting the loss of civic virtue that is both its cause and effect. Stewart has noted that this lament can be coupled to the tragic civic heroism of Glendenning in *King*. As he outlines, one way of understanding Glendenning's story is that his hallucinatory mental decline in §48 suggests that his subjective coherence as the advocate for renewed civic life has symbolically shattered under the pressure of the corporate model of citizenship ushered in by the neoliberal reforms of the 1980s.[24] In the historical narrative of Wallace's fiction, the heroic failure of Glendenning's project of civic renewal results in the epic tragedy of *Jest*'s world of privatized, corporatized decay, as is exemplified by the private sponsorship of time, the United States' creation of the Great Concavity, and the depression and loneliness of Hal in the novel. Without the civic virtue that Glendenning argues for in *King*, the aggressively individualizing impulse of the 1980s tax reforms will create the dystopian world found in *Jest*.

The Institutionalization of Citizenship

The theme of the renewal of republican citizenship in Wallace's work arguably takes on a different – and more ambivalent – emphasis when considered in relation to the representation of civic institutions in his fiction. David Hering has argued that Wallace's fiction has a consistent preoccupation with the "rapacious nature of the institution" and its "figurative and cultural geographical colonizing" of the space outside itself, with examples including the imposition of the G.O.D. on Wayne National Forest in *The Broom of the System*, the absorption of the Midwest landscape by the classroom in *Girl with Curious Hair*, and the "progressive institutionalization" depicted in *Jest* and *Brief Interviews*.[25] Hering summarizes this dynamic as "an ambivalent anxiety central to Wallace's fiction: the institutional site will come, both figuratively and literally, to dominate, subsume and exterminate the space outside of itself."[26]

[24] Stewart, "Modern Myth," 68–69.   [25] Hering, *Fiction and Form*, 53, 55–56, 62, 78.
[26] Ibid., 51.

Here, perhaps one important addition to Hering's claim is that the institutions with which Wallace is concerned are largely ones that administer and produce the life of the *citizen*. This is evident in *BS*'s focus on the Shaker Heights Nursing Home, site of the administration of the life of the nation's elderly population; *Girl*'s focus on the lives of civic, institutional figures such as senators, lawyers and television show hosts; *Jest*'s consistent comparisons of the institutional space of the tennis academy to the nation-state and the positioning of Alcoholics Anonymous as a model institution; *Brief Interviews*' ambivalent concern about the institutional (re)production of violent citizens; *Oblivion*'s documentation of the brutality that develops in the absence of the civic virtue of republican institutions; and *The Pale King*'s focus on the offices of the Internal Revenue Service and their role in shaping the life of the American citizen. Wallace's fiction hinges on its concern about the role of the institution in shaping the life and identity of the citizen.

In Wallace's fictions, institutions colonize the space outside themselves, and this act of incorporation is one that his texts are deeply ambivalent about. Mark McGurl argues that Wallace was a writer shaped by institutions – "a Program Man if ever there was one" – particularly the university and the knowledge it produces, and that his fictions lead readers indoors, into the institution, as in *The Pale King*'s move from the vista of the Midwest into the offices of the IRS.[27] Yet, as Hering has noted, there is an ambivalence in Wallace's text about this move indoors; *Broom* concludes with Lenore "escap[ing] from the novel itself" after "negotiating five apparently 'tightly locked' monadic environments," while "the englobing image in 'Lyndon' indirectly indicates a centripetal global subjugation to US territory."[28] In *Infinite Jest*, the institution is a safe space from the polluted world outside, which itself is polluted by ONAN's institutions, while the imprisoned, imprisoning narratives of *Brief Interviews* are mirrored in the institutional confinement of their protagonists, as with "interview #59 [with] a male character in [the] 'Harold R and Phyllis N. Engleman Institute for Continuing Care.'"[29] In Wallace's writing, the institution might provide shelter, but it is also stultifying and claustrophobic in its envelopment of the world outside.

If institutions are the space of the citizen in Wallace's work, they also enact a disconcerting incorporation of that which is outside them. Here, Hering's observation that the spatial dynamic of institutions in Wallace represents "an ambivalent anxiety central to [his] fiction" can help to

[27] McGurl, "Institution," 77.   [28] Hering, *Fiction and Form*, 52, 59.   [29] Ibid., 69.

illuminate the conflicted concept of citizenship in Wallace. If we acknowledge that institutions in Wallace are spaces that produce and administer the life of the citizen, then we can understand this ambivalence about institutional expansion as related to the figure of the citizen. That is, in Wallace's fiction, the institutional establishment of norms for the citizen mirrors the geographical expansiveness of the institution, since it likewise works to "dominate, subsume and exterminate" that which is outside itself.[30] As the institution expands, more and more aspects of life are subsumed by the norms of citizenship.

On first glance, Wallace's dialogic, republican citizenship seems to avoid establishing itself as an enveloping, institutionalizing norm; citizenship in his work is relational rather than ontologically static, made through dialogue rather than preexisting it. However, a closer analysis of the conditions under which such dialogue can take place reveals the establishment of a number of norms that circumscribe participation. This is evident in §19 of *King*, where Glendenning consistently acts as a disciplining voice. He condescends to the other participants ("Did your school have civics when you were a boy? Do you even know what civics is?"), and this paternal dynamic structures the ongoing conversation.[31] Each of the challenges made by the other participants – the Vietnam War, the Civil Rights movements of the 1960s, the patriarchal whiteness of the slave-owning founding fathers – to Glendenning's narrative is rationalized by him. The conversation is thus not so much a performance of the dialogic ideal, as it is a demonstration of the coerciveness of the public sphere that the scene – and Glendenning – are advocating for. Objections to Glendenning's vision float around the passage as disconnected voices, only drawn together by his narration of the events they reference. Glendenning thus establishes the norm of the conversation, which is an ability to narrate, with rhetorical persuasiveness, the world-historical significance of American political history within the discourse that he sanctions and polices.

In this scene, the precondition of dialogic republican citizenship is willingness to submit to the discursive disciplining of Glendenning and the version of American history he legitimizes. As the "primal scene" of citizenship in Wallace's work, what this suggests is that civic participation is inescapably circumscribed by (often subtly coercive) norms. As a representative of the institutions of civic virtue for which he advocates, Glendenning's role in the conversation demonstrates the way that

[30] Ibid., 51.   [31] Wallace, *TPK*, 133.

institutions insist on translating dialogue into a register that they have sanctioned. The scene thus demonstrates that comprehension and comprehensibility via institutional norms are the preconditions of participation in civic, dialogic exchange, and that the gently coercive power of rhetoric still operates within it. The republican, dialogic ideal of Wallace's fiction is in fact circumscribed by norms that discipline speech into institutionally acceptable forms of meaning-making.

This runs through Wallace's novels. *Broom* is focalized through Lenore coming to realize that language functions via a collectively agreed set of norms; *Jest* is focalized through Don Gately's recovery and his absorption of the wisdom of the "Crocodiles";[32] *King* is focalized through Chris Fogle's conversion and Glendenning's heroic failure to restore civic virtue to the polity. In each case, norms are established as the precondition of dialogue – the necessity of understanding the norms that condition the functioning of language (and thus dialogue) in *Broom*; the norms of the recovery narrative in AA in *Jest*; and the norms of institutionally legitimate historical and political knowledge in *King*.

"I Could, If You'd Let Me, Talk and Talk"

The anxiety about institutions in Wallace's fiction extends to those that shape the practice of creative writing in America. Hering argues that "the subsumption and containment of the Illinois countryside in 'Westward' [occurs] via the institutional environment of the creative writing workshop," as the Midwestern landscape is increasingly enveloped across the stories in *Girl*, culminating with the writing workshop in "Westward."[33] This is to say, then, that while Wallace's fiction advocates for reviving the engaged, deliberative citizen, it is also aware of writing's institutionalizing, normalizing effect. As he remarked of the development of Euro-American metafiction in the aftermath of the Second World War, "after the pioneers always come the crank turners [. . . who] capitalize for a while on sheer fashion, and they get their plaudits and grants and buy their IRAs [investment retirement accounts]."[34] What is interesting here is that the "crank turners" are institutional figures, who "get their plaudits and grants." Wallace is concerned that institutions create norms that circumscribe writing, and, by association, dialogue and citizenship.

In this sense, Wallace's short fiction might hold more radical political potential than his novels. Wallace's novels demand that their reader

[32] Wallace, *IJ*, 278.   [33] Hering, *Fiction and Form*, 56–59.   [34] McCaffery, "Interview," 30.

become a "citizen" of them; their "norm" is that one must be imbued with knowledge of their encyclopedic characters, events and settings before one can speak about them. The short fiction does not make this demand with such intensity, and might thus be understood as less "institutionalizing" than Wallace's novels, insofar as engagement with it is less dependent on the "norm" of the exhaustive knowledge that is arguably required by the latter.

Here, we might also try to stay with the failure of Glendenning's civic renewal and the resultant inferno that is the world in *Infinite Jest*.[35] Perhaps, rather than attempting to renew citizenship, which inevitably brings failure and the risks of institutionalization, the task is simply to talk. At the opening of *Jest*, which we might understand as the revealing of the world produced by the failure of civic renewal in *King*, Hal declares, "I could, if you'd let me, talk and talk."[36] He is illegible to the institution of the tennis academy here, who look upon him with "horror."[37] Rather than being concerned with the renewal of institutions and the norms they establish that circumscribe civic dialogue, Hal simply wants to talk. It is perhaps this speech, the unknown chatter of *Jest*'s cast of minor characters, who just want to talk – "Let's talk about anything," as Hal pleads – that offers a way to survive the decay and decline of the polity that is the backdrop of Wallace's work.[38]

In the absence of institutional renewal, and with the danger of institutional normalization, there is the chatter of characters such as Clenette in *Jest*, which does not register at the level of the institution, but which is nonetheless the unspoken engine of the novel. As Daniel Roach observes, Clenette "serves as the vector by which the Entertainment moves from ETA to Ennet House," which leads to Marathe's infiltration of it.[39] Clenette is vital to the narrative, then, yet in some way excluded from it, as Shapiro has discussed in Chapter 28. Roach notes that, in the one passage that represents Clenette's thought, "In contrast to most of the novel, a narrator does not intervene or mediate [. . .] either in the discourse or in endnotes."[40] While she is part of the recovery house, Clenette's voice is not mediated through the program – the institution – of recovery, nor of the narrator. Her speech exists outside the institution, unincorporated into the norms necessary for its dialogue.

When considering Clenette's role in the narrative, Roach highlights that her speech "becomes a marker of difference that leads to negative narrative

[35] On the use of Dante in *IJ*, see Higgins, "Narrative Infinity."   [36] Wallace, *IJ*, 12.
[37] Ibid., 12.   [38] Ibid.   [39] Roach, "Binding Commonalities," 79.   [40] Ibid., 78.

consequences." We might understand the "negative narrative consequences" of Clenette's speech – analogous to the civic destruction wrought
by the Entertainment cartridge that she brings to Ennet House – as the
destruction of the institutions of the citizen and their norms. Her sharing
that "Wardine be down at my crib cry say her momma aint treat her right,
and I go on with Reginald to his building where he live at, and Wardine be
sit deep far back in a closet in Reginald crib, and she be cry" contains none
of the narrator's mediation of interiority that is common to the Ennet
House characters in *Jest*.[41] While Clenette remains ensnared by the institution insofar as she is a character written by Wallace, who "reads like an
exhibitionist 'sampler' on black consciousness," produced in the institutional setting of the writing program, she is nonetheless suggestive of the
desire for some kind of life outside of the citizen and its institutions in
Wallace's work, which is nevertheless consistently folded back into it.[42]
In light of Glendenning's failure to renew civic virtue in *King*, and in
acknowledgment of the exclusionary danger of the institutional norms of
civil society that is present throughout Wallace's work, Clenette's chatter
perhaps represents the only available alternative. Perhaps what is to be
done is not to try and renew civic virtue, but rather to try and talk, "about
anything," in ways unmediated by the norms of civic institutions and
their citizens.

---

[41] Wallace, *IJ*, 37.   [42] Roach, "Binding Commonalities," 78–79.

CHAPTER 32

David and Dutch
Wallace, Reagan and the US Presidency
David Hering

In 1985, the political biographer and writer Edmund Morris told his publisher Random House that "I want to make literature out of Ronald Reagan."[1] Morris had been commissioned by the White House to write the president's official biography after the success of his 1979 book *The Rise of Theodore Roosevelt*. However, the making of literature out of Reagan proved to be surprisingly difficult. The book *Dutch* was eventually released in 1999, over a decade after the end of Reagan's tenure. Morris admitted that his writing problems were connected to the president's character, telling friends that:

> Ronald Reagan is a man of benign remoteness and no psychological curiosity [. . .]. He gives nothing of himself to intimates [. . .] believing that he has no self to give [. . .]. Any orthodox quest for the real "Dutch," then, is bound to be an exercise in frustration [. . .]. Since Reagan has been primarily a phenomenon of the American imagination [. . .] he can be re-created only by an extension of biographical technique.[2]

Instead of a conventional biography, Morris wrote a partly fictionalized memoir into which he wrote himself as a contemporary of Reagan. Morris' lateral approach to the depiction of the president – one that confronts the impossibility of faithfully or engagingly presenting him as anything other than cultural or psychological phenomenon – recalls J. G. Ballard's "Why I Want to Fuck Ronald Reagan" from *The Atrocity Exhibition*, in which the prepresidential Reagan is described in similar terms to Morris' depiction:

> Fragments of Reagan's cinetized postures were used in the construction of model psychodramas in which the Reagan-figure played the role of husband, doctor, insurance salesman, marriage counselor, etc. The failure of these roles to express any meaning reveals the nonfunctional character of

---

[1] Morris, *Dutch*, vii–viii. [2] Ibid., viii–ix.

Reagan. Reagan's success therefore indicates society's periodic need to re-conceptualize its political leaders. Reagan thus appears as a series of posture concepts.[3]

During Reagan's presidency, these "posture concepts" came, unsurprisingly, to fascinate certain postmodern theorists preoccupied with what Fredric Jameson famously referred to as "a new depthlessness."[4] Jean Baudrillard described Reagan's public image as a triumph of advertising: "Governing today means giving acceptable signs of credibility. It is like advertising and it is the same effect that is achieved – commitment to a scenario, whether it be a political or an advertising scenario. Reagan's is both at once."[5]

It is in the context of advertising and salesmanship that David Foster Wallace makes a lengthy reference to Reagan in his essay on John McCain, "Up, Simba," outlining the difference between two kinds of presidential candidate. The first figure, a "leader," has the ability, whatever their moral foibles, to "help us overcome the limitations of our own individual laziness and selfishness and weakness and fear and get us to do better, harder things than we can get ourselves to do on our own."[6] The second figure is a "salesman," whose "ultimate, overriding motivation," despite having the charisma of a leader, is "self-interest."[7] Wallace suggests that rather than being a leader, Reagan was instead "a great salesman" who was effective at selling "the idea of himself as a great leader."[8] Writing in 2000, over a decade after the end of Reagan's administration, Wallace believes that young voters can now "smell a marketer a mile away" because they came of age with the kind of political salesmanship that Reagan represents.[9] Back in the 1980s, though, his own sense of smell was not so acute. As Max reports in *Every Love Story Is a Ghost Story*, Wallace voted for Reagan in 1980.[10]

Between the 1980s and the early 1990s, Wallace's political position changed substantially. This shift is illustrated perhaps most directly in his comments about consumerism in a 2006 interview:

> America, as everybody knows, is a country of many contradictions, and a big contradiction for a long time has been between a very aggressive form of capitalism and consumerism against what might be called a kind of moral or civic impulse [. . .]. Sometime – I'm not sure whether it was the 1990s or 1980s in America – half of that conflict really sort of disappeared.[11]

---

[3] Ballard, *Atrocity*, 167. [4] Jameson, *Postmodernism*, 6. [5] Baudrillard, *America*, 109.
[6] Wallace, "Up," *CL*, 225. [7] Ibid., 226. [8] Ibid., 227. [9] Ibid.
[10] Max, *Every Love Story*, 259. [11] Karmodi, "Frightening Time."

This quotation is an amended rephrasing of the leader/salesman split raised in the McCain essay, and when one takes a long view of Wallace's career, it becomes increasingly evident how the acts of the Reagan administration exposed Wallace to a convergence between social conservatism and neoliberalism, one which formed the basis of much of Wallace's subsequent political writings, particularly those regarding the presidency and the question of leadership. Wallace's disquiet at this convergence manifests itself in the fiction as early as the mid-1980s, in the story "Lyndon," before becoming a more substantial critique of neoliberal economics in *The Pale King*, much of which takes place during Reagan's second term. However, this doesn't preclude Wallace retaining a socially conservative position on civics until the end of his career, one based upon a rather idealized image of a pre-neoliberal unified nation. Wallace's fiction also enacts Morris and Ballard's model of Reagan as a "nonfunctional character" with "no psychological curiosity"; this is staged by Wallace via a series of tangential portraits of Reagan or Reagan's America that do not directly depict the president, but instead exploring this nonfunctionality indirectly through analogy or parody. Wallace breaks with this tradition in his late and unfinished story "Wickedness," in which Reagan is at least nominally the subject.

"Lyndon": Reagan's Civic Failures

"Lyndon" is partly modeled on a true story: the life of Lyndon Johnson's aide Walter Jenkins, who resigned his post after an arrest for cottaging in 1964, an event homophobically exploited by Barry Goldwater in his unsuccessful election campaign against Johnson. Jenkins was, like David Boyd in "Lyndon," extremely close to the first family. "Lyndon" presents an alternative history of Johnson's presidency, with Wallace's most striking historical alteration being Johnson's death in 1968 on the eve of the election that he declined to contest (Wallace includes a fictional eulogy by Jack Childs), when in reality he died five years later in 1973.[12] The story's other major anachronism is the controversial decision to depict Boyd and his lover Duverger as suffering from AIDS at a time before the condition had been formally identified in the United States. "Lyndon" was most likely written during Reagan's second term as it was first published in *Arrival* in 1987, and I read it here as an analogy, at least in part, for the social legacy of Reagan's presidency. In "Lyndon," Johnson's fictional

[12] Wallace, "Lyndon," *GCH*, 108–9.

death in 1968 coincides with the election won by Nixon, which signaled the beginning of the end of the former's so-called Big Society, which was one of the final iterations of the New Deal in American politics.[13] While the New Deal didn't wither immediately upon Nixon's victory, the beginnings of deregulation gathered momentum under his administration. It was in Reagan's presidency, though, that neoliberalism really began to bloom. By writing about Johnson in the Reagan era, Wallace analogously situates an early version of the civic leader/salesman split at the political moment between the end of the New Deal and rise of neoliberalism.

Wallace also incorporates into "Lyndon" a largely unchallenged socially conservative political commentary on the counterculture of the 1960s. Watching Vietnam War protestors, Johnson suggests to Boyd that the youth of America have "had it too goddamn easy," and that people "need some suffering to even be Americans inside."[14] Suffering, an increasingly prevalent motif across Wallace's fiction, is often aligned with social responsibility, namely a commitment to certain civic tasks that are unpleasant to carry out, and which are important to understanding how societies should operate altruistically. Here Johnson defines protest as an empty, performative suffering when set against civic responsibility, and in a monologue unanswered by Boyd, he states that the protestors are complaining because they lack "genuine stimulation" due to "these careful domestic programs."[15] While this sentiment is in the mouth of a character, it's not the last time that Wallace voices disdain for the lack of responsibility in 1960s counterculture. In his controversial 1996 essay "Hail the Returning Dragon, Cloaked in New Fire," Wallace argues that the devastation wrought by AIDS could be the "salvation of sexuality" in the 1990s after what he sees as the legacy of the 1960s: "Civil Rights, rebellion as fashion, inhibition-killing drugs, the moral castration of churches and censors. Bikinis, miniskirts. 'Free love.' Sex could finally be unconstrained, 'Hang-up'-free, just another appetite: casual."[16] Wallace's queasy position on AIDS is strikingly socially conservative, incorporating a tin-eared equation of sincere and long-standing political positions and stylish poses; the Civil Rights Movement is made analogous here with "rebellion as fashion." Wallace places emphasis here on the importance of the individual's responsibility, framing suffering as the virtue of not being "casual,"

---

[13] Severs has produced the fullest analysis of Wallace's relationship to the New Deal in *Fictions of Value*, in which he believes that Wallace's interest relates to a time "when the nation relearned the meaning of monetary value and submitted to its profound intertwining with the civic" (63).
[14] Wallace, "Lyndon," *GCH*, 106.   [15] Ibid.   [16] Wallace, "New Fire," *BFN*, 170.

but retaining a civic duty to not infect your fellow citizens with a deadly virus. If we read "Hail the Returning Dragon" alongside the very different treatment of AIDS in "Lyndon," while considering Lyndon as a response to Reagan's presidency, we can begin to better understand the gradual development of the civic/salesman split in Wallace's writing.

The Reagan administration became notorious in its second term for its failure to acknowledge HIV and AIDS, which had by then developed into a full-blown national health crisis. Reagan famously only mentioned AIDS unprompted in a speech in 1986, around the time that Wallace was writing "Lyndon." By having the dying Johnson welcome the AIDS-stricken Duverger into his bed in a gesture of companionship at the climax of the story, Wallace implicitly positions the current president's negligent stance on AIDS as a failure of civic duty. Dr. Paul Volberding, who treated some of the first AIDS patients in America, excoriated Reagan for his slow response, believing that "it was a political calculation. This wouldn't sell to Republican voters."[17] While suffering itself might be a noble pursuit, letting those with AIDS suffer because it didn't play well with voters is, for Wallace, an unconscionable act. This is perhaps the first major example of the divergence between civic leadership and salesmanship in Wallace's writing, where the well-being of the population is subjugated to the saleable image and act of the presidency.

Performing Reagan: *Infinite Jest*

Johnny Gentle, the dysfunctional germophobe president of ONAN in *Infinite Jest*, is an amalgam of presidential caricatures, with elements of his character recalling the portraits of Nixon in Robert Coover's *The Public Burning* and Thomas Pynchon's *Gravity's Rainbow*, along with an explicit parody of George Bush Sr.'s infamous "read my lips – no new taxes" speech.[18] However, the emphasis on Gentle's former career as an entertainer allows Wallace to explore more directly the cultural dissemination of Jean Baudrillard's "synopsis of performance and enterprise"[19] that accompanied Reagan's presidency. The description of Gentle is littered with covert references to Reagan's career; his stewardship of the "Velvety Vocalists Guild" evokes Reagan's presidency of the Screen Actors Guild in the 1940s and 1950s, and the account of Gentle's bringing of General Electric "to heel"[20] recalls Reagan's tenure as spokesperson for General

---

[17] La Ganga, "First Lady."   [18] Wallace, *IJ*, 441.   [19] Baudrillard, *America*, 105.
[20] Ibid., *IJ*, 382.

Electric, a position that biographer Garry Wills credits with Reagan's transition from Democratic to Republican politics.[21] Finally, Gentle's promise of "novel sources of revenue" speaks to the "trickle-down" economic policies that Wallace would later critique in *The Pale King*.[22]

The future America depicted in *Infinite Jest* is suffused with indirect references to the amalgamation of entertainment, salesmanship and politics that characterized Reagan's vision. In the world of ONAN, this has become forcibly animated in national institutions; a simulated presidency has prefigured a simulated nation. The assassins of the AFR recall one of Reagan's most celebrated roles from the 1942 melodrama *King's Row*, in which his character Drake McHugh has his legs amputated after a train accident. McHugh's famous cry of "Where's the rest of me?" (which Reagan would subsequently use as the title of his autobiography) is also enacted in the repeated motifs of disembodiment throughout the novel. More broadly, the generational appeal of Reagan's pragmatic pre-method approach to acting, and his generic matinee-hero roles, is implicitly invoked in the pre-postmodern figure of action valorized by James Incandenza's father, who criticizes the way in which Marlon Brando ruined "two generations' relations with their own bodies."[23] One might also see Reagan in the heroic pre-postmodern screen idol of lawman Steve McGarrett in *Hawaii Five-O*, whose "field of action is bare of diverting clutter," according to Hal Incandenza's essay; Reagan was notable for almost exclusively playing heroes onscreen.[24]

This synthesis of enterprise and performance is most clearly stated when Gentle tells the citizens of ONAN to "sit back and enjoy the show," having promised that he will make "tough choices" on behalf of the nation.[25] Of course, making tough choices for us is not the same as asking us to suffer or to carry out those tough choices ourselves. In the McCain essay, Wallace explicitly associates this latter quality with his leader figures like JFK, who can inspire citizens to do better and more difficult things; Gentle, then, is a salesman writ large.[26]

---

[21] Wills, *Reagan's America*, 305.   [22] Wallace, *IJ*, 383.   [23] Ibid., 157.   [24] Ibid., 141.
[25] Ibid., 383.
[26] It is also useful to read Gentle's stewardship of ONAN in the context of Wallace's decision to vote for Ross Perot, who opposed the North American Free Trade Agreement (or NAFTA), which ONAN clearly parodies. While it was Clinton, and not Reagan, who implemented NAFTA, the movement toward international free-trade agreements that is lampooned in ONAN, and Wallace's vote for Perot, make it clear that in the mid-90s, he was still occupying a broadly conservative but anti-neoliberal position.

Reagan's Legacy: *The Pale King* and "Up Simba"

The Pale King and "Up, Simba" develop this view of the Reagan era as a desacralizing moment for American civics. However, what sets these works apart from *Infinite Jest* and "Lyndon" is that they approach it in a more explicitly dialogic fashion, with the McCain essay being constructed as an appeal to the young voter, and §19 of *The Pale King* taking the form of an extended dialogue on politics. In Wallace's later work, the question of suffering also takes on increased significance. Lyndon Johnson's suggestion that Vietnam protestors should "go be responsible for something for a second" is echoed in Wallace's portrait of McCain, who was a Vietnam POW for over four years.[27] Wallace holds up this suffering as a supreme example of behavior "opposed to [one's] own self-interest."[28] This quality, he suggests, could make an ideal leader, but Wallace's problem with McCain is that Wallace is unsure whether this campaign is genuinely based on altruism or on a strategy of cynically using McCain's suffering to sell him as a candidate.[29] That merging of political persona and neoliberal politics that concretized under Reagan has, Wallace implies, impaired our ability to gauge the sincerity of a presidential campaign, and essentially reduced voter choice to a leap of faith. This position also explains Wallace's tentative hopes about McCain, a politician who underwent suffering for a cause other than himself prior to the neoliberal era proper, and who therefore might somehow be immune to its excesses.

In *The Pale King*, set in Reagan's birth state of Illinois, the relationship between neoliberalism and civics forms the basic structure of the plot. Wallace dramatizes what he sees as a split between civic government and corporate-led government in the implementation of the fictional Spackman initiative, a neoliberal attempt to deregulate the IRS. This deregulation occurs – as Marshall Boswell, Richard Godden and Michael Szalay have argued – as a direct response to Reagan's first-term tax policy.[30] This policy, often referred to as trickle-down economics, suggests that cutting tax rates will encourage investment and growth due to job creation, which will lead to increased tax revenue. The failure of this policy instead created a massive deficit and subsequent recession, though Reagan

---

[27] Wallace, "Lyndon," *GCH*, 107.   [28] Wallace, "Up," *CL*, 164.

[29] On this score, Wallace's position on Vietnam seems not to have shifted too much since the late 1980s. He still seems more comfortable with the selflessness of the soldier, and in both this essay and in "Lyndon," Wallace doesn't spend significant time considering the plight of the Vietnamese citizen.

[30] See Godden and Szalay, "The Bodies in the Bubble"; and Boswell, "Trickle-Down Citizenship."

later took credit for the natural economic recovery by framing it as an outcome of his earlier plan. Garry Wills suggests that, through this "malign neglect of governmental machinery rather than legislative abolition of it," Reagan solidified post-Watergate public distrust as he "governed by discrediting government."[31]

Accordingly, while the distrust or hatred of government in "Lyndon" is staged as a failure by young voters to understand certain civic values held by the previous generation, the skepticism in *The Pale King* is directed at the *government's* failure to uphold those same civic values. The early signs of disillusionment with Reagan in "Lyndon" blossom in *The Pale King* into a full-throated critique of neoliberal deregulation, which Wallace frames as the very definition of self-interest. Most of this critique is rehearsed in §19 of the novel, which takes place in the months before Reagan's election in 1980. Wallace returns here to the matter of the Vietnam protests, but frames them now, in dialogic fashion, against the rise of neoliberalism:

> But how did this alienated small selfish make-no-difference thing result from the sixties, since if the sixties showed anything good it showed that like-minded citizens can think for themselves [. . .] there can be real change; we pull out of "Nam" [. . .].

> Because corporations got in the game and turned all the genuine principles and aspirations and ideology into a set of fashions and attitudes – they made Rebellion a fashion pose instead of a real impetus.[32]

The discussion then moves to the political candidate who can harness this moment:

> Look for us to elect someone who can cast himself as a Rebel, maybe even a cowboy [. . .] Look for a candidate who can do to the electorate what corporations are learning to do, so Government – or, better, Big Government, Big Brother, Intrusive Government – becomes the image against which this candidate defines himself.[33]

At which point another voice answers: "This describes Reagan even better than Bush."[34] This is a clear example of how Wallace's social conservatism has altered in his fiction since "Lyndon." Protest, unlike in the earlier story, is now depicted as holding a prelapsarian quality of civic citizenship, which has *then* become hopelessly compromised by incipient neoliberal deregulation. By placing the most explicitly political section of the novel in Reagan's election year, it's clear that Wallace sees 1980 as Year Zero for the

---

[31] Wills, *Reagan's America*, xxii.   [32] Wallace, *TPK*, 140.   [33] Ibid., 147.   [34] Ibid.

full-blown civic/salesmanship split in American politics, a point which is then made in flatly undramatized fashion:

> Of course the marvellous double irony of the Reduce Government candidate is that he's financed by the corporations [. . .] who are going to benefit enormously from the laissez-faire deregulation Bush-Reagan will enable the electorate to believe will be undertaken in their own populist interests.[35]

In *The Pale King*, Wallace's conservative squeamishness about 1960s protest migrates instead to the liberal culture of the 1970s, which is explored in highly ambivalent fashion in the chapter that depicts the perpetually stoned Chris Fogle and his parents' breakup. That "rebellion as fashion," which Wallace chides in "Hail the Returning Dragon," has now become manifest in the afterimages of the sixties counterculture, which are now, on Wallace's timeframe, more directly linked with the rise of neoliberalism.

Reagan as Character: "Wickedness"

Around the same time that Wallace was writing *The Pale King*, he was working on a short story called "Wickedness," which was to feature Reagan as a character. The draft of "Wickedness" is messily handwritten and is only eleven pages long, with no ending and no strong indication of a planned structure. What does exist tells the story of an undercover reporter, Chet Skyles, who is employed by a website named Filth.com. Skyles is being interviewed for a job at the San Placido Institute, where the Alzheimer's-afflicted Reagan is being cared for. Skyles is being paid by Filth.com to take photographs of Reagan for the website, a situation for which the institute have prepared by offering any employee who is approached by a media outlet a matching fee to preserve Reagan's privacy. The premise of a journalist meeting the ailing Reagan is so similar to the epilogue to *Dutch*, published the year before Wallace wrote "Wickedness," in which Edmund Morris visits a clearly unwell Reagan, that it is not unreasonable to suggest that it may have influenced this story.

Reagan's visibility, or lack of it, is central to "Wickedness," in which Nancy Reagan wants Reagan to "disintegrate in total private."[36] Historically, Reagan's Alzheimer's removed his primary presidential quality, the ability to perform publicly. Perhaps as a result of this, Reagan does

---

[35] Ibid., 149.   [36] Wallace, *TPK*, Draft Materials, Harry Ransom Center.

not himself appear in the story, and is referred to only through secondary reports, in a form that recalls the lateral descriptions by Ballard:

> The president no longer recognized loved ones. The president wept for hours at a time. The president threw fits and had to be restrained [. . .]. The president had bitten an RN. The president had become incontinent. The president sat cross-legged in the corner playing with his feet and making sounds like a litter of puppies.[37]

In a sense, "Wickedness" performs the same scenario as "Lyndon" – the relationship between a protagonist and a president in private. But Skyles' threat to make Reagan's indignity public changes the balance of power from that depicted in "Lyndon," where presidential idiosyncrasies are always presented firmly behind closed doors. In "Wickedness," the intimacy of Lyndon's final tableau, involving the dying president, is nonconsensually converted into public property in the world of the story.

In "Wickedness," Wallace draws together those motifs of suffering, responsibility and salesmanship in a new configuration. The story inverts the fixation on the necessary suffering of the citizen seen in "Lyndon" by giving Skyles the power to make public, unnecessarily, the suffering of the ex-president. It's clear that Wallace sees this public commodification – essentially, being a salesman of suffering – as a fundamental betrayal of the understanding and empathy that suffering affords. I suspect that one of the reasons that "Wickedness" remained unfinished is because Wallace found a better home for its concerns – the journalist protagonist, the public commodification of pain – in "The Suffering Channel."

However, in "The Suffering Channel," the images of pain are not focused around a single figure, and in conclusion, I want to suggest that the use of Reagan in "Wickedness" dramatizes the metastasizing of Reagan's salesmanship into all corners of public and private life. In the description of Filth.com, we can infer that the unregulated market that produces mercenaries like Skyles is at least, in part, a product of the Reagan era itself. Nobody knows "who or what owned Filth.com," and the institute is engaged in a continuous battle to prevent employees taking pictures of Reagan to be sold to the highest bidder.[38] In the story, the major tabloids have all refused to consider publishing photos of Reagan, but the Internet, which is presented here as effectively stateless and bodiless, offers a platform for publication. In effect, the publishing of photos of Reagan by Filth.com represents a complete separation between

[37] Ibid.   [38] Ibid.

civics and salesmanship, by positing the public debasement of the former head of state for money.

It would be glib to suggest that "Wickedness" is Wallace's revenge on Reagan for his facilitation of the slow separation between the civic and the neoliberal. Instead, to close, I think it's important that when we think about Wallace's "presidential" writing, we consider that separation as fundamental to Wallace's political ethics, and that Reagan is an immensely important figure in the development of those ethics. Reagan's victimhood in "Wickedness" is, on this view, *proof* of the inertia of neoliberal commodification and its erosion of the civic. While this position does not necessarily make Wallace a liberal, it does help us to understand how crucial the Reagan era is to his fiction and his ideas of political leadership.

CHAPTER 33

David Foster Wallace and Publishing

Tim Groenland

Given his interest in the many systems of capitalism, and the thread of salesmanship that David Hering has identified in Chapter 32, David Foster Wallace's own implication in these systems merits attention. Of particular interest to scholars considering his legacy are the systems of publishing through which Wallace's writing career was mediated. In his lifetime, Wallace published two novels (with Viking and Little, Brown), three collections of stories (the first with W. W. Norton, the others with Little, Brown), a coauthored book about rap music (with Ecco Press, an imprint of HarperCollins) and a compact history of infinity for W. W. Norton's "Great Discoveries" series. He published stories in – among others – *The Amherst Review, Conjunctions, Grand Street, McSweeney's Quarterly Concern, Mid-American Review, The New Yorker, The Paris Review, Playboy, Ploughshares, Rampike, Sonora Review, Tin House* and *Triquarterly*. His essays and non-fiction pieces were published in venues such as *The Atlantic Monthly, Esquire, Gourmet, Harper's, The Missouri Review, The New York Times, Premiere, Rolling Stone* and *Tennis*. Additionally, he wrote reviews for *The Harvard Book Review*, the *Los Angeles Times*, the *New York Times Book Review, The Philadelphia Enquirer, Rain Taxi, Science, Spin Magazine, The Washington Post* and others; guest edited an issue of *Review of Contemporary Fiction* (1996) and the *Best American Essays* 2007 volume; and gave interviews to a wide range of literary and popular magazines.

The aforementioned lists are alphabetical rather than chronological, and are not definitive; they do not include a variety of posthumous publications, one of which (*This Is Water*) has become one of his most widely quoted, and another (*The Pale King*) that deserves to be numbered among his major works. They do, however, give us a sense of Wallace's varied productivity over the roughly quarter-century span of his literary career, bespeaking a rare combination of interests as well as talents: few authors, surely, can claim to have been published in each of *The New Yorker*,

Playboy, Science and *Tennis.* Wallace's publication venues included national newspapers (*The New York Times*), men's magazines with long-standing commitments to fiction (*Esquire, Playboy*), small-audience literary journals (*Conjunctions*), glossy commercial publications (*Gourmet*), long-established bastions of literary culture (*Harper's*), and newer millennial ventures (*McSweeney's*). More importantly for my purposes here, the lists place Wallace within the context of the late twentieth- and early twenty-first-century publishing worlds. Indeed, it is notable that several of the publications listed earlier are no longer in existence (*Grand Street, Rampike, Tin House*), while another (*McSweeney's*) not only began publishing after Wallace was an established literary star but was also arguably saturated by its editor's admiration for Wallace.

Wallace's written output, then, spans a particular historical timeframe and exists within networks of production that underwent dramatic changes between the early 1980s and the time of his passing in 2008. The latter phase of his career, for example, saw the seismic shift from print toward digital in the magazine and newspaper industry, a process about which Wallace felt ambivalent at best.[1] Taken as a whole, Wallace's career also spans the second half of what Dan Sinykin has termed the Conglomerate Era, a period of several decades throughout which media conglomerates steadily purchased publishing houses and transformed the conditions under which publishers, editors and authors worked.[2] Waves of mergers and acquisitions swept through the industry in these decades, resulting in a present-day situation in which "what were once dozens of independent publishing firms now exist as imprints within a handful of enormous publishing companies" that are themselves "under the umbrellas of huge parent corporations."[3]

I contend not only that these changes impacted upon Wallace's work but also that he integrated an awareness of these shifts into his own writing – from his anxieties about the threats to literary culture from television in the 1980s, and his development of these fears in the spectacle of weaponized entertainment in *Infinite Jest*, to his sustained act of Information Age media archaeology in *The Pale King* in response to the corporate-dominated "Total Noise" of the twenty-first century. In what follows, I give a necessarily compressed overview of Wallace's publishing

[1] Max, *Every Love Story*, 295.
[2] Specifically, Sinykin dates the process from 1965 (when RCA purchased Random House) to 2007 (the year of the release of Amazon's Kindle), a time roughly coinciding with Wallace's lifetime. Sinykin, "The Conglomerate Era."
[3] Crosthwaite, *Market Logic*, 21.

history, noting some key pressures bearing upon his published output, and considering how these were incorporated into his writing. I focus primarily on his work against the background of conglomeration, with *Infinite Jest* and "The Suffering Channel" the key works here.

***

Wallace's first stories were published in 1984 in *The Amherst Review* ("The Planet Trillaphon as It Stands in Relation to the Bad Thing") and *The Allegheny Review* ("The Piano in the Pantechnicon"); the last new work published in his lifetime was "The Compliance Branch" in the February 2008 issue of *Harper's*. The trajectory indicated here from university literary journals to established New York-based national magazines is, of course, not untypical for a successful author. It indicates the institutional underpinnings of Wallace's career and of American fiction more generally, with the university support of the Program Era, to borrow Mark McGurl's term, existing alongside the long-established power of the New York publishing world (the "MFA vs. NYC" dichotomy influentially proposed by Chad Harbach in the essay of the same name).[4]

Wallace's movement between these worlds was unusually rapid, since his first novel, submitted as one of his undergraduate honors theses at Amherst, led directly to publication by a major house. On the advice of one of his teachers, Wallace sent a sample of the work to a number of literary agencies, receiving a positive response from Bonnie Nadell at the Frederick Hill agency. After taking him on as a client, she sent the novel to several editors, including Gerry Howard at Viking Penguin, whose enthusiasm led him to offer $20,000 for the novel, leaving Wallace – then twenty-four years old – in an enviable position. Within three years of his first published story, he was seeing his debut novel in print: In addition to this, however – and perhaps just as importantly – he had found a supportive agent and editor to enable him to navigate the world of publication. When Howard moved from Viking to Norton in 1988, Wallace decided to follow, and the lengthy delays caused by the legal vetting of *Girl with Curious Hair* came to an end with the collection's publication in August 1989.[5] To a large extent, these early years of publication and their contingencies would set the terms for the rest of his career. Nadell would remain his agent until his death in 2008, and his

[4] McGurl, *Program Era*; Harbach, "MFA vs NYC."   [5] Max, *Every Love Story*, 65–71, 106–9.

future editor Michael Pietsch had, by 1987, already noted the author's published stories and struck up a correspondence.

The late 1980s and early 1990s saw Wallace expanding his range of non-fiction writing. Along with *Signifying Rappers*, the cultural analysis of rap music coauthored with Mark Costello in 1990, he published a number of book reviews at the beginning of the decade, and began to work on the longer essays and reportage that would establish him as a cultural commentator. *Harper's* would be the venue for several important pieces throughout the 1990s, and his works of travel reportage in particular, with their linguistic and intellectual verve and distinctive authorial persona, did much to "lay the groundwork for his conquest" of the literary landscape with his second novel.[6] His work with Colin Harrison on these essays exemplifies the intensity with which Wallace would approach these assignments, as he routinely turned in pieces that far exceeded the possible word count and subsequently entered into detailed editorial back-and-forths that were often "insanely ornate."[7] Several of Wallace's editors (of both his fiction and non-fiction) have testified to similar experiences. In more than one instance, Wallace's virtuosity and ability to argue his case persuaded editors to bend and even break publication protocols for him. Several of his *Harper's* essays comfortably exceeded the original allocated word count and ran uninterrupted by advertisements in print; he persuaded *Esquire* to run "Adult World" as two separate stories divided by other pieces (a choice the editor would later come to regret), and successfully insisted on defying the *New York Times'* style rules in his use of the Oxford comma.[8] As Ralph Clare has noted earlier in this volume, Wallace also positioned himself in the context of literary rather than popular publications, especially including the now-famous 1993 issue of *The Review of Contemporary Fiction*.

***

During these years, Wallace was beginning to write (and, later, edit) his longest novel. He wrote most of the book under the auspices of Little, Brown, with whom he had signed a contract for $85,000 in 1992; his move away from Viking was motivated both by their significantly lower offer, and by a desire to work with Pietsch, with whom he had by then developed a friendship. Pietsch's enthusiasm for the novel was crucial both in enticing Wallace to work with him and in persuading his editorial board

---

[6] Boswell, *Wallace Effect*, 7.   [7] Nadell, *Editors on Wallace*.
[8] A. Miller, *Land of Men*; Max, *Every Love Story*, 290.

to pursue someone who he described as a key writer of his generation. For Wallace, the move represented an opportunity to reach an audience equal to his ambition and, as he put it to Pietsch, "to improve as a writer": his correspondence from this time shows an awareness of his own resistance to editorial intervention and his need for a new collaborator to challenge him.[9]

Wallace delivered the first (incomplete) draft of *Infinite Jest* to Pietsch in the summer of 1993, and the subsequent editorial process, which I have described in detail elsewhere, has come to acquire legendary status, representing a milestone in the career of both its author and editor.[10] The bulk of the labor took place from late 1994 to the summer of the following year. Pietsch's long and detailed suggestions for potential cuts were answered by equally intricate responses indicating acquiescence, impassioned defense or complex compromises involving the condensation or consolidation of individual scenes and the transfer of sections of text to endnotes. Max accurately describes the process as one of "playful combat," and while the duration of this combat evidently made it progressively more grueling, the process was one for which Wallace would express gratitude throughout the rest of his career.[11]

The steps taken as the book moved toward publication would be crucial ones, as Pietsch managed the various levers of the publishing apparatus required to bring it to readers. Pietsch's role in this respect was arguably every bit as important as his textual work on the novel, and the marketing of the book has come to acquire a similarly outsized importance: In the publishing world, the novel is considered a "case study in how to sell" ambitious literary fiction, while some critics have gone so far as to suggest that the novel owes its stature more to canny marketing than intrinsic literary merit.[12] The campaign for the novel involved a deliberate focus on the book's size and complexity, with teasing postcards and a string of ecstatic blurbs from Wallace's contemporaries generating the sense of a major literary event, positioning the novel as a signature achievement, and cementing its author's role as a figure of genius.[13]

Considering Wallace's position within the Conglomerate Era might, as Sinykin suggests, encourage us to read *Infinite Jest*, a novel saturated with anxiety over the hegemony of corporations in US life, as exhibiting "a complex formal response to changes in the publishing industry."[14] Sinykin

[9] Wallace, "Letter to Michael Pietsch," 1992, Harry Ransom Center.
[10] Groenland, *Art of Editing*, 115–42.   [11] Max, *Every Love Story*, 206.
[12] Kachka, "When"; Hungerford, *Making Literature Now*, 158–59.
[13] Max, *Every Love Story*, 211; Andersen, "Judging."   [14] Sinykin, "The Conglomerate Era," 463.

points out that Little, Brown had become a division of the new conglomerate Time Warner in 1989, three years before Wallace signed a contract to
publish his next novel with them; this conglomerate would itself be sold to
French publisher Hachette Livre in 2006. Wallace's work on the novel,
then – particularly the editorial work, an exchange that began before he
had completed the full first draft – was informed by an awareness of being
enmeshed in a publishing environment that gave an immediate urgency to
his concerns with corporate entertainment.

Broadly speaking, conglomeration has been associated with an increased
emphasis on shareholder value in major publishing houses, with fewer risks
being taken on "literary" fiction and an expectation that individual titles
will rapidly repay the capital invested in them. The ambitious literary
fiction writer, then, works in a context in which the risk of failure is high
and a degree of conscious complicity with market values is a necessary
precondition of publication. Wallace's comments to Don DeLillo in a
letter written during the editorial process, for example, show an acute
awareness of this complicity and how it might relate to the development of
his own work: "I am uncomfortable about making cuts for commercial
reasons – it seems slutty – but on the other hand L,B is taking a big gamble
publishing something this long and hard and I feel some obligation not to
be a p.-donna and fuck them over." Wallace was attempting to manage
this tension and, in Sinykin's words, "to seduce readers while ultimately
criticizing the culture of entertainment that Time Warner hoped to profit
from by the novel's publication."[15]

***

After the publication of *Infinite Jest*, Wallace's reputation was securely
established and his work in high demand. Indeed, with the emergence of
McSweeney's in 1998 and *The Believer* in 2003, the author could be said to
be having a perceptible influence on the publishing environment.[16]

In her 2020 memoir *In the Land of Men*, Adrienne Miller recounts her
excitement at acquiring the rights to publish one of Wallace's new stories,
"Adult World," near the beginning of her tenure as *Esquire's* fiction editor.
Wallace, it turned out, had submitted the story to numerous other venues

---

[15] Max, *Every Love Story*, 205; Sinykin, "The Conglomerate Era," 462–63.
[16] Boswell, *Wallace Effect*, 9–10; Konstantinou, *Cool Characters*, 193–203. This influence was so
apparent that it may have contributed to his decision to write for *McSweeney's* under a pseudonym.
"Mr. Squishy" was published in 2000 in the magazine's fifth issue under the name "Elizabeth
Klemm," an identity that seems to have fooled very few readers.

without success (due to its high level of difficulty); *Esquire*, though, was still prepared to pay $10,000 for the work, a sum that would come to seem remarkable a few years later as the magazine's fiction section dwindled to nothing. Miller's book frequently takes an elegiac tone when discussing the magazine business in the 1990s and early 2000s, shortly before the Internet transformed reading habits. She would publish several more stories by Wallace, but the final one ("Oblivion") was, despite a lengthy editorial process that cut the story by roughly half, "killed" by the magazine without explanation; the length of the story may still have been greater than was considered acceptable. *Esquire* won a National Magazine Award for Fiction in 2004, yet in the following year, as Miller describes, not a single short story was published in its pages, a circumstance that contributed to her resignation.[17]

In the Land of Men, as its title suggests, also concerns itself with the overwhelmingly patriarchal environment not only of the men's magazine in which Miller worked but also of the publishing industry as a whole during these years: She presents a damning indictment of a culture in which women are consistently undervalued, objectified and preyed upon.[18] Her account – which also deals with the romantic relationship with Wallace that proceeded from the first editorial exchange – does not exempt the writer from her critique.[19] While we may wish to separate author and work (and Miller does this herself to a degree, lavishing praise upon Wallace's ability and professional habits), it is impossible entirely to elide the context of these stories. The "boundary issues" she identifies with Wallace are, for this chapter, the salient point: It becomes clear, in reading Miller's account, that much of *Brief Interviews with Hideous Men*, the collection in which Wallace most directly confronts and anatomizes misogyny, was published in a context saturated with patriarchal power dynamics, and that the author consciously benefitted from these dynamics.[20] While there already exists a significant body of scholarship that reads

---

[17] A. Miller, *Land of Men*. The story would appear in the July 1998 issue.

[18] The catalogue of alleged abuse ranges from dismissive remarks and casual insults to sexual misconduct, harassment and specific material injustices. At one point, Miller recalls her surprise upon discovering that Dave Eggers, who was employed at *Esquire* as a journalist for a brief period during her tenure (and before he published his acclaimed debut novel), was being paid twice her salary.

[19] Numerous specific instances of cruelty, narcissism and manipulation support her claim that Wallace "was a person with poor impulse control and even poorer boundary issues, and without a doubt his sense of entitlement was extreme" (A. Miller, *Land of Men*, n.p.).

[20] A. Miller, *Land of Men*. While this is not the first allegation of misogynistic behavior on Wallace's part, it is notable, for my purposes, that the behavior described by Miller took place within the immediate context (and through the power dynamics) of the publishing world. See Hayes-Brady's

Wallace through a feminist lens, with which several earlier chapters in this
volume engage at length, particularly Chapters 20–23,[21] one mode of
reckoning with this troubling knowledge – although doing so is beyond
the scope of this chapter – might be to bring a more fine-grained focus to
the links between the writing and the gender dynamics of its immediate
cultural contexts, as Daniela Franca Joffe does by historicizing *Broom*
through an analysis of the impact of second-wave feminism on Wallace's
own campus of Amherst.[22]

***

The experience of working with New York magazines such as *Esquire*
clearly informed Wallace's work on "The Suffering Channel," the novella
in which he most explicitly depicts the publishing industry as well as the
landscape of conglomeration undergirding it.[23] "The Suffering Channel"
depicts the work of two very different creators – Brint Moltke, the savant
artist of fecal sculptures; and Skip Atwater, the "salaryman" writing
human-interest pieces for *Style* magazine – within the context of corporate
entertainment structures.[24]

Atwater's pieces run in a magazine described by the narrator as within
the niche of the "big soft glossy, with soft in turn meaning the very most
demotic kind of human interest."[25] While *Style* is clearly some distance
from the prestigious venues in which Wallace tended to publish, the
corporate structure in which it is nested contains obvious nods to the
reality of the publishing structures with which the author engaged directly.
Jeffrey Severs points out that Eckleschafft-Böd Medien AG, the "German
conglomerate that controls nearly 40 percent of all US trade publishing"
parodies Bertelsmann AG, owner of Knopf and Random House.[26] He also
observes that Wallace is going a step further in suggesting a possible merger
with AOL Time Warner, owner (at that point) of Little, Brown.[27] Wallace

---

"Reading Your Problematic Fave"; and "#MeToo Era" for summaries and responses to some of
these allegations.

[21] See, for example, Hayes-Brady's *Failures*; Holland, "By Hirsute Author"; Kelly, "Brief Interviews
with Hideous Men."

[22] Joffe, "The Last Word." A similar analysis could, perhaps, complement readings of race in Wallace's
work with a consideration of the well-documented persistence of racial hierarchies in the US
publishing industry. See McGrath, "Comping White."

[23] Indeed, Miller claims that the character of the unnamed executive intern is very loosely based
on her.

[24] As in *IJ*, the story, as Severs observes, "thus meditates on what distinguishes artistic fiction like
Wallace's from the products of a massive entertainment-and-data corporation" (188).

[25] Wallace, "Suffering," *OB*, 296.   [26] Ibid.   [27] Severs, *Balancing Books*, 187–88.

was, it seems, well aware of the corporate machinations at play during these years: in a 2003 letter to Pietsch, he alludes to rumors of Time Warner's impending sale of Little, Brown, suggesting that he would be prepared to follow his editor to a different publisher if Pietsch were to leave.[28]

Critics have tended to find in *Oblivion* a series of evocations of claustrophobia and paralysis, with characters and readers trapped within hermetic structures that threaten to overwhelm their sense of agency.[29] This sense of claustrophobia is linked in "The Suffering Channel" to the writer's enmeshment in corporate structures, as we follow a sequence of events that highlights contemporary developments in the publishing ecosystem. The plot hinges on a devious piece of corporate synergy arranged far from the groundwork of the "salaryman," as the executive intern (who has close links to the conglomerate's owners) arranges to combine the two stories that Atwater is pursuing: that of Moltke, the artist whose own agency is undermined to the point where he is completely bypassed in negotiations, and the titular television channel, itself already on the way into "the Eckleschafft-Böd pipeline" as a result of high-level financial machinations.[30] This arrangement not only exemplifies the way in which characters in Wallace's late fiction seem to be threatened by disappearance into corporate structures, but gestures metafictionally toward the diminished sense of agency of the conglomerate-era author.

***

The Pale King, which never advanced meaningfully toward publication until after Wallace's death, displays the author's continued engagement with the commercial conditions of his work's production.[31] The metafictional "Author here" sections, as Boswell has observed, draw obliquely on the legal ordeal that Wallace faced during the production of *Girl with*

---

[28] Wallace, "Letter to Michael Pietsch," 2003, Harry Ransom Center.
[29] Boswell, "Constant Monologue," 151–56. Hering sees *Oblivion* as performing the "progressive effacement of non-institutional space in Wallace's fiction" (*Fiction and Form*, 70), while Severs finds Wallace returning here "to the specter of writers idling and failing to free themselves of corporate frames" (188).
[30] Wallace, "Suffering," *OB*, 290, 306, 324.
[31] For a detailed discussion of Pietsch's role in the novel's posthumous construction and an analysis of what I see as an increasingly intense focus on the act of mediation in the draft material, see Groenland, *Art of Editing*, 143–74, 216–26.

Curious Hair, while their style indicates an attempt to reckon with his own "aggravating influence" upon literary culture.[32] The opening pages of the first of these sections, indeed, invite the reader to "flip back and look at the book's legal disclaimer," which the narrator ("David Wallace") claims has been inserted "to protect me, the book's publisher, and the publisher's assigned distributors from legal liability."[33] The result is to set up a complex interplay between fact and fiction that draws attention not just to these constructs as genres, but as genres in the literary marketplace.[34]

The metafictional sections, then, written late in the composition of the novel, frame the book's entire structure as a consequence of the publishing industry's response to a paradigm shift that appears largely technology-driven (by "web logs, reality television, cellphone cameras, chat rooms").[35] While definitive judgments upon the unfinished novel's structure are impossible, these sections suggest a provocative formal gambit – a "thematization of its own status as a legal fiction and corporate commodity," in Kelly's words – that gestures toward the mechanisms governing its creation, as well as prompting the reader to consider the value of literary fiction in an increasingly online culture.[36]

***

I have focused primarily here upon Wallace's publication history within his lifetime; it would be possible, of course, to expend significant attention upon his posthumous output.[37] Pietsch, who worked together with Wallace's estate to edit and frame these publications for readers, is once again a key figure here. The *David Foster Wallace Reader*, for example, was published in late 2014, during a period in which Pietsch was simultaneously leading a highly publicized struggle between Hachette and Amazon over the pricing of e-books.[38] The author's implication in

---

[32] Boswell, "Author Here."   [33] Wallace, *TPK*, 69–70.

[34] In one early draft, Wallace even names Pietsch and Little, Brown along with a fictional agent (see Groenland, *Art of Editing*, 224–25). Elsewhere in this chapter, it is suggested that the rise of the memoir as a genre has provided a specific profit motive for the impecunious "Wallace," an author who is well aware of the fact that the "cultural present of 2005" rewards the "public" and "performative" nature of autobiographical writing more than it does fiction.

[35] Wallace, *TPK*, 82–83. I discuss the composition of these section of the work in Groenland, *Art of Editing*, 218–26.

[36] Kelly, "Formally," 55.

[37] Apart from *TPK*, for example, we have also seen the publication of a volume of uncollected essays, *Both Flesh and Not* (2012), his Kenyon college commencement address, and his undergraduate philosophy thesis *Fate, Time, and Language* (2010).

[38] Streitfeld, "Amazon."

corporate publishing structures has, then, continued beyond his death, with his writings circulating in a changing marketplace in which the power balance among conglomerates has been challenged by the dramatic rise of "a company whose scale and scope defy description."[39] At present, Wallace's legacy (including any future publications that bear his name) remain linked to the fortunes of his publisher and those of Pietsch, his friend, editor and – at the time of writing – current Chief Executive Officer of Hachette Book Group. The author's published *oeuvre* is – given the existence of uncollected stories, archival material and letters – unlikely to yet be complete, and his writing will continue to reach readers in new forms as well as contexts.

[39] Glass, "Publishing," 361.

CHAPTER 34

Author Here, There and Everywhere
David Foster Wallace and Biography

Mike Miley

The 1993 interview with Larry McCaffery, the most quoted of Wallace's interviews, has formed the foundation of academic inquiries into Wallace for decades. In it, Wallace describes himself as "an exhibitionist who wants to hide, but is unsuccessful at hiding; therefore, somehow [he] succeed [s]."[1] The product of a series of written (and edited) exchanges, the interview is not the spontaneous conversation that it appears on the page to be (and that interviews in general are often taken for). Rather, it is a crafted work in itself, one that Wallace himself had a heavy hand in forming. What we see in this interview is a writer directing his readership on how he would like to be read. Academics have been quite willing to take this direction. For one thing, the quotes are just so good, as good as anything in Wallace's essays on popular entertainment. More importantly, the substance of the interview outlines and explicates Wallace's literary project and biography with a clarity that also provides scholars with multiple paths of inquiry into his work. But such inquiry runs the risk of being circular, in that scholars are seduced into explicating a version of Wallace's life put forward by Wallace himself. In doing so, the exhibition-ist certainly gets to be seen, but on his own terms, turning the spotlight on what he wants others to see, allowing those aspects less suitable for public display to fall into shadow.

As the voluminous amount of biographical writing about Wallace published since his death in 2008 demonstrates, for every aspect of Wallace on display in his non-fiction and interviews, another remains hidden from view. In many cases, one has difficulty discerning the degree to which the visible Wallace is constructed to conceal another Wallace from public knowledge and scrutiny. Through carefully selected (and sometimes fabricated) details and statements in fiction, essays and espe-cially interviews, Wallace crafts a literary and public persona that is a

[1] McCaffrey, "Interview," 43.

heavily curated version of his actual life. Naturally, Wallace is hardly unique among writers in this regard. After all, writers spend most of their professional lives constructing and shaping narratives both out of whole cloth and the details of their everyday lives. The Wallace of this curated biography has proven to be an enduring – and endearing – figure that many readers and scholars are reluctant to give up. However, the examination of Wallace the person as he relates to Wallace the literary figure happens to be occurring at time when the importance of the factual details about the artist to the invented elements of their art has come under review.

In recent years, we have seen the work of artists such as Woody Allen, Louis C. K., Joss Whedon and J. K. Rowling undergo popular and critical reevaluation as details about their personal lives and political opinions have become public, and the repercussions have ranged from the loss of book and movie deals or professional representation to a few days' worth of agitation on social media. Much of the debate about Wallace as a writer and public figure stems from a similar disconnect between the persona that he and the publishing industry presented to his readership, and the actual human who has emerged in the subsequent posthumous biographies, memoirs, testimonials, archives, tweets and think pieces. It seems that having a position on Wallace is, as Marshall Boswell quips in his book *The Wallace Effect*, "a grim cultural obligation for people who are committed to contemporary cultural literacy."[2] Even if one has not read Wallace – or refuses to, after Amy Hungerford[3] – one is expected to know how to appear culturally hip by using his name or the title of *Infinite Jest* as a punch line.[4]

In coming to look at Wallace as an author and the debate surrounding his place in letters, one can see literary and media culture shift and remake themselves in real time. The paratexts surrounding Wallace's biography depict the degree to which Wallace is a unique product of his time and place, a time and place that, only a few years later, is not entirely compatible with the present moment. The debate about Wallace is about more than Wallace and his work: It is also a reckoning with the (white male) author as a public figure of authority, genius and privilege. Latent in this debate is a discussion about what an author is (or should be) in the public discourse (such as it is). Viewing it, one looks through a window into literary study and American culture in transition during a time when

---

[2] Boswell, *Wallace Effect*, 131.   [3] See Chapters 2, 15, 23 and 25.
[4] Hungerford, "On Not Reading."

what one wants or expects out of literature and the human beings who produce it is, as I argue later, being reimagined. Wallace in many respects has become the catalyst for (and casualty of) this conversation. Different Wallaces have been battling for supremacy in the years since his death, to the extent that there is a dizzying array of David Foster Wallaces to contend with: sinner, saint, tormented genius, pathological misogynist and more. Which Wallace one chooses determines what one reads and gains from what Wallace wrote, and how his legacy will affect the course of contemporary fiction. Whatever form this new conception of the author takes, it is going to be made out of the rubble of Wallace by a multitude of architects with different visions of what they are building.

Wallace himself was the first to use his writing to construct a public biography and persona by asserting his presence strongly in his fiction and non-fiction, and by reinforcing that presence in interviews. As is to be expected, this persona exaggerates some elements of Wallace's life and downplays others in the pursuit of a good story both on and off the page (and in the interest of keeping embarrassing and unpleasant details quiet). The Wallace on display in his non-fiction reportage, best exemplified in his field reports for *Harper's* such as "A Ticket to the Fair" and "Shipping Out," is a journalistic rube stumbling through the bizarro world of American culture, with nothing to protect him but his keen powers of attention, a bandanna and a notebook with Barney the Purple Dinosaur emblazoned on the cover. This Wallace is comically endearing and intellectually inspiring, a stunningly average genius as bewildered as the reader by modern life, but also in possession of the critical and linguistic acumen to render contemporary life's unintelligibility intelligible. This Wallace is as brilliant as he is harmless, a victim of both his erudite cynicism (see "The View from Mrs. Thompson's") and his slack-jawed naïveté (his essay on tennis player Michael Joyce, for example, or "Consider the Lobster"). As many have noted, especially Jonathan Franzen, this Wallace and the events he reports on are often heavily doctored to suit Wallace's fictional desires.[5] As early as "Derivative Sport in Tornado Alley" and at least as late as "Big Red Son," Wallace plays fast and loose with the facts and the expectations of journalism (as Martin Eve notes in Chapter 7 of this volume), and this play often gets excused because it is deployed in service of an infectiously engaging persona, or simply because he is a genius.

---

[5] In an interview at the *New Yorker* Festival, Franzen alleged to David Remnick that Wallace's nonfiction pieces contained fabricated elements. See Dean, "Supposedly True."

As suggested earlier, Wallace defends and extends that persona most persuasively in his interviews. Some of these documents get quoted as much as his actual writing, if not more, as is the case with the McCaffrey interview. Self-effacingly sincere, cautiously invested in the significance of his work and its relationship to literature and philosophy, charmingly reluctant to being interviewed but not shy to make Big Pronouncements about the Culture, this Wallace mixes the erudition of the professor with the relaxed concern of the older brother in college. He dispenses carefully crafted aphorisms in a voice that expresses disdain for aphoristic speech, such as "literature is what it means to be a fucking *human being*."[6] This push and pull between having a Message and not wanting to be Someone with a Message endears Wallace to a Gen-X and post-Gen-X readership that craves authenticity and remains suspicious of authority figures, but yearns for someone and something to believe in. More importantly, it often makes anyone who raises questions about the authenticity of his work elsewhere, such as the veracity of his non-fiction, seem like they are mean spirited or, at best, missing "The Point."

Wallace's fiction establishes and advances the trademarks of his non-fiction and interview persona by inserting himself (or a barely concealed stand-in) into his fiction. Doing so allows him to merge the didacticism of his interviews and more serious essays (such as "E Unibus Pluram") with the picaresque humor of his reportage. However, as his career develops, Wallace comes to feel increasingly confined by those trademarks and longs for an escape. The Fiction-Writer of "Octet" who is paralyzed by the ethics of authenticity gradually becomes the David Wallace of "Good Old Neon," tragically paralyzed by the self-critical spiraling voice in his head, only to end up as the comically beleaguered David Wallace of *The Pale King* who struggles to prove that he is a real and singular human being capable of telling the truth in print. By the time he writes the David Wallace sections of *The Pale King* – the newest material in the novel – Wallace has created an alternate biography, complete with a new Social Security Number and birth year – to distinguish himself from "God only knew how many other David Wallaces running around out there, doing God knows what,"[7] only to arrive at the realization that there is no escaping his persona. He has become "a creature of the system," a system largely of his own design.[8]

Since his death in 2008, the number of David Wallaces running around out there has only increased, and they have, on the whole, not squared

[6] McCaffery, "Interview," 26.   [7] Wallace, *TPK*, 297, n. 48.   [8] Ibid., 548.

neatly with the David Wallace established in his fiction, non-fiction and interviews. The most prevalent David Wallace running around in the initial years following his death was certainly the most flattering. The flurry of tributes and obituaries published in major media outlets, from towering figures such as Don DeLillo, A. O Scott, Zadie Smith and George Saunders to more informal remembrances by former students and fans, crafted an image of Wallace as writer whose abundant empathy, sincerity and wisdom rendered him too good for this cynical world. Franzen, Wallace's friend and literary rival, succinctly dubbed this image "Saint Dave."[9] The Saint Dave image was bolstered by the publication of his 2005 Kenyon commencement address *This Is Water*. Printed in the style of a devotional book, with a single sentence on each of its pages, this speech distilled Wallace's literary mission down to under 200 easy-to-read sentences that repackaged – or, in Boswell's words, "defanged" – Wallace for the masses as some kind of modern-day "postmodern self-help" guru, what John Gallagher characterized as a "dudebro Confucius."[10] This little book led to an explosion in Wallace's readership and book sales and, along with James Ponsoldt's 2015 film *The End of the Tour* (based on David Lipsky's book *Although of Course You End Up Becoming Yourself*), ushered in a hagiography of Wallace that has won comparisons to that other Gen-X icon gone-too-soon, Kurt Cobain. The backlash against the Saint Dave caricature was inevitable and swift, however, and it came from those who knew Wallace best, most prominently Karen Green, Franzen and Jeffrey Eugenides.

A hideously fragile Wallace haunts Green's memoir *Bough Down*, a book that stands as a subtle-but-sharp rebuke to the impersonal, two-dimensional Saint Dave. There is no sainthood in Wallace's final days, no valiant or redemptive suffering, and Wallace is no martyr for single-entendre principles or anything else. In Green's account, Wallace is simply and painfully a tragically broken – and breaking – person crippled by depression. Green's characterization of him as a "shrapnel angel" who sometimes has "spinach caught between canine and gum" may seem to be aestheticizing his ordinary guyness, but her depiction of Wallace does not contain any sentimental flourishes such as a camera tilting up to the sky like the final shot of *The End of the Tour*. Rather, it is grounded in collapse, most vividly the collapse of his dead body after she cuts the rope that he hanged himself with.[11] By depicting a Wallace divorced from his

[9] Lipsky, "Lost Years."   [10] Boswell, *Wallace Effect*, 75–76; and Gallagher, "Cobainification."
[11] Green, *Bough Down*, 29, 34.

literary stardom, Green's book brings gravity to a life that threatened to be elevated to the point of triviality.

Like Green, Wallace's fellow writers Franzen and Eugenides confront Wallace's evolving (and ascending) literary reputation in an attempt to make sense of their own literary standing, and to counter a sanitized and tired narrative of Wallace as Tormented Saint or Tortured Genius. It is indeed a fierce reckoning, a battle in which these writers grapple with their own complicated feelings about Wallace, and fight to establish their position in a post-Wallace literary world. As a result, the Wallace that emerges is incredibly flawed, almost comically, pathetically so, rendered that way by each writer's impressive powers of observation and expression. At times, it seems as though his peers wish to treat Wallace and his towering influence the same way that Wallace dispatched John Barth in his story "Westward the Course of Empire Takes Its Way," In doing so, Franzen and Eugenides perhaps act as the "real lovers," as defined by Wallace in "Westward" in that they are lovers "who could hate enough to feel enough to love enough to perpetrate the kind of special cruelty *only real lovers can inflict*."[12] Their characterizations are more cutting than most takedowns of Wallace we have seen, yet it is apparent that each believes their work to ultimately be an act of love, a sign of their friendship, devotion and admiration. Through their cruel attack on Wallace, Franzen and Eugenides hope to demonstrate the depth, realness and superiority of their love.

Although it purports to be a eulogizing story about his quest to scatter his friend's ashes, Franzen's essay "Farther Away" shares more attributes with a negative profile or hit piece. Published in *The New Yorker* the same week that *The Pale King* appeared on bookshelves, the essay reveals to readers a Wallace as far away from a saint as one could ask to encounter. Franzen pans Wallace's life as a selfish existence devoid of genuine love or connection. According to Franzen, Wallace opted for "the adulation of strangers over the love of the people closest to him," by "kill[ing] himself, in a way calculated to inflict maximum pain on those he loved most."[13] Wallace's suicide becomes, in this depiction, the ultimate form of literary exhibitionism, "a career move" that transforms a three-dimensional person, complete with embarrassing flaws and frailties, "into a very public legend" that hides the problematic and unseemly from public view.[14] The hiding and the exhibitionism are inextricable from each other for Franzen's

[12] Wallace, "Westward," *SFT*, 332 (emphasis added).   [13] Franzen, "Farther Away," 38–39.
[14] Ibid., 38, 42.

Wallace: Afraid of intimacy and genuine love, Wallace chases – and obtains – a superficial validation that ensures he will never be seen as the unlovable, unloving person he truly is. Although Franzen does include praise for Wallace's fiction, he ultimately deems it as morally remote and bankrupt as its creator.

Eugenides casts Wallace in a similar, if smaller-scale, manipulative role as the womanizing Leonard Bankhead, who comprises one-third of the love triangle of his 2011 novel *The Marriage Plot*. Although he has denied that Bankhead was based on Wallace, Eugenides makes Bankhead into a caricature of the author, outfitting him with several of Wallace's trademarks: the bandanna, the chewing tobacco, the cunning intellect, the debilitating mental illness. Where Eugenides differs from Franzen is in the level of tenderness that he shows toward the Wallace figure, suggesting that the impulse to critique Wallace may, at least for Eugenides, come from a place of love and desire. In Eugenides' reckoning, both parties have some issues they need to work out, but the novel ends with Mitchell Grammaticus, the Eugenides stand-in, conceding that he is an inferior lover to Bankhead but a more ethical human. His depiction of Wallace does not allow him to hide his failings, nor does it require Eugenides to conceal his view that he has the aesthetic and ethical upper hand.

If Eugenides' rendition of Wallace is a comic depressive, the one that emerges in D. T. Max's and David Lipsky's non-fictional accounts is a tragic one that pivots from intense concealment to manic exhibitionism. Both depict Wallace as the ultimate exhibitionist-in-hiding who functions as his own worst enemy, and who is beset by the contradictions of his personal life and moral fiction. At each stage, Wallace appears as someone preoccupied with being seen – not just with whether or not he is being seen, but how, for what and in relation to whom. In Max's telling, Wallace is the victim of a brilliance not even he could measure up to. Whether he is attempting to surpass *Infinite Jest*, curb his penchant for lying and womanizing, or wean himself from a dependence on antidepressants, Wallace is depicted here as vacillating between ambition (he wants the world to recognize his talent) and fear (that both himself and others would find his achievements wanting). Lipsky's account, a direct transcript of his taped interactions with Wallace, also captures Wallace at the peak of his ambition and exhibitionism, and the picture is of a Wallace coveting concealment at every turn, largely driven by fear that he will not be able to control how he is seen once he is exposed. This Wallace, seeming less edited than he appears in the McCaffrey interview, is shown always to be in the process of editing, working overtime to control how he will come across in the interview. His fears of the trappings of fame and attention only highlight his preoccupation with them in his fiction and his life. The Lipsky interviews depict a very real and present fear of being found out and exposed by others, and while Wallace largely escaped this exposure in his lifetime, the years since his death have shown that the scrutiny does not end with the author's life, at least not in twenty-first-century entertainment culture.

Perhaps it is his stature, or the ardor of his fans, or the sheer size of his impact on contemporary literature, but whatever it is, the conversation about Wallace always has room for another angle, another take, another takedown. Wallace certainly did not invent the kind of public takedown of which he is frequently the target, but he did provide writers and readers alike with its most blistering templates, first in "Westward" and then in his unsparingly brutal review of John Updike's novel *Toward the End of Time*. The piece pretends to be a pan of the novel when it is actually a *coup de grâce* of Updike and, by extension, the most prominent men in postwar American fiction, whom Wallace refers to as the Great Male Narcissists.[15] Wallace's review is a fitting example for the large volume of writing that has positioned Wallace as a misogynist, abuser or predator, in that Wallace's main contention with the Great Male Narcissists – that their fiction evinces a sexual narcissism that the writer relentlessly inflicts upon an unconsenting reader – strongly resembles the substance of the pieces denouncing Wallace for his own narcissistic sexual domination.

There are almost too many of these pieces about Wallace to keep track of, and there will almost certainly be a half dozen more by the time this writing appears in print,[16] but the most prominent are Mary Karr's poems and tweets about her relationship with Wallace, Deirdre Coyle's 2017 personal essay "Men Recommend David Foster Wallace to Me" and Adrienne Miller's 2020 memoir *In the Land of Men*. The Wallace of Karr's account – portions of which also appear in Max's biography – is a far cry from the mindfulness guru of *This Is Water* or the cleverly self-effacing average bumbling dude of his non-fiction. Here we see allegations of Wallace as a stalker, a manipulator, an abuser, a potential murder, a truly hideous man "unable to bear the [mask] / of [his] own [face]."[17] Unlike many of the other accounts of Wallace's behavior, Miller's *In the Land of Men* is

---

[15] Wallace, "Consider," *OB*, 51.
[16] For example, Moreau's "Describing the Surface," in which he destroys his copy of *Infinite Jest*, appeared in *The New Critique* in between drafts of this chapter.
[17] Karr, "Suicide's Note," 10–11.

told from a perspective within the publishing industry, and claims to offer readers an inside look at how that industry enables and excuses boorish, predatory and abusive behavior as the prerogative of the (almost always male) genius, as Tim Groenland has noted in the previous chapter. In another time, these accounts would be primarily of interest to the biographer, who would include them as salacious details in the hopes of appealing to the reader's more sordid interests. They would be treated as gossip, dirty laundry, tales told out of school, juicy pull quotes that are interesting but ultimately trivial in relation to the Great Man and The Work. In another time, writers would frame these stories as secondary, "complication[s] to another story [. . .] the story of the romantically unruly genius of David Foster Wallace."[18]

As this suggests, as much as Wallace may have attempted to use his writing and interviews as a means to distance himself from the Great Male Narcissists of the previous generation, subsequent details and a shifting cultural conversation may reveal that the difference – or distance – between Wallace and the Great Male Narcissists is, to borrow a phrase Wallace borrowed for the title of one of his essays, greatly exaggerated. Rather than being part of a new breed of writers, perhaps Wallace is the last of an old one. Predation and abuse of women is, as Coyle writes, "par for the course, when the course is reading books and the par is the Western canon."[19] The more pressing issue, Coyle argues, is "having this man's work recommended to you, over and over, by men who have talked over you, talked down to you, coerced you into certain things, physically forced you into others, and devalued your opinion" in nearly every encounter.[20] What Coyle's essay demonstrates is the effect of valorizing Wallace as a genius and excusing his alleged behavior as a necessary burden that goes along with the gift of his brilliance: It allows others to believe that genius – even the genius of someone else – is something that can and should be forced on the unwilling. Such a sentiment threatens to invalidate – or at least severely undermine – the work of a writer who frequently focused on the importance of choice. If authorship today is, as Benjamin Widiss describes it, based in a present and accessible author figure that "cultivates within its readers a sense of intimacy," then that intimacy cannot be fostered through coercion.[21] Acknowledging the contradiction is an

---

[18] Garber, "Dangerous Romance."   [19] Coyle, "Men Recommend."   [20] Ibid.
[21] Widiss, *Obscure Invitations*, 3.

important first step toward resolving it, but, as Wallace himself writes in "Octet," and as Coyle asserts in her essay, self-awareness is not enough.

Miller implies that this dynamic depends upon a sort of Mutually Assured Deception between the celebrity and their admirers. As the person in the spotlight, Wallace "got to see humanity at its weirdest and most affected – everyone always performing for [him], presenting false versions of themselves, trying to please [him]. But the celebrity was, of course, expected to perform, too, and so in each encounter everyone had to meet everyone else in their falsity and pretend that the mask were real."[22] Miller sees the literary establishment as fostering a circle of exhibitionists trying to hide within their own visions of the author that they want to see, be seen as, and be seen by, and this author, in turn, is able to cloak his ugliest parts in their exhibitionism.

What is changing is the power of this kind of deception, and as its power wanes, we are coming to reconsider how we see, who is seen, and what we want to see from and in a writer.[23] As such, one must view Wallace as a contested site, a monument to the Great Male Narcissist and a test case for how authorship will be assessed and defined in the twenty-first century. Like many other contested sites, we still have not decided what to do with this one or where to put it. Reckoning with his complicated legacy is also a reckoning with a style of authorship and literary celebrity that has run its course, or is at the very least untenable in the current culture.

The contested state of his literary reputation provides us with an opportunity to redefine the writer's relationship to the broader world for a new era and culture. As Clare Hayes-Brady succinctly put it in an interview with Steve Paulson, "Wallace was an extremely talented writer and a very flawed human being [who] can teach us a lot about the culture he was writing about" as well as the one we currently inhabit.[24] Wallace's life and work deserve this kind of scrutiny because through his example we can observe the literary debates of our time: its contested grounds, its

---

[22] A. Miller, *Land of Men*, 211.

[23] The "Shitty Media Men" list, created by Moira Donegan, is a good example of the way that power in publishing is beginning to shift. Even if many Shitty Media Men still hold positions of power and prestige, it is clear from documents such as Donegan's that the industry is losing interest in enabling and keeping quiet about their behavior. See Donegan, "Media Men List."

[24] Paulson, "#MeToo Era."

preoccupations, its blind spots and so on. His failings will shape another generation of writers, critics and scholars as much or more than his successes. Because so much of Wallace's work grapples with the effects of media and sexual predation on a person's relationships and their sense of self, this debate is perhaps the best-case scenario for forging a stronger, more inclusive understanding of the writer's place in a society even more saturated with exploitative media than the one Wallace wrote about. And it's all happening in real time. Try to stay awake.

Works by David Foster Wallace

"100-Word Statement," *Rolling Stone Magazine*, December 30, 1999, p. 125.

"Adult World (I)," *Esquire*, July 1998, pp. 76–85.

"Adult World (II)," *Esquire*, July 1998, pp. 100–1.

"All That," *The New Yorker*, December 6, 2009, www.newyorker.com/magazine/2009/12/14/all-that-2.

"Another Example of the Porousness of Various Borders (VI): Projected but Not Improbable Transcript of Author's Parents' Marriage's End, 1971," *McSweeney's Quarterly Concern*, 3 (Summer/Autumn, 1999), n.p. Printed on spine.

"Asset," *The New Yorker*, June 21, 1999, www.newyorker.com/archive/1999/06/21/1999_06_21_093_TNY_LIBRY_00001844.

"The Best of the Prose Poem: An International Journal," *Rain Taxi*, 6.1 (Spring 2001), 22–24.

"Borges on the Couch," *The New York Times*, November 7, 2004, http://tinyurl.com/nxamww.

Brief Interviews with Hideous Men (Boston: Little, Brown, 1999).

"Brief Interviews with Hideous Men – What They Talk About When They Talk About Themselves," *Harper's Magazine*, October 1998, pp. 41–56.

The Broom of the System (New York: Penguin, 1987).

"The Compliance Branch," *Harper's Magazine*, February 2008, https://harpers.org/archive/2008/02/the-compliance-branch/.

Consider the Lobster: Essays (New York: Little, Brown, 2005).

"Crash of 69," *Between C&D Magazine*, Winter 1989, https://biblioklept.org/2010/11/29/crash-of-69-david-foster-wallace/.

The David Foster Wallace Reader, ed. Karen Green and Michael Pietsch (New York: Little, Brown, 2014).

"David Lynch Keeps His Head," *US Premiere Magazine*, September 1996, www.lynchnet.com/lh/lhpremiere.html.

References here are to first editions. While efforts have been made to ensure consistent pagination in citations, there may be small variations across editions.

"Deciderization 2007 – A Special Report," in Introduction to *The Best American Essays*, ed. David Foster Wallace (New York: Mariner-Houghton Mifflin, 2007), pp. xii–xxiv.

"Democracy and Commerce at the U.S. *Open*," *Tennis Magazine*, September 1996.

"The Depressed Person," *Harper's Magazine*, January 1998, https://harpers.org/wp-content/uploads/HarpersMagazine-1998-01-0059425.pdf.

"E Unibus Pluram: Television and US Fiction," *The Review of Contemporary Fiction*, 13.2 (Summer 1993), 151–94.

"The Empty Plenum: David Markson's *Wittgenstein's Mistress*," *The Review of Contemporary Fiction*, 10.2 (Summer 1990), 217–39.

Everything and More: A Compact History of ∞ (London: Orion Books, 2003).

"Exploring Inner Space: *War Fever* by J.G. Ballard," *The Washington Post*, April 21, 1991, http://tinyurl.com/l4ulya.

Fate, Time and Language: An Essay on Free Will, eds. Steven M. Cahn and Maureen Eckert (New York: Columbia University Press, 2011).

"Federer as Religious Experience," *New York Times*, August 20, 2006, http://tinyurl.com/rnhv9.

"Fictional Futures and the Conspicuously Young," *The Review of Contemporary Fiction*, 8.3 (Autumn 1988), 36–53.

"The Fifth Column – A Novel: Week Eleven," *The Village Voice*, March 26, 1996, p. 50.

"The Flexicon," *Parnassus*, 23.1–2 (1998), 180–94.

"F/X Porn," *Waterstone's Magazine*, Winter/Spring 1998.

Girl with Curious Hair (New York: W. W. Norton, 1989).

"God Bless You, Mr. Franzen," *Harper's Magazine*, September 1996.

"Good Old Neon," Handwritten Draft, David Foster Wallace Papers, Harry Ransom Center, The University of Texas at Austin, MS-5155, Container 24.2.

"Good People," *The New Yorker*, February 5, 2007, http://tinyurl.com/qbgzrl.

"Greeting Card to David Markson," David Foster Wallace Papers, Harry Ransom Center, The University of Texas at Austin, Container 3, Folder 3.

"High Regret Ink," *Puncture*, 35 (Spring 1996), 17–20.

"On His Deathbed, Holding Your Hand, the Acclaimed New Young Off-Broadway Playwright's Father Begs a Boon," in *Bestial Noise: The Tin House Fiction Reader* (London: Bloomsbury, 2003) pp. 347–71.

"H.L. Hix's Morte d'Author: An Autopsy," *Harvard Book Review* (Spring 1991), 2–3.

"The Horror of Pretentiousness: *The Great and Secret Show* by Clive Barker," *The Washington Post*, February 19, 1990.

"Host," *The Atlantic Monthly*, April 2005, www.theatlantic.com/doc/200504/wallace.

"Impediments to Passion," *Might Magazine*, 7, Winter 1996. Later published as "Hail The Returning Dragon, Clothed in New Fire" in *Shiny Adidas*

Tracksuits and the Death of Camp and Other Essays from Might Magazine (New York: Berkley Trade, 1998), pp. 14–17.

Infinite Jest (Boston: Little, Brown, 1996).

Infinite Jest, Draft Materials, David Foster Wallace Papers, Harry Ransom Center, The University of Texas at Austin, Containers 15.7, 16.6, 16.7.

"Inside," *The Amherst Review*, XIII, 1985, 63–70.

"Iris' Story: An Inversion of Philosophical Skepticism: *The Blindfold* by Siri Hustvedt," *The Philadelphia Inquirer*, May 24, 1992, p. M2.

"John Updike, Champion Literary Phallocrat, Drops One: Is This Finally the End for the Magnificent Narcissists?," *The New York Observer*, October 13, 1997, https://observer.com/1997/10/john-updike-champion-literary-phallocrat-drops-one-is-this-finally-the-end-for-magnificent-narcissists/.

"Joseph Frank's *Dostoevsky*," Handwritten and Typescript Drafts, Research Materials, David Foster Wallace Papers, Harry Ransom Center, The University of Texas at Austin, Container 4.12.

"Just Asking," *The Atlantic Monthly*, November 1997, www.theatlantic.com/doc/200711/wallace-safety.

"Kenyon College Commencement Address," *The Economist 1843 Magazine*, September 19, 2008 [2005], http://tinyurl.com/mfunbz.

"Late Night," *Playboy Magazine*, June 1988.

"Laughing with Kafka," *Harper's Magazine*, July 1998, www.harpers.org/archive/1998/07/0059612.

"Letter to Didier Jacob," David Foster Wallace Papers, Harry Ransom Center, The University of Texas at Austin, Container 1, Folder 1.1.

"Letter to Michael Pietsch," January 17, 1988, David Foster Wallace Papers, Harry Ransom Center, The University of Texas at Austin, Container 1, Folder 1.1.

"Letter to Michael Pietsch," June 22, 1992, Little, Brown and Company Collection of David Foster Wallace, Box 1–5, Harry Ransom Center, The University of Texas at Austin, Box 3, Folder 2.

"Letter to Michael Pietsch," April 2, 2003, Little, Brown and Company Collection of David Foster Wallace, Box 1–5, Harry Ransom Center, The University of Texas at Austin, Box 3, Folder 5.

"Matters of Sense and Opacity," Letter, *The New York Times*, August 2, 1987, sec. 7, p. 24.

McCain's Promise (New York: Back Bay Books, 2008).

"Michael Martone's *Fort Wayne Is Seventh on Hitler's List*," *Harvard Book Review* (Spring 1990), 12–13.

"Midwesternisms," Notebook, David Foster Wallace Papers, Harry Ransom Center, The University of Texas at Austin, Container 31.12.

"The Million-Dollar Tattoo: F.J. Fiederspiel's *Laura's Skin*," *New York Times Book Review*, May 5, 1991, p. 20.

"Mr. Costigan in May," *Clarion* (Spring 1985), 40.

"Mr. Squishy," pseudonym Elizabeth Klemm, *McSweeney's Quarterly Concern*, 5 (Autumn 2000), pp. 199–248.

"The Nature of the Fun," *Fiction Writer Magazine*, September 1998.
"Neither Adult Nor Entertainment," *US Premier*, September 11, 1998.
"Nothing Happened," *Open City*, 5 (1997), 63–68.
Oblivion: Stories (New York: Little, Brown, 2004).
"Order and Flux in Northampton," *Conjunctions*, 17 (Autumn 1991), 91–118.
"Other Math," *Western Humanities Review* (Summer 1987), pp. 287–89.
"Overlooked: Five Direly Underappreciated U.S. Novels>1960," *Salon*, April 12, 1999, www.salon.com/1999/04/12/wallace/.
The Pale King: An Unfinished Novel, ed. Michael Pietsch (New York: Little, Brown, 2011).
The Pale King, Draft Materials, David Foster Wallace Papers, Harry Ransom Center, The University of Texas at Austin, Box 39.5.
"Passion, Digitally," *New York Times Magazine*, September 29, 1996, www.nytimes.com/1996/09/29/magazine/passion-digitally.html.
"Peoria (4)," *TriQuarterly*, 112 (June 2002), 131–32.
"Peoria (9) 'Whispering Pines,'" *TriQuarterly*, 112 (June 2002), 132–34.
"The Planet Trillaphon As It Stands in Relation to The Bad Thing," *Tin House*, 40 (Summer 2009), 29–46.
"Pop Quiz," *Spelunker Flophouse*, 1.4 (1997), 30–41.
"Presley as Paradigm: *Dead Elvis: A Chronicle of Cultural Obsession* by Greil Marcus," *LA Times*, November 24, 1991, http://tinyurl.com/r5sydd.
"Quo Vadis – Introduction," *The Review of Contemporary Fiction*, 16:1 (Spring 1996), 7–8.
"Rabbit Resurrected," *Harper's Magazine*, August 1992, https://harpers.org/wp-content/uploads/HarpersMagazine-1992-08-0072766.pdf.
"A Radically Condensed History of Postindustrial Life," *Ploughshares*, Spring 1998, http://tinyurl.com/npa6sr.
"Richard Taylor's 'Fatalism' and the Semantics of Physical Modality", in Steven M. Cahn and Maureen Eckert (eds.), *Fate, Time, and Language: An Essay on Free Will* (New York: Columbia University Press, 2011), pp. 141–218.
"Rhetoric and Math Melodrama," *Science Magazine*, December 22, 2000, http://tinyurl.com/ksyebd.
"Self-Harm as a Sort of Offering," *Mid-American Review XVIII*, 2 (Spring 1998), 97–100.
"Several Birds," *The New Yorker*, June 27, 1994, http://tinyurl.com/lb43np.
"Shipping Out: On the (Nearly Lethal) Comforts of a Luxury Cruise," *Harper's Magazine*, January 1996, https://harpers.org/archive/1996/01/shipping-out/.
Signifying Rappers: Rap and Race in the Urban Present, Co-authored with Mark Costello (New York: Ecco Press, 1990).
"Solomon Silverfish," *Sonora Review*, 16 (Autumn 1987), 54–81. Republished in tribute edition, 55/56 (Summer 2009).
"The String Theory," *Esquire*, September 17, 2008 [1996], www.esquire.com/features/sports/the-string-theory-0796.

String Theory: David Foster Wallace on Tennis (New York: Library of America, 2016).

A Supposedly Fun Thing I'll Never Do Again: Essays and Arguments (Boston: Little, Brown, 1997).

"Tennis, Trigonometry, *Tornadoes,*" *Harper's Magazine*, December 1991, https://harpers.org/wp-content/uploads/HarpersMagazine-1991-12-0000710.pdf.

"Tense Present: Democracy, English, and the Wars over Usage," *Harper's Magazine*, April 2001, https://harpers.org/wp-content/uploads/HarpersMagazine-2001-04-0070913.pdf.

"Ticket to the Fair," *Harper's Magazine*, July 1994, https://harpers.org/wp-content/uploads/HarpersMagazine-1994-07-0001729.pdf.

This Is Water: Some Thoughts, Delivered on a Significant Occasion, about Living a Compassionate Life (New York: Little, Brown, 2009).

"Three Protrusions," *Grand Street*, 42 (Spring 1992), 102–14.

"Tragic Cuban Émigré and a Tale of 'The Door to Happiness': *The Doorman* by Reinaldo Arenas," *The Philadelphia Enquirer Book Review*, July 14, 1991.

"The Weasel, Twelve Monkeys, and the Shrub," *Rolling Stone Magazine*, April 13, 2000, www.rollingstone.com/politics/politics-features/david-foster-wallace-on-john-mccain-the-weasel-twelve-monkeys-and-the-shrub-194272/.

"Wiggle Room," *The New Yorker*, March 9, 2009, http://tinyurl.com/mf5dbl.

"Yet Another Instance of the Porousness of Certain Borders (VIII)," *McSweeney's Quarterly Concern*, 1 (Autumn 1998), 199–248.

"Yet Another Instance of the Porousness of Certain Borders (XII)," *Esquire*, November, 1998, n.p.

"Yet Another Instance of the Porousness of Certain Borders (XXI)," *Conjunctions*, 28 (Spring 1997), www.conjunctions.com/print/article/david-foster-wallace-c28. Collected as "Yet Another Instance of the Porousness of Certain Borders (XI)."

Bibliography of Secondary Sources

Abbott, Alison, "Merger of Glaxo Wellcome and SmithKline Beecham Creates Pharmaceutical Giant," *Nature*, 403 (2000), 232.

Abbott, Paul, "What Isn't Water: David Foster Wallace and the Ambiguity of a Punch Line," *The Explicator*, 75.4 (2017), 252–56.

Aczel, Amir D., "When Good Novelists Do Bad Science," *The Globe and Mail*, January 3, 2004, www.theglobeandmail.com/arts/when-good-novelists-do-bad-science/article740894/.

Adams, Hazard, *Critical Theory Since Plato* (New York: Harcourt, 1971).

Ahmed, Sara, *The Promise of Happiness* (Durham, NC: Duke University Press, 2010).

Ahn, Sunyoung, "New Sincerity, New Worldliness: The Post-9/11 Fiction of Don DeLillo and David Foster Wallace," *Critique: Studies in Contemporary Fiction*, 60.2 (2019), 236–50.

Andersen, Tore Rye, "Down with the Rebels! David Foster Wallace and Postironical Literature," *Cultural Text Studies*, 1 (2006), 197–208.

"Judging by the Cover," *Critique: Studies in Contemporary Fiction*, 53.3 (2012), 251–78.

"Pay Attention! David Foster Wallace and His Real Enemies," *English Studies*, 95.1 (2014), 7–24.

Andrew, Laurie McRae, "Technologically Constituted Spaces: David Foster Wallace, Martin Heidegger, and Technological Nostalgia," *Critique: Studies in Contemporary Fiction*, 61.5 (2020), 589–601.

Araya, Jorge, "Why the Whiteness? Race in *The Pale King*," in Philip Coleman (ed.), *Critical Insights: David Foster Wallace* (New York: Grey House Publishing/Salem Press, 2015), pp. 238–51.

Arden, Patrick, "David Foster Wallace Warms Up," in Stephen J. Burn (ed.), *Conversations with David Foster Wallace* (Jackson: University Press of Mississippi, 2012), pp. 94–100.

Ashbery, John, *Selected Poems* (New York: Viking, 1985).

Aubry, Timothy, *Reading as Therapy: What Contemporary Fiction Does for Middle-Class Americans* (Iowa City: University of Iowa Press, 2006).

Ballard, James Graham, *The Atrocity Exhibition* (San Francisco: Re/Search, 1990).

Banner, Olivia, "'They're Literally Shit': Masculinity and the Work of Art in the Age of Waste Recycling," *Iowa Journal of Cultural Studies*, 10.1 (2009), 74–90.

Barney, Rachel, "The Carpenter and the Good," in Douglas L. Cairns, Frit-Gregor Herrmann, and Terry Penner (eds.), *Pursuing the Good: Ethics and Metaphysics in Plato's Republic* (Edinburgh: Edinburgh University Press, 2007), pp. 293–319.

Baron-Cohen, Simon, Ofer Golan, and Emma Ashwin, "Can Emotion Recognition Be Taught to Children with Autism Spectrum Conditions?," *Philosophical Transactions of the Royal Society B – Biological Sciences*, 364.1535 (2009), 3567–74.

Bartlett, Christopher, "'An Exercise in Telemachry': David Foster Wallace's *Infinite Jest* and Intergenerational Conversation," *Critique: Studies in Contemporary Fiction*, 57.4 (2016), 374–89.

Baskin, Jon, "Coming to Terms: Franzen, Wallace and the Question of Realism," *The Point*, 5, January 15, 2012, https://thepointmag.com/criticism/coming-to-terms/.

"Death Is Not the End: David Foster Wallace, His legacy, and His Critics," *The Point*, 1, March 1, 2009, https://thepointmag.com/criticism/death-is-not-the-end/.

Ordinary Unhappiness: The Therapeutic Fiction of David Foster Wallace (Stanford, CA: Stanford University Press, 2019).

"Untrendy Problems: *The Pale King's* Philosophical Aspirations," in Robert K. Bolger and Scott Korb (eds.), *Gesturing toward Reality: David Foster Wallace and Philosophy* (London: Bloomsbury Academic, 2014), pp. 141–56.

Baudrillard, Jean, *America* (London: Verso, 1988).

Beauvoir, Simone de, "Literature and Metaphysics," in *Philosophical Writings*, ed. Margaret A. Simons, trans. Veronique Zaytzeff and Frederick M. Morrison (Chicago: University of Illinois Press, 2004), pp. 269–77.

Been, Eric, "David Foster Wallace: Genius, Fabulist, Would-Be Murderer," *The Atlantic*, September 6, 2012, www.theatlantic.com/entertainment/archive/2012/09/david-foster-wallace-genius-fabulist-would-be-murderer/261997/.

Bennett, Alice, *Afterlife and Narrative in Contemporary Fiction* (New York: Palgrave, 2012).

Contemporary Fictions of Attention: Reading and Distraction in the Twenty-First Century (London: Bloomsbury Academic, 2018).

Bennett, Andrew, "Inside David Foster Wallace's Head: Attention, Loneliness, Suicide and the Other Side of Boredom," in Robert K. Bolger and Scott Korb (eds.), *Gesturing toward Reality: David Foster Wallace and Philosophy* (London: Bloomsbury Academic, 2014), pp. 69–84.

Suicide Century: Literature and Suicide from James Joyce to David Foster Wallace (Cambridge: Cambridge University Press, 2017).

Benzon, Kiki, "Darkness Legible, Unquiet Lines: Mood Disorders and the Fiction of David Foster Wallace," in Richard Pine (ed.), *Creativity, Madness and Civilisation* (Newcastle: Cambridge Scholars Publishing, 2007), pp. 189–99.

"David Foster Wallace and Millennial America," in Philip Coleman (ed.), *Critical Insights: David Foster Wallace* (Ipswich, MA: Salem Press, 2015), pp. 29–45.

Berkeley, George, *The Works of George Berkeley, Bishop of Cloyne*, vol. VII, ed. Arthur Aston Luce (London: Thomas Nelson & Sons, 1955).

Berlant, Lauren, *Cruel Optimism* (Durham, NC: Duke University Press, 2011)

Berlin, Isaiah, and Ian Harris, *Liberty: Incorporating Four Essays on Liberty*, ed. Henry Hardy (Oxford: Oxford University Press, 2002).

Berryman, John, *The Dream Songs* (London: Faber & Faber, 1993).

Bhalla, Nita, "South Africa's #RhodesMustFall Founder Speaks Out on Statues That Glorify Racism," Thomson Reuters Foundation, June 17, 2020, www .globalcitizen.org/en/content/rhodes-must-fall-founder-racist-statues/.

Bird, Benjamin, "History, Emotion, and the Body: Mourning in Post-9/11 Fiction," *Literature Compass*, 4.3 (2007), 561–75.

Birkerts, Sven, *The Gutenberg Elegies: The Fate of Reading in an Electronic Age*, 2nd ed. (New York: Faber & Faber, 2006).

"The Sentence: David Foster Wallace," *Sonora Review*, 55–56 (2009), 7–12.

Blanchot, Maurice, and Jacques Derrida, *The Instant of My Death / Demeure: Fiction and Testimony*, trans. Elizabeth Rottenberg (Stanford, CA: Stanford University Press, 2000).

Bleakley, Alan, and Margaretta Jolly, "Writing Out Prescriptions: Hyperrealism and the Chemical Regulation of Mood," *Advances in Health Science Education*, 17.5 (2012), 779–90.

Blum, David, "Hollywood's Brat Pack," *New York Magazine*, June 10, 1985, https://nymag.com/movies/features/49902/, pp. 40–47.

Blumenbach, Ulrich, "Interview by Klaus Brinkbäumer," *Der Spiegel*, September 8, 2009, www.spiegel.de/kultur/literatur/zehn-wahrheiten-von-ulrich-blu menbach-ich-musste-das-falsche-richtig-falsch-uebersetzen-a-646947.html.

Bocharova, Jean, "David Foster Wallace's Catholic Imagination: 'The Depressed Person' and *Orthodoxy*," *Renascence*, 71.4 (2019), 233–46.

Bockmann, Lars-Frederik, "Freedom-from versus Freedom-to: A Dialectical Reading of David Foster Wallace's *Infinite Jest*," *Zeitschrift für Anglistik und Amerikanistick: A Quarterly of Language, Literature and Culture*, 65.1 (2017), 51–65.

Boddy, Kasia, "A Fiction of Response: *Girl with Curious Hair* in Context," in Marshall Boswell and Stephen Burn (eds.), *A Companion to David Foster Wallace Studies* (New York: Palgrave Macmillan, 2013), pp. 23–41.

Bolger, Robert K., and Scott Korb (eds.), *Gesturing toward Reality: David Foster Wallace and Philosophy* (London: Bloomsbury Academic, 2014).

Bono, Marta, "Reactions to Chaos Theory: The Mathematical References in the Notes of *Infinite Jest*," *Lettera Matematica*, 3.4 (2015), 295–98.

Boon, Marcus, *The Road of Excess: A History of Writers on Drugs* (Cambridge, MA: Harvard University Press, 2002).

Booth, Martin, *Opium: A History* (London: St. Martin's Press, 2013).

Boswell, Marshall, "Author Here: The Legal Fiction of David Foster Wallace's *The Pale King*," *English Studies*, 95.1 (2014), 25–39.

"'The Constant Monologue Inside Your Head': *Oblivion* and the Nightmare of Consciousness," in Marshall Boswell and Stephen J. Burn (eds.), *A Companion to David Foster Wallace Studies* (New York: Palgrave Macmillan, 2013), pp. 151–70.

Boswell, Marshall (ed.), *David Foster Wallace and "The Long Thing": New Essays on the Novels* (London: Bloomsbury, 2014).

"Heading Westward," *Sonora Review*, 55–56 (2009), 28–32.

"The Rival Lover: David Foster Wallace and the Anxiety of Influence in Jeffrey Eugenides's *The Marriage Plot*," *Modern Fiction Studies*, 62.3 (2016), 499–518.

"Slacker Redemption: Wallace and Generation X," in Ralph Clare (ed.), *The Cambridge Companion to David Foster Wallace* (Cambridge: Cambridge University Press, 2018), pp. 19–32.

"Trickle-Down Citizenship: Taxes and Civic Responsibility in *The Pale King*," in Marshall Boswell (ed.), *David Foster Wallace and "The Long Thing": New Essays on the Novels* (London: Bloomsbury Academic, 2014), pp. 209–25. First published in *Studies in the Novel*, 44.4 (2012), 464–79.

Understanding David Foster Wallace, Revised and Expanded Edition (Columbia: University of South Carolina Press, 2020 [2003]).

The Wallace Effect: David Foster Wallace and the Contemporary Literary Imagination (London: Bloomsbury Academic, 2019).

Boswell, Marshall, and Stephen J. Burn (eds.), *A Companion to David Foster Wallace Studies* (New York: Palgrave MacMillan, 2013).

Bourdieu, Pierre, *The Field of Cultural Production* (New York: Columbia, 1993).

Boyd, Brian, *Nabokov's Ada: The Place of Consciousness* (Ann Arbor, MI: Ardis Publishers, 1985).

Vladimir Nabokov: The Russian Years (Princeton, NJ: Princeton University Press, 1990).

Brenner, Leon S., "Creative Hyper-Activation in Depression," *Creativity Research Journal*, 31.4 (2019), 359–70.

Bresnan, Mark, "The Work of Play in David Foster Wallace's *Infinite Jest*," *Critique: Studies in Contemporary Fiction*, 50.1 (2008), 51–68.

Brick, Martin, "A Postmodernist's Progress: Thoughts on Spirituality across the David Foster Wallace Canon," *Christianity and Literature*, 64.1 (2014), 65–81.

Bruni, Frank, "The Grunge American Novel," *The New York Times Magazine*, March 24, 1996, pp. 38–41.

Bryce, Gordon, *The Red Hourglass: Lives of the Predators* (New York: Dell Publishing, 1998).

Büchner, Georg, "Lenz," in *Eight German Novellas*, trans. Michael Fleming (1835; repr. New York: Oxford University Press, 1997), 58–82.

Buell, Lawrence, *The Dream of the Great American Novel* (Cambridge, MA: Harvard University Press, 2014).

The Environmental Imagination: Thoreau, Nature Writing, and the Formation of American Culture (Cambridge, MA: Harvard University Press, 1995).

Burn, Stephen J., *Conversations with David Foster Wallace* (Jackson: University Press of Mississippi, 2012).

David Foster Wallace's Infinite Jest: A Reader's Guide, 2nd ed. (London: Continuum, 2012).

"Generational Succession and a Possible Source for the Title of David Foster Wallace's *The Broom of the System*," *Notes on Contemporary Literature*, 33.2 (2003), 9–11.

"The Machine-Language of the Muscles: Reading, Sport, and the Self in *Infinite Jest*," in Michael Cocchiarale and Scott D. Emmert (eds.), *Upon Further Review: Essays on American Sports Literature* (Westport, CO: Greenwood, 2004), pp. 41–50.

"'A Paradigm for the Life of Consciousness': Closing Time in *The Pale King*," *Studies in the Novel*, 44.4 (2012), 371–88.

"Second-Generation Postmoderns," in Brian McHale and Len Platt (eds.), *The Cambridge History of Postmodern Literature* (Cambridge: Cambridge University Press, 2016), pp. 450–64.

"Toward a General Theory of Vision in Wallace's Fiction," *English Studies*, 95.1 (2014), 85–93.

"'Webs of Nerves Pulsing and Firing': *Infinite Jest* and the Science of Mind," in Marshall Boswell and Stephen J. Burn (eds.), *A Companion to David Foster Wallace Studies* (New York: Palgrave Macmillan, 2013), pp. 59–85.

Burris, Stanley, and H. P. Sankappanavar, *A Course in Universal Algebra* (Ontario: University of Ontario Press, 2012).

Burroughs, William S., *Junky* (New York: Grove Press, 2003).

Butler, Judith, *Gender Trouble: Feminism and the Subversion of Identity* (New York: Routledge, 2006).

Precarious Life (London: Verso, 2004).

Cahn, Steven M., and Maureen Eckert (eds.), *Freedom and the Self: Essays on the Philosophy of David Foster Wallace* (New York: Columbia University Press, 2015).

Camus, Albert, "The Fall," in *The Plague, The Fall, Exile and the Kingdom, and Selected Essays*, trans. Justin O'Brien (New York: Everyman's Library, 2004), pp. 273–56.

The Rebel: An Essay on Man in Revolt, trans. Anthony Bower (New York: Vintage, 1991).

Cantor, Georg, *Über unendliche, lineare Punktmannigfaltigkeiten: Arbeiten zur Mengenlehre aus den Jahren 1872–1884* (Leipzig: Springer-Verlag, 1984).

Caracciolo, Marco, *The Experientiality of Narrative: An Enactivist Approach* (Berlin: De Gruyter, 2017).

Carcasson, Martin, "Ending Welfare as We Know It: President Clinton and the Rhetorical Transformation of the Anti-Welfare Culture," *Rhetoric and Public Affairs*, 9.4 (2006), 655–92.

Carlisle, Greg, *Elegant Complexity: A Study of David Foster Wallace's Infinite Jest* (Los Angeles, CA: Sideshow Media Group Press, 2007).

Nature's Nightmare: Analyzing David Foster Wallace's Oblivion (Los Angeles, CA: Sideshow Media Group Press, 2013).

"Wallace's Infinite Fiction," *Sonora Review*, 55–56 (2009), 33–37.

Carroll, Hamilton, *Affirmative Reaction: New Formations of White Masculinity* (Durham, DC: Duke University Press, 2011).

"Desire, Self, and Other: Wallace and Gender," in Stephen J. Burn and Mary K. Holland (eds.), *Approaches to Teaching the Works of David Foster Wallace* (New York: Modern Language Association, 2019), pp. 169–79.

Castiglia, Christopher, and Glenn Hendler, "Introduction," in Christopher Castiglia and Glenn Hendler (eds.), *Walt Whitman, Franklin Evans, or The Inebriate* (Durham, NC: Duke University Press, 2007), pp. ix–lviii.

Cavell, Stanley, "The Availability of Wittgenstein's Later Philosophy," in *Must We Mean What We Say? A Book of Essays*, updated ed. (Cambridge: Cambridge University Press, 2002 [1976]), pp. 41–67.

The Claim of Reason: Wittgenstein, Morality, Skepticism, and Tragedy (Oxford: Oxford University Press, 1979).

Conditions Handsome and Unhandsome: The Constitution of Emersonian Perfectionism (Chicago: The University of Chicago Press, 1990).

Little Did I Know: Excerpts from Memory (Stanford, CA: Stanford University Press, 2010).

Philosophy the Day After Tomorrow (Cambridge, MA: The Belknap Press of Harvard University Press, 2005).

In Quest of the Ordinary: Lines of Skepticism and Romanticism (Chicago: University of Chicago Press, 1989).

Centers for Disease Control and Prevention, "Understanding the Epidemic," 2021, www.cdc.gov/drugoverdose/epidemic/index.html.

Certeau, Michel de, *The Practice of Everyday Life*, trans. Steven F. Rendall (Los Angeles: University of California Press, 1984).

Childs, Jason, and Denise Gigante (eds.), *The Cambridge History of the British Essay* (Cambridge: Cambridge University Press, forthcoming).

Chodat, Robert, "The Advanced U.S. Citizenship of David Foster Wallace," in *The Matter of High Words: Naturalism, Normativity, and the Postwar Sage* (New York: Oxford University Press, 2017), pp. 238–303.

Cioffi, Frank Louis, "'An Anguish Become Thing': Narrative as Performance in David Foster Wallace's *Infinite Jest*," *Narrative*, 8.2 (2000), 161–81.

Clancy, Tom, *The Sum of All Fears* (New York: G. P. Putnam's Sons, 1991).

Clapham, Christopher, and James Nicholson, *The Concise Oxford Dictionary of Mathematics*, 5th ed. (Oxford: Oxford University Press, 2014).

Clare, Ralph (ed.), *The Cambridge Companion to David Foster Wallace* (Cambridge: Cambridge University Press, 2018).

Clare, Ralph, "Introduction," in Ralph Clare (ed.), *The Cambridge Companion to David Foster Wallace* (Cambridge: Cambridge University Press, 2018).

"The Politics of Boredom and the Boredom of Politics in David Foster Wallace's *The Pale King*," *Studies in the Novel*, 44.4 (2012), 428–46.

Clegg, Brian, *A Brief History of Infinity: The Quest to Think the Unthinkable* (London: Robinson, 2003).

Cockfield, Arthur J., "David Foster Wallace on Tax Policy, How to Be an Adult and Other Mysteries of the Universe," *Pittsburgh Tax Review*, 12 (2015), 89–109.

Cohen, Joshua, *Attention! A (Short) History* (London: Notting Hill Editions, 2013).

Cohen, Samuel, "The Whiteness of David Foster Wallace," in Len Platt and Sara Upstone (eds.), *Postmodern Literature and Race* (Cambridge: Cambridge University Press, 2015), pp. 228–43.

"To Wish to Try to Sing to the Next Generation: Infinite Jest's History," in Samuel Cohen and Lee Konstantinou (eds.), *The Legacy of David Foster Wallace* (Iowa City: University of Iowa Press, 2012), pp. 59–79.

Cohen, Samuel, and Lee Konstantinou (eds.), *The Legacy of David Foster Wallace* (Iowa City: University of Iowa Press, 2012).

Coleman, Philip (ed.), *Critical Insights: David Foster Wallace* (Ipswich, MA: Salem, 2015).

Collignon, Fabienne, "USA Murated Nation, or, the Sublime Spherology of Security Culture," *Journal of American Studies*, 49.1 (2015), 99–123.

Comentale, Edward P., "Database Regionalism in *Infinite Jest* and *Open City*," *Australasian Journal of American Studies*, 36.2 (2017), 79–114.

Connell, Liam, *Precarious Labour and the Contemporary Novel* (London: Palgrave Macmillan, 2017).

Copi, Irving M., Carl Cohen, and Kenneth McMahon, *Introduction to Logic*, 14th ed. (London: Pearson Education Limited, 2013).

Coughlan, David, "'Sappy or No, It's True': Affect and Expression in *Brief Interviews with Hideous Men*," in Philip Coleman (ed.), *Critical Insights: David Foster Wallace* (New York: Grey House Publishing/Salem Press, 2015), pp. 160–75.

Courtwright, David T., *Dark Paradise: A History of Opiate Addiction in America* (Cambridge, MA: Harvard University Press, 2001).

Coyle, Deirdre, "Men Recommend David Foster Wallace to Me," *Electric Literature*, April 17, 2017, https://electricliterature.com/men-recommend-david-foster-wallace-to-me/.

Crannell, Annalisa, Marc Frantz, and Fumiko Futamura, *Perspective and Projective Geometry* (Princeton, NJ: Princeton University Press, 2019).

Crosthwaite, Paul, *The Market Logics of Contemporary Fiction* (Cambridge: Cambridge University Press, 2019).

Crystal, David, *The Language of Stories* (Woodstock, NY: The Overlook Press, 2004).

Curtis, Paul M., "'Yo Man So What's Your Story': The Double Bind and Addiction in David Foster Wallace's *Infinite Jest*," *Mosaic: An Interdisciplinary Critical Journal*, 49.4 (2016), 37–52.

Cvetkovich, Ann, *Depression: A Public Feeling* (Durham, NC: Duke University Press, 2012).

Daalder, Jurrit, "'A Place to Fear and Love': The Imagined Heartland of David Foster Wallace's *The Broom of the System*," in Robert Primeau (ed.), *Midwestern Literature* (Ipswich, MA: Salem, 2013), pp. 94–108.

Darling, Matthew J., "David Foster Wallace and the Athlete's War with the Self," in Michael Cocchiarale and Scott D. Emmert (eds.), *Critical Insights: American Sports Fiction* (Ipswich, MA: Salem, 2013), pp. 209–30.

Dauben, Joseph Warren, *Georg Cantor: His Mathematics and Philosophy of the Infinite* (Princeton, NJ: Princeton University Press, 1990).

Davis, N. Ann, "Invisible Disability," *Ethics*, 116.1 (2005), 153–213.

Dawson, Paul, *The Return of the Omniscient Narrator* (Columbus: Ohio State University Press, 2013).

Dazzle Communication, "Le Conversazioni 2006," *YouTube*, May 26, 2007, www.youtube.com/watch?v=MsziSppMUS4.

Dean, Michelle, "A Supposedly True Thing Jonathan Franzen Said about David Foster Wallace," *The Awl*, October 11, 2011, www.theawl.com/2011/10/a-supposedly-true-thing-jonathan-franzen-said-about-david-foster-wallace/?utm_source=feedburner&utm_medium=feed&utm_campaign=Feed:+TheAwl+(The+Awl.

De Bourcier, Simon, "Forms, Punch Cards and LETTERS: Self-Reference, Recursion and (Un)self-Consciousness in *The Pale King*'s Representation of Bureaucracy," *English Studies* 95.1 (2014), 40–58.

"'They All Sound Like David Foster Wallace': Syntax and Narrative in *Infinite Jest, Brief Interviews with Hideous Men, Oblivion* and *The Pale King*," *Orbit: A Journal of American Literature*, 5.2 (2017), 1–30, https://orbit.openlibhums.org/article/id/439/.

Defossez, Ellen, "Unending Narrative, One-sided Empathy, and Problematic Contexts of Interaction in David Foster Wallace's 'The Depressed Person,'" *Journal of Medical Humanities*, 39.1 (2018), 15–27.

DeLillo, Don, *White Noise* (London: Picador, 2011 [1984]).

Denning, Michael, *Mechanic Accents: Dime Novels and Working-Class Culture in America* (New York: Verso, 1987).

De Quincey, Thomas, *Confessions of an English Opium-Eater and Other Writings* (New York: Oxford University Press, 2008 [1821]).

Derdeyn, LeeAnn, "Love the Jackalope: Historicity, Relational Identity, and Naming in David Foster Wallace's 'Lyndon,'" *College Literature*, 45.4 (2018), 747–72.

Derrida, Jacques, "The Rhetoric of Drugs," trans. Peggy Kamuf, *Points ... Interviews 1974–1994* (Stanford, CA: Stanford University Press, 1995), pp. 228–54.

DeWeerdt, Sarah, "Tracing the US Opioid Crisis to Its Roots," *Nature*, 573.7773 (2019), S10–S12.

Diakoulakis, Christoforos, "'Quote Unquote Love ... A Type of Scotopia': David Foster Wallace's *Brief Interviews with Hideous Men*," in David Hering (ed.),

Consider David Foster Wallace: Critical Essays (Los Angeles, CA: Sideshow Media Group Press, 2010), pp. 147–55.

Diamond, Jason, "Sex, Drugs, and Bestsellers: The Legend of the Literary Brat Pack," *Harper's Bazaar*, November 2, 2016, www.harpersbazaar.com/cul ture/art-books-music/a18422/literary-brat-pack-donna-tartt-jay-mcinerney.

Dickinson, Emily, *The Poems of Emily Dickinson*, ed. R. W. Franklin (Cambridge, MA and London: The Belknap Press of Harvard University Press, 2003).

Di Leo, Jeffrey, "Sovereignty of the Dead: Authors, Editors, and the Aesthetic Text," *Comparatist*, 36 (2012), 123–36.

Dolo, Eva, "Too Much Fun: Endnotes in *Infinite Jest*," *Symbolism*, 15 (2015), 75–100.

Donegan, Moira, "I Started the Media Men List. My Name Is Moira Donegan," *The Cut*, January 10, 2018, www.thecut.com/2018/01/moira-donegan-i-started-the-media-men-list.html.

Dorson, James, "Critical Posthumanism in the Posthuman Economy: The Case of 'Mister Squishy,'" in Catrin Gersdorf and Juliane Braun (eds.), *America After Nature: Democracy, Culture, Environment* (Heidelberg: Universitätsverlag, 2016), pp. 423–39.

"How (Not) to Be Liked: David Foster Wallace's Anti-Popular Aesthetic," in Martin Lüthe and Sascha Pöhlmann (eds.), *Unpopular Culture* (Amsterdam: Amsterdam University Press, 2016), pp. 61–79.

"The Neoliberal Machine in the Bureaucratic Garden: Pastoral States of Mind in David Foster Wallace's *The Pale King*," in Eric Erbacher, Nicole Maruo-Schröder, and Florian Sedlmeier (eds.), *Rereading the Machine in the Garden: Nature and Technology in American Culture* (Frankfurt-on-Main: Verlag, 2014), pp. 211–30.

Dostoevsky, Fyodor, *Notes from Underground*, trans. Richard Pevear and Larissa Volkhonsky (New York: Everyman's Library, 2004).

Douglas, Ann, *The Feminization of American Culture* (New York: Farrar, Straus and Giroux, 1998 [1977]).

Douglas, Christopher, "David Foster Wallace's Evangelicals: The Other Postsecularism," *Christianity and Literature*, 67.3 (2018), 548–58.

Dowling, William, and Robert Bell, *A Reader's Companion to Infinite Jest* (Bloomington, IN: Xlibris, 2005).

Dreyfus, Hubert, and Sean Dorrance Kelly, "David Foster Wallace's Nihilism," in *All Things Shining: Reading the Western Classics to Find Meaning in a Secular Age* (New York: Free-Simon, 2011), pp. 22–57.

Dulk, Allard den, "Beyond Endless 'Aesthetic' Irony: A Comparison of the Irony Critique of Søren Kierkegaard and David Foster Wallace's *Infinite Jest*," *Studies in the Novel*, 44.3 (2012), 325–45.

"Boredom, Anxiety and Irony: Wallace and the Kierkegaardian View of the Self," in Marshall Boswell (ed.), *David Foster Wallace and "The Long Thing"* (New York and London: Bloomsbury Academic, 2014), pp. 43–61.

Existentialist Engagement in Wallace, Eggers and Foer: A Philosophical Analysis of Contemporary American Literature (New York: Bloomsbury, 2015).

"Good Faith and Sincerity: Sartrean Virtues of Self-Becoming in David Foster Wallace's *Infinite Jest*," in Robert K. Bolger and Scott Korb (eds.), *Gesturing Toward Reality: David Foster Wallace and Philosophy* (New York: Bloomsbury Academic, 2014), pp. 205–27.

"The Transcendence of a Meaningful Life: The Portrayal of the Contemporary Self in David Foster Wallace's *Infinite Jest*," in Wessel Stoker and W. L. van der Merwe (eds.), *Looking Beyond? Shifting Views of Transcendence in Philosophy, Theology, Art, and Politics* (Amsterdam: Rodopi, 2012), pp. 413–29.

"Wallace and Wittgenstein: Literature as Dialogue Concerning the Real World," in Sébastian Hüsch (ed.), *Philosophy and Literature and the Crisis of Metaphysics* (Würzburg: Verlag, 2011), pp. 343–58.

Durantaye, Leland de la, "The Subsurface Unity of All Things, or David Foster Wallace's Free Will," in Robert K. Bolger and Scott Korb (eds.), *Gesturing Toward Reality: David Foster Wallace and Philosophy* (London: Bloomsbury Academic, 2014), pp. 19–29.

Eckert, Maureen, "Renewing the Fatalist Conversation," in Steven M. Cahn and Maureen Eckert (eds.), *David Foster Wallace, Fate, Time, and Language: An Essay on Free Will* (New York: Columbia University Press, 2011), pp. 135–39.

Eggers, Dave, "David Foster Wallace: Interview," *The Believer*, November 1, 2003, https://believermag.com/an-interview-with-david-foster-wallace/.

Elderon, Shannon, "The Shaping of Storied Selves in David Foster Wallace's *The Pale King*," *Critique: Studies in Contemporary Fiction*, 55.5 (2014), 508–21.

Eldridge, Richard (ed.), *Stanley Cavell and Literary Studies: Consequences of Skepticism* (London and New York: Bloomsbury, 2011).

Elie, Paul, "A Conversation with Author Jonathan Franzen," Berkeley Center for Religion, Peace and World Affairs at Georgetown University, YouTube, March 26, 2018, www.youtube.com/watch?v=78_UKtCYJ_s.

Eliot, T. S., *Selected Poems* (London: Faber & Faber, 1961).

Ellerhoff, Steve Gronert, "Proteus Bound: Pinning *Girl with Curious Hair* under Short Story Theory," in Philip Coleman (ed.), *Critical Insights: David Foster Wallace* (New York: Grey House Publishing/Salem Press, 2015), pp. 112–27.

Ellis, Bret Easton, "Looking for Cool in L.A.," *Vanity Fair*, November 1985, pp. 90–93, 118–19.

Ellison, David R., "Camus and the Rhetoric of Dizziness: *La Chute*," *Contemporary Literature*, 24.3 (1983), 322–48.

Emerson, Ralph Waldo, *Emerson's Prose and Poetry*, eds. Joel Porte and Saundra Morris (New York and London: W. W. Norton, 2001).

Essays and Lectures, ed. Joel Porte (New York: Library of America, 1983).

The Essential Writings of Ralph Waldo Emerson (New York: Random House, 2000).

The End of the Tour, Film, dir. James Ponsoldt (Los Angeles, CA: Anonymous Content, 2015).

Englade, Emilio, "The Birth of the Reader: Inside the Final Edits to *Infinite Jest*," *Critique: Studies in Contemporary Fiction*, 60.5 (2019), 613–26.

English, Lyn D., *Mathematical Reasoning: Analogies, Metaphors, and Images* (New York and London: Routledge, 2009).

Ercolino, Stefano, "'End of the End of the Line': The Broken Temporality of David Foster Wallace's *Infinite Jest*," in Cindy Weinstein (ed.), *A Question of Time: American Literature from Colonial Encounter to Contemporary Fiction* (Cambridge: Cambridge University Press, 2019), pp. 293–311.

"The Killing Vision: David Foster Wallace's Infinite Jest," in Stefano Ercolino, Massimo Fusillo, Mirko Lino, and Luca Zenobi (eds.), *Imaginary Films in Literature* (Leiden: Brill, 2016), pp. 18–34.

The Maximalist Novel: From Thomas Pynchon's Gravity's Rainbow to Roberto Bolaño's 2666 (New York: Bloomsbury Academic, 2014).

Erickson, Paul, "Erotica," in Joanna Levin and Edward Whitley (eds.), *Walt Whitman in Context* (Cambridge: Cambridge University Press, 2018), pp. 136–45.

Eve, Martin Paul, "Equivocationary Horseshit: Post-Correlationist Aesthetics and Post-Critical Ethics in the Works of David Foster Wallace," *Open Library of Humanities*, 6.1 (2020), 1–29, https://olh.openlibhums.org/articles/10.16995/olh.538/.

"Preferential Consideration: Bartleby, Class, and Genocide in David Foster Wallace's 'Consider the Lobster,'" *C21 Literature: Journal of 21st-Century Writings*, 5.3 (2017), 1–23, https://c21.openlibhums.org/article/id/529/.

"Review of Andrew Piper, Enumerations: Data and Literary Study," *Modern Philology*, 117.1 (2019), E12–14.

"Thomas Pynchon, David Foster Wallace and the Problems of 'Metamodernism': Post-Millennial Post-postmodernism?," *C21*, 1.1 (2012), 7–25.

Faludi, Susan, *Stiffed: The Betrayal of the American Man* (New York: Perennial, 2000).

Faulkner, William, *As I Lay Dying*, ed. Michael Gorra, Norton Critical Edition (New York: W. W. Norton, 2010).

Felski, Rita, "Fin de Siècle, Fin du Sexe: Transsexuality, Postmodernism, and the Death of History," in Susan Stryker and Stephen Whittle (eds.), *The Transgender Studies Reader* (London: Routledge, 2006), pp. 565–73.

Ferguson, Kevin L., "Youth Culture on the Skids: Generation X and Brat Pack Fiction," in D. Quentin Miller (ed.), *American Literature in Transition: 1980–1990* (New York: Cambridge University Press, 2018), pp. 13–26.

Fest, Bradley J., "The Inverted Nuke in the Garden: Archival Emergence and Anti-Eschatology in David Foster Wallace's *Infinite Jest*," *Boundary 2*, 39.3 (2012), 125–49.

"'Then Out of the Rubble': The Apocalypse in David Foster Wallace's Early Fiction," *Studies in the Novel*, 44.3 (2012), 284–303.

Fischer, Molly, "Why Literary Chauvinists Love David Foster Wallace," *The Cut*, August 12, 2015, www.thecut.com/2015/08/david-foster-wallace-beloved-author-of-bros.html.

Fitzpatrick, Kathleen, *The Anxiety of Obsolescence: The American Novel in the Age of Television* (Nashville, TN: Vanderbilt University Press, 2006).

Flaherty, Colleen, "Junot Díaz, Feminism and Ethnicity," *Inside Higher Ed*, May 29, 2018, www.insidehighered.com/news/2018/05/29/rift-among-scholars-over-treatment-junot-d%C3%ADaz-he-faces-harassment-and-misconduct.

Fordham, Finn, "Katabasis in Danielewski's *House of Leaves* and Two Other Recent American Novels," in Joe Bray and Alison Gibbons (eds.), *Mark Z. Danielewski* (Manchester: Manchester University Press, 2011), pp. 33–51.

Foster, Graham, "A Blasted Region: David Foster Wallace's Manmade Landscapes," in David Hering (ed.), *Consider David Foster Wallace: Critical Essays* (Los Angeles, CA: Sideshow Media Group Press, 2010), pp. 37–48.

"A Deep Insider's Elegiac Tribute: The Work of Don DeLillo in David Foster Wallace's *Infinite Jest*," *Orbit: A Journal of American Literature*, 4.2 (2016), 1–20, https://orbit.openlibhums.org/article/id/470/.

Foucault, Michel, *The History of Sexuality*, vol. I, trans. Robert Hurley (New York: Pantheon Books, 1976).

Society Must Be Defended: Lectures at the College de France, 1975–76, trans. David Macey (New York: Picador, 2002).

Frank, Joseph, *Dostoevsky: The Miraculous Years, 1865–1871* (Princeton, NJ: Princeton University Press, 1995). In Harry Ransom Center, David Foster Wallace Library, Container 4.12.

Frankenberg, Ruth, "Cracks in the Façade: Whiteness and the Construction of 9/11," *Social Identities*, 11.6 (2005), 553–71.

Frantzen, Mikkel Krause, "Finding the Unlovable Object Lovable: Empathy and Depression in David Foster Wallace," *Studies in American Fiction*, 45.2 (2018), 259–79.

Franzen, Jonathan, "Farther Away: 'Robinson Crusoe,' David Foster Wallace and the Island of Solitude," *The New Yorker*, April 18, 2011, www.newyorker.com/magazine/2011/04/18/farther-away-jonathan-franzen.

"Mr. Difficult," in *How to Be Alone* (London: Fourth Estate, 2010), pp. 238–69.

Frascina, Francis, "The New York Times, Norman Rockwell and the New Patriotism," *Journal of Visual Culture*, 3.2 (2003), 99–130.

Fraser, Benjamin, "On the (In)Visibility of Cognitive Disability," in *Cognitive Disability Aesthetics: Visual Culture, Disability Representations, and the (In)Visibility of Cognitive Difference* (Toronto: University of Toronto Press, 2018), pp. 29–48.

Frazer, T. C., "An Introduction to Midwest English," in W. Wolfram and B. Ward (eds.), *American Voices: How Dialects Differ from Coast to Coast* (Malden, MA: Blackwell, 2006), pp. 101–5.

Freudenthal, Elizabeth, "Anti-Interiority: Compulsiveness, Objectification, and Identity in *Infinite Jest*," *New Literary History*, 41.1 (2010), 191–211.

Frost, Laura Catherine, *The Problem with Pleasure: Modernism and Its Discontents* (New York: Columbia University Press, 2013).

Gallagher, John, "The Cobainification of David Foster Wallace," *The New Statesman*, December 16, 2013, www.newstatesman.com/cultural-capital/2013/12/cobainification-david-foster-wallace.

Gandert, Sean, "A Short Meditation on the Whiteness of David Foster Wallace's Writing," *The International David Foster Wallace Society*, July 15, 2017, www.dfwsociety.org/2017/07/15/a-short-meditation-on-the-whiteness-of-david-foster-wallaces-writing/.

Garber, Megan, "David Foster Wallace and the Dangerous Romance of Male Genius," *The Atlantic*, May 9, 2018, www.theatlantic.com/entertainment/archive/2018/05/the-world-still-spins-around-male-genius/559925/.

Garland-Thomson, Rosemarie, "Building a World with Disability in It," in Anne Waldschmidt, Hanjo Berressem, and Moritz Ingwersen (eds.), *Culture – Theory – Disability: Encounters between Disability Studies and Cultural Studies* (Bielefeld: Transcript Verlag, 2017), pp. 51–62.

Extraordinary Bodies: Figuring Physical Disability in American Literature and Culture (New York: Columbia University Press, 1997).

Gelpi, Albert, *A Coherent Splendor: The American Poetic Renaissance, 1910–1950* (Cambridge: Cambridge University Press, 1987).

Genette, Gerard, *Paratexts: Thresholds of Interpretation* (Cambridge: Cambridge University Press, 1997).

Gerdes, Kendall, "Habit-Forming: Humility and the Rhetoric of Drugs," *Philosophy and Rhetoric*, 48.3 (2015), 337–58.

Giles, Paul, "Sentimental Posthumanism: David Foster Wallace," *Twentieth-Century Literature*, 53.5 (2007), 327–44.

Gilmore, Michael T., *American Romanticism and the Marketplace* (Chicago: University of Chicago Press, 1985).

Ginsburg, Faye, and Rayna Rapp, "Disability Worlds," *Annual Review of Anthropology*, 42 (2013), 53–68.

Glass, Loren, "Publishing in the Age of Amazon," in Rachel Greenwald Smith (ed.), *American Literature in Transition, 2000–2010* (Cambridge: Cambridge University Press, 2018), pp. 360–69.

Gödel, Kurt, *On Formally Undecidable Propositions of Principia Mathematica and Related Systems*, trans. B Meltzer (New York: Dover, 1962).

Godden, Richard, and Michael Szalay, "The Bodies in the Bubble: David Foster Wallace's *The Pale King*," *Textual Practice*, 28.7 (2014), 1273–322.

Goeke, Joseph F., "'Everyone Knows It's About Something Else, Way Down': Boredom, Nihilism, and the Search for Meaning in David Foster Wallace's *The Pale King*," *Critique: Studies in Contemporary Fiction*, 58.3 (2017), 191–213.

Goerlandt, Iannis, "'Put the Book Down and Slowly Walk Away': Irony and David Foster Wallace's *Infinite Jest*," *Critique: Studies in Contemporary Fiction*, 47.3 (2006), pp. 309–28.

"'Still Steaming as Its Many Arms Extended': Pain in David Foster Wallace's 'Incarnations of Burned Children,'" *Sprachkunst*, 37.2 (2006), 297–308.

Goldberg, Emma, "Do Books by Men Implicated by #MeToo Belong in the Classroom?," *The New York Times*, October 7, 2019, www.nytimes.com/2019/10/07/us/metoo-schools.html.

Goldfarb, Michael, "The Connection: David Foster Wallace" in Stephen J. Burn (ed.), *Conversations with David Foster Wallace* (Jackson: University Press of Mississippi, 2012), pp. 136–51.

Goodman, Nelson, *Ways of Worldmaking* (Indianapolis, IN: Hackett Publishing Company, 1978).

Goodwin, Jonathan, "Wallace's *Infinite Jest*," *Explicator*, 61.2 (2003), 122–24.

Gould, Timothy, *Hearing Things: Voice and Method in the Writing of Stanley Cavell* (Chicago: The University of Chicago Press, 1998).

Gourley, James, "Kafkaesque Laughter in the Face of Bureaucracy: David Foster Wallace's *The Pale King*," *English Studies*, 99.8 (2018), 944–59.

Gowers, Timothy, June Barrow-Green, and Imre Leader (eds.), *The Princeton Companion to Mathematics* (Princeton, NJ: Princeton University Press, 2008).

Graeber, David, *Bullshit Jobs: A Theory* (London: Allen Lane, 2018).

Grassian, Daniel, *Hybrid Fictions: American Literature and Generation X* (Jefferson, NC: McFarland, 2003).

Green, Karen, *Bough Down*, (Los Angeles, CA: Siglio, 2013).

Green, Lisa J., *African American English: A Linguistic Introduction* (Cambridge: Cambridge University Press, 2002).

Greenberg, Scott, "Taxes on the Rich Were Not Much Higher in the 1950s," *Tax Foundation*, August 4, 2017, https://files.taxfoundation.org/20170804133536/Average-Effective-Tax-Rate-on-the-Top-1-Percent-of-U.S.-Households.png.

Grewal, Inderpal, "Transnational America: Race, Gender and Citizenship after 9/11," *Social Identities* 9.3 (2003), 535–61.

Griffin, Charles J. G., "The 'Washingtonian Revival': Narrative and the Moral Transformation of Temperance Reform in Antebellum America," *Southern Communication Journal* 66.1 (2000), 67–78, DOI: 10.1080/10417940009373187.

Groenland, Tim, *The Art of Editing: Raymond Carver and David Foster Wallace* (London: Bloomsbury Academic, 2019).

"'The Fragment': 'Cede,' Ancient Rome, and *The Pale King*," *The Journal of David Foster Wallace Studies*, 1.2 (2019), 131–65.

"'A Recipe for a Brick': *The Pale King* in Progress," *Critique: Studies in Contemporary Fiction*, 58.4 (2017), 365–76.

Gross, Terry, "David Foster Wallace: The 'Fresh Air' Interview", *NPR*, August 14, 2015, www.npr.org/2015/08/14/432161732/david-foster-wallace-the-fresh-air-interview?t=1615298754891.

Haddad, Vincent, "Conjuring David Foster Wallace's Ghost: Prosopopeia, Whitmanian Intimacy and the Queer Potential of *Infinite Jest and The*

Pale King," *Orbit: A Journal of American Literature*, 5.2 (2017), 1–28, https://orbit.openlibhums.org/article/id/447/.

Halberstam, Jack, *The Queer Art of Failure* (Durham, NC: Duke University Press, 2011).

Hamilton, Robert C., "'Constant Bliss in Every Atom': Tedium and Transcendence in David Foster Wallace's *The Pale King*," *Arizona Quarterly: A Journal of American Literature, Culture, and Theory*, 70.4 (2014), 167–90.

Harbach, Chad, "MFA vs NYC," *n +1*, 10, Fall 2010, pp. 1–12.

Harris, Charles B., "The Anxiety of Influence: The John Barth/David Foster Wallace Connection," *Critique: Studies in Contemporary Fiction*, 55.2 (2014), 103–26.

"David Foster Wallace: 'That Distinctive Singular Stamp of Himself,'" *Critique: Studies in Contemporary Literature*, 51.2 (2010), 168–76.

"David Foster Wallace's Hometown: A Correction," *Critique; Studies in Contemporary Fiction*, 51.3 (2010), 185–86.

Harris, Michael, "A Sometimes Funny Book Supposedly about Infinity: A Review of Everything and More," *Lettera Matematica*, 3.4 (2015), 259–65. First published in *Notices of the American Mathematical Society*, 51.6 (2004), 632–38.

Harry Ransom Center, "Biographical Sketch," David Foster Wallace: An Inventory of His Papers at the Harry Ransom Center, The University of Texas at Austin, https://norman.hrc.utexas.edu/fasearch/findingAid.cfm?eadid=00503.

Hawkins, Anne Hunsaker, *Reconstructing Illness: Studies in Pathography*, 2nd ed. (West Lafayette, IN: Purdue University Press, 1999).

Hayes-Brady, Clare, "'I Kept Saying Her Name': Naming, Labels, and Power in David Foster Wallace," *Orbit: A Journal of American Literature*, 5.2 (2017), 1–26, https://orbit.openlibhums.org/article/id/457/.

"'. . .': Language, Gender, and Modes of Power in the Work of David Foster Wallace," in Marshall Boswell and Stephen J. Burn (eds.), *A Companion to David Foster Wallace Studies* (New York: Palgrave Macmillan, 2013), pp. 131–50.

"'Palely Loitering': On Not Finishing (in) The Pale King," in Ralph Clare (ed.), *The Cambridge Companion to David Foster Wallace* (Cambridge: Cambridge University Press, 2018), pp. 142–56.

"'Personally I'm Neutral on the Menstruation Point': David Foster Wallace and Gender," in Philip Coleman (ed.), *Critical Insights: David Foster Wallace* (Ipswich, MA: Salem, 2015), pp. 63–77.

"Reading Your Problematic Fave: David Foster Wallace, Feminism and #metoo," *Honest Ulsterman*, June 2018, https://humag.co/features/reading-your-problematic-fave.

The Unspeakable Failures of David Foster Wallace: Language, Identity, and Resistance (London: Bloomsbury Academic, 2016).

Hayles, N. Katherine. "The Illusion of Autonomy and the Fact of Recursivity: Virtual Ecologies, Entertainment, and *Infinite Jest*," *New Literary History*, 30.3 (1999), 675–97.

Hegel, Georg Wilhelm Friedrich, *Introductory Lectures on Aesthetics*, trans. Bernard Bosanquet (London: Penguin Books, 1993).

Hemingway, Ernest, *Green Hills of Africa* (New York: Simon & Schuster, 2015 [1935]).

Henry, Casey Michael, "'Sudden Awakening to the Fact That the Mischief Is Irretrievably Done': Epiphanic Structure in David Foster Wallace's *Infinite Jest*," *Critique: Studies in Contemporary Fiction*, 56.5 (2015), 480–502.

"'Way Closer to the Soul than Mere Tastelessness Can Get': David Foster Wallace and Transcendent Extra-Textuality," in *New Media and the Transformation of Postmodern American Literature: From Cage to Connection* (London: Bloomsbury Academic, 2019), pp. 105–59.

Hering, David (ed.), *Consider David Foster Wallace: Critical Essays* (Los Angeles, CA: Sideshow Media Group Press, 2010).

Hering, David, *David Foster Wallace: Fiction and Form* (London: Bloomsbury Academic, 2016).

"Oblivion," in Ralph Clare (ed.), *The Cambridge Companion to David Foster Wallace* (Cambridge: Cambridge University Press, 2018), pp. 97–110.

"Reading the Ghost in David Foster Wallace's Fiction," *Orbit: A Journal of American Literature*, 5.1 (2017), 1–30, https://orbit.openlibhums.org/article/id/465/.

"Theorising David Foster Wallace's Toxic Postmodern Spaces," *US Studies Online*, 18 (2011), www.baas.ac.uk/issue-18-spring-2011-article-2/.

Hertzberg, Hendrik, "The Short Happy Life of the American Yuppie," *Esquire*, February 1, 1988, pp. 100–9.

Hetman, Jaraslaw, "Fragmentation in David Foster Wallace's Fiction," in Vanessa Guignery and Wojiech Drag (eds.), *The Poetics of Fragmentation in Contemporary British and American Fiction* (Delaware: Vernon, 2019), pp. 123–34.

Higgins, Frances, "Narrative Infinity in the Encyclopedic Novel: Manipulations of Dante Alighieri's Divina Commedia in David Foster Wallace's Infinite Jest," Unpublished MA thesis, University of North Carolina (2006).

Himmelheber, Rachel Haley, "'I Believed She Could Save Me': Rape Culture in David Foster Wallace's 'Brief Interviews with Hideous Men #20,'" *Critique: Studies in Contemporary Fiction*, 55 (2014), 522–35.

Hirt, Stefan, "An Existentialist Reading of Infinite Jest," in *The Iron Bars of Freedom: David Foster Wallace and the Postmodern Self* (Stuttgart: Ibidem Press, 2014), pp. 11–119.

Hoberek, Andrew, "The Novel After David Foster Wallace," in Marshall Boswell and Stephen J. Burn (eds.), *A Companion to David Foster Wallace Studies* (New York: Palgrave Macmillan, 2013), pp. 211–28.

"Wallace and American Literature," in Ralph Clare (ed.), *The Cambridge Companion to David Foster Wallace* (Cambridge: Cambridge University Press, 2018), pp. 33–48.

Hodson, Jane (ed.), *Dialect and Literature in the Long Nineteenth Century* (New York: Taylor & Francis, 2017).

Hodson, Jane, *Dialect in Film and Literature* (New York: Palgrave Macmillan, 2014).

Hogg, Emily J., "Subjective Politics in *The Pale King*," *English Studies*, 95.1 (2014), 59–69.

Holland, Mary K., "The Art's Heart's Purpose: Braving the Narcissistic Loop of David Foster Wallace's Infinite Jest," *Critique: Studies in Contemporary Fiction*, 41.3 (2004), 218–42.

"'By Hirsute Author': Gender and Communication in the Work and Study of David Foster Wallace," *Critique: Studies in Contemporary Fiction*, 58.1 (2016), 65–78.

"David Foster Wallace's 'Octet' and the 'Atthakavagga,'" *The Explicator*, 74.3 (2016), 165–69.

"*Infinite Jest*," in Ralph Clare (ed.), *The Cambridge Companion to David Foster Wallace* (Cambridge: Cambridge University Press, 2018), pp. 127–41.

Succeeding Postmodernism: Language and Humanism in Contemporary American Literature (New York: Bloomsbury, 2013).

"'Your Head Gets in the Way': Reflecting (on) Realism from Barth to Wallace," in Gabrielle Dean and Charlie B. Harris (eds.), *John Barth: A Body of Words* (Victoria, TX: Dalkey, 2016), pp. 201–31.

Holloway, Emory, *Free and Lonesome Heart* (New York: Vantage Press, 1960).

Honohan, Iseult, "Liberal and Republican Conceptions of Citizenship," in Ayelet Shachar, Rainer Bauböck, Irene Bloemraad, and Maarten Peter Vink (eds.), *The Oxford Handbook of Citizenship* (Oxford: Oxford University Press), pp. 83–106.

Houser, Heather, "*Infinite Jest*'s Environmental Case for Disgust," in Samuel Cohen and Lee Konstantinou (eds.), *The Legacy of David Foster Wallace* (Iowa City: Iowa University Press, 2012), pp. 118–42.

"Managing Information and Materiality in *Infinite Jest* and Running the Numbers," *American Literary History*, 26.4 (2014), 742–64.

Horkheimer, Max, and Theodore W. Adorno, "The Culture Industry: Enlightenment as Mass Deception," in *Dialectic of Enlightenment*, trans. John Cumming (New York: Herder & Herder, 1972), pp. 120–67.

Howard, Gerry, "I Know Why Bret Easton Ellis Hates David Foster Wallace," *Salon*, September 7, 2012, www.salon.com/2012/09/07/i_know_why_bret_easton_ellis_hates_david_foster_wallace/.

Hudson, Cory M., "David Foster Wallace Is Not Your Friend: The Fraudulence of Empathy in David Foster Wallace Studies and 'Good Old Neon,'" *Critique: Studies in Contemporary Fiction*, 59.3 (2018), 295–306.

Huehls, Mitchum, "Coda – Accounting 101: Reading the Exomodern," in *After Critique: Twenty-First Century Fiction in a Neoliberal Age* (New York: Oxford University Press, 2016), pp. 159–68.

Hungerford, Amy, "On Not Reading," *The Chronicle Review*, September 11, 2016, www.chronicle.com/article/on-not-reading.

"On Not Reading DFW," in *Making Literature Now* (Stanford, CA: Stanford University Press, 2016), pp. 141–67.

Hurley, Jessica, "War as Peace: Afterlives of Nuclear War in David Foster Wallace's *Infinite Jest*," in Michael Blouin, Morgan Shipley, and Jack Taylor (eds.), *The Silence of Fallout: Nuclear Criticism in a Post-Cold War World* (Cambridge: Cambridge Scholars, 2013), pp. 192–210.

Hyde, Lewis, *The Gift: Creativity and the Artist in the Modern World*, 25th anniversary ed. (New York: Vintage, 2007).

Inglis, Lucy, *Milk of Paradise: A History of Opium* (New York: Pegasus Books, 2019).

Irigaray, Luce, "Body Against Body: In Relation to the Mother," in *Sexes and Genealogies*, trans. Gillian C. Gill (New York: Columbia University Press, 1993), pp. 7–21.

Jackson, Edward, *David Foster Wallace's Toxic Sexuality: Hideousness, Neoliberalism, Spermatics* (London: Bloomsbury Academic, 2020).

Jacobs, Timothy, "American Touchstone: The Idea of Order in Gerard Manley Hopkins and David Foster Wallace," *Comparative Literature Studies*, 38.3 (2001), 215–31.

"The Brothers Incandenza: Translating Ideology in Fyodor Dostoevsky's *The Brothers Karamazov* and David Foster Wallace's *Infinite Jest*," *Texas Studies in Literature and Language*, 49.3 (2007), 265–92.

"Wallace's *Infinite Jest*," *Explicator*, 58.3 (2000), 172–75.

James, William, *A Pluralistic Universe* (Lincoln: University of Nebraska Press, 1996 [1909]).

The Principles of Psychology, 2 vols. (Boston: Harvard University Press, 1981 [1890]).

The Varieties of Religious Experience (New York: Mentor, 1958 [1902]).

Jameson, Fredric, "Postmodernism, or The Cultural Logic of Late Capitalism," *New Left Review*, 1.146 (1984), 53–92.

Postmodernism, or, The Cultural Logic of Late Capitalism (Durham, NC: Duke University Press, 1991).

Jansen, Brian Douglas, "'On the Porousness of Certain Borders': Attending to Objects in David Foster Wallace's *Infinite Jest*," *ESC: English Studies in Canada*, 40.4 (2014), 55–77.

Joffe, Daniela Franca, "'The Last Word': Sex-Changes and Second-Wave Feminism in *The Broom of the System*," *The Journal of David Foster Wallace Studies*, 1.1 (2018), 151–84.

Johnson, Walter, and Robin E. Kelley (eds.), *Race Capitalism Justice* (Cambridge, MA: MIT Press, 2017).

Jones, Gavin, *Strange Talk: The Politics of Dialect Literature in Gilded Age America* (Oakland: University of California Press, 1999).

Kachka, Boris, "When Did Books Get So Freaking Enormous? The Year of the Very Long Novel," *Vulture*, May 19, 2015, www.vulture.com/2015/05/year-of-the-very-long-novel.html.

Kaiser, Wilson, "David Foster Wallace and the Ethical Challenge of Posthumanism," *Mosaic: An Interdisciplinary Critical Journal*, 47.3 (2014), 53–69.

"Humor after Postmodernism: David Foster Wallace and Proximal Irony," *Studies in American Humor*, 3.28 (2013), 31–44.

Kakutani, Michiko, "Maximized Revenue, Minimized Existence," *The New York Times*, March 31, 2011, www.nytimes.com/2011/04/01/books/the-pale-king-by-david-foster-wallace-book-review.html.

Karmodi, Ostap, "'A Frightening Time in America': An Interview with David Foster Wallace," *The New York Review of Books*, June 13, 2011, www .nybooks.com/daily/2011/06/13/david-foster-wallace-russia-interview/, *Live Journal*, June 13, 2011, http://ostap.livejournal.com/799511.html.

Karnicky, Jeffrey, "Kinds of Stasis in David Foster Wallace," in *Contemporary Fiction and the Ethics of Modern Culture* (New York: Palgrave, 2007), pp. 91–124.

Karr, Mary, "Suicide's Note: An Annual," *Poetry*, September 2012, www .poetryfoundation.org/poetrymagazine/poems/55744/suicides-note-an-annual.

Katz, Josh, and Margot Sanger-Katz, "'The Numbers Are So Staggering.' Overdose Deaths Set a Record Last Year," *The New York Times*, November 29, 2018, www.nytimes.com/interactive/2018/11/29/upshot/fen tanyl-drug-overdose-deaths.html.

Keely, Karen A., "Sexual Slavery in San Francisco's Chinatown: 'Yellow Peril' and 'White Slavery' in Frank Norris's Early Fiction," *Studies in American Naturalism*, 2.2 (2007), 129–49.

Kelly, Adam, "Brief Interviews with Hideous Men," in Ralph Clare (ed.), *The Cambridge Companion to David Foster Wallace* (Cambridge: Cambridge University Press, 2018), pp. 82–96.

"David Foster Wallace: The Critical Reception," in Philip Coleman (ed.), *Critical Insights: David Foster Wallace* (Ipswich, MA: Salem Press, 2015), pp. 46–62.

"David Foster Wallace: The Death of the Author and the Birth of a Discipline," *Irish Journal of American Studies*, 2 (2010), http://ijas.iaas.ie/article-david-foster-wallace-the-death-of-the-author-and-the-birth-of-a-disci pline/.

"David Foster Wallace and the New Sincerity in American Fiction," in David Hering (ed.), *Consider David Foster Wallace: Critical Essays* (Los Angeles, CA: Sideshow Media Group Press, 2010), pp. 130–46.

"Development through Dialogue: David Foster Wallace and the Novel of Ideas," *Studies in the Novel*, 44.3 (2012), 267–83.

"Dialectic of Sincerity: Lionel Trilling and David Foster Wallace," *Post 45*, October 17, 2014, http://post45.org/2014/10/dialectic-of-sincerity-lionel-trilling-and-david-foster-wallace/.

"Formally Conventional Fiction," in Rachel Greenwald Smith (ed.), *American Literature in Transition, 2000–2010* (Cambridge: Cambridge University Press, 2018), pp. 46–60.

"The New Sincerity," in Jason Gladstone, Andrew Hoberek, and Daniel Worden (eds.), *Postmodern/Postwar and After: Rethinking American Literature* (Iowa City: University of Iowa Press, 2016), pp. 197–208.

"Sincerity, Discipline, and Good Posture: David Foster Wallace at Mid-Career," Conference Paper, May 2014, "Philosophy, Literature, America", University College Dublin.

Kennedy, Hugh, and Geoffrey Polk, "Looking for a Garde of Which to Be Avant: An Interview with David Foster Wallace," in Stephen J. Burn (ed.), *Conversations with David Foster Wallace* (Jackson: The University Press of Mississippi, 2012), pp. 11–20.

Kierkegaard, Søren, *The Concept of Irony, with Continual Reference to Socrates/ Notes of Schelling's Berlin Lectures*, trans. Howard V. Hong and Edna H. Hong (Princeton, NJ: Princeton University Press, 1989).

Either/Or, Part II, trans. Howard V. Hong and Edna H. Hong (Princeton, NJ: Princeton University Press, 1987).

Kimmel, Michael, *Manhood in America: A Cultural History*, 3rd ed. (Oxford: Oxford University Press, 2012).

King, Kyle R., "The Spirituality of Sport and the Role of the Athlete in the Tennis Essays of David Foster Wallace," *Communication and Sport*, 6.2 (2018), 219–38.

King, Stephen, *The Stand* (New York: Doubleday, 1978).

Kinlaw III, Dennis F., "'A Strange Kind of Slavery': David Foster Wallace's Enslaved Selves," in Robert Sirvent and Duncan B. Reyburn (eds.), *Theologies of Failure* (Eugene: Cascade, 2019), pp. 133–40.

Knausgaard, Karl Ove, *My Struggle, Book 2*, trans. Don Bartlett (New York: Archipelago, 2014).

My Struggle, Book 6, trans. Don Bartlett and Martin Aitkin (New York: Archipelago, 2018).

So Much Longing in So Little Space: The Art of Edvard Munch, trans. Ingvild Burkey (London: Penguin, 2019).

Konstantinou, Lee, *Cool Characters: Irony and American Fiction* (Harvard, MA: Harvard University Press, 2016).

"How to Be a Believer," in *Cool Characters: Irony and American Fiction* (Cambridge, MA: Harvard University Press, 2016), pp. 163–216.

"No Bull: David Foster Wallace and Postironic Belief" in Samuel Cohen and Lee Konstantinou (eds.), *The Legacy of David Foster Wallace* (Iowa City: University of Iowa Press, 2012), pp. 83–112.

"Wallace's 'Bad' Influence," in Ralph Clare (ed.), *The Cambridge Companion to David Foster Wallace* (Cambridge: Cambridge University Press, 2018), pp. 49–64.

"The World of David Foster Wallace," *boundary 2*, 40.3 (2013), 59–86.

Kozin, Alexander, "On the Elementals and Their Qualities in David Foster Wallace's 'Derivative Sport in Tornado Alley,'" *Palgrave Communications* 3.18 (2017), 1–8.

Krishnan, Nikhil, "*The Topeka School* by Ben Lerner Review: A Fine, Exacting Novel about How to Raise a Good Son," *The Telegraph*, November 4, 2019, www.telegraph.co.uk/books/what-to-read/topeka-school-ben-lerner-review-fine-exacting-novel-raise-good/.

Kušnír, Jaroslav, "Fiction and Commercialization in David Foster Wallace's 'Westward the Course of Empire Takes Its Way,'" *American, British and Canadian Studies*, 10 (2008), 209–21.

"From Descriptive to (Meta)Meta-fictional: Form and Meaning in David Foster Wallace's Short Fiction," *AAA: Arbeiten aus Anglistik und Amerikanistik*, 32.2 (2007), 319–31.

Lackey, Ryan, "David Foster Wallace and Postsecularism," in Michael McGowan and Martin Brick (eds.), *David Foster Wallace and Religion: Essays on Faith and Fiction* (New York: Bloomsbury, 2019), pp. 149–62.

La Ganga, Maria L., "The First Lady Who Looked Away: Nancy and the Reagans' Troubling Aids Legacy," *The Guardian*, March 11, 2016, www.theguardian.com/us-news/2016/mar/11/nancy-ronald-reagan-aids-crisis-first-lady-legacy.

Lago, Edouard, "A Brand New Interview with David Foster Wallace," *Electric Lit*, November 16, 2018 [2000] https://electricliterature.com/a-brand-new-interview-with-david-foster-wallace/.

Lambert, Stephanie, "'The Real Dark Side, Baby': New Sincerity and Neoliberal Aesthetics in David Foster Wallace and Jennifer Egan," *Critique: Studies in Contemporary Fiction*, 61.4 (2020), 394–411.

LeClair, Tom, "The Prodigious Fiction of Richard Powers, William Vollmann, and David Foster Wallace," *Critique: Studies in Contemporary Fiction*, 38 (1996), 12–37.

Lerner, Ben, *10:04* (London: Picador, 2014).

Lessing, Doris, "Preface," in *The Golden Notebook* (London: HarperCollins, 2007 [1962]).

Letzler, David, *The Cruft of Fiction: Mega-Novels and the Science of Paying Attention* (Lincoln: University of Nebraska Press, 2017).

Levey, Nick, "'Analysis Paralysis': The Suspicion of Suspicion in the Fiction of David Foster Wallace," *M/C Journal*, 15.1 (2012), https://journal.media-culture.org.au/index.php/mcjournal/article/view/383.

Maximalism in Contemporary American Literature: The Uses of Detail (New York: Routledge, 2017).

Levin, Joanna, and Edward Whitley, "Bohemianism," in Joanna Levin and Edward Whitley (eds.), *Walt Whitman in Context* (Cambridge: Cambridge University Press, 2018), pp. 136–45.

Lewis, C. S., *The Screwtape Letters* (London: Geoffrey Bles, 1942).

Lipsky, David, *Although of Course You End Up Becoming Yourself: A Road Trip with David Foster Wallace* (New York: Broadway Books, 2010).

"The Lost Years and Last Days of David Foster Wallace" in Stephen J. Burn (ed.), *Conversations with David Foster Wallace* (Jackson: Mississippi University Press, 2012), pp. 161–83.

Lodge, David, *Consciousness and the Novel: Connected Essays* (London: Penguin Books, 2003).

Loja, Ema, Maria Emília Costa, Bill Hughes, and Isabel Menezes, "Disability, Embodiment and Ableism: Stories of Resistance," *Disability & Society*, 28.2 (2013), 190–203.

Lowe, Lisa, *The Intimacies of Four Continents* (Durham, NC: Duke University Press, 2015).

Mahon, Áine, "Difficulties of Reality in David Foster Wallace and Cora Diamond," in Philip Coleman (ed.), *David Foster Wallace: Critical Insights* (Hackensack, NJ: Salem Press, 2015), pp. 252–67.

The Ironist and the Romantic: Reading Richard Rorty and Stanley Cavell (London: Bloomsbury, 2014).

Makari, George, *Soul Machine: The Invention of the Modern Mind* (New York: W. W. Norton, 2015).

Mann, Bonnie, *Sovereign Masculinity: Gender Lessons from the War on Terror* (Oxford: Oxford University Press, 2014).

Markovits, Elizabeth, *The Politics of Sincerity: Plato, Frank Speech, and Democratic Judgment* (University Park: Pennsylvania State University Press, 2008).

Markson, David, *Reader's Block* (Normal, IL: Dalkey Archive Press, 1996).

Marsh, Stephen Taylor, "Self-Sacrifice in the Autobiographical Narration of David Foster Wallace's *The Pale King*," *Biography*, 39.2 (2016), 111–28.

Marx, Leo, *The Machine in the Garden* (Oxford: Oxford University Press, 2000 [1964]).

Mashaal, Maurice, *Bourbaki: a Secret Society of Mathematicians*, trans. Anna Pierrehumbert (Providence, RI: American Mathematical Society, 2006).

Masiero, Pia, "The Case of 'Think' in *Brief Interviews with Hideous Men*. Is Dialogism Possible?," *The Journal of David Foster Wallace Studies*, 1.2 (2019), 93–130.

Matthews, Christopher M., "A Different Dow Emerges Following Merger with DuPont," *The Wall Street Journal*, April 1, 2019, www.wsj.com/articles/a-different-dow-emerges-following-merger-with-dupont-11554150629.

Matthiessen, Francis Otto, *American Renaissance: Art and Expression in the Age of Emerson and Whitman* (Oxford: Oxford University Press, 2006 [1941]).

Max, D. T., "David Foster Wallace in Recovery," *The New Yorker*, September 4, 2012, www.newyorker.com/books/page-turner/david-foster-wallace-in-recovery-an-excerpt-from-the-new-biography.

Max, D. T., *Every Love Story Is a Ghost Story: A Life of David Foster Wallace* (New York: Viking, 2012).

"Why David Foster Wallace Should Not Be Worshipped as a Secular Saint," *The Guardian*, October 9, 2015, www.theguardian.com/books/2015/oct/09/david-foster-wallace-worshipped-secular-saint.

Mayo, Rob, *Depression and Dysphoria in the Fiction of David Foster Wallace* (London: Routledge, 2021).

"'That's My Sad, It's Not Your Sad': Love, Loneliness, and Communication in *The Broom of the System* by David Foster Wallace," *Critique: Studies in Contemporary Fiction*, 61.1 (2020), 67–78.

McAdams, James, "'I Did a Nice Thing': David Foster Wallace and the Gift Economy," *ESC: English Studies in Canada*, 42.3 (2016), 119–33.

McCaffery, Larry, "An Expanded Interview with David Foster Wallace," in Stephen J. Burn (ed.), *Conversations with David Foster Wallace* (Jackson: University Press of Mississippi, 2012), pp. 21–52. First published in *The Review of Contemporary Fiction*, 13.2 (Summer 1993), 127–50.

McClanahan, Annie, "Future's Shock: Plausibility, Preemption, and the Fiction of 9/11," *symplokē*, 17.1–2 (2009), 41–62.

McCumber, John, "From Scientific Revolutions to Boston AA: Philosophy and the Speaking of Matter," in *On Philosophy: Notes from a Crisis* (Stanford, CA: Stanford University Press, 2013), pp. 22–46.

McGowan, Michael, "Conclusion: The Religious Worlds of David Foster Wallace," in Michael McGowan and Martin Brick (eds.), *David Foster Wallace and Religion: Essays on Faith and Fiction* (New York: Bloomsbury, 2019), pp. 187–200.

McGowan, Michael, and Martin Brick (eds.), *David Foster Wallace and Religion: Essays on Faith and Fiction* (New York: Bloomsbury Academic, 2019).

McGrath, Laura B., "Comping White," *Los Angeles Review of Books*, January 21, 2019. www.lareviewofbooks.org, www.lareviewofbooks.org/article/comping-white/.

McGurl, Mark, "The Institution of Nothing: David Foster Wallace in the Program," *boundary 2*, 41.3 (2014), 27–54.

The Program Era: Postwar Fiction and the Rise of Creative Writing (Cambridge, MA: Harvard University Press, 2009).

McHale, Brian, *The Cambridge Introduction to Postmodernism* (Cambridge: Cambridge University Press, 2015).

McKergow, Mark, and Dierolf, Kirsten, "Enactivism and the Nature of Mind: Interview with Daniel D. Hutto," *InterAction*, 8.2 (2016), 44–54.

McLaughlin, Robert L., "After the Revolution: US Postmodernism in the Twenty-First Century," *Narrative*, 21.3 (2013), 284–95.

"Post-Postmodern Discontent: Contemporary Fiction and the Social World," *symplokē*, 12.1–2 (2004), 53–68.

"Post-Postmodernism," in Joe Bray, Alison Gibbons, and Brian McHale (eds.), *Routledge Companion to Experimental Literature* (London: Routledge, 2012), pp. 212–23.

"Wallace's Aesthetic," in Ralph Clare (ed.), *The Cambridge Companion to David Foster Wallace* (Cambridge: Cambridge University Press, 2018), pp. 159–72.

Medin, Daniel L., *Three Sons: Franz Kafka and the Fiction of J.M. Coetzee, Philip Roth, and W.G. Sebald* (Evanston, IL: Northwestern University Press, 2010).

Melamed, Jodi, *Represent and Destroy: Rationalizing Violence in the New Racial Capitalism* (Minneapolis: University of Minnesota Press, 2011).

Melville, Herman, *The Confidence Man: His Masquerade*, in Harrison Hayford, Hershel Parker, and G. Thomas Tanselle (eds.), *The Writings of Herman*

Melville, Vol. X (Evanston, IL and Chicago: Northwestern University Press and the Newberry Library, 1984).

Michaelson, Christopher, "Accounting for Meaning: On §22 of David Foster Wallace's *The Pale King*," *Critical Perspectives on Accounting*, 29 (2015), 54–64.

"Business in the Work and World of David Foster Wallace," *Journal of Management Inquiry*, 25.2 (2016), 214–22.

Miley, Mike, ". . . And Starring David Foster Wallace as Himself: Performance and Persona in *The Pale King*," *Critique: Studies in Contemporary Fiction*, 57.2 (2016), 191–207.

"Desperately Seeking David: Authorship in the Early Works of David Foster Wallace," *Orbit: A Journal of American Literature*, 7.1 (2019), 1–26, https:// orbit.openlibhums.org/article/id/813/.

"'This Muddy Bothness': The Absorbed Adaptation of David Lynch by David Foster Wallace," *Literature/Film Quarterly*, 48.1 (2020), https://lfq.salisbury .edu/_issues/48_1/this_muddy_bothness_the_absorbed_adaptation_of_david_ lynch_by_david_foster_wallace.html.

Miller, Adam S., *The Gospel According to David Foster Wallace: Boredom and Addiction in an Age of Distraction* (New York: Bloomsbury, 2016).

Miller, Adrienne, *In the Land of Men* (New York: HarperCollins, 2020).

Miller, Laura, "Interview with David Foster Wallace," in Stephen J. Burn (ed.), *Conversations with David Foster Wallace* (Jackson: University Press of Mississippi, 2012), pp. 58–65.

Mitchell, David, and Sharon Snyder, "Narrative Prosthesis," in Lennard Davis (ed.), *The Disability Studies Reader*, 4 ed. (New York: Routledge, 2013), pp. 232–35.

Moi, Toril, "Describing My Struggle," *The Point*, December 27, 2017, https:// thepointmag.com/criticism/describing-my-struggle-knausgaard/.

Moon, Michale, *Disseminating Whitman: Revision and Corporeality in Leaves of Grass* (Cambridge, MA: Harvard University Press, 1993).

Moore, Brian, *Catholics* (Middlesex: Penguin, 1977).

Moore, Steven, "The First Draft of Infinite Jest," in *My Back Pages* (Los Angeles, CA: Zerogram, 2017), pp. 684–712.

"In Memoriam David Foster Wallace," *Modernism/Modernity*, 16.1 (2009), 1–3.

The Novel, An Alternate History: Beginnings to 1600 (New York: Continuum, 2011).

Moran, Alexander, "The Importance of Habits in Meredith Rand and Shane Drinion's 'tête-à-tête' in The Pale King," *Orbit: A Journal of American Literature*, 5.2 (2017), 1–25, https://orbit.openlibhums.org/article/id/391/.

Moreau, Nathan, "Describing the Surface: David Foster Wallace and Postcritical Reading," *New Critique*, August, 2020, https://newcritique.co.uk/2020/08/ 01/essay-describing-the-surface-david-foster-wallace-and-postcritical-reading- nathan-moreau/.

Morris, David, "Lived Time and Absolute Knowing: Habit and Addiction from *Infinite Jest* to the *Phenomenology of Spirit*," *Clio*, 30 (2001), 374–415.

Morris, Edmund, *Dutch: A Memoir of Ronald Reagan* (London: HarperCollins, 1999).

Morrissey, Tara, and Lucas Thompson, "'The Rare White at the Window': A Reappraisal of Mark Costello and David Foster Wallace's *Signifying Rappers*," *Journal of American Studies*, 49.1 (2015), 77–97.

Morrison, Toni, *Playing in the Dark: Whiteness and the Literary Imagination* (Cambridge, MA: Harvard University Press, 1992).

Morse, Chuck, "Capitalism, Marxism, and the Black Radical Tradition: An Interview with Cedric Robinson," *Perspectives on Anarchist Theory*, 3.1 (Spring 1999), 1, 6–8.

Morsia, Elliott, "The Composition of 'The Depressed Person,'" *Textual Cultures*, 9.2 (2015), 79–99.

Mortenson, Erik R., "Xmas Junkies: Debasement and Redemption in the Work of William S. Burroughs and David Foster Wallace," *Dionysos: Journal of Literature and Addiction*, 9.2 (1999), 37–46.

Mott, Frank Luther, *A History of American Magazines, 1741–1850* (Cambridge, MA: Harvard University Press, 1957).

Moulier-Boutang, Yann, *Cognitive Capitalism*, trans. Ed Emery (Cambridge: Polity Press, 2012).

Mulhall, Stephen, "Quartet: Wallace's Wittgenstein, Moran's Amis," in *The Self and Its Shadows: A Book of Essays on Individuality as Negation in Philosophy and the Arts* (Oxford: Oxford University Press, 2013), pp. 283–319.

Mullins, Matthew, "Rewriting Language," in *Postmodernism in Pieces: Materializing the Social in U.S. Fiction* (New York: Oxford University Press, 2016), pp. 103–36.

   The Self and Its Shadows: A Book of Essays on Individuality as Negation in Philosophy and the Arts (Oxford: Oxford University Press, 2013).

Mullins, Ryan David, "Theories of Everything and More: Infinity is Not the End," in Robert K. Bolger, Scott Korb (eds.), *Gesturing Toward Reality: David Foster Wallace and Philosophy* (London: Bloomsbury Academic, 2014), pp. 221–44.

Mullins, Matthew, "Wallace, Spirituality, and Religion," in Ralph Clare (ed.), *The Cambridge Companion to David Foster Wallace* (Cambridge: Cambridge University Press, 2018), pp. 190–204.

Mulvey, Laura, "Visual Pleasure and Narrative Cinema," in Leo Braudy and Marshall Cohen (eds.), *Film Theory and Criticism: Introductory Readings* (New York: Oxford University Press, 1999), pp. 833–44.

Mura, David, "White Writing Teachers (or David Foster Wallace vs. James Baldwin)," *Journal of Creative Writing Studies*, 1.1 (2016), 1–15.

Nabokov, Vladimir, *The Annotated Lolita*, ed. Alfred Appel, Jr. (New York: Vintage, 1991 [1955]).

   Speak, Memory (New York: Vintage, 1967).

   Strong Opinions (New York: Vintage, 1973).

Nadel, Ira B., "Consider the Footnote," in Samuel Cohen and Lee Konstantinou (eds.), *The Legacy of David Foster Wallace* (Iowa City: University of Iowa Press, 2012), pp. 218–40.

Nadell, Bonnie, "Editors on Wallace," Harry Ransom Center, The University of Texas, Austin, May 14, 2012, www.youtube.com/watch?v=IAfuZRryjHk& feature=youtube_gdata_player.

Nash, Woods, "Narrative Ethics, Authentic Integrity, and an Intrapersonal Medical Encounter in David Foster Wallace's 'Luckily the Account Representative Knew CPR,'" *Cambridge Quarterly of Healthcare Ethics*, 24 (2015), 96–106.

Natalini, Roberto, "David Foster Wallace and the Mathematics of Infinity," *Lettera Matematica*, 3.4 (2015), 245–53. First published in Burn (ed.), *A Companion to David Foster Wallace Studies* (London: Palgrave MacMillan, 2013), pp. 43–57.

Nealon, Jeffrey, *Post-Postmodernism: or, The Cultural Logic of Just-in-Time Capitalism* (Stanford, CA: Stanford University Press, 2012).

Newton, Richard, *The Little Book of Thinking Big* (New York: Wiley, 2014).

Nichols, Catherine, "Dialogizing Postmodern Carnival: David Foster Wallace's *Infinite Jest*," *Critique: Studies in Contemporary Fiction*, 43.1 (2001), 3–16.

Ng, Audrey, "Darkenfloxx™ for Two: Kantian Morality and the Presentations of Suicide in George Saunders's *Tenth of December* and David Foster Wallace's 'Good Old Neon,'" *Interdisciplinary Literary Studies*, 21.2 (2019), 191–217.

Ngai, Sianne, *Our Aesthetic Categories: Zany, Cute, Interesting* (Cambridge, MA: Harvard University Press, 2012).

Nørretranders, Tor, *The User Illusion: Cutting Consciousness Down to Size*, trans. Jonathan Sydenham (London: Allen Lane Penguin Press, 1998).

Norris, Andrew (ed.), *The Claim to Community: Essays on Stanley Cavell and Political Philosophy* (Stanford: Stanford University Press, 2016).

North, Michael, "A More Than Infinite Jest," in *Machine Age Comedy* (Oxford: Oxford University Press, 2009), pp. 163–83.

Nyamnjoh, Anye, "The Phenomenology of Rhodes Must Fall: Student Activism and the Experience of Alienation at the University of Cape Town," *Strategic Review for Southern Africa*, 39.1 (2017), 256–77.

O'Connell, Michael J., "'Your Temple Is Self and Sentiment': David Foster Wallace's Diagnostic Novels," *Christianity and Literature*, 64.3 (2015), 266–92.

O'Connor, Flannery, *Everything That Rises Must Converge* (New York: Farrar, Strauss and Giroux, 1965)

O'Donnell, Patrick, "Beyond the Limit: Teaching Wallace and the Systems Novel," in Stephen J. Burn and Mary K. Holland (eds.), *Approaches to Teaching the Works of David Foster Wallace* (New York: The Modern Language Association of America, 2019), pp. 113–22.

Oliver, Michael, *Understanding Disability: From Theory to Practice* (New York: Palgrave, 1996).

Olsen, Lance, "Termite Art, or Wallace's Wittgenstein," *Review of Contemporary Fiction*, 13.2 (1993), 199–215.

O'Sullivan, Michael, "David Foster Wallace, Loneliness, and the 'Pretty Much Nothing' the University Teaches," *Literature Compass*, 14.7 (2017), 1–11.

Oxoby, Marc, "The Mediated Trauma of September 11, 2001, in William Gibson's *Pattern Recognition* and David Foster Wallace's 'The Suffering Channel,'" in Veronique Bragard, Christophe Dony, and Warren Rosenberg (eds.), *Portraying 9/11: Essays on Representations in Comics, Literature, Film and Theatre* (Jefferson, NC: McFarland, 2011), pp. 102–17.

Palvashay (@Palvashits), Tweet, May 5, 2018, https://twitter.com/Palvashits/status/992688850127478784?s=20.

Panzani, Ugo, "'Mathematically Uncontrolled but Humanly Contained': Narrative Iteration in *Infinite Jest*," *Lettera Matematica*, 3.4 (2015), 289–93.

Paramananda, *Change Your Mind: Practical Guide to Buddhist Meditation*, trans. Jerome K. Rothenberg (Cambridge: Windhorse Publications, 2005).

Parker, Hershel, *Herman Melville: A Biography Vol. II 1851–1891* (Baltimore and London: The Johns Hopkins University Press, 2002).

Patterson, James, *Restless Giant: The United States from Watergate to Bush v. Gore* (Oxford: Oxford University Press, 2005).

Paulson, Steve, "To the Best of Our Knowledge: Interview with David Foster Wallace," in Stephen J. Burn (ed.), *Conversations with David Foster Wallace* (Jackson: University Press of Mississippi, 2012), pp. 127–35.

"David Foster Wallace in the #MeToo Era: A Conversation with Clare Hayes-Brady," *Los Angeles Review of Books*, September 10, 2018, https://lareviewofbooks.org/article/david-foster-wallace-in-the-metoo-era-a-conversation-with-clare-hayes-brady/.

Pease, Donald E., "*Moby-Dick* and the Cold War," in Donald E. Pease and Walter Benn Michaels (eds.), *The American Renaissance Reconsidered* (Baltimore: The Johns Hopkins University Press, 1989 [1985]), pp. 113–55.

Pietsch, Michael, "Editor's Note," in David Foster Wallace, *The Pale King* (New York: Little, Brown, 2011), pp. ix–xiv.

Piper, Andrew, *Enumerations: Data and Literary Study* (Chicago: The University of Chicago Press, 2018).

Pire, Beatrice, and Pierre-Louis Patoine (eds.), *David Foster Wallace: Presences of the Other* (Brighton: Sussex Academic Press, 2017).

Pitari, Paolo, "The Influence of Leo Tolstoy's What Is Art? On David Foster Wallace's Literary Project," *Critique: Studies in Contemporary Fiction*, 62.1 (2021), 69–83.

"The Influence of Sartre's "What Is Literature?" on David Foster Wallace's Literary Project," *Critique: Studies in Contemporary Fiction*, 61.4 (2020), 423–39.

Platts, Charlie, "David Foster Wallace and the Search for New Male Identities," *Medium*, August 11, 2020, https://medium.com/@charlieplatts1996/david-foster-wallace-and-the-search-for-new-male-identities-48b56ffd15c9.

Poirier, Richard, *Poetry and Pragmatism* (Boston: Harvard University Press, 1992).

Polsgrove, Carol, "Magazines and the Making of Authors," in David Paul Nord, Joan Shelley Rubin, and Michael Schudson (eds.), *A History of the Book in*

America: Volume 5: The Enduring Book: Print Culture in Postwar America (Chapel Hill: University of North Carolina Press, 2014), pp. 256–68.

Price, Devon, "A Brief on Hideous Things About David Foster Wallace," *Medium*, May 6, 2018, https://medium.com/@devonprice/a-brief-on-hideous-things-about-david-foster-wallace-72034b20de94.

Prout, Matt, "Reading Others / Reading Texts: The Hermeneutics of Suspicion in *Brief Interviews with Hideous Men*," *Critique: Studies in Contemporary Fiction*, 61.5 (2020), 602–16.

Putnam, Walter, *Paul Valéry Revisited* (New York: Twayne, 1994).

Pynchon, Thomas, *Gravity's Rainbow* (London: Vintage, 2000 [1973]).

Quayson, Ato, *Aesthetic Nervousness: Disability and the Crisis of Representation* (New York: Columbia University Press, 2007).

Raban, Jonathan, "Divine Drudgery: A Review of *The Pale King*," *New York Review of Books*, May 12, 2011, www.nybooks.com/articles/2011/05/12/divine-drudgery/.

Ragde, Prabhakar, "Mathematical Errata for '*Everything and More: A Compact History of* ∞', by David Foster Wallace, Atlas/Norton, 2003, 1st Hardcover Edition," 2003, www.thehowlingfantods.com/dfw/images/enmerrata.pdf.

Rando, David P., "David Foster Wallace and Lovelessness," *Twentieth Century Literature*, 59.4 (2013), 575–95.

Rawls, John, *A Theory of Justice* (Cambridge, MA: The Belknap Press of Harvard University Press, 1971).

Redgate, Jamie, "David Foster Wallace's Treatment of Therapy after Postmodernism," *Critique: Studies in Contemporary Fiction*, 59.3 (2018), 284–94.

Wallace and I: Cognition, Consciousness, and Dualism in David Foster Wallace's Fiction (New York: Routledge, 2019).

Ribbat, Christoph, "Being 'Stresslessly Invisible': The Rise and Fall of Videophony in David Foster Wallace's *Infinite Jest*," *Bulletin of Science, Technology, and Society*, 30.4 (2010), 252–58.

Roach, Daniel Thomas Zachary, "Binding Commonalities: The Chronotopes of *Infinite Jest*," unpublished BA thesis, Wesleyan University (2017).

Roache, John, "'The Realer, More Enduring and Sentimental Part of Him': David Foster Wallace's Personal Library and Marginalia," *Orbit: A Journal of American Literature*, 5.1 (2017), 1–35, https://orbit.openlibhums.org/article/id/410/.

Roberts, Joel, and Edward Jackson, "White Guys: Questioning *Infinite Jest's* New Sincerity," *Orbit: A Journal of American Literature*, 5.1 (2017), 1–28, https://orbit.openlibhums.org/article/id/429/.

Robinson, Cedric, *Black Marxism: The Making of the Black Radical Tradition* (Chapel Hill: University of North Carolina Press, 1983).

Robinson, Sally, *Marked Men: White Masculinity in Crisis* (New York: Columbia University Press, 2000).

Robinson, William I., *A Theory of Global Capitalism: Production, Class, and State in a Transnational World* (Baltimore: Johns Hopkins University Press, 2004).

Rocca, Alexander, "'I Don't Feel Like a Genius': David Foster Wallace, Trickle-Down Aesthetics, and the MacArthur Foundation," *Arizona Quarterly: A Journal of American Literature, Culture, and Theory*, 73.1 (2017), 85–111.

Rodin, Musée, "The Thinker," 1903, *Rodin Museum*, www.musee-rodin.fr/en/collections/sculptures/thinker-0.

Rogers, Heather, *Gone Tomorrow: The Hidden Life of Garbage* (New York: New Press, 2005).

Rorty, Richard, *Contingency, Irony, and Solidarity* (Cambridge: Cambridge University Press, 1989).

   Philosophy and the Mirror of Nature, 30th anniversary ed. (Princeton, NJ: Princeton University Press, 2009 [1979]).

   Philosophy and Social Hope, new ed. (New York: Penguin, 1999).

Rose, Arthur, "Asbestos Populism in David Foster Wallace's *Infinite Jest*," *Safundi*, 21.3 (2020), 339–54.

Ross, Thomas, "Whiteness after 9/11," *Washington University Journal of Law and Policy*, 18 (2005), 223–43.

Rother, James, "Reading and Riding the Post-Scientific Wave: The Shorter Fiction of David Foster Wallace," *Review of Contemporary Fiction*, 13.2 (1993), 216–34.

Rousseau, Jean-Jacques, *Of the Social Contract and Other Political Writings*, ed. Christopher Bertram, trans., Quintin Hoare (London: Penguin, 2012).

Rucker, Rudy, "Infinite Confusion," *Science*, 303.5656 (2004), 313–14.

Russell, Emily, *Reading Embodied Citizenship: Disability, Narrative, and the Body Politic* (London: Rutgers University Press, 2011).

   "Some Assembly Required: The Embodied Politics of *Infinite Jest*," *Arizona Quarterly: A Journal of American Literature, Culture, and Theory*, 66.3 (2010), 147–69.

Ryan, Judith, "David Foster Wallace's Infinite Jest," in *The Novel After Theory* (New York: Columbia, 2012), pp. 192–97.

Ryerson, James, "Introduction: A Head That Throbbed Heartlike: The Philosophical Mind of David Foster Wallace," in Steven M. Cahn and Maureen Eckert (eds.), *Fate, Time, and Language: An Essay on Free Will* (New York: Columbia University Press, 2011), pp. 1–33.

Ryle, Gilbert, *The Concept of Mind* (London: Penguin, 2000 [1949]).

Salaita, Steven George, "Beyond Orientalism and Islamophobia: 9/11, Anti-Arab Racism, and the Mythos of National Pride," *The Centennial Review*, 6.2 (2006), 245–66.

Santel, James, "On David Foster Wallace's Conservatism," *The Hudson Review*, 66.4 (2014), 625–34.

Sartre, Jean-Paul, *Being and Nothingness. An Essay on Phenomenological Ontology*, trans. Hazel E. Barnes (London: Routledge, 2010).

   The Transcendence of the Ego: A Sketch for a Phenomenological Description, trans. Andrew Brown (London: Routledge, 2004).

Sayers, Philip, "Representing Entertainment(s) in *Infinite Jest*," *Studies in the Novel*, 44.3 (2012), 346–63.

Saylor, Colton, "Loosening the Jar: Contemplating Race in David Foster Wallace's Short Fiction," *The Journal of David Foster Wallace Studies*, 1.1 (2018), 119–50.

Schiff, James, "John Updike and David Foster Wallace: Of Binaries, Sports Writing, and Transcendence," *Critique: Studies in Contemporary Fiction*, 59.1 (2018), 15–26.

Schmeidel, Stacey, "Brief Interview with a Five-Draft Man," *Amherst Magazine*, Spring 1999, www.amherst.edu/amherst-story/magazine/extra/node/66410.

Schwarz, Alan, *ADHD Nation: The Disorder. The Drugs. The Inside Story* (New York: Little, Brown, 2016).

Scocca, Tom, "David Foster Wallace," in Stephen J. Burn (ed.), *Conversations with David Foster Wallace* (Jackson: University Press of Mississippi, 2012), pp. 82–88.

Searle, John R., "The Logical Status of Fictional Discourse," in *Expression and Meaning: Studies in the Theory of Speech Acts* (Cambridge: Cambridge University Press, 1979), pp. 58–76.

Sedgwick, Eve Kosofsky, *Tendencies* (Durham, NC: Duke University Press, 1993).

Seguin, Robert, "Form, Voice, and Utopia in David Foster Wallace," *Criticism*, 62.2 (2020), 219–41.

Severs, Jeffrey, "'Blank as the Faces on Coins': Currency and Embodied Value(s) in David Foster Wallace's *The Pale King*," *Critique: Studies in Contemporary Fiction*, 57.1 (2016), 52–66.

"Collision, Illinois: David Foster Wallace and the Value of Insurance," *Modern Fiction Studies*, 62.1 (2016), 136–56.

"Cutting Consciousness Down to Size: David Foster Wallace, Exformation, and the Scale of Encyclopedic Fiction," in Michael Tavel Clarke and David Wittenberg (eds.), *Scale in Literature and Culture* (Cham: Palgrave Macmillan, 2017), pp. 281–304.

David Foster Wallace's Balancing Books: Fictions of Value (New York: Columbia University Press, 2017).

"David Foster Wallace, James Wood, and a Source for 'Irrelevant' Chris Fogle," *The Explicator*, 73.2 (2015), 129–32.

"Wallace's Nonfiction," in Ralph Clare (ed.), *The Cambridge Companion to David Foster Wallace* (Cambridge: Cambridge University Press, 2018), pp. 111–125.

"'We've Been Inside What We Wanted All Along': David Foster Wallace's Immanent Structures," in Brynnar Swenson (ed.), *Literature and the Encounter with Immanence* (Leiden and Boston: Brill Rodopi, 2017), pp. 8–29.

Shapiro, Mary, "The Poetic Language of David Foster Wallace," *Critique: Studies in Contemporary Fiction*, 60.1 (2019), 24–33.

"The Textually Aware Text: Recursive Self-consciousness in *Infinite Jest*'s Filmography," *Orbis Litterarum*, 75.1 (2020), 24–33.

Wallace's Dialects (London: Bloomsbury Academic, 2020).

Shapiro, Stephen, "From Capitalist to Communist Abstraction: *The Pale King*'s Cultural Fix," *Textual Practice*, 28.7 (2014), 1249–71.

Shields, David, *Reality Hunger* (New York: Vintage, 2011).

Shippey, Tom, *J. R. R. Tolkien: Author of the Century* (London: HarperCollins, 2000).

Shorrocks, Graham, "Non-Standard Dialect Literature and Popular Culture," *Bamberger Beitrage Zur Englischen Sprachwissenschaft*, 38 (1995), 385–411.

Shusterman, Richard, "Putnam and Cavell on the Ethics of Democracy," *Political Theory*, 25.2 (2007), 193–214.

Silverblatt, Michael, "David Foster Wallace: *Infinite Jest*," *Bookworm*, April 11, 1996, www.kcrw.com/culture/shows/bookworm/david-foster-wallace-infinite-jest.

Silvers, Anita, and Leslie Pickering Francis, "Justice through Trust: Disability and the 'Outlier Problem' in Social Contract Theory," *Ethics*, 116.1 (2005), 40–76.

Simon, Herbert, "Designing Organizations for an Information-Rich World," in Martin Greenberger (ed.), *Computers, Communications and the Public Interest* (Baltimore: The Johns Hopkins University Press, 1971), pp. 37–53.

Sinykin, Dan N., "The Conglomerate Era: Publishing, Authorship, and Literary Form, 1965–2007," *Contemporary Literature*, 58.4 (2017), 462–91.

Sloane, Peter, *David Foster Wallace and the Body* (London: Routledge, 2019).

Smith, James K. A., *You Are What You Love: The Spiritual Power of Habit* (Grand Rapids, MI: Brazos Press, 2016).

Smith, Zadie, "The Difficult Gifts of David Foster Wallace," in *Changing My Mind* (London: Penguin, 2009), pp. 255–97 (New York: Hamish Hamilton, 2009), pp. 257–300.

"Zadie Smith," *Five Dials*, 10 (2008), p. 14.

Sontag, Susan, "Literature Is Freedom," in *At the Same Time: Essays and Speeches* (New York: Farrar, Straus, and Giroux, 2007), pp. 192–209.

Spampinato, Erin, "How Does the Literary Canon Reinforce the Logic of the incel?," *The Guardian*, June 4, 2018, www.theguardian.com/books/2018/jun/04/incel-movement-literary-classics-behind-misogyny.

Sprauge, Rosamond Kent, *Plato's Philosopher-King* (Columbia: University of South Carolina Press, 1976).

Staes, Toon, "The Coatlicue Complex in David Foster Wallace's *Infinite Jest*," *The Explicator*, 72.1 (2014), 67–71.

"'Only Artists Ccan Transfigure': Kafka's Artists and the Possibility of Redemption in the Novellas of David Foster Wallace," *Orbis Litterarum*, 65.6 (2010), 459–80.

"Rewriting the Author: A Narrative Approach to Empathy in *The Pale King* and *Infinite Jest*," *Studies in the Novel*, 44.4 (2012), 409–27.

"Work in Process: A Genesis for *The Pale King*," *English Studies*, 95.1 (2014), 70–84.

Stein, Lorin, "Letter to the Editor," *The New Yorker*, January 10, 2013, www.nytimes.com/2013/01/13/books/review/faith-and-fiction.html.

Steinberg, Ted, *Down to Earth: Nature's Role in American History* (New York: Oxford University Press, 2009).

Steinhilber, Dominik, "The Perils of Self-Consciousness: Heinrich von Kleist's 'Über das Marionettentheater' in David Foster Wallace's *Infinite Jest*," *Critique: Studies in Contemporary Fiction*, 58.5 (2017), 548–57.

Stewart, Matthew Ryan, "Modern Myth and Ideology in David Foster Wallace's The Pale King," unpublished MA thesis, Missouri State University (2016).

Stock, Richard, "Beyond Narratology: David Foster Wallace's *Infinite Jest*," *Prague Journal of English Studies*, 2.1 (2013), 31–51.

Streitfeld, David, "Amazon and Hachette Resolve Dispute," *The New York Times*, November 13, 2014, www.nytimes.com/2014/11/14/technology/amazon-hachette-ebook-dispute.html.

Taylor, Mark C., "Speed: David Foster Wallace (1962–2008): The Pale King, 'Good Old Neon,'" in *Last Works: Lessons in Leaving* (New Haven, CT: Yale University Press, 2018), pp. 227–51.

Taylor, Richard, "Fatalism," in Steven M. Cahn and Maureen Eckert (eds.), *David Foster Wallace, Fate, Time, and Language: An Essay on Free Will* (New York: Columbia University Press, 2011), pp. 41–51. First published in *The Philosophical Review*, 71.1 (1962), 56–66.

Taylor, Stuart James, "The Making of Wallace's Everything and More: an interview with Erica Neely," *Lettera Matematica*, 3 (2015), 269–73.

Terranova, Tiziana, "Attention, Economy and the Brain," *Culture Machine*, 13 (2012), 1–19.

Thomas, Calvin, "Art Is on the Way: From the Abject Opening of *Underworld* to the Shitty Ending of *Oblivion*," in Rina Arya and Nicholas Chare (eds.), *Abject Visions: Powers of Horror in Art and Visual Culture* (Manchester: Manchester University Press, 2016), pp. 162–90.

Thomas, Dylan, *The Collected Poems: The New Centenary Edition*, ed. John Goodby (London: Weidenfeld & Nicolson, 2014).

Thomas, Eric A., "'Psychotic Depression' and Suicide in David Foster Wallace's *Infinite Jest*," *Critique: Studies in Contemporary Fiction*, 54.3 (2013), 276–91.

Thompson, Bob, "*New Yorker* Publishes Part of Unfinished Wallace Novel," *Washington Post*, March 2, 2009, www.washingtonpost.com/wpdyn/content/article/2009/03/01/AR2009030101774.html.

Thompson, John B., *Merchants of Culture: The Publishing Business in the Twenty-First Century*, 2nd ed. (Cambridge: Polity, 2012).

Thompson, Lucas, "'Books Are Made Out of Books': David Foster Wallace and Cormac McCarthy," *The Cormac McCarthy Journal*, 13.1 (2015), 3–26.

"David Foster Wallace and 'Blurbspeak,'" *Los Angeles Review of Books* (2015), https://lareviewofbooks.org/article/david-foster-wallace-and-blurbspeak/.

"David Foster Wallace's Germany," *Comparative Literature Studies*, 56.1 (2019), 1–30.

Global Wallace: David Foster Wallace and World Literature (New York: Bloomsbury Academic, 2016).

"Programming Literary Influence: David Foster Wallace's 'B.I. #59,'" *Texas Studies in Literature and Language*, 56.2 (2014), 113–34.

"'Sincerity with a Motive': Literary Manipulation in David Foster Wallace's *Infinite Jest*," *Critique: Studies in Contemporary Fiction*, 57.4 (2016), 359–73.

"Wallace and Race," in Ralph Clare (ed.), *The Cambridge Companion to David Foster Wallace* (Cambridge: Cambridge University Press, 2018), pp. 204–19.

Thomson, Philip, *The Grotesque* (London: Methuen, 1972).

Thoreau, Henry David, "Walking," in Elizabeth Hall Witherell (ed.), *Collected Essays and Poems* (New York: Literary Classics of the United States, 2001), pp. 225–55.

Toal, Catherine, "Corrections: Contemporary American Melancholy," *Journal of European Studies*, 33.3–4 (2003), 305–22.

Toh, Justine, "The White Fireman and the American Heartland in the Memory of 9/11," *Critical Race and Whiteness Studies*, 10.2 (2014), 1–17.

Tolkien, J. R. R., *The Letters of J. R. R. Tolkien*, eds. Humphrey Carpenter and Christopher Tolkien (London: HarperCollins, 2006 [1981]).

Tolkien, J. R. R., *The Lord of the Rings* (London: HarperCollins, 2008 [1955]).

The Monsters and the Critics and Other Essays (London: HarperCollins, 2007)

Tracey, Thomas, "The Formative Years: David Foster Wallace's Philosophical Influences and *The Broom of the System*," in Robert K. Bolger and Scott Korb (eds.), *Gesturing Toward Reality: David Foster Wallace and Philosophy* (New York: Bloomsbury Academic, 2014).

Traister, Bryce, "Academic Viagra: The Rise of American Masculinity Studies," *American Quarterly*, 52.2 (2000), 274–304.

Traubel, Horace, *With Walt Whitman in Camden*, vol. 3 (New York: Rowman & Littlefield, 1961).

Treisman, Deborah, "Deborah Treisman Reads David Foster Wallace," *The New Yorker Fiction Podcast*, April 1, 2020, www.newyorker.com/podcast/fiction/deborah-treisman-reads-david-foster-wallace.

Trilling, Lionel, "Reality in America," in *The Liberal Imagination: Essays on Literature and Society* (New York: The New York Review of Books Classics, 2007 [1950]), pp. 3–21.

Sincerity and Authenticity (Harvard: Harvard University Press, 1973).

Tubbs, Robert, *Mathematics in Twentieth-Century Literature and Art: Content, Form, Meaning* (Baltimore: Johns Hopkins University Press, 2014).

Turnbull, Daniel, "This Is Water and the Ethics of Attention: Wallace, Murdoch and Nussbaum," in David Hering (ed.), *Consider David Foster Wallace: Critical Essays* (Los Angeles, CA: Sideshow Media Group Press, 2010), pp. 209–17.

Tysdal, Dan, "Inarticulation and the Figure of Enjoyment: Raymond Carver's Minimalism Meets David Foster Wallace's 'A Radically Condensed History of Postindustrial Life,'" *Wascana Review of Contemporary Poetry and Short Fiction*, 38.1 (2003), 66–83.

Updike, John, *Picked-Up Pieces* (New York: Alfred A. Knopf, 1976).

US Department of Defence, "National Defense Budget Estimates for FY 2015," April 2014, http://comptroller.defense.gov/Portals/45/Documents/defbud get/fy2015/FY15_Green_Book.pdf.

Valdré, Rossella, "'The End of the Tour': A Journey into the Mind of David Foster Wallace: A Psychoanalytic and Artistic Reflection Through the Film," *International Journal of Psychoanalysis*, 98.3 (2017), 909–25.

Van Ewijk, Petrus, "'I' and the 'Other': The Relevance of Wittgenstein, Buber and Levinas for an Understanding of AA's Recovery Program in David Foster Wallace's *Infinite Jest*," *English Text Construction*, 2.1 (2009), 132–45.

Van Zee, Art, "The Promotion and Marketing of Oxycontin: Commercial Triumph, Public Health Tragedy," *American Journal of Public Health*, 99.2 (2009), 221–27.

Veggian, Henry, "Anachronisms of Authority: Authorship, Exchange Value, and David Foster Wallace's *The Pale King*," *boundary 2*, 39.3 (2012), 97–124.

Vermeulen, Pieter, "In the Fishtank: The Biopolitical Imagination in David Foster Wallace's *This Is Water* and *The Pale King*," *Image and Narrative*, 14.1 (2013), 63–75.

Vidal, Fernando, and Francisco Ortega, "Approaching the Neurocultural Spectrum: An Introduction," in Francisco Ortega and Fernando Vidal (eds.), *Neurocultures: Glimpses into an Expanding Universe* (Frankfurt am Main: Peter Lang, 2011), pp. 7–27.

Violaris, Elena, "The Semiotics of Emoji: *Infinite Jest* and the Yellow Smiley Face," *Critique: Studies in Contemporary Fiction*, 61:2 (2020), 193–205.

Waldstein, Edmund, "The Dialectics of Individualism and Totalitarianism in Charles de Koninck and David Foster Wallace," 2016, https://sancrucensis.files.wordpress.com/2016/05/the-dialectics-of-individualism-and-totalitarianism.pdf.

Warner, Michael, "Whitman Drunk," in Betsy Erkkila and Jay Grossman (eds.), *Breaking Bounds: Whitman and American Cultural Studies* (New York: Oxford University Press, 1996), pp. 30–43.

Warren, Andrew, "Narrative Modeling and Community Organizing in *The Pale King* and *Infinite Jest*," *Studies in the Novel*, 44.4 (2012), 389–408. Republished in Marshall Boswell (ed.), *David Foster Wallace and "The Long Thing"* (London: Bloomsbury, 2014), pp. 61–82.

"Wallace and Politics," in Ralph Clare (ed.), *The Cambridge Companion to David Foster Wallace* (Cambridge: Cambridge University Press, 2018), pp. 173–89.

Watt, Ian, *The Rise of the Novel: Studies in Richardson, Fielding, Defoe* (London: Pimlico, 2000 [1957]).

Weinberger, Eliot, "Notes on Susan," *The New York Review of Books*, August 16, 2007, www.nybooks.com/articles/2007/08/16/notes-on-susan/.

Weissman, Benjamin, "A Sleek and Brilliant Monster: David Foster Wallace Comes Clean," *L.A. Weekly*, April 28, 1999, www.laweekly.com/a-sleek-and-brilliant-monster/.

Welsh, Irvine, "Up From the Street," *The Guardian*, March 14, 2009, www
.theguardian.com/books/2009/mar/14/iceberg-slim-pimp-irvine-welsh.

Werner, Clay, *Gospel Brokenness: The Unexpected Path to Deep Joy* (Eugene, Oregon: Wipf and Stock, 2019).

West, Cornel, *The American Evasion of Philosophy: A Genealogy of Pragmatism* (Basingstoke: Macmillan, 1989).

West, Mark, "'Observacion of these Articles': Surveillance and the 1970s in David Foster Wallace's *The Pale King*," *Critique: Studies in Contemporary Fiction*, 59.2 (2018), 223–34.

Wheeler, R. S., "Attitude Change Is Not Enough: Disrupting Deficit Grading Practices to Disrupt Dialect Prejudice," *Proceedings of the Linguistic Society of America*, 4.10 (2019), 1–12.

White, Christopher T., "Narrative Crisis and Renewal in the Age of Information: David Foster Wallace's 'Mister Squishy,'" *Critique: Studies in Contemporary Fiction*, 61.5 (2021), 617–30.

Whitman, Walt, *Franklin Evans, or the Inebriate* (Durham, NC: Duke University Press, 2007 [1842]).

Journalism, Vol. 1, eds. Herbert Bergman, Douglas A. Noverr, and Edward J. Recchia (New York: Peter Lang, 1998).

The Portable Walt Whitman (New York: Penguin, 2004).

Widiss, Benjamin, *Obscure Invitations: The Persistence of the Author in Twentieth-century American Literature* (Stanford, CA: Stanford University Press, 2011).

Wiegman, Robyn, "Whiteness Studies and the Paradox of Particularity," *boundary 2*, 26.3 (1999), 115–50.

Wilberding, James, "David Foster Wallace on Dumb Jocks and Athletic Genius," *Journal of the Philosophy of Sport*, 44.1 (2017), 108–22.

Williams, Iain, "(New) Sincerity in David Foster Wallace's 'Octet,'" *Critique: Studies in Contemporary Fiction*, 56.3 (2015), 299–314.

"'Something Real American': David Foster Wallace and Authenticity," unpublished PhD thesis, University of Edinburgh, 2015.

Williams, William Carlos, *Collected Poems, Volume II: 1939–1962*, ed. Christopher MacGowan (London: Paladin, 1991).

Wills, Garry, *Reagan's America: Innocents at Home* (London: Penguin, 2000).

Wilson, Timothy D., *Strangers to Ourselves: Discovering the Adaptive Unconscious* (Cambridge, MA: The Belknap Press of Harvard University Press, 2002).

Winningham, Thomas, "'Author Here': David Foster Wallace and the Post-metafictional Paradox," *Critique: Studies in Contemporary Fiction*, 56.5 (2015), 467–79.

Wittgenstein, Ludwig, "A Lecture on Ethics," *The Philosophical Review*, 74.1 (1965), 3–12.

Wohlmann, Anita, "The Illness Is You: Figurative Language in David Foster Wallace's Short Story 'The Planet Trillaphon,'" in Heike Hartung (ed.), *Embodied Narration: Illness, Death, and Dying in Modern Culture* (Bielefeld: Transcript, 2018), pp. 203–25.

Woodend, Kyle, "Irony, Narcissism, and Affect in David Foster Wallace's *Infinite Jest*," *Critique: Studies in Contemporary Fiction*, 60.4 (2019), 462–74.

Woods, Aengus, "Early-Morning Uncertainties: Anxiety, Abstraction, and Infinity in Everything and More: A Compact History of ∞," in Philip Coleman (ed.), *Critical Insights: David Foster Wallace* (Ipswich, MA: Salem Press, 2015), pp. 268–85.

Wouters, Conley, "'What Am I, a Machine?' Humans and Information in *The Pale King*," in Marshall Boswell (ed.), *David Foster Wallace and "The Long Thing": New Essays on the Novels* (London: Bloomsbury Academic, 2014), pp. 169–86. First published in *Studies in the Novel*, 44.4 (2012), 447–63.

Yeats, W. B., *The Poems*, ed. Daniel Albright (London: Everyman's Library, 1990).

Yeats, W. B., and Dorothy Wellesley, *Letters on Poetry: From Yeats to Dorothy Wellesley* (Oxford: Oxford University Press, 1964).

Young, Stephen, "Searching for the Author: A Performative Reading of Legal Subjection in David Foster Wallace's *The Pale King*," *Law and Humanities*, 13.2 (2019), 247–68.

Ziegler, Heide, "John Barth and David Foster Wallace: An Abortive Patricide," *Anglia*, 137.3 (2019), 449–62.

Index

Printed in the United States
by Baker & Taylor Publisher Services